Lecture Notes in Computer Science   12671

More information about this subseries at http://www.springer.com/series/7411

Oliver Hohlfeld · Andra Lutu ·
Dave Levin (Eds.)

Passive and Active Measurement

22nd International Conference, PAM 2021
Virtual Event, March 29 – April 1, 2021
Proceedings

 Springer

Editors
Oliver Hohlfeld 🆔
Brandenburg University
of Technology (BTU)
Cottbus, Germany

Andra Lutu
Telefonica Research
Barcelona, Spain

Dave Levin
Iribe Center
University of Maryland
College Park, MD, USA

ISSN 0302-9743   ISSN 1611-3349   (electronic)
Lecture Notes in Computer Science
ISBN 978-3-030-72581-5   ISBN 978-3-030-72582-2   (eBook)
https://doi.org/10.1007/978-3-030-72582-2

LNCS Sublibrary: SL5 – Computer Communication Networks and Telecommunications

This Springer imprint is published by the registered company Springer Nature Switzerland AG
The registered company address is: Gewerbestrasse 11, 6330 Cham, Switzerland

Preface

We are excited to present the proceedings of the 22nd annual Passive and Active Measurement (PAM) conference. After more than two decades, PAM continues to provide an important venue for emerging and early-stage research in network measurement – work that seeks to better understand complex, real-world networked systems in the wild and provide critical empirical foundations and support to network research. In light of a still ongoing global COVID-19 pandemic, this 22nd edition of PAM was again organized as a virtual conference from March 29 to 31st 2021. This year's edition benefited from experiences gathered by measuring the participant's experience of PAM 2020.

This year's proceedings demonstrate the import and extent to which measurements pervade systems – from protocols to performance to security. In total, we received 75 double-blind submissions from authors representing 132 unique institutions, of which the Technical Program Committee (TPC) selected 33 for publication – making this year's PAM program the largest in its history. Particular attention was paid to ensuring that the TPC was as broadly representative as possible, including both junior and senior researchers. We are indebted to this hard-working TPC, which ensured that each paper received three reviews, and carried out a lively (and in several cases spirited) online discussion to arrive at the final program. TPC members were asked to provide constructive feedback, bearing in mind PAM's focus and goals that recognize promising early work. This year at PAM we also implemented a Review Task Force (RTF), following the model used by USENIX Security and ACM IMC. The RTF included senior, experienced researchers in the community who are also great mentors. The engagement of such a group ensured that all the TPC's feedback met high standards of technical correctness, specific critiques, and a positive, constructive tone. To ensure the quality of the program and equanimity of the presented results, each paper was assigned a shepherd from the TPC who reviewed the paper. We are delighted with the final set of 33 papers and hope the readers find them as valuable and provocative as we do.

We would be remiss not to thank the Steering Committee for help while organizing the conference, Georgios Smaragdakis for handling the publication process, Pedro Casas for publicity, Taejoong "Tijay" Chung for managing the conference web site, Sebastian Böhm for designing the logo, and the Computer Networks group at Brandenburg University of Technology including Sebastian Böhm, Helge Reelfs, Stefan Mehner, Joachim Paschke, and Katrin Willhöft for their support in the organization and running of PAM 2021. Last, we thank all of the researchers who make PAM such an interesting and important conference year after year.

March 2021

Oliver Hohlfeld
Andra Lutu
Dave Levin

Organization

General Chair

Oliver Hohlfeld   Brandenburg University of Technology, Germany

Program Committee Chairs

Andra Lutu   Telefónica, Spain
Dave Levin   University of Maryland, USA

Publication Chair

Georgios Smaragdakis   TU Berlin, MPI-Informatics, Germany

Publicity Chair

Pedro Casas   Austrian Institute of Technology, Austria

Web Chair

Taejoong Chung   Virginia Tech, USA

Steering Committee

Marinho P. Barcellos   University of Waikato, New Zealand
Fabián E. Bustamante   Northwestern University, USA
Anja Feldmann   Max Planck Institute for Informatics, Germany
Jelena Mirkovic   University of Southern California, USA
Michalis Faloutsos   University of California, Riverside, USA
Steve Uhlig   Queen Mary University of London, UK

Program Committee

Özgü Alay   University of Oslo, Norway
Marcelo Bagnulo   University Carlos III of Madrid, Spain
Muhammad Bashir   ICSI, USA
Theophilus Benson   Brown University, USA
Zachary Bischof   IIJ Research Lab, Japan
Anna Brunstrom   Karlstad University, Sweden
Randy Bush   IIJ Research Lab & Arrcus, Inc, Japan
Fabián Brunström   Northwestern University, USA
Timm Böttger   Facebook, USA

Contents

COVID-19

Video Conferencing and Flow-Rate Fairness: A First Look at Zoom
and the Impact of Flow-Queuing AQM 3
   Constantin Sander, Ike Kunze, Klaus Wehrle, and Jan Rüth

Characterizing Service Provider Response to the COVID-19 Pandemic
in the United States. 20
   Shinan Liu, Paul Schmitt, Francesco Bronzino, and Nick Feamster

A First Look at COVID-19 Domain Names: Origin and Implications 39
   Ryo Kawaoka, Daiki Chiba, Takuya Watanabe, Mitsuaki Akiyama,
   and Tatsuya Mori

Web Security

Clairvoyance: Inferring Blocklist Use on the Internet. 57
   Vector Guo Li, Gautam Akiwate, Kirill Levchenko,
   Geoffrey M. Voelker, and Stefan Savage

Our (in)Secure Web: Understanding Update Behavior of Websites
and Its Impact on Security 76
   Nurullah Demir, Tobias Urban, Kevin Wittek, and Norbert Pohlmann

Winding Path: Characterizing the Malicious Redirection in Squatting
Domain Names. 93
   Yuwei Zeng, Xunxun Chen, Tianning Zang, and Haiwei Tsang

Video Streaming

An Empirical Measurement Study of Free Live Streaming Services. 111
   Sina Keshvadi and Carey Williamson

A Data-Driven Analysis and Tuning of a Live Hybrid CDN/V2V Video
Distribution System. 128
   Ishani Sarkar, Soufiane Roubia, Dino Martin Lopez-Pacheco,
   and Guillaume Urvoy-Keller

Too Late for Playback: Estimation of Video Stream Quality in Rural
and Urban Contexts. 141
   Vivek Adarsh, Michael Nekrasov, Udit Paul, Alex Ermakov, Arpit Gupta,
   Morgan Vigil-Hayes, Ellen Zegura, and Elizabeth Belding

TLS

Measurement and Analysis of Automated Certificate Reissuance.   161
  Olamide Omolola, Richard Roberts, Md. Ishtiaq Ashiq,
  Taejoong Chung, Dave Levin, and Alan Mislove

Revocation Statuses on the Internet.   175
  Nikita Korzhitskii and Niklas Carlsson

Measuring DNS over TLS from the Edge: Adoption, Reliability,
and Response Times   192
  Trinh Viet Doan, Irina Tsareva, and Vaibhav Bajpai

Staying Connected

Long-Lasting Sequences of BGP Updates   213
  Lorenzo Ariemma, Simone Liotta, Massimo Candela,
  and Giuseppe Di Battista

Inferring Cloud Interconnections: Validation, Geolocation,
and Routing Behavior   230
  Alexander Marder, K. C. Claffy, and Alex C. Snoeren

On the Resilience of Internet Infrastructures in Pacific Northwest
to Earthquakes   247
  Juno Mayer, Valerie Sahakian, Emilie Hooft, Douglas Toomey,
  and Ramakrishnan Durairajan

DoS

New Kids on the DRDoS Block: Characterizing Multiprotocol
and Carpet Bombing Attacks   269
  Tiago Heinrich, Rafael R. Obelheiro, and Carlos A. Maziero

DDoS Never Dies? An IXP Perspective on DDoS Amplification Attacks. . . .   284
  Daniel Kopp, Christoph Dietzel, and Oliver Hohlfeld

A Peek into the DNS Cookie Jar   302
  Jacob Davis and Casey Deccio

Performance

What You Need to Know About (Smart) Network Interface Cards   319
  Georgios P. Katsikas, Tom Barbette, Marco Chiesa, Dejan Kostić,
  and Gerald Q. Maguire Jr.

Scouting the Path to a Million-Client Server.   337
   Yimeng Zhao, Ahmed Saeed, Mostafa Ammar, and Ellen Zegura

Building Out the Basics with Hoplets   355
   Prathy Raman and Marcel Flores

Network Security

NATting Else Matters: Evaluating IPv6 Access Control Policies
in Residential Networks.   373
   Karl Olson, Jack Wampler, Fan Shen, and Nolen Scaife

Plight at the End of the Tunnel.   390
   John Kristoff, Mohammad Ghasemisharif, Chris Kanich,
   and Jason Polakis

An Online Method for Estimating the Wireless Device Count
via Privacy-Preserving Wi-Fi Fingerprinting.   406
   Pegah Torkamandi, Ljubica Kärkkäinen, and Jörg Ott

DNS

Cache Me Outside: A New Look at DNS Cache Probing.   427
   Arian Akhavan Niaki, William Marczak, Sahand Farhoodi,
   Andrew McGregor, Phillipa Gill, and Nicholas Weaver

Can Encrypted DNS Be Fast?.   444
   Austin Hounsel, Paul Schmitt, Kevin Borgolte, and Nick Feamster

Fragmentation, Truncation, and Timeouts: Are Large DNS Messages
Falling to Bits?.   460
   Giovane C. M. Moura, Moritz Müller, Marco Davids, Maarten Wullink,
   and Cristian Hesselman

Capacity

On the Accuracy of Tor Bandwidth Estimation.   481
   Rob Jansen and Aaron Johnson

Comparison of TCP Congestion Control Performance over
a Satellite Network   499
   Saahil Claypool, Jae Chung, and Mark Claypool

Throughput Prediction on 60 GHz Mobile Devices for High-Bandwidth,
Latency-Sensitive Applications   513
   Shivang Aggarwal, Zhaoning Kong, Moinak Ghoshal, Y. Charlie Hu,
   and Dimitrios Koutsonikolas

Exposing Hidden Behaviors

Characterizing the Security of Endogenous and Exogenous Desktop
Application Network Flows   531
  Matthew R. McNiece, Ruidan Li, and Bradley Reaves

Zeroing in on Port 0 Traffic in the Wild   547
  Aniss Maghsoudlou, Oliver Gasser, and Anja Feldmann

A Study of the Partnership Between Advertisers and Publishers   564
  Wenrui Ma and Haitao Xu

Author Index   581

COVID-19

Video Conferencing and Flow-Rate Fairness: A First Look at Zoom and the Impact of Flow-Queuing AQM

Constantin Sander[✉], Ike Kunze, Klaus Wehrle, and Jan Rüth

Communication and Distributed Systems,
RWTH Aachen University, Aachen, Germany
{sander,kunze,wehrle,rueth}@comsys.rwth-aachen.de

Abstract. Congestion control is essential for the stability of the Internet and the corresponding algorithms are commonly evaluated for interoperability based on flow-rate fairness. In contrast, video conferencing software such as Zoom uses custom congestion control algorithms whose fairness behavior is mostly unknown. Aggravatingly, video conferencing has recently seen a drastic increase in use – partly caused by the COVID-19 pandemic – and could hence negatively affect how available Internet resources are shared. In this paper, we thus investigate the flow-rate fairness of video conferencing congestion control at the example of Zoom and influences of deploying AQM. We find that Zoom is slow to react to bandwidth changes and uses two to three times the bandwidth of TCP in low-bandwidth scenarios. Moreover, also when competing with delay aware congestion control such as BBR, we see high queuing delays. AQM reduces these queuing delays and can equalize the bandwidth use when used with flow-queuing. However, it then introduces high packet loss for Zoom, leaving the question how delay and loss affect Zoom's QoE. We hence show a preliminary user study in the appendix which indicates that the QoE is at least not improved and should be studied further.

1 Introduction

The stability of the Internet relies on distributed congestion control to avoid a systematic overload of the infrastructure and to share bandwidth. Consequently, protocols that make up large shares of Internet traffic, such as TCP and QUIC, feature such congestion control mechanisms.

The COVID-19 pandemic and subsequent actions to limit its spread have now caused a drastic increase in traffic related to remote-working [16]. Of particular interest is the increasing share of video conferencing software which typically bases on UDP to conform to the inherent low-latency and real-time requirements which cannot be provided by TCP [8,14]. Yet, UDP features no congestion control, meaning that the video conferencing software has to implement it on the application layer. While this allows for adapting the video conference to the specific network conditions [11,14], such implementations can introduce unknown effects and undesired behavior when interacting with "traditional" congestion

© Springer Nature Switzerland AG 2021
O. Hohlfeld et al. (Eds.): PAM 2021, LNCS 12671, pp. 3–19, 2021.
https://doi.org/10.1007/978-3-030-72582-2_1

control. Especially in light of the now increased share of the overall traffic, these tailored implementations can potentially pose a threat to Internet stability.

Thus, we investigate the interaction of real-world video conferencing software and traditional congestion control. For our study, we choose Zoom as it has seen an enormous increase in traffic share by at least one order of magnitude from being marginally visible up to surpassing Skype and Microsoft Teams at certain vantage points [16]. We focus on how Zoom reacts to loss and how it yields traffic to competing TCP-based applications. We also study the impact of Active Queue Management (AQM) on the bandwidth sharing as it is of growing importance. Specifically, our work contributes the following:

- We present a testbed-based measurement setup to study Zoom's flow-rate when competing against TCP CUBIC and BBRv1.
- Comparing different bandwidths, delays, and queue sizes, we find that Zoom uses a high share on low-bandwidth links and that there are high queuing delays, even despite TCP congestion control trying to reduce it (e.g., BBR).
- We show that flow-queuing AQM reduces queuing delay and establishes flow-rate equality to a certain degree reducing Zoom's and increasing TCP's rate by dropping Zoom's packets, where the former is probably beneficial but the latter is probably detrimental for Zoom's QoE. Our preliminary user study shows that users do not see QoE improvements with flow-queuing AQM.

Structure. Section 2 discusses the definition of fairness, as well as related work on general and video conferencing specific congestion control fairness analyses. Section 3 describes the testbed for our flow-rate equality measurements. Section 4 shows our general results on Zoom and the impact of AQM on flow-rate equality, packet loss, and delay. A preliminary user study evaluating the impact of AQM on the QoE can be found in the appendix. Finally, Sect. 5 concludes this paper.

2   Background and Related Work

The interaction of congestion control algorithms, especially regarding fairness, is a frequent focus of research. It has been thoroughly investigated for common TCP congestion control algorithms. However, the definition of fairness itself has also been investigated and discussed.

Fairness Definition. Most work relies on the conventional flow-rate definition of fairness: competing flows should get an equal share of the available bandwidth [19]. However, there are compelling arguments that flow-rate fairness is not an optimal metric [7,27] and new metrics such as harm [27] propose to also consider the demands of applications and their flows. We agree that flow-rate equality is no optimal metric for fairness as it ignores specific demands and the impact of delay, thus making it an outdated fairness estimate.

On the other hand, the notion of harm is hard to grasp as it requires (potentially wrong) demand estimates. Further, techniques such as AQM are demand unaware and flow-queuing even specifically aims at optimizing flow-rate equality, ignoring any actual application demands. Hence, given the prevalence of flow-rate equality in related work and AQM techniques, we explicitly use flow-rate equality as our fairness metric to evaluate the precise impact of this metric on the application performance. That is, we want to, e.g., see the impact on video conferencing when flow-queuing is used. This naturally also means that results depicting an "unfair" flow-rate distribution are not necessarily bad.

TCP Congestion Control. Many of the congestion control studies have especially looked at CUBIC [17] and BBR [10] and found that BBR dominates in under-buffered scenarios causing packet loss and making CUBIC back off, while it is disadvantaged in over-buffered scenarios [18,23,26,28]. Here, CUBIC, as a loss-based algorithm, fills the buffer and increases the queuing delay which makes BBR back off. Introducing AQM, these behavior differences vanish.

Impact of AQM. AQM mechanisms come with the potential of giving end-hosts earlier feedback on congestion, thus helping to reduce queuing delays, and there have been extended studies regarding their fairness (for a survey see [6]). While some AQM algorithms are specifically designed to enable a fair bandwidth sharing (see [13] for an overview and evaluation), generally, any AQM can be made to fairly share bandwidth with the help of fair queuing [15]. Today, this idea is most commonly implemented through a stochastic fair queuing (SFQ) which performs similar to a true fair queuing when the number of flows is limited. In fact, several works (e.g., [22,23]) show that AQM using this SFQ (often called flow-queuing) can create flow-rate fairness while effectively limiting congestion, even though there are no comprehensive studies available in literature.

2.1   Congestion Control for Video Conferencing

Loss-based congestion control, such as CUBIC, is not favorable to delay-sensitive real-time applications. Hence, research has proposed several congestion control algorithms tailored to the needs of video conferencing. However, in contrast to general-purpose congestion control, there is only limited research on its interaction mostly focusing on proposed algorithms with known intrinsics.

Known Algorithms. For example, the Google Congestion Control (GCC) [11], used in Google Chrome for WebRTC, was tested for flow-rate fairness [11,12]. The results indicate that GCC shares bandwidth equally with CUBIC when using a tail-drop queue and also subject to the CoDel and PIE AQM algorithms.

There are similar findings for the Self-Clocked Rate Adaptation for Multimedia (SCReAM) [20] congestion control algorithm. It achieves an approximately equal share with a long-lived TCP flow on a tail-drop queue and yields bandwidth when using CoDel [21]. Contrasting, the Network-Assisted Dynamic Adaptation (NADA) congestion control [32] shares bandwidth equally when using a tail-drop queue, but uses bigger amounts when being governed by an AQM algorithm.

Unknown Algorithms in Video Conferencing Software. However, many actually deployed real-world congestion control algorithms in video conferencing software are unknown and closed-source. Thus, similar to our work, research also studies the externally visible behavior of video conferencing software.

De Cicco et al. [14] investigate the behavior of Skype's congestion control and find that it is generally not TCP-friendly and claims more than its equal share. Interestingly, Zhang et al. [29] found that Skype yields a bigger share to competing TCP flows, but only after exceeding a certain loss threshold. However, in contrast to work on TCP congestion control, these studies only consider limited scenarios and generally do not provide extensive evaluations (e.g., no AQM).

Other works focus even more only on aspects impacting the video conference, e.g., how the audio and video quality evolve subject to packet loss with unlimited rates [24,30] or very specific wireless settings [31].

Takeaway. *Studies on general congestion control are not applicable to video conferencing. Research on video conferencing software, on the other hand, mostly focuses on the concrete impact on its quality while the number of evaluation scenarios and the context to the general congestion control landscape is scarce.*

We thus identify a need for a more thorough evaluation of real-world video conferencing congestion control that also considers the impact of different bandwidths, buffer sizes, or AQM on fairness. For this purpose, we devise a methodology that centers around a configurable testbed which allows us to evaluate the behavior of the congestion control of Zoom.

3   Measurement Design

Research on congestion control fairness is often done using simulations or isolated testbeds to focus on the intrinsics of the algorithms. In contrast, our work on Zoom forbids such an approach as the Zoom clients interact with a cloud-based backend that is responsible for distributing audio and video traffic. Thus, to fully grasp the real-world performance of Zoom, we devise a testbed that connects to this backend while still letting Zoom's traffic compete with a TCP flow over a variety of network settings. While we consequently have to take potential external effects into account, our testbed still allows us to control parameters, such as bottleneck bandwidth, queuing, and delay.

3.1   Preliminaries

For our investigations, we set up two Zoom clients which then connect to a joint Zoom conference via the Zoom backend running in a data center. We find that free Zoom licenses use data centers operated by Oracle in the US, while our University license mostly connects to data centers operated by AWS in Europe. We generally see that connections are established to at least two different AWS data centers, one in Frankfurt (Germany) and one in Dublin (Ireland). As our upstream provider peers at DE-CIX in Frankfurt, we choose to focus on these connections to reduce the number of traversed links, thus minimizing the probability of external effects, such as changing routes or congestion.

3.2   Testbed Setup

As shown in Fig. 1, our testbed uses a dumbbell topology and consists of five dedicated machines. In the center, one machine serves as the configurable bottleneck link over which Zoom Client 1 (ZC 1) connects to the Zoom backend to

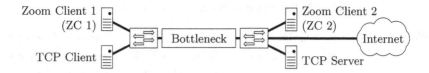

Fig. 1. Testbed setup representing a dumbbell topology

join a conference with Zoom Client 2 (ZC 2). Our two remaining machines (TCP Client, TCP Server) operate a concurrent TCP flow to assess competition.

Testbed Interconnection. All our machines are interconnected using 1 Gbps Ethernet links. The uplink to our university's network is 10 Gbps which in turn connects to the German Research Network (DFN) via two 100 Gbps links. The DFN then peers at DE-CIX with, e.g., AWS. We can thus be reasonably sure that our configurable bottleneck machine represents the overall bottleneck.

Shaping the Bottleneck. We configure our bottleneck using Linux's traffic control (TC) subsystem similar to [25] to create network settings with different bandwidths, delays, queue sizes, and queue management mechanisms. For rate-limiting, we use token bucket filters with a bucket size of one MTU (to minimize bursts) on the egress queues in both directions. Similarly, we also configure the AQM on the egress queues. Delay is modeled on the ingress queues using intermediate function blocks (ifbs) and netem. We first create an additional ingress qdisc via ifb and add the delay to the egress of this ifb via netem. This technique is necessary as netem is not directly compatible with AQM qdiscs [1] and usage of netem on the end-hosts would cause issues due to TCP small queues [9]. Further, we add no artificial jitter, as this causes packet reorderings, as such, jitter is only introduced through the flows filling the queue itself.

Balancing RTTs. Our testbed compensates for differing RTTs and ensures that the Zoom and the TCP flow have the same RTT, a requirement for the common flow-rate equality definition. For this, we first measured the average delay between different AWS hosts and ZC 1 as well as between TCP Client and TCP Server prior to our experiments. We then adapted the netem delay accordingly such that the TCP flow and the flow between ZC 1 and AWS have about the same RTT when the queue is empty. By adapting the delay prior to our experiments, we avoid skewing the initial RTT of flows which we presume to be important for Zoom's congestion control, but accept a potential bias due to changing hosts at AWS which we cannot predict prior to establishing our video conferences. However, the relative error of this bias should be insignificant as we emulate rather large artificial RTTs.

3.3 Fairness Measurement Scenarios and Procedure

With our measurements, we aim to represent video conferences from a low-speed residential access where Zoom's video flow and a TCP flow (e.g., a movie download) compete. The used parameters are shown in Table 1.

Table 1. Parameter configuration for our testbed

BW [Mbps]	RTT [ms]	QSize [BDP]	AQM	CC	Order	Direction
0.5, 1, 2, 4	30, 50	0.5, 2, 10	Tail-Drop	CUBIC	Zoom first	Downlink
			(FQ_)CoDel	BBRv1	TCP first	Uplink

The lowest bandwidth (0.5 Mbps) falls slightly below Zoom's requirements of 0.6 Mbps [2]. Yet, we argue that it also has to behave sound in out-of-spec cases.

We shape the bandwidth symmetrically, which is atypical for a residential connection, but study the up- and downlink separately. We also adjust and balance the minimum RTT (min-RTT) symmetrically as described before. As queue sizes, we use multiples of the BDP, i.e., 0.5, 2, and 10× the BDP. When investigating AQM, we use 2×BDP as AQM algorithms require headroom to operate, and adopt the TC Linux defaults for CoDel (target 5 ms and interval 100 m s). Further, we vary which flow starts first to investigate late-comer effects.

Overcoming Transient States. For our measurements, we want to avoid transient phases. As such, we usually wait in the order of half a minute after activating each flow to stabilize. We then start a 60 s measurement period in which we capture all exchanged packets, measure the queuing delay, and also observe the queue sizes at the bottleneck using a small eBPF program.

Video Conference. The Zoom video conference itself is established between ZC 2 and ZC 1 (ensuring connectivity via AWS in Frankfurt). As their video feeds, both clients simulate a webcam via `v4l2loopback` [3]. To rule out effects of video compression on the congestion control behavior of Zoom, we ensure a constant video data rate by using uniform noise as our video input.

Every scenario is repeated 30 times and retried where, e.g., Zoom restarts due to high loss. The measurements were made from July 2020 to October 2020 on Linux `5.4.0-31` with Zoom version `5.0.408598.0517`. To observe variations, we sort the points in the following scatterplots chronologically from left to right.

Equality Metric. We measure flow-rate equality using the metric of our prior work [25]. In contrast to, e.g., Jain's fairness index [19], this metric shows which flow over-utilizes the bottleneck by how much. The metric is defined as:

$$\text{flow-rate equality} = \begin{cases} 1 - \frac{bytes(TCP)}{bytes(Zoom)}, & \text{if } bytes(Zoom) \geq bytes(TCP) \\ -1 + \frac{bytes(Zoom)}{bytes(TCP)}, & \text{otherwise} \end{cases}$$

flow-rate equality lies in the interval of $[-1, 1]$. With 0 both flows share the bandwidth equally, while $1/-1$ means that Zoom/TCP monopolizes the link.

Please note that flow-rate equality is likely *not* the desired metric to depict a fair service enablement. For example, Zoom simply needs a certain data-rate to deliver its service, as such flow-rate equality should likely not be used to establish fairness, e.g., in an AQM. Nevertheless, we still opted for this metric to i) judge what happens when an AQM tries to utilize this metric, and ii) investigate the bandwidth demand and the ability of the congestion controller to seize the required bandwidth as well as the side effects in doing so.

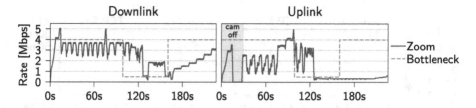

Fig. 2. Zoom video flow behavior for a 50 ms RTT and a 10×BDP tail-drop queue. Bandwidth (dashed) is varied from 4 Mbps to 0.5 Mbps and back to 4 Mbps.

4   Zoom Inter-Protocol Fairness Results

In the following we present our findings on the behavior of Zoom by first analyzing its general congestion reaction (Sect. 4.1). We then discuss how ZC 1 competes with a TCP flow in scenarios without AQM at low bandwidths subject to different queue sizes (Sect. 4.2). We further evaluate the effects of using CoDel (Sect. 4.3) and FQ_CoDel (Sect. 4.4) AQM. Lastly, we show results of a small-scale user study that investigates the effects of FQ_CoDel on the actual QoE, which can be found in the appendix to this work (Appendix A).

Before conducting our experiments, we first verify the standalone throughput of TCP and Zoom in our scenarios. We find that TCP achieves a utilization above 80% in almost all cases except for 3 outliers out of 4800 runs. Similarly, Zoom's throughput for the AQM scenarios only changes by at most 10%. The following differences in flow-rate equality are thus mainly due to the interaction of the congestion control algorithms and not rooted in our settings.

4.1   General Observations on Zoom's Behavior

We first observe the behavior of a single Zoom flow without competition in a scenario with a 50 ms RTT and a 10×BDP tail-drop queue. Figure 2 shows Zoom's video send rate when varying the bandwidth (dashed) from 4 Mbps to 0.5 Mbps and back. At first, Zoom's backend (left) sends at slightly less than 4 Mbps while the Zoom client (right) sends at ∼2.5 Mbps. In both cases, the queue is empty. Similar to BBR [10], Zoom seems to repeatedly probe i) the bandwidth by increasing its rate and ii) the min-RTT by reducing its rate.

Once we reduce the bandwidth to 0.5 Mbps, both Zoom entities keep sending at ∼3.5 Mbps, thus losing many packets and filling the queue. After ∼30 s, Zoom reduces its rate to 0.5 Mbps. Surprisingly, the backend again increases the rate by a factor of 4 shortly thereafter. After resetting the bandwidth to 4 Mbps, Zoom slowly increases its rate on the uplink and faster on the downlink.

Packet loss and increased queuing delays do not seem to directly influence Zoom's sending behavior. However, Zoom occasionally restarted the video conference completely, stopping sending and reconnecting to the backend with a new bandwidth estimate not overshooting the bottleneck link. We filtered these occurrences from the following results as the time of reconnecting would influence our metric and also the meaning of our "Zoom first" scenario.

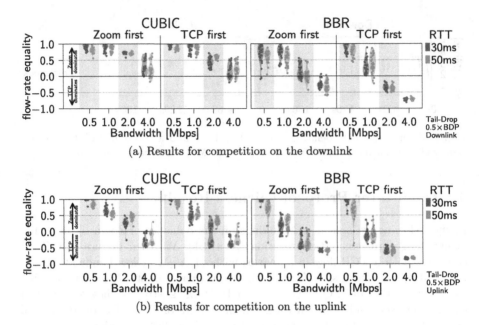

(a) Results for competition on the downlink

(b) Results for competition on the uplink

Fig. 3. Flow-rate equality for Zoom competing at a 0.5 × BDP queue with TCP.

We also changed the min-RTT from 50 ms to 500 ms instead of the bandwidth. We did not see any obvious reaction, although we expected that Zoom backs off to wait for now delayed signaling information or to reduce potential queuing.

To summarize, Zoom handles up- and downlink differently and does not seem to directly react on increased queuing or loss, instead reacting slowly which leads to big spikes of loss. We next investigate how this impacts competing flows.

4.2 Competition at Tail-Drop Queues

Undersized Tail-Drop Queue. We first examine Zoom's behavior when competing at a 0.5×BDP tail-drop queue against TCP CUBIC and BBR. The scatterplots in Fig. 3 show our flow-rate equality for downlink (a) and uplink (b).

Downlink. Zoom uses a disproportionate bandwidth share on the downlink with bottleneck bandwidths ≤ 1 Mbps. The flow-rate equality is mostly above 0.5, i.e., Zoom's rate is more than twice the rate of the TCP flow. For higher bandwidths, Zoom yields more bandwidth. Additionally, we can see that TCP flows starting first result in slightly better flow-rate equality. For CUBIC, equality values of around 0 can be first seen at 4 Mbps. For BBR, equality values of around 0 can already be seen at 2 Mbps. However, when being started first and at 4 Mbps, BBR disadvantages Zoom significantly.

Uplink. For the uplink, the equality values are comparable, but in total lower. This means that the TCP flows claim more bandwidth (especially with

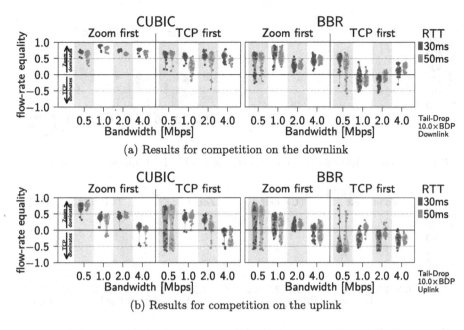

(a) Results for competition on the downlink

(b) Results for competition on the uplink

Fig. 4. Flow-rate equality for Zoom competing at a $10 \times$ BDP queue with TCP.

BBR) and Zoom seems to act less aggressive. We posit that Zoom's congestion control might be adapted to the asymmetric nature of residential access links.

The queuing delays on the down- and uplink mostly exceed 50% of the maximum (not shown). We attribute this to the TCP flows as i) CUBIC always fills queues, and ii) BBR overestimates the available bandwidth when competing with other flows [28] and then also fills the queue plus iii) Zoom reacting slowly.

Slightly Oversized Tail-Drop Queues. When increasing the buffer size to 2×BDP, the results are surprisingly similar (and thus not visualized). CUBIC can gather a slightly larger bandwidth share, which we attribute to its queue-filling behavior. However, Zoom still holds twice the bandwidth of the TCP flows at links with ≤1 Mbps, i.e. the equality values mostly exceed 0.5. Only on faster links, CUBIC can gain an equal or higher bandwidth share. For BBR, equality values are closer to 0 for bandwidths below 2 Mbps, i.e., Zoom as well as BBR dominate less. For higher bandwidths, the results are equivalent to before. Also the avg. queuing delay rises to about 75% due to filled queues as before.

Overlarge Tail-Drop Queues. Next, we study the flow-rates for large queues of 10×BDP. Figure 4 shows the results for downlink (a) and uplink (b).

Downlink. Contrary to our expectation, there is no significant improvement in flow-rate equality for the downlink. Zoom still uses a high bandwidth share and CUBIC's queue-filling behavior does not result in a larger share. Compared to the previous scenarios, the equality values are not decreasing significantly when Zoom starts first and it even uses more bandwidth than before for the 4 Mbps

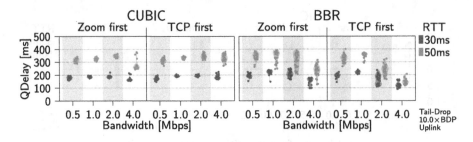

Fig. 5. Queuing delay for Zoom competing at a 10 × BDP queue on the uplink.

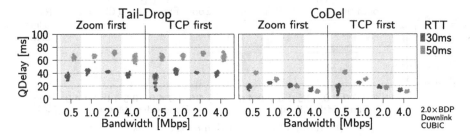

Fig. 6. Queuing delay for Zoom+CUBIC competing at a tail-drop/CoDel queue.

setting. For TCP CUBIC starting first, equality values now spread around 0.5, regardless of the bandwidth. For Zoom starting first, BBR barely reaches values below zero.

Uplink. The scenario looks completely different for the uplink. Zoom yields bigger parts of the bandwidth to CUBIC and even reduces on one third of the bandwidth when BBR starts first. This is surprising, as BBR is known to be disadvantaged in this overbuffered scenario [18]. We also checked if changes between the BBR code used in [18] and our Linux Kernel 5.4 could explain this difference, but the basic principle *seems* to be unaltered. Still, we remark that the BBR codebase has seen significant changes since [18] and we are not aware of any investigations how these changes affect BBR's properties.

The queuing delay, shown in Fig. 5 for the uplink, still reaches about 75% of the maximum queuing delay for CUBIC and BBR in low-bandwidth scenarios where delay is slightly smaller on the uplink than on the downlink. BBR seems to be able to reduce queuing delay in the higher bandwidth region, but we expected that BBR would reduce the queuing delay more strongly in all scenarios.

Takeaway. *We can see that Zoom is unfair w.r.t. flow-rate to CUBIC in low-bandwidth scenarios with 1.0 Mbps and less, although Zoom is less aggressive on the uplink. As BBR is more aggressive, it gains higher rates in these situations – also on the downlink. However, all scenarios have in common that the queuing delay is significantly increased being detrimental to video conferencing.*

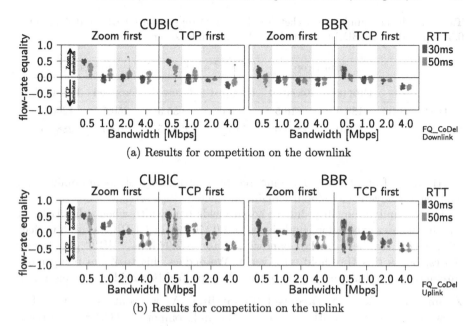

(a) Results for competition on the downlink

(b) Results for competition on the uplink

Fig. 7. Flow-rate equality for Zoom competing with TCP at an FQ_CoDel queue

4.3 Competition at CoDel Queues

Using AQM might be beneficial, given the increased queuing delays. Hence, we study Zoom and TCP flows competing at CoDel queues. We expect significant changes in flow-rate equality as CoDel drops packets early to signal congestion.

Yet, our results are very similar to the 2×BDP tail-drop queue, thus we do not show them here. They only slightly shift towards CUBIC. However, CoDel keeps its promise of reduced queuing delays, as shown in Fig. 6: The queuing delay of Zoom competing with CUBIC (BBR looks similar) at 2×BDP queues roughly halves when CoDel is used at 0.5 Mbps. For higher bandwidths, the effect is even stronger. This is potentially beneficial for real-time applications.

Takeaway. *All in all, CoDel does not significantly alter the flow-rate distribution. However, it keeps its promise of reducing the experienced queuing delays.*

4.4 Competition at FQ_CoDel Queues

To enforce flow-rate equality, we next apply FQ_CoDel to the queue. FQ_CoDel adds stochastic fair-queueing to CoDel, i.e., it isolates flows into subqueues, applies CoDel individually, and then serves the queues in a fair manner.

While the queuing delays are equivalent to CoDel and thus not shown, our flow-rate equality metric significantly shifts towards TCP in most conditions as shown in Fig. 7 for uplink (a) and downlink (b). For example, the downlink results

Table 2. Median number of packets received and dropped for CUBIC and Zoom at a 0.5 Mbps, 50 ms, 2×BDP bottleneck on the downlink (Zoom started first).

	Tail-Drop		CoDel		FQ_CoDel	
	Dropped	Received	Dropped	Received	Dropped	Received
TCP CUBIC	188.0	816.5	190.0	935.5	250.5	1260.5
Zoom	331.0	2824.0	515.5	2852.5	903.5	2880.5

mostly range from 0.3 to −0.3 compared to prior findings of Zoom dominating. The biggest advance for Zoom remains in the 0.5 Mbps setting.

On the uplink, equality differs. Zoom yields bandwidth when using BBR in mostly all cases except for bandwidths ≤ 1.0 Mbps. For CUBIC, also no perfect equalization can be seen. For bandwidths above 2.0 Mbps CUBIC gets bigger shares, below this threshold, vice versa. We deduct this to Zoom being more careful on the uplink and not using the whole probed bandwidth, leaving a gap.

Zoom's Reaction to Targeted Throttling. As we could see, FQ_CoDel allows to share bandwidth between Zoom and competing TCP flows after a bottleneck more equally. However, it is unclear whether Zoom reduces its rate or whether the AQM is persistently dropping packets, specifically in the low-bandwidth scenarios. We hence show the dropped and sent packets for CUBIC and Zoom over 60 s in Table 2 for the 0.5 Mbps bottleneck with 2×BDP queue and 50 ms RTT. We can see that Zoom does not reduce its packet-rate from a tail-drop queue up to FQ_CoDel. Instead, the AQM drops packets increasingly. **Takeaway.** *In combination with flow-queuing, CoDel can reduce the experienced queuing delay, which is probably beneficial for Zoom's QoE, while equalizing the bandwidth share with TCP. However, in low-bandwidth scenarios this share is still not perfectly equal. Zoom does not reduce its rate but CoDel and FQ_CoDel increasingly drop Zoom's packets which might affect Zoom's QoE negatively. A preliminary user study shows that FQ_CoDel does, indeed, not improve QoE and can be found in the appendix.*

5   Conclusion

In this work, we recognize the impact of video conferencing on Internet stability and investigate congestion control fairness in combination with Zoom. Flow-rate equality as fairness measure is well researched for TCP's congestion control and for real-world TCP flows in the Internet. However, for congestion control of video conferencing software it is not – specifically regarding different scenarios. Hence, we investigate Zoom as increasingly popular real-world deployment of video conferencing. We find that Zoom uses high shares of bandwidth in low-bandwidth scenarios yielding it when more bandwidth is available. Adding AQM, such as CoDel, alone does not improve the bandwidth sharing, but reduces latency which is probably beneficial for Zoom. Only when also using flow-queuing, more equal bandwidth sharing can be achieved with FQ_CoDel. However, this fair sharing comes at the price of reduced bandwidth and packet loss for Zoom, potentially reducing its QoE. Our small-scale user study found that FQ_CoDel did not improve the QoE. For future work, we imagine a more thorough user study to evaluate Zoom's QoE with AQM such as FQ_CoDel in more detail. Further, testing Zoom's reaction on ECN and multiple Zoom flows competing could give interesting information on its behavior on backbone congestion.

Acknowledgments. This work has been funded by the Deutsche Forschungsgemeinschaft (DFG, German Research Foundation) under Germany's Excellence Strategy – EXC-2023 Internet of Production – 390621612. We would like to thank the center for teaching- and learning services at RWTH Aachen University for issuing further Zoom Licenses. We further thank the anonymous reviewers and our shepherd Mirja Kühlewind for their valuable comments.

Appendix

In the following, we present results of a small-scale user study which we conducted to analyze whether our findings regarding packet loss but also improvements regarding delay have positive or negative impact on Zoom's subjective quality. However, as our study was performed with a limited number of participants due to COVID-19 restrictions, we had to restrict the number of scenarios that we could investigate. Thus, the results and their generalizability are limited and this study should be regarded as an initial step in understanding how QoE, queuing and Zoom interact.

A   QoE Impact of Flow-Queuing AQM

As we have shown in Sect. 4.4, flow-queuing AQM can achieve more equal flow-rates and reduce latency when Zoom and TCP share a bottleneck. However, this means lower bandwidths for Zoom, so likely worse video quality. In contrast, lower latencies should probably mean better interactivity. As the exact correlation w.r.t. perceived experience is hard to grasp, we perform a small-scale user study to capture the influence of flow-rate equality and AQM reduced latency on Zoom's QoE.

Limitations of this Study. However, our study is limited, as we had to limit the number of participants ($n = 10$) due to COVID-19 restrictions. As such, we also restricted the number of scenarios to keep the individual study duration to roughly 25 min. Additionally, we had to switch from synthetically generated videos (noise to maximize bandwidth utilization) that we used throughout Sect. 4 to real video-conferences. This makes it difficult to compare the video-flows' demands from our synthetic evaluation to this user study as the bandwidth demand varies with the compression rate (higher compression for actual webcam video). In summary, our study should only be regarded as an initial step.

In the following, we introduce the design and stimuli of our study and which metrics we are interested in. Subsequently, we present the results.

A.1   User Study Design

We perform a video conference where the subject interacts with an experiment assistant via Zoom focusing on interactivity and understandability to rate the quality and whether potentially degraded quality is acceptable when a concurrent download is active. The assistant reads short paragraphs of texts and the subject shortly summarizes them once the paragraph ended. This way, we test whether the video conference allowed for easy understanding but also represent the typical condition where conference attendees interrupt each other unintentionally. After 5 repetitions of summarizing, the subject and assistant alternately count to 10 to get a feeling for the delay, as proposed by the ITU [4]. Lastly, the assistant reads random numbers and the subject stops the assistant at a given number (unknown to the assistant) for the same reasons.

Quality Rating. After every run, the subject rates the overall, audio, video, and interactivity quality on a seven-point linear scale [5] (c.f., y-axis in Fig. 8). Moreover, the subject decides (yes/no) if communicating was challenging, whether the connection was acceptable at all, whether the quality was acceptable if they were downloading a file during a business or private call or when someone else was downloading documents or watching movies in parallel.

Test Conditions. We test 3 different scenarios using our previously described testbed; for all conditions, we shape the subject's link to 0.5 Mbps, adjust the min. RTTs to 50 ms and use a queue size of 10×BDP. The scenarios differ in whether an extra flow competes on the downlink and whether the queue is managed. In detail, in Scenario 1 (Tail-Drop) only Zoom is active using a tail-drop queue. Scenario 2 (Tail-Drop + Flow) adds a TCP CUBIC flow on the downlink, representing, e.g., a movie download. Scenario 3 (FQ_CoDel + Flow) adopts the TCP flow, but switches to the flow-queuing variant of CoDel.

Study Details. We perform a "within subject" lab study: each subject rates every test condition selected from a latin square to randomize the order. Each experiment takes about 5 min and is repeated for the 3 scenarios plus a training phase at the start using Scenario 1. In total, the 4 experiments plus rating take about 25 min. Although conducting studies with members familiar to the study is discouraged [4], we stick to the same experiment assistant to reduce variations.

Subject Recruitment. Our subjects are 10 colleagues from our institute which volunteered to take part and are strongly familiar with Zoom. We limited our study to these participants to reduce contacts during the pandemic. As such we were able to hold the conferences in the participant's first language.

A.2   Results

Figure 8a shows the mean opinion score and 95% confidence intervals of the quality rating (distributions checked for normality via a Shapiro-Wilk test). The confidence intervals are computed via the t-distribution due to our small sample

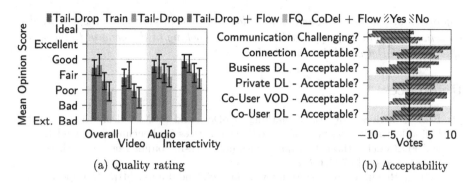

Fig. 8. User study quality rating and votes

size. Further, Fig. 8b shows the distributions of "Yes" (positive, to the right) and "No" (negative, to the left) answers for the different questions.

Generally looking at the plots we can see that the worst results stem from using FQ_CoDel, while using a tail-drop queue with no concurrent flow results in the best quality ratings. For the overall quality of the video conference and the video quality this difference is statistically significant as the confidence intervals do not overlap. However, for the scenarios where Zoom competes with TCP flows, the results are statistically insignificant and allow no statement. Similar, all audio quality and interactivity votes allow no statistically significant statement.

Flow-Queuing AQM Induced QoE Changes. Hence, interpreting these results is complex. What can be said is that CoDel's positive effect of reducing the queuing delay was not perceived by the users. On the other hand, also the reduction in bandwidth did not yield any statistically significant quality reduction. However, a trend against using FQ_CoDel is visible, but it cannot be statistically reasoned. Only following the trend, it might be not worth using FQ_CoDel due to its potentially worse QoE. Otherwise, only few users considered the connection unacceptable (c.f. Fig. 8b), surprisingly uncorrelated to whether FQ_CoDel was used or whether a concurrent flow was actually started. I.e., some users considered our scenarios generally as unacceptable regardless of FQ_CoDel.

Influence of Concurrent Downloads on Acceptability. Surprisingly, users also consider the quality unacceptable when imagining a concurrent download of documents in business or private conversations. We expected that users accept deteriorations, as they would not pay attention to the video conference, but want their download to complete. However, specifically in the business case, our users did not. Also quality deteriorations induced by other users downloading movies or documents were not seen more disturbing. I.e., independent of self-inflicted or not, some users do not accept quality deteriorations at all, while others do.

Takeaway. *Unfortunately, our study did not yield statistically conclusive results with respect to how participants perceive the difference in Zoom quality between using a tail-drop queue and FQ_CoDel when a flow competes. Also regarding acceptance, users did not see strong differences and either disliked the quality* *regardless of possible concurrent downloads as reasons or just accepted it, disagreeing on a generally applicable statement. Looking at the general trend of our study, FQ_CoDel could decrease QoE.*

References

1. Best Practices for Benchmarking CoDel and FQ CoDel. https://www.bufferbloat.net/projects/codel/wiki/Best_practices_for_benchmarking_Codel_and_FQ_Codel/#the-netem-qdisc-does-not-work-in-conjunction-with-other-qdiscs. Accessed 07 Oct 2020
2. System Requirements for Windows, macOS, and Linux. https://support.zoom.us/hc/en-us/articles/201362023-System-requirements-for-Windows-macOS-and-Linux. Accessed 07 Oct 2020
3. v4l2loopback. https://github.com/umlaeute/v4l2loopback Accessed 07 Oct 2020
4. ITU-T Recommendation P.920: Interactive test methods for audiovisual communications. Technical Report, ITU (2000)
5. ITU-T Recommendation P.851: Subjective quality evaluation of telephone services based on spoken dialogue systems. Technical Report, ITU (2003)
6. Adams, R.: Active queue management: a survey. IEEE Commun. Surv. Tutorials **15**(3), 1425–1476 (2013). https://doi.org/10.1109/SURV.2012.082212.00018
7. Briscoe, B.: Flow rate fairness: dismantling a religion. SIGCOMM CCR **37**(2), 63–74 (2007). https://doi.org/10.1145/1232919.1232926
8. Brosh, E., Baset, S.A., Misra, V., Rubenstein, D., Schulzrinne, H.: The delay-friendliness of TCP for real-time traffic. IEEE/ACM Trans. Networking. **18**(5), 1478–1491 (2010). https://doi.org/10.1109/TNET.2010.2050780
9. Cardwell, N.: BBR evaluation with netem. https://groups.google.com/d/msg/bbr-dev/8LYkNt17V_8/xyZZCwcnAwAJ (2017). Accessed 07 Oct 2020
10. Cardwell, N., Cheng, Y., Gunn, C.S., Yeganeh, S.H., Jacobson, V.: BBR: congestion-based congestion control: measuring bottleneck bandwidth and round-trip propagation time. Queue **14**(5), 20–53 (2016). https://doi.org/10.1145/3012426.3022184
11. Carlucci, G., De Cicco, L., Holmer, S., Mascolo, S.: Congestion control for web real-time communication. IEEE/ACM Trans. Networking **25**(5), 2629–2642 (2017). https://doi.org/10.1109/TNET.2017.2703615
12. Carlucci, G., De Cicco, L., Mascolo, S.: Controlling queuing delays for real-time communication: the interplay of E2E and AQM algorithms. SIGCOMM CCR **46**(3), 1–7 (2018). https://doi.org/10.1145/3243157.3243158
13. Chatranon, G., Labrador, M.A., Banerjee, S.: Fairness of AQM schemes for TCP-friendly traffic. In: Global Telecommunications Conference (GLOBECOM), vol. 2 (2004). https://doi.org/10.1109/GLOCOM.2004.1378056
14. De Cicco, L., Mascolo, S., Palmisano, V.: Skype video congestion control: an experimental investigation. Comput. Networks **55**(3), 558–571 (2011). https://doi.org/10.1016/j.comnet.2010.09.010
15. Demers, A., Keshav, S., Shenker, S.: Analysis and simulation of a fair queueing algorithm. In: SIGCOMM. ACM (1989). https://doi.org/10.1145/75246.75248
16. Feldmann, A., et al.: The lockdown effect: implications of the COVID-19 pandemic on internet traffic. In: Internet Measurement Conference IMC 2020. ACM (2020)
17. Ha, S., Rhee, I., Xu, L.: CUBIC: a new TCP-friendly high-speed TCP variant. SIGOPS Oper. Syst. Rev. **42**(5), 64–74 (2008). https://doi.org/10.1145/1400097.1400105

18. Hock, M., Bless, R., Zitterbart, M.: Experimental evaluation of BBR congestion control. In: International Conference on Network Protocols (ICNP) (2017). https://doi.org/10.1109/ICNP.2017.8117540
19. Jain, R.K., Chiu, D.M.W., Hawe, W.R.: A Quantitative Measure of Fairness and Discrimination for Resource Allocation in Shared Computer System. DEC Research Report TR-301 (1984)
20. Johansson, I., Sarker, Z.: Self-Clocked Rate Adaptation for Multimedia. RFC 8298, RFC Editor (December 2017)
21. Johansson, I.: SCReAM: Update and Test Case Results. https://www.ietf.org/proceedings/96/slides/slides-96-rmcat-0.pdf. [IETF-96 RMCAT]
22. Khademi, N., Ros, D., Welzl, M.: Evaluating CoDel, FQ_CoDel and PIE: how good are they really? https://www.ietf.org/proceedings/88/slides/slides-88-iccrg-4.pdf. [IETF-88 - ICCRG]
23. Kunze, I., Rüth, J., Hohlfeld, O.: Congestion control in the wild-investigating content provider fairness. IEEE Trans. Network Serv. Manage. **17**, 1224–1238 (2020). https://doi.org/10.1109/TNSM.2019.2962607
24. Liotta, A., Druda, L., Menkovski, V., Exarchakos, G.: Quality of experience management for video streams: the case of skype. In: 10th International Conference on Advances in Mobile Computing and Multimedia (MoMM 2012). ACM (2012). https://doi.org/10.1145/2428955.2428977
25. Rüth, J., Kunze, I., Hohlfeld, O.: An empirical view on content provider fairness. In: Network Traffic Measurement and Analysis Conference (TMA) (2019). https://doi.org/10.23919/TMA.2019.8784684
26. Scholz, D., Jaeger, B., Schwaighofer, L., Raumer, D., Geyer, F., Carle, G.: Towards a deeper understanding of TCP BBR congestion control. In: IFIP Networking Conference (IFIP Networking) and Workshops (2018). https://doi.org/10.23919/IFIPNetworking.2018.8696830
27. Ware, R., Mukerjee, M.K., Seshan, S., Sherry, J.: Beyond Jain's fairness index: setting the bar for the deployment of congestion control algorithms. In: Workshop on Hot Topics in Networks (HotNets 2019). ACM (2019). https://doi.org/10.1145/3365609.3365855
28. Ware, R., Mukerjee, M.K., Seshan, S., Sherry, J.: Modeling BBR's interactions with loss-based congestion control. In: The Internet Measurement Conference (IMC 2019). ACM (2019). https://doi.org/10.1145/3355369.3355604
29. Zhang, X., Xu, Y., Hu, H., Liu, Y., Guo, Z., Wang, Y.: Profiling skype video calls: rate control and video quality. In: INFOCOM. IEEE (2012). https://doi.org/10.1109/INFCOM.2012.6195805
30. Xu, Y., Yu, C., Li, J., Liu, Y.: Video telephony for end-consumers: measurement study of Google+, IChat, and Skype. In: Internet Measurement Conference (IMC 2012). ACM (2012). https://doi.org/10.1145/2398776.2398816
31. Zhu, J.: On traffic characteristics and user experience of Skype video call. In: International Workshop on Quality of Service (2011). https://doi.org/10.1109/IWQOS.2011.5931328
32. Zhu, X., Pan, R.: NADA: a unified congestion control scheme for low-latency interactive video. In: International Packet Video Workshop (2013). https://doi.org/10.1109/PV.2013.6691448

Characterizing Service Provider Response to the COVID-19 Pandemic in the United States

Shinan Liu[1]([☒]), Paul Schmitt[2], Francesco Bronzino[3], and Nick Feamster[1]

[1] University of Chicago, Chicago, USA
{shinanliu,feamster}@uchicago.edu
[2] Princeton University, Princeton, USA
pschmitt@cs.princeton.edu
[3] Université Savoie Mont Blanc, Chambéry, France
francesco.bronzino@univ-smb.fr

Abstract. The COVID-19 pandemic has resulted in dramatic changes to the daily habits of billions of people. Users increasingly have to rely on home broadband Internet access for work, education, and other activities. These changes have resulted in corresponding changes to Internet traffic patterns. This paper aims to characterize the effects of these changes with respect to Internet service providers in the United States. We study three questions: (1) How did traffic demands change in the United States as a result of the COVID-19 pandemic?; (2) What effects have these changes had on Internet performance?; (3) How did service providers respond to these changes? We study these questions using data from a diverse collection of sources. Our analysis of interconnection data for two large ISPs in the United States shows a 30–60% increase in peak traffic rates in the first quarter of 2020. In particular, we observe traffic downstream peak volumes for a major ISP increase of 13–20% while upstream peaks increased by more than 30%. Further, we observe significant variation in performance across ISPs in conjunction with the traffic volume shifts, with evident latency increases after stay-at-home orders were issued, followed by a stabilization of traffic after April. Finally, we observe that in response to changes in usage, ISPs have aggressively augmented capacity at interconnects, at more than twice the rate of normal capacity augmentation. Similarly, video conferencing applications have increased their network footprint, more than doubling their advertised IP address space.

1 Introduction

The COVID-19 pandemic has resulted in dramatic shifts in the behavioral patterns of billions of people. These shifts have resulted in corresponding changes in how people use the Internet. Notably, people are increasingly reliant on home broadband Internet access for work, education, and other activities. The changes in usage patterns have resulted in corresponding changes in network traffic

© Springer Nature Switzerland AG 2021
O. Hohlfeld et al. (Eds.): PAM 2021, LNCS 12671, pp. 20–38, 2021.
https://doi.org/10.1007/978-3-030-72582-2_2

demands observed by Internet service providers. Many reports have noted some of the effects of these changes from service provider networks [1,5], application providers [19,23], and Internet exchange points [20]. Generally, previous findings and conventional wisdom suggest that while overall traffic demands increased, the Internet responded well in response to these changing demands.

Previous work has shed light on the nature of the resulting changes in traffic patterns. In Europe, Internet exchange points saw a 15–20% increase in overall traffic volumes [3], in some cases resulting in peaks in round trip latency in some countries (e.g., Italy) that were approximately 30% higher than normal [12]. For cellular networks in the UK [16], because users were less mobile, downlink traffic volume decreased by up to 25%. While some of the characteristics of shifting traffic demands are known, and certain aspects of the Internet's resilience in the face of the traffic shifts are undoubtedly a result of robust design of the network and protocols, some aspects of the Internet's resilience are a direct result of providers' swift responses to these changing traffic patterns. This paper explores these traffic effects from a longitudinal perspective—exploring traffic characteristics during the first half of 2020 to previous years—and also explores how service providers *responded* to the changes in traffic patterns.

Service providers and regulatory agencies implemented various responses to the traffic shifts resulting from COVID-19. AT&T and Comcast have made public announcements about capacity increases in response to increases in network load [1,5]. The Federal Communications Commission (FCC) also announced the "Keep Americans Connected" initiative to grant providers (such as AT&T, Sprint, T-Mobile, U.S. Cellular, Verizon, and others) additional spectrum to support increased broadband usage [9]. Web conferencing applications Zoom and WebEx were also granted temporary relief from regulatory actions [9]. These public documents provide some perspectives on responses, but to date, there are few independent reports and studies of provider responses. This paper provides an initial view into how some providers responded in the United States.

We study the effects of the shifts in Internet traffic resulting from the COVID-19 pandemic response on Internet infrastructure. We study three questions:

- *How did traffic patterns change as a result of COVID-19?* Traffic volumes and network utilization are changing as a reaction to changes in user behaviors. It is critical to measure the exact alterations in a long time span.
- *What were the resulting effects on performance?* Considering an expected surge around the dates when states issued stay-at-home orders or declared states of emergency, we seek to observe possible changes in the latency and throughput of network traffic across locations. Further, different ISPs also have different capacity and provisioning strategies, which provides us a finer granularity based on these differences.

– *How did ISPs and service providers respond?* Finally, to deal with the usage boosts and performance degradations during the COVID-19 response, operations and reactions of ISPs and service providers were taken which may explain the changes in network performance. The answer to this question informs us of the networks robustness and their effective disaster provisioning strategies. These questions have become increasingly critical during the COVID-19 pandemic, as large fractions of the population have come to depend on reliable Internet access that performs well for a variety of applications, from video conferencing to remote learning and healthcare.

To answer these questions, we study a diverse collection of datasets about network traffic load, through granular measurements, proprietary data sharing agreements, and user experiences, as well as extensive baseline data spanning over two years.

Summary of Findings. First, we study the traffic pattern changes in the United States (Sect. 4) and find that, similar to the changes previously explored for European networks, our analysis reveals a 30–60% increase in peak traffic volumes. In the Comcast network in particular, we find that downstream peak traffic volume increased 13–20%, while upstream peak traffic volume increases by more than 30%. Certain interconnect peers exhibit significant changes in the magnitude of traffic during the lockdown. Second, we observe a temporary, statistically significant increase in latency lasting approximately two months (Sect. 5). We observe a temporary increase of about 10% in average latency around the time that stay-at-home orders were issued. Typical latency values returned to normal a few months after these orders were put in place. We also find heterogeneity between different ISPs. Finally, we explore how service providers responded to this increase in traffic demands by adding capacity (Sect. 6). ISPs aggressively added capacity at interconnects, more than 2x the usual rates. On a similar note, application service providers (e.g., video conferencing apps) increased the advertised IP address space by 2.5–5x to cope with the corresponding 2–3x increase in traffic demand.

2   Related Work

The pandemic response has modified people's habits, causing them to rely heavily on the Internet for remote work, e-learning, video streaming, etc. In this section, we present some previous efforts in measuring the effects of COVID-19 and past disaster responses on networks and applications.

Network Measurements During COVID-19. Previous work has largely focused on aggregate traffic statistics surrounding the initial COVID-19 lockdowns. Traffic surged about 20% in Europe for broadband networks [12]. In the United States, a blog post [18] reveals that the national downstream peak traffic has recently stabilized, but in the early weeks of the pandemic, it showed a growth of 20.1%. For wireless networks in the US, volume increases of up to 12.2% for voice and 28.4% for data by the top four providers were shown in an industry report [6]. Mobile networks in the UK reported roughly 25% drops in downlink data traffic volume [16]. Industry operators have self-reported on their network responses largely through blog posts [1,5,14,17].

For traffic performance changes, different patterns appear in different regions. Facebook shows that less-developed regions exhibited larger performance degradations through their analysis of edge networks [2]. Network latencies were approximately 30% higher during the lockdown in Italy [12]. According to an NCTA report, networks in the United States saw less congestion [18]. Due to decreased user mobility, cellular network patterns have shifted [16]: The authors found a decrease in the average user throughput as well as decreased handoffs. Feldmann et al. [12] observed that the fixed-line Internet infrastructure was able to sustain the 15–20% increase in traffic that happened rapidly during a short window of one week.

Our work differs from and builds on these previous studies in several ways: First, this study extends over a longer time frame, and it also uses longitudinal data to compare traffic patterns *during* the past six months to traffic patterns in previous years. Due to the nascent and evolving nature of COVID-19 and corresponding ISP responses, previous studies have been limited to relatively short time frames, and have mainly focused on Europe. Second, this work explores the ISP *response* to the shifting demands and traffic patterns; to our knowledge, this work is the first to begin to explore ISP and service provider responses.

Application Measurements During COVID-19. Previous work has also studied application usage and performance, such as increases in web conferencing traffic, VPN, gaming, and messaging [12]. Favale et al. studied ingress and egress traffic from the perspective of a university network and found that the Internet proved capable of coping with the sudden spike in demand in Italy [8]. Another paper used network traffic to determine campus occupancy at the effect of COVID-19 related policies on three campus populations across Singapore and the United States [25]. The cybercrime market was also statistically modeled during the COVID-19 era to characterize its economic and social changes [24].

Network Measurements of Other Disasters. While COVID-19 responses are ongoing and evolving, making measurement efforts incomplete, network responses under other disastrous events can be informative. In 2011, the Japan earthquake of Magnitude 9.0 caused circuit failures and subsequent repairs within a major ISP. Nationwide, traffic fell by roughly 20% immediately after the earthquake. However, surprisingly little disruption was observed from outside [4]. In 2012, Hurricane Sandy hit the Eastern seaboard of the United States and caused regional outages and variances over the network [15]. For human-caused disasters such as the September 11th attacks, routing, and protocol data were analyzed to demonstrate the resilience of the Internet under stress. Their findings showed that although unexpected blackouts did happen, they only had a local effect [21]. Oppressive regimes have also caused Internet outages, such as a complete Internet shutdown due to censorship actions during the Egypt and Libya revolts [7], where packet drops and BGP route withdrawals were triggered intentionally.

Although there have been several preliminary measurements of the effects of the COVID-19 response, none have holistically studied traffic data, performance analysis, routing data, and ISP capacity information together, as we do in this paper. It is crucial to collect and correlate such information to better understand the nature of both traffic demands, the effects of these changes on performance, and the corresponding responses. This paper does so, illuminating the collaborative view of responses of service providers in the United States.

3   Data

We leverage multiple network traffic datasets to facilitate our study:

Traffic Demands and Interconnect Capacity: Internet Connection Measurement Project. We leverage a dataset that includes network interconnection statistics for links between 7 anonymized access ISPs and their neighboring partner networks in the United States [11]. These access networks contain about 50% of broadband subscribers across all states within America. At each interconnect interface connecting a neighboring partner network, the access ISP collects IPFIX data. The dataset contains roughly 97% of links (paid peering, settlement-free peering, and ISP-paid transit links) from all participating ISPs. All of the links represented in the dataset are private (i.e., they do not involve public IXP switch fabrics). The dataset consists of flow-level statistics over five-minute intervals, including: timestamp, region (as access ISPs may connect to a partner network in multiple geographic regions), anonymized partner network, access ISP, ingress bytes, egress bytes, and link capacity. In terms of either bytes or packets over a period of time, each five-minute interval provides the sum of the utilization of traffic flows that were active during that interval. We also calculate secondary statistics from the dataset, including: timestamp for the peak ingress and egress hour for each day on each link in terms of usage, ingress/egress peak hour bytes, and daily 95th and 99th percentile usage.

Performance Data: Federal Communications Commission Measuring Broadband America (MBA). We analyze the FCC's ongoing nationwide performance measurement of broadband service in the United States [10]. The raw data is collected from a collection of distributed measurement devices (named Whiteboxes) placed in volunteer's homes across all states of America and operated by SamKnows. The sample includes tiers composed by the top 80% of the subscriber base for each ISP and is representative. Measurements are conducted on an hourly basis. The dataset includes raw measurements of several performance metrics, such as timestamp, unit ID, target server, round trip time, traffic volume, etc. Each Whitebox also includes information pertaining to its ISP, technology, and state where it is located. We also define dates related to the status of the pandemic response (e.g., stay-at-home orders, state of emergency declaration, etc.). Based on these, we can compute more statistics for specified groups (e.g., break into ISPs): average and standard deviation among Whiteboxes, daily 95th and 99th percentile latency/throughput.

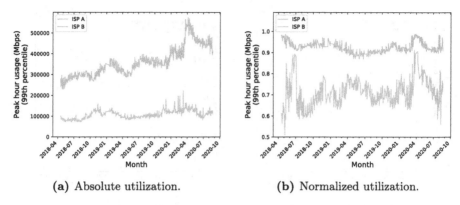

(a) Absolute utilization.   **(b)** Normalized utilization.

Fig. 1. 99th percentile interconnect link utilization for two ISPs.

To keep the network capacity consistent and to record eventual changes solely based on utilization factors, we pre-process the MBA dataset with several filters. First, we filter the non-continuous data within the dates of interest (Dec. 1st, 2019 to June, 30th 2020, and the previous year) to capture successive shifts. Then, we eliminate the Whiteboxes which do not aggregate a statistically significant amount of data, such as some states, ISPs, and technologies with limited data (e.g., satellite). Finally, we choose the measurements from Whiteboxes to the top 10 most targeted servers across the United States to represent the overall US performance. We take this decision because servers with less measurements will have higher variance in sample, and introduce unexpected errors when tracked across time. These servers are sparsely located in major cities of the US and they have the most Whiteboxes (over 200 for each ISP) connecting with them.

IP Prefix Advertisements: RouteViews. To gain insight into changes in IP address space, we parse Internet-wide BGP information globally from several locations and backbones via RouteViews. Raw RIBs (Routing Information Bases) files were obtained from RouteViews [22] data on a weekly basis. The average of each Tuesday is computed to represent that week. The RIBs are then parsed to obtain IPv4 Prefix-to-Autonomous System (AS) relationships, including mappings of IP prefix, prefix length, paths of AS numbers. In Sect. 6.2, we compute the total advertised IPv4 spaces for AS numbers associated with two popular video conferencing applications: Zoom and Cisco WebEx [9].

4 How Did Traffic Demands Change?

Because most previous studies [3,12,16] focus on Europe, we begin our explorations by validating whether similar traffic changes are observed in the United States. We consider peak hour link utilization from the Interconnect Measurement Project as a measure of traffic demand. We pre-process the interconnect dataset and remove anomalous data points that are caused by failures in the

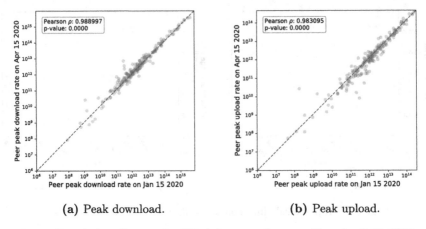

(a) Peak download.   (b) Peak upload.

Fig. 2. Peer link utilization for ISP A between January 15 to April 15, 2020.

measurement system. In particular, we do not analyze dates that are greater than two standard deviations outside of a 60-day rolling mean for each link. Due to confidentiality reasons, we present the results in aggregation for the United States as a whole.

Figure 1 shows both the absolute utilization and the utilization normalized against the link capacity for two anonymized ISPs. For each ISP, we plot the value corresponding to the 99th percentile link utilization for a given day. We observe from Fig. 1a that ISP A saw a dramatic increase in raw utilization at roughly the same time as the initial COVID-19 lockdowns (early March 2020), with values tapering off slightly over the summer of 2020. ISP B, on the other hand, saw a smaller raw increase in utilization for its 99th percentile links. To better understand whether ISP B's smaller increase is a byproduct of different operating behaviors, we explore possible trends in the normalized data (Fig. 1b). Here we see that both ISPs experienced significant increases in utilization in March and April 2020.

We also investigated how traffic patterns changed between ISP A and each of its peers, in both the upstream and downstream directions. For this analysis, we focused on the dates around the utilization peaks shown in Fig. 1. We compared the peak hour download and upload rates on all of ISP A's interconnects on (1) January 15, 2020, and (2) April 15, 2020 (Fig. 2). In general, we see that traffic patterns to peers do not vary greatly between the two dates. We do see, however, that traffic volumes to (and from) some peers change significantly—some by several orders of magnitude. The identities of the peers are anonymous in the dataset, but some patterns are nonetheless clear: For example, some peers show an increase of upstream utilization by two or three orders of magnitude. Such drastic changes may be attributable to users working from home and connecting to services that would cause more traffic to traverse the peer link in the upstream direction. We confirmed these results with the operators at ISP A and report that they observed that streaming video traffic decreased from 67 to 63% of the

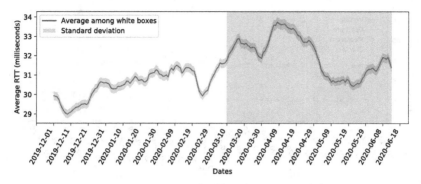

Fig. 3. Daily changes of latency from Dec. 2019 to June 2020. The lockdown period is marked in red. Change in average latency across the non-satellite ISPs in the FCC MBA program reflect a small (2–3 ms) but significant increase in overall average latency. (Note: y-axis does not start at zero.)

total traffic, but video conferencing increased from 1% to 4% as a percentage of overall traffic.

5   What Was the Effect on Performance?

The surge in interconnect utilization poses a challenge for service providers, as high utilization of interconnects can potentially introduce high delays for inter-active traffic, packet loss, or both. These effects can ultimately be observed through changes in latency (and, potentially, short-term throughput). To examine whether we can observe these effects, we look into the latency and throughput reported by the Measuring Broadband America (MBA) dataset [10]. We explore these effects over the course of several years to understand whether (and how) performance anomalies that we observe during COVID-19 lockdown differ significantly from performance anomalies observed during other time periods.

5.1   How Performance Changed After Lockdown

To better understand how performance changed during the COVID-19 lockdown in the United States, we explored how latency evolved over the course of 2020. To establish a basis for comparison, we show the time period from late 2019 through mid-2020. The Appendix also contains a similar analysis for the 2018–2019 time period. We compute the average latency per-Whitebox per-day, and subsequently explore distributions across Whiteboxes for each ISP. (As discussed in Sect. 3, we consider only Whiteboxes in fixed-line ISPs for which there are an adequate number of Whiteboxes and samples.) We use March 10th[1], the average declaration of emergency date [13], to mark the beginning of the COVID-19 pandmic phase (red shaded for figures).

---

[1] Note that this is also the launch date of Call of Duty Warzone.

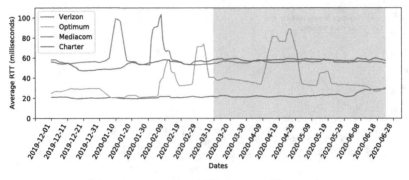

(a) 95th percentile of ISP latency (Group 1).

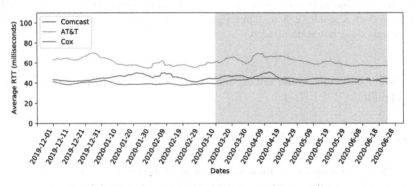

(b) 95th percentile of ISP latency (Group 2).

Fig. 4. Latency (95th percentile) for different ISPs.

Longitudinal Evolution of Aggregate, Average Round-Trip Latency.
Figure 3 shows a seven-day moving average of average round-trip latencies
between all Whiteboxes in this study. We observe an increase in average round-
trip latency by as much as 10%, this increase in mean latency is significant,
corresponding to 30x standard deviation among all Whiteboxes. At the end of
April, latencies return to early 2020 levels. It is worth noting that, although this
increase in average latency is both sizable and significant, similar deviations and
increases in latency have been observed before (see the Appendix for comparable
data from 2018–2019). Thus, although some performance effects are visible during the COVID-19 lockdown, the event and its effect on network performance are
not significantly different from other performance aberrations. Part of the reason for this, we believe, may be the providers' rapid response to adding capacity
during the first quarter of 2020, which we explore in more detail in Sect. 6.

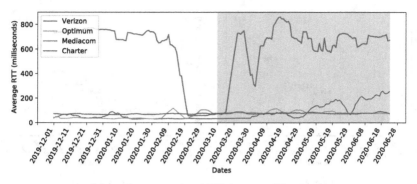

(a) 99th percentile of ISP latency (Group 1).

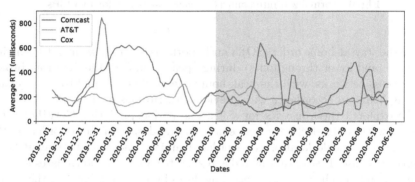

(b) 99th percentile of ISP latency (Group 2).

Fig. 5. Latency (99th percentile) for different ISPs.

Longitudinal Evolution of Per-ISP Latencies. In addition to the overall changes in performance, we also explored per-ISP latency and throughput effects before and during the COVID-19 lockdown period. Figures 4 and 5 show these effects, showing (respectively) the 95th and 99th percentiles of average round-trip latency across the Whiteboxes. These results show that, overall 95th percentile latency across most ISPs remained stable; 99th percentile latency, on the other hand, did show some deviations from normal levels during lockdown for certain ISPs. Notably, however, in many cases the same ISPs experienced deviations in latency during other periods of time, as well (e.g., during the December holidays).

5.2 Throughput-Latency Relationship

High latencies can sometimes be reflected in achieved throughput, given the inverse relationship between TCP throughput and round-trip latency. To explore whether latency aberrations ultimately result in throughput effects, as well as how those effects manifest at different times of day, we explored the distribution of latencies before COVID-19 emergency declarations (ED), after the ED but

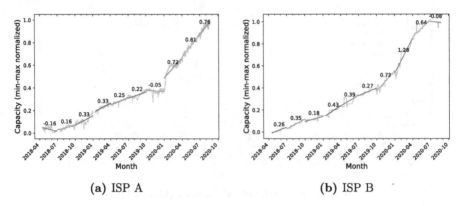

Fig. 6. Normalized interconnect capacity increases for two ISPs.

before the stay-at-home order (SO). Our hypothesis was that we might see higher latencies (and lower throughputs) during "peak hours" of the day from broadband access networks, with the peak hours effectively expanded to the weekday working hours, in accordance with previous descriptions of these effects [5].

We explored these metrics for a baseline period predating COVID-19, the time between state declaration of emergency and stay at home ordered [13], after stay-at-home declarations were ordered, and two months after stay-at-home ordered. Because these dates differed across states, we used known dates for each state [13] and matched the corresponding dates for each state against the known location of the Whiteboxes.

Figure 11 shows the distribution throughput and latency distributions across all Whiteboxes for four time intervals, plotted in four-hour intervals. From Fig. 11a, it is clear that the quantiles, median, and maximum latencies all exhibit effects that correlate with these time periods, which are consistent with the latency changes in Fig. 3.

The period between ED and SO corresponds to abrupt routing changes, and the latency data thus reflects a corresponding degradation during this time interval, perhaps at least partially due to the fact that providers cannot immediately respond after the initial emergency declaration (we discuss the timeframes during which capacity was added to the networks in Sect. 6). As the transition continues, SO appears to be a point in time where latency stabilizes. Figure 11b shows that distributions of throughput measurements are more robust, although the upper end of the distribution is clearly affected, with maximum achieved throughputs lower. The median and minimum have negligible changes during time periods in late April suggesting (and corresponding to) aggressive capacity augmentation, which we discuss in more detail in Sect. 6.

6   How Did Service Providers Respond?

In this section, we study how service providers responded to the changes in traffic demands. We focus on the capacity changes during lockdown by inspecting two data sources: (1) to understand how ISPs responded by adding capacity to interconnects, we study the interconnect capacity of two large ISPs in the United States; and (2) to understand how video service providers expanded their network footprints in response to increasing demand, we analyze IPv4 address space from two major video conference providers—WebEx and Zoom—and find that both providers substantially increased advertised IP address space.

6.1   Capacity Increases at Interconnect

We begin by exploring how ISPs responded to changing traffic demands by adding network capacity at interconnect links. To do so, we use the Interconnect Measurement Project dataset. We calculate the total interconnect capacity for each ISP by summing the capacities for all of the links associated with the ISP. To enable comparison between ISPs that may have more or less infrastructure overall, we normalize the capacity values for each using min-max normalization. We again filter out date values that are beyond two standard deviations from a rolling 60-day window mean. To show aggregate infrastructure changes over time, we take all of the data points in each fiscal quarter and perform a least-squares linear regression using SciKit Learn. This regression yields a slope for each quarter that illustrates the best-fit rate of capacity increases over that quarter. We scale the slope value to show what the increase would be if the pace was maintained for 365 days (i.e., a slope of 1 would result in a doubling of capacity over the course of a year). Figure 6 shows the resulting capacity plots.

The overall trend shows how these two ISPs in the United States aggressively added capacity at interconnects—at more than twice the rate at which they were adding capacity over a comparable time period in the previous year. Second, both ISPs significantly added capacity in the first quarter of 2020—at a far greater rate than they were adding capacity in the first quarter of 2019. Recall from the usage patterns shown in Fig. 1, ISP A tends to operate their links at nearly full capacity, in contrast to ISP B, where aggregate utilization is well below 90%. Both ISPs witnessed a jump in usage around the lockdown; the response of aggressively adding capacity appears to have mitigated possible adverse effects of high utilization rates. The increase in capacity was necessary to cope with the increased volume: although network performance and utilization ratios returned to pre-COVID-19 levels, the *absolute* traffic volumes remain high.

6.2   Increased Advertised IP Address Space

To cope with abrupt changes caused by COVID-19, application service providers also took action to expand their infrastructure. Previous work has observed shifted traffic in communication applications (such as video conferencing apps, email, and messaging) after lockdown [12]. It has been reported informally that many application providers expanded serving infrastructure, changed the routes of certain application traffic flows, and even altered the bitrates of services to cope with increased utilization.

While not all of these purported responses are directly observable in public datasets; however, RouteViews makes available global routing information, which can provide some hints about routes and infrastructure, and how various characteristics of the Internet routing infrastructure change over time. This data can provide some indication of expanding infrastructure, such as the amount of IPv4 address space that a particular Autonomous System (AS) is advertising. In the case of video conference providers, where some of the services may be hosted on cloud service providers or where the video service is a part of a larger AS that offers other services (e.g., Google Meet), such a metric is clearly imperfect, but it can offer some indication of response.

To understand how service providers announced additional IPv4 address space, we parsed BGP routing tables from RouteViews [22]. For each route that originates from ASes of certain application providers, we aggregate IP prefixes and translate the resulting prefixes into a single count of overall IPv4 address space. We focus on two popular video conferencing applications, Zoom and WebEx, since they are two of the largest web conference providers in the United States—as also recognized by the FCC in their recent order for regulatory relief [9]. We track the evolution of the advertised IP address space from the beginning of 2019 through October 2020.

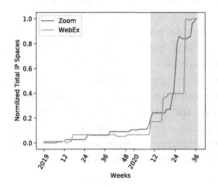

Table 1. Advertised IPv4 space.

App	Min	Max
Zoom	9,472	46,336
WebEx	110,080	265,728

Fig. 7. Normalized advertised IPv4 space. Red: COVID-19 pandemic phase.

Figure 7 demonstrates how each provider increased the advertised IPv4 address space from before the pandemic through October 2020. After the beginning of the COVID-19 pandemic, both Zoom and WebEx rapidly begin to advertise additional IPv4 address space. Table 1 enumerates the absolute values of advertised IP address space: Zoom and WebEx increased the advertised IP address space by about 4x and 2.5x respectively, as we observe a roughly corresponding 2–3x increase in video conferencing traffic.

7   Conclusion

This paper has explored how traffic demands changed as a result of the abrupt daily patterns caused by the COVID-19 lockdown, how these changing traffic patterns affected the performance of ISPs in the United States, both in aggregate and for specific ISPs, and how service providers responded to these shifts in demand. We observed a 30–60% increase in peak traffic rates for two major ISPs in the US corresponding with significant increases in latency in early weeks of lockdown, followed by a return to pre-lockdown levels, corresponding with aggressive capacity augmentation at ISP interconnects and the addition of IPv4 address space from video conferencing providers. Although this paper presented the first known study of interconnect utilization and service provider responses to changes in patterns resulting from the COVID-19 pandemic, this study still offers a somewhat limited viewpoint into these effects and characteristics. Future work could potentially confirm or extend these findings by exploring these trends for other ISPs, over the continued lockdown period, and for other service providers.

Acknowledgements. This research was funded in part by NSF Award CNS-2028145 and a Comcast Innovation Fund grant. We also thank CableLabs for their help with acquisition of data from ISP interconnects.

Appendix A   Longitudinal Latency Evolution for 2018–2019 (Previous Year)

This section provides a basis for performance comparison in Sect. 5. Following the same analysis, we choose the exact same time period in the previous year (i.e., late 2018 to mid-2019) in the United States. We compute the average latency per-Whitebox per-day, and subsequently explore distributions across Whiteboxes for each ISP.

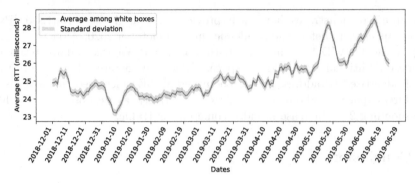

Fig. 8. Daily changes of latency from Dec. 2018 to June 2019. (Note: y-axis does not start at zero.)

Longitudinal Evolution of Aggregate, Average Round-Trip Latency. Figure 8 shows the aggregate average latency per-Whitebox per-day. The previous year has an overall latency of about 6ms lower than 2020. We observe that the latency keeps stable until the end of April, where a deviation of about 2 ms is shown. The rate of increase is of about 10%, echoing similar effects around lockdown.

Longitudinal Evolution of per-ISP Latencies. We further break the aggregate results into the granularity of ISPs. We report both 95th and 99th percentile latencies here. Note that in the 95th percentile plot, we show the groups differently, mainly because of major differences of latency for Mediacom and AT&T compared to other ISPs. From Fig. 9, we find that the majority of ISPs performed stably, while Mediacom has a large variance in the average RTT. They both have a tail that contributes to what we observed in Fig. 8. Figure 10 is grouped the same as Fig. 5, which shows that for certain ISPs, they experience similar deviations in latency during similar periods of different years.

Appendix B   Throughput-Latency Relationship

We put a supplementary figure referred to in Sect. 5 in this appendix. It shows the distributional changes in latency and throughput on a 4-h basis. Detailed explanations are in the main text.

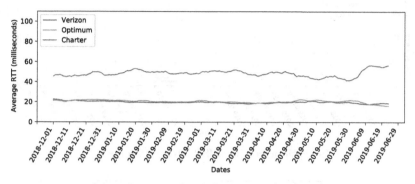

(a) 95th percentile of ISP latency (Group 1)

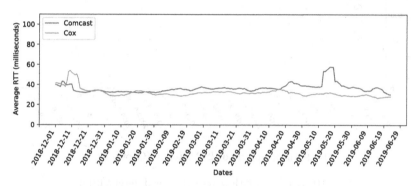

(b) 95th percentile of ISP latency (Group 2)

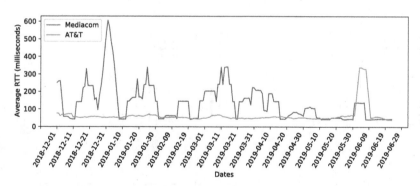

(c) 95th percentile of ISP latency with unstable changes (Group 3)

Fig. 9. Latency (95th percentile) for different ISPs.

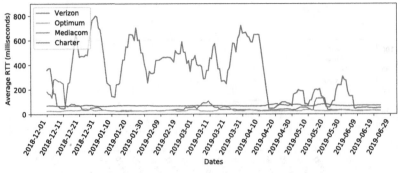

(a) 99th percentile of ISP latency (Group 1)

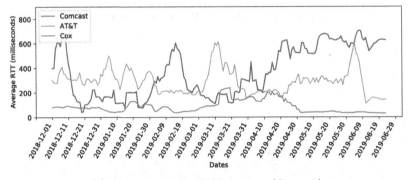

(b) 99th percentile of ISP latency (Group 2)

Fig. 10. Latency (99th percentile) for different ISPs.

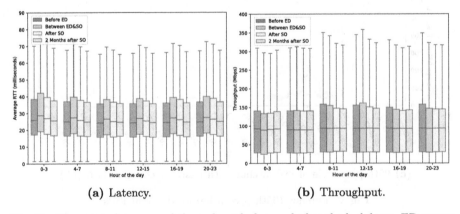

(a) Latency.   (b) Throughput.

Fig. 11. Changes in latency and throughput before and after the lockdown. ED means "Emergency is declared" SO means "Stay-at-home Ordered".

References

1. AT&T: COVID-19: Our Response. https://about.att.com/pages/COVID-19.html. Accessed Oct 2020
2. Böttger, T., Ibrahim, G., Vallis, B.: How the internet reacted to COVID-19 - a perspective from facebook's edge network. In: ACM IMC (2020)
3. Candela, M., Luconi, V., Vecchio, A.: Impact of the COVID-19 pandemic on the internet latency: a large-scale study. arXiv preprint arXiv:2005.06127 (2020)
4. Cho, K., Pelsser, C., Bush, R., Won, Y.: The Japan earthquake: the impact on traffic and routing observed by a local ISP. In: Proceedings of the Special Workshop on Internet and Disasters, pp. 1–8 (2011)
5. Comcast: COVID-19 Network Update. https://corporate.comcast.com/covid-19/network/may-20-2020. Accessed Oct 2020
6. CTIA: The Wireless Industry Responds to COVID-19: Network Performance. https://www.ctia.org/homepage/covid-19#network-performance. Accessed Oct 2020
7. Dainotti, A., et al.: Analysis of country-wide internet outages caused by censorship. In: Proceedings of the 2011 ACM SIGCOMM Conference on Internet Measurement Conference, pp. 1–18 (2011)
8. Favale, T., Soro, F., Trevisan, M., Drago, I., Mellia, M.: Campus traffic and e-learning during COVID-19 pandemic. Computer Networks (2020)
9. FCC: Keep Americans Connected. https://www.fcc.gov/keep-americans-connected. Accessed Oct 2020
10. FCC: Measuring Broadband Raw Data Releases. https://www.fcc.gov/oet/mba/raw-data-releases. Accessed Oct 2020
11. Feamster, N.: Revealing utilization at internet interconnection points. TPRC (2016)
12. Feldmann, A., et al.: The lockdown effect: Implications of the covid-19 pandemic on internet traffic. In: Internet Measurement Conference (IMC 2020) (2020)
13. Foundation, W.: U.S. state and local government responses to the COVID-19 pandemic. https://en.wikipedia.org/wiki/U.S._state_and_local_government_responses_to_the_COVID-19_pandemic. Accessed Oct 2020
14. Google: Keeping our network infrastructure strong amid COVID-19. https://blog.google/inside-google/infrastructure/keeping-our-network-infrastructure-strong-amid-covid-19/. Accessed Oct 2020
15. Heidemann, J., Quan, L., Pradkin, Y.: A preliminary analysis of network outages during hurricane sandy. University of Southern California, Information Sciences Institute (2012)
16. Lutu, A., Perino, D., Bagnulo, M., Frias-Martinez, E., Khangosstar, J.: A characterization of the covid-19 pandemic impact on a mobile network operator traffic. In: ACM IMC (2020)
17. McKeay, M.: Parts of a Whole: Effect of COVID-19 on US Internet Traffic. https://blogs.akamai.com/sitr/2020/04/parts-of-a-whole-effect-of-covid-19-on-us-internet-traffic.html.Accessed Oct 2020
18. NCTA: COVID-19: How Cable's Internet Networks Are Performing: Metrics, Trends & Observations. https://www.ncta.com/COVIDdashboard. Accessed Oct 2020
19. Nokia: Network traffic insights in the time of COVID-19: April 9 update. https://www.nokia.com/blog/network-traffic-insights-time-covid-19-april-9-update/. Accessed Oct 2020

20. OECD: Keeping the Internet up and running in times of crisis. https://www.oecd.org/coronavirus/policy-responses/keeping-the-internet-up-and-running-in-times-of-crisis-4017c4c9/. Accessed Oct 2020
21. Partridge, C., et al.: The internet under crisis conditions: learning from September 11. Comput. Commun. Rev. **33**(2), 1–8 (2003)
22. RouteViews: University of Oregon Route Views Project. http://www.routeviews.org/routeviews/. Accessed Oct 2020
23. Sandvine: COVID-19 Global Internet Trends. https://www.sandvine.com/covid-19-trends/. Accessed Oct 2020
24. Vu, A.V., et al.: Turning up the dial: the evolution of a cybercrime market through set-up, stable, and COVID-19 eras. In: ACM IMC (2020)
25. Zakaria, C., Trivedi, A., Chee, M., Shenoy, P., Balan, R.: Analyzing the impact of COVID-19 control policies on campus occupancy and mobility via passive wifi sensing. arXiv preprint arXiv:2005.12050 (2020)

A First Look at COVID-19 Domain Names: Origin and Implications

Ryo Kawaoka[1] , Daiki Chiba[2] , Takuya Watanabe[2], Mitsuaki Akiyama[2] ,
and Tatsuya Mori[3(✉)]

[1] Waseda University, Tokyo, Japan
k-hsw119@nsl.cs.waseda.ac.jp
[2] NTT Secure Platform Laboratories, Musashino, Japan
daiki.chiba@ieee.org, watanabe@nsl.cs.waseda.ac.jp, akiyama@ieee.org
[3] Waseda University/NICT/RIKEN AIP, Tokyo, Japan
mori@seclab.jp

Abstract. This work takes a first look at domain names related to COVID-19 (Cov19doms in short), using a large-scale registered Internet domain name database, which accounts for 260 M of distinct domain names registered for 1.6 K of distinct top-level domains. We extracted 167 K of Cov19doms that have been registered between the end of December 2019 and the end of September 2020. We attempt to answer the following research questions through our measurement study: **RQ1:** *Is the number of Cov19doms registrations correlated with the COVID-19 outbreaks?*, **RQ2:** *For what purpose do people register Cov19doms?* Our chief findings are as follows: (1) Similar to the global COVID-19 pandemic observed around April 2020, the number of Cov19doms registrations also experienced the drastic growth, which, interestingly, pre-ceded the COVID-19 pandemic by about a month, (2) 70% of active Cov19doms websites with visible content provided useful information such as health, tools, or product sales related to COVID-19, and (3) non-negligible number of registered Cov19doms was used for malicious purposes. These findings imply that it has become more challenging to distinguish domain names registered for legitimate purposes from others and that it is crucial to pay close attention to how Cov19doms will be used/misused in the future.

Keywords: COVID-19 · Domain names · Phishing · Blocklist

1 Introduction

Several researchers have conducted Internet measurement studies to understand how the COVID-19 pandemic affected the Internet and user behaviors [2,4,8,9, 15]. Favale et al. and Feldmann et al. [8,9] explored the changes in Internet traffic, Lutu et al. [15] explored the changes in traffic and its impact on user mobility in mobile operators, Candela et al. [4] analyzed the impact of Internet traffic changes

© Springer Nature Switzerland AG 2021
O. Hohlfeld et al. (Eds.): PAM 2021, LNCS 12671, pp. 39–53, 2021.
https://doi.org/10.1007/978-3-030-72582-2_3

on network latency, and Boettger et al. [2] analyzed the changes in social media access patterns and the implications. The details of these studies will be discussed in Sect. 5.

To the best of our knowledge, there has been no academic study that has analyzed the impact of COVID-19 in terms of registered domain names. This work takes a first look at domain names related to COVID-19 (Cov19doms in short), using a large-scale set of registered domain names. We note that the only literature we have been able to find on this subject is a blog article [6], which analyzed the domain names associated with COVID-19. The article reported that the number of COVID-19 domain name registrations has spiked in mid-March 2020, with some days seeing the registration of more than 5,000 Cov19doms. However, we found that the data used in the article contained many false positives due to the naive string match heuristics. Also, this data is no longer updated since May 2020, so we cannot perform a longer-term analysis using the data. In this study, we attempt to extract Cov19doms accurately and analyze how it changes over a long period of time.

With so many of us keeping an eye on COVID-19 and spending more and more of our time online, it is crucial to understand the origins and implications of Cov19doms. Given these backgrounds in mind, we attempt to answer the following research questions:

RQ1: *Is the number of Cov19doms registrations correlated with the COVID-19 outbreaks?*

RQ2: *For what purpose do people register Cov19doms?*

To address the research questions, we compiled an exhaustive list of Cov19doms using a large-scale registered Internet domain name database [7], which accounted for 260 M of distinct domain names registered for the 1.6 K of top-level domains. Using the dataset, we found that at least 167 K of distinct Cov19doms containing strings such as "covid" or "corona" have been registered from the end of December 2019 to the end of September 2020. We attempt to study how domain name registration behavior changed with the emergence of COVID-19; i.e., we examine whether or not the time-series of COVID-19 infections is correlated with the time series of domain name registrations.

Next, from the 167K of Cov19doms, we extracted active websites that used Cov19doms by checking DNS A record and HTTP/HTTPS response. We then randomly sampled 10,000 of the Cov19doms websites to study how Cov19doms are used in the wild. By applying cluster analysis to the screenshots, we systematically classified 10 K websites. For the remaining general websites, we performed manual inspection with the aid of three evaluators. We also leveraged online virus-testing services to check whether some Cov19doms were used for malicious activities.

Our chief findings are as follows:

- Similar to the global COVID-19 pandemic observed around April 2020, the number of Cov19doms registrations also experienced drastic growth, which, surprisingly, preceded the COVID-19 pandemic by about a month.

- 70% of active Cov19doms websites with visible content provided useful information such as health, tools, or product sales related to COVID-19.
- Non-negligible number (roughly 4%) of registered Cov19doms have been used for malicious purposes such as phishing or malware distribution.

These findings imply that it has become more challenging to distinguish between domain names registered for legitimate purposes and those that are not. It was also indicated that it is necessary for researchers who analyze domain names, and even operators and blacklisters who take security measures based on domain names to pay close attention to how Cov19doms currently parked or in preparation will be used/misused in the future.

2   Data

2.1   Collecting Cov19doms

To collect registered Cov19doms, we used a large-scale commercial domain name database, domainlist.io [7]. This database contains snapshots of approximately 260M domain names taken from 1.6K of different TLDs, and we continued to retrieve data daily from 27 December 2019 to 20 September 2020. Of the $98,940,555$ domain names that have been newly registered since December 27, 2019, we first extracted the domain names that contained "covid" or "corona" as a substring. As a result, we obtained a total of $170,846$ Cov19doms. We note that this approach could include false positives such as "covideo.co.uk", for instance. However, we can safely ignore the effect of false positives in the following analysis, as our manual inspection of the randomly sampled data showed that the occurrence of such false positives was extremely rare as these words are. We believe that these words, especially in the COVID-19 era, are mostly used in the context of a specific purpose, i.e., "severe acute respiratory syndrome coronavirus 2," resulting in fewer false positives.

To study the characteristics of the Cov19doms, it is essential that we can get information about the creation date of the domain names. Therefore, we used the WHOIS information for the extracted Cov19doms to obtain information on the date and time the domain name was created. If the creation date of a domain name was older than December 27, 2019, those domain names were excluded from the following analysis. This resulted in a total of 166,825 Cov19doms, as shown in Table 1. To ensure that domains registered before December 27, 2019 were not related to COVID-19, we manually checked on them and found it be correct. In fact, most of them were related to Coronado city in California, U.S.

We investigated where the specific words related to COVID-19, i.e., "covid" and "corona", are located in the left-most labels of Cov19doms (e.g., "covidcare" in `covidcare[.]example`) and confirmed that (a) 59.6% are at the beginning, (b) 24.2% are at the end, and (c) 16.2% are in the middle of them. The patterns (a) and (b) mean that the left-most labels of Cov19doms were generated by concatenating any character at the beginning or end of the COVID-19-related words such as "covid". We believe that patterns (a) and (b) are less likely to cause

Table 1. Statistics of extracted Cov19doms data.

	Orig. Cov19doms	WHOIS check	DNS check	HTTP/HTTPS check
# of domain names	170,846	166,825	144,522	77,333

false positives than pattern (c). We further investigated the extent to which similar COVID-19-related words, "covid", "covid19", and "covid-19", are included in Cov19doms and found that they are 41,718, 32,671, and 10,120 Cov19doms, respectively. These numbers do not overlap, because we checked Cov19doms that contain "covid19" and "covid-19" earlier. It is interesting that "covid19" is more common in Cov19doms than its formal name of the desease, "covid-19". Among these, "covid" was most frequently included in Cov19doms, and as far as we manually checked, the majority of cases (about 40%) were used in the context of the COVID-19. One of the reasons why "covid" is included in Cov19doms in large numbers is that there are cases where various numbers are added to the end of "covid" (e.g., covid-2019, covid-2020, and covid-2021). We expect those domain names to have been acquired for speculative purposes.

We looked into what country registered Cov19doms firstest by usinig WHOIS registrant information. Of the 165,185 Cov19doms we extracted, 153,243 domains had valid WHOIS registrant country information. Among the countries, United States was the first to register Cov19doms. The top-5 countries registered Cov19doms were United States (85,970), Canada (17,229), Panama (6,781), Germany (4,533) and United Kingdom (4,237).

2.2 Collecting Active Websites Using Cov19doms

With the aim of studying the usage of Cov19doms, we extract the active websites that are operating using Cov19doms. To extract active websites, we first check the DNS A record to determine if an IP address is assigned to the extracted Cov19doms. We then send an HTTP/HTTPS request to the domain name where the DNS A record exists, and record the response. Specifically, we check if a connection can be established to Port 80 and Port 443 of each host that had a Cov19dom. Next, if a connection with either port can be established, we made an HTTP/HTTPS request to those hosts and checked whether the content could be retrieved from them. This step removes websites that caused connection timeouts and/or TLS errors such as invalid certificate. These steps resulted in a total of 77,333 of active websites that use Cov19doms, as shown in Table 1.

3   Measurement Study

Figure 1 presents an overview of the measurement processes. We first study the correlation between the number of COVID-19 infections and the number of Cov19doms registrations (Sect. 3.1). For this analysis, we used the statistics on the number of COVID-19 infections by country, provided by WHO [22]. We then study how Cov19doms are used for various websites (Sect. 3.2). The classification

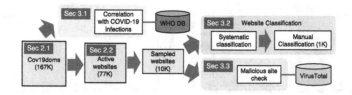

Fig. 1. Overview of the measurement processes.

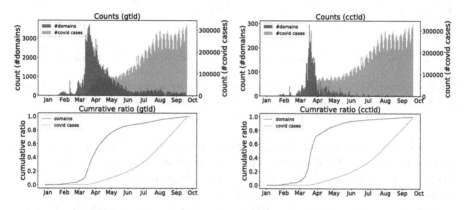

Fig. 2. Number of COVID-19 infections and Cov19doms registrations over time. Cases for gTLD (left) and ccTLD (right).

of active websites operated using Cov19doms was manually performed by three evaluators. Due to the large number of websites to be analyzed, we conducted a random sampling study. Finally, we report the analysis of Cov19doms that have been used for malicious activities (Sect. 3.3). We used VirusTotal [1] to investigate the presence of malicious sites using Cov19doms.

3.1 Number of New Infections and Cov19doms Registrations

We analyze the online behavior of people around the world in response to the unprecedented event of COVID-19 through the lens of DNS. Specifically, we examine whether or not the time series of COVID-19 infections is correlated with the time series of domain name registrations.

First, we investigate the time series of new registrations of Cov19doms and the number of new COVID-19 infections worldwide. We take all Cov19doms and split them into groups of gTLDs (e.g., `.com`) and ccTLDs (e.g., `.uk`). We obtained information on the number of COVID-19 infections from the official WHO website [22]. Figure 2 shows the time series of the number of new COVID-19 infections and the number of new registrations in Cov19doms (gTLD and ccTLD). These figures show that similar to the situation of the COVID-19 pandemic outbreak around the world around April 2020, Cov19doms saw a significant increase in its new registrations as well. Surprisingly, the number of new domain name

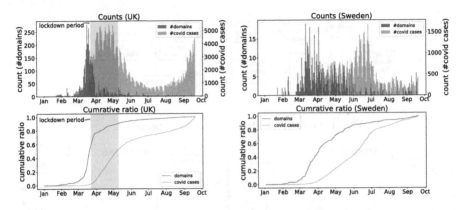

Fig. 3. Number of COVID-19 infections and Cov19doms registrations over time. Cases for UK (left) and SE (right). In Sweden, no lockdown enforcement was taken.

registrations peaked around March 2020, about a month ahead of the peak in the number of new COVID-19 infections. Subsequently, the number of new registrations of Cov19doms has reached a stable daily registration rate, but the number of COVID-19 infections has still increasing as of October 2020.

Second, we focus on the Cov19doms of ccTLDs and investigate the relationship between the number of new registrations of Cov19doms per ccTLD and the number of new COVID-19 infections in the country corresponding to the ccTLD over time. Our Cov19doms data included only four ccTLDs: United Kingdom (.uk), Sweden (.se), Niue (.nu), and Australia (.au). We excluded .nu, for which no information on the number of WHO infected people existed there, and .au, for which we were unable to obtain the full domain name registration date from the WHOIS data, and conducted a survey of 4,766 .uk and 549 .se Cov19doms. Figure 3 shows the time-series change in the number of new infections of Cov19doms and COVID-19 in the UK and Sweden, respectively. Since the lockdown was implemented in the UK, the period is also shown in .uk graph. In both cases, Cov19doms registrations tend to be more likely to be ahead of the COVID-19 infection explosion. Furthermore, we find that registration of Cov19doms moves faster and clearer in the UK than in the Sweden case.

Our results obtained so far above indicate two things: (1) events like COVID-19 that affect so many people's lives will create a massive demand for domain names and (2) people are anticipating such demand and taking the action of registering domain names at an amazingly early stage. In subsequent sections, we will clarify for what purpose people are registering these Cov19doms.

3.2   Understanding the Usage of Cov19doms

In general, automatic website classification is not an easy task as the modern web is composed of rich and complex multimedia, making it difficult to automatically analyze its contents using simple data processing scheme. Therefore, instead of fully automating the website classification process, this work adopted manual inspection to ensure the quality of the classification. However, the number of Cov19doms we have collected is so large that it is infeasible to inspect them all manually. Therefore, we took the approach of applying random sampling to reduce the number of domains/websites to be analyzed. As shown in Figure 1, we randomly sampled 10 K of websites from 77 K active Cov19doms websites to reduce the number of samples to be classified by human. For the 10K of randomly sampled Cov19doms websites, we took the following two-stage approach.

In the first stage, we aim to systematically classify websites into the following categories: *Empty, Error, Parked, Hosted,* and Has content, where *Empty* represents cases in which HTTP/HTTPS requests were responded to, but the data was empty, *Error* represents the websites responded with error codes such as 404 or 501, *Parked* represents the domain parking websites, *Hosted* represents cases where the domain name has been purchased, but the website only shows the initial page after installation of Apache, WordPress, etc., and *Has content* represents the remaining Cov19doms websites that have some content. In the second stage, three evaluators manually classify the websites classified as "Has content." In the following, we present the details of the analysis to be performed at each stage and the results obtained.

Stage 1: Systematic Classification. We classify websites into the five classes defined above based on HTTP/HTTPS response codes and screenshot information. Among the five classes, the classification of empty and error is simple. They can be classified by analyzing the size of the data retrieved and the response code. For the remaining classes parking and hosted, we use cluster analysis. For parking, we could use domain name registrar information in some cases, however, our preliminary study shows that we cannot do a comprehensive study due to the existence of so many different domain parking companies. The key idea is that the majority of websites that are accessed for parking and hosted are similar in appearance. Therefore, we apply cluster analysis to the screenshot images and classify the websites by determining whether each cluster is *Parked* or *Hosted* or *Has content.* With this approach, we can streamline the classification.

To perform clustering of screenshot images, we need to calculate the distance between images; i.e., it is necessary to compute the similarity of images. There are several methods for computing the similarity of images, and in this paper, we adopt the perceptual hash (pHash) [23], which computes close hash values for two similar images. pHash is widely used to discover copyright infringement and is known to be effective in discovering resemblances to certain images.

We first accessed 10K of randomly sampled active websites and extract HTML, screenshots, and other metadata by navigating Google Chrome[1] using Selenium [18]. The language was set to English, and the User-Agent was set to Windows 10 Google Chrome. To not halm the websites set to be investigated, access to the IP address corresponding to each Cov19dom is limited twice (HTTP

---

[1] We used the version of 81.0.4044.129.

Table 2. Result of systematic classification.

Category	# of active websites	Fraction (%)
Empty	609	6.1
Error	1,663	16.6
Parked	2,138	21.4
Hosted	1,402	14.0
Has contents	4,188	41.9
Total	10,000	100.0

and HTTPS). Next, we computed the pHash values for the 10,000 screenshots we collected, using imageHash [3]. We then grouped the corresponding Cov19doms with the same value of pHash and HTTP status code pairs into the same cluster. Table 2 presents the classification result of the Cov19dom websites. From the table, we can see that many of the Cov19doms websites resulted in either domain parking or errors, and that 40% of the websites (classified as "Has content") requires detailed manual inspection. We note that 60% of the websites categorized as other than "Has content" do not currently provide any useful content, however, they might start providing some content in the future, so we need to pay attention to them. In the following, we will classify the websites categorized as "Has content."

Stage 2: Manual Classification. In the second stage, we will classify the Cov19doms websites marked as "Has content" in the Stage 1. Since 4K of websites are too many to analyze manually, further random sampling is performed and 1,000 general websites will be carefully classified by three evaluators. Through the Stage 1 classification, the classification categories for Stage 2 were predetermined and provided to the evaluators with detailed explanations. Figure 4 presents a screenshot image of a tool developed by the authors to help evaluators efficiently classify websites. Although the evaluators made a classification based on screenshot image and metadata, there are cases that cannot necessarily be determined by screenshot or metadata. For example, if the evaluators could not understand the language used in the web content, they also leveraged external resources such as a search engine.

Three evaluators used the tool to classify 1,000 of websites marked as "General" taking 4.8 h on average, resulting in 477 websites where the three evaluators agreed, 423 websites where the two evaluators agreed, and 100 websites where they all disagreed. That is, for 90% of the websites, at least two evaluators' classification results were consistent. The result of calculating the Fleiss' kappa coefficient, which is a quantitative measure of inter-rater agreement, was 0.50, which can be interpreted as moderate agreement [13]. The results of the interviews with the three evaluators revealed that the primary reason for the disagreement was the difference in the decisions they made when they were unsure of their classification. One

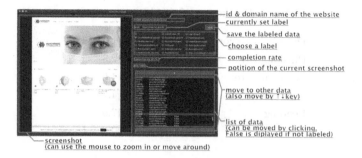

Fig. 4. A screenshot of the website classification tool we developed for our analysis.

Table 3. Results of manual classification.

Category	Description	#sites
Health	Websites providing information on health*	405
Sales	Websites selling products related to COVID-19	109
Tools	Websites providing apps/maps/dashboards of COVID-19	123
Activities	Websites dedicated to people's activities to address COVID-19**	72
Social security	Websites regarding to social security	2
Unrelated	Websites unrelated to COVID-19	139
Login	Websites showing a login page	26
Index of	Websites showing the "Index of /" page	24
Unknown	Websites with discrepancies between the evaluators' classifications	100
Total	–	1,000

* hospitals, infection testing, sterilization, and other health-related topics.
**Fundraising, volunteering, business, and political movements regarding COVID-19.

of the evaluators reported that he categorized all of his confusion as "activities for COVID-19." Discrepancies in judgments also arose because of the existence of websites that could be classified into multiple categories. For example, a website that displays medical products (masks, face shields) may be categorized as both Health and Sales. Apart from such discrepancies, the classifications were generally consistent and the manual classification results can be considered reasonable. In the final classification, a majority vote was adopted. Websites with discrepancies between the three evaluators' classification results were marked as "Unknown."

Table 3 presents the classification results. About 70% of the websites were related to COVID-19. Those websites were medical services, selling products, providing COVID-19 information such as apps, maps and dashboards, supporting people's activities related to COVID-19, and social security. As would be expected from the nature of COVID-19, the majority of the websites (40%) were medical-related. Many of these health-related websites are critical sources of information in countering COVID-19 pandemic and should never be blocked. The remaining 30% were completely irrelevant websites, websites with no content displayed, and "Unknown," which we defined earlier.

Table 4. Breakdown of the detection results.

Detected category	# detections	fraction (%)
Phishing site	117	32.8
Malicious site	52	14.6
Malware site	17	4.7
Pending	171	47.9
Total	357	100.0

3.3   Malicious Activities Using Cov19doms

Finally, we investigate whether Cov19dom websites were involved in any malicious activities. To achieve this goal, we utilize VirusTotal, a large-scale online virus scanning service. As shown in Figure 1, we target 10K of active websites that had Cov19doms. Of the 10 K websites, 6,362 of the websites were detected as malicious by at least one or more scanners. This is an alarming number, but when we analyzed the detection results, we found that one online scanner detected 6,256 websites as malicious, and that the majority of them (about 98.7%) were classified as phishing sites. Although we cannot determine from our data whether or not these detections were correct, the result does suggest that there may be a non-negligible number of malicious sites that use Cov19doms. On the other hand, one of the reasons why online scanners may falsely detect Cov19doms as a phishing site is likely to be naïve detection using keyword matching. For example, a scheme that increases the probability of detecting a website with a domain name containing the strings corona or covid-19 as a malicious site could be employed. However, such an approach might have the risk of blocking websites that provide important information about COVID-19.

To reduce the effect of false positives from individual scanners, we examined websites that were detected as malicious by at least two online scanners. We note that this approach is consistent with the best practice used in many papers that make use of multiple engines/vendors of VirusTotal for the labeling task [16]. As a result, we found that the number was 357, which accounted for roughly 4% of the active Cov19doms websites. The detection categories of those detected by two or more online scanners are summarized in Table 4. Note that a website may be detected as a different category (e.g., phishing site and malware site) by several online scanners . In such cases, the category is decided by majority vote, and if the category is not uniquely determined, the category is marked as "pending". It can be seen that once again, phishing sites have the highest number of detections, but the number of other malicious sites is also very close.

4   Discussion

4.1   Limitations

This study aims to understand the Cov19doms in the wild. In order to ensure the accuracy of the results, two heuristics were applied to extract such domain names, as described in Sect. 2. The first heuristic was to limit the domain search words to "covid" and "corona." Such limitation will miss several cases where domain names contain other keywords such as "virus" or "mask," which could bring false positives as we discussed. We also limited our search to the e2LD part; the limitation will eliminate the cases where an FQDN contains the substrings in its hostname. Another heuristic was to constrain the registration date for domain names.

Our analysis also excluded websites that did not include keywords in their domain name but were COVID-19-related in their website content. Such websites existed on both malicious and benign sites. Another limitation that we are aware of is that the URL path is not taken into account when creating a URL from an FQDN. We only retrieved web content from the top directory on a website in the web-crawling process. Exploring the URL path might reduce the errors shown in the Table 2, however we may miss web content if a website does not configure the setting of index file. Addressing these issues is left for future study.

4.2 Detecting Malicious Cov19doms

As we have shown in this work, simply using a list of Cov19doms as a blocklist may result in false positives, and this introduces the risk of blocking information that is useful for COVID-19 countermeasures. In order to determine if a detected Cov19dom is malicious, we need to monitor a domain name when it is being abused and examine the content in a timely manner. The Trademark Clearinghouse (TMCH) is a global database of trademarks and provides this information to registries and registrars during the domain name registration process to thwart unwanted domain name registrations by third-parties. This is effectively used by trademark owners to fight against a trademark infringement using fake domain names. Unfortunately, this countermeasure is not effective against domain names piggybacking on global crises including COVID-19, due to the fact that there is no right owner of such corresponding keywords. Szurdi and Christin proposed the anti-bulk registration policy such as dynamic pricing to make bulk domain registrations expensive [19], which is a potential countermeasure against bulk-registered COVID-19 domain names.

4.3 Ethical Considerations

Our study analyzed publicly available DNS records and web content corresponding to the domain names without collecting personally-identifiable information. In our web-crawling process, we sent the minimum amount of legitimate requests to websites, i.e., two requests (HTTP and HTTPS) per site, and left them and their users unharmed.

5   Related Work

In this section, we present several related works and clarify how our work differs.

Internet Measurement Driven by COVID-19. Favale et al. [8] analyzed the impact of the lockdown enforcement on a campus network in Italy. Through analyzing Internet traffic statistics, they revealed that while incoming traffic was reduced by a factor of 10 during the lockdown, outgoing traffic increased by 2.5 times, driven by more than 600 daily online classes, with around 16,000 students per day. They concluded that the campus network infrastructure is robust enough to successfully cope with the drastic changes while maintaining the university operations. Feldmann et al. [9] conducted similar analysis using traffic data collected at one ISP, three IXPs, and one educational network. They reported on changes in Internet traffic in various perspectives and concluded that the Internet infrastructure has been able to deliver the increased Internet traffic without significant impact.

Candela et al. [4] conducted a large-scale analysis of Internet latencies, which could be affected by the increased amount of online activities during the lockdown. By leveraging the measurement data collected with the RIPE Atlas platform [17], they analyzed Internet latencies focusing on Italy, where people experienced more than a month of lockdown. They reported that the increase in online activity led to an increase in the variability of Internet latencies, a trend that intensified in the evening due to the increase in the entertainment traffic.

Event-Driven Domain Name Registration. The strategy of early acquisition of domain names associated with ongoing events has been a well-known approach in the domain name business community. In fact, a patent of such a technique was filed by an Internet domain registrar [14]. Although event-driven domain registration is a widely known best practice in the domain name business community, to the best of our knowledge, there has been little research on the topic in the research community. One of the few available studies is that Coull et al. [5] derived rules to describe topics, such as ongoing events, from popular Google search queries with the aim of characterizing the registration of speculative domain names and empirically evaluated the feasibility of domain acquisition based on such a method. While they attempted to extract current events using Google search, COVID-19 is a unique phenomenon, and researchers have not had an opportunity to study domain names for such a case.

Tombs et al. [21] tried to determine the level of credibility of a top-level coronavirus-related website that purport to be government websites, and find out the purpose of non-governmental entity or company register a top-level coronavirus-related domain name by analyzing data collected from 303 websites which domains related to COVID-19 between April 5 and April 6, 2020. They found that 80% of websites presented as government websites cannot be verified the authenticity. Additionally, about 30% of websites collected had unverified information and nearly half were squatting domains or "under construction." Government websites providing critical information about coronaviruses should not be subject to ambiguous in their authenticity, and therefore should not share the top-level domain name space with non-governmental entity or company. Their findings are important in establishing trusted communication channel between government and their citizens during this crisis.

Malicious Domain Names and Websites. Much research has been conducted on ways to observe the registration and early activity of malicious domain names [10,12,20]. Hao et al. [10] unveiled that DNS infrastructures and early DNS lookup patterns for a newly registered malicious domain name differ significantly from those with a legitimate domain name. Korczynski et al. [12] collected WHOIS information, web content, and DNS records for corresponding malicious domain names provided from 11 distinct abuse feeds and observed a growing number of spam domains in new gTLDs, indicating a shift from legacy gTLDs to new gTLDs. We conducted our measurement by referring to the ways practiced in these existing studies. While these studies analyzed fake domain names containing strings related to brand names having specific owners, our study focuses on domain names containing strings related to generic crisis having no specific owners, which makes it be challenging to distinguish between malicious and legitimate domain names.

There are few academic studies so far on detection of malicious domain names related to COVID-19. Ispahany and Islam developed a machine learning model using lexical features to detect malicious domain names and examined registered domain names in April 2020 [11]. The purpose of our study is not to detect malicious Cov19doms, but to investigate the usage of Cov19doms. Furthermore, our study utilized a long-term dataset obtained from the end of December 2019 to the end of September 2020.

6   Conclusion

Through the analysis of 167K of Cov19doms we collected, we found that a month before the global COVID-19 pandemic hit in April 2020, there was a flood of domain name registrations. This phenomenon can be attributed to a variety of people registering domain names for the purpose of COVID-19 countermeasures, speculative domain name business, or to generate phishing sites, as they predicted the high impact of COVID-19. Such a global, high-impact phenomenon is unprecedented in the past and is a remarkable event from the perspective of Internet measurement. In conventional measures against the registration of unwanted domain names targeting brands, distinguishing between an original domain name and a fake domain name has been relatively straightforward since the brand owner has been determined. In the case of the Cov19doms, on the other hand, there is no concept of a brand owner, and many different players have registered Cov19doms to benefit society. Therefore, it is not feasible to apply traditional domain name analysis methods. As this study revealed, majority of Cov19doms (about 60%) are not active. Even if Cov19doms are uesd for active websites, many of them are parked or hosted, and it is not clear how these domain names will change in the future. Addressing these problems is a challenge for the future. We plan to release our dataset and tools used for our analyses at https://github.com/cov19doms/cov19doms.

References

1. VirusTotal. https://www.virustotal.com/
2. Boettger, T., Ibrahim, G., Vallis, B.: How the Internet reacted to COVID-19. In: Proceedings of the Internet Measurement Conference 2020 (Nov 2020)
3. Buchner, J.: imagehash - A Python Perceptual Image Hashing Module. https://github.com/JohannesBuchner/imagehash (2020)
4. Candela, M., Luconi, V., Vecchio, A.: Impact of the COVID-19 pandemic on the internet latency: a large-scale study. Comput. Networks **182**, 107495 (2020)
5. Coull, S.E., White, A.M., Yen, T.F., Monrose, F., Reiter, M.K.: Understanding domain registration abuses. In: Rannenberg, K., Varadharajan, V., Weber, C. (eds.) Security and Privacy - Silver Linings in the Cloud, pp. 68–79. Springer, Berlin, Heidelberg (2010)
6. Cyber Threat Coalition: 2020–05-26 Weekly Threat Advisory (2020). https://www.cyberthreatcoalition.org/advisories/2020-05-26-weekly-threat-advisory
7. DOMAINLISTS.IO: Lists of all domains updated daily. https://domainlists.io/ (2020)
8. Favale, T., Soro, F., Trevisan, M., Drago, I., Mellia, M.: Campus traffic and e-learning during covid-19 pandemic. Comput. Networks **176**, 107290 (2020). https://doi.org/10.1016/j.comnet.2020.107290
9. Feldmann, A., et al.: The lockdown effect: implications of the COVID-19 pandemic on internet traffic. In: Proceedings of the Internet Measurement Conference 2020 (Nov 2020)
10. Hao, S., Feamster, N., Pandrangi, R.: Monitoring the initial DNS behavior of malicious domains. In: Proceedings of the 2011 ACM SIGCOMM Conference on Internet Measurement Conference IMC 2011, pp. 269–278, Association for Computing Machinery, New York, NY, USA (2011). https://doi.org/10.1145/2068816.2068842
11. Ispahany, J., Islam, R.: Detecting malicious URLs of COVID-19 pandemic using ML technologies (2020)
12. Korczynski, M., Wullink, M., Tajalizadehkhoob, S., Moura, G.C.M., Noroozian, A., Bagley, D., Hesselman, C.: Cybercrime after the sunrise: a statistical analysis of DNS abuse in new gTLDs. In: Proceedings of the 2018 on Asia Conference on Computer and Communications Security (ASIACCS 2018), pp. 609–623, Association for Computing Machinery, New York, NY, USA (2018). https://doi.org/10.1145/3196494.3196548
13. Landis, J.R., Koch, G.G.: The measurement of observer agreement for categorical data. Biometrics, pp. 159–174 (1977)
14. Lee, Y.: Generating domain names relevant to current events. US Patent 20100146119A1, Dec 2008
15. Lutu, A., Perino, D., Bagnulo, M., Frías-Martínez, E., Khangosstar, J.: A characterization of the COVID-19 pandemic impact on a mobile network operator traffic. In: Proceedings of the Internet Measurement Conference 2020 (Nov 2020)
16. Peng, P., Yang, L., Song, L., Wang, G.: Opening the blackbox of virustotal: analyzing online phishing scan engines. In: Proceedings of the Internet Measurement Conference (IMC 2019), pp. 478–485, Association for Computing Machinery, New York, NY, USA (2019). https://doi.org/10.1145/3355369.3355585
17. RIPE NCC: RIPE Atlas (2020). https://atlas.ripe.net/
18. Selenium: Selenium - A browser automation framework and ecosystem (2020). https://github.com/SeleniumHQ/selenium

19. Szurdi, J., Christin, N.: Domain registration policy strategies and the fight against online crime. In: Proceedings (online) of the Fourteenth Workshop on the Economics of Information Security (WEIS). Innsbruck, Austria (Jun 2018)
20. Tian, K., Jan, S.T.K., Hu, H., Yao, D., Wang, G.: Needle in a haystack: Tracking down elite phishing domains in the wild. In: Proceedings of the Internet Measurement Conference 2018 (IMC 2018), pp. 429–442, Association for Computing Machinery, New York, NY, USA (2018). https://doi.org/10.1145/3278532.3278569
21. Tombs, N., Fournier-Tombs, E.: Ambiguity in authenticity of top-level coronavirus-related domains. In: Special Issue on COVID-19 and Misinformation 1 the Harvard Kennedy School (HKS) Misinformation Review (2020). https://doi.org/10.37016/mr-2020-036
22. World Health Organization (WHO): WHO Coronavirus Disease (COVID-19) Dashboard (2020). https://covid19.who.int/
23. Zauner, C.: Implementation and benchmarking of perceptual image hash functions (2010). https://www.phash.org/

Web Security

Clairvoyance: Inferring Blocklist Use on the Internet

Vector Guo Li[1], Gautam Akiwate[1(✉)], Kirill Levchenko[2],
Geoffrey M. Voelker[1], and Stefan Savage[1]

[1] University of California, San Diego, USA
gul027@eng.ucsd.edu, gakiwate@cs.uscd.edu
[2] University of Illinois Urbana-Champaign, Champaign, USA

Abstract. One of the staples of network defense is blocking traffic to
and from a list of "known bad" sites on the Internet. However, few organizations are in a position to produce such a list themselves, so prag-
matically this approach depends on the existence of third-party "threat
intelligence" providers who specialize in distributing feeds of unwelcome
IP addresses. However, the choice to use such a strategy, let alone which
data feeds are trusted for this purpose, is rarely made public and thus
little is understood about the deployment of these techniques in the wild.
To explore this issue, we have designed and implemented a technique to
infer proactive traffic blocking on a remote host and, through a series of
measurements, to associate that blocking with the use of *particular* IP
blocklists. In a pilot study of 220K US hosts, we find as many as one
fourth of the hosts appear to blocklist based on some source of threat
intelligence data, and about 2% use one of the 9 particular third-party
blocklists that we evaluated.

1 Introduction

Over the last decade, the use of threat information sharing—commonly labeled
"threat intelligence"—has become a staple in any discussion of network defense.
Based on the premise that by broadly sharing information about known threats,
organizations can better protect themselves, a burgeoning industry has emerged
to collect, aggregate and distribute such information [6,40], largely consisting
of lists of IP addresses, domain names or URLs thought to be associated with
particular classes of threats (a.k.a., *indicators of compromise*).

However, despite all the promises, it is far from clear how people actually
adopt threat intelligence data, especially for proactive traffic blocking, commonly
called "blocklisting". Proactively blocking traffic based on threat intelligence
data is uniquely attractive to a defender, since, if effective, it can foreclose threats
without requiring attention from a human analyst. However, it is also a strong
action, and recent work by Li et al. [23] has shown that threat intelligence
feeds can be far from comprehensive and may include significant numbers of
false positives that might cause an organization to inadvertently block benign

© Springer Nature Switzerland AG 2021
O. Hohlfeld et al. (Eds.): PAM 2021, LNCS 12671, pp. 57–75, 2021.
https://doi.org/10.1007/978-3-030-72582-2_4

sites. Given this, it is important to understand the extent to which network administrators are using such data to block network traffic in practice.

Motivated by this issue, our work seeks to infer if online hosts use threat intelligence IP feeds (IP blocklists) to proactively block network traffic. The principal challenge in pursuing this question is that such decisions are largely invisible: a network choosing to block IP address A or not is indistinguishable from a third vantage point, as this vantage point does not have access to either the network or IP address A. Moreover, for operational security reasons, few organizations are willing to publicly document the details of their network defenses.

In this paper, we describe an inference technique, based on the IP ID increment side-channel (inspired by previous work focused on censorship detection [11,29]), to detect network-layer blocklisting. Our design is both specialized to the unique characteristics of IP blocklists (e.g., dynamic, overlapping membership) and is designed to be conservative with respect to common sources of network measurement error (hence a finding of blocking is robust). To evaluate this technique, we test against known ground truth data and then conduct a large-scale pilot study with over 220K U.S. hosts and against 9 popular IPv4 blocklists. In the two cases where network operators were willing to share their blocking configuration with us, they were in perfect agreement with our findings.

Across our pilot study, we identified 4,253 hosts (roughly 2% of the hosts we surveyed), consistently using at least one of the 9 lists that we tested against. We also established that a larger fraction (roughly a fourth) of the hosts we surveyed make use of some form of security-related blocking and reliably block traffic to at least some subset of the IP addresses in our lists. This significant level of security-related blocking is particularly surprising as our pilot study is biased towards older machines with minimal traffic (a cohort that we would not have associated with organizations having an aggressive network security posture).

2   Background

There is a large body of literature concerning the use of various kinds of "threat intelligence" (not always using that term). One popular focus among these is evaluating their effectiveness, including works that analyze coverage and accuracy of spam blocklists [30,37], phishing blocklists [35], and malware domain blocklists [20]. Others have explored techniques to better populate such lists, including Ramachandran et al.'s work on inferring botnet IP addresses from DNSBL lookups [33], and the work of Hao et al. for predicting future domain abuse [13,14] (among others). More recently, Thomas et al. explored the value of sharing threat intelligence data across functional areas (e.g., mail spam, account abuse, search abuse) and found limited overlap and significant numbers of false positives [39]. Many of these results are echoed by Li et al. [23].

However, there is comparatively little work focused on understanding how threat intelligence data is being used in practice. Indeed, the literature that exists is primary driven by surveys [31,34] and not validated by any empirical measurement.[1]

There also has been significant empirical exploration of Internet connection blocking in the setting of Internet freedom and access. Indeed, there are a range of studies that measure connection block in the context of Internet censorship [2,4, 10,28,43], geo-blocking [1,25,27], and Tor blocking [18,36]. Most of these studies rely on vantage points sited in the target networks being studied, and so are not directly helpful in our work. However, recent work by Ensafi et al. [11] and Pearce et al. [29] has removed this requirement using an indirect side channel technique to test connectivity between pairs of remote hosts. While our approach differs in a number of ways from theirs, it is inspired by the same idea of using IP ID to infer if a remote host sent an IP packet.

The *IP ID traffic side channel* has been well-known since mid 1990s. In particular, the Identification (ID) field of an IPv4 packet is a 16-bit value in the IP packet header, designed to support fragmentation by providing a unique value that can be used to group packet fragments belonging to the same IP datagram [32]. The simplistic approach using a per-host global counter to ensure unique IP ID values implicitly encodes the *number* of packets sent. Thus, by probing a host multiple times one can use the value of the returned IP ID to infer how many packets have been sent by the remote host *between* the two probes. This side channel has been employed for a wide variety of measurement purposes, including anonymous port scanning [3], host alias detection [38] and enumerating hosts behind NATs [5] among others. While most operating systems no longer use such a simple approach, it is still reasonably common across the Internet. For example, all versions of Windows up to version 7 used the global increment algorithm [19].

3   Methodology

In this section, we first describe our inference technique, using the IP ID side channel (Sect. 2), that determines if a particular host uses a known blocklist. The intuition here is that if a *reflector*—a host suitable for our technique—blocks all blocklist IPs from one particular blocklist, then it is likely that the particular blocklist is being used for blocking traffic at the network-layer. Next, we detail criteria of suitable reflectors (Sect. 3.2), and our criteria when sampling blocklist IPs (Sect. 3.3). Finally, we discuss additional validation measures (Sect. 3.4) and ethical concerns (Sect. 3.5).

3.1   Technique Overview

To measure if a reflector is blocking a particular IP from a blocklist, we send a train of packets (here we use SYN-ACK packets) from our measurement machine

---

[1] One exception is the recent work of Bouwman et al. [7] which has explored aspects of this question through the interview of over a dozen security professionals.

to the reflector. The packet train consists of packets whose source address is the blocklist IP (spoofed), bracketed by packets whose source address is our measurement machine, as illustrated in Fig. 1. If a firewall in the reflector's network blocks packets from the blocklist IP, the reflector will not receive packets with the blocklisted source address. It will only receive packets with our measurement machine's source address. On the other hand, if there is no blocking, the reflector will receive the entire packet train.

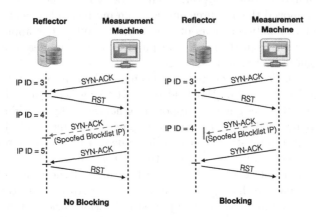

Fig. 1. The basic method to detect network-layer blocking using the IP ID side channel. When there is no blocking in place (left), the measurement machine will see an IP ID gap in two RST responses: the second IP ID will increase by two. Whereas if there is network blocking (right), then the two IP IDs will be consecutive without a gap.

In an ideal world, where there is no packet loss during transmission and no extra traffic on the reflector, we expect the reflector to send a RST response for each SYN-ACK packet we send, and we will receive the responses for the SYN-ACK with our measurement machine's source address. The IP IDs of these received RST packets will reflect the number of packets sent by the reflector. If the reflector did not receive the SYN-ACK packets with the blocklist IP as source addresses (being blocked by a firewall), the IP ID sequence in the RST responses will be an increasing sequence without gaps (the "Blocking" case in Fig. 1). On the other hand, if the reflector did receive the SYN-ACK packets with the blocklist IP, it would have sent a RST in response to each such packet, incrementing the IP ID counter each time. While we will not see the RST packets sent to the blocklist IP, we *will* observe the increments in the IP ID sequence. More specifically, we would see a gap in the IP ID sequence of packets received by our measurement machine (the "No Blocking" case in Fig. 1). These two cases allow us to determine whether a particular blocklist IP is blocked by some network device, such as a firewall, somewhere between the measurement host and the reflector.

In previous works [11,29], the technique relies on sending spoofed SYN packets to the sites (equivalent to our *blocklist IPs* here), with the source IPs equal to reflector IPs. The sites then reply with SYN-ACK packets to the reflectors. By monitoring the reflectors' IP ID changes during this process, the authors can determine whether the reflectors are blocking the tested sites. To use this strategy, however, one requires both reflectors and sites to be active hosts that reply to SYN/SYN-ACK probes. Unfortunately, in our case there is no guarantee that blocklist IPs will reply to TCP probes. In fact, we found that on average only about 24% of IPs on a blocklist reply to TCP probes. Using only blocklist IPs that reply would dramatically reduce the candidate IPs we can sample from a blocklist, especially for small blocklists that only have a few hundred IPs. We already have many constraints when sampling IPs from a blocklist (Sect. 3.3), and this extra requirement could leave us with not enough candidates for a measurement.

Therefore, in our technique, we directly send SYN-ACK packets to reflectors, with no involvement of hosts behind blocklist IPs. The disadvantage here is that we cannot detect outbound blocking—wherein the spoofed packet reaches the reflectors but the responses are blocked when going out of the network. Based on our experience talking with several security companies, most customers deploy inbound or bi-directional traffic blocking, so we believe missing outbound blocking is not a major concern.

In this section, we explain how the technique works on a theoretical level. The actual implementation needs to handle potential packet loss and other extraneous traffic at reflectors. We list the full implementation of the technique and false positive and false negative analyses in Appendix A.

3.2   Criteria for Reflectors

At a high level, our technique relies on the presence of the IP ID side channel. Keeping that in mind, listed below are the criteria for suitable reflectors.

- **RST packet generation:** The reflectors must reply with a RST packet to a TCP SYN-ACK packet without an established connection. Hosts that drop incoming SYN-ACK packets without a corresponding SYN packet are not suitable for our methodology. We use SYN-ACK packets instead of SYN because it does not create an intermediate state on the reflectors and the connection is terminated in one go.
- **Shared monotonic increasing IP ID counter:** The reflector should have a monotonically increasing globally shared IP ID counter, so all network traffic from the host uses the same IP ID counter counter and the number of packets generated by the host between two measurements is implicit in the difference of IP IDs.
- **Low traffic:** Our technique relies on a clear observable difference in IP ID. As such, hosts must have low traffic volumes since a high traffic volume makes it infeasible to observe the IP ID changes triggered by our probing packets.
- **No ingress filtering:** We send spoofed packets to reflectors to infer traffic blocking. However, some network providers use ingress filtering techniques and drop packets once they detect the packets are not from the networks

they claimed to originate. This filtering would cause our spoofed packets being dropped and give us a false signal of traffic blocking.

- **No stateful firewall blocking:** Some networks deploy a stateful firewall that blocks access from a source IP after receiving too many repetitive packets. One example is to defend against SYN floods [21]. While we try to keep the number of our probing packets as low as possible, if our spoofed packets trigger such firewall rules and then we are blocked by the firewall, we will incorrectly conclude that the reflector uses a blocklist to block that IP.

Our goal is to discover if online hosts are using IP blocklists to block traffic. But when looking at the problem on a global scale, there are many policy related reasons why a host blocks network traffic, such as censorship. These alternate sources of blocking could disrupt our experiments. To simplify the problem, and for ethical considerations, in this paper we only test the hosts located in the United States.

3.3 Sampling Blocklist IPs

To determine if a reflector uses a particular IP blocklist, we use a sample of IPs from a blocklist, as it would be infeasible for us to test all blocklist IPs. Further, to obtain a definitive signal from our experiment, we need to adhere to the following constraints when sampling blocklist IPs to avoid possible noise:

- **Exclusive:** A blocklist can share part of its contents with other blocklists. To reasonably infer whether a reflector is using a specific blocklist, we need to test with IPs unique to that blocklist—IPs that are only in this blocklist but no others.
- **Stable:** IPs on a blocklist change over time. To reliably measure if a reflector blocks IPs from a certain blocklist, we need the sampled IPs to stay in the list throughout one experiment. This cannot be enforced beforehand, so we discard the cases where a blocklist IP does not remain on the list for the duration of the experiment.
- **Routable:** IP blocklists can contain unroutable IPs [23]. Sending packets with an unroutable source address results in a large portion of packets being dropped, as we have observed (which could potentially happen at end ISPs or transient links). Packet drops due to unroutable IPs would create noise in the experiment. Therefore, when sampling IPs from blocklists we ensure that the IPs are routable.
- **Geo-location diversified:** Besides blocklisting, another common reason for traffic blocking is geo-blocking, where a host blocks all traffic coming from a certain country or region. To minimize the effect of geo-blocking, we prioritize IPs that are from the United States when sampling IPs, assuming a host in the US will not geo-block traffic from the US. For IPs in other countries, we try to increase the diversity of IP locations, making sure the sampled IPs are not concentrated in only a few countries when possible.

– **Not from reflectors' network (AS disjoint):** We observed that not many networks have implemented ingress filtering (we saw less than 2% of the total hosts we scanned showing this behavior). However, many networks drop spoofed packets when the spoofed source addresses are within their own network. So when selecting blocklist IPs, we make sure that these IPs are not from the same ASes as one of our reflectors.

3.4 Control Group

To further validate our technique, every time we test a set of blocklist IPs against each reflector, we also include a control group of 20 randomly chosen IPs that are BGP routable, geo-located in the United States and not blocklisted (see Sect. 4.2). The control group represents a random set of IPs that are unlikely to be blocked in bulk by a reflector. We use US IPs to avoid the potential problem of geo-blocking. If a reflector does block a significant fraction of control IPs, it is probably because the reflector is not suitable for this technique (one reason can be that our ingress-filtering step did not catch these IPs), and we should discard all the results associated with this reflector.

3.5 Ethical Considerations

In our experiments, we send spoofed packets to reflectors impersonating traffic from other IPs to infer the presence of network-layer blocking based on IP blocklists. A key ethical concern with this kind of measurement is the extent to which either receiving such packets or being seen to have received such packets would put the recipients at undue risk. Indeed, this is particularly problematic in censorship measurements [11,29] because of the potential to inadvertently cause a host to be associated with content that is politically dangerous in their country. However, our work operates in a context that is substantially less risky, and we have further designed multiple aspects of our protocol to minimize the likelihood of risk. In particular, our methodology incorporates the following approaches to minimize risk:

Restriction in Scope: We have specifically restricted our measurements to only reflectors within the United States, which affords relatively robust free speech rights and considerable transparency around criminal proceedings. Indeed, from our conversations with both network operators and law enforcement, we are unaware of a realistic scenario where the mere receipt of a packet has led to criminal or civil liability.

Conventional Sources: Unlike in censorship studies, the source IP addresses being spoofed in our measurement are those that have been used to mount wide-spread abusive activity such as spamming, port scanning, etc. and these represent precisely the kinds of traffic that a typical host on the Internet would *expect* to receive.

Inbound, Connection-Free Probes: Our measurements are constructed to be inbound only and connection free; that is, a network monitor could witness traffic consistent with an *external* scan of one of their hosts, but will never witness a completed connection or any data transmission. From our discussions with network operators and network security vendors, we could not identify a scenario where the mere receipt of the packets we send would be sufficient to drive an incident response team to action.

Minimal Use of End-Host Resources: Our scans are purposely constructed with SYN-ACK packets to ensure that no state is created on the reflector. Moreover, our peak probing rate per reflector is 6 min-sized packets per second (see appendix for more details). But even that rate only persists for two seconds in each test, and in the following pilot study, we probe each reflector no more than once every 3 mins.

4   Pilot Study Implementation

With the technique discussed in the previous section, one can then infer if an online host (reflector) satisfying the selection criteria outlined above is blocking traffic using a specific IP blocklist. To evaluate our inference technique, we conducted a pilot study over a large number of reflectors to infer their blocklist usage. In this section, we explain in detail the implementation of our experiment, including reflector selection, blocklist selection, sampling IPs from blocklists and measurement setup.

4.1   Reflector Selection

We start our selection of reflectors using a snapshot of Censys [9] scanning data from November 8, 2019, consisting of over 40 million IPv4 hosts with open ports in the US. We then send multiple probes to each host targeting an open port from different source addresses, checking the IP IDs of responses to identify the ones with the IP ID side channel. We further run tests to make sure they meet the criteria listed in Sect. 3.2 (see Appendix A). If one host has multiple open ports, we randomly pick one to probe.

Table 1. The number of reflectors (IP addresses) identified in the United States, and the corresponding count of /24 prefixes and Autonomous Systems.

Category	Count
IP addresses	222,782
/24 Count	128,712
Autonomous Systems	3,371

We identified 222,782 IP addresses in the US that meet our criteria. For the purpose of this paper, we treat each individual IP address as a distinct reflector. Table 1 counts these addresses at different network aggregations. By construction, the set of reflectors we use will necessarily have certain biases. To understand what fraction of networks of potential interest to others this might cover, we queried the Alexa top 100K domains as of Dec. 17th, 2019 for their A records and MX records and obtained their corresponding IP addresses. Of these, we identified a total of 94,846 IPs that are located in the US, covering 34,083 /24 s. While we made no attempt to find reflectors in these networks *a priori*, our selection methodology identified at least one reflector in 16.9% of these /24 s. When only looking at the top 10K domains, our data set covers 13.2% of US /24 s.

We also checked the WHOIS record of each reflector and identified all hosts associated with education institutions. In total, our data set includes 4,370 education IPs, ranging across 181 different institutions, and covers 40 out of the top 100 US universities based on the US News ranking [42]. Thus, while there may be networks without a suitable reflector for one reason or another, our technique is applicable to a large number of existing networks.

4.2   Choosing Blocklists and Sampling IPs

For the pilot study, we choose candidate blocklists from public IPv4 blocklists. We use the FireHOL IP blocklist collection [12], which aggregates over 100 public IP blocklists every day. However, we cannot reasonably test against all the blocklists and so, for the purposes of this paper, we select the most popular public IP blocklists and then do a more detailed measurement on them.

For each of the public IP blocklists, we sample five IPs (using the criteria in Sect. 3.3) from each list and test how many reflectors block all sampled blocklist IPs in each blocklist. The goal of this step is to roughly estimate how widely used these blocklists might be, so that we can pick the most prevalent ones for more detailed measurements later in Sect. 5. We repeat the measurement twice and select the top 9 blocklists:

1. **Spamhaus DROP**: Spamhaus Don't Route Or Peer Lists
2. **Spamhaus EDROP**: An extension of the Spamhaus DROP list
3. **DShield Top Blocklist**: DShield.org recommended top 20 /24 s to block
4. **ET Compromised**: EmergingThreats.net recorded compromised hosts
5. **Snort IP Filter List**: labs.snort.org supplied IP blocklist
6. **BDS IP Ban List**: Binary Defense System ban list
7. **Feodo IP Blocklist**: Abuse.ch Feodo tracking list
8. **Blocklist De Blocklist**: Blocklist.de blocklist IPs
9. **Tor IP Blocklist**: IPs that belong to the Tor network (not just exit nodes)

When sampling IPs from blocklists to test, we use the criteria listed in Sect. 3.3. To find the exclusive IPs on each blocklist, we use the public IP blocklists collected by FireHOL, as mentioned earlier, and calculate the unique part of each target blocklist. For the stable IP requirement, we collect all the target blocklists hourly, and ensure the sampled IPs are in the blocklist through the duration of the experiment. To satisfy the routable requirement, we use daily RouteView data [41] to identify BGP routable IPs. For geo-location diversity, we use NetAcuity [26] to make sure for each experiment the sampled IPs cover as many different countries as the data allows.

4.3 Measurement Setup

Having selected the reflectors and blocklists, we can now conduct the experiment to infer which reflectors use which specific blocklist.

For a particular experimental run, we randomly selected **25** IPs from each blocklist that satisfy the requirements defined in Sect. 3: exclusive, stable, routable, geo-diversified, and AS disjoint. Then we evaluated the blocking behavior for all 220K reflectors against the 225 blocklist IPs sampled from the 9 blocklists. To handle cases where reflectors might take time to update and start blocking the newest IPs on the blocklist, we ensure the sampled IPs have appeared in the blocklist at least 2 weeks before our experiment. During post-processing, we remove blocklist IPs from consideration that did not remain on the list for the duration of the experiment. Furthermore, we conducted three experimental runs, each time using a different set of 25 IPs from each blocklist. We then conclude that a reflector is using a blocklist if and only if all experiment runs show that it blocked all the sampled IPs from that blocklist.

We conducted our measurements from December 3–23rd, 2019. During this period, we tested in total 96,067,051 distinct (`reflector, blocklist IP`) pairs. (In the first two experiments, we tested against all reflectors. In the last experiment, we only tested the ones that have shown blocking behavior in the first two tests.) Among these pairs, 894,570 pairs display a clear signal indicating "blocking".

5 Pilot Study Overall Results

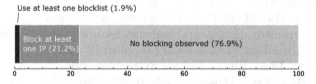

Fig. 2. Breakdown of reflector blocking based on three experimental runs. We identified 4,253 reflectors that use at least one blocklist (Sect. 5.1). We also found a large number of reflectors blocking at least some IPs in blocklists (Sect. 5.2).

Figure 2 presents the overall blocking behavior of all 222,782 reflectors we tested partitioned into four categories: those reflectors that we conclude use at least one of the public blocklists (1.9%), reflectors that block at least one blocklist IP

(21.2%), and reflectors that do not block any blocklist IPs (76.9%). Note that given the attributes of hosts to be reflectors, such as running old OS versions, it is not surprising a large percentage shows no blocking of the blocklist IPs: they already have attributes anti-correlated with high degrees of security hygiene. The following sections explores each of these categories of reflector blocking behavior in more detail.

Table 2. Breakdown of reflectors we conclude using each of the nine blocklists.

Blocklist (abbr.)	Reflectors	/24s	ASes
Spamhaus DROP (DROP)	4,142	1,782	50
Spamhaus EDROP (eDROP)	1,272	362	25
DShield Top Blocklist (DTop)	223	69	18
ET Compromised (ET)	116	58	15
BDS IP Ban List (BDS)	85	41	3
Feodo IP Blocklist (Feodo)	64	26	16
Snort IP Filter List (Snort)	52	20	11
Blocklist De Blocklist (DE)	36	18	8
Tor IP Blocklist (Tor)	24	9	8
Total Unique	4,253	1,827	77

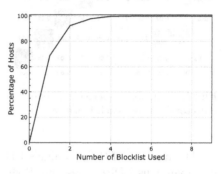

Fig. 3. CDF of the number of blocklists used by reflectors.

5.1 Reflectors Using Blocklists

We identified 4,253 (1.9%) reflectors that use at least one of the 9 public blocklists. Table 2 shows the number of reflectors using each of the nine different blocklists, as well as the number of unique /24 s and ASes those reflectors appear in. Spamhaus DROP is by far the most popular blocklist in our collection, followed by Spamhaus EDROP. The remaining blocklists have a comparatively small number of reflectors using them. Since many aspects of our method and experiment make conservative choices, these results should be considered a lower bound.

Figure 3 shows the cumulative distribution of the number of blocklists these reflectors use. For the 9 public blocklists we studied, over 68.6% use just one blocklist, 23.8% use two or more, and 7.6% use three or more. One reflector used 6 of the 9 blocklists.

For these reflectors, though, there are interesting patterns to the multiple blocklists used. Figure 4 shows the use of multiple blocklists with a heatmap. Rows and columns correspond to blocklists, and each cell of the heatmap shows the fraction of the reflectors using the blocklist in row R that are also using the blocklist in column C. For example, the first cell for ET Compromised shows that 78% of the reflectors that use ET also use the Spamhaus DROP blocklist. Diagonal cells are 1.00 since they show blocklists compared with themselves. Blocklists are ordered in the same order as in Table 2.

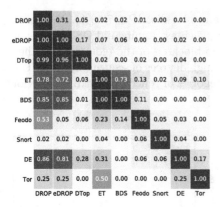

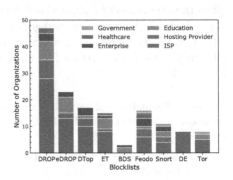

Fig. 4. Pair wise intersection between reflectors that use each blocklist.

Fig. 5. Breakdown of the number of organizations covered by each blocklist.

The first cell of the Spamhaus EDROP row indicates that all reflectors that use Spamhaus EDROP also use Spamhaus DROP. Since the eDROP list is an extension of the DROP list, the behavior is strongly consistent with expectations. Moreover, the many significant values in the first two columns show that reflectors that use any of the other blocklists very often also use Spamhaus DROP and eDROP. At least for the hosts that we select for, these results underscore the popularity of Spamhaus lists and indicate that, if a reflector blocks traffic using blocklists, it very likely uses Spamhaus.

Ultimately the blocklist use and blocking behavior of the reflectors is strongly tied to the organization to which they belong. While inferring the exact organization behind an IP is difficult, we can still explore some high-level organizational aspects of blocklists. We first identify the AS for every reflector, then use the CAIDA AS-to-Organization dataset [8] to map the AS to an organization. Then, we manually partition the organizations into six categories: ISPs (e.g., Comcast), Hosting Providers (e.g., GoDaddy web hosting, AWS cloud computing), Education (e.g., universities), Healthcare (e.g., hospitals), Government (e.g., state and federal agencies), and Enterprise (individual companies owning the IPs).

Figure 5 shows the number of organizations using each blocklist, and their breakdowns by organization category. Most blocklists are used by a wide variety of organizations. Feodo IP Blocklist is the most diverse blocklist in our study, as organizations from all six categories use it. From the perspective of organizations, Educational institutions cover 8 of the 9 blocklists we selected, suggesting a potential preference among universities on using public blocklists.

Validation: Based upon the locations of blocking reflectors, we reached out to two universities that we concluded are using blocklists. In both cases, the blocklists we inferred matched the blocklists they reported using, validating the technique in these two cases. More specifically, University A confirmed our findings that they use BDS IP Ban List, ET Compromised, Spamhaus DROP and

Spamhaus EDROP. University B confirmed our findings that they use Spamhaus DROP and Spamhaus EDROP.

5.2 Partial Blocking

Partial blocking is when a reflector blocks some of the blocklist IPs but not all of them. There are many reasons, unrelated to the use of a blocklist, why a reflector may block a blocklist IP. A host may have internal policies that deny access from some network providers, or network administrators may add IPs into their firewall on an ad-hoc basis based on an organization's own policies. These alternate blocking behaviors could overlap with the blocklist IPs we sampled, leading to partial blocking behavior.

Geo-blocking is one cause of partial blocking we identified, where a reflector drops all traffic from a particular country. DShield Top Blocklist, for example, had over 50% of its IPs on January 25, 2020 geo-located in the Netherlands. If a reflector blocks traffic from the Netherlands, then we would observe that the reflector is partially blocking DShield Top Blocklist. To identify whether a reflector uses geo-blocking, we check whether the reflector *consistently* blocks IPs from a particular country. For all countries related to blocklist IPs we tested, we sample IP addresses from those countries based on four IP location services: MaxMind [24], IP2Location [15], IPDeny [16], and IPIP.net [17], and test against our reflectors. Overall, we identified a small number of reflectors, 614 (0.28%), that consistently block traffic from at least one country.

After removing the geo-blocking reflectors from partial blocking cases, we noticed that a small percentage of reflectors consistently blocked a significant subset of blocklist IPs, but not all, in *every experiment*. This consistency suggests that there is a large overlap between the blocklist and the blocking policy of the reflector. If a reflector blocks over 50% of sampled IPs from a blocklist *every time* we test, we regard the reflector as exhibiting *significant partial blocking* over a blocklist. In total we identified 871 (0.4%) such reflectors. These hosts are probably using a source that is very similar to the blocklists we tested, as previous work has shown that commercial products can aggregate data from public blocklists, and then conduct post-processing to eliminate some content [23]. It is also possible that they are using an older version of the same list, where the content is mostly the same.

Besides these cases, an additional fifth of reflectors demonstrate blocking behavior, as evidenced in Fig. 2. Although we do not know the exact reason for the blocking, the result suggests that security-related network blocking is relatively prevalent even among low security hygiene hosts such as these reflectors.

Finally, we had originally hypothesized that network layer blocking would be primarily implemented in border devices (e.g., firewalls, gateways) and thus affect whole network blocks identically. However, when checking reflectors within the same /24 s, we find that reflectors under the same /24 frequently do not block the same set of IPs. We refer to this as *inconsistent blocking*. Our experiment found 8,909 (`/24, blocklist`) pairs where multiple reflectors under that /24 block some IPs in that specific blocklist. Among them, 3,263 (36.6%) pairs show inconsistent blocking behavior. This result implies there is considerable intra-network diversity in blocking policy. More analyses and details on the methodology can be found in Chap. 4 in [22].

6 Conclusion

Our paper proposes, implements and tests a technique for inferring the deployment of network-layer blocklists and, further, for attributing the use of particular blocklists by particular hosts. While our technique depends on hosts that are largely quiescent (not sending or receiving much traffic) and use a global increment strategy for IP ID generation (typically those with older operating systems), both of these limitations may be addressable to some extent. Hosts with modest levels of traffic are likely still amenable to testing by using larger sample sizes and more sophisticated statistical testing regimes. As well, while many modern hosts purposely obfuscate the generation of IP ID values, recent work by Klein and Pinkas [19] has demonstrated attacks on these algorithms (in Windows and Linux in particular) which may provide purchase for using the IP ID side channel with more contemporary machines. Future work could leverage these methods to apply our technique to more blocklists with a broader set of reflectors.

Our pilot study covered 220K US hosts, identified blocking behavior in roughly a fourth of all reflectors, but only 2% show clear use of the blocklists we tested against. This difference is puzzling on multiple fronts. It suggests that even among older quiescent hosts that there are significant network security controls in place. Also, it indicates that there may be far more diversity in blocklist usage than we had initially imagined.

A   Inference Technique Details

Our technique, while simple in theory, needs to handle real-world scenarios, including packet losses, packet reordering during transition, and other traffic on reflectors. The inference method needs to be *efficient*, *accurate*, and have *low overhead*. Blocklists can change frequently, leaving a short window to infer a stable behavior. As such, for the measurement to finish in a reasonable amount of time requires an efficient inference method. Additionally, the method should also have low false positive and false negative rates so that we can be confident about the result. Finally, it should require as few packets as possible to reduce potential impact on reflectors.

The first step is to find reflectors suitable to our measurement technique. Recall that a suitable reflector should have minimal background traffic, and not be part of a network doing ingress filtering for spoofed packets. To find quiescent hosts, reflectors with low background traffic, we send 24 probes to each candidate host, 1 per second, and repeat the experiment 5 times at different times of the day. We then only select hosts where at least 30% of their IP ID increases are equal to 1 per second—the host did not receive any extra traffic in that one second. We use the 30% threshold to select hosts that are largely "quiet", and thus more likely to yield a perfect signal in the experiment. Next, to identify hosts behind ingress filtering, we acquired 7 vantage points around the world to exercise different paths to the reflector. We sent spoofed packets from our measurement machine to the hosts with spoofed source addresses corresponding to the 7 vantage points, and then collected responses at each vantage point. We only select the hosts that send responses to all 7 vantage points, meaning they did not drop spoofed packets on any of the exercised network paths.

Next, we describe how we infer if a given reflector blocks an IP using multiple *trials*. We define a *trial* as a single experiment that tests if a reflector blocks one blocklist IP. Figure 6 shows the process of one trial. For each trial, the measurement machine sends five consecutive *probe packets* to the reflector, with each packet being sent one second apart. In our experiment, the probe packets are TCP SYN-ACK packets and we get IP IDs from response RST packets. Between the third and fourth probe packets, the measurement machine sends five *spoofed packets*, also TCP SYN-ACK, with source IPs equal to the blocklist IP. And between the fourth and the fifth probe packets, it sends another five spoofed packets. We send the five spoofed packets 0.15 s apart consecutively each time, spreading them across the one-second window between two probes.

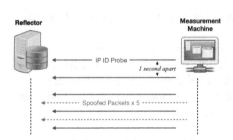

Fig. 6. Blocking inference methodology. Solid blue lines are *probe packets*, dashed red lines are *spoofed packets*. (Color figure online)

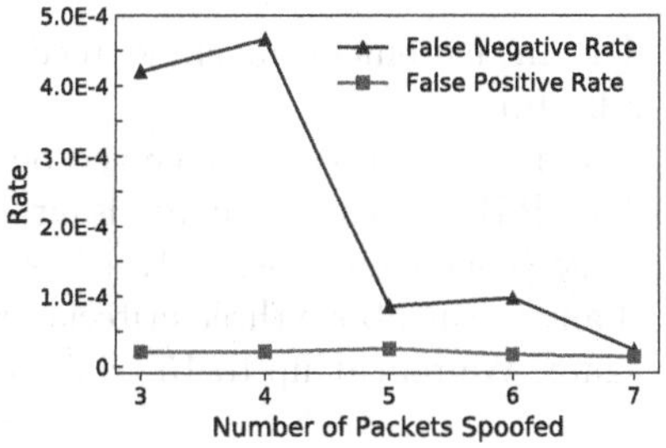

Fig. 7. Experiment design and false positive and false negative analysis

We then inspect the increases between the IP IDs in the packets received by the measurement machine. Ideally, assuming no additional traffic and no packet loss, the IP ID should increase by exactly one between consecutive probes. For the last two deltas, since we send the spoofed packets in between our probe packets, the final IP ID increases will be different based on the host's blocking behavior.

If the reflector does not block the blocklist IP, then we will observe an IP ID increase sequence in our received RST responses that is: [+1, +1, +6, +6]. Here the last two deltas are +6 since the reflector does not block the blocklist IP and thus responds to spoofed packets, causing IP ID to increase by 5, and our probe packet causes it to increase by another 1, which together make +6.

On the other hand, if the reflector blocks the blocklist IP, then we will see an IP ID increase sequence that is: [+1, +1, +1, +1]. Here the last two deltas are +1 since the reflector blocks the blocklist IP, leading to no extra change in IP ID.

The first three probes—corresponding to the first two IP ID deltas—act as a control. The last two "probe and spoof" patterns perform the actual experiment. Seeing the initial two "+1" indicates this host is in a quiet period (no extra network traffic). Therefore, we can be more confident that the following IP ID jump ("+6" in our case) is because of our experiment. While the choice of the numbers in the experiment may seem arbitrary, there is a rationale behind the choice which we will discuss in following sections.

A.1   Inference Criteria

We now look at the criteria to infer if a reflector blocks a blocklist IP or not. Our limited vantage point from the measurement machine limits our information to the IP IDs seen from the reflector. Moreover, we desire to be conservative when inferring blocking. Thus, our approach is to try the same trial, between a reflector and a blocklist IP, until we get a "perfect signal"—a response which matches all the criteria below:

1. The measurement machine received exactly five RST responses from the reflector.
2. The five responses are received one second apart consecutively.
3. The IP ID increase sequence is either [+1, +1, +6, +6], which we will conclude as no blocking, or [+1, +1, +1, +1], which we will conclude as blocking.
4. If any of the above three criteria are not met, we repeat the same experiment again. We repeat up to 15 trials before giving up.

The first requirement ensures no packet loss. The second requirement ensures responses we received reflect the real IP ID changes in the reflector. The Internet does not guarantee the order of packet arrival. Although we send one probe packet per second, these packets might not arrive at the reflector in the same order. Thus, the IP ID sequence from the response packets might not represent the real order of IP ID changes at the host. Hence, by requiring that the response packets cannot be less than 0.85 or more than 1.15 s apart we can minimize the probability of reordered packets.

The third requirement is the core of our inference logic. Since we ignore everything other than an IP ID increase sequence of [+1, +1, +1, +1] or [+1, +1, +6, +6], we can assure that our inference of blocking is conservative. If we saw a sequence of [+1, +1, +1, +1] but the reflector does not block the blocklist IP, that would mean all 10 spoofed packets were lost. On the other hand, if we see [+1, +1, +6, +6] and the reflector actually blocks the blocklist IP, that would mean there are exactly five extra packets generated by the reflector during each of the last two seconds. Both cases are very unlikely, which we will demonstrate next with an analysis of false positives and false negatives.

A.2   False Positive and False Negative Analysis

For our experiment, a *false positive* is when a reflector is not blocking a blocklist IP, but we mistakenly conclude it is blocking. On the other hand, a *false negative* is when a reflector is blocking a blocklist IP, but we mistakenly conclude it is not. To evaluate false positive and false negative rates, we conduct experiments on *all* the reflectors under consideration and measure the false positive and false negative rates.

For false positive evaluation, we first acquire a list of IPs that are verifiably not being blocked by reflectors. Since we own these IPs, we can easily verify by directly probing reflectors from these IPs. We acquired and tested 1,265 IPs from five different /24s. Then we probe reflectors and send the spoofed packets with source addresses set to these pre-selected IPs. Since these IPs are not being blocked, if we observe an IP ID increase sequence of [+1, +1, +1, +1], then we know it is a false positive.

For false negatives, we run the experiment with only probe packets, and no spoofed packets. This scenario is equivalent to the one where the reflector blocks the spoofed IP. If we observe an IP ID increase sequence of [+1, +1, +6, +6], then we know it was due to the background traffic at the reflector and hence is a false negative.

Although we present the experiment design with five spoofed packets in each of the last two seconds, we also experimented with a range of numbers and calculated their false positive and negative rates. We tested 15 times with spoofed packets equal to 3, 4, 5, 6, and 7 with every reflector, and we repeated the experiment again on a different day. The final results are shown in Fig. 7.

We need to trade off between keeping false positive and negative rates low while generating as little traffic as possible. We choose 5 spoofed packets as a balance. By sending 5 spoofed packets, we get a false positive rate of 2.5e-5, and a false negative rate of 8.5e-5. Furthermore, we also experimented with strategies where we send 4 probe packets, from which we get 3 IP ID deltas, and sending 6 probe packets, from which we get 5 IP ID deltas. With only 3 deltas we suffer a higher false negative rate, as it is easier for the reflector to show the same IP ID increase sequence with extra traffic. With 6 probes, on the other hand, we prolong the experiment, making it harder to get a "perfect signal". Thus, our choice of 5 probe packets with 5 spoofed packets in between is a good balance between competing factors.

References

1. Afroz, S., Tschantz, M.C., Sajid, S., Qazi, S.A., Javed, M., Paxson, V.: Exploring Server-side Blocking of Regions. Tech. rep, ICSI (2018)
2. Anderson, D.: Splinternet behind the great firewall of China. Queue **10**(11), 40–49 (2012)
3. antirez: new TCP scan method. https://seclists.org/bugtraq/1998/Dec/79
4. Aryan, S., Aryan, H., Halderman, J.A.: Internet censorship in iran: a first look. In: Proceedings of the 3rd USENIX Workshop on Free and Open Communications on the Internet (FOCI) (2013)

5. Bellovin, S.M.: A Technique for Counting NATted Hosts. In: Proceedings of the 2nd Internet Measurement Conference (IMC), pp. 267–272 (2002)
6. Bhutani, A., Wadhwani, P.: Threat Intelligence Market Size By Component, By Format Type, By Deployment Type, By Application, Industry Analysis Report, Regional Outlook, Growth Potential, Competitive Market Share and Forecast, 2019–2025 (2019)
7. Bouwman, X., Griffioen, H., Egbers, J., Doerr, C., Klievink, B., van Eeten, M.: A Different cup of TI? the added value of commercial threat intelligence. In: Proceedings of the 29th USENIX Security Symposium (USENIX Security), pp. 433–450, August 2020
8. CAIDA: Inferred AS to Organization Mapping Dataset. https://www.caida.org/data/as_organizations.xml
9. Censys - Public Internet Search Engine. https://censys.io/
10. Clayton, Richard., Murdoch, Steven J., Watson, Robert N.M.: Ignoring the great firewall of China. In: Danezis, George, Golle, Philippe (eds.) PET 2006. LNCS, vol. 4258, pp. 20–35. Springer, Heidelberg (2006). https://doi.org/10.1007/11957454_2
11. Ensafi, Roya., Knockel, Jeffrey., Alexander, Geoffrey, Crandall, Jedidiah R.: Detecting intentional packet drops on the internet via TCP/IP side channels. In: Faloutsos, Michalis, Kuzmanovic, Aleksandar (eds.) PAM 2014. LNCS, vol. 8362, pp. 109–118. Springer, Cham (2014). https://doi.org/10.1007/978-3-319-04918-2_11
12. FireHOL IP Lists - All Cybercrime IP Feeds. http://iplists.firehol.org/
13. Hao, S., Kantchelian, A., Miller, B., Paxson, V., Feamster, N.: PREDATOR: proactive recognition and elimination of domain abuse at time-of-registration. In: Proceedings of the ACM SIGSAC Conference on Computer and Communications Security (CCS), pp. 1568–1579. ACM (2016)
14. Hao, S., Thomas, M., Paxson, V., Feamster, N., Kreibich, C., Grier, C., Hollenbeck, S.: Understanding the Domain Registration Behavior of Spammers. In: Proceedings of the ACM Internet Measurement Conference (IMC), pp. 63–76. ACM (2013)
15. IP2Location: IP Address to Identify Geolocation. https://www.ip2location.com/
16. IPdeny IP country blocks. https://www.ipdeny.com/
17. IPIP.net: The Best IP Geolocation Database. https://en.ipip.net/
18. Khattak, S., et al.: Do you see what i see? differential treatment of anonymous users. In: Proceedings of the Network and Distributed System Security Symposium (NDSS) (2016)
19. Klein, A., Pinkas, B.: From IP ID to device ID and KASLR bypass. In: Proceedings of the 28th USENIX Security Symposium (USENIX Security), pp. 1063–1080 (2019)
20. Kührer, Marc., Rossow, Christian, Holz, Thorsten: Paint it black: evaluating the effectiveness of malware blacklists. In: Stavrou, Angelos, Bos, Herbert, Portokalidis, Georgios (eds.) RAID 2014. LNCS, vol. 8688, pp. 1–21. Springer, Cham (2014). https://doi.org/10.1007/978-3-319-11379-1_1
21. Lemon, J.: Resisting SYN Flood DoS attacks with a SYN Cache. In: Proceedings of the BSD Conference (BSDCon), pp. 89–97. USENIX Association, USA (2002)
22. Li, G.: An Empirical Analysis on Threat Intelligence: Data Characteristics and Real-World Uses. Ph.D. thesis, UC San Diego (2020)
23. Li, V.G., Dunn, M., Pearce, P., McCoy, D., Voelker, G.M., Savage, S.: Reading the Tea leaves: a comparative analysis of threat intelligence. In: Proceedings of the 28th USENIX Security Symposium (USENIX Security), pp. 851–867, August 2019
24. MaxMind: IP Geolocation and Online Fraud Prevention. https://www.maxmind.com/

25. McDonald, A., et al.: 403 forbidden: a global view of CDN Geoblocking. Proc. Internet Measurement Conf. **2018**, 218–230 (2018)
26. NetAcuity. https://www.digitalelement.com/solutions/
27. OpenNet Initiative: Survey of Government Internet Filtering Practices Indicates Increasing Internet Censorship, May 2007
28. Park, J.C., Crandall, J.R.: Empirical study of a national-scale distributed intrusion detection system: backbone-level filtering of HTML responses in China. In: IEEE 30th International Conference on Distributed Computing Systems (ICDCS), pp. 315–326. IEEE (2010)
29. Pearce, P., Ensafi, R., Li, F., Feamster, N., Paxson, V.: Augur: internet-wide detection of connectivity disruptions. In: Proceedings of the IEEE Symposium on Security and Privacy (SP), pp. 427–443. IEEE (2017)
30. Pitsillidis, A., Kanich, C., Voelker, G.M., Levchenko, K., Savage, S.: Taster's choice: a comparative analysis of spam feeds. In: Proceedings of the ACM Internet Measurement Conference (IMC), pp. 427–440. Boston, MA, November 2012 (2012)
31. Ponemon Institute LLC: Third Annual Study on Changing Cyber Threat Intelligence: There Has to Be a Better Way (January 2018)
32. Postel, J.: RFC0791: Internet Protocol (1981)
33. Ramachandran, A., Feamster, N., Dagon, D.: Revealing Botnet Membership Using DNSBL Counter-Intelligence. SRUTI **6** (2006)
34. Shackleford, D.: Cyber Threat Intelligence Uses, Successes and Failures: The SANS 2017 CTI Survey. Technical Report, SANS (2017)
35. Sheng, S., Wardman, B., Warner, G., Cranor, L.F., Hong, J., Zhang, C.: An empirical analysis of phishing blacklists. In: Proceedings of the Conference on Email and Anti-Spam (CEAS) (2009)
36. Singh, R., et al.: Characterizing the nature and dynamics of tor exit blocking. In: Proceedings of the 26th USENIX Security Symposium (USENIX Security), pp. 325–341 (2017)
37. Sinha, S., Bailey, M., Jahanian, F.: Shades of grey: on the effectiveness of reputation-based "blacklists". In: Proceedings of the 3rd International Conference on Malicious and Unwanted Software (MALWARE), pp. 57–64. IEEE (2008)
38. Spring, N., Mahajan, R., Wetherall, D.: Measuring ISP topologies with Rocketfuel. ACM SIGCOMM Comput. Commun. Rev. (CCR) **32**(4), 133–145 (2002)
39. Thomas, Kurt., Amira, Rony., Ben-Yoash, Adi., Folger, Ori., Hardon, Amir., Berger, Ari., Bursztein, Elie, Bailey, Michael: The abuse sharing economy: understanding the limits of threat exchanges. In: Monrose, Fabian, Dacier, Marc, Blanc, Gregory, Garcia-Alfaro, Joaquin (eds.) RAID 2016. LNCS, vol. 9854, pp. 143–164. Springer, Cham (2016). https://doi.org/10.1007/978-3-319-45719-2_7
40. Tounsi, W., Rais, H.: A survey on technical threat intelligence in the age of sophisticated cyber attacks. Comput. Secur. **72**, 212–233 (2018)
41. University of Oregon Route Views Project. http://www.routeviews.org/routeviews/
42. Best National University Rankings. https://www.usnews.com/best-colleges/rankings/national-universities, January 2020
43. Zittrain, J., Edelman, B.: Internet filtering in China. IEEE Internet Computing **7**(2), 70–77 (2003)

Our (in)Secure Web: Understanding Update Behavior of Websites and Its Impact on Security

Nurullah Demir[1]([✉]), Tobias Urban[1], Kevin Wittek[1,2], and Norbert Pohlmann[1]

[1] Institute for Internet Security—if(is), Westphalian University of Applied Sciences Gelsenkirchen, Gelsenkirchen, Germany
{demir,urban,wittek,pohlmann}@internet-sicherheit.de
[2] RWTH Aachen University, Aachen, Germany

Abstract. Software updates take an essential role in keeping IT environments secure. If service providers delay or do not install updates, it can cause unwanted security implications for their environments. This paper conducts a large-scale measurement study of the update behavior of websites and their utilized software stacks. Across 18 months, we analyze over 5.6M websites and 246 distinct client- and server-side software distributions. We found that almost all analyzed sites use outdated software. To understand the possible security implications of outdated software, we analyze the potential vulnerabilities that affect the utilized software. We show that software components are getting older and more vulnerable because they are not updated. We find that 95 % of the analyzed websites use at least one product for which a vulnerability existed.

Keywords: Updates · Vulnerabilities · Security · Web measurement · Web security

1 Introduction

Nowadays, we use the Web for various tasks and services (e.g., talking to our friends, sharing ideas, to be entertained, or to work). Naturally, these services process a lot of personal and valuable data, which needs to be protected. Therefore, web services need to be hardened against adversaries, for example, due to imperfections of software. An essential role in every application's security concept is the updating process of the used components [9]. Not updating software might have severe security implications. For example, the infamous *Equifax* data breach that affected 143 million people was possible because the company used software with a known vulnerability that has already been fixed in a newer version [26].

However, keeping software up to date is not always easy and, from the security perspective, not always necessary (i.e., not every update fixes a security issue). Modern applications require a variety of different technologies (e.g., libraries, web servers, databases, etc.) to operate. Updating one of these technologies might have unforeseeable effects and, therefore, updates might create potentially high overhead (e.g., if an update removes support of a used feature). More specifically, service providers might object to install an update because they do not directly

O. Hohlfeld et al. (Eds.): PAM 2021, LNCS 12671, pp. 76–92, 2021.
https://doi.org/10.1007/978-3-030-72582-2_5

profit from the new features (e.g., changes in an unused module). Hence, it is reasonable not always to install every available update (e.g., to ensure stability).

In this work, we show that this challenge can have grave implications. To understand how up to date the utilized software on the Web is and to understand its possible security implications, we conduct a large-scale measurement. Previous work also analyzed update behavior on the Web (e.g., [19,23]) but – to the best of our knowledge – our measurement is more comprehensive than the previous studies. While we analyze over 5.6M sites and nearly 250 software (SW) products, other work in this field often only analyzed one specific type of software or a small subset. Therefore, our results are more generalizable and provide a better overview of the scale of the problem.

To summarize, we make the following contributions:

1. We conduct a large-scale measurement that evaluates 246 software products used on 5.6M websites over a period of 18 months, to determine update behavior and security impact of not updating.
2. We show that 96 % of the analyzed websites run outdated software, which is often more than four years old and is getting even older since no update is applied.
3. We show that a vast majority of the analyzed websites (95%) use software for which vulnerabilities have been reported, and the number of vulnerable websites is increasing over time.

2 Background

In this section, we discuss the principles of how web applications work and how known vulnerabilities are publicly managed, both necessary to appreciate our work.

2.1 Preliminaries

We start by introducing key terminology. In this work, we use the term *site* (or *website*) to describe a registerable domain, sometimes referred to as *eTLD+1* ("extended Top Level Domain plus one"). Examples for sites are foo.com and bar.co.nz. Each site may have several *subdomains* (e.g., news.foo.com and sport.foo.com). Following the definition of RFC 6454 [1], we call the tuple of protocol (e.g., HTTPS), subdomain (or hostname), and port *origin*. This distinction is important since the well-known security concept *Same-Origin Policy* (SOP) guarantees that pages of different origins cannot access each other. We use the term *page* (or *webpage*) to describe a single HTML file (e.g., a webpage hosted at a specific URL).

2.2 Web Technologies and Updating

To implement modern web applications, service providers rely on a diverse set of server-side (e.g., PHP or MySQL) and client-side technologies (e.g., HTML or JavaScript). This combination of different technologies often results in a very complex and dynamic architecture, not always under full control of the service provider (e.g., usage of third parties [8]). Furthermore, the update frequency of web technologies is higher compared to desktop software [20]. Web applications are commonly composed of different modules that rely on each other to perform a given task. Hence, one vulnerability in any of these modules might undermine the security of the entire web app, depending on the severity of the vulnerability. Once a vulnerability of an application is publicly known or privately reported to the developers (see also Sect. 2.3), the provider of that application (hopefully) provides an update to fix it. Therefore, service providers need to check the availability of updates of the used components and their dependencies and transitive dependencies regularly. However, it should be noted that not all updates fix security issues, and, therefore, it is not necessary or desired (e.g., for stability reasons) to install all updates right away.

2.3 Common Vulnerabilities and Exposures

Once vulnerabilities in software systems are discovered, reported to a vendor, or shared with the internet community publicly, they are published in vulnerability database platforms (e.g., in the *National Vulnerability Database* (NVD)). The NVD utilizes the standardized *Common Vulnerabilities and Exposures* (CVE) data format and enriches this data. Each CVE entry is provided in a machine-readable format and contains details regarding the vulnerability (e.g., vulnerability type, vulnerability severity, affected software, and version(s)). The primary purpose of each CVE entry is to determine which software is affected by a vulnerability and helps to estimate its consequences. Each entry in the NVD database is composed of several data fields, of which we now describe the one most important for our work. In the NVD database, the field ID of a CVE entry uniquely identifies the entry and also states the year when the vulnerability was made public, followed by a sequence number (e.g., CVE-2020-2883), the field CVE_data_timestamp indicates when the CVE entry was created. Furthermore, each CVE entry also includes a list of known software configurations that are affected by the vulnerability (field configurations), formally known as *Common Platform Enumeration* (CPE). CPE defines a naming scheme to identify products by combining, amongst other values, the vendor, product name, and version. For example the CPE (in version 2.3) cpe:2.3:a:nodejs:node.js:4.0.0:*[...]* identifies the product node.js provided by the vendor *nodejs* in version 4.0.0. Furthermore, the configurations field lists all conditions under which the given vulnerability can be exploited (e.g., combination of used products). Finally, the field impact describes the practical implications of the vulnerability (e.g., a description of the attack vector) and holds a score, the *Common Vulnerability Scoring System* (CVSS), ranging from 0 to 10, which indicates the severity of the CVE (with ten being the most severe). Again, it is worth noting that it not definite that if one uses a software product – for which a vulnerability exists – that it is exploitable by an attacker. For example, if an SQL-Injection is possible via the comment function of a blog, it can only be exploited if the comment function is enabled. Thus, our results can be seen as an upper bound.

3 Method

In this work, we want to assess the update behavior of web applications, measure if they use outdated software, and test the security implications of using the vulnerable software. To accomplish that, we collect the used modules (software and version) of the websites present in the *HTTPArchive* [4] over a period of 18 month, extract known vulnerabilities from the *National Vulnerability Database* database, and map them against the used software versions of the analyzed sites.

Identifying Used Software. To assess the update behavior of websites, we need to identify the software versions of the software in use. To do so, we utilized data provided by *HTTPArchive* [6], which includes all identified technologies used by a website. HTTPArchive crawls the landing page of millions of popular origins (mobile and desktop) based on the *Chrome User Experience Report* (CrUX) [3] every month, since January 2019. In CrUX, Google provides publicly metrics like load, interaction, layout stability of the websites that are visited by the Chrome web browser users on a monthly basis. This real-world dataset includes popular and unpopular websites [5]. In our study, we analyze all websites provided in HTTPArchive. Hence, we can use 18 data points in our measurement (M#1 – M#18). The data provided by HTTPArchive includes, among other data: (1) the date of the crawl, (2) the visited origins, and (3) identified technologies (software including its version). HTTPArchive uses *Wappalyzer* [24] to identify the used software, which uses different information provided by a site to infer the user version and technology stack. In order to make version changes comparable, we converted the provided data to the *semantic versioning* (SemVer) standard (i.e., `MAJOR.MINOR.PATCH`) [14] and validate also the version information from HTTPArchive as well as from NVD and check if provided versions are in a valid SemVer format. This unification allows us to map the observed versions of the known vulnerabilities. If we find an incomplete SemVer string, we extended it with ".0" until it fits the format.

Identifying Vulnerable Software. To better understand the security impact of updates, we map the software used by an origin to publicly known vulnerabilities. We collect the vulnerabilities from the *National Vulnerability Database* (NVD)[1]. Each entry in the NVD holds various information, but only three are essential to our study: (1) the date on which it was published, (2) a list of systems that are affected by it, and (3) the impact metrics how it can be exploited and its severity. In this work, we only focus on vectors that can be exploited by a remote network adversary.

---

[1] We used the database published on 04/07/20.

3.1   Dataset Preparation and Enrichment

Here, we describe the steps taken to enrich our dataset to make it more reliable.

Release History. To get a firm understanding of the update behaviour of websites, it is inevitable to know the dates on which different versions of a software were released ("release history"). To construct the list of release dates of each software product, we used *GitHub-API* for the official repositories, on *GitHub*, of the products and extracted the date on which a new version was pushed to it and store the corresponding SemVer. If a product did not provide an open repository on *GitHub*, we manually collected the official release dates from the product's official project webpages, if it's published.

Dataset Preparation. Since the Web is constantly evolving and Web measurements tend to be (strongly) impacted by noise, we only analyzed software products on a site for which we found version numbers in at least four consecutive measurements. Furthermore, we dropped all records with polluted data (e.g., blank, invalid versions, duplicates, dummy data) from our dataset. Finally, in order to make a valid match between CVE entries and software in our dataset, we manually assigned each software in our dataset their CPE (naming scheme) using the *CPE Dictionary* [12] provided by NVD.

3.2   Analyzing Updating Behavior and Security Implications

In this section, we describe how we measure update behavior and identify vulnerable websites.

Updating Behavior. To understand update behavior in our dataset, one needs to measure the deployed software's version changes over time. Utilizing the release dates of each software product, we know, at each measurement point in our dataset, whether a site/origin deploys the latest software version of a product or if it should be updated. If we found that an outdated product is used, we check if it was updated in the subsequent measurements (i.e., if the SemVer increases). This approach allows us to test if a product is updated after all and to check how long this process took. In our analysis, we call an increasing SemVer an *update* and decreasing version number a *downgrade*. In this analysis, we compare the `MINOR` and `PATCH` part of a product's SemVer, utilizing the release dates of each version, and not the `MAJOR` section because service providers might not use the latest major release due to significant migration overhead. For example, we would consider that an origin is "up to date" if it runs version 1.1.0 of a product even if version 2.1.0 (major release change) is available. However, if version 1.1.1 would be available, we consider it "out of date".

Identifying Vulnerable Websites. One way to measure the impact of an update on the security of a site is to test if more or less vulnerabilities exists for the new version, in contrast to the old version. To identify vulnerable software on a website, we retrieve the relevant CVEs for the identified software and then check if it is defined in these CVE entries – with consideration of *version-Start[Excluding/Including]* and *versionEnd[Excluding/Including]* settings. We map a vulnerability to a crawled origin if and only if (1) it uses a software for which a vulnerability exists and (2) if it was published before the crawl was conducted. Utilizing the *Common Vulnerability Scoring System* (CVSS) of each vulnerability, we can also assess the theoretical gain in security.

4   Results

After describing our approach to analyze the update behavior of websites and its possible security impact on websites, this section introduces the large-scale measurement results. Overall, we observed 8.315.260 origins on 5.655.939 distinct domains using 342 distinct software products. After filtering, we were left with 8.205.923 origins (99%) on 5.604.657 domains (99%) using 246 (72%) software products. We collected 31.909 releases for 246 software products. Furthermore, we collected 147.312 vulnerabilities of which 2.793 (2%) match to at least one identified product. Overall, we found an exploitable vulnerability for 148 (60%) of the analyzed software products. Note that products with no public release history are excluded from analyzing update behavior and security analysis if they don't have a known vulnerability. Note also we have full access to all the segments of the `MAJOR.MINOR.PATCH` for 98.5% of our data. In total, we identified 12.062.618 software updates across all measurements. Table 1 provides an overview of all evaluated records of each measurement run.

4.1   Update Behavior on the Web

In the following, we analyze the impact of adoption of releases on the Web on website level and from software perspective.

Update Behavior of Websites. The first step to understand the update behavior of websites is to analyze the fraction of used software products that are fully patched, according to our definitions. Remember that we assume that a software product should be updated if a newer minor version or patch is available (i.e., we exclude the major version (see Sect. 3.2)). In our dataset, we identified a median of 3 (min: 1, max: 17, avg: 3.37) evaluable software products for each website. Overall, we identified that across all measurement points, on average, 94% of all observed websites were *not* fully updated (i.e., at least for one software product exists a newer version). Only 6% of the observed sites used only up to date software while 47% entirely relied on outdated software types. The mean fraction of out of date software products is 74% for each observed website across our measurement points. These numbers show that websites often utilize outdated software. While at domain granularity, almost all analyzed sites use outdated software, it is interesting to analyze if subdomains show different update behavior. Figure 1 compares the fraction of up to date software utilized

Table 1. Overview of all measurement points.

M.	Date	#Sites	#Origins	#Products	#dist. Ver.	#Updates	#Vuln.
M#1	01/19	2.5M	3.4M	208	15,436	—	2,201
M#2	02/19	2.3M	3.1M	204	15,178	0.4M	2,224
M#3	03/19	2.3M	3.1M	205	15,390	0.5M	2,235
M#4	04/19	2.7M	3.5M	205	16,145	0.6M	2,291
M#5	05/19	2.8M	3.6M	216	16,741	0.4M	2,298
M#6	06/19	2.8M	3.6M	217	17,013	0.7M	2,310
M#7	07/19	3.0M	3.9M	215	17,438	0.6M	2,286
M#8	08/19	3.0M	3.9M	215	17,474	0.5M	2,316
M#9	09/19	3.0M	3.9M	215	17,682	1.0M	2,390
M#10	10/19	3.0M	3.8M	217	17,873	0.8M	2,424
M#11	11/19	3.0M	3.8M	217	17,958	1.0M	2,468
M#12	12/19	3.0M	3.8M	216	18,122	1.0M	2,478
M#13	01/20	2.9M	3.8M	217	18,173	0.8M	2,502
M#14	02/20	2.7M	3.4M	211	17,558	0.4M	2,526
M#15	03/20	3.1M	3.9M	217	18,558	0.4M	2,412
M#16	04/20	3.3M	4.2M	217	19,321	0.6M	2,467
M#17	05/20	3.1M	4.0M	220	19,353	0.8M	2,460
M#18	06/20	3.4M	4.4M	218	20,118	0.6M	2,475

on subdomains (e.g., *bar.foo.com*) against the root domains (e.g., *foo.com*), along our measurement points. In the figure, zero means that all software is up to date and one means that all software is outdated. Our data shows that most software products are not updated to the newest release, but it is still interesting to analyze the update cycles websites use in the field. On average, we observed 0.7M version changes between two measurement runs. 97 % of them were upgrades (i.e., the SemVer increased) and consequently 3 % were downgrades.

Update Behavior from a Software Perspective. Previously, we have shown that websites tend to use outdated software. In the following, we take a closer look at the used software to get a better understanding if the type of used software has an impact on its update frequency. Across all measurements, the software used on the live systems is 44 months old (M#1: 40, M#18: 48), and the trend during the measurement is that it gets even older (18 days each month on average). To determine how the average age changes by software types, we measured the average age of the top ten used software types for all measurement points. These top ten account for 65 % of all analyzed software types. In Fig. 2 we show the corresponding results. Our finding clarifies that client-side software (e.g., JavaScript Libraries) is older than server-side software (e.g., Web Servers). A closer observation of the releases SW shows that the server-side software has shorter release cycles than client-side

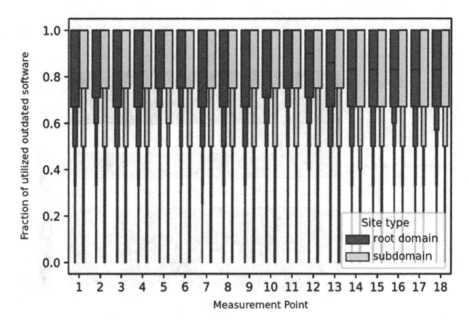

Fig. 1. Fractions of utilized outdated software products on the analyzed domains in comparison to their subdomains (1 = no product is up-to-date).

software in the measured period (e.g., *nginx* has 18 and *jQuery* only has 6 releases). While the age of the software itself is not necessarily a problem per se, it is notable that the average number of months a utilized software is behind the latest patch is 48. The ANOVA test ($\alpha = 0.05$) showed no statistical evidence that the popularity of a website, according to the *Tranco* list [11], has an impact on the age of the used software (i.e., popular and less popular websites use outdated software alike). Using software that is four years old might be troubling, given that on average 41 newer version exists, because the software might have severe security issues. We have shown that overall mostly outdated software is used. However, it is interesting to understand if this applies to all types of software alike or if specific products are updated more frequently.

Adoption of Software Releases. To get a better understanding of the update behavior of websites, we observe the adoption of releases. We find that every month, on average, 67 % of the software used has a new release. However, our observations show that only a few service providers install the release promptly. We record that on average, only 7 % of available updates are processed (min: 4 %, max: 11 %). The mean time between two updates for any of the used software on one website is 3.5 months (SD: 5.4). To get a more in-depth understanding of the adoption of software releases, we measure it in a time span of 30 days after the release. Figure 3 shows the fraction of processed updates by websites in that time span for the top eight software types. The top eight types account

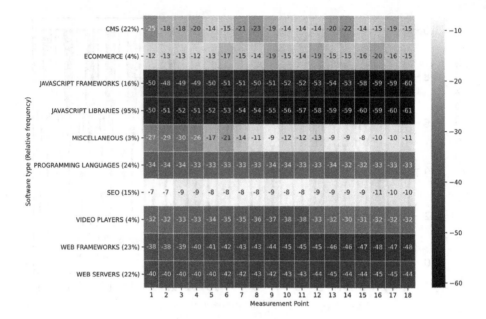

Fig. 2. Average age (in month) of top utilized 10 software types for all measurement points.

for 60 % of all used software. In general, we see that PATCH level releases are processed most frequently. Furthermore, we observe that the adoption of release types differ based on the software types. E-Commerce software process PATCH releases most frequently and search engine optimization software (SEO) MAJOR releases respectively. We assume that integrated automatic background updates play an important role why specific software types are updated. For example *WordPress* and *Shopware*, two popular content management systems, provide an auto update functionality [17, 25].

Summary. Based on our dataset, we have shown that the used software on the Web is often very old and not updated frequently. While differences in the update behavior between different types of software exist, the majority of all times is still not updated. However, the impact of this not-updating is not clear and needs more investigation.

4.2 Security Impact of *Not* Updating

Experts agree that updating is one of the most critical tasks one should do to harden a system or to avoid data leaks [15]. Therefore, we are interested in the security impact of the identified tend to use outdated software.

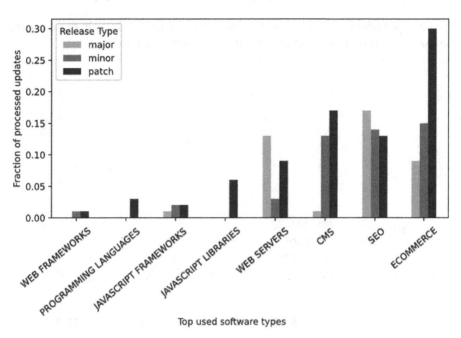

Fig. 3. Fraction of processing a new release for top used eight software types.

Vulnerability of Websites. Towards understanding the threats that result from the usage of outdated software, we first analyze the scope of affected websites. On average, 94 % of the analyzed websites contain at least one potential vulnerable software, which was slightly increasing over the course of our measurements (M#1: 92 % to M#18: 95 %). We also record that each analyzed software has on average 8 vulnerabilities and that websites are affected, on average, by 29 (min: 0, max: 963). Our data shows that the number of exploitable vulnerabilities is decreasing over time for both per software (0.4 per month) and per websites (0.14 per month). Hence, overall the number of websites that have at least one vulnerability increases but the amount of vulnerabilities per site decreases.

Each vulnerability has a different security impact on a website, and, therefore, the number of identified vulnerabilities does not directly imply the severeness of them. The NVD assigns a score to each vulnerability to highlight its severeness (i.e., the CVSS score). Figure 4 shows the mean CVSS scores for the analyzes websites their rank. By inspecting the figure, one can see that less popular sites (the rank is higher) are affected by more severe vulnerabilities. The Spearman test ($\alpha = 0.05$) showed a statistical significant correlation between the rank and the mean CVSS score of the identified vulnerabilities (p-value < 0.007). Table 2, in Appendix A lists the most common vulnerabilities in our last measurement point (M#18). A stunning majority of websites (92 %) is theoretically vulnerable to *Cross-site Scripting* (XSS) attacks. In our dataset, *jQuery* is the software that is most often affected by a CVE (92 %). A list of the most prominent CVEs is given in Appendix C. Given the wide occurrence of vulnerabilities in our dataset, the question arises which threats websites and users actually face.

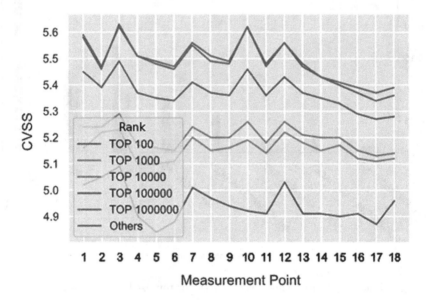

Fig. 4. AVG CVSS by popularity of websites. Vulnerability severity is significantly lower for high-ranked websites.

Analysis of Available Vulnerabilities. Figure 5, shows the distribution of severity of identified vulnerabilities on websites based on the *Common Vulnerability Scoring System* (CVSS). Our results show that the number of websites with the most severe vulnerability (CVSS: 10) steadily decreases. The average number of vulnerable websites with a severity "HIGH" (CVSS: 7–10) is decreasing (M#1: 43 %, M#18: 39 %), while the number of vulnerable websites with "MEDIUM" (CVSS: 4–7) remains almost constant (M#1: 47 %, M#18: 49 %). For this analysis, we only used the most severe vulnerability for each website.

Given the result that the average age of used software depends on its type (see Fig. 2), we find that older software has more dangerous vulnerabilities. For example, the average CVSS/age of JavaScript-Frameworks was 4/50 in M#1 and 6/62 in M#18, while the score and age for programming languages go from 9/34 to 8/33. This confirms that older software *does* have more vulnerabilities and highlights the need for better update processes of websites. Furthermore, our analysis shows that performing updates has a significant impact on the security of software. The average value of CVSS for software for which an update is available is 6.4 ("MEDIUM"). However, after applying the update(s), the CVSS is lowered to 2.4 ("LOW").

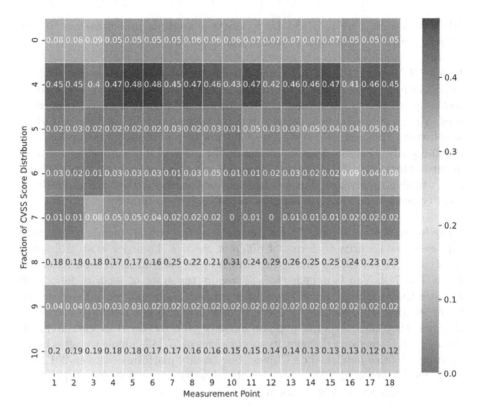

Fig. 5. Fraction of CVSS score distribution on websites for all measurement points (10 = Critical, 0 = No Vulnerability).

5 Limitations

Although we have put a great effort while preparing our dataset, our study is impacted by certain limitations. Our approach comes with the limitation that, on the one hand, *HTTPArchive* only crawls landing pages and does not interact with the website, which might hide the complexity of an origin [21], and, on the other hand, *Wappalyzer* might not detect all used software for the website. Although NVD is one of the most popular vulnerability databases, there are some discussions around the accuracy of the data provided by NVD e.g., [13,16]. In our study, we assume that software utilized by a website is vulnerable if the NVD provides a CVE entry for it. For ethical reasons, we did not validate if successful exploitation of the CVE requires any interaction or enabled functions. We also don't examine any mechanism for the validity of CVE entries.

6 Related Work

To the best of our knowledge, our study is the first one that measures update behavior and security implications by evaluating all utilized server and client-side software on a website and by conducting multiple measurements. In the following, we discuss studies related to our research.

Update Behavior. Update behavior of software has been previously studied. Tajalizadehkhoob et al. [19] measure the security state of software provided by hosting providers to understand the role of hosting providers for securing websites. Vaniea et al. [23] conduct a survey to understand the update behaviour of software. They ask 307 survey respondents to provide software update stories and analyze these stories to determine the possible motivations for software updates. Stock et al. [18] examine the top 500 websites per year between 1997 and 2016 utilizing archive.org dataset. In their measurement, they mainly evaluate security headers and analyse usage of outdated *jQuery* libraries.

Security Implications. Prior literature has proposed various techniques to measure websites' security in terms of different metrics. Lauinger et al. [10] study widely used 72 client-side JavaScript libraries usage and measure security across Alexa Top 75k. Van Goethem et al. [2] report the state of security for 22,000 websites that originate in 28 European countries. Their analysis is based on different metrics (e.g., security headers, information leakage, outdated software). However, they use only a few popular software products for their measurement. Huang et al. [7] measure the security mechanisms of 57,112 chinese websites based on vulnerabilities published on Chinese bug bounty platforms between 2012 and 2015. Van Acker et al. [22] scrutinize the security state of login webpages by attacking login pages of websites in the Alexa top 100k.

7 Discussion and Conclusion

In this work, we measured the update behavior and possible security implications of software products utilized on more than 5.6M websites. Our measurement highlights the current state of the Web and shows the update behavior of websites over the course of 18 month. We show that most of the Web's utilized software is outdated, often by more than four years. Running outdated software is not a security problem per se because the old software might not be vulnerable. However, we found several sites that use software products for which vulnerabilities have been reported. Furthermore, we show that the number of vulnerable websites increases over time while the average severity of identified vulnerabilities decreases. For instance, we record that 95 % of websites *potentially* contain at least one vulnerable software. It has to be noted that the identified vulnerabilities in our work must be seen as an upper bound because utilizing a product for which vulnerabilities exist does not automatically mean that it can be exploited (e.g., the vulnerable module of the product is deactivated or not used). Our results still highlight that website providers need to take more care about their update processes, even if this comes with a potential overhead, to protect their users and services.

Acknowledgment. This work was partially supported by the Ministry of Culture and Science of North Rhine-Westphalia (MKW grant 005-1703-0021 "MEwM" and "connect.emscherlippe") and by the Federal Ministry for Economic Affairs and Energy (grant 01MK20008E "Service-Meister").

A   Overview of the Top Identified CWEs

In this appendix, we show our findings related to identified CWEs. Table 2 lists the most common CWEs on websites that we identified in the last measurement run (June 2020). While the vulnerability *Cross-site Scripting* (XSS) occurs in almost all websites, a closer analysis of the same measurement point (M#18) shows that only 28% of software is vulnerable to this vulnerability.

Table 2. Top 10 vulnerabilities in our last measurement point (M#18) by relative frequency on websites.

Vulnerability type (CWE)	Relative frequency
CWE-79 Improper Neutralization of Input During Web Page Generation ('Cross-site Scripting')	0.92
CWE-20 Improper Input Validation	0.32
CWE-400 Uncontrolled Resource Consumption	0.27
CWE-200 Exposure of Sensitive Information to an Unauthorized Actor	0.24
CWE-476 NULL Pointer Dereference	0.24
CWE-601 URL Redirection to Untrusted Site ('Open Redirect')	0.22
CWE-125 Out-of-bounds Read	0.22
CWE-119 Improper Restriction of Operations within the Bounds of a Memory Buffer	0.20
CWE-787 Out-of-bounds Write	0.19
CWE-190 Integer Overflow or Wraparound	0.17
CWE-284 Improper Access Control	0.17

Table 3. Some examples of vulnerabilities identified on analyzed websites that run outdated software.

Software	CVE	CVE Publication	CWE	CVSS	Public exploit	Vuln. Websites	Total usage
jQuery	CVE-2020-11023	04.2020	XSS	4.3	✗	3.98M	4M
Apache	CVE-2017-7679	06.2017	Buffer Over-read	7.5	✓	0.26M	0.46M
PHP	CVE-2015-8880	05.2016	Double free	10	✓	0.45M	0.46M
PHP	CVE-2016-2554	03.2016	Buffer Over-read	10	✓	0.23M	0.46M
WordPress	CVE-2018-20148	12.2018	Deserialization of Untrusted Data	7.3	✓	0.18M	0.46M
WordPress	CVE-2019-20041	12.2019	Improper Input Validation	7.3	✗	0.31M	0.46M

B   Average age of the 20 used software by website-ranking

Figure 6 shows the most popular software types, their average age (in month), and the rank of the websites on which they are used. We record that most of the widely used software on the web is often very old. We also found that the average age of utilized software on a website is unrelated to its popularity, according to the *Tranco* list [11].

C   Case Studies

Table 3 illustrates the most common CVE entries identified in our study. *CVE-2020-11023* is the most common vulnerability with the severity "MEDIUM" – based on our last measurement. Some of the vulnerabilities require certain functions or enabled functions (e.g., CVE-2017-7679 for *Apache* requires *mod_mime*

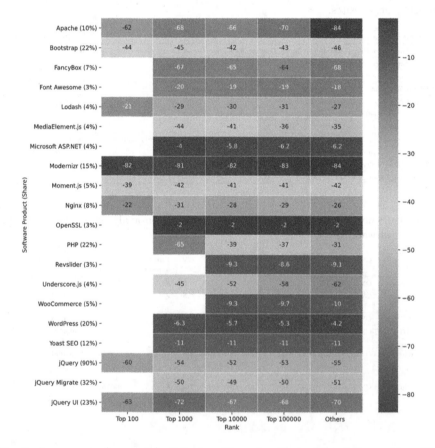

Fig. 6. Average age (in month) of the top 20 used software by website ranking. The share of software in our dataset is shown in brackets – Blank cells: no website identified in the corresponding ranking.

and CVE-2016-2554 for *PHP* requires file uploading functionality) In some cases, the running software requires interaction between more than one component to abuse an exploit. The listed vulnerabilities for *WordPress* and vulnerability CVE-2015-8880 for *PHP* do not require any interaction or enabled features and can be exploited directly.

References

1. Barth, A.: The Web Origin Concept. RFC 6465, Internet Engineering Task Force (2011). https://tools.ietf.org/html/rfc6454
2. van Goethem, T., Chen, P., Nikiforakis, N., Desmet, L., Joosen, W.: Large-scale security analysis of the web: challenges and findings. In: Holz, T., Ioannidis, S. (eds.) Trust 2014. LNCS, vol. 8564, pp. 110–126. Springer, Cham (2014). https://doi.org/10.1007/978-3-319-08593-7_8
3. Google Inc.: Chrome User Experience Report | Tools for Web Developers (2020). https://developers.google.com/web/tools/chrome-user-experience-report?hl=de. Accessed 08 June 2020
4. HTTP Archive: About HTTP Archive (2020). https://httparchive.org/about. Accessed 20 Oct 2020
5. HTTP Archive: Methodology—The Web Almanac by HTTP Archive (2020). https://httparchive.org. Accessed 18 Jan 2021
6. HTTP Archive: The HTTP Archive Tracks How the Web is Built (2020). https://httparchive.org. Accessed 20 Oct 2020
7. Huang, C., Liu, J., Fang, Y., Zuo, Z.: A study on web security incidents in China by analyzing vulnerability disclosure platforms. Comput. Secur. **58** (2016). https://doi.org/10.1016/j.cose.2015.11.006
8. Ikram, M., Masood, R., Tyson, G., Kaafar, M.A., Loizon, N., Ensafi, R.: The chain of implicit trust: an analysis of the web third-party resources loading. In: International Conference on World Wide Web, WWW, International World Wide Web Conferences Steering Committee (2019). https://doi.org/10.1145/3308558.3313521
9. Kula, R.G., German, D.M., Ouni, A., Ishio, T., Inoue, K.: Do developers update their library dependencies? Empirical Softw. Eng. **23**(1), 384–417 (2017). https://doi.org/10.1007/s10664-017-9521-5
10. Lauinger, T., Chaabane, A., Arshad, S., Robertson, W., Wilson, C., Kirda, E.: Thou shalt not depend on me: analysing the use of outdated javascript libraries on the web. In: Symposium on Network and Distributed System Security, NDSS (2017). https://doi.org/10.14722/ndss.2017.23414
11. Le Pochat, V., Van Goethem, T., Tajalizadehkhoob, S., Korczyński, M., Joosen, W.: Tranco: a Research-oriented top sites ranking hardened against manipulation. In: Symposium on Network and Distributed System Security, NDSS (2019). https://doi.org/10.14722/ndss.2019.23386
12. National Institute of Standards and Technology: Official Common Platform Enumeration (CPE) Dictionary (2020). https://nvd.nist.gov/products/cpe. Accessed 19 Oct 2020
13. Nguyen, V.H., Massacci, F.: The (un)reliability of NVD vulnerable versions data: an empirical experiment on Google Chrome vulnerabilities. In: ACM Symposium on Information, Computer and Communications Security, AsiaCCS (2013). https://doi.org/10.1145/2484313.2484377

14. Preston-Werner, T.: Semantic Versioning 2.0.0 (2020). https://semver.org/. Accessed 20 Oct 2020
15. Redmiles, E.M., Kross, S., Mazurek, M.L.: How I learned to be secure: a census-representative survey of security advice sources and behavior. In: ACM Conference on Computer and Communications Security, CCS (2016). https://doi.org/10.1145/2976749.2978307
16. Shahzad, M., Shafiq, M.Z., Liu, A.X.: A large scale exploratory analysis of software vulnerability life cycles. In: International Conference on Software Engineering, ICSE (2012). https://doi.org/10.5555/2337223.2337314
17. shopware AG: Updating Shopware (2020). https://docs.shopware.com/en/shopware-5-en/update-guides/updating-shopware. Accessed 20 Oct 2020
18. Stock, B., Johns, M., Steffens, M., Backes, M.: How the web tangled itself: uncovering the history of client-side web (in)security. In: USENIX Security Symposium, SEC (2017). https://doi.org/10.5555/3241189.3241265
19. Tajalizadehkhoob, S., et al.: Herding vulnerable cats: a statistical approach to disentangle joint responsibility for web security in shared hosting. In: ACM Conference on Computer and Communications Security, CCS (2017). https://doi.org/10.1145/3133956.3133971
20. Torchiano, M., Ricca, F., Marchetto, A.: Are web applications more defect-prone than desktop applications? Int. J. Softw. Tools Technol. Transf. **13**(2), 151–166 (2011). https://doi.org/10.1007/s10009-010-0182-6
21. Urban, T., Degeling, M., Holz, T., Pohlmann, N.: Beyond the front page: measuring third party dynamics in the field. In: International Conference on World Wide Web, WWW (2020). https://doi.org/10.1145/3366423.3380203
22. Van Acker, S., Hausknecht, D., Sabelfeld, A.: Measuring login webpage security. In: Symposium on Applied Computing, SAC, pp. 1753–1760 (2020). https://doi.org/10.1145/3019612.3019798
23. Vaniea, K., Rashidi, Y.: Tales of software updates: the process of updating software. In: Conference on Human Factors in Computing Systems, CHI (2016). https://doi.org/10.1145/2858036.2858303
24. Wappalyzer: Identify technology on websites–Wappalyzer (2020). https://www.wappalyzer.com. Accessed 08 July 2020
25. WordPress: Configuring Automatic Background Updates (2019). https://wordpress.org/support/article/configuring-automatic-background-updates. Accessed 20 Oct 2020
26. Zou, Y., Mhaidli, A.H., McCall, A., Schaub, F.: "I've got nothing to lose": consumers' risk perceptions and protective actions after the equifax data breach. In: Symposium on Usable Privacy and Security, SOUPS (2018). https://doi.org/10.5555/3291228.3291245

Winding Path: Characterizing the Malicious Redirection in Squatting Domain Names

Yuwei Zeng[1,2], Xunxun Chen[1,3], Tianning Zang[1,2(✉)], and Haiwei Tsang[4]

[1] Institute of Information Engineering, Chinese Academy of Sciences, Beijing, China
{zengyuwei,zangtianning}@iie.ac.cn
[2] School of Cyber Security, University of Chinese Academy of Sciences, Beijing, China
[3] National Computer Network Emergency Response Technical Team/Coordination Center of China, Beijing, China
[4] Jilin University, Changchun, China

Abstract. An increasing number of adversaries tend to cover up their malicious sites by leveraging the elaborate redirection chains. Prior works mostly focused on the specific attacks that users suffered, and seldom considered how users were exposed to such attacks. In this paper, we conduct a comprehensive measurement study on the malicious redirections that leverage squatting domain names as the start point. To this end, we collected 101,186 resolved squatting domain names that targeted 2,302 top brands from the ISP-level DNS traffic. After dynamically crawling these squatting domain names, we pioneered the application of performance log to mine the redirection chains they involved. Afterward, we analyzed the nodes that acted as intermediaries in malicious redirections and found that adversaries preferred to conduct URL redirection via imported JavaScript codes and iframes. Our further investigation indicates that such intermediaries have obvious aggregation, both in the domain name and the Internet infrastructure supporting them.

Keywords: Domain squatting · URL redirection

1 Introduction

URL redirection has been widely used since its inception. With this technique, website administrators are able to provide more customized navigation services for visitors by specifying certain parameters in the URL (e.g., language). Instead of directly typing the lengthy URL into the browser's address bar, users can walk through diverse web resources easily with the help of URL redirection. However, this technique is now being abused by adversaries to circumvent static web security checks [18]. Compared with directly delivering malicious content to any visitor, this method is able to ensure the targeted delivery of malicious content by conducting multi-layer verification during the process of visitors being

© Springer Nature Switzerland AG 2021
O. Hohlfeld et al. (Eds.): PAM 2021, LNCS 12671, pp. 93–107, 2021.
https://doi.org/10.1007/978-3-030-72582-2_6

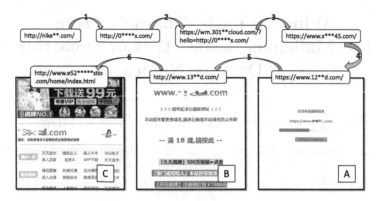

Fig. 1. An example of malicious redirection. The domain name of the start URL is a combo squatting of 'nike.com'.

redirected [13,25]. For instance, the adversary checks whether the current visitor is a static crawler by inspecting the 'User-Agent' field of HTTP request header.

Although an elaborate redirection chain can boost the stealth of the malicious site to some extent, it lowers the accessibility of that site as well. Therefore, in order to get more traffic, some adversaries have targeted the squatting domain names [23]. Domain squatting refers to the impersonation of particular brands at the domain level, so as to confuse visitors. For instance, 'bauidu.com' is a typo squatting of 'baidu.com', which targets the user who extra types a character 'u' while entering 'baidu.com'. By exploiting these squatting domain names as the start node of redirection chains, adversaries can arbitrarily control the direction of careless visitors, and even determine the malicious behavior to be performed based on the profile of visitors.

To facilitate the understanding of such malicious redirections, we present a real-world example in Fig. 1, which abuses a combo squatting domain name of 'nike.com' as the start node. To prevent the relevant malicious domain names from being further spread, we have hidden some characters in Fig. 1. This example contains 7 URLs and 6 hops, of which the first hop uses the HTTP-based redirection with 302 status code, while the remaining five hops are all performed via certain JavaScript codes. Before reaching the fifth URL, there is nothing displayed on the page. After rendering the HTML content returned by the fifth URL, a loading bar and a button appear on the page (Page A). If the user does not click the button within a given time, this page will auto-redirect the user to the next page (Page B), which lists several links to illegal gambling sites. Similarly, if the user does not interact with this page within a given time, he will be redirected to the final URL, which serves an illegal pornographic site (Page C).

Prior works have analyzed various types of squatting domain names. However, all of these works focus on the specific malicious behaviors involved in such domain names (e.g., phishing) [14,23]. So far, nobody has paid attention to how visitors are transferred from the squatting domain names to the sites that actually conduct malicious activities. In this paper, we first lift the veil of such malicious intermediaries in malicious activities, namely the relay nodes in malicious redirections. To this end, we make the following contributions: First, we measure the typical squatting domain names in Chinese DNS traffic; Second, we pioneered the application of performance log to mine malicious redirection chains; Third, we accurately analyze the redirection method abused by malicious intermediaries; Fourth, we profile the sharing of such intermediaries in malicious redirections.

2 Background

2.1 Domain Squatting Abuse

Domain squatting abuse refers to the malicious preemptive registration of domain names that are similar to well-known brands. According to prior works, there are six types of commonly-seen domain squatting abuse in the Internet today, comprising typo [7,22], bit [20], homograph [11], combo [15], level [10], and wrong-TLD [23]. Here, we use the real-world examples listed in Table 1 to explain the definition of each squatting type.

Table 1. Examples of different squatting types.

#	Domain	Target	Type
1	bauidu.com	baidu.com	typo
2	taocao.com	taobao.com	bit
3	xvide0s.com	xvideos.com	homograph
4	nikeav.com	nike.com	combo
5	weixin.qq.com.powlau.kunxiangrunhe.com.cn	qq.com	level
6	cnki.xyz	cnki.net	wrong-TLD

- Typo: Users may request incorrect domain names due to the careless typing. Typo squatting leverages this "fat finger" phenomenon of users when they are typing the domain names, which involves the following four typo scenarios: insertion, omission, permutation, and replacement. The first sample in Table 1 is a typo squatting of 'baidu.com', which additionally inserts a character 'u' between 'a' and 'i' ('u' is adjacent to 'i' on the keyboard).
- Bit: The bit may be flipped during the transmission due to some external reasons. Bit squatting leverages such bit-flip phenomenon occurring in domain names. As the second sample in Table 1, which flips the lowest bit of 'b' (01100010) from 0 to 1 to get the character 'c' (01100011).
- Homograph: Homograph squatting refers to the replacement of characters in target brands with other visually indistinguishable ones. Take the third sample in Table 1, the squatter uses the digit '0' to imitate the character 'o'.

- Combo: Combo squatting is to combine the target brand with other words to form a new domain name. Compared with the other five types, combo squatting is capable of maintaining the integrity of target brands to the greatest extent, so as to resort to their reputations to attract users. For example, the fourth sample attaches the word 'av' to the tail of 'nike' to form an easy-to-remember domain name of an adult site.
- Level: As opposed to the above four squatting types that tampering with the 2LD, level squatting focuses on its own subdomain. That is, adversary uses the intact target domain name as its subdomain. For example, the fifth sample in Table 1 directly uses 'weixin.qq.com' as its subdomain. In certain cases where the complete domain name cannot be displayed because of space limitation, users can only see the prefix part of the domain name, thus mistaking it for Tencent's authoritative domain name.
- Wrong-TLD: Wrong-TLD squatting refers to replacing the TLD of target domain name while maintaining the remainder of this domain name unchanged. As the last sample shown in Table 1, it impersonates the target domain name by replacing the TLD '.net' with '.xyz'. Compared with the above five squatting types, this type is the most confusing to users.

2.2 URL Redirection

URL redirection technique has been widely used in a variety of web activities, making the Internet users navigate between various web resources without manually typing the lengthy target URL into the address bar. There are three main types of redirection approaches at present, namely HTTP-based, JavaScript-based, and HTML-based. Table 2 lists some examples to illustrate these redirection approaches.

Table 2. Illustration of the URL redirection approaches.

Redirection	Example
HTTP	Status Code: 30X Location: http://domain.com/
	Refresh: 2; url = http://domain.com/
JavaScript	document.location = 'http://domain.com/'
	window.location = 'http://domain.com'
HTML	<meta http-equiv="refresh" content="2; url = http://domain.com/">
	<a href="http://domain.com/">

- HTTP-based: HTTP-based redirection has two forms: 1). When the requested resource is migrated to a brand new URL, to ensure the old URL is still available, the server will write the current URL of the requested resource in the 'Location' field of corresponding HTTP response message, and set the status code to 30X; 2). The server fills in the 'Refresh' field of the HTTP

Response Header to command the client to request the given URL after a given time. For example, the second sample in Table 2 indicates that the current page will be navigated to "http://domain.com" right after 2 s.

- JavaScript-based: This approach refers to rewriting the 'location' attribute of current document (or window) object to target URL through JavaScript scripts, and then redirecting the current page to the target URL. Compared with HTTP-based redirection, this approach gives developers more autonomy, enabling the redirection to be triggered only when certain conditions are met.
- HTML-based: HTML-based redirection mainly refers to the user's active click on the <a> tag on current page to perform the page jump. The 'href' field of <a> tag indicates the destination of the page jump. Besides, there is another case of HTML-based redirection, that is, by adding a <meta>-refresh tag below the <head> tag. In specific, by setting the 'http-equiv' attribute of <meta> to 'refresh', and specifying the waiting time and target URL in its 'content' attribute. The browser will automatically jump to the specified URL after parsing the <head> tag.

3   Measurement Methodology

This section first introduces the approach we employ to collect resolved squatting domains from real DNS traffic. Then, we describe the dynamic crawling strategy we use to get the redirection chain behind these domains.

3.1   Measuring Squatting Domains

Intuitively speaking, the higher the popularity of target domain names, the greater the probability of relevant squatting domains being visited. Therefore, we first collected the domain name of target brands from three authoritative data sources:

- Alexa Category List: Alexa provides 17 category lists, such as arts, business, and computers. Each of them lists the 50 most visited domain names in the category [3]. We crawled this site and finally obtained a total of 850 candidate brand domain names.
- Alexa Top List: Alexa maintains a domain popularity ranking based on the daily traffic of each domain name [1]. We extracted the Top-1000 from this list as candidates.
- CN Top List: Since our experiment was conducted on a Chinese network environment, it is clear that we can observe more squatting domains specifically targeting Chinese brands. Therefore, we got domain names of the Top-1000 Chinese sites from an authoritative organization [4].

Due to the day-to-day fluctuation of the domain top List [21], here we obtained the Alexa Lists for 8 consecutive days from [2] (the dates of these lists are consistent with the dates of DNS traffic we use), and extracted the

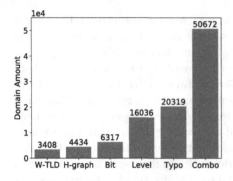 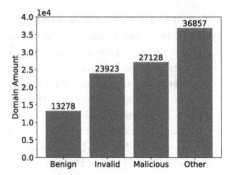

Fig. 2. Breakdown of different squatting types.

Fig. 3. Breakdown of the labeling results.

1000 domains with the highest overall ranking. We aggregated the above list and merged the domain names that had the same 2LD (e.g., 'tmall.com' and 'login.tmall.com'). Finally, we got a total of 2,302 distinct brand domain names. Next, we asked for the resolver-to-client DNS traffic from a local Internet service provider (ISP) for 8 consecutive days, ranging from 04/27/2019 to 05/04/2019. These traffic records all DNS packets returned from local recursive DNS servers to clients. We used these data to build a passive DNS (pDNS) database. Due to the tremendous volume of data, we only reserved the A-type resource records and filtered the resource records with no resolved values (NXDomain) to alleviate the storage overhead. Each entry in the database consists of four columns, namely the client's IP address, the queried domain name, the timestamp, and the resolved IP addresses. In addition, to protect the privacy of users, we have hashed the IP addresses of all clients. Eventually, we got a pDNS database with more than fourteen billion entries, averaging about seventy million entries per hour.

After the above preparations, according to the definition introduced in Sect. 2.1, we generated a large number of squatting domains based on the 2,302 brand domain names and verified their survival in the DNS traffic. Due to space limitation, we omit the description of generating candidate squatting domain names here. The specific generation steps can refer to the references mentioned in Sect. 2.1. In the end, we found 101,186 successfully resolved squatting domain names from the pDNS database. Figure 2 shows a breakdown of the six squatting types. Due to space limitation, 'wrong-TLD' and 'homograph' are abbreviated as 'w-TLD' and 'h-graph', respectively. The bars in this figure have been arranged in the ascending order of domain amount. We can see that combo squatting is absolutely dominant, accounting for more than 50.1% of all our collected squatting domain names. Followed by typo and level squatting, accounting for 20.1% and 15.8% of the total, respectively. While the remaining three types add up to only 14%. The above measurement results are basically consistent with the description in [23,27], reflecting the representativeness of the DNS traffic we use.

3.2   Crawling Strategy

In order to understand the abuse intention of these squatting domain names, we need to further analyze the specific behaviors they conduct. To this end, we crafted a dynamic crawler to automatically query these domain names and accurately record all events triggered during each querying. Specifically, we use Selenium [5], a Chrome-based tool, to build this crawler. Compared with the traditional static crawlers that can only return the HTML content of the website, Selenium is able to simulate all the operations that a user performs in the browser, such as mouse clicks.

Here, we employed the headless mode of Selenium, which allows us to run it in bulk on the backend of the server, and set its User-Agent to 'iPhone 6/7/8 Plus' to disguise as a mobile user. To prevent Selenium from crashing at runtime, we performed the crawler task in groups of five samples. We restarted the tool and cleared the cache right after each crawling (5 samples). In order to successfully capture all events triggered during the page loading, we waited 30 s for each sample. For each sample, we saved the HTML content, the screenshot, and the performance log.

Table 3. Explanation of typical methods in the performance log.

Method	Explanation
requestWillBeSent	Initiate an HTTP request for a specific URL
responseReceived	HTTP response about a specific URL
frameScheduledNavigation	Navigate to another document for certain reasons
frameAttached	Load the 'iframe' (or 'frame') in current document
navigatedWithinDocument	Navigate to an anchor within current document

The performance log of Chrome is absolutely the treasure we found in this work, which records all the events during the page loading with the dictionary form, including the requests for page resources and the operations performed by users. Compared with previous methods relying on the analysis of network traffic and HTML content, directly analyzing the entries in performance log is obviously much more efficient. There are mainly five methods in the performance log involving the request and receive of page resources, which are shown in Table 3. Among them, 'requestWillBeSent' and 'responseReceived' appear in pair, representing the request and response for specific page resources. The followed two methods, 'frameScheduledNavigation' and 'frameAttached', are used to reflect the request type of new document, where the former indicates the reason of certain navigation, and the latter indicates that the requested URL is the 'src' of certain <iframe> tag. The last method does not involve any requests for new resources, and it is only used to indicate the navigation to the target anchor within current document. In most cases, the requested URLs are derived from the 'src' field of HTML tags. While there are some exceptions, such as the requests initiated via embedded JavaScript snippets. Fortunately, in addition to completely recording the browser events, the performance log provides many assistant fields in each entry, which can precisely indicate the cause of this request (e.g., script initiated), the type of the requested resource (e.g., Document), and the most important, the initiator of this request (namely the parent URL).

Moreover, we also maintained a dataset to record the start time, the end time, the start URL, the end URL, and the title of final page of each crawling. After completing the crawling task, we extracted the entries involving resource requests from the performance log of each sample and rebuilt the URL request tree. Finally, we extracted the redirection chain from the rebuilt tree, that is, a path between the root node (i.e., start URL) and the end node (i.e., end URL). Note that, if an 'iframe' (or 'frame') occupies more than 80% of the current screen area, we consider it as an additional redirection. The reason lies in the fact that even though the URL in the address bar has not changed, 'iframe' is essentially another document. Any interaction a user makes in an 'iframe' is not restricted by the current document.

Next, we divided these samples into three equal parts and employed three well-trained volunteers to label them. To ensure the objectivity of the labeling results, each volunteer was responsible for two parts of the samples. They mainly resorted to the following six features during the labeling, namely the start URL, end URL, hop counts, and the title, screenshot, and HTML content of the final page. Due to the large number of samples, our labeling process lasted for more than two weeks. The samples were classified into four categories, namely benign, malicious, invalid, and other. Specifically, if a sample is ultimately navigated to a malicious site, distributes illegal contents or involves the drive-by download, we consider it to be malicious. Because pornography, gambling, lottery, and surrogacy are all illegal in China, we also regard the relevant sites as malicious sites here. If a sample returns an invalid page (e.g., 404 status code), we label it as invalid. If three volunteers disagree on the labeling result of one sample, we consider that sample as 'other'. Additionally, we found that a large number of samples were redirected to parked domain names. Even though we have not found that these samples involve malicious activities, some prior works have pointed out the potential threat of parked domain names [8,24]. Accordingly, in a comprehensive consideration, we classified all such samples as 'other'. Figure 3 shows the breakdown of labeling results, where the bars have been sorted based on the domain amount. Unsurprisingly, the proportion of benign samples is the least here. Some benign samples directly navigated users to the original task domain names. The remaining benign samples were used to support their own legitimate web services, which did not involve any illegal content. Besides, we can clearly see that the 'other' type occupies the most share of samples, accounting for about 36.4%. The vast majority of these 'other' samples were labeled due to being navigated to parked domain names, while only a few were labeled for the disagreements among volunteers. The 'malicious' type makes up 26.8% of the total. According to our investigations, which will be expounded in Sect. 4, most malicious samples participated in the distribution of pornographic or gambling services. Moreover, these samples tend to embed illegal content into the 'iframe' to evade the general static analysis [12,17,26].

4   Malicious Redirection Analysis

After the collection and labeling of malicious squatting domain names, we need to understand how these domains are leveraged to conduct malicious activities. In this section, we shed light on the redirection behavior involved in our collected squatting domain names. First, we compared the differences of URL redirection in malicious samples and benign samples. Next, we investigated the URLs acting as intermediaries in redirection chains. Finally, we analyzed the Internet infrastructures that held these intermediaries.

4.1   Benign Redirection vs. Malicious Redirection

Based on the discussion in Sect. 3.2, we know that most malicious squatting domain names will navigate users to illegal websites, while the benign ones tend to redirect users back to original domain names. Thus, it is necessary to figure out whether the redirection mode will change significantly for different destinations.

Table 4. Statistics of the samples conducting URL redirections.

Category	Domain amount	Redirection	Oversize iframe
Benign	13,278	7,071 (53.3%)	36 (0.3%)
Malicious	27,128	20,079 (74.0%)	11,158 (41.1%)

To this end, we extracted all the samples conducting URL redirections. Note again that if an 'iframe' occupies more than 80% of the current window, we treat it as one redirection. Table 4 lists the statistics of the samples. Obviously, URL redirection is a widely abused technique in malicious squatting domain names, accounting for up to 74%. Moreover, 41.1% of the malicious samples employ the oversize 'iframe's to display illicit information. It is worth noting that more than half of the benign samples performed redirections as well, which is absolutely a high proportion, but only 0.3% of them employed the oversize 'iframe's. These statistics are somewhat unexpected, that is, the disparity in the proportion of redirection between benign samples and malicious samples, although 20.7% is not a small gap, is not as significant as supposed.

In order to mine more useful characteristics, we extracted the redirection chain from each sample and further characterized the malicious redirection from two aspects, namely the distribution of both hop counts and redirection method. Table 5 shows the hop counts distribution of chains. Interestingly, even though 53.3% of the benign samples applied URL redirections, 87.5% of which had

Table 5. Hop counts distribution of the samples conducting URL redirection.

Category	Hop counts distribution										
	1	2	3	4	5	6	7	8	9	10	>10
Benign	87.5%	9.4%	2.5%	0.4%	0.1%	0.0%	0.0%	0.0%	0.0%	0.0%	0.0%
Malicious	31.1%	35.3%	13.7%	8.4%	4.5%	1.3%	0.7%	0.3%	0.2%	0.2%	4.3%

only one hop. However, some benign samples also reached five hops, which is already a relatively high hop counts. We investigated the samples that suffered five hops and found that these samples had a common characteristic, namely verifying the identity of visitors. In this case, visitors will be redirected to the login page or guest page if they are found to have no login account. In contrast, the hop counts distribution of malicious samples is relatively flat. Most malicious samples experienced two hops, while the corresponding proportion is only 35.3%. As shown in the last column of Table 5, 4.3% of the malicious samples were redirected more than 10 times. It is worth noting that, several malicious samples performed an astonishing 26 times of URL redirection and eventually landed on the same illegal fundraising site.

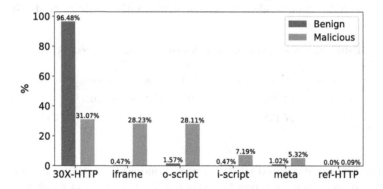

Fig. 4. Distribution of different redirection types.

Then, we measured the specific redirection methods used in the collected chains. According to the introduction in Sect. 2.2, URL redirection can be divided into three types based on the source of redirection command, namely HTTP-based, JavaScript-based, and HTML-based. More specifically, the HTTP-based redirection can be further subdivided into two cases: 30X-status-code-based and refresh-field-based (denoted as '30X-HTTP' and 'ref-HTTP', respectively). In addition, JavaScript-based redirection can also be subdivided into two cases, inner and outer, in the light of the source of snippets. In particular, the inner type (denoted as 'i-script') refers to the JavaScript codes that are hard-coded inside the <script> tags, while the outer type (denoted as 'o-script') refers to the JavaScript codes imported by assigning the 'src' field of <script> tags.

Figure 4 exhibits the distribution of redirection types. One can find that almost all benign samples employed '30X-HTTP' to perform URL redirection, accounting for 96.48% of the total. It is reasonable that legitimate web services tend to solve problems on the server-side. Compared with other redirection methods, '30X-HTTP' is able to minimize the computational overhead on the client. Here, we once again examined the benign samples mentioned in the previous paragraph that experienced five hops, and found that all the hops were performed based on the 30X status code of HTTP response message. However, '30X-HTTP' only accounted for 31.07% of the malicious samples. Besides, as we can see from Fig. 4, the redirection methods leveraged by adversaries are much more diverse. There is almost no difference among the utilization frequency of '30X-HTTP', 'iframe', and 'o-script' in malicious samples. Nevertheless, Fig. 4 still reveals the adversary's preference for JavaScript-based redirection [16,19,28]. Combining the proportions of 'o-script' and 'i-script', we can find that the JavaScript-based method accounts for 35.3% of the total. Moreover, in terms of the usage of redirection snippets, adversaries are obviously more inclined to import them from external files (i.e., o-script), rather than directly hard-coding them into the HTML content (i.e., i-script). In this way, adversaries can circumvent the static analysis of HTML content by security personnel to some extent.

4.2 Intermediary Sharing

We have presented in the previous subsection that there are some malicious samples that end up pointing to the same URL. That is, some samples start at different points but end at the same point. For instance, an adversary manages multiple squatting domain names, and forces them to navigate the visitors to an illegal gambling site under his control. Inspired by this, we speculated that there were certain samples that not only had the same destination, but also shared the same intermediary. To verify this conjecture, we aggregated all redirection chains in malicious samples to investigate whether there were common relay nodes.

Table 6. Measurements of the commonly used URL, domain names, and effective 2LDs in the malicious redirection chains.

	Total	Commonly used		Involved sample	
		#	%	#	%
URL	72,538	4,117	5.68%	15,593	57.48%
Domain name	40,525	3,634	8.97%	16,899	62.29%
effective 2LD	33,532	3,558	10.61%	17,060	62.89%

We first measured the URLs that appeared in multiple redirection chains. It should be noted that what we did here was an exact match of URL, including complete parameters and fragments. The second row in Table 6 shows the statistics of the commonly used URLs. In this case, we got a total of 72,538 distinct URLs, where 4,117 URLs appeared in at least two redirection chains, accounting for about 5.68% of the total. In addition, these commonly used URLs involved 15,593 malicious samples. That is to say, 57.48% of the malicious squatting domain names have business sharing among them, which is indeed a large proportion.

Next, we turn our attention to the commonly used domain names in malicious redirections. Compared with the commonly used URLs, commonly used domain names obviously own much higher coverage. Because in this case, we no longer need to match various URL parameters and URL fragments as before. Also, we ignored the port field when extracting domain names from URLs. Table 6 lists the corresponding measurement results in the third row. We obtained 40,525 distinct domain names from the redirection chain of malicious samples, of which 3,634 domain names were leveraged by more than one sample, accounting for 8.97% of the total. Moreover, there were about 62.29% of the malicious samples shared these intermediary domain names in common.

However, we found during the measurement process that although some relay nodes have different domain names, the difference only exists in their subdomain names. In other words, these relay nodes have the same effective 2LD (e2LD). Based on this, we further digged deep into the e2LD level and found that 10.61% of e2LDs appeared in multiple malicious redirection chains. However, compared with the commonly used domain names, the coverage of the commonly used e2LDs has not increased significantly. In general, there were only 161 more involved samples in this case.

4.3 Infrastructure Sharing

This part focuses on our investigation on the Internet infrastructures holding such intermediary domain names. Concretely, we will discuss the abuse of Internet infrastructures by malicious redirections from the bottom up in terms of three aspects, namely IP, BGP, and AS.

We have introduced the sharing of e2LDs in malicious redirections in Sect. 4.2. Here, we matched the associated IP addresses of those 33,532 e2LDs from the built pDNS database, which yielded 27,396 distinct IP addresses. This result indicates that numerous e2LDs are being resolved to the same IP address. We then found out these IP addresses that supported multiple e2LDs from the pDNS database. The second row of Table 7 lists the relevant statistics, from which we can see that 8.38% of these IP addresses are responsible for the resolution of multiple malicious intermediaries at the same time. Furthermore, 41.93% of the malicious samples involved the sharing of IP addresses during their redirections.

With these matched IP addresses, we moved our attention to their BGP prefixes. Here, we resorted to a third-party Python extension module, called 'pyasn' [9], to lookup the BGP prefix of an IP address based on a daily updated public BGP archive [6]. Ultimately, we got a total of 8,932 BGP prefixes, of which 4,817 were abused by at least two malicious intermediaries. Moreover, it is shocking that these BGPs have provided resolution services for 92.54% of

Table 7. Measurements of the commonly used IP addresses, BGP prefixes, and ASes in the malicious redirection chains.

	Total	Commonly used		Involved sample	
		#	%	#	%
IP	27,396	2,296	8.38%	11,375	41.93%
BGP	8,932	4,817	53.93%	25,104	92.54%
AS	754	424	56.23%	26,608	98.08%

the malicious squatting domain names, directly or indirectly. In addition to the lookup of BGP prefix, 'pyasn' also provides the lookup of AS number. In this way, we further measured the AS that claimed the ownership of those abused BGPs. The fourth row of Table 7 shows the statistics of AS. We can see that the 8,932 BGPs are eventually aggregated into 754 ASes, and 424 of them have been exploited by more than one malicious intermediaries, accounting for 56.23% of the total. More importantly, 98.08% of the malicious samples involved the abuse of these 424 ASes during their redirections.

The above measurements reveal an important role that the Internet Infrastructure playing in malicious redirection activities. Because different countries (or regions) have different attitudes towards the grey Internet services, adversaries tend to select such ISP with weaker Internet supervision to set up their network services. This leads to the measurement results in this subsection, that is, the vast majority of malicious intermediary domain names aggregate in the same Internet infrastructure.

5   Limitation

This paper focuses on the malicious redirections that stem from squatting domain names, but the domain types employing such malicious services in the wild are far more than just squatting domain names. Besides, we only considered the domain rankings when selecting target brands, but missed some hot terms at that time, making the squatting domain names we generated lack timeliness to some extent. For example, a large number of pandemic-related squatting domain names have emerged in early 2020. In addition to the sharing of Internet infrastructures, we found that many malicious domain names also exhibit obvious aggregation in the requested web resources. That is, we can leverage this sharing phenomenon to mine more suspicious domain names involving such malicious sharing resources. Moreover, we have not shed much light on the specific working mechanism of the malicious redirection in this paper, especially the JavaScript-based method. In terms of the experiment background, our measurements are all conducted in the Chinese network environment, which makes us unclear about the abuse URL redirections in other regions. Solving the above problems plays an important role in understanding the target victims, working mechanism, and monetization of malicious redirection, and we will leave them for future work.

6   Conclusion

In this paper, we give the first insight into the malicious redirections which start with squatting domain names. By crawling these domain names and analyzing their performance logs, we identified 20,079 squatting domain names leveraged URL redirection to navigate visitors to malicious sites. The investigation of corresponding redirection chains shows that adversaries prefer to perform malicious redirections via imported JavaScript codes or iframes. More importantly, our further measurements reveal that there is a very common phenomenon of resource sharing among various malicious redirection chains.

Acknowledgment. We thank the anonymous reviewers for their comments on this paper. We would also like to thank Ignacio Castro for shepherding this paper. This work was partially supported by the National Key Research and Development Program of China under grant No. 2016QY05X1002 and the Strategic Priority Research Program of Chinese Academy of Sciences under grant No. XDC02030100.

References

1. Alexa Top 1M Sites. https://www.alexa.com/topsites
2. Alexa Top 1M Sites Archive. https://toplists.net.in.tum.de/archive/alexa/
3. Alexa Top Category Sites. https://www.alexa.com/topsites/category
4. CN Top Sites. http://www.alexa.cn/siterank/
5. Selenium. https://www.selenium.dev/
6. University of Oregon Route Views Archive Project. http://archive.routeviews.org/
7. Agten, P., Joosen, W., Piessens, F., Nikiforakis, N.: Seven months' worth of mistakes: a longitudinal study of typosquatting abuse. In: Proceedings of the 22nd Network and Distributed System Security Symposium (NDSS 2015). Internet Society (2015)
8. Alrwais, S., Yuan, K., Alowaisheq, E., Li, Z., Wang, X.: Understanding the dark side of domain parking. In: 23rd {USENIX} Security Symposium ({USENIX} Security 2014), pp. 207–222 (2014)
9. Asghari, H.: pyasn. https://github.com/hadiasghari/pyasn
10. Du, K., et al.: TL;DR hazard: a comprehensive study of levelsquatting scams. In: Chen, S., Choo, K.-K.R., Fu, X., Lou, W., Mohaisen, A. (eds.) SecureComm 2019. LNICST, vol. 305, pp. 3–25. Springer, Cham (2019). https://doi.org/10.1007/978-3-030-37231-6_1
11. Holgers, T., Watson, D.E., Gribble, S.D.: Cutting through the confusion: a measurement study of homograph attacks. In: USENIX Annual Technical Conference, General Track, pp. 261–266 (2006)
12. Huang, L.S., Moshchuk, A., Wang, H.J., Schecter, S., Jackson, C.: Clickjacking: attacks and defenses. In: Presented as part of the 21st {USENIX} Security Symposium ({USENIX} Security 2012), pp. 413–428 (2012)
13. Invernizzi, L., Thomas, K., Kapravelos, A., Comanescu, O., Picod, J.M., Bursztein, E.: Cloak of visibility: detecting when machines browse a different web. In: 2016 IEEE Symposium on Security and Privacy (SP), pp. 743–758. IEEE (2016)
14. Khan, M.T., Huo, X., Li, Z., Kanich, C.: Every second counts: quantifying the negative externalities of cybercrime via typosquatting. In: 2015 IEEE Symposium on Security and Privacy, pp. 135–150. IEEE (2015)

15. Kintis, P., et al.: Hiding in plain sight: a longitudinal study of combosquatting abuse. In: Proceedings of the 2017 ACM SIGSAC Conference on Computer and Communications Security, pp. 569–586 (2017)
16. Li, Z., Alrwais, S., Wang, X., Alowaisheq, E.: Hunting the red fox online: understanding and detection of mass redirect-script injections. In: 2014 IEEE Symposium on Security and Privacy, pp. 3–18. IEEE (2014)
17. Mavrommatis, N.P.P., Monrose, M.: All your iframes point to us. In: USENIX Security Symposium, pp. 1–16. USENIX Association (2008)
18. Mekky, H., Torres, R., Zhang, Z.L., Saha, S., Nucci, A.: Detecting malicious http redirections using trees of user browsing activity. In: IEEE INFOCOM 2014-IEEE Conference on Computer Communications, pp. 1159–1167. IEEE (2014)
19. Nikiforakis, N., et al.: You are what you include: large-scale evaluation of remote javascript inclusions. In: Proceedings of the 2012 ACM Conference on Computer and Communications Security, pp. 736–747 (2012)
20. Nikiforakis, N., Van Acker, S., Meert, W., Desmet, L., Piessens, F., Joosen, W.: Bitsquatting: exploiting bit-flips for fun, or profit? In: Proceedings of the 22nd International Conference on World Wide Web, pp. 989–998 (2013)
21. Scheitle, Q., et al.: A long way to the top: significance, structure, and stability of internet top lists. In: Proceedings of the Internet Measurement Conference 2018, pp. 478–493 (2018)
22. Szurdi, J., Kocso, B., Cseh, G., Spring, J., Felegyhazi, M., Kanich, C.: The long "taile" of typosquatting domain names. In: 23rd {USENIX} Security Symposium ({USENIX} Security 2014), pp. 191–206 (2014)
23. Tian, K., Jan, S.T., Hu, H., Yao, D., Wang, G.: Needle in a haystack: tracking down elite phishing domains in the wild. In: Proceedings of the Internet Measurement Conference 2018, pp. 429–442 (2018)
24. Vissers, T., Joosen, W., Nikiforakis, N.: Parking sensors: analyzing and detecting parked domains. In: Proceedings of the 22nd Network and Distributed System Security Symposium (NDSS 2015), pp. 53–53. Internet Society (2015)
25. Wang, D.Y., Savage, S., Voelker, G.M.: Cloak and dagger: dynamics of web search cloaking. In: Proceedings of the 18th ACM Conference on Computer and Communications Security, pp. 477–490 (2011)
26. Yang, G., Huang, J., Gu, G.: Iframes/popups are dangerous in mobile webview: studying and mitigating differential context vulnerabilities. In: 28th {USENIX} Security Symposium ({USENIX} Security 2019), pp. 977–994 (2019)
27. Zeng, Y., Zang, T., Zhang, Y., Chen, X., Wang, Y.: A comprehensive measurement study of domain-squatting abuse. In: ICC 2019–2019 IEEE International Conference on Communications (ICC), pp. 1–6. IEEE (2019)
28. Zhou, Y., Evans, D.: Understanding and monitoring embedded web scripts. In: 2015 IEEE Symposium on Security and Privacy, pp. 850–865. IEEE (2015)

Video Streaming

An Empirical Measurement Study
of Free Live Streaming Services

Sina Keshvadi[(✉)] and Carey Williamson

University of Calgary, Calgary, AB, Canada
`sina.keshvadi1@ucalgary.ca, carey@cpsc.ucalgary.ca`

Abstract. Live streaming is one of the most popular Internet activities. Nowadays, there has been an increase in free live streaming (FLS) services that provide unauthorized broadcasting of live events, attracting millions of viewers. These opportunistic providers often have modest network infrastructures, and monetize their services through advertising and data analytics, which raises concerns about the performance, quality of experience, and user privacy when using these services. In this paper, we measure and analyze the behaviour of 20 FLS sports sites on Android smartphones, focusing on packet-level, video player, and privacy aspects. In addition, we compare FLS services with two legitimate online sports networks. Our measurement results show that FLS sites suffer from scalability issues during highly-popular events, deliver lower QoE than legitimate providers, and often use obscure and/or suspicious tracking services. Caution is thus advised when using FLS services.

Keywords: Network traffic measurement · Free live streaming · Quality of Service (QoS) · Quality of Experience (QoE) · Privacy.

1 Introduction

In 1995, a company called Progressive Networks[1] broadcast the first live sports streaming event on the Internet, featuring a baseball game between the Seattle Mariners and the New York Yankees [26]. Since then, the growing adoption of smartphones and the emerging mobile Internet (i.e., 4G, 5G, and LTE technologies) have enabled users to watch live events from anywhere without much difficulty. Mobile video streaming, including live streaming, currently accounts for 75% of total mobile data traffic [6]. This high demand for video streaming is both an opportunity and a challenge for network service providers.

For users, the Quality of Experience (QoE) for video streaming is important [10]. Measuring QoE can be done either with a subjective approach in which human viewers rate video sessions on a Mean Opinion Score (MOS) scale, or an objective approach that collects information from different protocol layers and uses mathematical models to estimate QoE for the video content [27]. Since

---

[1] https://www.realnetworks.com.

© Springer Nature Switzerland AG 2021
O. Hohlfeld et al. (Eds.): PAM 2021, LNCS 12671, pp. 111–127, 2021.
https://doi.org/10.1007/978-3-030-72582-2_7

measuring QoE is challenging, there are several studies that map network-level Quality of Service (QoS) parameters to user QoE [23]. This paper focuses on network-level and video QoS parameters that impact QoE.

The growth in popularity for live sports streaming has led to the emergence of many free live streaming (FLS) sites. However, using these unauthorized and unregulated providers raises concerns about QoS, QoE, and user privacy. For instance, these FLS sites may not have adequate network infrastructure to deliver scalable services, and as a consequence, both QoS and QoE may suffer. Furthermore, many of these FLS sites recoup their operational costs through advertising and data analytics, which raises concerns about what user-level information is collected by these sites, and where such information is sent.

Prior research efforts have focused on blocking live broadcasting sites [21,29], or detecting security leaks in FLS sites [25]. However, many Internet users still seek out these free sites despite their awareness of security concerns, and the number of FLS sites and users continues to proliferate [1].

In this paper, our basic premise is that users should be aware of the many tradeoffs associated with video streaming sites, including performance (i.e., QoS and QoE) as well as security and privacy. We study live sports streaming from both free and legitimate sites, doing so from these different viewpoints. The purpose of our study is to provide better insight into how video providers deliver their services, and what QoS is provided. Based on these insights, users can make better-informed decisions about using these services or not.

The research questions in our work are the following:

– What are the performance characteristics of FLS providers?
– What is the network and video QoS provided by FLS services?
– Are these services scalable for popular events?
– What privacy risks are associated with these services?

To study live sports streaming, we collected network traffic measurement datasets from several FLS sports sites during NHL, NBA, NFL, and UEFA (soccer) games in the 2019–2020 season. To capture video streaming sessions, we customized an existing mobile video streaming measurement tool [18] to study these services from different viewpoints. Also, we compared the FLS results with streaming from two popular monthly-paid service providers (TSN and DAZN). This comparison is motivated in part by the well-known adage: "If you are not paying for the service, then YOU are the product being sold".

The main contributions of this paper are as follows:

– We conduct a network traffic measurement study of FLS sports sites during selected NHL, NBA, NFL, and UEFA games in the 2019–2020 season.
– We measure and analyze the delivered network and video QoS for FLS services on a smartphone.
– We compare the live video streaming from FLS Web sites with two well-known monthly paid online sports networks.
– We investigate privacy concerns when using FLS services on smartphones.

The rest of this paper is organized as follows. Section 2 provides background on FLS. Section 3 describes our experimental methodology, measurement environment, and data collection process. Section 4 presents our measurement results. Section 5 summarizes prior related work. Section 6 concludes the paper.

2   Free Live Streaming

FLS services provide an infrastructure that allows Internet users to watch live events for free. Users can access live streams (usually without the owner's permission) even without registration [13]. In these services, the channels are neither catalogued nor listed in directories, and are not searchable via the Web site. Instead, the channel owner usually shares the channel links in online social network communities in order to reach viewers. One example is Reddit, a popular online social network on which users discuss, share, and rate Web content.

There are five major players in the FLS ecosystem: *Media Providers* that provide and stream the media content; *Channel Providers* that receive live streams from media providers and serve them to users; *Aggregators* that provide a list of available streams for users to browse; *Advertisers* that support the foregoing three entities through ads and overlays; and *Users* that watch their favourite live stream events found via the aggregators [1].

Sports streaming services are popular and constantly evolving [25,30]. In this paper, we study Web-based sports FLS services from a vantage point in Canada.

3   Measurement Methodology

Analyzing live video streaming on smartphone devices faces many challenges [8]. Video streaming characteristics such as QoE have to be observed to see how the user might react. Also, a multimedia stream may be encoded using different video codecs, devices may receive different resolutions and bitrates, depending on their screen size, location, end-to-end network status, membership type, etc. Processing and analyzing the captured traffic is another challenge, because of the voluminous network traffic involved. Furthermore, encryption makes measurement and analysis more difficult.

We used MoVIE [18], an open-source mobile video streaming analyzer, to capture and analyze live video sessions on an Android smartphone. MoVIE provides a multi-level view of video streaming by intercepting and analyzing all incoming/outgoing network traffic of a smartphone. MoVIE analyzes video streaming at the packet-level, flow-level, and video player level. We extended the existing MoVIE tool by adding a Privacy View component to its Traffic Interceptor component. We leveraged EasyList[2] from the ad-blocker community to investigate the generated flows to find potential ads, trackers, and malicious connections.

Figure 1 illustrates the architecture of MoVIE, which consists of seven components: Traffic Interceptor, Packet Tracer, Player View, Privacy View, Mapper, Main, and Graphical User Interface. For more details about MoVIE, see [18].

---

[2] https://www.easylist.to.

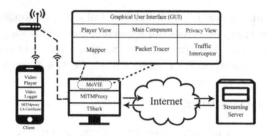

Fig. 1. System structure of MoVIE tool for Mobile Video Information Extraction

3.1 Experimental Setup

We set up a controlled measurement environment similar to Fig. 1 to capture the transmitted packets, flows, and video player activities during live streaming events. Table 1 shows our system specifications. The mobile device and the PC were set up to use the same WiFi access point. We ran MoVIE on a Linux PC running MITMproxy [7] to intercept the network traffic, and Wireshark to capture traces of the Internet traffic generated by the smartphone. MoVIE captured all video player activities using an Android application that exploits the Google Chrome media feature.

Table 1. Experimental setup for measurements

Device	OS	CPU	Cores	RAM	Video Player
Smartphone	Android 8.1.0	2.15 GHz	4	4 GB	Google Chrome v 71
PC	Ubuntu 18.4	3.6 GHz	8	8 GB	Google Chrome v 79.0.3945

All video streaming sessions were streamed using the Google Chrome browser. We performed a factory reset to ensure that other software or previous experiments do not impact our experiments. In addition, we updated the OS and pre-installed apps to the latest versions. We cleared the browser history and cache before each streaming session. During each session, the Chrome browser played video streams on the smartphone, while Wireshark and MoVIE were running on the PC to capture network traffic at the packet level. For each FLS Web site, we captured a video streaming session of 1–5 min in duration.

Since MITMproxy v4.0 is not able to decrypt HTTPS traffic from an updated Android device, we designed our setup to decrypt Android traffic on a single smartphone under test. To do this, we rooted the Android mobile device by using the Magisk tool. Rooting allows a user to have root access to the Android operating system with privileged access to modify code or install software that the vendor would not normally allow. Then we installed Xposed version 90-beta3 to install the Charles proxy certificate in system mode. Finally, we installed a CA

Certificate on the mobile device. Charles proxy[3] version 4.2.8 was installed on the PC to capture and decrypt all SSL connections generated from the smartphone. We used this setup to provide more data for privacy analysis.

Once the measurement environment was set up, we started the data collection tools on the PC and the video streaming on the mobile device. After capturing all network traffic, we used MoVIE to analyze the data.

3.2   Data Collection

To collect our dataset, we focused on FLS Web sites that are shared in sports-themed sections on Reddit. We monitored these forums during the NHL, NBA, NFL, and UEFA Champions League 2019–2020 season to find popular FLS providers.

Reddit has subreddits, which are like a Web forum in which users discuss and share content. Reddit differs from other social networks like Twitter, Instagram, or Facebook in that subreddits are openly accessible. The shared content is not limited to registered users, members, or friends. Users can access shared content and links without logging in. Ayers et al. [1] analyzed the data gathered from Alexa and SimilarWeb[4] and observed that the Reddit community receives up to 86 million visits a month from users looking for sports streams.

We observed that free sports streams are usually aggregated and shared in a few popular subreddits. In these subreddits, users can like or dislike shared FLS Web sites. Web sites with more likes increase in popularity and rise to the top of the Web page, and have a higher chance to attract even more visitors. Although there are approaches to automatically crawl and discover aggregator Web sites using online search engines [1], we found that most FLS pages are not reachable via search engines. Furthermore, service providers delete pages after the events. For these reasons, we manually selected the top-5 most popular FLS Web sites based on user votes for each of NHL, NBA, NFL, and UEFA events.

To compare the performance of FLS services with legitimate providers, we considered several features from the packet-level to the application-level. Since streaming sports events are geo-restricted and specific sports events are available only through specific online sports channels within each region, we subscribed to two Canadian online sports channels. The main sports provider in Canada is *TSN* (The Sports Network), which holds the Canadian rights to the top sports events. We also study *DAZN*, a relatively new sports streaming service in Canada.

Our collected dataset is composed of the top-5 popular (according to the likes from users) FLS Web sites in four popular sports, as gathered from the Reddit community, along with the two subscription-based sports streaming services. All videos are captured with the experimental setup mentioned in the previous subsection. We analyzed the captured data of an NBA game in December 2019, the NFL SuperBowl in February 2020, a UEFA playoff game in February 2020, and an NHL game in March 2020. All captured events are before the

---

[3] https://www.charlesproxy.com.

[4] https://www.similarweb.com.

global shutdown of sports events due to the COVID-19 pandemic in 2020. All captured network data, video streaming log, and player activities are available online [17]. We used the `traceroute` command to determine the geographic locations of streaming sessions. In general, UEFA events were streaming from European countries, while the NBA, NHL, and NFL events were streaming from North America. However, some of the FLS sites use CDNs, and we could not find their originating locations.

4   Measurement Results

To gain a comprehensive view of FLS, we evaluated video streaming from four different viewpoints, namely Network QoS, Video QoS, QUIC, and privacy.

4.1   Network Quality of Service (QoS) Analysis

Since most FLS providers record live events from a legitimate streaming service and broadcast them simultaneously [1], the quality of these services is unknown. In order to evaluate the network QoS provided by FLS Web sites, we analyze the packet-level traffic transferred during the streaming sessions.

Throughput. Several studies have proposed intelligent throughput-aware bitrate selection and adaptation algorithms for video players to improve the QoE in adaptive streaming techniques [32]. These algorithms predict the throughput and determine the bitrate for the next chunk of the video. High throughput variation could result in quality switches or stalls during the video playback [15]. Figure 2(a) shows boxplots of the average throughput for the FLS and legitimate providers. The legitimate sites had throughputs of 4–9 Mbps, compared to 1–6 Mbps for the FLS sites. The FLS throughputs were higher for the NFL and NHL sites, and lower for the UEFA and NBA sites. The FLS sites had problems during popular games, such as the 2019 NBA Finals, in which a Canadian team won the championship for the first time in NBA history. During this event, the FLS Web sites were not always able to deliver video, and some rejected new users with the message "Viewer limit reached". Table 2 in the Appendix provides further details for each service provider, and time-series graphs of throughput are available on our project Web site [17].

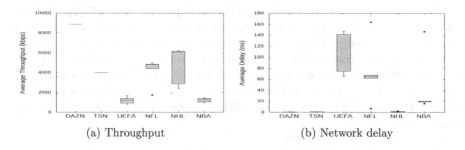

(a) Throughput   (b) Network delay

Fig. 2. Quality of Service (QoS) measurement results for live sports streaming sites

Delay. Network packet delay is an important performance characteristic of a computer network [3,28]. We used ping to estimate the average delay of service providers. We set the ping packet size based on the average packet size of a video streaming session. We conducted the ping test during the games when the server was broadcasting and users were streaming. As shown in Fig. 2(b), the average network delay for FLS sites tends to be much higher than the legitimate sites, and vary much more widely, though it does depend on their geographic location (e.g., some NHL streaming sites are in Calgary). Table 2 in the Appendix presents more detailed results for each service provider.

Packet Loss. We used the ping flood technique to study the packet loss. We observed that packet loss for the legitimate Web sites is about 0%, while it is between 1% and 4% for FLS providers. The higher loss can indicate problems in the network. Zennaro et al. [33] observed that packet loss below 1% is good, 1%–2.5% is acceptable, 2.5%–5% is poor, 5%–12% is very poor, and packet loss in excess of 12% is bad. Their observations showed that above 5% of packet loss, video conferencing becomes irritating and incomprehensible. The number of packet losses for each streaming site is shown in Table 2 in the Appendix.

4.2 Video Quality of Service (QoS) Analysis

In this section, we analyze the video QoS for our sports streaming Web sites.

Startup Time. Startup time is the elapsed time between when the user requests a video stream and the start of playback. This metric includes network delays (e.g., RTT, DNS, CDN) and the initial buffering delay [9]. Previous studies have shown that startup time is important, though it has only a small impact on QoE [20,34]. As shown in Fig. 3(a), the legitimate Web sites start playing a video about 1 to 2 s faster than the FLS sites. We observed 8 to 16 s of startup delay when streaming from NBA FLS providers.

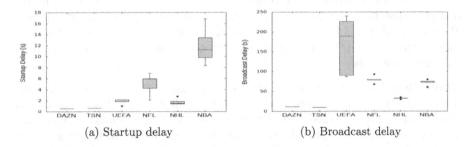

(a) Startup delay   (b) Broadcast delay

Fig. 3. Quality of Experience (QoE) measurement results for live sports streaming sites

Broadcast Delay. Broadcast delay is an intentional delay (often 7 s) inserted by live broadcasters to prevent mistakes or unacceptable content during live events. To calculate the real-time broadcast delay, we used information from two auxiliary Web sites to determine the actual time elapsed in a sports game: FlashScore.com and Bet365.com. FlashScore.com provides the fastest live and detailed stats of thousands of competitions in more than 30 sports, and Bet365 is one of the world's leading online gambling companies worldwide that covers over 30 different sports. As shown in Fig. 3(b), DAZN had a broadcast delay of around 12 s for UEFA competitions. The FLS services that deliver UEFA games had between 1 and 4 min of broadcasting delay. This delay could be due to the time for recording and broadcasting the video. Due to the nature of live sports events, immediacy is extremely valuable. In general, live events streamed from FLS Web sites are not always truly "live" streams.

Some of the FLS Web sites, and in particular NHL aggregators, have a broadcasting delay around 30–35 s. By reviewing video player activities, we observed that these FLS services use channel providers like Wstream or Vimeo to deliver live streaming while recording videos. We also used the `traceroute` tool to locate the source of streaming, but found that these channel providers use CDNs like Akamai to deliver videos to users. Pandey et al. [24] also noted the use of Akamai CDNs by 4 of 12 illegal sports and news streaming providers studied. The most likely reason for using CDNs is to reduce latency for users.

Visual Quality. This metric indicates the average video resolution received by the video player, particularly when the streaming rate and quality level are dynamically adapted to the available bandwidth, such as in DASH (Dynamic Adaptive Streaming over HTTP) [31]. In our experiment, the two legitimate Web sites and several FLS Web sites (except NBA providers) provide HD video quality. However, we observed that the transferred data for the same duration of the same video streaming on a legitimate Web site is higher than the FLS Web sites.

Quality Switches. The number of quality changes is another video QoS factor that affects QoE [23]. The number of quality switches is calculated by counting the number of video resolution changes over the duration of the video session. We observed that 11 out of 20 FLS sites experienced two or more quality switches. We also found that a few FLS providers did not switch to lower resolution when video stalls occurred. We did not observe any quality switches in streaming from legitimate Web sites.

Stalls. Rebuffering is the most noticeable streaming artifact for users [9]. If the player does not find sufficient new data in the buffer, it causes a pause during the playback that is called a *stall*. Studies show that the number of stalls has the highest impact on QoE [9]. From our (fast) campus network, our measurement tool never showed any stalls with legitimate sports streaming Web sites. Although all NHL FLS providers experienced quality switches, none of them stalled during video playback. However, the vast majority of the other FLS service providers suffered from several stalls. Table 3 in the Appendix shows the number of rebuffering events observed for each streaming site studied.

4.3   QUIC

TCP is the prevailing transport-layer protocol used by FLS services. TCP is amenable to video streaming, and is widely used for Web and mobile applications. For example, MPEG-DASH is an HTTP-based adaptive bitrate streaming technique to deliver high-quality streaming of media content over the Internet.

We observed that 18 out of 20 FLS Web sites deliver their services over TCP. One of the FLS providers used UDP and another one used the Datagram Transport Layer Security (DTLS) protocol to deliver video streaming. DTLS is similar to the TLS protocol that provides security guarantees over UDP. Interestingly, the two legitimate providers both deliver live streaming via UDP-based solutions. We observed that TSN delivers live video streams using QUIC [19].

Experimental Setup. In this section, we describe our tests to evaluate the impact of QUIC on the performance of live streaming in different network settings. Google by default enables support for the QUIC protocol in the Chrome browser. To compare QUIC with TCP, we disable this feature in Chrome to stream live video over TCP. Although TCP Cubic is the default congestion control algorithm in QUIC [14], the congestion control algorithm used by QUIC version 50 on the TSN site was unknown to us. To test different network settings, we introduce delay, packet loss, and bandwidth limits by using the network emulation (netem) functionality of the traffic control (`tc`) Linux command. Metrics of interest are the startup delay, the average received throughput, and the number of quality switches.

We conducted all measurements on the described Linux PC with the Google Chrome browser for live streaming in both Wired and WiFi settings. Figure 4 shows selected results from our experiments, while the full results appear in Table 4 in the Appendix. The results report the averages from 10 video streaming sessions, from TSN provider, each lasting 100 s, with the browser's cache and history cleared before each session. We observed that all video streaming were streamed from the same IP address. Since recent studies show that QUIC provides minimal improvements for video streaming in networks with low delay and loss [2], we set high latency and loss to highlight the impacts of using QUIC.

Network Type. Here we study the behavior of QUIC/TCP live video streaming in wired and WiFi networks. When the device is connected to a stable wired connection, enabling QUIC does not have an impact on startup time, but the average received throughput is slightly better than with TCP. When using the WiFi network, the QUIC protocol had a lower average startup time than TCP. However, the received throughput of video sessions using TCP was slightly higher than with the QUIC protocol.

Delay. We applied 500 ms of delay to both wired and WiFi network connections. In this scenario, QUIC started playing the video with a lower startup delay than TCP over both wired and WiFi connections. The behavior of live streaming over

TCP in the WiFi network was significantly worse than QUIC, with higher startup time, much lower throughput, and more quality switches. This experiment shows that QUIC works better than TCP over the WiFi network with high delay.

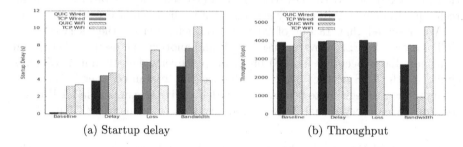

(a) Startup delay   (b) Throughput

Fig. 4. QUIC vs TCP measurement results for live sports streaming sites

Loss. We added 25% random packet loss to both wired and WiFi connections. The packet loss drastically reduces the throughput in both QUIC and TCP live streaming. However, QUIC achieved a higher throughput. That is, QUIC was able to receive videos with higher resolution while TCP streamed with lower quality. This could be a key advantage of streaming via QUIC during popular games that induce network congestion and packet loss.

Bandwidth. We reduced the available network bandwidth to 8 Mbps. In this condition, the received throughput over TCP connections in both wired and WiFi networks are higher than the QUIC-based video streaming. The captured traces show that the server sends the data using three concurrent TCP connections on different ports, with the transferred data almost balanced over each connection. On the other hand, QUIC experienced worse performance in comparison to TCP. In the WiFi network with limited bandwidth, QUIC's startup time is higher, with lower received throughput, and more quality switches.

4.4   Privacy Analysis

The results from the Privacy View of FLS sports Web sites are summarized in Fig. 5, as well as Table 5 in the Appendix. We discuss selected results next.

HTTP vs. HTTPS. While the two legitimate sports streaming sites deliver their services over HTTPS, most of the FLS sites use HTTP rather than HTTPS. There may be several reasons why FLS providers do not upgrade to HTTPS on their Web site, such as the costs to purchase and install SSL certificates on the server, the extra CPU processing required for encryption, and the fact that some FLS providers frequently change their Web domains. For these reasons, they may just simply opt to deliver their services over HTTP.

Ad and Tracking Services. To recognize advertisement and tracking services, we leveraged the EasyList and EasyPrivacy filter lists provided by the ad-blocker community. We used Privacy Badger[5] to distinguish malicious ads from other ads. By investigating the generated HTTP(S) requests/responses, we observed that both FLS and legitimate Web sites connect users to advertising and tracking services (see Fig. 5(a)). However, the legitimate Web sites mostly connect to known tracking domains, such as Facebook and Google analytics, while the FLS sites expose users to malicious trackers like onclicksuper.com, which is known to redirect browsers to many unwanted advertisements. In addition, we observed that some tracking services like google-analytics.com appear in both FLS and legitimate sports streaming Web sites.

Overlay Ads and Offered Applications. During the data collection phase, we observed that FLS Web sites use different techniques to show overlay and pop-up ads. Some of these overlay ads cover part of the video player, and trick users into pushing a fake close button, which then pops up multiple overlay ads. These ads violate the online advertising standards [12], degrade the video streaming QoE, and also lure users to numerous potentially malicious ads. Clicking on misleading ads can lead to computer viruses such as ransomware, trojans, crypto-mining, etc. In addition, we observed that some FLS Web sites offer a complimentary application to watch free live sport streams on the mobile device. Prior work has shown that these applications contain an advertising package, display ads without user consent, and trigger potential ad fraud [25].

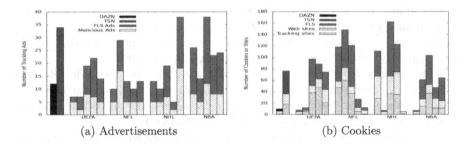

(a) Advertisements   (b) Cookies

Fig. 5. Privacy and security measurement results for live sports streaming sites

Browser Security. Sandboxing is often used to run a Web browser in a low-permission mode that limits malware access to vulnerable aspects of the operating system. However, some users bypass these security warnings when accessing FLS sites [1]. Also, tools like ad-blockers can protect the user from deceptive ads linked to scams and malware [22]. However, some FLS providers use anti-ad-blocking techniques, or simply refuse to serve users with ad-blockers installed.

Cookies. We observed that both FLS and legitimate Web sites install third-party advertising and tracking cookies on user systems. Since cookies contain a history of the user's actions, they may be exploited or misused to track the user's behavior. Figure 5(b) shows the number of third-party cookies observed for each Web site in our dataset. For instance, we observed that visiting the

---

[5] https://www.privacybadger.org.

TSN site results in 76 cookies from 38 different third-party Web sites, 18 of which are third-party tracking sites. Unlike TSN, DAZN alerts users about the use of cookies on its Web site, and installs a few cookies on user systems. In general, FLS Web sites trigger more advertising and tracking on user systems. In addition, some FLS Web sites set zombie cookies, which can automatically re-create themselves from stored data even after being deleted.

Data Leaks. By investigating POST requests, we observed that some FLS sites send user information such as IP address, ISP, city, area, device name, OS, browser version, and graphic card model to tracking Web sites. In addition, we discovered TSN uses a new approach, wherein a single POST method was used to perform multiple GET and POST requests. To do this, it inserts several GET and POST requests in a JSON-like format, and then sends all of these using one GET request to its server. One of the POST requests was 16,029 bytes long, and contained 18 GET and 3 POST requests, each addressing a tracking/advertisement service. This approach can hide requests from browsers, ad-blockers, and other security tools. An example of these POST requests is available on our project Web site [17].

5   Related Work

One early work that mentioned free live sports streaming was the epilogue of the *Globalization and Football* book [11], in which the authors discussed the impact of emerging FLS platforms on 'the global game'. Later, Birmingham et al. [4] studied FLS for England's Premier League of soccer, and noted parallels to the music industry, which faced similar piracy issues in the 1990s.

FLS services have grown tremendously over the past decade. Rafique et al. [25] explored the FLS ecosystem by investigating those infringing upon sports streaming Web sites. In addition, they analyzed the advertising content that the FLS Web sites expose during the live broadcasts.

Ayers et al. [1] offered a solution to automatically crawl and discover aggregator Web pages through the Google search engine. Then they studied FLS services by collecting and investigating 500 illegal live streaming domains. They observed that despite the improvement in the privacy mechanisms by ad-blockers and browsers, users are still using illegal streaming and exposing themselves to scams and deceptive ads. Kariyawasam et al. [16] studied the copyright concerns in the FLS ecosystem by analyzing the legal landscape for live sports streaming.

Bronzino et al. [5] developed models that derive video quality metrics from encrypted video streaming services. Biernacki et al. [3] conducted a thorough video streaming simulation study with different network conditions and video bitrates. Their study showed that QoS metrics significantly impact the QoE metrics for video streaming. In many cases, however, the buffering strategies implemented by a player client are able to mitigate unfavourable network conditions and further improve QoE.

The main novelty of our own work is the focus on performance tradeoffs in live sports streaming (i.e., QoS and QoE), as well as on user privacy and security.

Furthermore, we provide multiple observational viewpoints at different layers of the protocol stack, using a customized version of the MoVIE tool.

6   Conclusion

In this paper, we presented a measurement study of FLS sites to identify tradeoffs in performance (i.e., network QoS and video QoS) as well as privacy and security. Our measurements were made using an extended version of an open-source video measurement tool called MoVIE [18]. We also conducted measurements of two legitimate sports streaming Web sites to provide a basis for comparison.

Our main results can be summarized as follows. We observed a long broadcasting delay in free live streams. The throughput, streaming quality, and packet loss rate differ greatly across FLS sites. TSN delivers live video streaming using QUIC. We observed that QUIC's benefits are larger in WiFi networks with higher delay and loss. Similar to previous studies, we also noted that the FLS ecosystem continues to flourish. Although FLS is free, you always "get what you pay for": the user pays the cost of FLS by dealing with the uncertainty of the streaming services, and the inherent privacy/security risks.

Ethical Considerations

There are several ethical issues associated with studying illegal FLS services. First, many countries have Fair Dealing exceptions that authorize the use of copyrighted materials for specific purposes. In Canada, these purposes include "research, private study, education, parody, satire, criticism, review, or news reporting". Second, we studied Web sites that millions of users visit monthly, despite the copyright law and potential malicious behaviours. We do not crawl automatically through the FLS providers, and our study has minimal impact on visit numbers. In addition, there is a chance that any increased views triggered by our study will be suitably moderated by the increased awareness of FLS users. Finally, to study privacy issues, it was necessary to decrypt the device's network traffic to see the incoming and outgoing flows. However, our measurements and experiments were conducted on a single device in a controlled lab environment. We collected neither personal data nor the device traffic from other users. All captured data are publicly available for future studies [17].

Acknowledgements. The authors thank the PAM 2021 reviewers and shepherd David Choffnes for their feedback and suggestions. Financial support for this research was provided by Canada's Natural Sciences and Engineering Research Council (NSERC).

Appendix

The following four tables provide the detailed results from our active and passive measurement experiments with live sports streaming sites. In Table 2, Table 3, and Table 5, the rows correspond to the different legitimate and FLS providers

Table 2. Network Quality of Service (QoS) metrics for live sports streaming Web sites.

Type		Provider	HTTP(S)	Protocol	Avg Throughput	Trace SYN RTT	Trace Loss		TCP Retrans	Ping Avg RTT	Ping SD Delay	Ping Loss
							%	pkts				
Paid	UEFA NFL	DAZN	HTTPS	UDP	8,899 kbps	-	-	-	-	1.046 ms	0.975 ms	0%
	NHL NBA	TSN	HTTPS	QUIC	4,021 kbps	-	-	-	-	1.252 ms	1.119 ms	0%
FLS	UEFA	P1	HTTP	TCP	1,676 kbps	59.061 ms	0.8%	114	69 pkts	65.544 ms	7.439 ms	2%
		P2	HTTP	TCP	1,212 kbps	137.900 ms	0.8%	75	24 pkts	141.688 ms	12.368 ms	3%
		P3	HTTP	TCP	918 kbps	135.949 ms	0.7%	49	29 pkts	141.759 ms	31.675 ms	2%
		P4	HTTP	UDP	1,413 kbps	-	-	-	-	74.548 ms	16.54 ms	2%
		P5	HTTP	TCP	766 kbps	155.932 ms	0.9%	74	40 pkts	147.422 ms	46.860 ms	4%
	NFL	P6	HTTP	TCP	4,833 kbps	53.793 ms	0.0%	11	11 pkts	66.500 ms	12.062 ms	7%
		P7	HTTP	TCP	1,763 kbps	145.940 ms	0.1%	16	12 pkts	164.126 ms	38.925 ms	0%
		P8	HTTP	TCP	4,990 kbps	150.393 ms	0.1%	105	43 pkts	62.496 ms	7.896 ms	0%
		P9	HTTP	TCP	4,428 kbps	179.007 ms	0.1%	53	46 pkts	67.876 ms	12.212 ms	4%
		P10	HTTP	TCP	4,877 kbps	7.248 ms	0.0%	23	26 pkts	7.351 ms	7.440 ms	0%
	NHL	P11	HTTP	UDP	2,412 kbps	-	-	-	-	1.359 ms	1.476 ms	0%
		P12	HTTP	TCP	2,888 kbps	-	0.0%	12	26 pkts	1.570 ms	1.612 ms	0%
		P13	HTTP	TCP	6,195 kbps	15.331 ms	0.0%	3	10 pkts	2.597 ms	2.661 ms	0%
		P14	HTTP	TCP	6,168 kbps	-	0.0%	17	10 pkts	0.943 ms	0.845 ms	0%
		P15	HTTP	TCP	6,073 kbps	7.923 ms	0.0%	11	18 pkts	1.160 ms	1.256 ms	0%
	NBA	P16	HTTP	TCP	1,380 kbps	47.015 ms	0.1%	25	21 pkts	19.739 ms	1.195 ms	0%
		P17	HTTP	TCP	1,481 kbps	10.748 ms	0.1%	50	60 pkts	19.495 ms	0.557 ms	0%
		P18	HTTP	TCP	1,332 kbps	21.159 ms	0.0%	16	18 pkts	20.216 ms	0.748 ms	0%
		P19	HTTPS	TCP	1,050 kbps	311.496 ms	0.0%	11	25 pkts	146.680 ms	3.192 ms	0%
		P20	HTTP	TCP	960 kbps	28.848 ms	0.1%	17	22 pkts	16.482 ms	2.164 ms	0%

Table 3. Video QoS metrics for live sports streaming Web sites.

Type	Sports	Provider	Startup Time	Resolution	Rebuffering	Quality Switches	Broadcast Delay
Paid	UEFA NFL	DAZN	0.62 s	1280 × 720	0	0	12 s
	NHL NBA	TSN	0.64 s	1280 × 720	0	0	10 s
FLS	UEFA	P1	2.21 s	1280 × 720	2	0	87 s
		P2	2.17 s	1280 × 720	1	0	189 s
		P3	1.02 s	1280 × 720	4	0	90 s
		P4	1.83 s	960 × 540	0	0	226 s
		P5	2.18 s	1280 × 720	4	0	240 s
	NFL	P6	2.11 s	1024 × 576	5	0	93 s
		P7	4.24 s	1280 × 720	0	0	78 s
		P8	6.97 s	1024 × 576	3	0	80 s
		P9	5.91 s	1024 × 576	3	0	78 s
		P10	5.97 s	896 × 504	0	3	68 s
	NHL	P11	2.75 s	1280 × 720	0	2	32 s
		P12	1.44 s	1280 × 720	0	2	30 s
		P13	1.40 s	1280 × 720	0	2	32 s
		P14	1.43 s	1280 × 720	0	3	33 s
		P15	1.83 s	1280 × 720	0	2	35 s
	NBA	P16	8.39 s	640 × 360	6	5	74 s
		P17	16.82 s	986 × 504	4	4	80 s
		P18	9.81 s	640 × 360	8	4	75 s
		P19	11.21 s	512 × 288	6	2	72 s
		P20	13.40 s	512 × 288	7	2	61 s

Table 4. Comparison of QUIC and TCP in network emulation experiments.

Network Setting		QUIC			TCP		
Limitation	Type	Startup time (s)	Throughput	Quality Switch	Startup time (s)	Throughput	Quality Switch
None	Wired	0.169	3925 kbps	0	0.161	3720 kbps	0
	WiFi	3.233	4239 kbps	0	3.4054	4475 kbps	0
Delay = 500 ms	Wired	3.8624	3982 kbps	1	4.4692	4018 kbps	1
	WiFi	4.800	3978 kbps	3	8.755	2026 kbps	5
Loss Rate = 25%	Wired	2.189	4058 kbps	1	6.082	3928 kbps	2
	WiFi	7.514	2892 kbps	1	3.324	1095 kbps	0
Bandwidth = 8 Mbps	Wired	5.545	2734 kbps	2	7.686	3789 kbps	1
	WiFi	10.213	970 kbps	2	3.939	4789 kbps	0

Table 5. Privacy view of live sports streaming Web sites.

Type	Sports	Provider	Tracking ad	Malicious ad	Offering apps	Encryption Scheme	Anti ad-blocker	Cookie Consent	# 3rd-party cookies	# 3rd-party Web sites set cookies	# 3rd-party tracker sites set cookies
Paid	UEFA NFL	DAZN	12	0	No	CENC	No	Yes	10	6	1
	NHL NBA	TSN	34	0	No	CENC	No	No	76	36	18
FLS	UEFA	P1	7	5	Yes	N/A	No	No	8	5	1
		P2	7	2	No	N/A	No	No	12	7	5
		P3	19	8	Yes	N/A	No	No	97	50	38
		P4	22	7	No	N/A	No	No	88	62	47
		P5	14	5	No	N/A	No	No	74	44	21
	NFL	P6	10	5	No	N/A	No	No	118	58	47
		P7	29	17	Yes	N/A	No	Yes	148	82	59
		P8	13	5	No	N/A	No	Yes	121	49	37
		P9	10	5	No	N/A	No	No	27	12	5
		P10	13	5	No	N/A	No	No	12	7	1
	NHL	P11	13	5	No	N/A	No	No	111	67	28
		P12	10	5	No	N/A	No	No	7	5	0
		P13	19	7	Yes	N/A	Yes	Yes	162	67	36
		P14	5	2	No	N/A	No	No	123	74	35
		P15	38	18	Yes	N/A	No	No	5	5	2
	NBA	P16	26	8	Yes	N/A	No	No	7	5	1
		P17	14	5	Yes	N/A	Yes	No	61	27	14
		P18	38	12	Yes	N/A	No	Yes	103	52	37
		P19	23	8	Yes	N/A	No	No	47	28	11
		P20	24	8	Yes	N/A	No	No	64	24	11

studied, while the columns represent different performance metrics for network QoS, video QoS, and privacy, respectively. Table 4 provides results for the QUIC experiments, which structurally differ from the other measurement results.

References

1. Ayers, H., Hsiao, L.: The Price of Free Illegal Live Streaming Services, p. 10. arXiv:1901.00579, January 2019
2. Bhat, D., Rizk, A., Zink, M.: Not so QUIC: a performance study of DASH over QUIC. In: Proceedings of the 27th Workshop on Network and Operating Systems Support for Digital Audio and Video (NOSSDAV), Taipei, Taiwan, pp. 13–18, June 2017

3. Biernacki, A., Tutschku, K.: Performance of HTTP video streaming under different network conditions. Multimedia Tools Appl. **72**(2), 1143–1166 (2014)
4. Birmingham, J., David, M.: Live-streaming: will football fans continue to be more law abiding than music fans? Sport Soc. **14**(1), 69–80 (2011)
5. Bronzino, F., Schmitt, P., Ayoubi, S., Martins, G., Teixeira, R., Feamster, N.: Inferring streaming video quality from encrypted traffic: practical models and deployment experience. Proc. ACM Meas. Anal. Comput. Syst. **3**(3), 1–25 (2019)
6. Cisco.: Cisco Annual Internet Report (2018–2023) White Paper, Accessed 9 Mar 2020
7. Cortesi, A., Hils, M., Kriechbaumer, T., Contributors: MITMproxy: A Free and Open Source Interactive HTTPS Proxy (2010). https://MITMproxy.org/ [ver. 4.0]
8. Crovella, M., Krishnamurthy, B.: Internet Measurement: Infrastructure, Traffic and Applications. John Wiley & Sons, New York (2006)
9. Dimopoulos, G., Leontiadis, I., Barlet-Ros, P., Papagiannaki, K.: Measuring video QoE from encrypted traffic. In: Proceedings of ACM Internet Measurement Conference (IMC), Santa Monica, California, USA, pp. 513–526, November 2016
10. Duanmu, Z., Zeng, K., Ma, K., Rehman, A., Wang, Z.: A quality-of-experience index for streaming video. IEEE J. Sel. Top. Signal Process. **11**(1), 154–166 (2016)
11. Giulianotti, R., Robertson, R.: Globalization and Football. Sage Publications, London (2009)
12. IAB Technology Lab: Digital Video In-Stream Ad Format Guidelines, Accessed 8 Jan 2016
13. Ibosiola, D., Steer, B., Garcia-Recuero, A., Stringhini, G. Uhlig, S., Tyson, G.: Movie pirates of the caribbean: exploring illegal streaming cyberlockers. In: Proceedings of 12th International AAAI Conference on Web and Social Media, Palo Alto, California, US, pp. 131–140, June 2018
14. Iyengar, J., Swett, I.: QUIC Loss Recovery and Congestion Control, draft-tsvwg-quic-loss-recovery-01. IETF Internet draft. https://tools.ietf.org/html/draft-tsvwg-quic-loss-recovery-01
15. Junchen, J., Sekar, V., Milner, H., Shepherd, D., Stoica, I., Zhang, H.: CFA: a practical prediction system for video QoE optimization. In: Proceedings of 13th USENIX Symposium on Networked Systems Design and Implementation (NSDI), Boston, MA, USA, pp. 137–150, March 2017
16. Kariyawasam, K., Tsai, M.: Copyright and live streaming of sports broadcasting. Int. Rev. Law Comput. Technol. **31**(3), 265–288 (2017)
17. Keshvadi, S.: An Empirical Measurement Study of Free Live Streaming Services. https://www.cpsc.ucalgary.ca/~sina.keshvadi1/FLS
18. Keshvadi, S., Williamson, C.: MoVIE: a measurement tool for mobile video streaming on smartphones. In: Proceedings of the ACM/SPEC International Conference on Performance Engineering, Edmonton, Canada, pp. 230–237, April 2020
19. Langley, A., et al.: The QUIC transport protocol: design and internet-scale deployment. In: Proceedings of ACM SIGCOMM Conference, Los Angeles, CA, USA, pp. 183–196, August 2017
20. Mok, R., Chan, E., Luo, X., Chang, R.: Streaming from user-viewing activities. In: Proceedings of the First ACM SIGCOMM Workshop on Measurements Up the Stack, Toronto, Ontario, Canada, pp. 31–36, August 2011
21. National Intellectual Property Rights Coordination Center, "Homeland Security Investigations Curbing Illegal Streaming: The Investigation and the Case", Anti-Piracy and Content Protection Summit. https://bit.ly/3oDj4nQ

22. Nithyanand, R., et al.: Ad-blocking and counter blocking: a slice of the arms race. In: Proceedings of 6th USENIX Workshop on Free and Open Communications on the Internet (FOCI), Austin, Texas, USA, pp. 1–7, August 2016

23. Pal, D., Vanijja, V.: Effect of network QoS on user QoE for a mobile video streaming service using H. 265/VP9 Codec. Procedia Comput. Sci. **111**(C), 214–222 (2017)

24. Pandey, P., Aliapoulios, M., McCoy, D.: Iniquitous cord-cutting: an analysis of infringing IPTV services. In: IEEE European Symposium on Security and Privacy Workshops (EuroS&PW), Stockholm, Sweden, pp. 423–432, June 2019

25. Rafique, M., Goethem, T., Joosen, W., Huygens, C., Nikiforakis, N.: It's Free for a reason: exploring the ecosystem of free live streaming services. In: Proceedings of the 23rd Network and Distributed System Security Symposium (NDSS), San Diego, CA, pp. 1–15, February 2016

26. RealNetworks Incorporation History. http://goo.gl/IxHQRB

27. Skorin-Kapov, L., Varela, M., Hoßfeld, T., Chen, K.: A survey of emerging concepts and challenges for QoE management of multimedia services. ACM Trans. Multimedia Comput. Commun. Appl. (TOMM) **14**(2), 1–29 (2018)

28. Upadhyay, R., Bhatta, U., Chouhana, N., Sarsodia, T.: Computation of various QoS parameters for FiWi access network. Procedia Comput. Sci. **78**, 172–178 (2016)

29. Walker, C.: A La Carte Television: A Solution to Online Piracy. CommLaw Conspectus **20**, 471–494 (2011)

30. Wong, D.: The EPL drama-paving the way for more illegal streaming? Digital piracy of live sports broadcasts in Singapore. Leisure Stud. **35**(5), 534–548 (2016)

31. Yarnagula, H., Juluri, P., Kiani Mehr, S., Tamarapalli, V., Medhi, D.: QoE for mobile clients with segment-aware rate adaptation algorithm (SARA) for DASH video streaming. ACM Trans. Multimedia Comput. Commun. Appl. (TOMM) **15**(2), 1–23 (2019). Article No. 36

32. Yin, X., Jindal, A., Sekar, V., Sinopoli, B.: A control-theoretic approach for dynamic adaptive video streaming over HTTP. In: SIGCOMM'15: Proceedings of ACM SIGCOMM Conference, London, UK, pp. 325–338, August 2015

33. Zennaro, M., Canessa, E., Sreenivasan, K., Rehmatullah, A., Cottrell, R.: Scientific measure of africa's connectivity. Inf. Technol. Int. Dev. **3**(1), 55–64 (2006)

34. Zhai, G., Cai, J., Lin, W., Yang, X., Zhang, W., Etoh, M.: Cross-dimensional perceptual quality assessment for low bit-rate videos. IEEE Trans. Multimedia **10**(7), 1316–1324 (2008)

A Data-Driven Analysis and Tuning of a Live Hybrid CDN/V2V Video Distribution System

Ishani Sarkar[1,2]([✉]), Soufiane Roubia[1], Dino Martin Lopez-Pacheco[2], and Guillaume Urvoy-Keller[2]

[1] Easybroadcast, Nantes, France
ishani.sarkar@easybroadcast.fr
[2] Université Côte d'Azur, CNRS, I3S, Nice, France

Abstract. Video live streaming now represents over 34.97% of the Internet traffic. Typical distribution architectures for this type of service heavily rely on CDNs that enable to meet the stringent QoS requirements of live video applications. As CDN-based solutions are costly to operate, a number of solutions that complement CDN servers with WebRTC have emerged. WebRTC enables direct communications between browsers (viewers). The key idea is to enable viewer to viewer (V2V) video chunks exchanges as far as possible and revert to the CDN servers only if the video chunk has not been received before the timeout. In this work, we present the study we performed on an operational hybrid live video system. Relying on the per exchange statistics that the platform collects, we first present an high level overview of the performance of the system in the wild. A key performance indicator is the fraction of V2V traffic of the system. We demonstrate that the overall performance is driven by a small fraction of users. By further profiling individual clients upload and download performance, we demonstrate that the clients responsible for the chunk losses, i.e. chunks that are not fully uploaded before the deadline, have a poor uplink access. We devised a work-round strategy, where each client evaluates its uplink capacity and refrains from sending to other clients if its past performance is too low. We assess the effectiveness of the approach on the Grid5000 testbed and present live results that confirm the good results achieved in a controlled environment. We are indeed able to reduce the chunk loss rate by almost a factor of two with a negligible impact on the amount of V2V traffic.

1 Introduction

By 2022, the global video traffic in the Internet is expected to grow at a compound annual growth rate of 29%, reaching an 82% share of all IP traffic [2]. The video content is usually delivered to the viewers using a content delivery network (CDN). The huge amount of users puts a high pressure on the CDN networks to ensure a good Quality of Experience (QoE) to the users. It also leads to huge cost for the content owner. This is where a hybrid CDN/V2V (viewer-to-viewer) architecture plays an important role. It allows sharing of the data between different viewers (browsers) while maintaining the QoE for the users.

© Springer Nature Switzerland AG 2021
O. Hohlfeld et al. (Eds.): PAM 2021, LNCS 12671, pp. 128–140, 2021.
https://doi.org/10.1007/978-3-030-72582-2_8

This paper focuses on a commercial hybrid V2V-CDN system that offers video live streaming channels, where each channel is encoded in different quality levels. More precisely, we focus on the operations of the library that acts as a proxy for fetching the video chunks for the video player. The library strives to fetch the video chunks from other viewers watching the same content and reverts to the CDN in case the chunk is not received fast enough. This operation is fully transparent to the player, which is **independent from the library** and decides the actual quality level based on the adaptive bitrate algorithm it implements, according to the network conditions and/or the buffer level occupancy.

Our hybrid V2V-CDN architecture uses Web-RTC [3] for direct browser communication and a central manager, see Fig. 1. The library is downloaded when the user lands on the Web page of the TV channel. It first uses the Internet Communication Exchange (ICE) protocol along with the STUN and TURN protocols to find its public IP address and port. The library then contacts the central manager using the session description protocol (SDP) to provide its unique ID, ICE data which includes reflexive address (public IP and port), and its playing quality.

The manager sends to the library a list of viewers watching the same content at the same quality level. Those candidate neighbors, called a swarm, are chosen in the same Internet Service Provider (ISP) and/or in the same geographic area as far as possible. The viewer will establish Web-RTC [3] channels with up to 10 neighbors. This maximum swarm size value of 10 in our production system offers

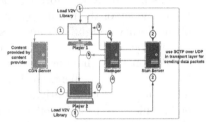

Fig. 1. Overall hybrid V2V-CDN architecture

a good trade-off between the diversity of video chunks it offers and the efforts needed to maintain those channels active.

When the video player asks for a new video chunk, the library selects the source from which the chunk will be downloaded, either another viewer or a CDN server if the chunk is not available in the swarm. We allow viewers to download data from other viewers within a specified time period which is generally in the order of the size of one video chunk. For example, in the channel used in this paper, the size of one chunk is 6 s for the three different encoding rates.

In terms of global synchronization of the live stream, there is no mechanism to enforce that clients stay synchronized within a given time frame, but a new video client, upon arrival, always asks for the latest available chunk whose id is in the so-called manifest file (list of available chunks, materialized as URLs) that the viewer downloads from the CDN server. Users have the possibility to roll back in time. For the channel we profile, the last 5 h of content is available from the CDN servers. The library maintains a history of the last 30 chunks, corresponding to about 3 min of content.

Although hybrid V2V-CDN systems offer a cost effective alternative to a pure CDN architecture, they need to achieve a trade-off between maintaining video quality and a high fraction of video chunks delivered in V2V mode. Those requirements are somehow contradicting as the V2V content delivery is easier when the content (video chunks) is smaller in size, i.e. for lower video quality.

The contributions of this paper are as follows:

(i) We present detailed statistics of a 3-day period – with over 34,000 clients and 6.TB of data exchanged – for a popular channel serviced by our commercial live video distribution. We follow an event-based rather than a time-based approach to select those days. Indeed, as the audience of a TV channel varies greatly over time depending on the popularity of the content that is broadcasted, we choose this 3-day period to offer a variety of events, in terms of connected viewers.

(ii) We question the efficiency of the system using three metrics: V2V Efficiency, which is the fraction of content sent in V2V mode, (application level) Throughput and Chunk Loss Rate (CLR) which is the number of chunks not received before the deadline. These metrics allow to evaluate the efficiency of the library operations. They are specific to the evaluation of the library and differ from classical metrics used at the video player like the number of stalled events and quality level fluctuations.

(iii) We demonstrate that the root cause of the high observed CLR rate lies at the uplink of some clients, rather than the actual network conditions. This allows us to devise a mitigation strategy that we evaluate in a controlled environment, to prove its effectiveness and then deploy on the same channel that we initially analyzed. We demonstrate that we are able to reduce the observed chunk loss rate by almost 50% with a negligible impact on the fraction of V2V traffic.

2   State of the Art

Several studies have demonstrated that Web-RTC can be successfully used for live video streaming, e.g. [5,6]. The V2V protocol used in this work relies on a mesh architecture to connect different viewers together [4]. The V2V content delivery protocol used applies a proactive approach, which means that the information is disseminated in the V2V network as soon as a single viewer downloads the information. The information is sent to other viewers by using the same Web-RTC channel with a message called *downloaded*. So even if a viewer has not yet requested the resource, it still has the information about all the resources present in its V2V network.

There have been some large scale measurement studies on live video systems done in the past. One of the most popular studies done on a P2P IPTV system is [7] dates back to 2008. In this paper, the authors demonstrate that the current Internet infrastructure was already able to support large P2P networks used to distribute live video streams. They analysed the downloading and uploading bitrate of the peers. They show that there is a lot of fluctuation in the upload and download bitrate. They also found that the popularity of the content does affect the number of viewers and how easy or difficult it is to find other viewers.

In [8], the authors focused on the problems caused by P2P traffic to ISP networks. This concern is in general addressed in hybrid V2V-CDN architectures through a central manager that can apply simple strategies like offering to a viewer neighbors in the same ISP or geographic location.

3   Overall Channel Profiling

The TV channel we profile in this study is a popular Moroccan channel serviced by our hybrid V2V-CDN system, that offers regular programs like TV series and extraordinary events like football matches. Almost 50% of the clients are in Morocco. The second most popular country is France which represents 15% of the viewers. Italy, Spain, Netherlands, Canada, United States, Germany, Belgium each hosts approximately 4% of the viewers, for a total of about 28% of users. Watching the channel is free of charge. It is accessible using a Web browser only (all browsers now support WebRTC), and not through a dedicated application as can be the case of other channels. On average, 60% of the users use mobile devices to view this channel, whereas 40% of the users use fixed devices.

3.1   Data Set

Our reference data set aggregates three days (from Oct. 2020) of data. Two days have no special events thus the distribution and size of the clients throughout the day remains the same whereas on the third day there is an important event which changes the distribution and size of the clients throughout the day. The channel can be watched at three different quality levels corresponding to 3.5 Mb/s for the smallest quality, 7 Mb/s for the intermediate quality and around 10 Mb/s for the highest quality. These quality levels are selected by the content owner, not the library. Over these three days, we collected information on 34,816 client sessions. On a standard day, the total amount of data downloaded (in CDN or V2V mode) varies between 1.5 and 2 TB whereas in case of big events, the amount of data downloaded is between 6 and 6.5 TB. Figure 2 reports the instantaneous aggregate bit rate over all the clients connected to the channel. The average is at 34 MB/s (372 Mb/s) while for the peak event (a football match), the aggregate throughput reaches 479 MB/s (3,8 Gb/s).

The V2V library reports to the manager detailed logs for all the resource exchanges made by each viewer every 10 s. Over the 3 days, 4,615,045 chunks have been exchanged. The manager later stores those records in a back-end database. Each exchange is labelled with the mode (V2V or CDN) and in case of V2V, the id of the remote viewer. We also have precise information about the time it took to download the chunk or alternatively if a chunk loss event occurred. In addition to per chunk exchange record, we also collect various player level information as well like watching time, video quality level, operating system (OS), browser, city, country, Internet service provider (ISP), etc. We also collect

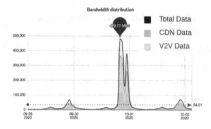

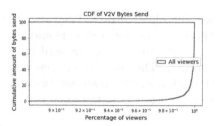

Fig. 2. Initial 3-day period   **Fig. 3.** V2V size bytes distribution

various other viewer information as well like to how many viewers a viewer is connected to simultaneously (swarm size), how many consecutive uploads to the other viewer has been done, rebuffering time, rebuffering count etc.

3.2 Clients Profiling and V2V Efficiency

The V2V paradigm directly inherits from the P2P paradigm where a significant problem was the selfishness of users [1]. We are not in this situation here as on one side, the V2V library is under our control and second, the choice of a viewer to request a chunk from, is done at random among the peers possessing this chunk. Still, we observe a clearly biased distribution of viewers contribution with 1% of the viewers responsible for over 90% of the bytes exchanged, as can be seen from Fig. 3. This bias in the contribution is in fact related to the time actually spent by the user watching the channel. We report session times in Fig. 4. Since most of the V2V data is sent by only 1% of the viewers, we compare the session time of all the viewers with these 1% of most active viewers. We can readily observe in Fig. 4 that the top 1% active viewers feature a bimodal distribution of session time with around 25% of clients staying less than 1 min and the rest staying in general between 30 min and a few hours. In contrast, the overall distribution (all users) is dominated by short session times with 60% of users staying less than 10 min.

Another factor that is likely to heavily affect the viewer ability to perform effective V2V exchanges is its network access characteristics. As part of the content is downloaded from the CDN servers which are likely to be close to the client and feature good network performance, the average throughput achieved during chunks downloads from the CDN provides a good hint on the network access capacity of the user. Note that as a chunk is several MB large, the resulting throughput should be statistically meaningful.

As we see from Fig. 6, there is a significant difference between the CDN bitrates of the overall viewers and most active 1% viewers, which experience way higher throughputs. The correlation coefficients between CDN bitrate and chunk loss rate (CLR) for overall viewers is -0.47 and for most active top 1% viewers, it is -0.7. Ideally, one expects this value to be indeed negative as the better the access link of the user is, the less likely it is to miss the deadline when sending or receiving a chunk. From this perspective, the CLR is highly correlated with the CDN throuhgput performance for the top 1% of users, hinting that this metric is a good estimator of the reception quality.

The actual chunk lost rate (CLR) of the overall viewers and most active viewers are reported in Fig. 5. We can clearly observe that for the most active 1% of users, the distribution is skewed to the left. Indeed, over 50% of these users experience less than 20% CLR, while the others experience a CLR roughly uniformly distributed between 20 and 75%.

To further understand the observed CLR, and how to reduce it, we carry a detailed study the CLR in the next section.

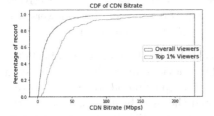

Fig. 4. Watching time distribution

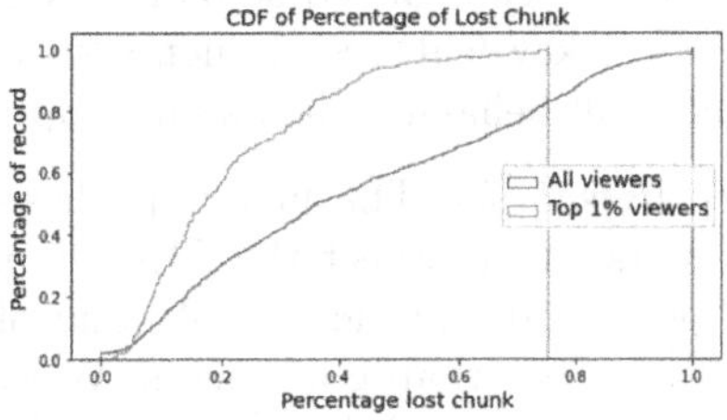

Fig. 5. Lost chunk rate distribution

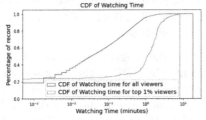

Fig. 6. CDN bandwidth distribution

Fig. 7. Viewer's neighbour set size

4 Detailed Analysis of Chunk Loss Rate (CLR)

We focus in this section on the 1% most active users viewers with more than 1 min session time. We formulated hypotheses to identify the root causes behind the observed lost data chunks:

- H_1: The swarm size affects the lost chunk rate of a viewer, because the bigger the swarm size, the more control messages you receive, thus more network traffic resulting in a higher CLR.
- H_2: The type of client access affects the lost chunk rate. Ideally, we would like to know the exact type of network access the client is using: Mobile, ADLS, FTTH. The library is not able (allowed) to collect such information. We can however classify clients as mobile or fixed lines clients based on the user-agent HTTP string.

- H_3: The network access link characteristics directly affects the CLR. We already studied the download rate of the users using the transfers made with the CDN servers. The download and especially the upload rates achieved during V2V exchanges can also be used to understand the characteristics of the client access link.

Based on the observation we made on Fig. 5, we form two groups of users (for the top 1%) that we term good or bad. The viewers with less than 20% CLR are categorised as good viewers while viewers with more than 60% CLR values are categorised as bad viewers. The rationale behind this approach is to uncover key features of clients that can lead to small and large CLR so as to isolate ill-behaving clients and improve the V2C efficiency.

H_1 *Hypothesis.* The first hypothesis states that the neighbour set size of the viewers should affect the CLR. Figure 7 presents the CDF of the peer set size of good and bad viewers. We can observe that bad peers tend to have smaller peer set size than good peers. While this could hint towards the fact that bad peers have more difficulties to establish links with other viewers, we believe that the actual session times play a key role, as the longer the session, the more likely a peer is to establish more connections. This is indeed the case here as bad peers have an average session time of 22 min while it is 160 min for the good peers. We however also found that the correlation coefficient between neighbour set size and CLR is only 0.05 and 0.07 for good and bad peers respectively. Thus although we observe distinct distributions for good and bad viewers, the neighbour set size does not seem to have any direct correlation with the CLR.

H_2 *Hypothesis.* The second hypothesis is to check if the type of device affects the CLR. We have two families of devices: desktop devices and mobile devices. As a mobile (resp. desktop) device can send to a desktop or mobile device, we have 4 possible combinations to consider. We plotted the distributions of CLR for the good and bad viewers for all the four combinations in Figs. 8 and 9 respectively. For the good users, the type of device does not seem to play a significant role[1]. For the bad viewers, we have very few cases of desktop senders, which is understandable as the worse network conditions are likely to be experienced on mobile devices. This hints towards putting the blame on the user access link that we investigate further with hypothesis H_3.

H_3 *Hypothesis.* We now investigate the impact on the CLR of the access link characteristics of the users that we indirectly estimate based on the bandwidth achieved during transfers with CDN servers and other viewers. From Fig. 10, we observe that 50% of the bad viewers have just 10Mbps of CDN bandwidth whereas 50% of the good viewers have about 25Mbps of CDN bandwidth. The coefficients of correlation between CLR and CDN bandwidth for the good viewers and bad viewers are −0.45 and −0.4 respectively.

---

[1] Note that the good users in Fig. 8 can experience CLR higher than 20% for some categories, as the threshold of 20% applies to the average CLR and not per category.

Looking at the V2V download rates should enable to estimate the uplink of the users as it is likely to be the bottleneck of the path. From Fig. 11, we clearly see that the V2V downloading rate of good viewers is far better than the one of bad viewers. It thus appears that a key factor that explains the observed CLR is the uplink capacity of the peers. In the next section, we leverage this information to devise a simple algorithm, that can be applied independently at each viewer and helps reducing the CLR.

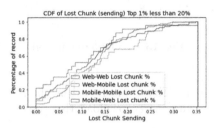

Fig. 8. CLR of good viewers

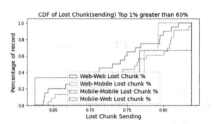

Fig. 9. CLR of bad viewers

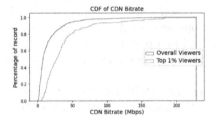

Fig. 10. CDN bandwidth distribution

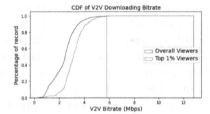

Fig. 11. V2V bandwidth distribution

5   CLR Mitigation Algorithm

Our objective is to achieve a trade-off between CLR reduction and a decrease of V2V traffic. Indeed, a simple but not cost effective way to reduce the CLR is to favor CDN transfers at the expense of V2V transfers. Results of the previous section have uncovered that a key (even though probably not the only one) explanation behind high CLRs is the weakness of the uplink capacity of peers. We thus devised a simple approach that allows viewers to identify themselves as good or bad viewers by monitoring their chunk upload success rate. The algorithm checks every second the CLR, and if it goes above a threshold of $th\%$, the viewer stops sending the so-called *downloaded* control messages, which indicate to its neighbors that it has a new available chunk. As the viewers won't send a *downloaded* message, they will not receive a request for that resource, which will reduce their lost data rate. Note that viewers can still request and

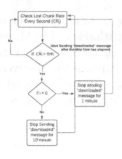
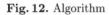

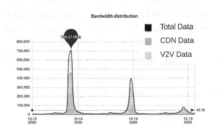

Fig. 12. Algorithm   **Fig. 13.** Second 3-day period

receive chunks in V2V mode from other viewers. This is motivated by the fact that the access links tend to be asymmetric with more download than upload capacity.

The algorithm (Fig. 12) implements a backoff strategy where the viewer alternates between full V2V (receiving and sending) and partial V2V (only receiving) mode to account for possible channel variations or varying congestion in the network. The first time the threshold th is reached, the viewer stops sending *downloaded* messages for 10^0 min and then starts again monitoring the CLR every second for one minute afterwards. If a second consecutive period of CLR over the threshold is observed, the viewer stops sending downloaded messages for 10^1 min and so on (i consecutive events lead to a period of 10^i minutes long silence period). In between silence periods, the test periods, where the viewer is allowed again to upload, last one minute.

In the next section, we report on tests performed with our CLR mitigation algorithm on a test-bed and in production in the live channel used in Sect. 3.

6 Evaluation

We evaluate our CLR mitigation algorithm first in a controlled environment which features 60 viewers and second in our production environment. While modest in size, the controlled environment is useful as it enables to : (i) perform functional tests as the client code in the same as the one in production, (ii) emulate a variety of client network conditions by tuning the upload and download rate of clients, even though we cannot reproduce the full diversity of network conditions observed in the wild and (iii) perform reproducible tests, which is unfeasible in the wild.

6.1   Test-Bed Results

Our test-bed was deployed on 4 physical servers on the Grid'5000 experimental platform [9] which uses KVM virtualisation. Each server hosts 4 virtual machines with 15 viewers per VM, for a total of 60 unique viewers. The viewers are connected to a forked version of the channel presented in Sect. 3, where they operate in isolation, i.e. they can only contact the CDN server and the local viewers.

We relied on Linux namespaces to create isolated viewers. The download capacity of each virtual node is around 325 Mb/s. Each experiment lasts 40 min. To emulate bad viewers, we capped their upload capacity, using the Netem module of Linux, to 3 Mb/s, a value smaller than the smallest bitrate, corresponding to smallest video quality of the channel. In contrast, we impose no constraints on their uplink. We created three different scenarios: (i) Scen. 1: 15 bad viewers and 45 good viewers, (ii) Scen. 2: 30 bad viewers and 30 good viewers and (iii) Scen. 3: 45 bad viewers and 15 good viewers.

Table 1 reports the fraction of chunks downloaded from the CDN or in V2V mode as well as the CLR for the three scenarios with the CLR mitigation algorithm on and off. Clearly, the V2V efficiency is not affected (it even increases) when the algorithm is turned on while the CLR significantly decreases. The CLR does not reach 0 as when the bad peers are in their test periods (in between silence periods) they can be picked as candidates by the good peers.

Table 1. CDN V2V and LCR rate For V2V protocol with and without algorithm

	No Algorithm			Algorithm		
	CDN%	V2V%	LCR	CDN%	V2V%	LCR
Scen. 1	36.7	63.3	7.85	36.37	63.3	3.38
Scen. 2	46.72	53.28	13.52	55.78	64.21	5.58
Scen. 3	66.4	33.6	38.7	53.51	46.49	7.75

6.2   Results in the Wild

We now present the result of a 3-day evaluation for the same channel as in Sect. 3 where the CLR mitigation algorithm is deployed. Figure 13 represents the evolution of aggregated traffic over the three days. We used a conservative approach and used a threshold $th = 80\%$ for this experiment, as we test on an operational channel.

The three days picked for the initial analysis in Sect. 3 were in fact chosen so as to offer a similar profile (with at least one major event) as the period where the algorithm was deployed. This enables to compare the two sets of days, even if we can not guarantee reproducibility due to the nature of the experiment.

We first focus on the V2V efficiency which is the most important factor for the broadcaster. We want the algorithm to reduce the CLR but not the

V2V efficiency as far as possible. The aggregated V2V efficiency for the days without the CLR mitigation algorithm is 28.98% whereas it is 30.61% when it is turned on. The scale of the events does affect the V2V % for both the algorithms. For a small (resp. large) scale event where the total data download remains less than 1.5 TB (over 6TB), the V2V protocol without mitigation algorithm has 32.5% (resp. 27.47%) of V2V efficiency whereas the V2V protocol with algorithm features an efficiency of 28.9% (resp. 32.55%). This suggests that when the protocol has enough viewers with good download capacity, there is no big performance impact on V2V efficiency. Even in the case of less viewers, the V2V efficiency percentage is reduced by only 4%.

The second metric we consider is the CLR. The overall (over the three days) CLR without the algorithm was 24.7% whereas it fell to 13.0% when the algorithm was turned on. Thus overall, the algorithm reduced the CLR by almost a factor of 2.

We further compared the distributions of the CLR for good viewers and bad viewers, using the same definition as in Sect. 3, for the two periods of 3 days in Figs. 14 and 15 respectively. We clearly observe the positive impact of the CLR mitigation algorithm on both the good and bad peers with more mass on the smaller CLR values, e.g. almost 22% of the good viewers do not loose any data at all.

As explained in the introduction, the library operations are transparent to the video player. One can however question if our CLR mitigation algorithm can adversely impact the video player by indirectly influencing the video quality level it picks. As a preliminary assessment of the interplay between the library and the player, we report in Table 2 the fraction of sessions at each quality level observed, per day, for the two periods of interest for the top 1% of viewers. We observe no noticeable difference in the distributions of client sessions at each quality level for the two periods, which suggests that the CLR mitigation algorithm has no collateral effect.

Table 2. Video quality levels distribution (top 1% viewers)

	Period 1 (no algo.)			Period 2 (algo.)		
	Low Q. %	Medium Q. %	High Q. %	Low Q. %	Medium Q. %	High Q. %
Day 1	27	30	44	33	29	38
Day 2	33	25	42	30	25	45
Day 3	30	35	35	28	34	38

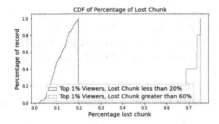

Fig. 14. CLR **No** mitigation alg.

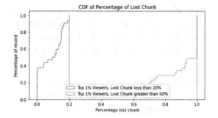

Fig. 15. CLR **With** mitigation alg.

7   Conclusion and Future Work

In this work, we have presented an in-depth study of a live video channel operated over the Internet using a hybrid CDN-V2V architecture. For such an architecture, the main KPI is the fraction of chunks delivered in V2V mode. The chunk loss rate (CLR) metric is another key factor. It indicates, when it reaches high values, that some inefficiencies exist in the system design since some chunks are sent but not delivered (before the deadline) to the viewers that requested them.

We have followed a data driven approach to profile the clients and relate the observed CLRs to other parameters related to the neighborhood characteristics, the type of clients (mobile or fixed) or the access link characteristics. The latter is inferred indirectly using the throughput samples obtained when downloading from the CDN or uploading to other peers. We demonstrated that, in a number of cases, the blame was to put on the access links of some of the viewers. We devised a mitigation algorithm that requires no cooperation between clients as each client individually assesses its uplink capacity and decides if it acts as server for the other peers or simply downloads in V2V mode. We demonstrated the effectiveness of the approach in a controlled testbed and then in the wild, with observed gains close to 50% with a negligible impact on the V2V efficiency. As our library is independent from the actual viewer, and simply acts as a proxy between the CDN server and the video player by re-routing requests for the content to other viewers if possible, our study provides a way to optimise any similar hybrid V2V architecture.

The next steps for us will be to devise an adaptive version of our CLR mitigation algorithm and test at a larger scale on the set of channels operated by our hybrid CDN-P2P live delivery system. We also want to study in more detail the relation between our QoS metrics at the library level and the classical QoE metrics used at the video player level.

References

1. Cohen, B.: Incentives build robustness in BitTorrent. In: Workshop on Economics of Peer-to-Peer systems, vol. 6 (2003)
2. Alex Bybyk **2**(5) (2020). https://restream.io/blog/live-streaming-statistics/. Accessed 18 Oct 2020

3. Bergkvist, A., Burnett, D.C., Jennings,C., Narayanan, A., Aboba, B.: Webrtc 1.0: Real-time commu- nication between browsers. Working draft, W3C (2012)
4. Sarkar, I., Rouibia, S., Pacheco, D.L., Urvoy-Keller, G.: Proactive Information Dissemination in WebRTC-based Live Video Distribution. In: IWCMC, pp. 304–309 (2020)
5. Bruneau-Queyreix, J., Lacaud, M., Négru, D.: Increasing End-User's QoE with a Hybrid P2P/Multi-Server streaming solution based on dash.js and webRTC (2017). ffhal-01585219f
6. Rhinow, F., Veloso, P.P., Puyelo, C., Barrett, S., Nuallain, E.O.: P2P live video streaming in WebRTC. In: World Congress on Computer Applications and Information Systems (WCCAIS), Hammamet, vol. 2014, pp. 1–6 (2014). https://doi.org/10.1109/WCCAIS.2014.6916588
7. Hei, X., Liang, C., Liang, J., Liu, Y., Ross, K.: A measurement study of a large-scale P2P IPTV system. IEEE Trans. Multimedia 9, 1672–1687 (2008). https://doi.org/10.1109/TMM.2007.907451
8. Silverston, T., Jakab, L., Cabellos-Aparicio, A., Fourmaux, O., Salamatian, K., et al.: Large-scale Measurement Experiments of P2P-TV Systems Insights on Fairness and Locality. Signal Process. Image Commun. 26(7), 327–338 (2011). ff10.1016/j.image.2011.01.007ff. ffhal-00648019f
9. Bolze, R., et al.: Grid'5000: a large scale and highly reconfigurable experimental grid testbed. Int. J. High Perform. Comput. Appl. 20(4), 481–494 (2006)

Too Late for Playback: Estimation of Video Stream Quality in Rural and Urban Contexts

Vivek Adarsh[1(✉)], Michael Nekrasov[1], Udit Paul[1], Alex Ermakov[1],
Arpit Gupta[1], Morgan Vigil-Hayes[2], Ellen Zegura[3],
and Elizabeth Belding[1]

[1] University of California, Santa Barbara, Santa Barbara, USA
{vivek,mnekrasov,u_paul,aermakov,arpitgupta,ebelding}@cs.ucsb.edu
[2] Northern Arizona University, Flagstaff, USA
morgan.vigil-hayes@nau.edu
[3] Georgia Tech, Atlanta, USA
ewz@cc.gatech.edu

Abstract. The explosion of mobile broadband as an essential means of Internet connectivity has made the scalable evaluation and inference of quality of experience (QoE) for applications delivered over LTE networks critical. However, direct QoE measurement can be time and resource intensive. Further, the wireless nature of LTE networks necessitates that QoE be evaluated in multiple locations per base station as factors such as signal availability may have significant spatial variation. Based on our observations that quality of service (QoS) metrics are less time and resource-intensive to collect, we investigate how QoS can be used to infer QoE in LTE networks. Using an extensive, novel dataset representing a variety of network conditions, we design several state-of-the-art predictive models for scalable video QoE inference. We demonstrate that our models can accurately predict rebuffering events and resolution switching more than 80% of the time, despite the dataset exhibiting vastly different QoS and QoE profiles for the location types. We also illustrate that our classifiers have a high degree of generalizability across multiple videos from a vast array of genres. Finally, we highlight the importance of low-cost QoS measurements such as reference signal received power (RSRP) and throughput in QoE inference through an ablation study.

Keywords: QoE · Video streaming · Network measurement · LTE · Digital divide

1 Introduction

More than 60 million people reside in rural regions in the United States [18]. However, cellular deployment is often guided by economic demand, concentrating deployment in urban areas and leaving economically marginalized and sparsely populated areas under-served [27]. Few prior studies have focused on assessing mobile broadband in rural areas of the U.S.; there is a lack of accessible datasets that are not only comprehensive (include network-level and application-level

© Springer Nature Switzerland AG 2021
O. Hohlfeld et al. (Eds.): PAM 2021, LNCS 12671, pp. 141–157, 2021.
https://doi.org/10.1007/978-3-030-72582-2_9

traces) but also representative and inclusive of rural demographics. As a result of the COVID-19 pandemic, the assessment of the quality of experience (QoE) for applications delivered over mobile broadband has become urgent as stay-at-home orders and rapid movement to online schooling and work-from-home protocols increase the demand for applications that are known to be sensitive to network quality, such as video streaming and interactive video chat [50]. As a result, communities without access to usable, high speed broadband, such as many rural communities, are particularly disadvantaged [8,32].

Unfortunately, the evaluation of user quality of experience for video streaming applications accessed over LTE in regions where people are most likely to be smartphone dependent [27,28,34] poses a significant scalability challenge. QoE metric collection over LTE networks in a geographic area requires time and resource intensive measurements for each network provider. As a result, experiments at a single geographic point can be quite lengthy. Moreover, in rural areas, obtaining LTE Internet measurements in places where people are likely to use mobile broadband (e.g., at their homes or along local transportation corridors) can be challenging [49], as places of interest are far apart (requiring more resource intensive targeted measurement campaigns) and less densely populated (prohibiting representative crowd-sourcing measurement efforts). It is in this context that we ask the following research question: *How can we infer the QoE for video streaming applications over LTE at scale?*

While there are few to no existing datasets that measure QoE in rural communities, there are many public and proprietary datasets that report quality of service (QoS) metrics, such as reference signal received power (RSRP) or throughput. These metrics are typically reported independently and are measured over LTE networks in a wide range of locations throughout the U.S. and globally [46,51–53,59,63]. We argue that the wealth of LTE-QoS data points across the U.S. represents a key resource that can be leveraged to broadly assess QoE: while measuring QoE at scale in LTE networks presents significant challenges, measuring QoS at scale in LTE networks has already been demonstrated to be feasible. Hence, *our goal, and key contribution, is a methodology that can leverage low-cost QoS measurements to predict QoE.*

To study the correlation between mobile QoS and QoE performance, a diverse set of network measurements that are representative of a wide-range of conditions is needed. As such, we undertook an extensive measurement campaign to collect 16 datasets comprised of network traces from the Southwestern U.S. for four major telecom operators: AT&T, Sprint, T-Mobile and Verizon. Our datasets vary along two primary axes: population density, and network load. To obtain data from varied population densities, we collected LTE network measurements within multiple rural and urban communities. For variable network load, we collected LTE network traces from crowded events in urban locations that resulted in atypically high volumes of network utilization [5] and, as a result, congestion. We also collected traces from the same urban locations during typical operating conditions as a baseline. Our datasets have broad spatial and temporal variability, but can be classified into three primary categories: under-provisioned (rural), congested (congested urban), and well-provisioned (baseline urban).[1] We lever-age these varied datasets to demonstrate the generality of the inference method. Based on our analysis, we show that predictive models can be used to infer video QoE metrics using low-cost QoS measurements, so that QoE can be more easily and scalably determined within difficult to assess regions.

Our key contributions and findings include:

- We collected sixteen measurement datasets[2] from twelve locations through an extensive ; ground measurement campaign within the Southwestern U.S. Our data points are representative of three different network conditions: under-provisioned (rural), congested urban and well-provisioned urban, and include over 32 Million LTE packets. (Sect. 2);
- We develop and evaluate a comprehensive set of predictive models that infer video QoE from low-cost QoS measurements such as RSRP and throughput. Our analysis reveals that predictive models can infer video QoE with an accuracy of at least 80% across all locations and network types (Sect. 3);
- We validate our models across multiple video types from a wide variety of genres. Further, we demonstrate the utility of low-cost RSRP measurements for inferring video QoE (Sect. 3).

2   Methodology and Datasets Overview

QoS metrics, such as received signal strength, latency, throughput, and packet loss, capture the state of network connectivity. However, while QoS provides an indication of network state, there can be a disconnect between QoS and user experience. QoS network metrics are not Pareto-optimal; one element can get better or worse without affecting the other. Consequently, estimation of user experience requires the incorporation of multiple network measures, which may be unique to time, space and application. Note that while the definition of QoE can vary depending on the vantage point from which measurements are taken, we only focus on application-level QoE. Our measurements are active end-user device/passive user as defined in [61].

2.1   QoS and QoE Metrics

In this section, we describe the QoS and QoE metrics we collected (and esti-mated) for this measurement study, as summarized in Table 1.

Quality of Service Metrics: We collect *reference signal received power (RSRP)* and *throughput* synchronously on the same user equipment (UE). RSRP is defined as the linear average over the power contributions (in Watts) of the

---

[1] Through extensive analysis, we verified that our datasets are representative of the network characteristics we anticipated: well-provisioned, congested, and/or under-provisioned. We omit that analysis from this paper due to space constraints.

[2] The subset of our dataset that we have permission to release is available at [4].

Table 1. Overview of QoS and QoE metrics at each location, aggregated across available providers.

Type	Metric	Test Interval	Number of Datapoints	Tools
QoS	RSRP	1 second	2160	Network Monitor
	Throughput	1 second	2160	iPerf
QoE	Video resolution	1 second	2160	Selenium, iframe API
	Resolution switches	1 second	2160	Selenium, iframe API
	Rebuffering events	1 second	2160	Selenium, iframe API

resource elements that carry cell-specific reference signals within the measurement frequency bandwidth [2] and, as illustrated by [7], is widely accessible through mobile operating systems. We record instantaneous RSRP readings from the UEs every one second through the Network Monitor application [43]. We measure throughput by fetching a pre-specified 500 MB file from an AWS instance in Virginia using iPerf over TCP to download the file. The large file size allows the data traffic to fill the pipe and to minimize the effect of slow start. We log the packet traces at the client during the iPerf tests in order to sample throughput at 1 s intervals.

Quality of Experience Metrics: We focus on streaming video, currently the most heavily used QoE-centric service in mobile networks [36]. Internet video streaming services typically use Dynamic Adaptive Streaming over HTTP (DASH) [60] to deliver a video stream. DASH divides each video into time intervals known as segments or chunks, which are then encoded at multiple bit rates and resolutions. To analyze video stream quality, we gather two QoE metrics: *resolution switches* and *rebuffering events*. For resolution switches, we compute the number of consecutive samples that had a different resolution as a percentage of the total number of samples collected during the video. We measure at one-second granularity, which captures resolution switches that happen between video *chunks* that are typically 4–5 s long [15]. Finally, a rebuffering event occurs when video pauses while the application buffer waits to accumulate enough content to resume playback. We record the video state (rebuffering event or normal playback) every second.

2.2   Measurement Suite

We run our measurement suite on Lenovo ThinkPad W550s laptops, each of which are tethered to their own Motorola G7 Power (Android 9) via USB in order to measure cellular performance. The cellular plans on all our cellular user equipment (UE) have unlimited data and are hot-spot enabled to effectively achieve the same level of performance as we would on the mobile device. We run our measurement suite on laptops tethered to phones; this configuration gives us the same application performance while facilitating ease of programming, data extraction, and unification of application-level measurements.

We choose YouTube as the streaming platform because of its popularity in the U.S., capturing over 88% of the mobile market [62]. To collect video QoE metrics, we run a 3-min clip of a Looney Tunes video [64], three times across each of the four LTE providers at each location; we exclude from our results the sessions that experienced playback errors during execution. We chose this particular video due its mix of high and low action scenes, which result in variable bitrates throughout the video (typically, high action scenes have a higher bitrate than low action scenes). After testing multiple playback duration, we observed that a 3-min window was adequate for the playback to reach steady state, while long enough to capture rebuffering and/or resolution switches that occur. To infer video QoE, we collect the input features (RSRP and throughput) synchronously, on a separate device so as not to bias the video streaming measurements. Synchronous measurements of throughput, RSRP and QoE metrics are required to train learning algorithms to infer video QoE for a future time instance. We use different servers for throughput and YouTube tests so that we can obtain concurrent QoS and QoE measurements. Our setup reflects the real world scenario where throughput test servers and YouTube servers are separate while simultaneously affected by varying conditions from *within* the cellular network [6]. In LTE, each bearer (connection from a UE) enjoys a relatively isolated data tunnel before the egress from the packet gateway, located inside the core [1]. This reduces contention among UEs competing for resources at a single eNodeB, and as a result we can accurately record QoS and QoE metrics on two separate devices.

To execute this experiment, we first automate the loading and playback of the YouTube video on the Chrome browser using Selenium [58]. The video resolution is set to auto. Then we use YouTube's iframe API [65] to capture playback events reported by the video player. The API outputs a set of values that indicate player state (not started, paused, playing, completed, buffering) using the getPlayerState() function. The API also provides functions for accessing information about play time and the remaining buffer size.

2.3 Description of Datasets

We collect 16 datasets from 12 locations across the Southwestern U.S. Eight of the datasets were collected from rural locations that had sparse cellular deployment.

An additional eight datasets were collected from four urban locations. In each urban location, we collect two datasets: one during a large event or gathering, in which we expect cellular network congestion to occur (these datasets are marked with _Cong); and a second during typical operating conditions. We call the latter dataset the baseline for that location (these datasets are marked with _Base). Hence, our 16 traces are broadly classified into three categories: rural, congested urban, and baseline urban. The details of each dataset are summarized in Table 2. The designation of each location as rural or urban is based on Census Bureau data [57]. Through these measurement campaigns, we collect and analyze over 32.7 Million LTE packets. Note that the "Number of Datapoints" column shown in Table 1 indicates the QoS/QoE datapoints gathered by the application, while the "# LTE Packets" column in Table 2 refers to the number of packets collected in the trace files.

Table 2. Summary of datasets

Location	Date	# LTE Packets	Type	Carriers*
Rural_1	May 28 2019	3.18 Million	Rural	V,A,T,S
Rural_2	May 29 2019	1.38 Million	Rural	V,T
Rural_3	May 28 2019	2.03 Million	Rural	V,A,T,S
Rural_4	May 30 2019	2.16 Million	Rural	V,A,T,S
Rural_5	May 30 2019	2.27 Million	Rural	V,A,T,S
Rural_6	May 31 2019	2.33 Million	Rural	V,A,T,S
Rural_7	May 31 2019	1.26 Million	Rural	V,T
Rural_8	Jun 01 2019	2.83 Million	Rural	V,A,T,S
Urban_1_Cong	Sep 22 2019	2.25 Million	Urban, Congested	V,A,T,S
Urban_1_Base	Sep 28 2019	1.92 Million	Urban, Baseline	V,A,T,S
Urban_2_Cong	Sep 29 2019	2.51 Million	Urban, Congested	V,A,T,S
Urban_2_Base	Sep 30 2019	1.97 Million	Urban, Baseline	V,A,T,S
Urban_3_Cong	Sep 21 2019	2.65 Million	Urban, Congested	V,A,T,S
Urban_3_Base	Sep 30 2019	2.13 Million	Urban, Baseline	V,A,T,S
Urban_4_Cong	Sep 25 2019	2.18 Million	Urban, Congested	V,A,T,S
Urban_4_Base	Sep 26 2019	2.08 Million	Urban, Baseline	V,A,T,S

*This column lists mobile carriers in each data set (some areas had no coverage for particular network operators). V: Verizon, A:AT&T, T:T-Mobile, S: Sprint.

2.4   Video QoE Measurement Scalability Challenges

Collection of *ground-truth* cellular network measurements, as we explore further in Sect. 4, is a challenging task for multiple reasons. First, it requires physical placement of measurement device at the location to be studied. While there are many large, publicly accessible datasets that incorporate some QoS measurements, QoE measurements, particularly in remote regions, are much more difficult. Second, gathering ground truth data to assess video QoE requires an active connection to stream a large encoded video file. This consumes a substantial amount of bandwidth, computational power, memory, and battery, due to the simultaneous use of LTE modems, display, CPU, and GPU [21] on the user device. For instance, streaming applications consume memory to load the video and require accelerated processing to decode and display the stream from the video server. Unlike QoS metrics, which can often be collected in the background through execution by back-end scripts, the high resource cost of QoE measurements for the end user makes this data difficult to crowd-source. In Fig. 1 we show the resource consumption during one hour of RSRP and throughput (QoS) measurements, compared to one hour of video streaming (QoE), on our data collection phones. As can be seen in the figure, the resources consumed by the QoE measurements were significantly higher, both preventing background data collection and more rapidly draining the device battery.

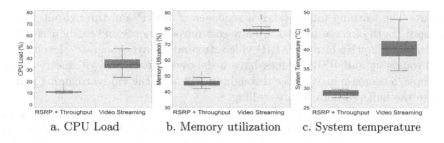

a. CPU Load   b. Memory utilization   c. System temperature

Fig. 1. Device resource consumption during either RSRP and throughput measurements only, or during video streaming.

Rural regions span large geographic areas with terrain that is often hard to access. QoS data from public sources already struggles to cover these areas. In particular, crowd-sourced datasets are data-rich in regions where there are higher density populations. These regions tend to be either urban areas, or other areas frequented by travelers (i.e. highways, national parks, etc.). Rural communities, by contrast, with their lower population densities, are often under-represented in crowd-sourced datasets. Yet it is exactly these regions where under-provisioned networks typically exist and hence where data is urgently needed. In order to effectively assess QoE in these remote areas, we need a method to improve QoE measurement scalability. We address this challenge in the next section, where we show how predictive models can use the less resource expensive QoS measurements to infer QoE for streaming video on mobile broadband networks in a variety of environments.

3   Inferring QoE Metrics for Video

As discussed in Sect. 2.4, the collection of QoS measurements is less resource consumptive, and hence more scalable, than video QoE measurements. We now describe our approach to infer QoE metrics for video streaming sessions using low-cost QoS metrics.

3.1   Learning Problem

Our learning problem's goal is to infer QoE metrics using a sequence of throughput and RSRP (QoS metrics) data input. The objective is to build models with appreciable performance that would work in a wide variety of network conditions and different region types (e.g., rural and urban locations). These models could be used to predict application QoE (in our case, video streaming) at a particular location. We use supervised learning to train two different binary classifiers. The first classifier infers whether the video's state is stalled or normal; the second infers whether there is any change in video resolution. Both models perform the classification task every one second.

Input: The learning model takes a sequence of RSRP and throughput values as input. Both of these metrics are low-cost measurements and easily accessible. Given how adaptive bitrate (ABR) video streaming players operate, the changes in throughput and RSRP values have a delayed impact on QoE metrics. For example, a decrease in available throughput will force the video streaming player to use the buffered data before stalling.

As part of feature engineering, we had to determine how many RSRP and throughput values to use as input for the learning model. Intuitively, the use of longer sequences will improve accuracy. However, longer sequences also increases the complexity of the learning model, which requires more training data to avoid over-fitting. After varying $n = 0 \rightarrow 180$ (total playback time of a session), we found that using a sequence of *three* throughput/RSRP values enabled us to strike a balance between model complexity and accuracy. A typical approach to assessing throughput would be to log continuous measurements for a long duration of time and analyze the resulting mean/mode of the distribution. However, our results (Sect. 3.3) indicate that we can infer the video quality from only a 3-s sample. This has the added benefit of reducing the resource utilization at the client device, such as data consumption and battery drainage, while accurately inferring the video stream quality.

Output: We train two separate binary classifiers to predict the video state and change in resolution at the granularity of one second. Predicting QoE metrics at such fine granularity enables opportunities to infer QoE with limited training data. Given the input features, our models infer how likely it is for the video stream to experience either a video stall or a resolution change in the next instant.

Training Data: Our dataset consists of 32,596 data points. Each data point has input values: a sequence of three RSRP and throughput values, as well as two boolean labels: video state (playing or stalled) and resolution switches (yes–resolution will change; no–resolution will not change). We collected this dataset through our measurement campaign by conducting a total of 181 video streaming sessions across multiple locations (Sect. 2.3). For each classifier, we label the output training samples into either of the two classes: class 0 is when playback is normal and devoid of any event (rebuffering or resolution switch), and class 1 is when there is an event. We carried out the classification task by splitting the entire dataset into a ratio of 70:30 training to test sets, as described in Table 3. We split the overall training dataset into training and validation sets (80:20). We chose the samples proportionate to the size of each dataset category (rural, congested urban, and baseline urban). We present the models' performance per location, where we train the models on specific locations and then test on others not included in the training. We do not make any distinctions between operators since an operator-agnostic evaluation is a more comprehensive reflection of coverage and QoE at a particular location.

Table 3. Breakdown of training and test set samples for both classifiers.

Classifier Type	Target Metric	Training Set		Test Set	
		Class 0	Class 1	Class 0	Class 1
Classifier 1	Rebuffering Event	22,175	642	9,504	275
Classifier 2	Resolution Switching	22,490	327	9,639	140

3.2   Learning Algorithm

We now present the learning models we used for the learning problem, our model training approach, and the method for addressing the inherent class-imbalance.

Learning Models: We trained a wide range of off-the-shelf classifiers for this learning problem in order to identify the classifier that strikes the best balance between performance (precision, recall, etc.) and generalizability. First, we trained simpler classifiers, such as gradient boosting [29], bagging [13], random forest [14], ARIMA [12], AdaBoost [30], etc. These classifiers offer better generalizability at the cost of performance. We also trained neural-network (NN)-based classifiers, such as a convolutional neural network (CNN) [41] and recurrent neural network (RNN) [37] (in particular, LSTMs [35] and GRUs [23]), that offer higher accuracy but require considerable training data to avoid over-fitting.

Setup: We ran all the classifiers on a local machine that runs Ubuntu 18.04, powered by a 4-core i7-7700 CPU (3.60 GHz) with 64,GB RAM and 8 GB NVIDIA RTX 2080 GPU. We implemented the simpler classifiers using the scikit-learn 0.21 [56] library of Python, and NN-based models using Keras with Tensorflow backend [24]. We used four fully-connected layers for the NN-based classifiers. For *RNN-LSTM-Focal* (see Table 4), the network utilized 64, 32, and then 16 hidden neurons, in addition to a final output layer with hyperbolic tangent activation function. We used Grid Search [25] to determine the ideal hyper-parameter configuration for each neural network. To avoid over-fitting, we use a dropout of 0.4 while training with the Adam gradient descent optimizer [39]. We ran the RNN-LSTM model for 120 iterations with a batch size of 64.

Class-Imbalance Problem: As rebuffering and changes in the resolution are rare, most of our data points are normal, i.e., they do not have any rebuffering or resolution switching events. As a result, our dataset has the class-imbalance problem, typical for most anomaly detection problems. To address this issue, we applied the sampling technique SMOTE [19] to balance the classes artificially. However, such an approach reduces the number of data points that we can use for training the classifier, which in turn affects the accuracy. With SMOTE, we observed no improvements in accuracy with simpler learning models (e.g., SVM, random forest, etc.), and lower accuracy for NN-based classifiers. Therefore, for the NN-based classifiers, we adapted a new technique that has proven to increase classification accuracy in datasets that suffer from the class-imbalance issue for the object detection problem [42]. This technique addresses the class-imbalance problem by reshaping the standard cross entropy loss in such a way that it lowers the weights for the majority class [42]. It also introduces the concept of *focal loss* that prevents the majority class from overwhelming the classifier during training. The focal loss can be represented as:

$$FL(p_j) = \alpha(1 - p_j)^\gamma log(p_j) \qquad (1)$$

Here, FL is the focal loss function, and p_j is the softmax probability of the jth class for a particular observation. α and γ are two regularizing parameters. This loss function adds more importance when the network predicts a minority sample as opposed to the overly represented sample—making it ideal for performing classification on an imbalanced dataset.

3.3 Results

We now present the performance of the different classifiers we used for this learning problem. For those that performed well, we also quantify their performance across different locations and video types. Finally, we quantify the contribution of an LTE-specific QoS metric, RSRP, in improving the accuracy of our learning models.

Table 4. Performance metrics of the classification models.

Models	Rebuffering Events			Resolution Switching		
	Accuracy	Precision	Recall	Accuracy	Precision	Recall
Boosting	0.87	0.88	0.88	0.84	0.85	0.84
Bagging	0.80	0.82	0.82	0.71	0.73	0.72
Random Forest	0.85	0.87	0.86	0.79	0.80	0.80
ARIMA	0.81	0.81	0.81	0.77	0.78	0.78
Decision Trees	0.80	0.80	0.98	0.75	0.75	0.75
Extra Randomized Tree	0.77	0.78	0.77	0.72	0.73	0.72
AdaBoost	0.62	0.60	0.63	0.51	0.55	0.53
Support Vector Machine	0.72	0.72	0.73	0.70	0.71	0.70
K-nearest neighbors	0.60	0.56	0.62	0.58	0.57	0.49
CNN	0.72	0.73	0.73	0.68	0.69	0.69
CNN - Focal	0.84	0.85	0.84	0.81	0.81	0.81
RNN - LSTM	0.82	0.83	0.83	0.80	0.79	0.80
RNN - LSTM - Focal	0.89	0.89	0.89	0.86	0.86	0.87
RNN - GRU	0.82	0.82	0.84	0.80	0.82	0.82
RNN - GRU - Focal	0.86	0.86	0.85	0.83	0.84	0.84

Performance: We analyze the performance of learning models in terms of accuracy, precision, recall, and training time. Table 4 summarizes the performance of all classifiers we explored. We observe that the accuracy of the rebuffering-event classifier is better than the resolution-switching one, as depicted in Fig. 2. This difference is attributable to the smaller number of anomalous data points (resolution switches) in the data (see Table 3). In terms of accuracy, *RNN-LSTM-Focal* performs best. This is expected as this model makes the best use of the sequence of throughput and RSRP values and is best suited to handle the class imbalance problem. On the other hand, though *RNN-LSTM-Focal* has the highest accuracy, the accuracy gains are marginal when compared to simpler learning models, especially *Boosting*. Given these marginal gains and the complexity of training NN-based classifiers (5 vs. 214 s), we use the *Boosting* classifier to characterize the performance across different network and video types.

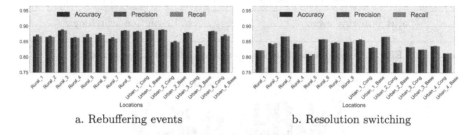

a. Rebuffering events   b. Resolution switching

Fig. 2. Performance of *Boosting* across different locations.

Generalizability: We now quantify the generalizability of the *Boosting* classifier. First, we show how its performance varies across different network types. Figure 2 depicts the performance of inferring video rebuffering using *Boosting* at each location. We observe that the performance differences across different network types are marginal (<2% deviation between categories). We saw similar trends for the *Boosting*-based classifier when inferring resolution switching.

Our initial measurements only collected the QoE metrics for the Looney Tunes video. To verify that our results generalize for other video types, we collected the QoS/QoE data for 108 additional video streaming sessions (a total of 48,825 new data points) at our research facility (baseline-urban). We selected 18 different videos from seven genres: action (trailers/movie clips), music videos, sports, online learning content, news, documentary, and animation (including the original Looney Tunes video) [16]. We selected top trending videos for each genre. Given that the videos were of varying duration, we capped each measurement to a maximum of ten minutes. We streamed each video over three different telecom providers (AT&T, T-Mobile, and Verizon); we were not able to obtain Sprint measurements because of closures of Sprint retail outlets due to the COVID-19 pandemic. Figure 3 shows the performance of *Boosting* for both video rebuffering and resolution switching. We observe marginal variations (<1.5% and <3% deviation for rebuffering and resolution switching, respectively) in accuracy across different video genres, implying that our learning model generalizes reasonably well to different video types. Note that we do not claim that these results generalize for other video players (e.g., Hulu, Netflix), client platforms or devices; we plan to quantify the performance of our learning models for other platforms, devices and non-YouTube videos in the future. Finally, we do not claim to have developed models that generalize across other locations or network conditions – rather we use this study to demonstrate the feasibility of inferring video QoE *at scale* within a limited, but diverse, dataset.

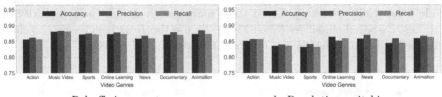

a. Rebuffering events   b. Resolution switching

Fig. 3. Performance of *Boosting* across different video genres.

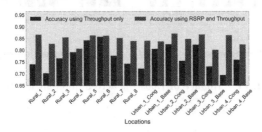

Fig. 4. Inferring video rebuffering using *Boosting* with and without RSRP as an input feature.

Ablation Study: To better understand the impact of an LTE-specific metric (i.e., RSRP) in inferring QoE metrics, we performed an ablation study. Figure 4 compares the accuracy of the *Boosting* classifier in inferring rebuffer events with and without the RSRP values. We observe that the average increase in accuracy, with RSRP as an input, is 9.28%, while the maximum gain is 18.61%. This result could be attributed to the exposition of the relationship, by the non-linear models, between RSRP and throughput to identify the target metrics at any given location successfully. This study highlights the importance of LTE-specific RSRP measurements in accurate prediction of rebuffering and resolution switching.

4 Related Work

Prior work most similar to ours, which focuses on quantifying the user experience, typically infers the QoE of video streaming from QoS of fixed broadband networks [22,31,38]. In contrast, our work focuses on mobile broadband, which often exhibits a wide variation in performance over time and space. Some past work on mobile broadband, such as [3,11,20,54], has examined metrics solely from the application and network layers. [15,26,33,40,44,45] require direct access to (encrypted or unencrypted) network traffic to infer video QoE. In contrast, our approach is independent of network traces and incorporates low-cost signal and throughput measurements for rapid QoE prediction. Few publicly available QoS datasets include synchronous RSRP measurements. [17,48,63] analyze network traces that contain performance indicators captured during streaming sessions, and experiment metadata from mobile broadband networks. All of these datasets, however, have limited types of datapoints (primarily from dense, urban locations); the datasets have minimal to no measurements from networks that are under-provisioned or located in remote regions. We believe it is challenging to uti-lize existing prior datasets (from primarily urban scenarios) to evaluate diverse network conditions in the context of the measurements examined in this work, either due to non-overlapping and non-scalable nature of prior measurements or lack of a comprehensive and representative dataset. Further, the accuracy of our models, given the inexpensive measurements, indicates the feasibility and scalability of our approach.

Prior work that has focused on charting the relationship between RSRP and QoE has important limitations. For instance, [10] presents a mapping of RSRP and video QoE that is derived using only simulated experiments. The authors of [47] explore the effect of radio link quality, such as RSRP, on streaming video QoE. The presented results are limited in scope as their setup streams a custom video hosted on their own server; by omitting evaluation of a popular streaming service, such as YouTube or Netflix, the work does not accurately capture the application and network performance experienced by actual users. [9] undertakes a study similar to ours, however, with a modest dataset that is limited to a small portion of a local transit route and is thus difficult to generalize.

5 Conclusion

Through an extensive measurement campaign, we collect 16 datasets with widely varying performance profiles. Our dataset includes representation of: i) the vari-ability of mobile broadband performance as a consequence of either sparse deploy-ments or network congestion, and ii) the communities most likely to be dependent on mobile broadband (rural areas). Through our analysis, we highlight the chal-lenges of quantifying QoE metrics at scale, particularly in remote locations. To address this challenge, we develop learning models that use low-cost and easily accessible QoS data (LTE-specific RSRP and throughput) to predict QoE metrics. Our models can be generalized to video content from different genres, as well as to other locations that share network characteristics similar to those of our dataset. The observed efficacy of the models indicates that video QoE can be more easily and scalably determined within difficult to assess regions, using low-cost QoS mea-surements. For instance, given the increased load on video streaming platforms during COVID-19 [50], cellular operators could employ our approach to detect sectors with possible bottlenecks without having to rely on user feedback/com-plaints, particularly in remote locations. This has the potential to lead to faster turnaround times for network troubleshooting [55], and therefore may lower out-age periods for users heavily dependent on video streaming.

Acknowledgments. Our work would not have been possible without the incredible support of Jerrold Baca. We wish to thank our shepherd, Marco Fiore and the anony-mous PAM reviewers for their valuable feedback on the paper. This work was funded through the National Science Foundation Smart & Connected Communities award NSF-1831698.

References

1. 3GPP TR 29.281: LTE General Packet Radio System (GPRS) and Tunnelling Protocol User Plane (GTPv1-U), July 2018
2. 3GPP TS 136.214: Evolved Universal Terrestrial Radio Access (E-UTRA); Physical layer - Measurements, April 2010
3. Abdellah, S., Sara, M., El-Houda, M.N., Samir, T.: QoS and QoE for mobile video service over 4G LTE network. In: IEEE Computing Conference, pp. 1263–1269. IEEE (2017)
4. Adarsh, V.: Dataset for QoE Analysis (2021). https://github.com/videostream-ML/urban_rural_qoe
5. Adarsh, V., Nekrasov, M., Zegura, E., Belding, E.: Packet-level overload estimation in LTE networks using passive measurements. In: Proceedings of the Internet Measurement Conference, pp. 158–164 (2019)
6. Adarsh, V., Schmitt, P., Belding, E.: MPTCP performance over heterogenous subpaths. In: 28th International Conference on Computer Communication and Networks (ICCCN), pp. 1–9. IEEE (2019)
7. Alimpertis, E., Markopoulou, A., Butts, C., Psounis, K.: City-wide signal strength maps: prediction with random forests. In: The World Wide Web Conference, pp. 2536–2542. WWW (2019)
8. Amanda Holpuch (The Guardian): US's Digital Divide 'is going to kill people' as COVID-19 exposes inequalities. https://www.theguardian.com/world/2020/apr/13/coronavirus-covid-19-exposes-cracks-us-digital-divide. Accessed 05 Oct 2020
9. Anchuen, P., Uthansakul, P.: Investigation into user-centric QoE and network-centric parameters for YouTube service on mobile networks. In: Proceedings of the 7th International Conference on Communications and Broadband Networking, pp. 28–32 (2019)
10. Awad, N., Mkwawa, I.: The impact of the reference signal received power to quality of experience for video streaming over LTE network. In: Annual Conference on New Trends in Information Communications Technology Applications (NTICT), pp. 192–196 (2017)
11. Begluk, T., Husić, J.B., Baraković, S.: Machine learning-based QoE prediction for video streaming over LTE network. In: 17th International Symposium Infoteh-Jahorina (InfoTeh), pp. 1–5. IEEE (2018)
12. Box, G.E., Pierce, D.A.: Distribution of residual autocorrelations in autoregressive-integrated moving average time series models. J. Am. Stat. Assoc. **65**(332), 1509–1526 (1970)
13. Breiman, L.: Bagging predictors. Machine Learn. **24**(2), 123–140 (1996)
14. Breiman, L.: Random forests. Machine Learn. **45**(1), 5–32 (2001)
15. Bronzino, F., Schmitt, P., Ayoubi, S., Martins, G., Teixeira, R., Feamster, N.: Inferring streaming video quality from encrypted traffic: practical models and deployment experience. In: Proceedings of the Measurement and Analysis of Computing Systems (2019)
16. Bärtl, M.: YouTube channels, uploads and views: a statistical analysis of the past 10 years. Convergence **24**(1), 16–32 (2018)
17. Casas, P., et al.: Predicting QoE in cellular networks using machine learning and in-smartphone measurements. In: 9th International Conference on Quality of Multimedia Experience (QoMEX), pp. 1–6 (2017)
18. Census Bureau: Differences Between Urban and Rural Populations (2016). https://www.census.gov/newsroom/press-releases/2016/cb16-210.html

19. Chawla, N.V., Bowyer, K.W., Hall, L.O., Kegelmeyer, W.P.: SMOTE: synthetic minority over-sampling technique. J. Artif. Intell. Res. **16**, 321–357 (2002)
20. Chen, H., Yu, X., Xie, L.: End-to-end quality adaptation scheme based on QoE prediction for video streaming service in LTE networks. In: 11th International Symposium and Workshops on Modeling and Optimization in Mobile, Ad Hoc and Wireless Networks (WiOpt), pp. 627–633. IEEE (2013)
21. Chen, X., Ding, N., Jindal, A., Hu, Y.C., Gupta, M., Vannithamby, R.: Smartphone energy drain in the wild: analysis and implications. In: Proceedings of the ACM SIGMETRICS International Conference on Measurement and Modeling of Computer Systems. SIGMETRICS (2015)
22. Chen, Y., Wu, K., Zhang, Q.: From QoS to QoE: a tutorial on video quality assessment. IEEE Commun. Surv. Tutor. **17**(2), 1126–1165 (2014)
23. Cho, K., et al.: Learning phrase representations using RNN encoder-decoder for statistical machine translation. arXiv preprint arXiv:1406.1078 (2014)
24. Chollet, F.: Keras (2019). https://github.com/keras-team/keras
25. Cournapeau, D.: Tuning the Hyper-Parameters of an Estimator (2019). https://scikit-learn.org/stable/modules/grid_search.html
26. Dimopoulos, G., Leontiadis, I., Barlet-Ros, P., Papagiannaki, K.: Measuring video QoE from encrypted traffic. In: Proceedings of the Internet Measurement Conference. IMC (2016)
27. Federal Communications Commission: Broadband Deployment Report, February 2018. https://www.fcc.gov/reports-research/reports/broadband-progress-reports/2018-broadband-deployment-report
28. Federal Communications Commission: Broadband Deployment Report, May 2019. https://www.fcc.gov/reports-research/reports/broadband-progress-reports/2019-broadband-deployment-report
29. Freund, Y., Schapire, R., Abe, N.: A short introduction to boosting. Japanese Society Artif. Intell. **14**(771–780), 1612 (1999)
30. Freund, Y., Schapire, R.E.: A desicion-theoretic generalization of on-line learning and an application to boosting. In: Vitányi, P. (ed.) EuroCOLT 1995. LNCS, vol. 904, pp. 23–37. Springer, Heidelberg (1995). https://doi.org/10.1007/3-540-59119-2_166
31. Goran, N., Hadžialić, M.: Mathematical bottom-to-up approach in video quality estimation based on PHY and MAC parameters. IEEE Access **5**, 25657–25670 (2017)
32. Grant Samms (Forbes): As Cities Face COVID-19, The Digital Divide Becomes More Acute, April 2020. https://www.forbes.com/sites/pikeresearch/2020/04/02/as-cities-face-covid-19-the-digital-divide-becomes-more-acute/#277c93e558c5. Accessed 05 Oct 2020
33. Gutterman, C., et al.: Requet: real-time QoE detection for encrypted YouTube traffic. In: Proceedings of the 10th ACM Multimedia Systems Conference, pp. 48–59 (2019)
34. Hansi Lo Wang (NPR): Native Americans On Tribal Land Are 'The Least Connected' To High-Speed Internet, December 2018. https://www.npr.org/2018/12/06/673364305/native-americans-on-tribal-land-are-the-least-connected-to-high-speed-internet
35. Hochreiter, S., Schmidhuber, J.: Long short-term memory. Neural Comput. **9**(8), 1735–1780 (1997)

36. Hoßfeld, T., Seufert, M., Sieber, C., Zinner, T.: Assessing effect sizes of influence factors towards a QoE model for HTTP adaptive streaming. In: 6th International Workshop on Quality of Multimedia Experience (QoMEX), pp. 111–116. IEEE (2014)
37. Jordan, M.I.: Attractor dynamics and parallelism in a connectionist sequential machine. In: Artificial Neural Networks: Concept Learning, pp. 112–127 (1990)
38. Kim, H.J., Choi, S.G.: A study on a QoS/QoE correlation model for QoE evaluation on IPTV service. In: 12th International Conference on Advanced Communication Technology (ICACT), vol. 2, pp. 1377–1382. IEEE (2010)
39. Kingma, D., Ba, J.: Adam: a method for stochastic optimization. In: International Conference on Learning Representations (2014)
40. Krishnamoorthi, V., Carlsson, N., Halepovic, E., Petajan, E.: BUFFEST: predicting buffer conditions and real-time requirements of HTTP (S) adaptive streaming clients. In: Proceedings of the 8th ACM on Multimedia Systems Conference, pp. 76–87 (2017)
41. Krizhevsky, A., Sutskever, I., Hinton, G.E.: ImageNet classification with deep convolutional neural networks. In: Advances in Neural Information Processing Systems, pp. 1097–1105 (2012)
42. Lin, T., Goyal, P., Girshick, R.B., He, K., Dollár, P.: Focal Loss for Dense Object Detection. CoRR abs/1708.02002 (2017). http://arxiv.org/abs/1708.02002
43. Lubek, B.: Network Monitor. https://github.com/caarmen/network-monitor
44. Mangla, T., Halepovic, E., Ammar, M., Zegura, E.: MIMIC: using passive network measurements to estimate HTTP-based adaptive video QoE metrics. In: 2017 Network Traffic Measurement and Analysis Conference (TMA) (2017)
45. Mangla, T., Halepovic, E., Ammar, M., Zegura, E.: eMIMIC: estimating HTTP-based video QoE metrics from encrypted network traffic. In: 2018 Network Traffic Measurement and Analysis Conference (TMA) (2018)
46. Midoglu, C., Moulay, M., Mancuso, V., Alay, O., Lutu, A., Griwodz, C.: Open video datasets over operational mobile networks with MONROE. In: Proceedings of the 9th ACM Multimedia Systems Conference, pp. 426–431 (2018)
47. Minovski, D., Åhlund, C., Mitra, K., Johansson, P.: Analysis and estimation of video QoE in wireless cellular networks using machine learning. In: 11th IEEE International Conference on Quality of Multimedia Experience (QoMEX), pp. 1–6 (2019)
48. MONROE: MONROE Video Dataset (2018). https://doi.org/10.5281/zenodo.1230448
49. Nekrasov, M., et al.: Evaluating LTE coverage and quality from an unmanned aircraft system. In: Proceedings of the 16th IEEE International Conference on Mobile Ad-Hoc and Smart Systems (2019)
50. Nielsen Insights: Streaming Consumption Rises in U.S. Markets With Early Stay-at-home Orders During COVID-19 (2020). https://www.nielsen.com/us/en/insights/article/2020/streaming-consumption-rises-in-u-s-markets-with-early-stay-at-home-orders-during-covid-19/
51. Ookla: Mobile Speedtest Intelligence Data (2019). https://www.speedtest.net/reports/united-states/
52. Open Signal: Open Signal 3G and 4G LTE Cell Coverage Map (2016). http://opensignal.com
53. OpenCelliD: The World's Largest Open Database of Cell Towers (2020). https://opencellid.org/

54. Orsolic, I., Pevec, D., Suznjevic, M., Skorin-Kapov, L.: A machine learning approach to classifying YouTube QoE based on encrypted network traffic. Multimedia Tools Appl. **76**(21), 22267–22301 (2017)
55. Paul, U., Ermakov, A., Nekrasov, M., Adarsh, V., Belding, E.: #Outage: detecting power and communication outages from social networks. In: Proceedings of The Web Conference, pp. 1819–1829. WWW (2020)
56. Pedregosa, F., et al.: Scikit-learn: machine learning in Python. J. Machine Learn. Res. **12**, 2825–2830 (2011)
57. Ratcliffe, M., Burd, C., Holder, K., Fields, A.: Defining rural at the US census bureau. Am. Community Surv. Geogr. Brief **1**(8) (2016)
58. Selenium: The Selenium Browser Automation Project. https://www.selenium.dev/documentation/en/
59. Skyhook: Skyhook Coverage Area (2019). https://www.skyhook.com/coverage-map
60. Sodagar, I.: The MPEG-DASH standard for multimedia streaming over the internet. IEEE Multimedia **18**(4), 62–67 (2011)
61. Sousa, I., Queluz, M.P., Rodrigues, A.: A survey on QoE-oriented wireless resources scheduling. J. Netw. Comput. Appl. **158**, 102594 (2020)
62. Statista: Most Popular Video Streaming Services in the US (2019). https://www.statista.com/statistics/910895/us-most-popular-video-streaming-services-by-reach/
63. Wamser, F., Wehner, N., Seufert, M., Casas, P., Tran-Gia, P.: YouTube QoE monitoring with YoMoApp: a web-based data interface for researchers. In: Network Traffic Measurement and Analysis Conference, pp. 1–2. IEEE (2018)
64. YouTube: Looney Tunes Summer Vacation! WB Kids (2018). https://www.youtube.com/watch?v=8fKNkiJl_Ro
65. YouTube: YouTube Player API Reference for iframe Embeds (2019). https://developers.google.com/youtube/iframe_api_reference

TLS

Measurement and Analysis of Automated Certificate Reissuance

Olamide Omolola[1(✉)], Richard Roberts[2], Md. Ishtiaq Ashiq[3],
Taejoong Chung[3], Dave Levin[2], and Alan Mislove[4]

[1] University of Vienna, Vienna, Austria
olamide@omolola.xyz
[2] University of Maryland, College Park, USA
[3] Virginia Tech, Blacksburg, USA
[4] Northeastern University, Boston, USA

Abstract. The Transport Layer Security (TLS) Public Key Infrastructure (PKI) is essential to the security and privacy of users on the Internet. Despite its importance, prior work from the mid-2010s has shown that mismanagement of the TLS PKI often led to weakened security guarantees, such as compromised certificates going unrevoked and many internet devices generating self-signed certificates. Many of these problems can be traced to manual processes that were the only option at the time. However, in the intervening years, the TLS PKI has undergone several changes: once-expensive TLS certificates are now freely available, and they can be obtained and reissued via automated programs.

In this paper, we examine whether these changes to the TLS PKI have led to improvements in the PKI's management. We collect data on *all* certificates issued by Let's Encrypt (now the largest certificate authority by far) over the past four years. Our analysis focuses on two key questions: First, *are administrators making proper use of the automation that modern CAs provide for certificate reissuance?* We find that for certificates with a sufficiently long history of being reissued, 80% of them did reissue their certificates on a predictable schedule, suggesting that the remaining 20% may use manual processes to reissue, despite numerous automated tools for doing so. Second, *do administrators that use automated CAs react to large-scale compromises more responsibly?* To answer this, we use a recent Let's Encrypt misissuance bug as a natural experiment, and find that a significantly larger fraction of administrators reissued their certificates in a timely fashion compared to previous bugs.

1 Introduction

The Transport Layer Security (TLS) public key infrastructure (PKI) is an essential component of the modern Internet: it allows users to communicate over the Internet in a trusted and confidential manner. However, previous work [2,3,8,13,21] has demonstrated that despite its importance, the *management* of the TLS PKI is often not compliant with recommended security practices. For example, systems administrators often fail to revoke or even reissue certificates when private keys are compromised [20], many internet-of-things devices

© Springer Nature Switzerland AG 2021
O. Hohlfeld et al. (Eds.): PAM 2021, LNCS 12671, pp. 161–174, 2021.
https://doi.org/10.1007/978-3-030-72582-2_10

generate self-signed certificates (sometimes even with identical keys) [13], and domains sometimes share private keys with third parties due to limitations in the PKI itself [2].

Many of these management issues can be traced to inadequate tools for system administrators. For example, in the wake of the Heartbleed [11] bug in 2014, a significant fraction of web servers potentially had their private keys exposed; as a result, administrators should have revoked their old certificates and reissue new ones. At the time, doing so was a largely manual process: because certificates were typically valid for up to 5 years, many administrators presumably eschewed automating the infrequent process of obtaining and installing new certificates. As a result, it took over a *week* before even 10% of the vulnerable web servers had reissued their certificates [21]. Similarly, in the DNSSEC PKI, it has been observed that inadequate tools—in the case of DNSSEC, a manual process of uploading DS records—has lead to poor adoption of secure protocols [4].

However, the TLS PKI has changed dramatically since 2014. While previously expensive, TLS certificates are now free with the advent of certificate authorities such as Let's Encrypt [14] (which is now, by far, the most popular CA [16]). More importantly, these free CAs often have much shorter certificate lifetimes (90 days for Let's Encrypt), encouraging the automation of the process of certificate reissuance and installation (as it happens every three months, rather than every five years). Open-source protocols (e.g., ACME) and tools (e.g., `certbot`, `acme.sh`, cPanel) now allow administrators to automate the entire process.

In this paper, we examine whether the presence of these tools and services has led to better TLS certificate reissuance. To understand the effects of automated tools in certificate reissuance, we focus on certificates issued by Let's Encrypt. We chose Let's Encrypt as it is by far the largest ACME-based CA [16], and it has the longest history of operation (and hence, the highest likelihood of having domain sets that have a long history of reissues). We use Certificate Transparency (CT) [12] logs to obtain a list of *all* 1.03B certificates Let's Encrypt issued over the past four years. We group certificates in this list by the set of domains they contain (similar to prior work [21], we refer to this as a *domain set*), enabling us to measure how often certificates are reissued.

We also use a recent bug discovered by Let's Encrypt as a natural experiment. In brief, in early 2020, Let's Encrypt discovered that over 3M certificates had been issued improperly, as they had failed to check for Certificate Authority Authorization (CAA) [19] records properly before issuance [5]. Because they were improperly issued, Let's Encrypt announced that they planned to revoke the certificates one week later, informing all system administrators that they needed to reissue their certificates. This serves as a natural experiment, as we can examine whether administrators took the necessarily manual action of reissuing their certificates, rather than simply relying on their automated reissuance.

Our paper makes two contributions: *First*, we examine the behavior of system administrators reissuing TLS certificates with the advent of free CAs such as Let's Encrypt. We find that approximately 80% of domain sets with a sufficiently long history of being reissued, did reissue their certificates on a predictable schedule. In addition, 60% of all domain sets show a median reissuance period of 60 days (the default recommended by Let's Encrypt [14] and used by many ACME tools [6, 23] for automated certificate reissuance).

Second, we use the Let's Encrypt bug mentioned above to explore whether system administrators now respond more quickly and completely when manual intervention *is* required. We focus on the subset of the 2M domain sets with a misissued certificate, and identify 98,652 domain sets that show a regular period of reissuance with at least one new certificate issued after the bug was discovered on February 29, 2020.[1] We demonstrate that, of these domain sets, at least 28% appear to have taken the manual steps necessary to reissue their certificates within a week, suggesting that, indeed, system administrators are better able to reissue certificates securely today when compared to previous incidents requiring certificate reissuance.

2 Background

We begin with an overview of the TLS certificate ecosystem and related work.

2.1 Certificates

TLS is based on certificates, which are bindings between identities (typically domain names) and public keys. Certificates are signed by *certificate authorities* (CAs), who verify the identity of the requestor. Certificates have a well-defined validity period, which is expressed as `NotBefore` and `NotAfter` fields in the certificate; clients will refuse to accept certificates outside of their validity period. As a result, certificate owners have to periodically *reissue* their certificate by contacting their CA (or another CA) and obtaining a new certificate.

While certificates originally only contained a single identity (domain name), this often made the administration difficult for web servers that served multiple domains. Today, certificates can carry multiple identities (domain names) via a `Subject Alternate Names` list. In essence, the owner of the certificate's public key has been verified by the CA to control *all* of the identities (domains).

Finally, domain owners may wish to limit the set of CAs who are authorized to issue certificates for a given domain. They can now do so by publishing Certificate Authority Authorization (CAA) records, which are DNS records that specify a list of CAs that are/are not allowed to issue certificates (if no such record exist, all CAs are implicitly authorized). CAs today are required to check for the CAA records for domains before issuing certificates.

2.2 Let's Encrypt

For a long time, TLS certificates were relatively expensive to obtain (typically $50 or more) and were valid for multiple years (typically 3–5) [13]. The cost and

---

[1] Because of the way the bug manifested itself, the misissued certificates are *not* a random sample of all certificates. We explore this in Sect. 3.

extended validity ended up having two effects: the overall adoption of HTTPS was relatively low (as administrators had to spend significant money to obtain the necessary certificates), and the system administrators who did purchase certificates were not incentivized to automate the infrequent reissuance process. Additionally, the certificate issuance and renewal processes were manual, administratively burdensome, and technically cumbersome.

In 2015, Let's Encrypt disrupted the TLS certificate business model by offering *free* certificates that were valid for 90 days. Other free CAs have also been created such as ZeroSSL[2] and Buypass[3], and the TLS ecosystem has since changed dramatically: the fraction of web connections using HTTPS has increased from ~27% in early 2014 to ~85% in 2020 [16], and Let's Encrypt is now the largest CA, with over 1B certificates issued and over 35% of the Alexa top 1M sites using Let's Encrypt certificates [1]. Importantly, while prior CAs often required certificates to be requested/reissued via web forms, Let's Encrypt is entirely automated via the ACME protocol; several popular ACME clients exist, including `certbot`, `acme4j`, and `acme.sh`.

In February 2020, Let's Encrypt announced that they discovered a bug in the Boulder software they used to issue certificates [5]. Specifically, the software failed to properly check for CAA records in requested certificates if (a) a certificate was requested for multiple domains, and (b) Let's Encrypt had previously checked the domain control validations (DCV) for these domains in the preceeding 30 days. While Let's Encrypt was supposed to re-check the CAA record for all domain names included in the certificate within 8 h of issuing the certificate, under these circumstances, it only picked one domain name among the multiple domains in the certificate and ran the CAA check n times (equivalent to the number of domains in the certificate). Let's Encrypt originally announced on February 29, 2020 that it planned to revoke all these certificates on March 5, 2020, and it emailed all affected domain administrators. On March 5, 2020, Let's Encrypt reversed their decision and decided to not revoke en-masse [15].

2.3   Related Work

Improvements in the ability to scan the Internet [10] in 2013 have led to a better understanding of the entire TLS ecosystem [9]. Researchers have unfortunately found that TLS clients and servers are often incorrectly managed [13], leading to reduced security for internet users. In the aftermath of the Heartbleed bug, it became evident that manual revocation and reissuance of certificates is a major security problem: most administrators failed to revoke or even reissue, and those that did sometimes reissued using the same key pair [8,21]. Similar behavior had been observed years prior when a bug in Debian caused many domains the need to reissue certificates [20]. Some domains have chosen to outsource certificate management to third-parties such as content delivery networks (CDNs); while this improves certificate management, it often requires sharing private keys [2].

---

[2] https://zerossl.com/features/certificates/.

[3] https://www.buypass.com/ssl/products/acme.

To the best of our knowledge, there has not been significant study of automated certificate reissuance in the TLS PKI. Previous work by Matsumoto et al. proposed a decentralized audit-based system: Instant Karma PKI (IPK) to promote automation among HTTPS domains [18]. The recent development of CAA records also provides a useful tool for automation as the domain name holders or DNS operators can use CAA records to control which CAs that they would like to get a certificate from [19].

3 Methodology

We now describe the datasets we collected and our methodology to determine a set of certificates that have been reissued.

3.1 Certificates

Our goal is to see how certificates have been (re)issued by the system administrators. We focus on Let's Encrypt as it is the largest free CA, and it has the longest history of operation. To this end, we obtain *all* certificates issued by Let's Encrypt by leveraging the Certificate Transparency (CT) logs; when issuing a certificate, Let's Encrypt publishes the certificate to one of the CT logs managed by Google.[4] Thus, to obtain a nearly complete view of the certificates issued by Let's Encrypt, we first fetch all certificates from all of the CT log servers managed by Google,[5] obtaining 5.3B certificates in total from September 9, 2014 to May 18, 2020. We then identify the certificates issued by Let's Encrypt according to their Issuer field, which leaves us with 1.03B certificates.[6]

3.2 Let's Encrypt CAA Bug List

On February 29th, 2020, Let's Encrypt announced the CAA issuance bug in their certificate issuance process (see Sect. 2.2). Let's Encrypt publicly released a list of the certificates impacted by this bug [5] containing serial numbers of 3,048,289 certificates, some of which were potentially misissued (i.e., the CAA records for some of domains in the certificate may have not permitted Let's Encrypt to issue a certificate, even though they did). We use this list to study how the impacted certificates have been *reissued* by administrators.

---

[4] In order for a certificate to be "CT qualified" in modern browsers such as Chrome, it has to be logged on multiple CT log servers and one of them has to be from a Google log [7].

[5] aviator, icarus, argon2018~2023, xenon2019~2023, pilot, rocketeer, skydiver.

[6] We intentionally exclude pre-certificates from the analysis (which Let's Encrypt has published as well since 2018 [17]) as they do not guarantee the issuance of their actual (final) certificates.

3.3 Defining Certificate Reissuances

While it is easy to identify when certificates are issued, there is a bit of subtlety to determining when they are *reissued*. In particular, we face two challenges: *First*, CT logs do not contain any identifier of the client such as IP address that sent a Certificate Signing Request (CSR), thus making it hard to identify if the certificate has been reissued from the same client; thus, we first link the certificates that share the same `Subject Alternate Name` (SAN) list.[7] We refer to this set of domains in the SAN list as the *domain set*. *Second*, we do not know when the client has replaced the old certificate with the new one; thus, we use the logging timestamp on the CT log server as a proxy.

In summary, we group certificates by their domain set and order them based on their timestamp on the CT logs; we refer to any certificates other than the first as reissued certificates. Using this, methodology we obtain 188M unique domain sets and 1.03B corresponding certificates issued during our measurement period. Out of the 188M domain sets, we find that 67M (35.7%) domain sets have no reissued certificates, 23M (12.2%) domain sets have reissued once and, 14M (7.8%) domain sets have reissued twice. One limitation of relying on CT logs alone worth noting is that we are unable to quantify how domain sets change, as we would need a way to "link" domain sets which is unavailable to us [2]. In these cases, the modified domain set would be considered a separate domain set in our analysis.

4 Results

We analyze the reissuance behaviors of certificates issued by Let's Encrypt. We aim to understand reissuance behavior of two types: reissuance that is likely done *automatically* (e.g., via a `cron` job) and reissuance that is likely done *manually* (e.g., directly invoked by a system administrator). We begin by describing how we distinguish these two cases.

4.1 Automated Reissuance

One of Let's Encrypt's key principles is that it makes it possible to automate obtaining and reissuing certificates. A new user of Let's Encrypt need only set up the first certificate issuing process with any ACME client of choice, then they can create a `cron` job to continually check if the certificate is still valid and request a new certificate once the current certificate nears expiry.

We first need to identify when we believe a certificate has been reissued via an automated process. As discussed previously we are not privy to Let's Encrypt's internal logs, so we can only rely on publicly available data from the CT logs. To do so, we group all Let's Encrypt certificates by the domain set present in them, and then sort these lists by the time in the CT log timestamp. We then examine the amount of time that passes between each pair of successive reissues.

---

[7] Thus, if the same client adds or removes one domain, it changes the SAN list. Therefore, ACME processes it as a separate certificate request, not a reissuance, thereby supporting our methodology of grouping by domain sets.

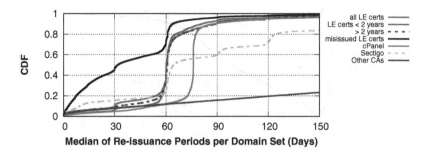

Fig. 1. Distribution of median reissuance period per domain set for all Let's Encrypt certificates with or without lifetimes and misissued certificates. For comparison, we also include the median reissuance period per domain set for a few other CAs: Sectigo, cPanel, and other top 10 CAs (we plot cPanel and Sectigo separately as they show different behavior than the others).

In Fig. 1, we plot the cumulative distribution of the median of these reissue time lists in the line labeled "all LE certs." We immediately observe a large "spike" around 60 days, and observe that over 55% of domain sets have a median reissue time between 55 and 65 days. This lines up with the reissuance policy recommended by Let's Encrypt, which recommends reissuing certificates that are within 30 days of their expiry (i.e., are at least 60 days old) [14]. Moreover, this timing lines up well as the default policies of many ACME clients: `cerbot` [6] and `acme.sh` [23] both default to renewing within 30 days of expiry. We also observe that the "spike" does not happen *entirely* at the 60 day mark; this is likely because the renewal occurs the first time the `cron` job runs after reaching the mark. Finally, we observe a much smaller spike around 30 days, which is likely the behavior of a different ACME client or a system administrator who manually changed their client's behavior.

Next, we examine whether this median reissue period of 60 days is only present in domain sets that have a long history of being reissued (i.e., that have been around a long time) or if it is also present in newer domain sets. To do so, we divide the "all LE certs" line into those first issued greater than two years ago, and those first issued within the past two years; these are both plotted in Fig. 1. We can observe the shapes of these curves are quite similar, suggesting that the behavior is relatively consistent between these two groups.

We also discover that roughly 10% of Let's Encrypt domain sets in all categories had a median re-issuance period of *greater than* 90 days, meaning the certificates were more often than not renewed after expiry. This behavior could occur if the administrator did not set up a `cron` job, incorrectly set up a `cron` job to run very infrequently, or if the system was not always online. We leave a deeper exploration of these domain sets to future work.

Finally, we also briefly compare the Let's Encrypt domain set behavior to that of other CAs. To do so, we extract the domain sets in the same manner from the CT logs for the top 10 CAs (other than Let's Encrypt), and compute

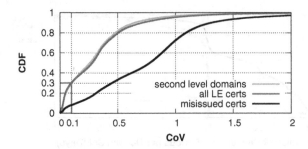

Fig. 2. Distribution of coefficient of variation (CoV) for all Let's Encrypt domain sets, second level domains, and the misissued certificates.

the median reissuance periods in the same manner per CA. We plot these as well in Fig. 1 under the lines "cPanel", "Sectigo", and "Other CAs"; we separate out cPanel and Sectigo as they show different behavior than the others. In brief, we see that most of the other top CAs show very long median reissuance periods, while cPanel shows a "spike" at 75 days and Sectigo at 60, 90, and 120 days.

Coefficient of Variation (CoV). While the median of the reissue time periods being so clearly at 60 days is suggestive that the administrators use automated software to reissue their certificates, it is not entirely definitive. Thus, we look for further evidence of automation by looking at how *similar* the reissuance periods of a given domain set are to each other. In other words, if a given domain set was using an automated process to reissue certificates, we would expect that the period between reissues would be highly consistent.

To do so, we calculate the *coefficient of variation* (CoV)—which is simply the standard deviation of a distribution over its mean—of the amounts of time between each successive reissuance. Automated reissuance would often lead to a consistent period between reissues, meaning that the CoV would be low i.e., 0.1 or smaller. We choose the CoV threshold of 0.1 as a cut-off as would allow, for example, a domain set with a mean reissuance time of 60 days to be classified as automated if the variance is less than 6 days (roughly one week). For this analysis, we only keep the domain sets where we have a sufficient reissue history of at least five reissues. Figure 2 plots the distribution of CoVs for the reissue time periods for each domain set under the "all LE certs" line. We can observe that many domain sets do show evidence of automation: 30.3% of domain sets have a CoV of less than 0.1.

We were concerned that particular domains with unusual patterns of reissuance may end up artificially shaping this curve, as our analysis is at the *domain set* level, rather than at the *system administrator* level. Thus, we additionally perform an aggregation to the second-level domain to see whether particular domains are skewing the results.

We aggregate domain sets into second-level domain through a weighted average: for each second-level domain S, we compute the average CoV for all domain sets that have at least one domain name from S. For domain sets that include

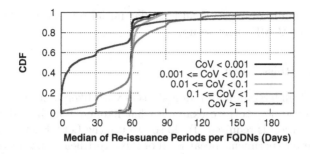

Fig. 3. Distribution of all Let's Encrypt domain set reissuances, divided across different CoV groups. We can see the groups with lower CoV tend to have a median reissuance period of 60 days.

domains from multiple second-level domains, we simply weigh the domain set's CoV by the fraction of domains that belong to S. The resulting cumulative distribution is also shown in Fig. 2, and we can observe that the distribution is quite similar to the analysis at the domain set level. Thus, we have some confidence that the (potentially odd) behavior of a small number of second-level domain sets is not dramatically altering the results.

Noticing that many domain sets tend to have a high CoVs, we next examine how well the CoV methodology identifies domain sets with regular reissuance patterns. We do so by dividing up domain sets by their CoV, and plotting the cumulative distribution of their median reissuance time in Fig. 3. We can immediately observed that the median reissuance time of certificates varies dramatically by CoV: we find that the median reissuance period of domain sets with a very low CoV (0.1 or smaller) is 60 days, while domain sets with a CoV greater than 1 are much less predictable. Further, Fig. 3 reveals that over 88% of domain sets with highly automated reissuance (CoV < 0.001) have a median reissue period of between 59 and 61 days (consistent with the reissue occurring during the first `cron` job to run after the 60 day period).

Initial Renewal Setup. Moving on, we hypothesize that the initial setup and use of ACME clients may result in multiple, irregular requests, which would affect our CoV calculation. To understand the effects, we focus on certificates that have at least five reissues, and make the assumption that most administrators would be comfortable with operating ACME clients after a year. Out of 188M unique domain sets, only 60M unique domain certificates have at least five reissues; these form the basis of the following analysis.

Roughly 48.2% of domain sets with at least five reissues have a CoV less than 0.1. However, if we also look at *subsequences* of reissues, ignoring the first set of reissues as long as at least five reissues remain, we can identify an *additional* 29.9% domain sets that have a subsequence of reissues with a CoV less than 0.1. In other words, 78% of domain sets with a subsequence of at least five reissues have a regular reissue cycle that begins at some point in their lifetimes. Thus, we have identified a limitation of the CoV metric, as it may be too conservative in cases where administrators have an irregular initial reissunce cycle before fully debugging their ACME client setup.

4.2 Manual Reissuance

Having a good understanding on domain sets with likely automated reissuance infrastructure, we now turn to examine what happens for these domains when manual intervention is required. To do so, we use the Let's Encrypt misissuance bug as a natural experiment: because all of these certificates need to be reissued, we have a collection of domain sets where we can study whether the system administrator did, in fact, reissue their certificate.

We first need to examine the set of certificates affected by the bug, which was announced on February 29, 2020. Let's Encrypt reported that over 3M certificates were affected; we collected all of these certificates and plotted their issue time in Fig. 4. We can see that these certificates went as far back as December 2, 2019, which would be expected given Let's Encrypt 90-day certificate lifetime. Importantly, the certificates appear to have been issued uniformly throughout the prior 90 days.

However, there are multiple reasons why these misissued certificates are *not* a random sample of all Let's Encrypt certificates. *First*, the bug only affected certificates with multiple domains in them, meaning any certificates with a single domain were not misissued. *Second*, and more importantly, it only affected domains *where the CAA record had been verified within the past 30 days*. As we observed previously, most certificates are reissued after *60* days, this means that the only certificates that were affected were ones that were either (a) not on a regular schedule to begin with, or (b) were on a regular schedule, but happened to be reissued in late 2019/early 2020 for another reason. This observation explains why the misissued certificates behave quite differently from all Let's Encrypt certificates in Figs. 1 and 2: due to the nature of the bug, domain sets that had regular, 60-day reissue periods were much less likely affected. In fact, such domain sets would only have been affected if one of the domains in the domain set happened to be in *another* domain set whose certificate was reissued in the previous 30-day time period, or where the administrator had manually reissued that domain set during that period.

Nevertheless, we need to identify when we believe a certificate was manually reissued from among the misissued certificates. Recall that we do not have access to Let's Encrypt's logs, so we can only rely on the timestamps public CT logs. We want to see how certificates affected by the bug were automatically reissued before the bug, but manually issued a new certificate in response to the bug. We therefore focus on those domain sets that (a) were affected by the Let's Encrypt bug, (b) were on a regular cycle prior to February 29, 2020, and (c) had at least one new certificate issued after February 29, 2020 (to see if the regular cycle continued). To see if a domain set was on a regular reissue cycle prior to February 29, 2020, we see if the five certificate reissues prior to the bug date had a CoV less than 0.1. In total, 98,652 domain sets satisfy these three criteria.

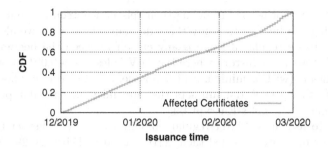

Fig. 4. Distribution of when the misissued certificates were issued.

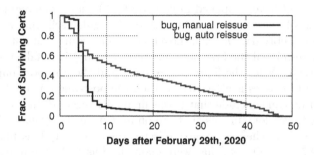

Fig. 5. Graph showing how long certificates "survived" after Let's Encrypt bug was announced. We plot (a) the 33,099 certificates that we inferred were manually reissued, and (b) the 66,553 certificates that we inferred were automatically reissued. We can see the manually reissued certificates we largely reissued quickly after the bug announcement.

Next, we calculate the CoV of the five reissues before the bug date *and* the first reissue after the bug date. If the CoV including the new certificate is high, then the first certificate after the Let's Encrypt bug could not have been automatically reissued; some form of manual intervention disrupted the issue cycle and caused the previously low CoV to increase. If the CoV including the new certificate remains low (<0.1), then the new certificate was likely issued on its expected regular schedule. It is also possible, though unlikely, that a new certificate was manually issued at the same time we would expect the next automatically reissued certificate. Of the 98,652 domain sets, 33,099 saw a significant CoV increase (i.e., likely had manual intervention) in the first reissue after the Let's Encrypt bug, and 65,553 likely did not.

We therefore focus on those domain sets with a low CoV (less than 0.1), which means the domain set has issued certificates previously on a *very* regular schedule. We refer to these domain sets as *misissued regular* domain sets, and we can identify 1,906 of them prior to February 29, 2020.

However, when examining the data, we observe a number of domain sets that appeared to have an irregular pattern initially, but then settled into a regular patter of reissuance as time went on. Presumably, these are cases where the system administrator needed to debug their reissuance `cron` job, but eventually got it working. To be able to study these domain sets as well, we also consider domain sets to be regular if there is any cut-off between the beginning of the domain set's reissuance history where the CoV is less than 0.001 for all reissues after the cut-off (with a minimum of 5 reissues). Using this methodology, we identify a further 10,905 domain sets that are misissued regular prior to the announcement of the Let's Encrypt bug.

We aim to use these 12,811 regular domain sets to see whether the system administrator promptly reissued their certificate after February 29, 2020. 2,068 domain sets had no reissues after Feb. 29, leaving us with 10,743. However, there is one final wrinkle: we need to be able to distinguish a manual reissue from a reissue that would have happened *anyway* on the domain set's regular schedule. Recall that all of these domain sets were on a regular schedule for at least 5 reissues prior to February 29, 2020; the 5 reissues preceding that date have a CoV <0.001. To determine if the first post-bug reissue would have fallen on-schedule, we compute the CoV for the 5 pre-bug reissues and the first post-bug reissue. If the CoV of all 6 reissues is above 0.001, then the post-bug reissue disrupted the schedule, and we can conclude that it was manually reissued. In other words, we only consider those domain sets that are on an extremely regular schedule who reissued well before when their next reissue was expected. This final grouping represents 4,873 domain sets that were manually reissued. The remaining 5,870 domain sets were reissued very close to their next scheduled time. It appears as though they were automatically reissued, though we cannot definitively say they were not manually reissued (it is possible they were manually reissued very close to when they were expected to automatically reissue anyway).

We now examine *how quickly* these 33,099 certificates were manually reissued after Let's Encrypt announced the bug, and emailed all administrators to tell them to reissue their certificates manually. Figure 5 plots the number of these certificates that survive in the line labeled "bug, manual reissue". We can observe that most certificates that are manually reissued are reissued quite quickly: within a week, over 84% of all certificates that we believe are manually reissued have been reissued. For comparison, we plot the same graph for the 66,553 certificates that were reissued close to their next reissue in the line labeled "bug, auto reissue". This group shows less-prompt reissuing than the manual reissues, as only 42% of likely-automatic reissues occurred in the 7 days following the bug announcement.

Recall from Sect. 2 that Let's Encrypt rescinded its decision to revoke certificates on March 5, 2020 (five days after the initial email stating they would be revoking certificates on March 5, 2020). Thus, there may be system administrators who intended to reissue but who delayed reissuing their certificates, only to decide it was no longer necessary after receiving the second message. While we cannot measure how large this group is, we believe it is likely small as Let's Encrypt decided sent out the second message on the day they originally announced as the deadline to reissue. Regardless, our results still serve as a lower bound on the number of system administrators who did take action.

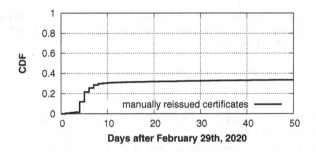

Fig. 6. Cumulative distribution of the manual reissues (CoV less than 0.1) after the announcement of the Let's Encrypt bug.

Finally, we plot the same data as in Fig. 5, but do so as a fraction of *all* misissued domain sets with a CoV less than 0.1 before the bug date. This graph is presented in Fig. 6, and it shows that among all the domain sets with a CoV less than 0.1 (those on a regular schedule before Feb. 29, 2020), at least 28% had reissued their certificate manually within a week of the bug announcement. This result is a significant improvement over prior incidents; with the Heartbleed bug, after a week, barely 10% of affected certificates had been reissued (and even fewer revoked) [22]. Even though circumstances between the two bugs differ significantly (such as notification of revocation), they both provide opportunities for natural experiments to see how the PKI is evolving over time, and the comparison suggests that system administrators may now be better managing the PKI.

5 Concluding Discussion

Over the past five years, the TLS PKI ecosystem has changed dramatically: largely due to new CAs such as Let's Encrypt, we have moved from primarily expensive, long-lived certificates to primarily free, short-lived certificates. In this paper, we examined whether this change in the nature of the certificate ecosystem has also improved the *management* of the TLS PKI, as it has been previously been observed that system administrators often fail to properly manage their certificates. Though we find significant evidence that most clients of Let's Encrypt have indeed set up automated processes for reissuing and installing their certificates using over four years of CT logs, a surprising fraction (20%) of clients with a sufficiently long history of being reissued still appear to use manual processes. Moreover, we find evidence that even when manual intervention is required, system administrators are more prompt in doing so when compared to studies from the 2014 Heartbleed bug and the 2009 Debian PRNG bug. Taken together, our results underscore the importance of reducing the burden of management of the TLS PKI, and how changes in the infrastructure and tools available to system administrators can lead to significant management improvements.

Acknowledgments. We thank the anonymous reviewers and our shepherd, Cecilia Testart, for their helpful comments. This research was supported in part by NSF grants CNS-1900879 and CNS-1901325.

References

1. Aas, J., et al.: Let's encrypt: an automated certificate: authority to encrypt the entire web. In: CCS (2019)
2. Cangialosi, F., et al.: Measurement and analysis of private key sharing in the HTTPS ecosystem. In: CCS (2016)
3. Chung, T., et al.: Measuring and applying invalid SSL certificates: the silent majority. In: IMC (2016)
4. Chung, T., et al.: Understanding the role of registrars in DNSSEC deployment. In: IMC (2017)
5. CAA Rechecking Bug. https://community.letsencrypt.org/t/2020-02-29-caa-rechecking-bug/114591
6. Certbot User Guide. https://certbot.eff.org/docs/using.html
7. Certificate Transparency in Chrome (2019). https://github.com/chromium/ct-policy/blob/master/ct_policy.md
8. Durumeric, Z., et al.: The matter of heartbleed. In: IMC (2014)
9. Durumeric, Z., Kasten, J., Bailey, M., Halderman, J.A.: Analysis of the HTTPS certificate ecosystem. In: IMC (2013)
10. Durumeric, Z., Wustrow, E., Halderman, J.A.: ZMap: fast internet-wide scanning and its security applications. In: USENIX Security (2013)
11. Heartbleed Bug. http://heartbleed.com
12. Laurie, B., Langley, A., Kasper, E.: Certificate Transparency. RFC 6962, IETF (2013). http://www.ietf.org/rfc/rfc6962.txt
13. Liu, Y., et al.: An end-to-end measurement of certificate revocation in the web's PKI. In: IMC (2015)
14. Let's Encrypt. https://letsencrypt.org
15. Let's Encrypt Community Support: 2020.02.29 CAA Rechecking Bug. https://community.letsencrypt.org/t/2020-02-29-caa-rechecking-bug/114591/3
16. Let's Encrypt Stats. https://letsencrypt.org/stats/
17. LetsEncrypt: Submit final certs to CT logs (#3640). https://github.com/letsencrypt/boulder/commit/1271a15be79b9717ee5b98e707b76e7ac86a9a0e
18. Matsumoto, S., Reischuk, R.M.: IKP: turning a PKI around with decentralized automated incentives. In: IEEE S&P (2017)
19. Scheitle, Q., et al.: A first look at certification authority authorization (CAA). CCR **48**(2), 10–23 (2018)
20. Yilek, S., Rescorla, E., Shacham, H., Enright, B., Savage, S.: When private keys are public: results from the 2008 debian OpenSSL vulnerability. In: IMC (2009)
21. Zhang, L., et al.: Analysis of SSL certificate reissues and revocations in the wake of Heartbleed. In: IMC (2014)
22. Zhang, L., et al.: Analysis of SSL certificate reissues and revocations in the wake of heartbleed. CACM **61**(3) (2018). https://cacm.acm.org/magazines/2018/3/225489-analysis-of-ssl-certificate-reissues-and-revocations-in-the-wake-of-heartbleed/fulltext
23. acme.sh. https://github.com/acmesh-official/acme.sh

Revocation Statuses on the Internet

Nikita Korzhitskii and Niklas Carlsson[✉]

Linköping University, Linköping, Sweden
niklas.carlsson@liu.se

Abstract. The modern Internet is highly dependent on the trust communicated via X.509 certificates. However, in some cases certificates become untrusted and it is necessary to revoke them. In practice, the problem of secure certificate revocation has not yet been solved, and today no revocation procedure (similar to Certificate Transparency w.r.t. certificate issuance) has been adopted to provide transparent and immutable history of all revocations. Instead, the status of most certificates can only be checked with Online Certificate Status Protocol (OCSP) and/or Certificate Revocation Lists (CRLs). In this paper, we present the first longitudinal characterization of the revocation statuses delivered by CRLs and OCSP servers from the time of certificate expiration to status disappearance. The analysis captures the status history of over 1 million revoked certificates, including 773K certificates mass-revoked by Let's Encrypt. Our characterization provides a new perspective on the Internet's revocation rates, quantifies how short-lived the revocation statuses are, highlights differences in revocation practices within and between different CAs, and captures biases and oddities in the handling of revoked certificates. Combined, the findings motivate the development and adoption of a revocation transparency standard.

1 Introduction

The modern Internet uses the Web Public-Key Infrastructure (WebPKI) as a foundation to establish trust between clients and servers. In WebPKI, Certificate Authorities (CAs) issue signed X.509 certificates that verify the mapping between public keys and public distinguished names, such as domain names.

In certain cases (e.g., a private key compromise, owner's request, or misissuance by a CA), certificates must be revoked; i.e., rendered invalid. To protect clients and servers from the use of revoked certificates, WebPKI supports several revocation protocols. Currently, revocation statuses of most certificates can be obtained via Online Certificate Status Protocol (OCSP) servers [28], but some CAs continue to support the traditional Certificate Revocation Lists (CRLs) [6] as a complementary option. However, these pull-based protocols raise many security, privacy, and performance issues. Therefore, many browser vendors do not utilize the protocols [23], but instead, they push a proprietary set of revocations to the users [2,11]. Yet, these push-based revocation mechanisms have their own limitations, which leave secure certificate revocation an open problem [4].

Furthermore, as of today, there does not exist any standardized mechanism in place (similar to Certificate Transparency (CT) [14,20,30] w.r.t. certificate

© Springer Nature Switzerland AG 2021
O. Hohlfeld et al. (Eds.): PAM 2021, LNCS 12671, pp. 175–191, 2021.
https://doi.org/10.1007/978-3-030-72582-2_11

issuance) to provide an immutable history of all revocations and corresponding revocation reasons. Consequently, there is no ability to easily study and detect revocation-related misbehavior by CAs (e.g., advertisement of wrong, or contradictory revocation statuses). While many novel WebPKI extensions, revocation protocols, architectures, and transparency schemes have been proposed to address this issue, none have been adopted so far [4]. Instead, we observe that the information about revocations is sparse and most revocation statuses disappear soon after certificate expiration.

In this paper, we make *a case for revocation transparency* by presenting a novel characterization study of the revocation rates on the Internet, the post-expiry life of revocation statuses, and the status-handling practices across CAs. First, we present a measurement methodology that allows us (i) to obtain nearly all revocations performed for the set of certificates expiring during a time window, and (ii) to track the certificate status (using both OCSP and CRL) of such sample sets over 100-day periods, starting at their respective expiration dates[1].

Second, we track all certificates from the Censys dataset [10] that expired between Mar. 2, 2020, and Apr. 1, 2020, and that were valid with respect to Apple's, Microsoft's, or Mozilla's root stores. This time period (see Fig. 1) is particularly interesting since the measurement was done prior to and during the mass-revocation event in which Let's Encrypt (LE), the largest CA, initially announced to revoke over 3 million certificates [22] due to a CAA-rechecking bug, but in the end, they revoked only 1.7 million certificates [21].

Third, and most importantly, we characterize the revocation-status-handling practices across CAs, including status lifetimes beyond the expiration date and handling differences across CAs and certificate types. We identify classes of behaviors, compare and contrast practices of different CAs, find revocation biases among different sets of certificates, and look closer at some odd CA behaviors (e.g., certificates that switch back to a "Good" status after being advertised as "Revoked"). Across our analysis, we observed highly heterogeneous behaviors among CAs and quick disappearance of revocation statuses. This highlights the lack of a global revocation transparency standard that would otherwise help to identify and improve odd revocation behaviors, similarly to CT, with its effect on the issuance process. Finally, we share our dataset [19].

Outline: After a brief overview of revocation protocols (Sect. 2), we present our methodology (Sect. 3) and characterization results (Sect. 4). Finally, related work (Sect. 5) and conclusions (Sect. 6) are presented.

2   Revocation Protocols

The two primary revocation protocols that CAs typically use are the following.

- **Online Certificate Status Protocol (OCSP):** Using OCSP, a client can request the status of a certificate by providing a serial number and the hashes of the issuer's name and key. The CA-Browser forum requires signed responses

---

[1] Currently, CAs must maintain revocation statuses only until certificate expiration [1].

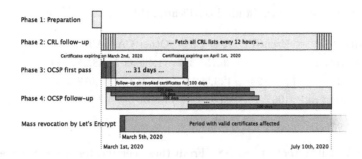

Fig. 1. Timeline of the measurement.

to be valid for at least 8 hours, and at most 10 days [1]. OCSP can be used in different ways. For example, *OCSP stapling* allows statuses to be delivered by a web-server, and the *OCSP Must-staple* extension prevents a client from making OCSP requests on their own and enforces a hard-fail policy if the status was not delivered by the web-server. The Must-staple extension is not widely adopted yet [5]. Instead, most browsers typically accept a certificate if they are unable to obtain revocation information [23].

– **Certificate Revocation List (CRL):** CAs maintain signed lists with the serial numbers of revoked certificates, and optionally, corresponding invalidation dates and reason codes for the revocations. CRLs can also be augmented using several extensions (e.g., CRL number, Authority Key Identifier, etc.) [6]. CRLs are required to be reissued at least once every 7 days [1].

Due to the security, privacy, and performance issues with OCSP and CRL, many browser vendors have disabled the above pull-based revocation protocols; instead, they periodically push limited sets of revocations to the clients (e.g., via software updates) [2,11]. However, this approach has some limitations; e.g., a delay introduced by scheduled updates, and a small coverage of all existing revocations.

WebPKI lacks revocation transparency, and no mechanism similar to CT has been adopted yet. In fact, CAs are not required to maintain revocation statuses for certificates beyond their expiration date [1], and as we show in this paper, most of the time, revocation statuses stop being advertised shortly after certificate expiration. The lack of a transparent and immutable history of revocations complicates keeping CAs accountable for their revocation mishandling.

3   Measurement Methodology

We conducted a four-phase measurement campaign (see Fig. 1).

1. Preparation: In the first phase, we collect all X.509 certificates (with their parent certificates) found in CT logs [20] and active scans that expire within a period starting from Mar. 2, 2020, to Apr. 1, 2020, using Censys [10]. For the analysis, we only select certificates that are valid with respect to Apple's,

Table 1. Summary of the studied certificates. (LE – Let's Encrypt).

Certificates	Event LE	Rest LE	Other CAs	All
Non-revoked	–	36,755,317	11,496,607	48,251,924
Revoked	773,128	129,552	174,712	1,077,390
Revocation rate	100%	0.35%	1.50%	2.18%

Microsoft's, or Mozilla's root stores [18]. From these certificates, we extract all OCSP responder URLs (used in phases 3 + 4) and CRL URLs (used in phase 2). For every remaining certificate, we then schedule an OCSP first pass (phase 3) 22 h before its expiration[2], and for every observed CRL, we schedule periodic CRL requests (phase 2).

2. CRL follow-up: During the second phase, we regularly (every 12 h) fetch all CRL lists using the URLs extracted in the first phase.

3. OCSP first pass: In the third phase, we perform an OCSP status lookup for each certificate 22 h before it expires. If a certificate is found to be revoked during its first pass, it gets scheduled for follow-up checks every 12 h (phase 4). In the case of an OCSP timeout or an error, the first pass is retried every minute until a revocation status is obtained or the certificate is expired.

4. OCSP follow-up: In the fourth phase, the revocation status of every revoked expired certificate is fetched every 12 h for 100 days (since the first pass of each individual certificate). We separate OCSP responses into four types: "Good", "Revoked", "Unauthorized", and "Unknown". The first two types ("Good" and "Revoked") are cryptographically-signed responses that definitively specify the status of a certificate. The third type ("Unauthorized") is an unsigned plaintext response. The final category ("Unknown") contains signed "Unknown" statuses (that some CAs deliver) and other unsigned responses.

External Effects on the Sampling Rate: Between May 12, 2020, and May 19, 2020, parallel processes running at our server have temporarily increased the average OCSP inter-request time from 12 h up to 21.7 h. Except for this short period, the average OCSP inter-request time was consistently 12 h ± a few minutes, up until June 21, 2020. Between June 21, 2020, and the end of our measurement period on July 20, 2020, the average inter-request time was roughly 24 h. Neither of the periods with increased OCSP inter-request times took place during the first month after the expiration date of any of the certificates; hence, the effects do not impact our conclusions.

---

[2] The interval of 22 h (slightly less than 24 h) was selected for performance reasons, after the initial evaluation of our measurement framework.

4   Characterization Results

4.1   High-Level Breakdown

In total, we collected OCSP status information for 49 million certificates. Table 1 provides a breakdown based on whether a certificate was revoked or not, whether the certificate was issued by Let's Encrypt (76.3% of the certificates) or a different CA (23.7%), and whether a Let's Encrypt certificate was part of the above-mentioned mass-revocation event (1.57%). For us to consider a certificate mass-revoked it needed to be (i) on the list of 3M certificates that Let's Encrypt publicized for the event [22] and (ii) to be revoked at the time it expired. We also found that 297,242 certificates from the list, with expiration dates falling on our first pass period, have never been revoked.

The timing of the mass-revocation event is particularly interesting since it provides a concrete example of the impact that such events can have on the revocation rate and the lifetime of revocation statuses. Finally, we note that the certificates affected by recent mass-revocation events have been disclosed through website postings of arbitrarily formatted datasets [8,9,22].

While the non-mass-revocation-rate of Let's Encrypt was much smaller than for the other CAs (0.35% vs 1.50%), the mass-revocation event increased Let's Encrypt's revocation rate for this period up to 2.40%. The effect is perhaps most noticeable when looking at the number of revoked certificates per day, based on their day of expiry, as shown in Fig. 2. Here, starting from Mar. 5, 2020, we can see the impact of the certificates associated with the mass-revocation event (gray in the figure). The other two classes of revocations (blue, orange) remained relatively stable throughout the measurement period.

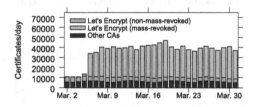

Fig. 2. Revoked certificates with a given expiration date.

We found large variations in the revocation rates of different CAs. Figure 3 shows the number of revoked (blue) and non-revoked (gray) certificates, broken down per CA. The orange markers show the number of revoked certificates listed in the CRLs, in addition to OCSP servers (discussed in Sect. 4.4). Here, we show all CAs with at least 100 revoked certificates in our dataset, ranked from the one with the most revocations to the one with the least. We also include the "other' category that combines the results for all other CAs. While most CAs have much fewer revoked certificates than non-revoked certificates, there are notable exceptions. Five CAs even had more revoked than non-revoked certificates: Actalis (92.5%), nazwa.pl (66.4%), SwissSign (59.9%), Plex (73.7%), Digidentify (100%). Among the most popular CAs (i.e., CAs with the highest gray/blue bars), GoDaddy also stands out with 34.5% being revoked before expiry.

4.2   Revocation Status Changes

The revocation statuses provided by OCSP servers often change from "Revoked" to some other status soon after certificate expiry. Figure 4 shows the time that the status remained "Revoked" after the revoked certificates had expired. Here, we filter out any temporary OCSP responses (e.g., unauthorized, unknown) and timeouts whenever we obtained at least one more "Revoked" response.

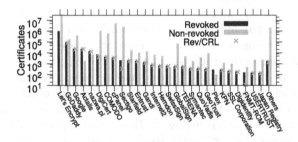

Fig. 3. Per-CA breakdown of the number of revoked (blue) and non-revoked (gray) certificates in the dataset. Revoked certificates found in CRLs are shown with ×. CAs are ordered by the number of revoked certificates, in descending order from left to right. In the following figures, the order is preserved. (Color figure online)

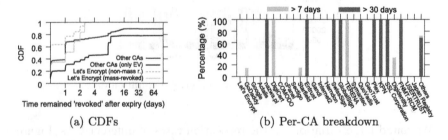

(a) CDFs   (b) Per-CA breakdown

Fig. 4. Time that the revoked certificates remained revoked after the expiration. (Color figure online)

Quickly Disappearing Revocation Statuses: Figure 4(a) shows the empirical Cumulative Distribution Functions (CDFs) for four classes of revoked certificates: 2 for Let's Encrypt certificates (mass-revoked and non-mass-revoked) and 2 for certificates by other CAs (with and without Extended Validation (EV)). All certificates by Let's Encrypt changed status within 3 days of expiration. Their mass-revoked certificates (gray) had longer status change times than the non-mass-revoked certificates (orange). The CDFs for the other CAs are relatively flat from about two weeks to 100 days. (Note the logarithmic y-axis.) On an encouraging note, the certificate class with the most long-lived revocation statuses is Extended Validation (EV) certificates (black). This class of certificates should typically endure the most scrutiny.

Some CAs Keep the State Longer: Figure 4(b) shows the fraction of the certificates issued by different CAs that maintained the revoked status for at least 1 week or 30 days. While many CAs maintained "Revoked" state for very short time periods after certificate expiry (e.g., blue CDF in Fig. 4(a) and CAs without any bars in Fig. 4(b)), most of the CAs that did keep the "Revoked" state beyond a week also kept this state beyond 30 days (brown bar).

Status Response Overview: For the revoked certificates, we performed more than 207 million OCSP status requests. Table 2 provides a per-category breakdown of the individual responses ("Resp." in the table) and the fraction of certificates ("Certs") with at least one such response.

All certificates started as "Revoked" and most eventually changed to an unauthorized response (100% of Let's Encrypt certificates and 76.43% of other CAs' certificates). While we only had timeouts for 0.04% of the status requests, the differences between the number of affected certificates were substantial between CAs: only 0.07% of the Let's Encrypt certificates had at least one timeout, compared to 13.98% of the other CAs' certificates. These fractions are non-negligible, since most browsers soft-fail on an OCSP timeout and continue to establish a potentially-insecure connection. A concerning observation is that 589 certificates issued by 13 CAs (0.34% in the other CA category) switched from "Revoked" status to "Good" (65,791 responses in total).

Table 2. Summary of different types of OCSP status responses.

	Revoked		Unauthorized		Unknown		Timeout		Good	
	Certs	Resp.	Certs	Resp.	Certs	Resp.	Certs	Resp.	Certs	Resp.
Mass rev. (LE)	100.00	2.83	100.00	97.10	12.37	0.07	1.43	0.01	–	–
Non-mass. LE	100.00	2.17	100.00	97.76	11.95	0.07	1.54	0.01	–	–
Other CAs	100.00	13.19	76.43	74.06	13.51	12.35	13.98	0.22	0.34	0.19
Total	100.00	4.43	96.18	93.43	12.50	2.07	3.48	0.04	0.05	0.03

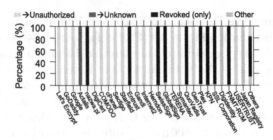

Fig. 5. Dominating status change behavior of different CAs.

Most Frequent Behaviors: Usually, public certification practice statements of CAs guarantee revocation status preservation for non-expired certificates, but do not specify the CAs' actions after that [13,15,33]. We next look at the most frequent CA behaviors. For this analysis, we filtered out temporary status changes whenever we observed the original state again. With this filtering, we observed the following dominating behaviors.

- Let's Encrypt almost always transition statuses from "Revoked" to "Unauthorized". This behavior was observed for 772,042 (99.86%) of the mass-revoked certificates and 129,400 (99.88%) of the other certificates revoked by Let's Encrypt. A possible explanation for this behavior is that they respond with code "Unauthorized" as soon as the status record has been removed [7]. Let's Encrypt's current certification practice statement only guarantees that "OCSP responses will be made available for all unexpired certificates" [15].
- Among the other CAs, we observed three dominating behaviors: 133,276 (76.28%) cases where the CA simply transitioned to "Unauthorized" (like Let's Encrypt), 21,816 (12.49%) cases where the status always changed to "Unknown", and 18,660 (10.68%) cases where the "Revoked" status remained for the duration of our measurement period.

Figure 5 breaks down the use of the dominating status change behaviors employed by the different CAs. In addition to the three behaviors mentioned above, we include the "other" behavior category. Most CAs have a dominating behavior that they employ for almost all of their certificates: 15 (out of 26) CAs almost always switch from "Revoked" to "Unauthorized" (pink bars), 9 (out of 26) CAs almost always keep the "Revoked" status for the full 100 day period, Actalis mainly switch certificates from "Revoked" status to "Unknown" (except for 91 cases, when the statuses were switched to "Good", following the intermediate "Unknown" status), Digidentify (who revoke all certificates) always start to timeout, and Japan Registry always switches statuses to "Good". As expected, the "other CA" category (not explicitly listed), contains a mix of behaviors. These results demonstrate the lack of a standard practice w.r.t. revocation statuses after certificate expiration. We have also observed some small differences in the weekly status-change patterns between CAs; however, compared to the differences in issuance timing, these differences are very small. See Appendix A.

Special Cases with the "Good" Status: 589 revoked certificates switched to status "Good". In almost all cases the servers kept the "Good" status until the end of the measurement period. In 349 of these cases, the status changed directly from "Revoked" to "Good" and in 91 cases an intermediate "Unknown" status was observed. All these cases provide strong motivation for transparent long-term recording of revocation information.

We note that Let's Encrypt and most of the other big CAs did not have any cases with the above strange behavior. Of the CAs with at least 100 revocations, only the following CAs had such cases: GoDaddy (117 cases), Actalis (91), Starfield (9), Entrust (5), and Japan Registry (135). Other CAs (not listed in our figures) with many cases include: "National Institute of Informatics" (91), "SECOM Trust Systems" (70), "ACCV" (54). (The rest of the non-listed CAs had five or fewer revoked certificates changing to status "Good".) Finally, a few certificates in this category stood out more than the others. For example, the list included three EV certificates: one by Entrust for "JPMorgan Chase and Co" ("Revoked" → "Good" → "Revoked"), one by GoDaddy for "Delmarva Broadcasting Company" ("Revoked" → "Unauthorized" → "Good"), and one by Actalis for "Pratiche.it" ("Revoked" → "Unknown" → "Good"). Otherwise, all the certificates in this class include RSA keys with the following key lengths: 1024 (9), 2048 (579), and 4096 (1). Furthermore, only 123 (out of 589) had Signed Certificate Timestamps (SCTs) embedded. We contacted all CAs with the above behavior. A summary of the responses is provided in Appendix B.

4.3   Biases in the Revocation Sets

Validity Period: We have found that the revoked certificates typically have longer validity periods. Figure 6(a) shows CDFs of the validity periods for both revoked (blue) and non-revoked (gray) certificates for all CAs other than Let's Encrypt. (Since Let's Encrypt always use a 90-day validity period, we kept these certificates separately.) Here, we note a clear shift between the two curves.

Figures 6(b) and (c) provide a similar comparison of the (b) revoked and (c) non-revoked certificates on a per-CA basis. Here, we plot the fraction of certificates with validity periods longer than 89 days, 90 days, 1 year (365 days), and 2 years (720 days), respectively. These choices are based on the observation that many CAs use validity periods of either 90 days or 398 days (e.g., steps in the CDFs in Fig. 6(a)). For almost all CAs, the fraction of certificates with long validity periods (darker colored bars) is larger among the revoked certificates (Fig. 6(b)) than among the corresponding CA's non-revoked certificates (Fig. 6(c)). This is in part an effect of CA/Browser Forum conventions [1] and decisions by individual browsers [3,12,24] forcing CAs to use shorter certificate validity periods. Another reason is that older certificates have had more time to become compromised. It could also be an indication that CAs apply increasingly stricter security policies (e.g., to comply with CT [20]).

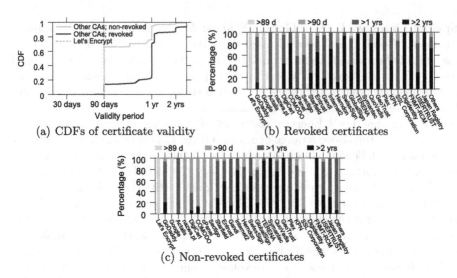

Fig. 6. Validity periods for different categories of revoked and non-revoked certificates. (Color figure online)

Public Key Types: The modern WebPKI relies on EC (Elliptic Curve) [17] and RSA (Rivest–Shamir–Adleman) [26] public-key cryptography. Here, we compare the use of different key types and key lengths. While RSA 2048 is the dominating public key among both revoked (90.44%) and non-revoked (80.81%) certificates, there are significant differences in the revocation rates of certificates including different key types. For example, certificates with RSA 3072 (4.55% revocation rate), EC 521 (80.49%) and RSA with key lengths other than the three most common lengths (6.67%) all have revocation rates well above average. In contrast, EC 256 (0.14%), EC 384 (0.62%) and RSA 4096 (1.48%) all have revocation rates below average. These differences are also present when looking at certificates of Let's Encrypt and other CAs separately. Table 3 summarizes the overall revocation rates (column 4) for each key type (column 1) and the key usage distributions seen for each of the three certificate groups: Let's Encrypt (columns 5 vs 6 vs 7), other CAs (columns 8 vs 9), and the aggregate over all certificates (columns 2 vs 3). Above/below average revocation rates are shown with italic/regular (column 4) and bold text indicates the sub-group with the highest relative representation (on a per-group basis). With this annotation, higher revocation numbers (bold) reflect revocation rate above average (italic).

SCT and EV Usage: To measure the CT compliance we looked at the use of Signed Certificate Timestamps (SCTs). While all certificates issued by Let's Encrypt have embedded SCTs, other CAs do not always embed the timestamps. Furthermore, among the certificates issued by other CAs, the fraction of certificates that do not contain SCTs was much greater among the revoked (10.04%)

Table 3. Key usage comparisons based on revocation vs non-revocation sets.

Key type	All certificates Revoked	Non-revoked	Revoked	Let's Encrypt (%) M-rev.	Rev.	Non.	Others (%) Rev.	Non.
RSA 2048	974,405 **(90.44%)**	38,996,600 (80.82%)	*2.44%*	88.75	**89.93**	80.79	**98.33**	80.91
RSA 3072	13,616 **(1.26%)**	285,636 (0.59%)	*4.55%*	**1.69**	0.43	0.78	**0.01**	0.00
RSA 4096	80,711 (7.49%)	5,382,669 **(11.16%)**	1.48%	8.70	8.85	**14.50**	**1.15**	0.47
RSA other	29 **(0.00%)**	406 (0.00%)	*6.67%*	–	–	**0.00**	**0.02**	0.00
EC 256	4,126 (0.38%)	2,873,827 **(5.96%)**	0.14%	0.36	0.45	**2.00**	0.45	**18.61**
EC 384	4,436 (0.41%)	712,770 **(1.48%)**	0.62%	0.52	0.34	**1.94**	**0.01**	0.00
EC 521	66 **(0.01%)**	16 (0.00%)	*80.49%*	–	–	–	**0.04**	0.00

than non-revoked certificates (1.91%). In addition to having longer validity periods, some of the older non-expired certificates lack embedded SCTs. Owners and issuers of these certificates may be replacing them with certificates that better meet recent browser requirements [3,25]. We have also observed significantly higher revocation rates among EV certificates. For example, 1,890 (10.77%) out of the 17,544 observed EV certificates were revoked. Furthermore, for CAs other than Let's Encrypt, 1.08% of the revoked certificates are EV certificates and 0.14% of the non-revoked certificates are EV certificates.

4.4 CRL-Based Analysis

For the 2,190 CRL URLs extracted from the certificates of interest, we collected 643,860 CRL snapshots. Combined, these snapshots included CRL entries for 169,911 (15.8%) of the revoked certificates found using OCSP. Let's Encrypt's decision not to implement CRL contributes to the small fraction. Here, we focus on the certificates with at least one CRL entry and one OCSP "Revoked" status.

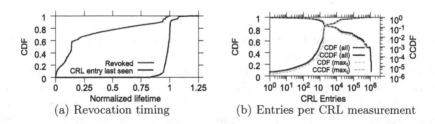

(a) Revocation timing   (b) Entries per CRL measurement

Fig. 7. Distributions for measured CRLs.

Timing Analysis: On average, revocation statuses disappear even faster from CRL lists than from OCSP responders. For example, only in 26.5% of the cases did we observe the revocation status in the CRLs after the expiration date of the certificates, and only for 2.9% did we observe the status being preserved longer than a week after expiration. This may be an attempt to reduce the size of the CRLs. However, since the majority of the revocations happen early in the lifetime of the certificates (e.g., the median normalized lifetime is 13.8%) there is still a significant time period over which certificates are included in the CRLs. This is illustrated in Fig. 7(a), which shows the normalized timing of revocations and when the CRL entries are last observed in our dataset. Here, all values are normalized relative to the total intended validity period (i.e., "NotBefore" and "NotAfter" corresponds to the values 0 and 1, respectively). As implied by Little's law, the average size of a CRL (e.g., measured as entries per CRL) is equal to the average time that the entries remain in the CRL (e.g., measured in days) times the average rate that certificates are being added to the CRL (e.g., revocations per day), CRL sizes therefore easily become very large. Indeed, the average CRL size was 7,362 entries and the largest CRL contained 1,139,538 entries at its peak. Figure 7(b) shows CDFs and CCDFs for both individual measurements (all) and when using the observed peak size ($\max_t$). We also observed some CRLs that did not appear to delete entries and roughly 0.94% of the certificates remained in the CRLs for the full duration of our measurement.

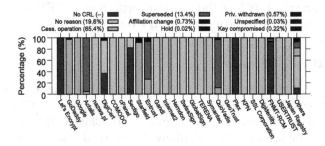

Fig. 8. Per-CA breakdown of CRL-listed reasons for revocation. (Color figure online)

Revocation Reasons: Figure 8 breaks down the percentage of certificates for which (i) we did not find any CRL entry (blue), (ii) we found CRL entries without revocation reason (gray), or (iii) we found a revocation reason for (orange, brown, black) on a per-CA basis. For simplicity, we only show the dominating reasons using colors (orange, brown) but provide the overall percentages (over all certificates with CRL entries) in the figure key. The four dominating CRL behaviors that we observed were: (i) some CAs did not use CRLs (Let's Encrypt, Plex) or only used it to a limited degree (e.g., Sectigo, FNMT-RCM), (ii) 17 CAs used CRLs for the majority of their revocations but did not provide any revocation reason, (iii) three CAs almost always used "Cessation Of Operation" as revocation reason (GoDaddy, Google, Starfield), and (iv) three CAs almost always specified "Superseded" as the revocation reason.

Overall, most revoked certificates are not included in CRLs and 19.6% of CRL entries contain no revocation reason. Our results show that the practices of CAs are highly heterogeneous and revocation statuses are not persistent; thus, we argue that the Internet would benefit from a revocation transparency standard.

5   Related Work

A number of studies have measured the revocation rates on the Internet. Liu et al. [23] performed several IPv4 HTTPS scans and found that a large fraction of served certificates was revoked (8%), while CRLSets [11] by Google was only covering 0.35% of all revocations. Chung et al. [5] evaluated the performance of OCSP responders by sending OCSP requests from geographically separated locations. They concluded that OCSP responders were not sufficiently reliable to support *OCSP Must-staple* extension. Zhu et al. [34] found OCSP latency to be "quite good", and showed that 94% of OCSP responses are served using CDNs. Moreover, only 0.3% of certificates were found to be revoked at that time (2015). Smith et al. [32] propose an efficient scheme to disseminate revocations. In the process, they measured revocation rates and found that in the absence of a mass-revocation event, the revocation rate on the Internet was 1.29%. This is similar to what we observed. The above works perform OCSP status checks before certificate expiration, while we check the certificates the day before their expiration and onward. Revocation effectiveness at the code-signing PKI was measured in [16], and a number of security problems related to revocations were identified. A recent survey and a comprehensive framework for comparison of implemented and proposed revocation/delegation schemes are provided in [4].

Other Community Efforts and Data Sources: The CA/Browser forum specifies some requirements that motivated our measurement design, including the requirement that "revocation entries on a CRL or OCSP Response MUST NOT be removed until after the Expiry Date of the revoked Certificate" [1]. We used the Censys search engine, backed by Internet-wide scanning [10], to obtain all certificates for our study. Some other online services also provide revocation statuses. For example, crt.sh [31] attempts to fetch and process every known CRL regularly (currently every 4 hours), while the OCSP requests are performed on-demand. Until late Aug. 2020, Internet Storm Center [27] was regularly fetching several CRLs; however, they did not monitor all CRLs present in our dataset and did not capture the mass-revocation by Let's Encrypt.

6   Conclusion

In this paper, we have presented the first characterization of the revocation status responses provided by OCSP and CRL responders from the time of certificate expiration and beyond. We described a measurement methodology, which allowed us to look at the revocation rates on the Internet from a new perspective; we quantified how short-lived the revocation statuses are, and highlighted differences in status handling practices of different CAs. We found that most CAs remove revocation statuses very soon after certificate expiration. Some

CAs do not provide CRL entries for all revoked certificates and/or remove entries from the CRLs before certificate expiration. The CA-dependent differences highlighted throughout the paper (e.g., revocation status lifetimes, usage of reason codes, and abnormal behavior of switching certificates from "Revoked" to "Good" status) capture a highly heterogeneous landscape that lacks a revocation transparency standard. Finally, we argue for the deployment of such a standard and demonstrate the global impact of the mass revocation event, which took place during our measurement campaign. We compared the characteristics of the mass-revoked certificates with the characteristics of other revoked and non-revoked certificates issued by Let's Encrypt and the rest of the CAs, and found a limited number of biases, e.g., the biggest differences in the revocation rates depend on the origin CA, key type, EV policy, and presence of embedded SCTs.

Acknowledgment. This work was supported by the Wallenberg AI, Autonomous Systems and Software Program (WASP) funded by the Knut and Alice Wallenberg Foundation.

Appendix A. Other CA-Based Behavior Comparisons

We have already seen that different CAs have different revocation-status-handling practices. To provide some additional insights, we obtained day-of-week distributions that capture *when* CAs change the "Revoked" status to something else (Fig. 9(a)); compare this to the distribution of the first certificate validity day (Fig. 9(b)). Perhaps, the most noticeable are the weaker weekly patterns. While more than half of the CAs issue significantly fewer certificates with start dates during weekends (dark areas for Sat/Sun in Fig. 9(b)), we did not observe such weekly patterns for the revocation status changes. Instead, only a few CAs have spikes of revocation status changes on a certain day (white squares in Fig. 9(a)). For example, Starfield, GoDaddy (part of Starfield), and Digidentify update most of their statuses on Friday, and Japanese Registry on Sunday (Monday Japanese time). The distributions suggest that the relation between last-status-change and certificate-validity-start days is not straightforward. Having said that, some of the CAs have even weekly distributions for both processes, which may suggest higher levels of automation (e.g., Let's Encrypt, Google, Actalis, cPanel, Gandi, Herndon). Among the large CAs, DigiCert stands out with their pronounced weekly patterns for both processes. Similarly, there are some differences in the daily (Fig. 10(a)) and hourly (Fig. 10(b)) distributions of the expiry times selected for certificates. Here, some of the large CAs (e.g., Let's Encrypt, GoDaddy, Google, GlobalSign) spread expiry times both across the week and the hours of the days, whereas other large CAs (e.g., DigiCert, Comodo, cPanel, Sectigo) always set certificates to expire at the same time of day. Although these differences may not have major security implications, perhaps, they demonstrate the lack of a standardized policy for managing the revocation status of expired certificates.

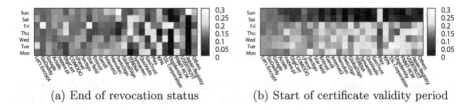

(a) End of revocation status   (b) Start of certificate validity period

Fig. 9. Weekly distribution of certificate-validity-start day for the revoked certificates and last-status-change day (from "Revoked" to something else).

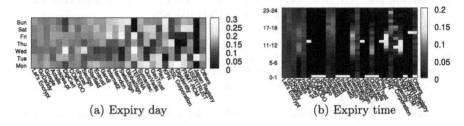

(a) Expiry day   (b) Expiry time

Fig. 10. Per-CA breakdown of expiry time of revoked certificates.

Appendix B: Responses by CAs

We contacted 8 organizations that operate the CAs for which we observed at least one status change from "Revoked" to "Good". However, we did not find a contact email for one CA that no longer operates: AT&T Wi-Fi Services. We received responses from 5 organizations: Starfield (GoDaddy), Japan Registry, Entrust, ACCV, and Atos. The CAs that responded confirmed that they had issued the certificates in question and provided varying explanations for their behavior. Two CAs argued that their use of "Good" statuses was motivated by RFC 6960 [29], which states that "at a minimum, this positive response [i.e., a "Good" response] indicates that no certificate with the requested certificate serial number currently within its validity interval is revoked." One of these two CAs also stated that they "are going to consult with the community to clarify the requirements, and then, [they will] follow it." We believe that CAs should avoid changing the status of revoked certificates to "Good" at any time.

References

1. Baseline Requirements for the issuance and management of publicly-trusted certificates, v1.7.2 (2020). https://cabforum.org/baseline-requirements-documents/
2. OneCRL (CA/Revocation Checking in Firefox) (2020) https://wiki.mozilla.org/CA:RevocationPlan#OneCRL
3. Apple: About upcoming limits on trusted certificates (2020). https://support.apple.com/en-us/HT211025

4. Chuat, L., Abdou, A., Sasse, R., Sprenger, C., Basin, D., Perrig, A.: SoK: delegation and revocation, the missing links in the Web's chain of trust. In: Proceedings of IEEE EuroS&P (2020)
5. Chung, T., et al.: Is the Web ready for OCSP must-staple? In: Proceedings of IMC (2018)
6. Cooper, D., Santesson, S., Farrell, S., Boeyen, S., Housley, R., Polk, W.: Internet X.509 Public Key Infrastructure certificate and Certificate Revocation List (CRL) profile. RFC 5280, May 2008
7. Deacon, A., Hurst, R.: The Lightweight Online Certificate Status Protocol (OCSP) Profile for High-Volume Environments. RFC Editor, RFC 5019, September 2007
8. DigiCert: DigiCert: Delay of revocation for EV audit inconsistency incident (2020). https://bugzilla.mozilla.org/show_bug.cgi?id=1651828
9. DigiCert: Inconsistent EV audits (2020). https://bugzilla.mozilla.org/show_bug.cgi?id=1650910
10. Durumeric, Z., Adrian, D., Mirian, A., Bailey, M., Halderman, J.A.: A search engine backed by Internet-wide scanning. In: Proceedings of ACM CCS (2015)
11. Google: CRLSets. https://dev.chromium.org/Home/chromium-security/crlsets. Accessed Sept 2020
12. Google: Certificate lifetimes (2020). https://chromium.googlesource.com/chromium/src/+/master/net/docs/certificate_lifetimes.md
13. Google Trust Services: Certificate Policy v1.3. https://pki.goog/GTS-CP-1.3.pdf, OID = 1.3.6.1.4.1.11129.2.5.3. Accessed 21 Jan 2021
14. Gustafsson, J., Overier, G., Arlitt, M., Carlsson, N.: A first look at the CT landscape: Certificate Transparency logs in practice. In: Proceedings of PAM, March 2017
15. Internet Security Research Group (ISRG): Certification Practice Statement, Version 3.0, October 2020. http://cps.letsencrypt.org. Accessed 21 Jan 2021
16. Kim, D., Kwon, B.J., Kozák, K., Gates, C., Dumitras, T.: The broken shield: measuring revocation effectiveness in the Windows code-signing PKI. In: Proceedings of USENIX Security, August 2018
17. Koblitz, N.: Elliptic curve cryptosystems. Math. Comput. 48(177), 203–209 (1987)
18. Korzhitskii, N., Carlsson, N.: Characterizing the root landscape of Certificate Transparency logs. In: Proceedings of IFIP Networking, June 2020
19. Korzhitskii, N., Carlsson, N.: Dataset for "Revocation Statuses on the Internet" PAM 2021 paper (2021). https://www.ida.liu.se/~nikca89/papers/pam21.html
20. Laurie, B., Langley, A., Kasper, E.: Certificate Transparency. RFC 6962 (2013)
21. Let's Encrypt: 2020.02.29 CAA Rechecking Bug, March 2020. https://community.letsencrypt.org/t/2020-02-29-caa-rechecking-bug/114591/3
22. Let's Encrypt: Download affected certificate serials for 2020.02.29 CAA Rechecking Incident, March 2020. https://letsencrypt.org/caaproblem/
23. Liu, Y., et al.: An end-to-end measurement of certificate revocation in the Web's PKI. In: Proceedings of IMC (2015)
24. Mozilla (2020). https://blog.mozilla.org/security/2020/07/09/reducing-tls-certificate-lifespans-to-398-days/
25. O'Brien, D.: Certificate Transparency Enforcement in Chrome and CT Day in London (2018). https://groups.google.com/a/chromium.org/d/msg/ct-policy/Qqr59r6yn1A/2t0bWblZBgAJ. Accessed Jan 2021
26. Rivest, R.L., Shamir, A., Adleman, L.: A method for obtaining digital signatures and public-key cryptosystems. Commun. ACM 21(2), 120–126 (1978)
27. SANS Internet Storm Center: SSL CRL activity. https://isc.sans.edu/crls.html. Accessed Sept 2020

28. Santesson, S., Myers, M., Ankney, R., Malpani, A., Galperin, S., Adams, C.: X.509 Internet public key infrastructure online certificate status protocol - OCSP. RFC Editor, RFC 6960, June 2013

29. Santesson, S., Myers, M., Ankney, R., Malpani, A., Galperin, S., Adams, C.: X. 509 internet public key infrastructure online certificate status protocol-ocsp. RFC 6960 (2013)

30. Scheitle, Q., et al.: The rise of Certificate Transparency and its implications on the Internet ecosystem. In: Proceedings of IMC (2018)

31. Sectigo: Certificate search. https://crt.sh. Accessed Sept 2020

32. Smith, T., Dickinson, L., Seamons, K.: Let's revoke: scalable global certificate revocation. In: Proceedings of NDSS (2020)

33. Starfield Technologies, LLC: Certificate Policy and Certification Practice Statement (CP/CPS), Version 4.9, October 2020. http://certificates.godaddy.com/repository/. Accessed 21 Jan 2021

34. Zhu, L., Amann, J., Heidemann, J.: Measuring the latency and pervasiveness of TLS certificate revocation. In: Proceedings of PAM (2016)

Measuring DNS over TLS from the Edge: Adoption, Reliability, and Response Times

Trinh Viet Doan$^{(\boxtimes)}$, Irina Tsareva, and Vaibhav Bajpai

Technical University of Munich, Munich, Germany
{doan,bajpaiv}@in.tum.de, irina.tsareva@tum.de

Abstract. The Domain Name System (DNS) is a cornerstone of communication on the Internet. DNS over TLS (DoT) has been standardized in 2016 as an extension to the DNS protocol, however, its performance has not been extensively studied yet. In the first study that measures DoT from the edge, we leverage 3.2k RIPE Atlas probes deployed in home networks to assess the adoption, reliability, and response times of DoT in comparison with DNS over UDP/53 (Do53). Each probe issues 200 domain name lookups to 15 public resolvers, five of which support DoT, and to the probes' local resolvers over a period of one week, resulting in 90M DNS measurements in total. We find that the support for DoT among open resolvers has increased by 23.1% after nine months in comparison with previous studies. However, we observe that DoT is still only supported by local resolvers for 0.4% of the RIPE Atlas probes. In terms of reliability, we find failure rates for DoT to be inflated by 0.4–32.2% points (p.p.) when compared to Do53. While Do53 failure rates for most resolvers individually are consistent across continents, DoT failure rates have much higher variation. As for response times, we see high regional differences for DoT and find that nearly all DoT requests take at least 100 ms to return a response (in a large part due to connection and session establishment), showing an inflation in response times of more than 100 ms compared to Do53. Despite the low adoption of DoT among local resolvers, they achieve DoT response times of around 140–150 ms similar to public resolvers (130–230 ms), although local resolvers also exhibit higher failure rates in comparison.

1 Introduction

The Domain Name System (DNS) faces various privacy-related issues such as fingerprinting or tracking [10,11,22,23,36] that affect DNS over UDP/53 (Do53). Consequently, DNS over TLS (DoT) was standardized in 2016 [19] to upgrade the communication [35]: The protocol establishes a TCP connection and TLS session on port 853, so that DNS messages are transmitted over an encrypted channel to circumvent eavesdropping and information exposure. DoT has gained increasing support since its standardization; e.g., it is supported on Android devices as "Private DNS" since Android 9 (August 2018) [24]. Similarly, Apple supports DoT and DNS over HTTPS (DoH) on their devices and services with the recent iOS 14 (September 2020) and MacOS Big Sur (November 2020) [38].

© Springer Nature Switzerland AG 2021
O. Hohlfeld et al. (Eds.): PAM 2021, LNCS 12671, pp. 192–209, 2021.
https://doi.org/10.1007/978-3-030-72582-2_12

Previous work [8,17,26] has studied the support and response times of DoT (and DoH). However, the studies performed response time measurements from proxy networks and data centers, which means that results might not appropriately reflect the latency of regular home users: The measured response times are likely overestimated due to the incurred latency overhead of proxy networks or underestimated due to the usage of well-provisioned data centers. We close this gap by measuring DoT from the end user [28] perspective for multiple DoT resolvers as the first study to do so, using 3.2k RIPE Atlas home probes deployed at the edge across more than 125 countries (Sect. 3). We issue DNS queries to 15 public resolvers, five of which support DoT, to analyze and compare the reliability and response times of Do53 and DoT resolvers. Our main findings are:

DoT Support (Sect. 2): We find DoT support among open resolvers to have increased by 23.1% compared to previous studies [8,26]. TLS 1.3 support [15,31] among these resolvers has increased by 15% points (p.p.), while support for TLS 1.0 and 1.1 is increasingly dropped. For RIPE Atlas (Sect. 4), we only find 13 (0.4%) of 3.2k home probes to receive responses over DoT from their local resolvers.

DoT Failure Rates (Sect. 4): While overall failure rates for Do53 are between 0.8–1.5% for most resolvers, failure rates for DoT are higher with 1.3–39.4%, i.e., higher by 0.4–32.2% points (p.p.) for individual resolvers. Failure rates are more varying across the continents for DoT, ranging from ≤1% up to >10%, with higher values primarily seen in Africa (AF) and South America (SA). On the other hand, Do53 failure rates are more consistent across most resolvers and continents (roughly 0.3–3%). Most failures occur due to timeouts (no response within 5 s), which we suspect is due to intervening middleboxes on the path that blackhole the connections by dropping packets destined for port 853.

DoT Response Times (Sect. 5): Comparing response times between Do53 and DoT, we find that most DoT response times are within roughly 130–230 ms, and are, therefore, slower by more than 100 ms, largely due to additional TCP and TLS handshakes. For most samples of well-known DNS services (such as Google, Quad9, or Cloudflare), response times of for Do53 are consistent across the continents, while other resolvers show larger regional differences. For DoT, only Cloudflare exhibits consistent response times across regions, whereas the remaining resolvers have highly varying response times. In cases where the local resolver does support DoT, response times are comparable to those of the faster public resolvers (140–150 ms) and similarly inflated compared to Do53.

We discuss limitations (Sect. 7) and compare our findings to previous work (Sect. 6) before concluding the study (Sect. 8). To facilitate reproducibility of our results [1], we share the created RIPE Atlas measurement IDs, analysis scripts, and auxiliary/supplementary files[1]. The measurements do not raise any ethical concerns.

---

[1] Repository: https://github.com/tv-doan/pam-2021-ripe-atlas-dot.

2 DoT Background: Adoption and Traffic Share

DoT Adoption Among Open Resolvers. Deccio and Davis [8] study and quantify the deployment of public DoT resolvers as of April 2019. Note that in the context of their study, a resolver refers to an IP endpoint, which may, therefore, include a replicated or anycasted service. They identify 1.2M open DNS resolvers in the public IPv4 address space, out of which 0.15% (1,747) support DoT. Of the DoT resolvers, 97% (1,701) support TLS 1.2 and 4.5% (79) support TLS 1.3, whereas older TLS versions (TLS 1.0 and 1.1) are not supported by 4.6% (80) of the resolvers. A similar number of open DoT resolvers (1.5k) was found by Lu *et al.* [26] (2019).

We repeat this scan from a research network at Technical University of Munich (TUM) in January 2020 (i.e., nine months after Deccio and Davis [8]) for the same set of open DNS resolvers. We find that the number of open resolvers supporting DoT has increased to 2,151, i.e., an increase by 23.1%. The share of resolvers supporting TLS 1.2 has increased to 99.9% (2,149 resolvers), while the percentage of TLS 1.3-supporting resolvers has increased to 20% even (433). Older versions of TLS are not supported anymore by 508 resolvers (24%), which altogether indicates that the adoption of DoT and newer TLS implementations is increasing.

DoT Traffic Share. To assess the usage of DoT in terms of traffic, we analyze public traffic traces collected from samplepoint-F of the WIDE backbone [7], which monitors a research network link in Japan. We aggregate the daily traffic traces of 2019 by month and inspect the traffic share of DoT, i.e., traffic on TCP/853. We observe that DoT accounts for roughly 2M out of 11.8B flows in the dataset, which means that DoT accounts for around 0.017% of all flows. On the other hand, the traffic share of Do53 is more than 135 times as much with 271.5M flows (2.3%), which indicates that DoT only contributes a very negligible amount of traffic overall.

3 Methodology

Measurement Platform and Probes. We use RIPE Atlas [32] to measure reliability and response times of Do53 and DoT from distributed vantage points; DoT measurements are performed over TLS 1.2, as RIPE Atlas probes do not fully support TLS 1.3 yet. For our experiment, we first select probes that are IPv4-capable and resolve A records correctly through the RIPE Atlas API. We exclude anchor probes to capture the Do53 and DoT behavior for end users more accurately. As older versions of RIPE Atlas probes (V1 and V2) exhibit load issues [2,14], we only consider V3 probes, ultimately finding 5,229 probes in total. For the analysis, however, we only take residential probes into account: We use RIPE Atlas user tags [3] for the identification of residential networks. Additionally, we issue `traceroute` measurements to an arbitrary public endpoint from all probes over IPv4: If the IP address of first hop on the path is private [30] and the IP address of the second hop is in the public address space (i.e., the probe is directly connected to the home gateway), we also identify the probe as residential. Combining the set of probe IDs determined from both these approaches, we identify 3,231 *home probes* overall. As the number of dual-stacked residential probes is significantly lower (roughly 700 globally), we decide to not perform measurements over IPv6: The low number of IPv6-capable probes overall limits the regional analysis, since such probes are primarily deployed in Europe (EU) and North America (NA), which would leave other continents largely underrepresented. Thus, we focus on IPv4 measurements exclusively in our study, although we suggest to repeat the measurements over IPv6 with increased deployment of probes having native IPv6 connectivity.

DNS Resolvers. We issue the resolution of 200 domains (A records) to 15 selected IP endpoints of different public DNS services once a day, repeated over a period of one week (July 03–09, 2019). Out of the 15 public DNS services, listed in Table 1, five support DoT: CleanBrowsing, Cloudflare, Google, Quad9, and UncensoredDNS. For these services, we additionally issue the same DNS lookups to the same IP endpoints using DoT for comparison. Moreover, we query the same 200 domains using the DNS resolvers provided by a probe's network configuration, which we will refer to as *local resolver* (typically operated by the ISP and assigned via DHCP) in the following; this allows us to study the support of DoT among ISPs. Note that probes may use multiple IP endpoints when resolving domains locally. In particular, probe hosts may use public resolvers as their local resolvers; thus, we exclude all occurrences of these public resolvers from the local resolver measurements, including alternative IP endpoints which these public DNS services may use. Among the 2,718 probes that receive at least one successful Do53 response from a local resolver, we find 2,257 probes to use an endpoint in their private network as local resolver (e.g., a CPE) and 572 probes to use an ISP resolver (public IP address) for local name resolution. However, as we do not see significant differences in terms of response times at the 5th percentiles of each probe (9.5 ms for CPE, 9.8 ms for ISP resolver), we do not further distinguish between both groups.

Domains. The 200 queried domains consist of 150 websites from Alexa Top 1M [33]: We split the Top 1M list into 10 equally-sized bins of 100k each (by rank order) and select the 15 first domains of each bin, resulting in 150 popularity-focused domains. The remaining 50 domains are selected from the country-based Alexa Toplists, for which we determine 10 countries across the continents with high numbers of probes (US, DE, GB, RU, NL, IT, JP, NZ, ZA, BR). We then pick 5 website domains from each Alexa Toplist of the associated Top-Level Domain (.us, .de, .co.uk, etc.), resulting in 50 region-focused domains. Note that sampling the entire 1M domains does not improve representativeness, since we repeat the measurements over a period of one week and expect records to be cached. Also, the known instability of the Alexa Toplist [33] does not substantially influence our measurements: We construct the list of overall 200 domains

Table 1. Overview of measured resolvers together with the number of failed requests, total requests, and failure rates for both Do53 and DoT. Failure rates for DoT are higher compared to Do53 for each resolver, with failure rates also being lower for public DNS services than local resolvers. Highlighted cells are referred to in Sect. 4.

Resolver Name	Do53			DNS over TLS		
	# Failures	# Total	Failure Rate	# Failures	# Total	Failure Rate
1) CZ.NIC ODVR	44,942	4,269,957	1.1%	—	—	—
2) CleanBrowsing	37,681	4,273,000	0.9%	430,401	4,163,095	10.3%
3) Cloudflare 1.1.1.1	107,841	4,273,000	2.5%	122,932	4,157,033	3.0%
4) Comodo Secure DNS	65,849	4,272,976	1.5%	—	—	—
5) DNS.WATCH	43,349	4,272,960	1.0%	—	—	—
6) Google Public DNS	38,670	4,272,587	0.9%	53,059	4,157,354	1.3%
7) Neustar UltraRecursive	4,190,474	4,269,365	98.2%	—	—	—
8) OpenDNS	34,826	4,273,051	0.8%	—	—	—
9) OpenNIC	61,077	4,266,712	1.4%	—	—	—
10) Oracle + Dyn	46,247	4,272,609	1.1%	—	—	—
11) Quad9	51,292	4,272,979	1.2%	110,404	4,157,340	2.7%
12) SafeDNS	37,291	4,269,648	0.9%	—	—	—
13) UncensoredDNS	62,175	4,269,656	1.5%	4,039,111	4,157,277	97.2%
14) VeriSign Public DNS	36,644	4,269,638	0.9%	—	—	—
15) Yandex.DNS	53,581	4,269,591	1.3%	—	—	—
16a) Local Resolver without DoT support	573,514	5,108,671	11.2%	—	—	—
16b) Local Resolver with DoT support	2,356	32,649	7.2%	13,737	34,839	39.4%
Total	5,487,809	69,209,049	7.9%	4,769,644	20,826,938	22.9%

(from July 01, 2019) to investigate whether there are larger differences between bins of more popular and less popular domains, or in terms of Top-Level Domain (TLD) and probe location. However, we do not find any significant deviations in terms of response times, neither regarding popularity rank nor TLD. Thus, we do not further distinguish between individual domains in the analysis.

With this experiment setup, we collect measurements for around 90M DNS requests from home probes in total (see Table 1).

4 Reliability

We investigate the reliability of Do53 and DoT by analyzing the *failure rate*, which we define as the relative number of failed queries to the total number of queries. A query is defined as failed if the domain lookup could not be sent to the resolver or the probe did not receive a response; in both cases, the RIPE Atlas API will return an error. Table 1 shows the overall failure rate, as well as the failure rate by resolver, for both Do53 and DoT. Note that we exclude 33 probes which failed nearly all of their DoT measurements (see *error analysis* below) from all following analyses. Further, only 2,718 probes of the 3.2k home probes successfully receive a Do53 response from local resolvers, i.e., the remaining probes cannot resolve a domain using a local resolver (but can with a public resolver). Considering DoT, we find that only 13 probes receive responses from their local resolver via DoT, which means that DoT is only supported by 0.4% of the local resolvers. We exclusively see these DoT-supporting local resolvers (discussed in more detail in Sect. 5) in EU (11 probes) and NA (2 probes). As such, we separate the queries to local resolvers (by probes with and without DoT-supported local resolvers) in Table 1 and this subsection.

Overall Failure Rates. The overall failure rate for Do53 is 7.9%, with individual failure rates of 0.8–1.5% for most resolvers, whereas the overall failure rate for DoT is much higher at 22.9%, i.e., a difference of 15.0% points (p.p.). However, the total failure rates are heavily influenced by a few resolvers exhibiting particularly high failure rates of close to 100%: For instance, 98.2% of the Do53 requests to Neustar UltraRecursive fail, accounting for 76.4% of the Do53 failure rate in total. For DoT, UncensoredDNS accounts for 84.7% of all DoT failures with an individual failure rate of 97.2%; local resolvers with DoT support have an overall DoT failure rate of 39.4%.

Individually, the Do53 failure rate is between 0.8% and 2.5% for all public resolvers when disregarding Neustar. Local resolvers encounter failures in 11.2% of the cases instead (7.2% for probes with DoT-supported local resolvers).

We observe an inflation of failure rates when moving from Do53 to DoT for all DoT resolvers: Inflations range from 0.4 and 0.5 p.p. for Google and Cloudflare, over 1.5 p.p. for Quad9 and 9.4 p.p. for CleanBrowsing, to 95.7 p.p. for UncensoredDNS; local resolvers with DoT support show an inflation toward the higher end with 32.2 p.p. Overall, these numbers suggest that DoT support on the paths is still experimental and, therefore, varying concerning reliability.

Error Analysis. Regarding the respective error messages, we find that most failures are attributed to timeouts (5 s), socket errors, and `connect()` errors (connection refused/reset, network unreachable). For Do53, nearly all failed requests toward Neustar (>99.9%) are due to timeouts. DoT measurements show a significant amount of `TUCONNECT` errors, which are exclusive to DoT and suggest TLS negotiation errors. To further investigate this, we count the number of `TUCONNECT` errors for each combination of probe and public resolver; we exclude UncensoredDNS from this analysis due to its high failure rate overall (which indicates server-side issues). For all combinations of 3.2k probes × 4 resolvers, we find repeated `TUCONNECT` errors for 33 probes across all resolvers where the probes fail nearly all scheduled 1.4k DoT measurements (200 domains × 7 days). This indicates blackholing of DoT packets closer to these probe (home router or in the ISP network). Although the number of affected probes is negligible (≈1%), we have excluded the affected 33 probes from the previous and following analyses. We further investigate `TUCONNECT` errors and find a higher number of probes failing nearly all DoT measurements for Cloudflare in particular, which affects 99 probes. The differential of 66 probes between these two groups show no errors for the other resolvers, suggesting DoT blackholing closer to Cloudflare

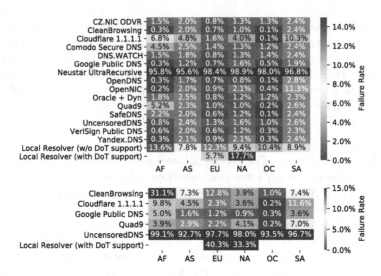

Fig. 1. Failure rates of resolvers by continent for Do53 (top) and DoT (bottom). Each cell represents the failure rate based on all failures relative to all queries for the specific resolver and continent. Most failure rates for Do53 are between 0.3–3%, whereas DoT failure rates are generally higher and more varying.

anycast instances that serve these probes, which in return causes a higher failure rate compared to other resolvers. CleanBrowsing, on the other hand, shows a similar failure rate regarding TUCONNECT errors as Google or Quad9; the majority of CleanBrowsing's overall DoT failures (10.3%) stem from timeouts instead.

The inflated failure rates for DoT in comparison with Do53 are less surprising, as DoT was only standardized in 2016 [19]: As such, DoT likely still faces issues with middleboxes along the path [16,29], which intervene with DoT packets (TCP/853) and result in timeouts.

Regional Comparison. To identify regional differences, Fig. 1 depicts the failure rates of Do53 (top) and DoT (bottom) by resolver and continent. Most resolvers exhibit similar Do53 failure rates across all continents, in the range of roughly 0.3–3%. Local resolvers show significantly higher failure rates (5.7–13.6%), which means that RIPE Atlas probes have less success in resolving domain names when using their local resolver (regardless of DoT support). Thus, Do53 resolutions are more reliable with public resolvers compared to local ones concerning RIPE Atlas measurements. Nevertheless, we find similarly high values for OpenNIC in SA (11.3%), and Cloudflare in AF (6.8%) and SA (10.3%). As mentioned, Neustar represents an outlier, as measurements fail in nearly all cases (95.6–98.9%). Probes in Oceania (OC) have the lowest failure rates for all resolvers when comparing different continents, with most resolvers having failure rates of at most 0.5%.

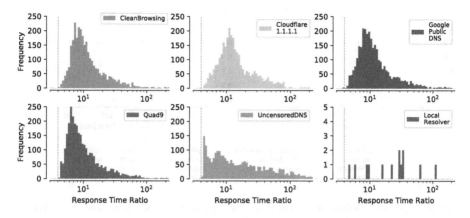

Fig. 2. Histograms of response time ratios (DoT to Do53) per probe for each resolver. The vertical dashed line represents the ratio of 4 RTTs for DoT (TCP handshake + TLS handshake + DNS lookup) to 1 RTT of Do53 (DNS lookup).

Regarding DoT, Google and Quad9 exhibit the lowest failure rates across all continents (<5% in most continents), although still higher than their respective Do53 failure rates. On the other hand, Cloudflare and CleanBrowsing show higher failure rates, especially in AF (9.8% and 31.1%) and SA (11.6% and 7.4%), with CleanBrowsing having a high failure rate in EU (12.8%) as well. Queries to UncensoredDNS fail in nearly all cases (92.7–99.1%). As multiple public DoT resolvers (even those with otherwise reliable services in other continents) have higher failure rates in AF and SA, these regions may be affected more heavily by ossification in terms of middleboxes. Local resolvers with DoT support also show high failure rates, with 40.3% in EU, and 33.3% in NA. In total, this indicates that the DoT reliability is highly dependent on the geographical location as well as the chosen DNS service.

5   Response Times

We aggregate the measurements by grouping distinct tuples of probe and resolver and, for each group, determine the 5th percentile in terms of response time (i.e., one value for each probe-resolver tuple across all measurements). We choose 5th percentiles to limit the analysis to responses for cached records, as those accumulate at the lower end of the distribution and represent best-case scenarios.

Background. Before discussing response times of the measurements, we elaborate on a technical limitation regarding DoT: By design, a DoT client would first establish a TCP connection and TLS session with the recursive resolver, then keep this session alive to reuse it for resolutions of multiple domains. Thus, the added delay due to the TCP and TLS handshake RTTs only apply once for

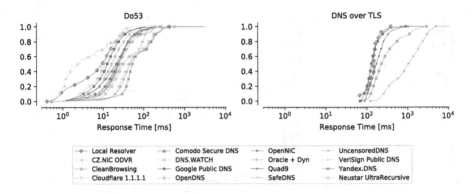

Fig. 3. CDF of resolver response time for successful Do53 (left) and DoT (right) requests (5th percentiles per probe). While most Do53 responses arrive within roughly 100 ms, the majority of DoT responses require more than 100 ms to return.

as long as the connection and session stay alive. For RIPE Atlas probes, however, DoT measurements do *not* keep the connection/session alive in between different measurements, which means that the additional RTTs required for the TCP and TLS handshakes apply to every DoT measurement. We contacted the RIPE Atlas support regarding specific protocol details: RIPE Atlas probes do not use TCP Fast Open or other extensions, so establishing the TCP connection will add 1 RTT to the response time. Further, probes typically use TLS 1.2 (2 additional RTTs), though some probes may use TLS 1.3 (1 additional RTT); however, the DoT measurement results do unfortunately not provide any information about the used TLS version for validation. As such, DoT measurements include 3 additional RTTs (2 in the best case) on top of the DNS lookup (1 RTT).

Considering we focus on cached responses (5th percentiles, see above) exclusively in this section, we argue that the lookup times are negligibly small (since results are simply returned from the cache). Thus, the response times largely consist of the RTTs between probe and resolver. Consequently, Do53 measurements resemble roughly 1 RTT, which we consider as the baseline RTT (cf. overall response times below), whereas DoT measurements resemble roughly 4 RTTs in total, plus time for connection/session management and processing on both probe and resolver. For approximation, we calculate the ratio between the 5th percentiles of the DoT and Do53 response times per probe for each resolver, shown in Fig. 2; the vertical dashed lines represent the outlined ratio of 4 RTTs to 1 RTT (i.e., DoT to Do53).

The minimum ratio across all resolvers is 3.11, which suggests usage of TLS 1.3 in these cases (1 RTT less than with TLS 1.2). Yet, these cases are rare (only four probe-resolver pairs), as the median ratio among the public resolvers is 10.5 (25th percentile 7.5); this suggests that besides the approx. 4 RTTs required for the handshakes, most samples require at least around 4 more RTTs for processing of the DoT request on probe and resolver side. However, this processing

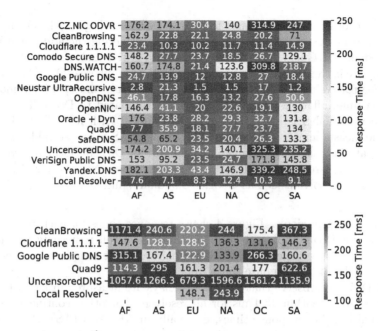

Fig. 4. Medians of the 5th percentile response times by continent and resolver for Do53 (top) and DoT (bottom). Do53 response times are mostly below 20–40 ms for most resolvers, whereas DoT response times are between roughly 120–180 ms instead.

overhead for DoT measurements cannot be accurately determined, as probes record the total response time only and, therefore, do not allow separation of different steps during the DoT lookup. Nevertheless, note that the handshake RTTs still account for a large fraction of the measured DoT response times overall. Recall that only 13 probes leverage DoT-supporting local resolvers, most of which have ratios toward the higher end (see Fig. 2, bottom right) due to very low Do53 response times (<10 ms) and likely early-stage DoT implementations.

Due to these limitations (also see Sect. 7), the following analyses describe the DoT response times as measured by RIPE Atlas, i.e., incl. TCP/TLS handshakes; observed inflations will only apply when initiating connections to DoT resolvers and, thus, represent upper bounds of response times for cached records.

Overall Response Times. The distributions of the 5th percentile response times for Do53 are shown in Fig. 3 (left). The fastest resolvers with medians of less than 15 ms are Neustar (median 2.4 ms), local resolvers (9.3 ms), Cloudflare (10.8 ms), and Google (12.6 ms). However, note that the sample size of Neustar measurements is much lower due to its high failure rate (see Sect. 4). Public resolvers that primarily serve clients of a specific country such as CZ.NIC (CZ, 41.2 ms) and Yandex (RU, 51.8 ms), as well as UncensoredDNS (44.9 ms) show response times toward the higher end. The remaining resolvers have response times in between (16–31.3 ms) over Do53.

On the other hand, response times for DoT (see Fig. 3, right) are much higher in comparison with Do53, as expected considering the additional RTTs. The medians for Google (129.3 ms), Cloudflare (131.9 ms), and local resolvers (147 ms) are in the same range of roughly 130–150 ms, whereas Quad9 (170.4 ms) and CleanBrowsing (227 ms) show higher response times, which indicates response time inflations of 150–200 ms when compared to Do53. The median for UncensoredDNS is an outlier at 1.06 s; coupled with its high DoT failure rate, the measurements suggest that UncensoredDNS is less suitable as a DoT resolver at this stage. Despite the low support of DoT by local resolvers, the response times are comparable to (and in some cases even better than) well-known public resolvers such as Google, Cloudflare, and Quad9.

Regional Comparison. Figure 4 shows response times for each resolver and continent for Do53 (top) and DoT (bottom); each cell represents the median value for the respective continent-resolver pair, with the sample values being the 5th percentiles of the response times from Fig. 3.

For Do53, we observe that the lowest delays are measured in EU, where the responses arrive within 43.4 ms for all resolvers. For other continents, we see occasionally higher response times, especially in AF, Asia (AS), OC, and SA, where some resolvers take more than 100 ms (up to 339.2 ms) to respond to a Do53 request. Local resolvers exhibit the lowest response times by far, with values ranging between 7.1–12.4 ms, similar to Google (10.2–23.4 ms); again, note that Neustar shows very low response times but is not fully comparable due to its lower sample size. Overall, we observe that the performance of well-known resolvers (Google, Quad9, Cloudflare) is consistent when comparing response times between different continents, i.e., regional differences for resolvers are marginal, while for other resolvers (with fewer points of presence around the globe) regional differences are higher.

Considering DoT (Fig. 4 bottom), we again find response times to be substantially higher than their Do53 counterparts for all cells. However, differences between the continents are much more varying compared to Do53, with the exception of Cloudflare which shows the least varying median response times (128.1–147.7 ms) across all continents. On the other hand, samples for Google are in between 122.9–315.1 ms (showing high response times in AF and OC), which is comparable to DoT-supported local resolvers in EU and NA (148.1 and 243.9 ms). Quad9 (114.3–622.6 ms) and CleanBrowsing (175.4–1,171.4 ms) show higher variance across the regions; responses from UncensoredDNS even require more than 1 s in most cases. Overall, response times for DoT are much more varying across different continents when compared to Do53.

Response Time Inflations by Individual Probes. To further investigate the actual difference between Do53 and DoT in terms of response time, we only consider resolvers that offer both protocols in the following. We calculate the individual deltas between Do53 and DoT for each probe-resolver tuple (i.e., the probe's inflation in response time to a specific resolver) by subtracting the 5th

percentile of a probe's DoT response times from the 5th percentile of its Do53 response times.

We find all deltas to be negative, which means that DoT is slower than Do53 in all cases. We observe the lowest inflations regarding response times to be around 66 ms (i.e., delta of -66 ms), although the interquartile range across all samples is $[-285.6; -114.8]$ ms. The medians of the deltas are highly varying across the continents (EU -145 ms, NA -164.9 ms, OC -188.4 ms, AS -234.4 ms, SA -330.5 ms, AF -367.3 ms). Regarding resolvers, Google (median -115.9 ms), Cloudflare (-121 ms), local resolvers (-143.8 ms), and Quad9 (-149.8 ms) show similar inflations in the range of roughly 120–150 ms; on the other hand, CleanBrowsing (-202.8 ms) and UncensoredDNS (-910.3 ms) exhibit much higher response time differences between Do53 and DoT.

Overall, while the observed overheads of DoT differ depending on continent and resolver, we still see differences of more than 100 ms for almost all samples in favor of Do53.

Local DoT Resolvers. To further examine local resolvers, we split the measurement of local resolvers with DoT support by individual resolvers. The 9 local resolvers that support DoT are operated by larger commercial ISPs, smaller associations that offer Internet services, cloud/DNS service providers, and academic institutions. However, note that they are only used by 13 probes (11 EU, 2 NA) in our study; DoT is not supported by *any* local probe resolver in AF, AS, OC, or SA. We find varying DoT response times for the different local resolvers in the range of 66.4–383.8 ms overall. XS4ALL (an ISP from NL) shows consistent response times (145.9–156.6 ms) for the five corresponding probes. Further, most of the remaining local resolvers respond within 104–223.2 ms; as such, the DoT response times of local resolvers are largely on par with those of public resolvers.

6 Related Work and Discussion

We contrast our results with those of recent studies: Deccio and Davis [8] find that DoT is supported by 0.15% (1.7k) of all publicly routable IPv4 resolvers, with most of them being assigned to CleanBrowsing (among some resolvers from Cloudflare, Google, and Quad9); our repetition of the experiment reveals that this number has increased by 23.1% within nine months (see Sect. 2).

Lu *et al.* [26] find a similar number of open DoT resolvers (1.5k) and measure response times for DoT and DoH from two residential proxy networks, covering 123k vantage points in total (30k global, 85k in China). In terms of reachability, 99% of the global users in their study can reach a DoT resolver. In their example, Cloudflare is reachable by 98.9% of the users due to the DoT failure rate being 1.1% only; for our results, we observe Cloudflare to fail in 3.0% for all DoT measurements, whereas Google only fails in 1.3%, ultimately resulting in roughly similar numbers in terms of reachability. However, they find much lower failure rates for Quad9 (0.15%, compared to our 2.7%). To contrast this with DoH, they find DoH failure rates of less than 1% from their global proxy network; overall, they observe DoH to have about equal or higher reachability than DoT.

Regarding response times, they find median response times for DoT without connection reuse to range between 349–1,106 ms based on location for Cloudflare, Google, and Quad9 resolvers; this includes overheads for TLS session negotiation, which are in the range of 77–470 ms. These response times are higher by as much as factors of 1.75–5.5 compared to the DoT response times (Sect. 5) of our RIPE Atlas measurements (median of all probe-resolver response time medians at 201 ms). This indicates that the residential proxy networks add a significant amount of latency to the measurements, which does not reflect the actual response times for home users. Nevertheless, the authors [26] find that connection reuse improves the average response times substantially. This suggests that our measurements represent a rough upper bound for the average DoT response times of home users.

Hounsel et al. [17] measure Do53, DoT, and DoH from five global vantage points through Amazon EC2 instances, using Cloudflare, Google, and Quad9. They compare the effects of the different DNS protocols on loading times of webpages and take advantage of the aforementioned connection reuse. For their DoT queries from Frankfurt (FRA), they observe most responses to return within 100 ms for Google and Cloudflare, although results for Quad9 are much more varying (only around 20% within 100 ms). These numbers are much lower compared to the RIPE Atlas 5th percentiles of roughly 130–150 ms that we discuss (Sect. 5), although this difference is likely related to the connection/session reuse as well as usage of well-provisioned data centers as vantage points (rather than home networks). Nevertheless, while DoT and DoH response times for individual queries are higher compared to Do53, the overall page loading times are lower when reusing the connection and session, showing that a switch from Do53 to DoT or DoH might be beneficial in terms of response times already.

7   Limitations and Future Work

We restrict the set of probes to home and V3 probes exclusively; note that these probes are deployed in 1.1k different ASes, with the top 10 ASes (0.9%) accounting for roughly 27.6% of all home probes. Although there is a potential bias toward overrepresented ASes, we decide not to normalize by ASes since network conditions and, hence, measurements are not guaranteed to be uniform across an AS either: Sampling "representative" probes for each AS would, therefore, introduce another bias into the dataset and analysis.

Furthermore, we cannot directly control the caching behavior of the measured resolvers, though the 200 selected domains are likely cached due to being highly ranked in Alexa Toplists and repeated measurements. Regarding response times, we further limit the analysis to the 5th percentiles for each probe. Note that measurements over RIPE Atlas cannot be guaranteed to run simultaneously or back-to-back due to scheduling and load balancing on the probe. Therefore, we cannot (for instance) pair Do53 and DoT measurements for a head-to-head comparison, and instead rely on the entire distribution (reliability, Sect. 4) and 5th percentiles (response times, Sect. 5) of the measurements.

Moreover, as RIPE Atlas does not keep the TLS session alive for reuse between different measurements, the presented response times represent the initial delays for the first DNS request. Thus, they estimate the upper bounds for DoT response times which end users would experience since subsequent DNS requests through the same TLS session do not require additional handshakes and will have lower response times as a result. Further, applications typically resolve multiple domains concurrently in real use cases, while measurements from RIPE Atlas are performed sequentially.

In the future, we plan to study the impact of different TLS versions, or the benefit of TLS session reuse, but also to study changes over time by repeating the measurements, including measurements over IPv6. To further investigate issues with middleboxes, `traceroute` measurements over UDP/53 and TCP/853 can complement the failure analysis of DNS requests by comparison to see where packets are dropped in the network. With the increasing adoption of DNSSEC and larger DNS responses, DNS measurements over TCP/53 can provide further insight about the adoption, reliability, and response times of DNS over TCP. Lastly, DoH measurements (which are not yet possible with RIPE Atlas) from home networks can contribute to ongoing research, as response times and reliability of DoH from the edge have not been widely studied yet.

8   Conclusion

We present first measurement results that compare Do53 and DoT w.r.t. reliability and response times in the context of residential networks, based on 90M domain lookups over both protocols from 3.2k RIPE Atlas home probes. We study the support of DoT among the local resolvers of the probes, finding that only 13 probes (i.e., 0.4%) have DoT-capable local resolvers, which indicates that the adoption of DoT is still very low. When comparing the failure rates for resolvers that respond to both Do53 and DoT queries, we observe that the DoT failure rate is higher by 0.4–32.2% points (p.p.) for these resolvers. In particular, the majority of failures occurs due to timeouts, which is likely seen due to middleboxes that drop packets associated with DoT on port 853. In terms of response times, we find that DoT is slower by more than 100 ms (in a large part due to connection and session establishment), with response times between 130–150 ms for the fastest resolvers and up to 230 ms when including slower ones. Although the support of DoT among local resolvers is low, some local resolvers achieve similar DoT response times (140–150 ms) to the faster public resolvers. Local resolvers further have the lowest latency over Do53, however, both their Do53 and DoT failure rates are higher compared to public resolvers.

With increasing support of DoT among mobile devices as shown by Android [24] and Apple [38], increasing support by local resolvers is important and necessary to avoid centralization of DNS traffic [27] to third parties besides the ISP: Although this can be worked around by cycling through several resolvers [12], this comes at the cost of higher resolution times (especially due to multiple connection and session establishments). As such, to reduce the information leakage through DoT [18] to additional parties while also keeping resolution times low, it is crucial for local resolvers to adopt encrypted DNS and be discoverable within home networks [6]; as seen, DoT response times are comparable between local and public resolvers.

Considering the issues with inflated failure rates for DoT due to ossification, one question that arises is whether to switch the development and deployment focus to DoH [5,13] instead: Just like HTTPS, DoH runs over TCP/443, which will make middlebox issues along the path less likely. Further, popular Web browsers such as Chrome [37] and Firefox [9] already support DoH. However, studies [34] have shown that DoH is more susceptible to fingerprinting attacks than DoT, and further drives centralization of DNS traffic [4,12,25,27]. As both DoT and DoH bring latency overheads, DNS over QUIC [20] might be another encrypted alternative with response times which are closer to Do53. Yet, legislation may discourage and hinder the deployment of encrypted DNS and similar protocols beyond the area of jurisdiction [21]. Thus, further advances and future follow-up studies on encrypted DNS are required to get a better understanding.

Acknowledgements. We thank Alexander Niedrist (TUM), Johan ter Beest and Philip Homburg (RIPE NCC), and the volunteering RIPE Atlas probe hosts for their valuable support regarding our measurement study. We also thank our shepherd Timm Böttger and the anonymous reviewers for their insightful feedback and suggestions.

References

1. Bajpai, V., et al.: The Dagstuhl beginners guide to reproducibility for experimental networking research. Comput. Commun. Rev. (CCR) **49**(1), 24–30 (2019). https://doi.org/10.1145/3314212.3314217
2. Bajpai, V., Eravuchira, S.J., Schönwälder, J.: Lessons learned from using the RIPE Atlas platform for measurement research. Comput. Commun. Rev. (CCR) **45**(3), 35–42 (2015). https://doi.org/10.1145/2805789.2805796
3. Bajpai, V., Eravuchira, S.J., Schönwälder, J., Kisteleki, R., Aben, E.: Vantage point selection for IPv6 measurements: benefits and limitations of RIPE Atlas tags. In: Symposium on Integrated Network and Service Management (IM), pp. 37–44. IEEE (2017). https://doi.org/10.23919/INM.2017.7987262
4. Bertola, V.: Recommendations for DNS privacy client applications. Internet-Draft draft-bertola-bcp-doh-clients-01, September 2019, Work in Progress. https://datatracker.ietf.org/doc/html/draft-bertola-bcp-doh-clients-01
5. Böttger, T., et al.: An empirical study of the cost of DNS-over-HTTPS. In: Internet Measurement Conference (IMC), pp. 15–21. ACM (2019). https://doi.org/10.1145/3355369.3355575

6. Boucadair, M., Reddy. K,T., Wing, D., Cook, N.: DHCP and router advertisement options for encrypted DNS discovery within home networks. Internet-Draft draft-btw-add-home-09, September 2020, Work in Progress. https://datatracker.ietf.org/doc/html/draft-btw-add-home-09

7. Cho, K., Mitsuya, K., Kato, A.: Traffic data repository at the WIDE project. In: USENIX Annual Technical Conference (ATC), Freenix Track, pp. 263–270. USENIX (2000). http://www.usenix.org/publications/library/proceedings/usenix2000/freenix/cho.html

8. Deccio, C.T., Davis, J.: DNS privacy in practice and preparation. In: Conference on Emerging Networking Experiments and Technologies (CoNEXT), pp. 138–143. ACM (2019). https://doi.org/10.1145/3359989.3365435

9. Deckelmann, S.: Mozilla Blog: firefox continues push to bring DNS over HTTPS by default for US users, February 2020. https://blog.mozilla.org/blog/2020/02/25/firefox-continues-push-to-bring-dns-over-https-by-default-for-us-users/. Accessed 13 Jan 2021

10. Greschbach, B., Pulls, T., Roberts, L.M., Winter, P., Feamster, N.: The effect of DNS on Tor's anonymity. In: Network and Distributed System Security Symposium (NDSS). ISOC (2017). https://www.ndss-symposium.org/ndss2017/ndss-2017-programme/e-effect-dns-tors-anonymity/

11. Herrmann, D., Banse, C., Federrath, H.: Behavior-based tracking: exploiting characteristic patterns in DNS traffic. Comput. Secur. **39**, 17–33 (2013). https://doi.org/10.1016/j.cose.2013.03.012

12. Hoang, N.P., Lin, I., Ghavamnia, S., Polychronakis, M.: K-resolver: towards decentralizing encrypted DNS resolution. In: Workshop on Measurements, Attacks, and Defenses for the Web (MADWEB) (2020). https://doi.org/10.14722/madweb.2020.23009

13. Hoffman, P.E., McManus, P.: DNS Queries over HTTPS (DoH). RFC 8484, pp. 1–21 (2018). https://doi.org/10.17487/RFC8484

14. Holterbach, T., Pelsser, C., Bush, R., Vanbever, L.: Quantifying interference between measurements on the RIPE Atlas platform. In: Internet Measurement Conference (IMC). ACM (2015). https://doi.org/10.1145/2815675.2815710

15. Holz, R., et al.: Tracking the deployment of TLS 1.3 on the Web: a story of experimentation and centralization. Comput. Commun. Rev. (CCR) **50**(3), 3–15 (2020). https://doi.org/10.1145/3411740.3411742

16. Honda, M., Nishida, Y., Raiciu, C., Greenhalgh, A., Handley, M., Tokuda, H.: Is it still possible to extend TCP? In: Internet Measurement Conference (IMC), pp. 181–194. ACM (2011). https://doi.org/10.1145/2068816.2068834

17. Hounsel, A., Borgolte, K., Schmitt, P., Holland, J., Feamster, N.: Comparing the effects of DNS, DoT, and DoH on web performance. In: The Web Conference (WWW), pp. 562–572. ACM/IW3C2 (2020). https://doi.org/10.1145/3366423.3380139

18. Houser, R., Li, Z., Cotton, C., Wang, H.: An investigation on information leakage of DNS over TLS. In: Conference on Emerging Networking Experiments and Technologies (CoNEXT), pp. 123–137. ACM (2019). https://doi.org/10.1145/3359989.3365429

19. Hu, Z., Zhu, L., Heidemann, J.S., Mankin, A., Wessels, D., Hoffman, P.E.: Specification for DNS over Transport Layer Security (TLS). RFC 7858 (2016). https://doi.org/10.17487/RFC7858

20. Huitema, C., Mankin, A., Dickinson, S.: Specification of DNS over dedicated QUIC connections. Internet-Draft draft-ietf-dprive-dnsoquic-01, October 2020, Work in Progress. https://datatracker.ietf.org/doc/html/draft-ietf-dprive-dnsoquic-01

21. Internet Society: Internet Society: Russia's Proposal Would Weaken the Internet, Make It Less Secure, September 2020. https://www.internetsociety.org/news/statements/2020/internet-society-russias-proposal-would-weaken-the-internet-make-it-less-secure/. Accessed 13 Jan 2021

22. Kirchler, M., Herrmann, D., Lindemann, J., Kloft, M.: Tracked without a trace: linking sessions of users by unsupervised learning of patterns in their DNS traffic. In: Workshop on Artificial Intelligence and Security (AISec), pp. 23–34. ACM (2016). https://doi.org/10.1145/2996758.2996770

23. Klein, A., Pinkas, B.: DNS cache-based user tracking. In: Network and Distributed System Security Symposium (NDSS). ISOC (2019). https://www.ndss-symposium.org/ndss-paper/dns-cache-based-user-tracking/

24. Kline, E., Schwartz, B.: DNS over TLS support in Android P Developer Preview (2018). https://android-developers.googleblog.com/2018/04/dns-over-tls-support-in-android-p.html. Accessed 13 Jan 2021

25. Livingood, J., Antonakakis, M., Sleigh, B., Winfield, A.: Centralized DNS over HTTPS (DoH) implementation issues and risks. Internet-Draft draft-livingood-doh-implementation-risks-issues-04, September 2019, Work in Progress. https://datatracker.ietf.org/doc/html/draft-livingood-doh-implementation-risks-issues-04

26. Lu, C., et al.: An end-to-end, large-scale measurement of DNS-over-encryption: how far have we come? In: Internet Measurement Conference (IMC), pp. 22–35. ACM (2019). https://doi.org/10.1145/3355369.3355580

27. Moura, G.C.M., Castro, S., Hardaker, W., Wullink, M., Hesselman, C.: Clouding up the Internet: how centralized is DNS traffic becoming? In: Internet Measurement Conference (IMC), pp. 42–49. ACM (2020). https://doi.org/10.1145/3419394.3423625

28. Nottingham, M.: The Internet is for End Users. RFC 8890, pp. 1–10 (2020) https://doi.org/10.17487/RFC8890

29. Papastergiou, G., et al.: De-ossifying the internet transport layer: a survey and future perspectives. Commun. Surv. Tutor. **19**(1), 619–639 (2017). https://doi.org/10.1109/COMST.2016.2626780

30. Rekhter, Y., Moskowitz, B.G., Karrenberg, D., de Groot, G.J., Lear, E.: Address Allocation for Private Internets. RFC 1918, pp. 1–9 (1996). https://doi.org/10.17487/RFC1918

31. Rescorla, E.: The Transport Layer Security (TLS) Protocol Version 1.3. RFC 8446, pp. 1–160 (2018). https://doi.org/10.17487/RFC8446

32. RIPE NCC: RIPE Atlas: a global internet measurement network. Internet Protoc. J. (IPJ) (2015). http://ipj.dreamhosters.com/wp-content/uploads/2015/10/ipj18.3.pdf

33. Scheitle, Q., et al.: A long way to the top: significance, structure, and stability of internet top lists. In: Internet Measurement Conference (IMC), pp. 478–493. ACM (2018). https://doi.org/10.1145/3278532.3278574

34. Siby, S., Juárez, M., Díaz, C., Vallina-Rodriguez, N., Troncoso, C.: Encrypted DNS ⇒ Privacy? A traffic analysis perspective. In: Network and Distributed System Security Symposium (NDSS). ISOC (2020). https://www.ndss-symposium.org/wp-content/uploads/2020/02/24301-paper.pdf

35. Sood, P., Hoffman, P.E.: Upgrading communication from stub resolvers to DoT or DoH. Internet-Draft draft-pp-add-stub-upgrade-02, June 2020, Work in Progress. https://datatracker.ietf.org/doc/html/draft-pp-add-stub-upgrade-02

36. Sun, M., Xu, G., Zhang, J., Kim, D.W.: Tracking you through DNS traffic: linking user sessions by clustering with Dirichlet mixture model. In: Conference on Modelling, Analysis and Simulation of Wireless and Mobile Systems, pp. 303–310. ACM (2017). https://doi.org/10.1145/3127540.3127567
37. The Chromium Projects: DNS over HTTPS (aka DoH): Auto-upgrade project (2020). https://www.chromium.org/developers/dns-over-https. Accessed 13 Jan 2021
38. WWDC 2020 - Apple Developer: Enable encrypted DNS (2020). https://developer.apple.com/videos/play/wwdc2020/10047. Accessed 13 Jan 2021

Staying Connected

Long-Lasting Sequences of BGP Updates

Lorenzo Ariemma[1]([⊠]) [iD], Simone Liotta[1], Massimo Candela[2] [iD],
and Giuseppe Di Battista[1] [iD]

[1] Roma Tre University, Rome, Italy
lorenzo.ariemma@uniroma3.it
[2] University of Pisa, Pisa, Italy

Abstract. The Border Gateway Protocol (BGP) is the protocol that
makes the various networks composing the Internet communicate to each
other. Routers speaking BGP exchange updates to keep the routing up-
to-date and allow such communication. This usually is done to reflect
changes in the routing configurations or as a consequence of link failures.
In the Internet as a whole it is normal that BGP updates are continuously
exchanged, but for any specific IP prefix, these updates are supposed
to be concentrated in a short time interval that is needed to react to
a network change. On the contrary, in this paper we show that there
are many IP prefixes involved in quite long sequences consisting of a
large number of BGP updates. Namely, examining ∼30 billion updates
collected by 172 observation points distributed worldwide, we estimate
that almost 30% of them belong to sequences lasting more than one week.
Such sequences involve 222 285 distinct IP prefixes, approximately one
fourth of the number of announced prefixes. We detect such sequences
using a method based on the Discrete Wavelet Transform. We publish an
online tool for the exploration and visualization of such sequences, which
is open to the scientific community for further research. We empirically
validate the sequences and report the results in the same online resource.
The analysis of the sequences shows that almost all the observation points
are able to see a large amount of sequences, and that 53% of the sequences
last at least two weeks.

Keywords: BGP instabilities · Discrete Wavelet Transform

1 Introduction

Interdomain routers exchange *BGP updates* [31] to adjust routing tables. This is
done to reflect changes in the network, such as link/router failures/restorations
and routing policy changes. In the Internet as a whole it is normal that BGP
updates are exchanged almost continuously, but for any specific *IP prefix*, these
updates are supposed to be concentrated in the short time intervals, say a couple
of minutes (e.g., [21,38]), that are needed to react to network changes.

On the contrary, looking at the updates received from a router, it is quite common to observe long-lasting sequences of updates involving the same prefix. This
is well known from the very beginning of the Internet, and several researchers

© Springer Nature Switzerland AG 2021
O. Hohlfeld et al. (Eds.): PAM 2021, LNCS 12671, pp. 213–229, 2021.
https://doi.org/10.1007/978-3-030-72582-2_13

discussed the reasons for that. E.g., [25] estimates that many BGP updates are "pathological" and not needed for the correct behaviour of the protocol.

In this paper we focus on the problem of finding and studying *long-lasting sequences of updates*, independently of their cause. This problem is, in our opinion, important from several perspectives: (1) Any study on long-lasting sequences of updates has to be well-founded on large sets of sequences detected with a rigorous method; this is true either to perform a root-cause analysis of such sequences or to analyse them to deepen the understanding of BGP dynamics. (2) Only a clear understanding of the quantity and of the features of long-lasting sequences can allow to state if such sequences can be a challenge for the scalability of inter-domain routing. However, the matter is complicated: (1) Giving a definition of long-lasting sequence is elusive. For example it can be arbitrarily said that a sequence is such if it contains a certain amount of updates for each consecutive day, hour, or minute. But all these pragmatic alternatives are questionable. (2) Currently, about 1 million prefixes (IPv4 + IPv6) are announced in the Internet. Studying from several observation points and within a large time-span the generated BGP updates, raises substantial computational issues.

We examine the updates collected by 172 observation points (*Collector Peers* or *CPs*) distributed around the world, for the entire Year 2019. The CPs are those of RRC00 of the RIPE RIS Project [6]. Since each CP has its own timing and its own visibility of the Internet, we process the updates received by each one independently. We show that almost 30% of the about 30 billion updates collected by the CPs belong to 434 790 sequences lasting more than one week and involving 222 285 distinct IP prefixes (i.e., approximately one fourth of the number of announced prefixes). We detect such sequences using a method based on the Discrete Wavelet Transform, we report and visualize them in a Web site [7] open to the scientific community for further research work. We inspect and validate a random sample of the sequences. The results of the validation are summarized in Sect. 4 and reported on the Web site. The analysis of the sequences shows that almost all the CPs are able to see a large amount of sequences, and that 53% of these sequences last at least two weeks.

The paper is organized as follows. In Sect. 2 we discuss the broad related work. In Sect. 3 we present a definition of long-lasting sequence and a methodology, based on the Discrete Wavelet Transform, to find such sequences. In Sect. 4 we apply the methodology to examine one year of BGP updates and discuss how the detected sequences are visualized. We also validate and analyse the sequences. Conclusions are in Sect. 5.

2   Related Work

In the past years various works have been published on the analysis of BGP data for the identification of anomalies and instabilities. In [25], the authors study BGP data exchanged between backbone service providers at US IXPs, in 1998. It classifies instabilities in five categories, and it estimates that 99% of the BGP data exchanged is redundant and pathologic (no topology changes).

The work in [26], some years later, re-evaluates the situation and sets to 16% the new rate of pathological BGP messages, most of which are redundant announcements. The reduction of the rate is attributed to software improvements introduced by router manufacturers. The rate of BGP messages has been analysed again in [18]. Contrarily to the previous estimations, they report that 40% is the amount of BGP messages redundant and not promoting topology changes (mostly re-announcements). The authors in [15] propose a solution for identifying BGP instabilities. Single features of the BGP updates are monitored every five minutes, and anomalies are identified based on statistical estimations on feature fluctuations observed by comparing different time windows of data for the same peer. In [39] is presented a technique for the identification of network events involving multiple prefixes. Such technique is based on the principal component analysis of BGP updates, which is used to identify temporal correlations among updates originated by different ASes. In [38], BGP updates involving the same CP-prefix pair are clustered together, and different events are detected based on changes in the frequency of the updates. The authors estimate that a normal event lasts around 200 s, events lasting longer should be considered anomalies. Similarly, in [29] a hard threshold of 46 updates/day for the same CP-prefix pair is adopted to differentiate between normal updates and anomalies. Such threshold is determined as the 1% of the CDF of the daily updates across all the CPs of Route Views [36]. The authors estimate that 80% of the prefixes in their dataset surpasses such threshold in 3 years. The paper [33] studies BGP updates in RIS and Route Views from different origin ASes and finds that many of them contain correlated information of events seen by many routers. The authors propose a methodology, based on the average distance between ASes in AS paths, able to distinguish such events in global or local ones.

Other works are based on statistical analyses. For example, in [19] the spatial and temporal correlation of BGP messages is analysed. In particular, the authors exclude long-range dependence (LRD) among BGP messages. A long-range dependence exists when data series have a strong time correlation and their auto-correlation function decays very slowly. This work is particularly important, because introduces the concept of LRD on BGP data that we also use in our analysis. However, a similar analysis [24] in 2015 concluded with the opposite result: BGP time series are long-range dependent. Additionally, BGP message rates are characterized as highly volatile, since peak rates exceed daily averages by several orders of magnitude. We believe the reason behind such different results is induced by the small observation time frame of the first work compared to the second one: they observe 3 days and 8.5 years, respectively. We also identify the long-range dependence in our work, this will be explained in the next sections. In [10], the authors look for a recurrent behaviour among BGP updates collected in five days by RIS' RRC03. They use auto-correlation, Fourier transform, and recurrence plots to analyse the time series and observe that BGP updates often repeat in time according to patterns. Recurrence plots [17] are drawings used to highlight recurring patterns in time series.

BGP data have been analysed also with the help of the Wavelet Transform [11]. In [30], the authors analyse two years of BGP data collected in an academic research network with the goal of detecting anomalies by identifying patterns such as self-similarity, power-law, or lognormal marginals. To investigate on the self-similarity they use the Discrete Wavelet Transform (DWT). Based on the result of the DWT, they exploit a *scalogram* which we also adopt and describe in Sect. 3. An anomaly detection tool called BAlet is presented in [27]. The tool is based on the observation that anomalies provoke abrupt increases of BGP updates. It uses the wavelet analysis for the identification of such anomalies. The authors confirm the property of self-similarity and LRD of interdomain routing data. In [13], the authors propose a methodology to classify BGP anomalies by considering the characteristic of multiple time scales. They propose a multi-scale long short-term memory model where the DWT is used to obtain temporal information on multiple scales. In [23] the author provide a complete taxonomy for BGP messages based on their effect on the routing process. Additionally, they provide a tool, named BLT, able to automatically classify BGP messages in such taxonomy. This classifier is later applied on Route Views data (LINX collector) to detect anomalies. The number of BGP messages labeled with the same class, in a specific time period, is the parameter monitored to detect deviation from usual rates. Finally, they apply such anomaly detection system on five well-known Internet events. However, none of the above papers focuses on identifying long-lasting sequences (way more than 200 s [38]) of BGP updates. Also, most of the used data is either collected inside a specific network, or it is geographically or temporally limited. Further, while several of the previous works identify anomalous phenomena, none of them provides a way to visually explore and analyse the related sequences.

3   Extracting Sequences from Time Series

BGP routers exchange messages called *BGP updates* (for brevity, *updates*). An update contains, among other information, a (possibly empty) set of announced prefixes, and a (possibly empty) set of withdrawn prefixes. Let u be an update, we denote by $reach(u)$ the set of prefixes announced by u and by $unreach(u)$ the set of prefixes withdrawn by u. We have that, for each update u, $reach(u) \cap unreach(u) = \emptyset$ and $|reach(u) \cup unreach(u)| \geq 1$. A *Route Collector* is a BGP router that collects the updates received by its peers (called CPs), and that labels each received update with the second in which the update is received, denoted by $time(u)$, and with the CP from which the update is received, denoted by $cp(u)$. A *Time Series of Updates* is the set of all the updates received by a Route Collector in a certain interval of time; we usually denote a time series with a capital letter, like U. Also, we denote by $U(n)$ the set of updates collected at second n. Given a time series U, we denote with $start(U)$ and $end(U)$ respectively the start and end seconds of its interval. Given a time series of updates U, we are interested in focusing on updates collected by a specific CP cp and containing a certain prefix ρ; we denote it $U_{cp,\rho}$.

Transforming a Time Series of Updates into a Signal. Given the time series $U_{cp,\rho}$, we associate to it a discrete time series $u_{cp,\rho}$ constructed as follows: we set $u_{cp,\rho}(n) = |U_{cp,\rho}(n)|$. Informally, $u_{cp,\rho}(n) = a$ means that at time n, collector peer cp received a updates containing ρ. As is, $u_{cp,\rho}$ is not suitable for a time-frequency analysis. In fact, the magnitude of $u_{cp,\rho}(n)$ at time n cannot be interpreted as the value of the signal, but it represents a value of frequency (number of updates) received at time n. Also, consider the maximum value $M = \max_{start(u_{cp,\rho}) \leq n \leq end(u_{cp,\rho})} u_{cp,\rho}(n)$, we have that the time series corresponds to a signal whose maximum frequency is M updates per second. Hence, in order to analyse the signal, we need to construct a *Hertzian* frequency representation of $u_{cp,\rho}$. According to the Nyquist-Shannon theorem [34], such a representation should contain samples taken with a *sampling time* $T_s < \frac{1}{2M}$, in a temporal range limited by $start(u_{cp,\rho})$ and $end(u_{cp,\rho})$. From the point of view of the sampling frequency f_s we have that $f_s > 2M$.

From $u_{cp,\rho}$ we construct a binary *code word* $w_{cp,\rho}$ composed by a rectangular pulse train that is the signal we are going to analyse. Each second n of $w_{cp,\rho}$ contains a sub-train of at least $2 \cdot u_{cp,\rho}(n)$ pulses. The pulses in the train are distributed in such a way to have a *duty-cycle* that is as much as possible equal to 50%. This duty-cycle requirement is imposed to improve the quality of the signal analysis in the frequency domain [35]. Formally, we have that each second n of $w_{cp,\rho}$ contains the following sub-train of pulses $w'_{cp,\rho}(n)$. Let $f_n = u_{cp,\rho}(n)$ be the *temporal frequency* value to represent at the second n and let $\omega_n = 2\pi \cdot f_n$ be the related *angular frequency* of the oscillation at the same time n. We have,

$$w'_{cp,\rho}(n) = \sum_{k=0}^{f_s-1} \frac{1 + \text{sgn}(\sin(\omega_n \cdot k \cdot T_s))}{2}$$

where $sgn(x) = -1, = 0$, and $= 1$ if $x < 0$, $x = 0$, and $x > 0$, respectively. In practice, we insert into the sequence $w_{cp,\rho}$ at least $2M$ time slots for each second of the sequence $u_{cp,\rho}$.

A Signal-Based Definition of Sequence. According to [24] when the signal obtained from a time series of updates has the burst presence of samples with a non-zero amplitude, it shows the features of a non-stationary and extremely volatile stochastic process. More importantly, it shows *long-term correlation* and *memory effects*. Similar features have been observed also by other authors (e.g., [8,30]), together with a self-similar behaviour. For these reasons, the sequences we are interested in can be distinguished from other sequences of updates because they exhibit such features.

The DWT Decomposition and the Multi-resolution Analysis. It has been observed in [9] that the *Discrete Wavelet Transform* or, more precisely, the *Discrete-Time Wavelet Transform* [11] (in what follows *DWT*) is a suitable method for searching sequences with the requested features. Hence, we analyse the signal $w_{cp,\rho}$ in the Wavelet domain performing a discrete multi-resolution analysis. The DWT permits to obtain a local representation of the signal, showing it in a time-frequency plane. The DWT series decomposition of the signal $w_{cp,\rho}(n)$ is defined as follows:

$$w_{cp,\rho}(n) = \sum_{k=0}^{K} c_{\ell,k}\phi_{\ell,k}(n) + \sum_{j=1}^{\ell}\sum_{k=0}^{K} d_{j,k}\psi_{j,k}(n)$$

where we have that $K+1$ is the number of samples of the signal. For the sake of simplicity we assume that $K = 2^{\ell} - 1$, with ℓ the number of the frequency bandwidth levels. Function ϕ is the *father wavelet* and ψ is the *mother wavelet* For a complete definition of the DWT see Appendix A.

Applying the DWT. Because of our definition of $w_{cp,\rho}$, we range k between $start(w_{cp,\rho})$ and $end(w_{cp,\rho})$. Also, we choose $f_s = 2M$ samples per second (limit case). Further, we select the range for j in such a way to capture the periodicities with a certain maximum value. Namely, suppose we are interested in signals with maximum periodicity λ we set ℓ to $\log_2(M\lambda)$.

As far as the father and the mother wavelet functions are concerned, we decided to use the *Haar* functions defined as follows:

$$\phi(n) = \begin{cases} 1 & 0 \leq n < 2, \\ 0 & \text{otherwise.} \end{cases} \qquad \psi(n) = \begin{cases} 1 & 0 \leq n < 1, \\ -1 & 1 \leq n < 2, \\ 0 & \text{otherwise.} \end{cases}$$

Other options are possible, e.g., we might use *Gaussian* kernel functions, typically modulated by several types of polynomials, *Daubechies*'s family functions, the *Biorthogonal* family one, etc. We opt for the Haar basis function because, even if it has slightly more uncertainty, it allows to compute the DWT faster, and this is crucial for the large amount of data we analyse.

Looking for Sequences Using the DWT. According to the above discussion we have to look for sequences that exhibit long term correlation and memory effects. We search them as follows. Given a DWT, a scalogram representation can be computed. Informally speaking (see Appendix A for more details), a scalogram representation is a matrix P, where $P[j,k]$ represents the percentage of the signal power at time k in the range of frequencies Δf_j defined below:

$$\Delta f_j = \left[\frac{f_s/2}{2^j}, \frac{f_s/2}{2^{j-1}}\right)$$

Given P, we compute for each second k, with $k \in [start(w_{cp,\rho}), \ldots, end(w_{cp,\rho})]$, the variance $\sigma^2_{X_k}$ of the power associated with the different frequencies of the decomposition:

$$\sigma^2_{X_k} = \frac{\sum_{j=1}^{\ell}(P[j,k] - \mu_{X_k})^2}{\ell} \qquad\qquad \mu_{X_k} = \frac{\sum_{j=1}^{\ell} P[j,k]}{\ell}$$

At a second k, a value of variance $\sigma^2_{X_k} = 0$ might indicate: (1) That in none of the levels of the scalogram there is any amount of power. This means that

instant k is not interesting for us since there is no signal. (2) That in all the
levels there is the same amount of power. This corresponds just to *white noise*,
that, again, is not interesting for us, since it is memory-less and it is completely
non-correlated in time. At a second k a value of variance $\sigma^2_{X_k} > 0$ indicates
that in such an instant there is some deviation with respect to the quiet state.
Hence, we consider the time series of the $\sigma^2_{X_k}$ from $start(w_{cp,\rho})$ to $end(w_{cp,\rho})$
and look for intervals of time $[k_s, k_e]$ such that for all k with $k_s \leq k \leq k_e$ we
have $\sigma^2_{X_k} > 0$. We say that such an interval is a *sequence* if the time elapsed
between k_e and k_s is at least one week. We consider a week a span sufficiently
large to solve temporary network outages.

An Efficiency-Accuracy Trade-Off. As described above, analysing a time
series with k updates with maximum frequency M would require to compute
the DWT on a signal with $2kM$ pulses. Since we analyse time series lasting one
year $k = |end(u_{cp,\rho}) - start(u_{cp,\rho})| = 31\,536\,000$. Also, following a study of the
updates captured by the CPs, we estimate that the typical value for M is around
10. Hence, in order to analyse each time series we have to process a signal with
about 600 million pulses. If we consider that we have to analyse a total amount
CP-prefix pairs that is given by the multiplication of the $\sim$800 000 announced
prefixes by 172 CPs (see Sect. 4) and that for each pair we have to perform a
DWT of a signal with 600 million pulses, we have that this could be unfeasible.
Hence, we use a slightly different approach. Namely, we apply a low pass filter
on each $w_{cp,\rho}$ before performing the DWT. The filter is set to a *cutoff frequency*
(maximum cut frequency) of 1 Hz. Also, before computing the DWT we perform
a downsampling of the series of a $\frac{1}{M}$ factor.
    This is equivalent to redefine $u_{cp,\rho}(n)$ as follows:

$$u_{cp,\rho}(n) = \begin{cases} 0 & \text{if } |U_{cp,\rho}(n)| = 0, \\ 1 & \text{if } |U_{cp,\rho}(n)| > 0, \end{cases}$$

adding a zero after each sample. The effects of applying the low pass filter and
the downsampling before performing the DWT are to set $M = 1$ and to have
an uncertainty in the order of seconds in detecting the start and the end of a
sequence. We see later how a larger uncertainty is due to the DWT itself.
    As an example, the upper part of Fig. 1 shows a time series $u_{cp,\rho}$ with $M = 1$
and the lower part shows the corresponding scalogram with 5 frequency bandwidth levels. Warmer colors correspond to larger percentages of energy.
    We do also another choice. We compute the DWT with $1 \leq j \leq 15$. Setting
to 15 the lowest bandwidth level of the DWT allows us to detect sequences whose
lowest frequency is at the smallest edge of the interval $\Delta f_{15} = \left[\frac{M}{32\,768}, \frac{M}{16\,384}\right)$.
Since $M = 1$, we have that our method is able to spot frequencies ranging from
one update per second to one update per 9 h. This is a reasonable choice for
detecting sequences that last at least one week.

Uncertainty in Determining Start and End Times of Sequences. A side-
effect of the joint time-frequency analysis of the DWT is that it is not possible
to define a mother wavelet function ψ that has both the following features: it has

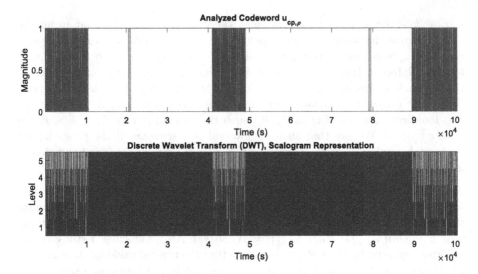

Fig. 1. An example of $u_{cp,\rho}$ and its scalogram representation. In this case $M = 1$ and we have 5 bandwith levels. The colors of the scalogram represent the percentage of energy in each second for each frequency bandwidth (wavelet coefficient).

energy that is highly localized in time, and it has a Fourier transform $\widehat{\psi}$ having energy concentrated in a small frequency interval. In fact, time and frequency energy concentrations are ruled by the Heisenberg uncertainty principle [28] stating that if the resolution of ψ is sharp in time, then the energy of $\widehat{\psi}$ must be spread over a relatively large domain and vice versa. More formally, the uncertainty principle theorem proves the following: $\sigma_t^2 \cdot \sigma_\omega^2 \geq \frac{1}{4}$.

This relationship can be represented in a time-frequency plane (t, ω) as the area of a rectangle (called *Heisenberg box*) with size $\sigma_t^2 \times \sigma_\omega^2$, where σ_t^2 and σ_ω^2 are the variances of ψ and $\widehat{\psi}$, respectively. This rectangle has a minimum surface that limits the joint time-frequency resolution: the larger σ_t, the more uncertainty there is concerning the time localization; and the larger σ_ω, the more uncertainty there is concerning its frequency distribution. At the equality, one of the two measures is exactly inversely proportional to the other one. However, this can be achieved only when the mother wavelet function ψ is chosen in the *Gaussian kernel* functions set. Since we are not using this family of functions, we are not able to match this limit case, so the uncertainty given by the Haar basis cannot be exactly defined. In particular, the σ_ω^2 can be evaluated for each level of the DWT, in order to know, for each frequency bandwidth Δf_j, the related time localization uncertainty. The highest is the frequency resolution expected, the lower is the time localization obtained. Hence, since in our context the maximum frequency bandwidth resolution σ_ω^2 is $\frac{1}{2^j}$, computed for $j = 15$, the related time uncertainty is $\sigma_t^2 > 8\,192$ s, that is $\sim$136 min.

4   One Year of BGP Sequences

We exploited the techniques of Sect. 3 to process the updates collected in the entire Year 2019 by RIPE RIS' RRC00 from all its 172 CPs (~1.2 TB of data). We choose RRC00 because it is both the largest in number of updates and the only one that has its CPs spread around the world in multihop peerings (see Appendix B for a list with locations). Notice that the number of RRC00 CPs reported in [5] is different from 172, for two reasons: (1) the set of the CPs changes over time and 172 is the number of CPs that were working in 2019 (not necessarily for the entire year); and (2) five of the CPs changed their AS number in 2019. Hence, the number of unique IPs of the considered CPs is 167.

We isolate 434 790 sequences containing more than 8 billion updates (i.e., 7 946 086 559 announcements and 368 546 514 withdrawals), which are a considerable 28.36% of all the updates collected by the RRC00 CPs in 2019.

Visualization. We present the extracted sequences in the Web site [7], publicly released to the research community.

First, for each sequence we show: (1) The involved prefix and the CP (IP, AS pair) that observed the sequence. (2) The start- and end-time. (3) The number of announcements and withdrawals. (4) The ASes that originated the prefix during the sequence. (5) The number of observed distinct AS-paths during the sequence. (6) The length of the longest common AS-path suffix, that gives a hint on how distant from the origin AS is the event that caused the sequence. (7) The number of occurrences of the most frequent announcement and its frequency, that gives an idea of the frequency of the event that originated the sequence. (8) A flag that says if the prefix corresponds to a known beacon. *Beacons* are BGP speakers that periodically announce and withdraw prefixes (widely used in experiments). The RIS beacons [2] and the RFD beacons [20] are well-known examples. (9) A flag that says if one or more updates have a value in the aggregator field (e.g., to check if all the announcements were sent from the same router of the origin AS). (10) Links to external resources to get more information on the sequence and its components (e.g., AsRank [1] and RIPEstat [4]).

Second, for each sequence, we display a chart that we call *sequence chart*, where the x-axis represents the time, the y-axis the number of updates over time, and vertical red lines are the start- and the end-time identified for the sequence. The same chart can show other sequences that we spot for the same CP-prefix pair, with gray lines. A sequence chart allows to easily understand if the sequence has been correctly identified.

Third, for each sequence, we visualize the *AS tree*, an alluvial diagram [32] showing the AS-paths involved in the sequence. The AS tree highlights the common suffix of the AS-paths. Also, each path has a thickness that is proportional to the number of updates containing that path.

Fourth, for each CP *cp* we show a chart, called *segment chart*, whose x-axis represents the time and each sequence detected from *cp* corresponds to a horizontal segment whose initial and final x-coordinates are its start- and end-times. The segments of sequences involving the same prefix have the same

y-coordinate. Segment charts highlight sequences that start and end at the same time, and that could be originated by the same event. Also, they allow to spot reboots (white vertical lines) and outages (white vertical strips) of the CPs.

Finally, we provide the *AB-BA-chart*, which shows the sequences containing updates with special types of AS-paths. Namely, in several papers (e.g., [14,22]) it has been observed that if a sequence of updates contains both AS-paths of the form $xAyBz$ and AS-paths of the form $uBvAw$ (where A and B are ASes and x, y, z, u, v, and w are, possibly empty, AS-paths), then that sequence might be caused by a so called *dispute wheel*. We call such sequences *AB-BA-sequences*. As an example, consider sequence with ID 5f070547a276df766c139bb3 reported in the Web site [7]. It contains the alternation of two AS-paths. One is 3333, 12859, *2914*, *1299*, 7473, 4761, 17451, 17451, 58495, 58495, 58495, 138068, 38527 and the other is 3333, 1273, *1299*, *2914*, 58463, 17451, 17451, 58495, 58495, 58495, 138068, 38527. In this case A is 2914 and B is 1299. Since finding dispute wheels in the wild is well-known to be a difficult task, we offer the community a method for visualizing the AB-BA-sequences with a temporal diagram which shows with a certain symbol the updates with $xAyBz$ AS-paths and with another symbol the updates with $uBvAw$ AS-paths.

Validation. We have given both a definition of long-lasting sequences and a method to find them (Sect. 3). Then, we applied such method on the 2019 BGP updates. However, in order to verify if our definition and method characterize what we expect from a long-lasting sequence, we manually inspect a random subset of the sequences. To do that we assign an ID to each sequence and randomize a sample of 280 IDs ($\sim$0.6‰ of the sequences). For the randomization we use the MongoDB function called $sample [3]. For each sampled sequence found by the method, having start time k_s and end time k_e, we perform the following checks, also exploiting the possibility of the sequence charts to be zoomed up to 5 min updates resolution: (1) Is the sequence correctly detected? Else, is the sequence a fragment of a longer sequence that has been incorrectly split into sub-sequences by the algorithm? If yes, how many fragments? If yes, what is the frequency of the updates between the fragments? (2) Does the prefix of the sequence correspond to a beacon? (3) If the sequence is correctly detected, are k_s and k_e the times of the first and of the last update of the sequence (with a tolerance of 136 min; see discussion in Sect. 3), respectively? If not, what is the absolute value of the time-distance between the actual starting (resp., ending) time of the sequence and k_s (resp., k_e)?

The sampled sequences and the results of the check performed on them are detailed in the Web site, what follows is a summary of the results: 91.7% of the sequences are correctly detected while 5.7% of them are fragments of a longer sequence that, on average, is split into 4.7 fragments. The remaining 2.6% of the sequences are just a portion of a partially detected sequence. None of the checked sequence is classified as a false-positive. In 78.9% of the correctly detected sequences, k_s is within the 136 min with respect to the correct start time; in the remaining cases it is on the average 189 min far from the correct start time. In 84% of the correctly detected sequences, k_e is within the 136 min with respect to the correct end time; in the other cases it is on the average 204 min far from the correct end time. Also, 31.2% of the fragmented sequences correspond to beacons. Detecting sequences originated by such beacons is a challenge for our technique. In fact all the RIPE RIS beacons have period of 4 h and a duty cycle of 50%, while the RFD beacons have a period of 4 h and a more complex behaviour within the period. Hence, beacons have a frequency that is in the lowest bandwidth levels of our DWT decomposition (Sect. 3). The validation indicates that our method does not produce false positives. Instead, we do not have an estimation of the total amount of false negatives. Our goal is the discovery of a phenomenon, a possible underestimation induced by false negatives does not affect our conclusions. In order to identify false negatives we would have to manually analyse terabytes of data, which would not be feasible. However, such analysis can be done in a known subset of unstable prefixes, the beacons. We are able to capture sequences for 60 of the 67 available beacons (39 RIS and 28 RFD). On average we find 118 sequences per beacon. We manually inspect the data for the undetected 7 beacons: 2 (RIS) were not active, 2 (RIS) were not visible from RRC00, 1 (RIS) was visible from only one RRC00 CP from Nov. 16 to Dec. and from 5 CPs from Dec. 20 to Dec. 30, and 2 (RFD) were active only from mid Sept. We consider the last three as false negatives.

Analysis. The analysis of the sequences shows what follows.

(i) (a) 59.86% of the sequences involve an IPv4 prefix, while 40.14% involve an IPv6 prefix. (b) Most of the sequences with an IPv4 prefix (55.3%) involve a /24 while most of the sequences with an IPv6 prefix (45.0%) involve a /48. Also, IPv4 /16 appear in 1.2% of all the sequences. (c) Fig. 2a shows how the sequences are distributed among such prefixes. We have that 90% of the 222 285 prefixes involved in sequences appear in at most 3 of them. Since our observation points are 172, the oscillation of a prefix is very often a phenomenon whose visibility is quite local. (d) Fig. 2b is a CDF showing the fraction of the prefixes announced by ASes that is involved in at least one sequence. For example, 64.7% of the ASes that announced at least one prefix in the Internet during year 2019 have no prefixes in any sequence, while, 85% of the ASes have less than 40% of the announced prefixes in a sequence.

(ii) (a) A fair amount of sequences – in the $(200; 2\,000)$ range – has been found in most CPs (see Fig. 2c), independently from their location. Two CPs (2a02:38::2 in AS 6881 and 194.50.19.4 in AS 202365) are outliers since they observed a large bulk of sequences. (b) On the other hand, the number of updates involved in the sequences (see Fig. 2c) is distributed evenly with most CPs having a number of updates in their sequences in the $(1M; 100M)$ range.

(iii) Fig. 2d shows the distribution of the duration of the sequences. We have that 47% of them last at most two weeks, and that 81% last less than 85 days. Also, 170 last the whole year. Notice the steps visible between 7 and 8 days and between 87 and 95 days. The first is due to ~100 000 sequences of about 8 days starting at mid March. All these sequences are visible from the above mentioned CP 194.50.19.4 of AS 202365 as it is apparent from the segment chart of this CP. The second step is due to ~65 000 sequences

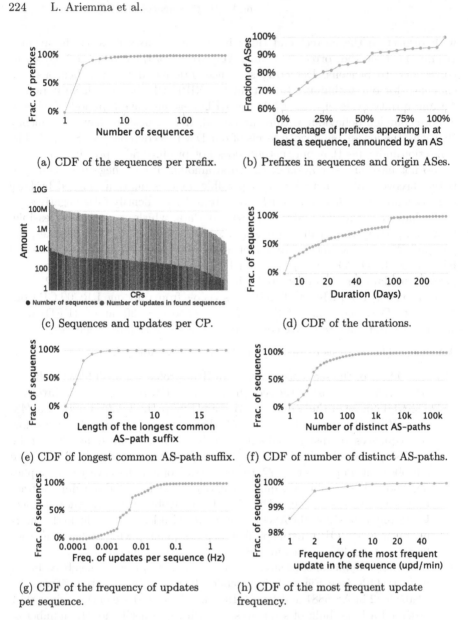

(a) CDF of the sequences per prefix.

(b) Prefixes in sequences and origin ASes.

(c) Sequences and updates per CP.

(d) CDF of the durations.

(e) CDF of longest common AS-path suffix.

(f) CDF of number of distinct AS-paths.

(g) CDF of the frequency of updates per sequence.

(h) CDF of the most frequent update frequency.

Fig. 2. Analysis of the sequences.

of about 90 days starting after the beginning of Oct. and ending at the end of the Year (when our data set finishes). All these sequences are visible from the above mentioned CP 2a02:38::2 of AS 6881 as it is apparent from the segment chart of this CP.

(iv) (a) The announcements involved in sequences were originated by 25 494 distinct ASes. (b) Additionally, in Fig. 2e we report the longest common

AS-path the identified instabilities have in common. We can see that 93% of the sequences involved in instabilities have less than 3 AS-hops in common, and that 40% have at least 1 AS-hop in common. The AS-paths do not include prepending. This may suggest that in several cases the events originating the sequences are far from the origin AS of the prefix. See, e.g., Sect. 4 in [12]. (c) In Fig. 2f we show the CDF of the number of the distinct AS-paths encountered in each sequence. We have that 80% of the sequences have less than 16 distinct AS-paths. On the other hand, there are sequences having an extremely high number of AS-paths.

(v) (a) We compute for each sequence the average frequency of the updates. The distribution of such frequencies is in Fig. 2g. We have that 18% of the sequences have an average frequency of 0.002 Hz, while 3.5% have more than 0.03 Hz. Notice the two sharp increases at around 0.02 Hz and at around 0.045 Hz. They are due to the two mentioned bulks of sequences. In each of these two large sets of updates, the sequences have almost the same average frequency. (b) We compute, for each sequence (Fig. 2h), the frequency of the announcement that appears more often. This may give a hint on the frequency of the event that caused the sequence. In fact, if the routing has one stable state periodically interleaved with some type of instability we may have that the most frequent announcement is the one corresponding to the stable state.

(vi) We find that only a few sequences (7 125, around 1.64%) correspond to beacons. Such sequences contain only 0.17% of the total sequences' updates.

(vii) We also count the sequences with special features. First, we find 31 602 AB-BA-sequences that may constitute an interesting data set for research on dispute wheels. Second, we find 44 302 sequences that contain at least one announcement where the BGP path aggregator attribute is populated, and 23 739 sequences that contain at least two announcement with different values for the aggregator attribute. This can be interesting from several points of view: (a) the announcements performed by beacons have such an attribute; and (b) the availability of different values for such attributes, for non beacons, might be used to distinguish updates exiting from different routers of the origin AS.

5   Conclusions

We release to the scientific community [7] a large set of long lasting sequences of BGP updates visible from the observation points of RIPE RIS during 2019. Such sequences can be individually analysed with the several visualization tools we developed. The sequences have been discovered with a Discrete Wavelet Transform based method that we devised and empirically validated.

Reproducibility. The data used in this study is publicly available at [6]. An indexed collection of sequences for the entire Year 2019 is available at [7]. The source code needed to reproduce the entire analysis is available on GitLab [37].

Appendices

A   The Discrete Wavelet Transform

The DWT series decomposition of the signal $w_{cp,\rho}(n)$ is defined as follows:

$$w_{cp,\rho}(n) = \sum_{k=0}^{K} c_{\ell,k}\phi_{\ell,k}(n) + \sum_{j=1}^{\ell}\sum_{k=0}^{K} d_{j,k}\psi_{j,k}(n)$$

Where $K+1$ is the number of samples of the signal. For the sake of simplicity we assume that $K = 2^{\ell} - 1$. Functions ϕ and ψ are the father and mother functions respectively. The j and k indexes represent the *scaling* and *translation* factors respectively. Each (j, k) pair gives a wavelet coefficient, which can also be seen as the cross-correlation at lag k between the signal function to be decomposed and the ψ wavelet basis function, described below, dilated by a scaling factor of 2^j. The coefficients $c_{\ell,k}$ are called *approximation coefficients* because derived by a low pass filtering, while the coefficients $d_{j,k}$ are called *detail coefficients* because derived by an high pass filtering. Function $\psi_{j,k}$ is defined as: $\psi_{j,k}(n) = 2^{-j/2}\,\psi(2^{-j}n - k)$, where ψ is the *mother wavelet* (also known as generic wavelet basis function) and can be chosen in a set of mother wavelet functions. For the duality principle the function ϕ is called *father wavelet*, or scaling function, because varying the j scaling index it gives a different resolution of the signal representation, creating a multi-resolution view of it. In the decomposition series formula above, $\phi_{\ell,k}$ represents $\phi_{j,k}$ computed in $j = \ell$, that describes the last resolution level of the signal decomposition.

Once the signal has been represented in the DWT domain, we can compute its *scalogram* representation, that describes the percentage of energy for each wavelet coefficient. The scalogram can be arranged in a matrix form, denoted by P, with ℓ rows and $K+1$ columns. Each element of P is denoted by $P[j, k]$.

Value $P[j, k]$ is the normalized power of coefficient $d_{j,k}$ that, to further generalize the DWT, we will briefly represent with the *Continuous Wavelet Transform* formalism

$$P[j, k] = \frac{1}{2\pi \cdot C \cdot 2^{2j}}|d_{j,k}|^2 \quad \text{where} \quad C = \int_{-\pi}^{\pi} \frac{|\widehat{\psi}(\omega)|^2}{|\omega|}d\omega$$

is a normalization constant regarding the *admissibility condition* of a mother wavelet ψ, with $\widehat{\psi}(\omega)$ denoting the *Fourier Transform* of $\psi(n)$.

Formally, the normalization is chosen so that $\sum_j \sum_k P[j, k] = 1$. This means that $P[j, k]$ represents the percentage of the signal power at time k in the range of frequencies Δf_j defined below. According to the Nyquist-Shannon rule:

$$\Delta f_j = \left[\frac{f_s/2}{2^j}, \frac{f_s/2}{2^{j-1}}\right)$$

where f_s is the sampling frequency.

B   The Collector Peers and their Locations

The locations of CPs are reported in Table 1.

Table 1. List of collector peers. Locations are retrieved from [16].

AS	Peer IP	Location	AS	Peer IP	Location
47422	45.12.70.254	Zürich, CH	8758	212.25.27.44	Zürich, CH
202365	2a07:59c6:e89a::100	DE	49752	2a09:11c0:f1:bbf8::2	
132825	43.251.115.197		210025	192.187.100.218	St. Louis, US
34800	194.50.99.254	Zürich, CH	37721	165.16.221.66	London, GB
49432	2a0b:5cc0:0:ffff::254	Feldkirch, AT	49134	2602:fed2:fc0:5e::1	Wichita, US
60371	94.177.122.243	Zürich, CH	395152	192.102.254.1	Vancouver, CA
205593	2a07:1c44:3100::1	AT	49752	141.98.136.105	Frankfurt, DE
205148	2a0d:f407:101:dead::1		202313	2a06:e881:121::4	Oxford, GB
49673	2a02:47a0:a::1	Novosibirsk, RU	34549	80.77.16.114	Frankfurt, DE
17639	2405:3200:0:23::		202365	44.164.66.20	Dronten, NL
206313	185.197.132.7	Frankfurt, DE	202365	2a00:1ca8:2a::e0	Dronten, NL
15562	165.254.255.2	Amsterdam, NL	396503	2602:fed2:fc0:5e::1	Wichita, US
202365	2a0a:54c0:0:32::2	London, GB	34872	2a0c:b640:ffff:194:28:98:32:37	BE
26073	23.139.160.84	Fremont, US	204092	89.234.186.6	Rennes, FR
20205	2001:4950::5		34549	2a01:360:0:6::2	DE
13830	192.34.100.0		49420	91.212.242.251	Gdańsk, PL
37989	2405:fc00::6	SG	35708	94.177.122.231	Wettingen, CH
852	2001:56a:8002:12::3		200334	2001:19f0:5001:53f:5400:1ff:fe9c:264e	
22652	2607:fad8::1:9	Barrie, CA	64050	182.54.128.2	Tokyo, JP
34681	193.228.123.1		174	130.117.255.1	Amsterdam, NL
35619	2a09:4c0:1:8b1c::6363		209152	2a0f:a300:bb:ff::ed6e	
14907	208.80.153.193	Carrollton, US	32097	2001:4858:251:b00b::3	US
34681	2a0e:46c7:1305::1		39351	193.138.216.164	Malmö, SE
60501	2a00:ae20:1:1::101		20514	217.151.205.144	Stockholm, SE
1836	2a01:2a8::3	Zürich, CH	35619	139.28.99.99	Zürich, CH
207968	2a0e:46c6::2		43607	94.177.122.244	Zürich, CH
3333	193.0.0.56	Amsterdam, NL	210234	2a0c:b641:60::1	
7018	12.0.1.63	US	57381	193.150.22.1	Oslo, NO
29608	79.143.241.12	Paris, FR	3257	213.200.87.254	Darmstadt, DE
49673	94.247.111.254	Kemerovo, RU	34854	2a01:4f8:c010:3ad0::	
38001	2406:f400:8:34::1	Singapore, SG	34927	2a0c:9a40:1030::1	
48147	185.142.156.156		205148	93.159.187.1	
48292	2001:19f0:5001:1cb5:5400:1ff:fed6:7f3f	US	396503	23.129.32.61	San Jose, US
139589	185.215.214.30	Nürnberg, DE	37989	203.123.48.6	SG
852	154.11.12.212		204092	2a00:5884::6	Rennes, FR
64271	161.129.32.1		202365	5.255.90.109	Dronten, NL
11708	72.22.223.9	Kansas City, US	55720	45.116.179.212	
263702	168.195.130.2		58057	2a09:4c0:0:8b1c::63fe	Zürich (Kreis 3), CH
58057	139.28.99.254	Zürich (Kreis 3), CH	59919	2a01:9ac0:0:ffff::	
29504	185.193.84.191	Prague, CZ	57199	2a0b:cbc0:2::1	
209152	45.154.32.1	Offenbach, DE	202365	2a03:3f40:32::365	NL
206499	185.215.214.1	Frankfurt, DE	20205	64.246.96.5	
13830	2001:506:30::		32097	69.30.209.253	Kansas City, US
58057	45.12.69.254	Zürich, CH	38001	202.150.221.37	Singapore, SG
35619	139.28.99.0	Zürich, CH	60474	94.177.122.241	Zürich, CH
131477	2a09:4bc7:d021::		204526	51.158.149.208	Stuttgart, DE
34800	2a0c:3b82:0:c232::63fe		202365	185.198.188.93	London, GB
205523	2a0c:b640:ffff:194:28:98:32:37	BE	200334	2001:19f0:5001:1cb5:5400:1ff:fed6:7f3f	US
50304	2a02:20c8:1f:1::4	NO	59919	5.178.95.254	Milan, IT
35619	2a09:4c0:1:8b1c::6300		49432	185.210.224.254	Feldkirch, AT
34854	116.203.251.34	Nürnberg, DE	57381	2001:67c:24e4:1::1	Hradec Králové, CZ
1403	198.58.198.254	Montréal, CA	44794	2a09:be40:c0de::1	Frankfurt, DE
60501	185.30.64.101		61292	2a02:ed03:ffff::1	
60474	2a0c:3b80:4348:5eb1::7afb	Zürich, CH	50300	176.12.110.8	London, GB
396503	23.129.32.65	Fremont, US	131477	103.102.5.1	
4608	203.119.104.1	Brisbane, AU	210025	2a09:b280:ffbf::cafe	
49420	2001:67c:24c::c		49134	23.129.32.61	San Jose, US
207968	141.98.136.107	Frankfurt, DE	58057	139.28.99.251	Zürich, CH
48292	194.50.19.65	Frankfurt, DE	29608	2a01:678::2	FR
209263	2.58.56.62	Neuss, DE	48821	185.138.53.0	Düsseldorf, DE
44794	2.56.8.1	Offenbach, DE	58057	2a09:4c0:0:8b1c::63fb	Zürich, CH
396503	2602:fed2:fc0::1	CA	206479	185.120.22.16	Frankfurt, DE
15562	2001:728:1808::2	GB	57264	2a0d:2640:1:1::1	
202409	185.215.214.6	Frankfurt, DE	50304	178.255.145.243	Oslo, NO
206499	2a06:1287:3308:cafe::1	AT	209263	2001:678:b0c:bb:49:211:1:1	
205523	194.28.98.37	Dronten, NL	29504	2a0a:3640:0:d::191	CZ
7018	2001:1890:111d:1::63	Boca Raton, US	210234	185.225.205.1	
57199	80.67.167.1	Saint-Denis, FR	17639	202.69.160.152	
8758	2001:8e0:0:ffff::9	Zürich, CH	206313	2a06:e881:2000:7::1	
48821	2a07:a40::	DE	45896	2001:df0:2e8:1000::1	Los Angeles, US
395766	98.159.46.1	Montréal, CA	43607	2a0c:3b80:4348:5eb1::7af4	
61292	185.152.34.255	Singapore, SG	61218	185.238.190.254	Frankfurt, DE
22652	45.61.0.85	Montréal, CA	57821	2001:67c:26f4::1	Luhansk, UA
3549	208.51.134.248		57381	193.150.22.240	Oslo, NO
205593	185.215.214.10	Frankfurt, DE	39351	2a03:1b20:1:ff01::5	Malmö, SE
50300	2a00:1c10:10::8	GB	14907	2620:0:860:ffff::2	
200334	95.179.155.193	Frankfurt, DE	174	2001:978:4::b	Amsterdam, NL
60474	2a0c:3b80:4348:5eb1::7af1		204072	2a02:38::2	Prague, CZ
61218	2a0c:3b80:4c49:b9ee::befe		263702	2803:3b80:1ee3:1000::1	Santiago, CL
55720	103.212.68.10		328474	102.67.56.1	
1836	146.228.1.3	Zürich, CH	328474	2c0f:ed60::1	
47422	2a0c:3b81:2d0c:46fe::		139589	2a07:59c6:ee00:9589::1	
57821	193.160.39.1	Frankfurt, DE	34872	194.28.98.37	Dronten, NL
26073	2602:fe19:1:f1cd:a1bf:0:84:1		6881	195.47.235.100	Liberí, CZ
57381	2001:67c:24e4:240::1	Oslo, NO	57264	194.156.180.1	Corsico, IT
202409	2a07:59c6:ee00:cafe::c0de	Frankfurt, DE	202365	194.50.19.4	Frankfurt, DE

References

1. CAIDA AS Rank. http://as-rank.caida.org/
2. Current RIS Routing Beacons - RIPE. https://www.ripe.net/analyse/internet-measurements/routing-information-service-ris/current-ris-routing-beacons
3. MongoDB Manual. https://docs.mongodb.com/
4. RIPEstat. https://stat.ripe.net
5. RIS RRC00 Collector Peers. https://www.ris.ripe.net/peerlist/rrc00.shtml
6. Routing Information Service - RIPE. https://www.ripe.net/analyse/internet-measurements/routing-information-service-ris/routing-information-service-ris
7. BGPie (2020). https://bgpie.net
8. Abry, P., Baraniuk, R., Flandrin, P., Riedi, R., Veitch, D.: Wavelet and multiscale analysis of network traffic. IEEE Signal Process. Mag. **19**(3), 28–46 (2002)
9. Abry, P., Flandrin, P., Taqqu, M.S., Veitch, D., et al.: Self-similarity and long-range dependence through the wavelet lens. In: Theory and Applications of Long-range Dependence, pp. 527–556 (2003)
10. Al-Musawi, B., Branch, P., Armitage, G.: Recurrence behaviour of BGP traffic. In: 2017 27th International Telecommunication Networks and Applications Conference (ITNAC), pp. 1–7 (2017)
11. Burrus, C.S., Gopinath, R.A., Guo, H.: Chapter 8: generalizations of the basic multiresolution wavelet systems. In: Introduction to Wavelets and Wavelet Transforms: A Primer, pp. 154–157. Prentice Hall, Upper Saddle River (1998)
12. Caesar, M., Subramanian, L., Katz, R.H.: Towards localizing root causes of BGP dynamics. Technical report UCB/CSD-03-1292, EECS Department, University of California, Berkeley (2003)
13. Cheng, M., Li, Q., Lv, J., Liu, W., Wang, J.: Multi-scale LSTM model for BGP anomaly classification. IEEE Trans. Serv. Comput. 1 (2018)
14. Cittadini, L., Di Battista, G., Rimondini, M., Vissicchio, S.: wheel + ring = reel: the impact of route filtering on the stability of policy routing. In: 2009 17th IEEE International Conference on Network Protocols, pp. 274–283 (2009)
15. Deshpande, S., Thottan, M., Ho, T.K., Sikdar, B.: An online mechanism for BGP instability detection and analysis. IEEE Trans. Comput. **58**(11), 1470–1484 (2009)
16. Du, B., Candela, M., Huffaker, B., Snoeren, A.C., claffy, k.: RIPE IPmap active geolocation: mechanism and performance evaluation. ACM SIGCOMM Comput. Commun. Rev. **50**(2), 3–10 (2020)
17. Eckmann, J.P., Kamphorst, S.O., Ruelle, D.: Recurrence plots of dynamical systems. Europhys. Lett. (EPL) **4**(9), 973–977 (1987)
18. Elmokashfi, A., Kvalbein, A., Dovrolis, C.: BGP churn evolution: a perspective from the core. IEEE/ACM Trans. Netw. **20**(2), 571–584 (2012)
19. Fukuda, K., Hirotsu, T., Akashi, O., Sugawara, T.: Time and space correlation in BGP messages. In: Kim, C. (ed.) ICOIN 2005. LNCS, vol. 3391, pp. 215–222. Springer, Heidelberg (2005). https://doi.org/10.1007/978-3-540-30582-8_23
20. Gray, C., et al.: BGP beacons, network tomography, and Bayesian computation to locate route flap damping. In: Proceedings of ACM Internet Measurement Conference. ACM, New York (2020)
21. Griffin, T.G., Premore, B.J.: An experimental analysis of BGP convergence time. In: Proceedings International Conference on Network Protocols, ICNP 2001, pp. 53–61 (2001)
22. Griffin, T.G., Shepherd, F.B., Wilfong, G.: The stable paths problem and interdomain routing. IEEE/ACM Trans. Netw. **10**(2), 232–243 (2002)

23. Kitabatake, T., Fontugne, R., Esaki, H.: BLT: a taxonomy and classification tool for mining BGP update messages. In: IEEE Conference on Computer Communications Workshops, pp. 409–414 (2018)
24. Kitsak, M., Elmokashfi, A., Havlin, S., Krioukov, D.V.: Long-range correlations and memory in the dynamics of internet interdomain routing. Plos One **10**, e0141481 (2015)
25. Labovitz, C., Malan, G.R., Jahanian, F.: Internet routing instability. In: Proceedings of the ACM SIGCOMM 1997 Conference on Applications, Technologies, Architectures, and Protocols for Computer Communication, SIGCOMM 1997, pp. 115–126. Association for Computing Machinery, New York (1997)
26. Li, J., Guidero, M., Wu, Z., Purpus, E., Ehrenkranz, T.: BGP routing dynamics revisited. SIGCOMM Comput. Commun. Rev. **37**(2), 5–16 (2007)
27. Mai, J., Yuan, L., Chuah, C.: Detecting BGP anomalies with wavelet. In: IEEE Network Operations and Management Symposium, pp. 465–472 (2008)
28. Mallat, S.: Chapter 2 - the Fourier kingdom. In: Mallat, S. (ed.) A Wavelet Tour of Signal Processing, 3rd edn., pp. 43–45. Academic Press, Boston (2009)
29. Oliveira, R.V., Izhak-Ratzin, R., Zhang, B., Zhang, L.: Measurement of highly active prefixes in BGP. In: GLOBECOM 2005. IEEE Global Telecommunications Conference, 2005, vol. 2, 5 pp. (2005)
30. Prakash, B.A., Valler, N., Andersen, D., Faloutsos, M., Faloutsos, C.: BGP-lens: patterns and anomalies in Internet routing updates. In: Proceedings of the 15th ACM SIGKDD International Conference on Knowledge Discovery and Data Mining, pp. 1315–1324 (2009)
31. Rekhter, Y., Li, T., Hares, S.: A Border Gateway Protocol 4 (BGP-4). RFC 4271, RFC Editor (2006)
32. Rosvall, M., Bergstrom, C.T.: Mapping change in large networks. PLoS ONE **5**(1), e8694 (2010)
33. Sapegin, A., Uhlig, S.: On the extent of correlation in BGP updates in the Internet and what it tells us about locality of BGP routing events. Comput. Commun. **36**(15), 1592–1605 (2013)
34. Shannon, C.E.: A mathematical theory of communication. Bell Syst. Tech. J. **27**(4), 623–656 (1948)
35. Smith, S.W.: The Scientist and Engineer's Guide to Digital Signal Processing, chap. 13: Continuous Signal Processing, 2nd edn., pp. 255–260. California Technical Publishing (1999)
36. University of Oregon: Route views (1997). http://www.routeviews.org/routeviews/
37. University of Roma Tre: BGPie source code repository (2020). https://gitlab.com/uniroma3/compunet/networks/bgpie
38. Wu, X., Yin, X., Wang, Z., Tang, M.: A three-step dynamic threshold method to cluster BGP updates into routing events. In: 2009 International Symposium on Autonomous Decentralized Systems, pp. 1–6 (2009)
39. Xu, K., Chandrashekar, J., Zhang, Z.L.: Principal component analysis of BGP update streams. J. Commun. Netw. **12**(2), 191–197 (2010). Conference Name: Journal of Communications and Networks

Inferring Cloud Interconnections: Validation, Geolocation, and Routing Behavior

Alexander Marder[1]($\boxtimes$), K. C. Claffy[1], and Alex C. Snoeren[2]

[1] CAIDA, UC San Diego, San Diego, USA
amarder@caida.org
[2] UC San Diego, San Diego, USA

Abstract. Public clouds fundamentally changed the Internet landscape, centralizing traffic generation in a handful of networks. Internet performance, robustness, and public policy analyses struggle to properly reflect this centralization, largely because public collections of BGP and traceroute reveal a small portion of cloud connectivity.

This paper evaluates and improves our ability to infer cloud connectivity, bootstrapping future measurements and analyses that more accurately reflect the cloud-centric Internet. We also provide a technique for identifying the interconnections that clouds use to reach destinations around the world, allowing edge networks and enterprises to understand how clouds reach them via their public WAN. Finally, we present two techniques for geolocating the interconnections between cloud networks at the city level that can inform assessments of their resilience to link failures and help enterprises build multi-cloud applications and services.

1 Introduction

The growing deployment of low-latency and high-throughput applications, the upfront and maintenance costs of computing resources, and constantly evolving security threats make it increasingly complex and costly for organizations to host services and applications themselves. Public cloud providers ease that burden by allowing organizations to build and scale their applications on networks and hardware managed by the cloud provider. At the core of cloud computing are virtual machines (VMs) and containers that run on physical hardware in a data center [47]. Clouds locate these data centers in globally distributed geographic regions [7,8,12]. The three major cloud providers, Amazon AWS, Microsoft Azure, and Google Cloud Platform (GCP), interconnect their regions using global backbones [6,9,52].

Public clouds fundamentally changed the Internet landscape from peer-to-peer to a cloud-centric model. According to a recent estimate [49], the ten highest-paying customers in AWS—all popular video and content generators— combine to spend over $100 million per month, and many enterprises store operations data and host internal applications in public clouds. Existing measurement platforms, with vantage points (VPs) located outside cloud networks, capture

© Springer Nature Switzerland AG 2021
O. Hohlfeld et al. (Eds.): PAM 2021, LNCS 12671, pp. 230–246, 2021.
https://doi.org/10.1007/978-3-030-72582-2_14

only a small fraction of the paths that connect public clouds to end users and enterprises, and the importance of the clouds necessitates that the Internet measurement community considers how to effectively capture this.

The goal of this paper is to evaluate and improve our ability to infer cloud connectivity, in the hope that it bootstraps Internet measurements and analyses that more accurately reflect the cloud-centric Internet. We also build on those inferences, identifying the interconnections that clouds use to reach destinations around the world. Such analysis enables edge networks and enterprises to understand how clouds reach them, and potentially respond to fallout from congestion on a cloud interconnection. Furthermore, we geolocate the interconnections between cloud networks at the city level, providing techniques that can inform assessments of their resilience to link failures and help enterprises build multi-cloud applications and services. We make the following contributions:

1. We validate the state-of-the-art in identifying network interconnections (bdrmapIT) on Azure, identifying path changes as a prominent source of error.
2. We demonstrate that changing the traceroute probing method to reduce the number of simultaneous traceroutes reduces the impact of path changes on the observed topology, and improves the accuracy of bdrmapIT's AS operator inferences for the interconnection addresses in our validation dataset by 8.6%.
3. We use traceroute to identify next-hop ASes for each Internet network from AWS, Azure, and GCP, finding that clouds still rely on tier 1 and tier 2 networks, and that next-hop ASes can be region-dependent.
4. We geolocate all observed AWS-Azure and Azure-GCP interconnections, and 34.4% of the AWS-GCP interconnections, discovering that clouds interconnect on every populated continent, and often interconnect in the same cities.

2   Background and Previous Work

Our work builds on prior work that inferred AS-links from BGP, identified network interconnections in traceroute paths, studied cloud backbone networks with traceroute, and geolocated network infrastructure.

BGP Route Announcements Reveal AS Connectivity. The public BGP route announcement collectors, Routeviews [4] and RIPE RIS [3], collect announcements received from the ASes that peer with the collectors (VP ASes), and researchers infer AS connectivity from adjacent ASes in collected AS paths [16,24]. We could infer cloud neighbors directly from the cloud networks through routes they propagate to public collectors, but cloud networks share few routes with public route collectors. We can also infer cloud connectivity indirectly from announcements that clouds originate into BGP, but VP ASes are unlikely to see cloud neighbors that enter into paid or settlement-free peering with the cloud [19,25,27,32,37,55,58]. Furthermore, VP ASes typically only propagate their chosen best-path for each prefix to collectors, and any VP AS that interconnects with a cloud network will likely select their direct interconnection as the best path to that cloud, and will not propagate alternate AS paths to the public collectors.

Inferring Router Ownership From Traceroute Paths. Substantial prior work attempted to infer AS interconnections from traceroute paths. Mao *et al.* [39,40] aligned traceroutes from VP ASes with BGP route announcements seen by that same AS to better determine address space ownership. Chen *et al.* [18] generalized and expanded Mao's methodology to align AS-level links seen in traceroute with those in BGP AS paths. Later work focused on inferring the AS operators of routers in traceroute paths. Huffaker *et al.* [30] used alias resolution to convert the IP address paths in traceroute to router graphs, and proposed and validated four techniques to map routers to AS operators. Marder *et al.* [44] and Luckie *et al.* [36] independently developed and validated heuristics to extract constraints from traceroute to more accurately infer AS operators. Marder and Luckie later integrated and extended their approaches, creating the current state-of-the-art bdrmapIT, and validated their bdrmapIT technique [43]. Most recently, Luckie *et al.* [38] used the AS operator inferences from Huffaker *et al.*'s technique and bdrmapIT as training data to learn regular expressions for extracting AS operators embedded in hostnames in the form of AS numbers.

Revealing Cloud Connectivity With Traceroute. VPs outside the cloud cannot reveal many of the paths and interconnections that clouds use to reach the Internet. Yeganeh *et al.* [56] conducted traceroutes from AWS to every /24 to reveal interconnected networks, using a new unvalidated approach to infer network interconnections. In subsequent work [57], they compared the quality of service of default interconnections between cloud networks and third-party transit between clouds, switching to bdrmapIT to perform interconnection IP addresses inferences. Arnold *et al.* [15] inferred directly connected networks from traceroute paths by converting traceroute IP addresses to ASes using longest-matching prefix in BGP route announcements and IXP participant IP addresses recorded in PeeringDB [2]. They then augmented the AS-level connectivity graph in CAIDA's AS Relationship dataset [1] with peer relationships between each cloud and the newly inferred neighbors, using the graph to estimate that clouds can avoid their transit providers listed in CAIDA's AS Relationship dataset to reach 76% of the Internet networks. They validated their neighbor inferences with feedback from Azure and GCP, with 11%–15% false neighbor inferences. Assuming nearly perfect accuracy for IXP participant addresses in PeeringDB, these false neighbor inferences almost entirely result from false private interconnection inferences.

We show that the traceroute technique used by prior studies is prone to path change corruptions, and we validate our cloud interconnection inferences (Sect. 4). Rather than use unvalidated AS interconnection inference techniques, we use the previously validated bdrmapIT tool to infer private interconnections between cloud public WANs and their neighbors, and perform additional validation to understand bdrmapIT's accuracy for cloud networks. Finally, while Arnold *et al.* speculated how clouds *could* reach other ASes [15], we report how clouds currently *do* reach other networks.

Geolocating Network Infrastructure. Commercial IP geolocation databases focus nearly exclusively on edge hosts, with poor accuracy for network infrastructure [22,26,48]. Some networks encode geographic information in router inter-face DNS hostnames, but the geographic codes are difficult to automatically extract and interpret, as they use a mix of IATA codes, CLLI codes, and com-mon location abbreviations. Rocketfuel includes the undns tool [51] that uses hand-crafted regular expressions to extract geolocations from hostnames. More general approaches avoid manually constructing regular expressions. DRoP [31] automatically learns rules to extract geolocation codes from hostnames, and HLOC [50] searches hostnames for geolocation codes. Other approaches use RTT to approximate distance between VPs and routers. Gueye *et al.* [28] and RIPE IPMap [45] triangulate RTTs to estimate location, and Katz-Basset *et al.* [33] refined RTT-based estimates using topology constraints. We use a combination of geolocation codes extracted from Azure DNS hostnames and traceroute paths to geolocate the interconnections between cloud providers.

3   Validating bdrmapIT With Azure Hostnames

Our analysis relies on bdrmapIT AS operator inferences to identify cloud inter-connections and neighbors, so we first validate bdrmapIT's inferences on Azure to gain confidence in its efficacy and look for opportunities to improve our techniques. bdrmapIT addresses the difficult problem of inferring the networks that operate each router observed in traceroute, but relies on general assump-tions of router configurations, internal traffic engineering, and network topol-ogy that might not hold in cloud WANs. Furthermore, prior bdrmapIT evalu-ations on transit interconnection inferences might not translate to cloud inter-connection inferences. Initial bdrmapIT evaluations used CAIDA's Ark tracer-outes and ground truth from ISP operators, and later experiments also val-idated bdrmapIT against pseudo ground truth derived from ISP DNS host-names [38,41,42]. Traceroutes from CAIDA's Ark VPs mostly reveal transit interconnections—those between providers and customers—so transit intercon-nections dominate their reported accuracy. Clouds primarily peer with other networks, and we expect that their peering interconnections vastly outnumber their transit interconnections. Importantly, bdrmapIT leverages the industry convention that transit providers supply the IP subnets for interconnection with customers, but no known convention exists for peering interconnections [35]. To date, no study has evaluated bdrmapIT's accuracy using traceroutes that originate in the cloud.

For this initial experiment, we created a VM in every Azure region and used Scamper [34], the traceroute tool used in prior cloud studies [15,56,57], to conduct traceroutes from every VM to each of the 11.5 M /24 s covered by a prefix in a BGP route announcement collected by RouteViews or RIPE RIS over 1–5 August 2020. Our choice of /24 granularity reflects our assumption that clouds are unlikely to receive many prefixes longer than /24. Each traceroute to a /24 targeted a random address to provide comprehensive coverage of Azure's neighboring networks, and we instructed Scamper to use Paris-style traceroute probes to prevent load-balancing from corrupting the traceroute paths.

To identify interconnection addresses between clouds and their neighbors, we used a combination of bdrmapIT AS operator inferences and IXP participant IP addresses listed in PeeringDB [2] and IXPDB [23] to map traceroute path IP addresses to ASes. In the event of a conflict between PeeringDB and IXPDB, a contact at both IXPDB and PeeringDB advised us to use the mapping in IXPDB, since IXP operators update information in IXPDB while IXP members populate information in PeeringDB, potentially causing stale entries. bdrmapIT requires AS address spaces as input, and we supplied prefix origin ASes derived from BGP announcements collected by RouteViews and RIPE RIS. For addresses with no covering prefix in BGP, we relied on the potentially stale longest matching prefix in RIR extended delegations. 0.8% of addresses did not have a covering prefix in BGP or RIR. We used whois [20] and RADb [46] to determine ownership for 53.4% of those addresses; this was the only manual step in this process (Fig. 1).

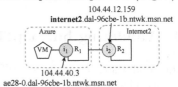

We used Azure DNS hostnames to provide pseudo ground truth for our interconnection inferences, and successfully resolved hostnames for 59.5% of the 5749 Azure IP addresses seen in our initial traceroutes. Azure tags many of its network interconnection address hostnames with the name of the neighboring network, and we used the tags visible in traceroute paths from Azure VMs to identify Azure addresses on routers operated by neighbors; e.g., in a traceroute starting from an Azure VM, the tag in internet2.dal-96cbe-1b.ntwk.msn.net

Fig. 1. In traceroute paths from Azure, the `internet2` tag indicates that `104.44.12.159` belongs to a router operated by Internet2. We use this as validation for bdrmapIT's router operator inferences from Azure traceroutes.

indicates that 104.44.12.159 belongs to an Internet2 router interconnected with Azure. Our evaluation focused on comparing bdrmapIT inferences to the tags extracted from Azure hostnames. We used the regular expression ([^-]*?)\..*\.ntwk\.msn\.net to extract the interconnection tags from Azure hostnames, finding 214 tags corresponding to 419 address hostnames. For each IP address with a hostname containing an interconnection tag, we manually validated that bdrmapIT's AS operator inference aligns with the name of the inferred AS or the organization that owns it. These tags are nearly always network names rather than AS numbers, preventing us from using Luckie, *et al.*'s technique [38] to identify the operating AS automatically.

3.1   Investigating as Operator Inference Errors

Our initial evaluation on Azure interconnections yielded 87.4% AS operator accuracy, with 53 errors. One source of error was that bdrmapIT occasionally filtered out valid neighboring ASes in favor of ASes seen adjacent to Azure in BGP AS paths. bdrmapIT relies heavily on AS connectivity inferred from BGP to constrain the choice of AS operator for a router, but the largely incomplete connectivity constraints led to six false inferences in our validation set. We modified bdrmapIT to remove these constraints only for the major cloud networks, but

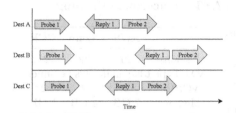

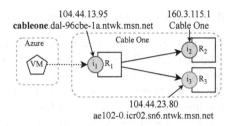

Fig. 2. Scamper increases efficiency by parallelizing traceroute probing across destinations, but a path change can corrupt all active traceroute paths.

Fig. 3. We observed the Azure address `104.44.23.80` after the border router in Cable One, likely indicating traceroute path corruption. This caused bdrmapIT to incorrectly conclude that Azure operates router R_1.

this change can apply to edge networks with largely incomplete neighbor constraints in BGP AS paths, like other cloud and content delivery networks. This change increased the AS operator inference accuracy to 88.8%, correcting all six of the AS operator inferences without introducing additional error.

Using an interface graph constructed from the traceroutes to investigate the remaining errors led us to conclude that path changes during traceroutes likely caused most of the errors. While Paris probes avoid corruptions due to load-balancing along a path, they cannot prevent corruptions due to path changes in router forwarding tables. Scamper probing is especially susceptible to corruptions caused by path changes. Like UNIX traceroute, Scamper waits for the response to the probe with Time to Live (TTL) i before sending the probe with TTL $i+1$, but for efficiency it parallelizes across traceroute destinations (Fig. 2). This concurrency enables rapid path discovery, necessary for temporally coherent snapshots of cloud topologies, but a path change can corrupt any of the traceroutes active at any given time.

To look for evidence of potential path changes, we generated a directed interface graph from the 355.8 M Azure traceroutes, creating directed edges between an address and every address that immediately followed it in a traceroute, but not when one or more unresponsive hops separate the addresses. We found 56 (13.4%) Azure interconnection addresses in our validation dataset followed by at least one Azure address in a traceroute. These interconnection addresses are on routers operated by neighboring networks, so an uncorrupted traceroute path would most likely not contain a subsequent Azure address. Figure 3 shows a potentially corrupted traceroute path, where we observed an Azure IP address following the interconnection with Cable One. Observing Azure addresses after routers in neighboring ASes does not necessarily indicate that path changes corrupted a traceroute, and can result from off-path addresses and load-balancing as well, so we conduct an additional experiment to rule out alternative explanations.

3.2   Fast and Straight Traceroute (FAST) Traceroute Probing

We developed a new traceroute tool, Fast
And Straight Traceroute (FAST), to test
our hypothesis that path changes corrupted
the cloud traceroute paths by mitigating
the impact of path changes on the observed
topology. FAST sends all probes from TTL
1 to 32 to a destination at a fixed packets per second (pps) rate, irrespective of
replies, before moving on to the next traceroute destination, and uses packet capture

	AWS	Azure	GCP
Regions	20	32	21
VM Type	t3a-small	B2s	e2-micro
vCPUs	2	2	2
Memory	2 GB	4 GB	1 GB

Fig. 4. We set up VMs in every cloud
region available to us using similar
VM types in each cloud.

to record probes and replies, allowing it to construct traceroute paths with accurate RTTs. Unlike similar tools such as Yarrp [17], FAST's guaranteed sequential
probing allows it to construct traceroute paths during probing while consuming
few resources on the cloud VMs.

To efficiently reveal traceroute paths, we
determined a probing rate for FAST that
balances topology discovery with probing
speed by conducting traceroutes from a VM
in every region of AWS, Azure, and GCP
(Fig. 4) to one address in 100,000 distinct
prefixes announced into BGP. Our results
(Fig. 5) indicate that probing at 5000 pps
reveals nearly all of the hops found by
probing at slower rates, but probing faster
induced rate-limiting in Azure. At 5000 pps,
FAST can complete probing to every routed
/24 in less than 21 h.

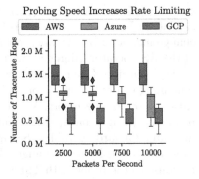

Fig. 5. We observed fewer traceroute hops for Azure probing above
5000 pps. GCP inflates probe TTLs
(Sect. 4.1), causing relatively few
responses for all probing rates.

To isolate the impact of path changes, we
changed only the traceroute tool from Scamper to FAST, but conducted traceroutes from
the same Azure regions to the same destina-
tions. Generating an interface-graph from the new set of traceroutes appears to
confirm our hypothesis that path changes corrupted the scamper traceroutes. In
the FAST traceroutes, we never observed an Azure address after a router known
to belong to a neighboring AS. Furthermore, path changes played a large role
in bdrmapIT's inaccurate AS operator inferences. bdrmapIT's inferences on the
FAST traceroutes were 97.4% accurate, compared to 88.8% with the Scamper
traceroutes.

Dest: 158.130.69.163			Dest: 146.97.33.5			Dest: 158.130.69.163		
1	128.91.238.217	[UPenn]	1	216.239.59.1	[GCP]	1	209.85.253.197	[GCP]
2	128.91.48.6	[UPenn]	2	172.253.65.167	[GCP]	2	172.253.65.176	[GCP]
			3	209.85.143.66	[GCP]	3	108.170.227.150	[GCP]
			4	108.170.246.168	[GCP]	4	108.170.248.11	[GCP]
			5	*		5	162.252.69.196	[I2]
			6	146.97.33.62	[JANET]	6	*	
			7	146.97.33.5	[JANET]	7	128.91.238.218	[I2]
						8	128.91.238.217	[UPenn]
						9	128.91.48.6	[UPenn]

(a) Los Angeles to UPenn.   (b) Los Angeles to JANET.   (c) Belgium to UPenn.

Fig. 6. A traceroute from GCP Los Angeles to the University of Pennsylvania (UPenn) revealed no GCP IP addresses (a), but traceroutes from Los Angeles to JANET in the UK (b), and Belgium to UPenn (c), each revealed GCP addresses.

4 Learning About Clouds from Interconnections

Armed with confidence in our interconnection inferences, we set up VMs in every region available to us for AWS, Azure, and GCP, the three largest cloud providers, and used FAST to conduct traceroutes from every VM to a random address in every routed /24. We configured our VMs to use the WAN as much as possible; Azure networking defaults to cold-potato routing and we selected GCP's premium network tier, but in AWS we used the default WAN behavior. We did not use AWS Global Accelerator [5], and we plan to investigate the affect of Global Accelerator in future work. These experiments derived routed address space using collected BGP route announcements from 1–5 October 2020. We used the same combination of bdrmapIT, PeeringDB, and IXPDB as in Sect. 3 to infer interconnection addresses, and used these interconnection inferences to analyze the neighboring networks that each cloud uses to reach public Internet networks, and to geolocate the interconnections between the three cloud providers.

4.1 GCP Inflates Traceroute Probe TTLs

One challenge for our analysis is that GCP, unlike AWS and Azure, inflates the TTL values of traceroute probes after they leave VMs such that the hop #1 traceroute address belongs to a later router in that path, rather than to the first router hop [13][1]. This behavior violates a core traceroute assumption that hop #1 corresponds to the first router probed. While invisible Multiprotocol Label Switching (MPLS) tunnels exhibit similar behavior, hiding router hops between the tunnel entry and exit routers [21,53,54], MPLS tunnels do not affect hop #1 since the probe with TTL 1 could not yet enter an MPLS tunnel. This practice of rewriting probe TTLs has likely caused researchers to incorrectly conclude that GCP routers do not respond to traceroute [29], or that hop #1 is a router just past the GCP border [57].

---

[1] We observed different behavior in February, 2021 (Appendix A).

Figure 6a shows the GCP TTL inflation with a traceroute from a VM in Los Angeles, where hop #1 reported an address that router configurations from Internet2 show belong to a University of Pennsylvania (UPenn) router [10], despite no direct interconnection between GCP and UPenn [11]. In fact, the UPenn router at hop #1 reported an interface address used to interconnect with Internet2 [10], indicating that the probes traversed Internet2 to reach UPenn, but the inflated TTL caused probes to expire only after reaching UPenn. Traceroutes from other GCP VMs to the same UPenn destination, such as in the Belgium region, exposed apparent GCP internal IP addresses, only reaching UPenn at hop 8 (Fig. 6c). All of our VMs use GCP's premium network tier, but not all revealed internal GCP addresses, contradicting reported behavior that only GCP's standard tier inflates traceroute TTLs [14]. Our ability to observe internal GCP addresses from the Belgium VM toward UPenn, and from the VM in Los Angeles toward JANET in the UK (Fig. 6b), suggests that the opportunity to view internal and interconnection GCP addresses depends on the combination of GCP region and traceroute destination. We leave an analysis of the interconnection information lost to GCP's TTL inflation for future work.

4.2 Inferring How Clouds Reach Internet Networks

We define the *cloud transit degree* for a cloud neighbor AS as the number of unique traceroute destination ASes for which the neighbor is the next-hop AS. This metric is an indication of the relative importance of that neighbor to the cloud network. In Fig. 7, the cloud network uses AS #1 to reach three ASes including AS #1, giving it a CTD of 3, while AS #2 has a CTD of 2. Here, the cloud uses both AS #1 and AS #2 to reach AS #3, so we count AS #3 once for each AS. This situation occurs when clouds choose different next-hop networks depending on the VM's region.

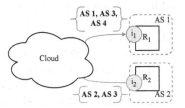

Fig. 7. AS #1 is the next-hop network in traceroute paths to three ASes, so its CTD = 3. AS #2 is the next-hop network for two ASes, so its CTD = 2.

We only used traceroutes with a cloud interconnection in the path to compute the CTDs, so we discarded any traceroute where an unresponsive hop separates the last hop inside the cloud network from the first hop outside the cloud network. Figure 8a shows the fraction of included traceroutes in each cloud. For every neighbor AS, we maintain a set of destination ASes reached through that neighbor, so at the first hop in the neighbor AS we add the traceroute's destination AS to that neighbor's set. Finally, we compute the CTD for each neighbor as the cardinality of its destination set.

Figure 8b shows the number of unique ASes for each cloud across their different regions. The different variances reflect the traffic engineering policies of each cloud. AWS uses hot-potato routing, so we not only saw different neighbors from each region, but we saw different numbers of neighboring ASes as well. Conversely, Azure uses cold-potato routing, so Azure transits packets destined

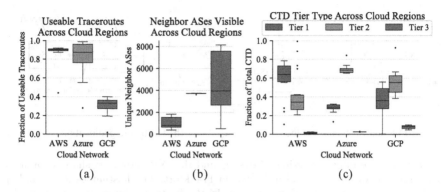

Fig. 8. We excluded many of the GCP traceroutes since the traceroute path often began outside GCP (a). Unlike AWS and GCP, we observed nearly all of the same neighbor ASes from every Azure region (b). All clouds rely on tier 1 and tier 2 networks, but AWS relies more heavily on tier 1s in most regions (c).

for a neighboring AS across its global backbone and hands them off to the neighbor directly. GCP also employs cold-potato routing, but certain regions included more internal routers in traceroute paths than others. We only included an AS as a neighbor when we saw a GCP interconnection address, as traceroute paths can start in unconnected networks (Fig. 6).

Figure 8c shows the fraction of the total CTD accounted for by tier 1, tier 2, and tier 3 networks. For the purposes of this analysis, we define tier 1 networks as the 19 ASes inferred to be at the top of the AS hierarchy in CAIDA's AS relationship dataset for October 1, 2020. Tier 2 networks include the 10,627 other ASes with at least one customer in the dataset, with the remaining networks classified as tier 3. Our analysis reveals that all three clouds rely heavily on ISPs, although we expect that the clouds primarily peer with these ISPs, rather than interconnect with them for Internet transit. AWS shows wide variance across regions, heavier reliance on tier 1 networks (due to hot potato routing), and heavy tier 2 network use in certain regions. Azure relies on tier 1 and tier 2 networks consistently across regions, and GCP appears better connected to edge networks.

In total, we discovered an order of magnitude more cloud neighbor ASes in our traceroutes from cloud VMs than were visible in RouteViews and RIPE RIS collections of BGP route announcements from 1–5 October, 2020 (Table 1). We also found that GCP appears to interconnect with more than twice as many networks as AWS and Azure. Importantly, our results indicate that

Table 1. We observed an order of magnitude more unique cloud AS neighbors traceroutes than in public BGP collections.

	AWS	Azure	GCP
Traceroute	4110	3889	8620
BGP	327	300	381

the visible connectivity of cloud networks, and their reliance on specific neighbors, is region-dependent. To properly measure and analyze the cloud requires gathering data from each region, and considering each region separately.

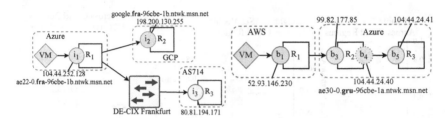

(a) IXP and hostname geolocation.   (b) Hostname geolocation.

Fig. 9. In (a) the interconnection address i_2 and the IXP address i_3 share a common predecessor, so we infer i_2 is also located in Frankfurt. The hostnames for i_2 and i_1 also indicate Frankfurt. In (b) we use **gru** in the hostname for b_4 to infer that the interconnection occurs in Sao Paulo. (Color figure online)

4.3 Geolocating Cloud Interconnections

Next, we use IXP location constraints and geolocation tags in Azure hostnames to infer the locations of interconnections between the clouds. For IXP constraints, we identify all addresses that preceded an interconnection address in a traceroute that also preceded an IXP address, and infer that the interconnection is located at the IXP location recorded in PeeringDB. Our reasoning follows from the fact that interconnected routers operated by two different networks are often located in the same facility or city. In Fig. 9a, bdrmapIT inferred that address 198.200.130.255 interconnects Azure and GCP, and the prior address 104.44.232.128 also preceded an address used for public peering at DE-CIX Frankfurt in a different traceroute, so we conclude that the interconnection using address 198.200.130.255 occurs in Frankfurt. Remote peering at IXPs, where a network participates at multiple IXPs through a port at a single IXP, creates the possibility that our method could identify multiple IXPs. We expect to more often observe local IXP peering than remote peering, so in the event our technique identified multiple IXPs, we select the most frequently appearing IXP city location.

We also used geographic locations embedded in Azure IP hostnames to geolocate interconnections involving Azure, such as the reference to Frankfurt in the hostname for 198.200.130.255, google.fra-96cbe-1b.ntwk.msn.net. We collected hostnames for three groups of addresses most likely to reside in the same city as the interconnection: (1) the interconnection address, (2) addresses that precede the interconnection address, and (3) the other address in the /31 subnet of addresses subsequent to the interconnection address. For the latter group, while the subsequent addresses might not reside in the interconnection city, we assume the other address in the point-to-point subnet likely belongs to the same router as the interconnection address. In Fig. 9b, we use the hostname for 104.44.24.40 which we infer belongs to the same router as the interconnection address 99.82.177.85, despite not appearing in the traceroutes. Using a hand-crafted regular expression, we extracted the geolocation codes, and mapped each code to a city. This technique always inferred a single city for each interconnection address. Using both

Cloud Interconnection Locations

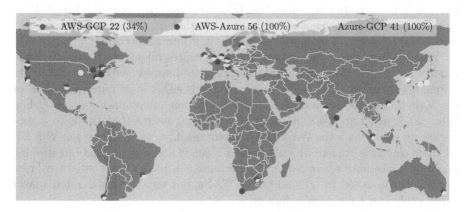

Fig. 10. Unique city locations for interconnections between the clouds. The clouds often interconnect in the same cities, indicated with pie-chart markers. We could only geolocate 22 of the 64 inferred AWS-GCP interconnections (34.4%).

techniques allowed us to infer geolocations for every Azure link, and the two techniques never inferred conflicting cities.

Our two geolocation strategies yielded the city locations in Fig. 10. We found that the clouds interconnect in all six populated continents and tend to interconnect in the same locations. The IXP constraints provided locations for 87.8% and 80.4% of the Azure-GCP and Azure-AWS interconnections respectively, but only geolocated 34.4% of the AWS–GCP interconnections, since many of their interconnection IP addresses did not share a common predecessor with an IXP address. Interconnections visible from AWS VMs rarely shared a predecessor with an IXP address, and the GCP traceroutes often lacked internal hops. The congruity between the two techniques indicates that these techniques can accurately geolocate many of the cloud interconnections visible in traceroute.

5 Limitiations

Our analysis performs inferences on top of inferences, and an error at any step can lead to false conclusions. Acknowledging the potential for compounding error, we validated as many of our interconnection and geolocation inferences as possible. In general, we expect our analysis to reflect the reality revealed by our traceroutes, despite imperfect accuracy.

One limitation of our validation is that we rely on the accuracy of Azure's DNS hostnames, but operators might not update them when an IP address switches from one router interface to another. While this might apply to our case, the 97.4% congruity between bdrmapIT AS operator inferences and the hostname tags suggests that Azure maintains its hostnames well. The coverage of our validation is a more fundamental limitation, as our validation dataset covers a single cloud network and only 30.3% of the total number of bdrmapIT inferred Azure private interconnection IP addresses. Our reported bdrmapIT AS operator accuracy might not generalize to the other Azure interconnections that bdrmapIT inferred, let alone to AWS and GCP interconnections.

When inferring cloud neighbors, our traceroutes might not reveal all of the interconnections between the cloud networks, and between the clouds and neighboring networks. In GCP, most traceroute paths either start outside of GCP or the VMs do not receive a reply from the apparent interconnection router hop (Fig. 8a). Specific to AWS, its hot-potato routing means that traffic to a connected AS might leave the WAN at a different neighbor closer to the the VM. For all three clouds, a traceroute only reveals a single active path, and our probing might miss alternate active paths. Furthermore, our probing can only reveal networks interconnected with cloud public WANs, but some networks interconnect with clouds in a more private fashion.

Yeganeh *et al.* [56] described cloud exchanges as multipoint-to-point interconnections that use address space provided by the exchange operator, and speculated that bdrmapIT cannot draw accurate AS operator inferences for routers at cloud exchanges. We do not expect cloud exchanges to pose problems for bdrmapIT's AS operator inferences, since it determines AS ownership by looking forward from a router to addresses seen subsequently in a traceroute. This allows bdrmapIT to determine ownership for IXP public peering addresses, and it should perform similarly for the cloud exchanges Yeganeh *et al.* described. A potential consequence of cloud exchanges is that our methodology for inferring next-hop networks might select the cloud exchange provider as the next-hop AS if the exchange does not use address space belonging to a cloud or list its address space in PeeringDB or IXPDB.

6 Conclusion

Public clouds play a central role in the modern Internet, but we know little about how they interconnect to each other or other networks. Understanding cloud connectivity is critical to studying the modern Internet, including for network planning and diagnosis, and resiliency assessments. This study lays a foundation for future analyses by validating and improving a technique to infer cloud interconnection IP addresses. We analyzed next-hop ASes that the clouds use to reach other networks and proposed techniques to geolocate interconnections between the clouds. We found that clouds interconnect with each other on all six populated continents, and that next-hop ASes can be region-dependent, indicating that properly analyzing cloud networks requires measurements from every region. We will make FAST and the code for our analysis available at https:// alexmarder.github.io/cloud-pam21/.

Acknowledgments. This work was supported by DARPA CA HR00112020014, NSF OAC-1724853, NSF CNS-1901517, and NSF CNS-1925729.

A   Recent GCP Traceroute Behavior

```
Dest: 158.130.69.163          Dest: 146.97.33.5
1 72.14.237.86    [GCP]       1 *              [GCP]
2 162.252.69.188  [I2]        2 *              [GCP]
3 *                           3 *              [GCP]
4 *                           4 *              [GCP]
5 128.91.238.218  [I2]        5 128.91.238.217 [UPenn]
6 128.91.238.217  [UPenn]     6 128.91.48.6    [UPenn]
7 128.91.48.6     [UPenn]
```

(a) Los Angeles to UPenn.   (b) Virginia to UPenn.

Fig. 11. Unlike the traceroute in October, 2020, the traceroute from GCP Los Angeles to UPenn in February, 2021 revealed an internal GCP IP addresses (a). The first responsive hop in the traceroute from Virginia was an address on a UPenn router, but the path contained unresponsive hops until that point (b).

We conducted the traceroutes in Sect. 4.1 in October, 2020. Revisiting our examples in February, 2021, we noticed a different behavior. Many paths still do not contain any internal GCP addresses, but the paths no longer appear to start in neighboring networks. As seen in the traceroute path from GCP Los Angeles to UPenn (Fig. 11a), hop #1 is an internal GCP address followed by the interconnection with Internet2 at hop #2 [10], rather than a UPenn address. The first responsive hop in the path from our GCP Virginia VM (Fig. 11b) is the same UPenn address that we previously observed as hop #1 in Sect. 4.1, but hop #1 is now an unresponsive address. This behavior makes interpreting GCP traceroutes more intuitive, as they follow conventional traceroute semantics, but observing GCP internal addresses still appears to depend on the combination of VM region and traceroute destination.

References

1. The CAIDA AS relationships dataset. https://www.caida.org/data/as-relation-ships/
2. PeeringDB. https://peeringdb.com/
3. Routing information service (RIS). https://www.ripe.net/analyse/internet-measure-ments/routing-information-service-ris
4. University of Oregon route views project. http://www.routeviews.org/routeviews/
5. AWS global accelerator, October 2020. https://aws.amazon.com/global-accel-erator
6. Azure global network, May 2020. https://azure.microsoft.com/en-us/global-infra-structure/global-network/
7. Azure regions, May 2020. https://azure.microsoft.com/en-us/global-infrastru-cture/regions/
8. Cloud locations, May 2020. https://cloud.google.com/about/locations

9. Global infrastructure, May 2020. https://aws.amazon.com/about-aws/global-infrastructure/
10. Internet2 - visible network raw data access, October 2020. https://vn.net.internet2.edu/xml/Internet2/2020/10/15/14/43/show_interfaces.gz
11. Pennnet network architecture (2020). https://upenn.app.box.com/v/RouterCoreDiagram
12. Regions and availability zones, May 2020. https://aws.amazon.com/about-aws/global-infrastructure/regions_az/
13. VPC network overview, May 2020. https://cloud.google.com/vpc/docs/vpc
14. Arnold, T., et al.: (How much) does a private wan improve cloud performance? In: IEEE INFOCOM 2020-IEEE Conference on Computer Communications, pp. 79–88. IEEE (2020)
15. Arnold, T., et al.: Cloud provider connectivity in the flat internet. IMC (2020)
16. Barabási, A.L., Albert, R.: Emergence of scaling in random networks. Science **286**(5439), 509–512 (1999)
17. Beverly, R.: Yarrp'ing the internet: Randomized high-speed active topology discovery. In: IMC, pp. 413–420 (2016)
18. Chen, K., et al.: Where the sidewalk ends: extending the internet as graph using traceroutes from P2P users. In: Proceedings of the 5th International Conference on Emerging Networking Experiments and Technologies, pp. 217–228 (2009)
19. Dimitropoulos, X., Krioukov, D., Fomenkov, M., Huffaker, B., Hyun, Y., Claffy, K., Riley, G.: As relationships: inference and validation. ACM SIGCOMM Comput. Commun. Rev. **37**(1), 29–40 (2007)
20. d'Itri, M.: whois. https://github.com/rfc1036/whois
21. Donnet, B., Luckie, M., Mérindol, P., Pansiot, J.J.: Revealing MPLS tunnels obscured from traceroute. ACM SIGCOMM Comput. Commun. Rev. **42**(2), 87–93 (2012)
22. Du, B., Candela, M., Huffaker, B., Snoeren, A.C., Claffy, K.: RIPE IPmap active geolocation: mechanism and performance evaluation. SIGCOMM Comput. Commun. Rev. **50**(2), 3–10 (2020)
23. Euro-IX: Ixpdb. https://ixpdb.euro-ix.net/en/
24. Faloutsos, M., Faloutsos, P., Faloutsos, C.: On power-law relationships of the internet topology. ACM SIGCOMM Comput. Commun. Rev. **29**(4), 251–262 (1999)
25. Gao, L.: On inferring autonomous system relationships in the internet. IEEE/ACM Trans. Netw. **9**(6), 733–745 (2001)
26. Gharaibeh, M., Shah, A., Huffaker, B., Zhang, H., Ensafi, R., Papadopoulos, C.: A look at router geolocation in public and commercial databases. In: Proceedings of the 2017 Internet Measurement Conference, pp. 463–469 (2017)
27. Giotsas, V., Luckie, M., Huffaker, B., Claffy, K.: Inferring complex as relationships. In: Proceedings of the 2014 Conference on Internet Measurement Conference, pp. 23–30 (2014)
28. Gueye, B., Ziviani, A., Crovella, M., Fdida, S.: Constraint-based geolocation of internet hosts. IEEE/ACM Trans. Netw. **14**(6), 1219–1232 (2006)
29. Haq, O., Raja, M., Dogar, F.R.: Measuring and improving the reliability of wide-area cloud paths. In: WWW, pp. 253–262 (2017)
30. Huffaker, B., Dhamdhere, A., Fomenkov, M., Claffy, K.C.: Toward topology dualism: improving the accuracy of AS annotations for routers. In: Krishnamurthy, A., Plattner, B. (eds.) PAM 2010. LNCS, vol. 6032, pp. 101–110. Springer, Heidelberg (2010). https://doi.org/10.1007/978-3-642-12334-4_11
31. Huffaker, B., Fomenkov, M., Claffy, K.: DRoP:DNS-based router positioning. ACM SIGCOMM Comput. Commun. Rev. **44**(3), 5–13 (2014)

32. Jin, Y., Scott, C., Dhamdhere, A., Giotsas, V., Krishnamurthy, A., Shenker, S.: Stable and practical AS relationship inference with ProbLink. In: 16th USENIX Symposium on Networked Systems Design and Implementation (NSDI 2019), pp. 581–598 (2019)
33. Katz-Bassett, E., John, J.P., Krishnamurthy, A., Wetherall, D., Anderson, T., Chawathe, Y.: Towards IP geolocation using delay and topology measurements. In: Proceedings of the 6th ACM SIGCOMM Conference on Internet Measurement, pp. 71–84 (2006)
34. Luckie, M.: Scamper: a scalable and extensible packet prober for active measurement of the Internet. In: IMC (2010)
35. Luckie, M., Dhamdhere, A., Clark, D., Huffaker, B., Claffy, K.: Challenges in inferring internet interdomain congestion. In: IMC (2014)
36. Luckie, M., Dhamdhere, A., Huffaker, B., Clark, D., Claffy, K.: bdrmap: inference of borders between IP networks. In: IMC (2016)
37. Luckie, M., Huffaker, B., Dhamdhere, A., Giotsas, V., Claffy, K.: As relationships, customer cones, and validation. In: Proceedings of the 2013 Conference on Internet Measurement Conference, pp. 243–256 (2013)
38. Luckie, M., Marder, A., Fletcher, M., Huffaker, B., Claffy, K.C.: Learning to extract and use ASNs in hostnames. In: Proceedings of the 2020 Internet Measurement Conference (2020)
39. Mao, Z.M., Johnson, D., Rexford, J., Wang, J., Katz, R.: Scalable and accurate identification of AS-level forwarding paths. In: IEEE INFOCOM 2004, vol. 3, pp. 1605–1615. IEEE (2004)
40. Mao, Z.M., Rexford, J., Wang, J., Katz, R.H.: Towards an accurate AS-level traceroute tool. In: Proceedings of the 2003 Conference on Applications, Technologies, Architectures, and Protocols for Computer Communications, pp. 365–378 (2003)
41. Marder, A.: Sharp snapshots of the internet's graph with HONE. Ph.D. thesis, University of Pennsylvania (2019)
42. Marder, A.: vrfinder: finding outbound addresses in traceroute. In: SIGMETRICS (2020)
43. Marder, A., Luckie, M., Dhamdhere, A., Huffaker, B., Claffy, K.C., Smith, J.M.: Pushing the boundaries with bdrmapIT: mapping router ownership at internet scale. In: IMC (2018)
44. Marder, A., Smith, J.M.: MAP-IT: multipass accurate passive inferences from traceroute. In: Proceedings of the 2016 Internet Measurement Conference, pp. 397–411. ACM (2016)
45. NCC, R.: RIPE IPMap. https://ipmap.ripe.net/
46. Network, M.: RADb: The Internet routing registry. https://www.radb.net/
47. Norton, W.B.: Cloud interconnections, September 2016. https://www.caida.org/workshops/wie/1612/slides/wie1612_wnorton.pdf
48. Poese, I., Uhlig, S., Kaafar, M.A., Donnet, B., Gueye, B.: IP geolocation databases: unreliable? ACM SIGCOMM Comput. Commun. Rev. 41(2), 53–56 (2011)
49. Saunders, B.: Who's using amazon web services? [2020 update], January 2020. https://www.contino.io/insights/whos-using-aws
50. Scheitle, Q., Gasser, O., Sattler, P., Carle, G.: HLOC: hints-based geolocation leveraging multiple measurement frameworks. In: 2017 Network Traffic Measurement and Analysis Conference (TMA), pp. 1–9. IEEE (2017)
51. Spring, N., Mahajan, R., Wetherall, D.: Measuring ISP topologies with rocketfuel. ACM SIGCOMM Comput. Commun. Rev. 32(4), 133–145 (2002)

52. Taneja, S., Pretzer, X.: Google cloud networking in depth: understanding network service tiers, May 2019. https://cloud.google.com/blog/products/networking/google-cloud-networking-in-depth-understanding-network-service-tiers
53. Vanaubel, Y., Luttringer, J.R., Mérindol, P., Pansiot, J.J., Donnet, B.: TNT, watch me explode: a light in the dark for revealing MPLS tunnels. In: 2019 Network Traffic Measurement and Analysis Conference (TMA), pp. 65–72. IEEE (2019)
54. Vanaubel, Y., Mérindol, P., Pansiot, J.J., Donnet, B.: Through the wormhole: tracking invisible MPLS tunnels. In: Proceedings of the 2017 Internet Measurement Conference, pp. 29–42. ACM (2017)
55. Xia, J., Gao, L.: On the evaluation of as relationship inferences [internet reachability/traffic flow applications]. In: IEEE Global Telecommunications Conference, 2004. GLOBECOM 2004, vol. 3, pp. 1373–1377. IEEE (2004)
56. Yeganeh, B., Durairajan, R., Rejaie, R., Willinger, W.: How cloud traffic goes hiding: a study of Amazon's peering fabric. In: IMC, pp. 202–216 (2019)
57. Yeganeh, B., Durairajan, R., Rejaie, R., Willinger, W.: A first comparative characterization of multi-cloud connectivity in today's internet. In: Sperotto, A., Dainotti, A., Stiller, B. (eds.) PAM 2020. LNCS, vol. 12048, pp. 193–210. Springer, Cham (2020). https://doi.org/10.1007/978-3-030-44081-7_12
58. Zhang, B., Liu, R., Massey, D., Zhang, L.: Collecting the internet as-level topology. ACM SIGCOMM Comput. Commun. Rev. 35(1), 53–61 (2005)

On the Resilience of Internet Infrastructures in Pacific Northwest to Earthquakes

Juno Mayer, Valerie Sahakian, Emilie Hooft, Douglas Toomey,
and Ramakrishnan Durairajan[✉]

University of Oregon, Eugene, USA
junom@cs.uoregon, {vjs,emilie,drt}@uoregon.edu,
ram@cs.uoregon.edu

Abstract. The U.S. Pacific Northwest (PNW) is one of the largest Internet infrastructure hubs for several cloud and content providers, research networks, colocation facilities, and submarine cable deployments. Yet, this region is within the Cascadia Subduction Zone and currently lacks a quantitative understanding of the resilience of the Internet infrastructure due to seismic forces. The main goal of this work is to assess the resilience of critical Internet infrastructure in the PNW to shaking from earthquakes. To this end, we have developed a framework called ShakeNet to understand the levels of risk that earthquake-induced shaking poses to wired and wireless infrastructures in the PNW. We take a probabilistic approach to categorize the infrastructures into risk groups based on historical and predictive peak ground acceleration (PGA) data and estimate the extent of shaking-induced damages to Internet infrastructures. Our assessments show the following in the next 50 years: ∼65% of the fiber links and cell towers are susceptible to a very strong to a violent earthquake; the infrastructures in Seattle-Tacoma-Bellevue and Portland-Vancouver-Hillsboro metropolitan areas have a 10% chance to incur a very strong to a severe earthquake. To mitigate the damages, we have designed a route planner capability in ShakeNet. Using this capability, we show that a dramatic reduction of PGA is possible with a moderate increase in latencies.

1 Introduction

Internet infrastructures—composed of nodes (e.g., data centers, colocation facilities, Internet eXchange Points or IXPs, submarine landing stations, cell towers, and points of presence or POPs) and links (e.g., short- and long-haul fiber-optic cables, and submarine cables)—play a crucial role in our day-to-day activities and public safety. For example, earthquake early warning systems such as ShakeAlert [1] rely on resilient Internet infrastructures to effectively detect, respond to, and recover from earthquakes. With 47% of trans-Pacific submarine cables in the west coast arriving onshore in Pacific Northwest (PNW)—37% in Oregon and 10% in Washington—a large presence of hyperscale cloud providers, and thousands of miles of metro- and long-haul fiber-optic cables [2–5], the PNW is undoubtedly a regional locus of critical Internet infrastructure.

Geographically, the PNW is the site of the Cascadia Subduction Zone (CSZ) known to create large magnitude (**M**) 9 subduction (megathrust) earthquakes, as well as more

© Springer Nature Switzerland AG 2021
O. Hohlfeld et al. (Eds.): PAM 2021, LNCS 12671, pp. 247–265, 2021.
https://doi.org/10.1007/978-3-030-72582-2_15

frequent deep earthquakes occurring within the subducting oceanic crust ("inslab"), and shallower earthquakes in the continental crust. This tectonic setting poses a significant hazard to the region, capable of producing several meters of rapid ground deformation, as well as strong ground accelerations from shaking. Seismic hazard describes the expected frequency of shaking in a region and is a combination of the region's tectonic activity (i.e., areas with faults that release more energy from earthquakes contribute to greater seismic hazard), as well as factors that affect levels of shaking (e.g., amplification from shallow sediment). Typically shown as the probability of exceeding a particular level of shaking, seismic hazard represents a long-term average of the maximum shaking that may be felt due to many faults (seismic sources). Shaking can be represented by intensity measures such as peak ground acceleration or PGA (i.e., in fractions of g, 9.81 m/s/s), or the qualitative Modified Mercalli Intensity (MMI) scale (e.g., severe, violent, etc.).

Recent global earthquakes have demonstrated that shaking and its associated hazards can have a large impact on telecommunications infrastructure and negatively affect post-disaster recovery (Sect. 2). For example, the 2016 **M**7.8 Kaikōura crustal and megathrust earthquake caused significant damage to buried fiber-optic cables and microwave towers on New Zealand's South Island, leading to outages for up to five days [6]. The **M**9 2011 Tohoku-Oki subduction earthquake resulted in connectivity losses for 2 days [7], and the **M**6.9 1995 Kobe crustal earthquake disconnected telecommunications infrastructure and isolated the cities of Kobe, Ashiya, and Nishinomiya [8]. In short, standard Internet infrastructures are not designed to be resilient to strong earthquake shaking.

To date, few studies [7, 9, 10] have considered how to assess and mitigate the effects of earthquake damage on Internet infrastructures, and none have investigated the potential impacts in the PNW. This is primarily due to two key issues. First is the paucity of high-quality Internet infrastructure maps that reveal dependencies between service providers and alerting systems, and the associated risks that are both intrinsic (e.g., infrastructure risks due to conduit sharing among providers [5]) as well as extrinsic (e.g., infrastructure outages due to natural disasters [4, 9–13]). Second is the interdisciplinary nature of the problem: that is, it is not fully known what the impacts of shaking and seismic hazard are on Internet infrastructure, even from past earthquakes, due to the lack of collaborative efforts between network measurements and earth science communities.

To address these issues, we design *ShakeNet*: a framework to study the impacts of earthquake-induced shaking on the Internet infrastructure. At the core of ShakeNet is the probabilistic approach to (a) categorize Internet infrastructure of varying types into risk groups (e.g., data centers in *very strong* shaking areas vs. colocation facilities in regions that might experience *violent* shaking) and (b) estimate the extent of potential shaking-induced damages to Internet infrastructures. Our approach is built atop ArcGIS [14] and their application to the following datasets: (a) probabilistic seismic hazard analysis (PSHA) estimates of shaking in the CSZ, for the highest level of peak ground acceleration (PGA) that may occur within the next 50 years, and (b) Internet infrastructure datasets from diverse network measurement efforts [3–5, 15].

Using ShakeNet, we seek answers to the following research questions: (a) How much infrastructure—both nodes and links—is susceptible to earthquake shaking and shaking-induced damages in the PNW? (b) What are the impacts of shaking-induced outages on society? and (c) How can we minimize the impacts of earthquakes on Internet infrastructure deployments? To answer these questions, we examine >40,000 miles of fiber, 59 colocation facilities, 422 POPs, 4 IXPs, 31 data centers, and 213,554 cell towers in the PNW. We find that 71% of metro fiber have a 2% chance of experiencing 0.34g of PGA (severe shaking) in the next 50 years, and 27,781 miles (65%) have a 10% chance of experiencing 0.18g PGA or greater (very strong shaking). Of the nodes, 14% are in locations with a 2% chance of exceeding 0.34g PGA, and a 10% chance of exceeding 0.18g PGA within the next 50 years. Besides these nodes, 66.5% of towers have a 2% chance of experiencing 0.34g PGA or greater, and 67% have a 10% chance of feeling 0.18g PGA within the next 50 years. Overall, the areas with the highest level of potential impact are the Seattle-Tacoma-Bellevue metro in Washington and the Portland-Vancouver-Hillsboro metro in Oregon as they contain the highest concentration of wired and wireless infrastructure as well as a 10% chance to incur very strong (0.29 average) to severe (0.39 average) shaking within the next 50 years.

Finally, we extend the ShakeNet framework with *route planner* capability to identify alternate fiber deployment routes that are geographically longer but are less susceptible to shaking vs. existing routes that are more prone to earthquake-induced shaking. While standard routing protocols employ backup paths to deal with connection interruptions e.g., due to outages, they are oblivious to this tradeoff space and are not robust to earthquakes and shaking risks. Identifying the alternative deployment locations by navigating this tradeoff space is the third contribution of this work. We show that route planner can be used to maximize the safety of infrastructure deployments and fiber networks. For example, data transfers between nodes in Seattle and Portland metros can be re-routed via the eastern PNW through Kennewick and Boise in the case that fiber running across the I-5 interstate is affected by damaging shaking. While this path is longer (i.e., ~1200 miles), it has the benefit of being even further away from the CSZ and less adverse to risk (PGA reduction of 0.11 g for 2% probability of exceedance in the next 50 years).

2   Background and Related Work

Seismic Hazard in the PNW. Seismic hazard is defined as the expected frequency of *shaking*, not the frequency of earthquakes; the shaking is what causes damage to infrastructures (e.g., power lines, fiber cables, right of ways, etc.). For any given location, seismic hazard is the shaking expected over integration of all possible sources and shaking, a combination of two factors: (1) The nearby sources of seismic energy (e.g., faults) and how much energy they release over time; seismic sources are determined based on geologic and geophysical studies of a region and are controlled by the tectonic setting [16]; and (2) The shaking expected from all these surrounding seismic sources. Larger magnitude earthquakes, and closer earthquakes both cause stronger shaking.

Expected shaking is represented by intensity measures (IMs) and is estimated from empirical ground-motion models (GMMs) [18]. IMs vary and include: the peak value of ground motion recorded such as the peak ground acceleration (PGA) reached, the peak spectral acceleration (peak shaking convolved with a damped oscillator of the given period), or maybe described qualitatively, such as by Modified Mercalli Intensity (MMI)

Table 1. PGA data (in fractions of g, 9.81 m/s/s) and earthquake risk categories based on the Modified Mercalli Index [17]. *Indicates where damage to buildings begins to occur.

PGA Value (g)	MMI Intensity	MMI-correlated perceived shaking
<0.0017	I	Not Felt
0.0017–0.014	II–III	Weak
0.14–0.039	IV	Light
0.039–0.092	V	Moderate
0.092–0.18*	VI*	Strong*
0.18–0.34	VII	Very Strong
0.34–0.65	VIII	Severe
0.65–1.24	IX	Violent
>1.24	X	Extremes

which categorizes ground-motion according to the perceived shaking experienced by an observer (shown in Table 1). In this study, we focus on PGA and MMI.

To represent the expected frequency of shaking, seismic hazard is typically reported for various "return periods" of interest, or for a probability of exceedance within a specified time interval. The specified time interval is chosen based on the application at hand—the typical life of a structure is considered to be ∼50 years—as such this is a common time interval in which to compute probabilities for exceeding a particular level of ground-motion [19]. Example maps produced by the US Geological Survey report the 2% or 10% probability of exceeding a particular level of shaking in the next 50 years, respectively equivalent to the maximum shaking expected for any earthquakes within a 2,475 and 475-year return period [15]. The reported shaking is, in fact, the median value of a distribution; the standard deviations represent the uncertainty on the estimate, based on unknowns in the seismic source or uncertainties in the GMMs. This statistical distribution of reported shaking forms the basis of our approach.

In the PNW, seismic hazard is controlled almost entirely by the Cascadia Subduction Zone (CSZ) system, where the Juan de Fuca, Gorda, and Explorer tectonic plates sink beneath the North American plate. Here, seismic energy comes from three main types of seismic sources or earthquakes. (1) Events that occur along the subduction zone interface itself (the "megathrust") [20]. This subduction system is very large (>1000 km long, extending 40 km beneath the Earth's surface). Earthquake magnitude increases with the area of fault that breaks, which means that earthquakes that rupture even a portion of the subducting interface can produce very large (>M8.5 or 9) earthquakes. (2) Deep (∼30 km or more down) earthquakes that occur within the subducting slab ("inslab" earthquakes) [21]. While these are not as large in size as megathrust events, they are often very energetic for their magnitude and can produce strong and damaging high frequency shaking. Because these happen at great depth within the downgoing plate, they tend to occur beneath the coastline or population centers in the PNW, such as the 2001 Nisqually earthquake beneath Seattle. (3) Shallow (<35 km deep) [22] earthquakes that occur within the overriding continental crust ("crustal" earthquakes). While these can be the smallest of the three types of events, because they occur much closer to the surface, they potentially cause strong shaking.

Although megathrust earthquakes are the only events that can produce large **M9** earthquakes with widespread strong shaking, inslab, and crustal earthquakes produce smaller, but more frequent earthquakes that occur closer to population centers. Such inslab and crustal earthquakes thus contribute significantly to seismic hazard, depending on the return period of interest. Overall, as most of these seismic sources are associated with the subduction zone, the greatest seismic hazard and possible ground-motions in the PNW are near the coast, and to the west of the Cascade mountains.

Internet Infrastructures and Earthquakes. Analyzing the resilience of infrastructures [23–35], fault detection/localization [36–38], and development of resilient routing protocols [39–43] has been the focus of many prior efforts. While studies analyzing the impact of natural disasters (such as hurricanes, wildfires, climate change, and storms) on the Internet are numerous [4,11,13,44–47], there are few that consider extensive levels of infrastructure damage due to earthquake shaking [7,9,10], and none in PNW. For example, the Kaikōura earthquake in New Zealand produced a maximum recorded PGA of 3.0g near the epicenter, and 1.3g more than 100 km away from the fault rupture. Two Internet eXchange Points were impacted: one sustained internal damages to equipment and required new hardware to return functionality in that region, while the other exchange was isolated due to damages to surrounding fiber connections, requiring 1km of replacement cable. Kaikōura's East Coast Link cable sustained 6 breakages and aerial fiber cables sustained stretch-induced damages across riverbanks [48]. Similarly, the Tohoku earthquake in Japan had a maximum recorded PGA of 2.99 near the epicenter, and 2.7 g at 75 km away from the fault [49]. A study on Japan's SINET4 R&E network showed that even with redundancies such as dual links between core nodes, full recovery of traffic volume took 5–6 weeks near the earthquake's epicenter [7]. While these comparisons *qualitatively* demonstrate the damage on infrastructure caused by strong shaking, there are no quantitative studies that detail the direct correlations between the two. This is a necessary avenue for future work, but one that we do not yet tackle here.

While seismic hazard in PNW is high, the CSZ is anomalously quiet. Seismicity here is unusually low for an active subduction zone, posing unique challenges to the region in terms of awareness to infrastructure resiliency. Internet infrastructure in the PNW has been installed for just a few decades, within which few significant earthquakes have occurred. This increases the challenge of understanding the full possible impact of a future earthquake. In Fig. 1), we show maps of shaking from earthquakes since 1990 with magnitudes greater than 4, for which the ground-motions do not exceed 0.34. The result is that the existing infrastructure has not yet been subject to destructive shaking or suffered severe damages.

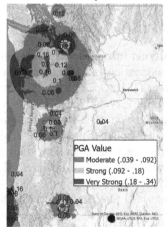

Fig. 1. PGA Values of historical earthquakes in the PNW.

There is, however, the unexplored potential that shaking from future earthquakes can have a significant impact on this infrastructure. In particular, these may affect fiber-optic cables, nodes, and cell towers. Terrestrial fiber-optic cables that carry Internet traffic provide protection from a variety of physical damages (e.g., fiber cut). They are packaged in conduits and are buried in trenches along existing right of ways [5]. We posit the following risks due to earthquakes in the region. The first is physical damage at the node level (e.g., cell towers), at link level (e.g., physical damage to fiber conduits), and at fiber termination points (i.e., colocation facilities and data centers). A majority of the submarine landing stations are near a seismically active region and terminate at the nearest colocation facility [50]. Ground accelerations beyond shaking thresholds published by infrastructure manufacturers will adversely impact fiber deployments: shaking-induced stress may cause state of polarization changes of the light traveling through cables leading to data loss. Furthermore, links may be severed at shaking levels produced by an M9 earthquake.

3   Design and Implementation of ShakeNet Framework

3.1   Overview of ShakeNet Framework

Motivated by above-mentioned impacts of earthquake-induced shaking on critical Internet infrastructures (Sect. 2), we design *ShakeNet*: a framework which brings probabilistic seismic hazard estimates to networking to assess and mitigate the impacts of seismic hazard on Internet infrastructure nodes and links. ShakeNet framework builds on top of a geographic information system (GIS) called ArcGIS and consists of capabilities to (a) categorize infrastructure of varying types (e.g., data centers, cell towers, submarine cables, etc.) into risk groups (e.g., severe, violent, etc.) (Sect. 3.3), (b) assess the extent of shaking-induced damages to those types (in Sect. 3.4), and (c) identify alternate strategies to mitigate the potential risks (in Sect. 3.5). We start by explaining the datasets used in this study, followed by each of these capabilities.

3.2   Datasets Used

Internet Infrastructure Datasets. ShakeNet uses Internet infrastructure datasets from a wide variety of network measurement and community efforts including Internet Atlas project [51], OpenCellID [52], and others [3–5]. The dataset is composed of nodes and links of varying types. Node types include data centers, colocation facilities, Internet exchange points (IXPs), submarine landing stations, wireless and microwave cell towers, and points of presence (POPs). Link types include short- and long-haul fiber cables and submarine cables. Our study focuses on Pacific Northwest (PNW) and considers a total of 59 colocation facilities, 422 POPs, 4 IXPs, and 31 data centers. We also examine 213,554 cell towers in the PNW area. Finally, we examine 42,516 miles of long- and short-haul fiber, and submarine cables terminating in CA, OR, and WA. Fiber cables are represented as polyline features and contain attributes such as provider info. and geodesic length. Nodes are represented as point features and contain attributes such as geographic coordinates and type (e.g., cell towers contain signal type as an attribute

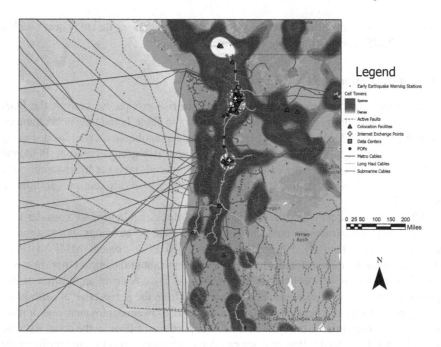

Fig. 2. Internet infrastructure overlap with mapped faults (yellow dotted lines) in PNW (Color figure online).

LTE, GSM, CDMA, UMTS). While the cable data is accurate in terms of location, there are instances where a cable is split into multiple polyline features; this does not impact the accuracy of our analyses.

Along the US west coast, there is much overlap between areas of high seismic hazard, and critical communications infrastructure. Figure 2 shows the close overlap between fiber-optic cables, colocation facilities, Internet exchange points, long-haul, metro, and submarine cables, cell towers, and mapped active faults. We hypothesize that earthquakes on these faults could be devastating to Internet infrastructure in PNW; here we apply probabilistic hazard assessment to describe that risk.

Earthquake Datasets. ShakeNet uses maps of peak ground acceleration (PGA), derived from probabilistic seismic hazard analyses (PSHA), to quantify the possible effects that future earthquakes may have on infrastructure deployments. We use two sets of probabilistic PGA data which encompass the CSZ: the values of PGA which have a 10% chance of being exceeded in the next 50 years (Fig. 5 in Appendix A.1) and the values which have a 2% probability of being surpassed in the next 50 years (Fig. 6 in Appendix A.1). These data sets were computed using the USGS national seismic hazard map software for the 2014 map edition [53], obtained as raster information, and converted to concentric polygons using *raster contouring* capabilities [54] in ArcGIS. They use the most up to date fault sources and expected earthquake rates in the western US. We choose 10% and 2% in 50 years as these are typical values considered in structural engineering applications, derived from the average life expectancy of a building

(50 years). These probabilities correspond to the average shaking that may occur within a 475 and 2,475 year return period, respectively.

3.3 Categorization of Risk Groups

To categorize infrastructures of varying types into risk groups, we convert the PGA datasets to Modified Mercalli Index (MMI) as shown in Table 1, and then break them up into risk categories. MMI provides a descriptive scale of earthquake's perceived shaking and potential damage. Categorizing infrastructure into risk groups based on PGA and MMI allows us to estimate the extent of shaking-induced damages by examining the percentage of infrastructure that may experience shaking, at different probabilities in the next 50 years.

After analyzing data using the overlap method discussed below, we consider how node and link infrastructures could be affected. Similar to buildings, we assume an infrastructure is potentially damaged if the expected PGA exceeds MMI VI (PGA 0.092). By marking these infrastructures, we can reason about the impact that structural damage and a loss of connectivity in that area could have. A novel application of this approach is the ability to view potential fiber routes from the perspective of earthquake shaking risks. Using this perspective, we can design risk-aware deployment and/or routing strategies: maximizing the traffic carried via portions of fiber in the areas with the lowest PGA values. Said differently, we can derive alternate ways to route traffic in the case that the shortest path, albeit with more earthquake risk, has been damaged. Here, we do not consider the fragility or performance of various types of infrastructure; rather, we assume a particular level of PGA will be equally damaging to all.

3.4 Assessment of Shaking-Induced Damages to Internet Infrastructure

We assess the extent of infrastructures damages incurred by earthquake shaking in two steps: (a) analyzing the risks of individual infrastructure types, and (b) combining these individual analyses to determine metropolitan statistical areas (MSAs) [3] with the greatest total risk. We explain these two steps below.

To determine earthquake risk to different infrastructure types, the PGA data is first *contoured*, creating a series of polygons which delineate areas of different minimum and maximum PGA values for the PNW area as shown in Figs. 5 and 6. The *intersect* tool [55] in ArcGIS is then used to assign these PGA values to the overlapping infrastructure. The tool takes two feature sets together and generates a new feature set composed of the intersecting geometry from both features. This allows ShakeNet to augment segments of fiber cable or individual nodes and cell towers with minimum and maximum PGA values depending on which PGA polygon the infrastructure in question overlaps with. Infrastructures are then placed into groups by PGA-MMI category and counted via a Python script written in ArcPy to determine the quantity of infrastructure at a given risk category. This script iterates through a given infrastructure dataset (which now contains a PGA value for every cable, node, or cell tower) and returns the quantity of infrastructure within the PGA ranges shown in Table 1. This script was used to create the tables described below. The count of infrastructure within a given group was divided over the total count within the PNW area to calculate percentage values.

To find the overall risk to different MSAs, we use the same overlap method described above, and augment a data set of MSAs in the PNW area with their experienced PGA level. We define polygons based on PGA values for a given probability map (2% or 10%). If an MSA falls on a polygon boundary, we take the average PGA of both polygons to represent the possible shaking at this site. We then use the *Summarize Within* tool [56] in ArcGIS to count the quantity of infrastructure per MSA. This allows us to assign MSAs a risk ranking based on their possible exceeded PGA, infrastructure quantity, and population density. Subsequently, a custom script—written using ArcPy [57]—is used to count and categorize overlap data into risk groups.

3.5 Mitigation of Infrastructure Risks

Mitigating the infrastructure risks is fraught with challenges. For one, network providers and state governments lack capabilities to (a) holistically combine risks and infrastructures together, (b) quantify risks to infrastructures and categorize them into different scenarios, and (c) identify alternate deployments for the identified scenarios. For example, if connectivity between two MSAs is disrupted by earthquake-induced shaking, how can traffic be dynamically re-routed via other alternate routes that have experienced less damage? Second, while IP routing allows the network infrastructures to dynamically detect and route around failures, shaking-related failure scenarios (like the ones depicted in Table 9) in particular, and natural disasters (e.g., [4,11,13,47,58]) in general, are shown to have localized effects (e.g., loss of connectivity) for extended periods of time. The main reasons for such localized and temporal Internet outages are typically a lack of geographic diversity in deployments and significant physical infrastructure sharing among providers [5].

To tackle these challenges, we extend the ShakeNet framework with a *route planner*: a scenario-based route planning capability to aid network providers and state governments to maintain the robustness and availability of infrastructures. Route planner is designed to identify alternate fiber deployment routes that are geographically longer but are less susceptible to shaking vs. existing routes that are more prone to earthquake-induced shaking. While network providers already employ backup routes for maintenance and safety purposes, unlike route planner, these backup routes may not explicitly minimize earthquake risk. Given a source and destination, alternate routes with likely lower shaking (PGA) levels are identified by examining the adjacent right of ways to (a) identify existing providers with infrastructure assets (for short-term peering and routing) or (b) deploy new infrastructure deployment locations (for long-term installation). Using route planner, network operators can enhance risk-awareness for deployments by determining routes that minimize predicted shaking and round trip time. The predictive nature of the probabilistic PGA data allows the route planner to be applied in the planning stages of new fiber deployments to harden the resiliency of future infrastructure.

4   Impacts of Earthquake Shaking on Infrastructures in PNW

4.1   How Much Infrastructure is Susceptible to Earthquakes?

Fiber Infrastructure Risk Groups. Using ShakeNet, we seek an answer to this question by analyzing the fiber infrastructure deployments in the PNW. Table 2 depicts the miles of long-haul and metro fiber infrastructures in PNW categorized based on the PGA-MMI mapping. The overlap of fiber miles is reported for both the expected PGA values for 10% and 2% probability of exceedance values in 50 years. Note that these miles of fiber represent the *minimum miles* that will experience, on average, the specified PGA or MMI. Because the hazard maps are derived from the average expected PGA within that return period, it is possible that lower levels of shaking may be surpassed within that time period (which may increase the miles of fiber affected).

Table 2. Miles of fiber categorized based on PGA-MMI mapping, for two different return periods or probabilities of exceedance. *This does not imply that no infrastructure will feel moderate shaking within the 2% in 50 years probability; rather, in this less likely scenario, the shaking at these infrastructure locations will surpass this level of shaking.

PGA (g)	MMI	Expected PGA - 10%	Expected PGA - 2%
0.039 < x <= 0.092	Moderate	681 (2%)	0*
0.092 < x <= 0.18	Strong	14054 (33%)	681 (2%)
0.18 < x <= 0.34	Very Strong	27782 (65%)	11246 (26%)
0.34 < x <= 0.65	Severe	0	27576 (65%)
0.65 < x <= 1.24	Violent	0	3015 (7%)

From Table 2, we observe that in the next 50 years, 65% of fiber infrastructures in the PNW have a 10% chance of experiencing *very strong* shaking (PGA between 0.18 and 0.34g), and 2% chance of experiencing *severe* shaking (0.34 and 0.65g). Over 3k miles of fiber have a 2% chance of being subjected to *violent* shaking in the next 50 years. This implies that there may be even greater shaking at these sites, though less likely. Further, this analysis suggests that infrastructure providers – with fiber assets in the very strong to violent risk groups – should consider alternate backup paths with fewer earthquake hazards.

Next, we seek to aid network operators in finding where multiple infrastructures are deployed and are prone to high PGA values. We convolve the probability of PGA with number of cables, since the ground motion side already is a probability distribution given by $P(PGA > x | 50 years)$. Specifically, we assign—without any lab-based tests—a qualitative "failure likelihood" (e.g., a number between 0 to 1, $p_{failure}$) to cables based on a given PGA they experience. We make a qualitative assumption that MMI VI, which is 10–20%g, will cause moderate damage, as this is also what causes damage on buildings and set $p_{failure} = 0.5$. Cables that experience 1g of ground motion will certainly be damaged/disrupted. Hence, we set $p_{failure} = 1.0$. For a given cable, the damage probability would then be: $DP = P(damage | 50 years, Y cable) =$

$P\left(PGA > x|50years\right) * P\left(p_{failure}|PGA\right)$. And then for a given region, we will use the damage probability (DP) to obtain the probability of failure/disruption given all the cables by multiplying the number of cables. The count of fiber cables and their failure likelihoods are are shown in Table 3. Similarly, the counts and the damage probabilities are shown in Table 4. The high-risk assets (e.g., 3 cables in the violent category) provide an opportunity to rethink earthquake monitoring using distributed acoustic sensing (DAS) and, more broadly distributed fiber optic sensing (DFOS) for detecting seismic events [59].

Table 3. Count of fiber cables categorized based on PGA-MMI mapping (and the corresponding probability of failure for that MMI, $p_{failure}$), for two different return periods or probabilities of exceedance. If a cable passes through multiple risk zones, it is counted for both. We assume that a PGA of 0.092 or below will not cause structural damage to cables. *This does not imply that no infrastructure will feel moderate shaking within the 2% in 50 years probability; rather, in this less likely scenario, the shaking at these infrastructure locations will surpass this level of shaking.

PGA (g)	MMI	$p_{failure}$	Count - PGA 10%	Count - PGA 2%
0.039 < x <= 0.092	Moderate	0	264	0*
0.092 < x <= 0.18	Strong	0.5	7449	241
0.18 < x <= 0.34	Very Strong	0.7	23061	8007
0.34 < x <= 0.65	Severe	0.9	0	22549
0.65 < x <= 1.24	Violent	1.0	0	3

Table 4. Count of fiber cables categorized based on PGA-MMI mapping, and their respective estimated damage probability (DP) in the next 50 years as a percentage, by convolving $p_{failure}$ with the probability of exceeding the level of PGA (2% or 0.02, or 10% or 0.1).

DP	1%	1.4%	1.8%	2%	5%	7%	9%	10%
Count	241	8007	22549	3	7449	23061	0	0

To complement Tables 2, 3, and 4, Figs. 7 and 8 (in Appendix A.2) show the fiber miles for individual providers for PGA values with 2% and 10% probability of exceedance within the next 50 years, respectively. From these figures, we see that Spectrum Business is at the highest risk as it has fiber assets in all higher PGA value bins, followed by Zayo and Integra. In the analysis of risk, we consider affected miles rather than percentages of a provider's total fiber in the PNW due to the proprietary nature of a provider's data.

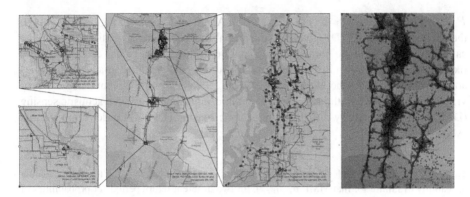

Fig. 3. Nodes proximal to CSZ. Red circles: POPs, green triangles: colos, yellow squares: data centers, white crosses: IXPs. (Color figure online)

Fig. 4. Cell towers in PNW.

Node Infrastructure Risk Groups. Next, we turn our attention to assess the node infrastructures that are susceptible to strong shaking. Unfortunately, as shown in Figs. 3 and 4, the nodes are not distributed uniformly across PNW. For example, the cell tower locations are highly distributed (see Fig. 4) whereas the rest of the nodes (as shown in Fig. 3) are located close to densely populated metro areas (e.g., Seattle, Portland, etc.). Hence, in our overlap analysis, we separate the cell towers from the rest of the nodes.

Tables 5 and 6 depict the raw count of node types (with percentages) under different risk groups with 10% and 2% probability of exceedance, respectively, in the next 50 years. From Table 5, we note that 39 colocation facilities, 371 POPs, and 29 data centers are prone to *very strong* shaking risk. These infrastructures are also susceptible to *severe* shaking risks if we consider with 2% probability of exceedance. The count (and percentage) of nodes falling into a given risk category in the 10% and 2% PGA is not coincidence. Note that areas with the highest predicted PGAs are also areas with some of the most concentrated infrastructures in the aforementioned metro areas. Meaning that in future earthquakes, these connectivity hubs would be the highest areas of concern.

Table 5. Count of nodes (with percentages) that are prone to earthquake shaking for expected PGAs with 10% probability of exceedance.

PGA	MMI	Colos	POPs	IXPs	Data centers
0.092 < x <= 0.18	Strong	20 (34.0%)	51 (12.0%)	1 (25.0%)	2 (6.0 %)
0.18 < x <= 0.34	Very Strong	39 (66.0%)	371 (88.0%)	3 (75.0%)	29 (94.0 %)

Table 6. Count of nodes (with percentages) that have a 2% chance of exceeding a specified level of shaking in the next 50 years.

PGA	MMI	Colos	POPs	IXPs	Data centers
0.18 < x <= 0.34	Very Strong	20 (34.0%)	51 (12.0%)	1 (25.0%)	2 (6.0 %)
0.34 < x <= 0.65	Severe	39 (66.0%)	371 (88.0%)	3 (75.0%)	29 (94.0 %)

Table 7. Percentage of cell towers (with percentages) that have a 10% chance of exceeding a specified level of shaking in the next 50 years.

PGA	MMI	LTE	CDMA	GSM	UMTS
0.039 < x <= 0.092	Moderate	2142 (1.75%)	378 (2.9%)	241 (1.94%)	688 (1.04%)
0.092 < x <= 0.18	Strong	40213 (32.92%)	3986 (30.57%)	3180 (25.54%)	18810 (28.53%)
0.18 < x <= 0.34	Very Strong	79596 (65.17%)	8636 (66.23%)	8995 (72.25%)	46353 (70.31%)
0.34 < x <= 0.65	Severe	190 (0.16%)	39 (0.3%)	34 (0.27%)	73 (0.11%)

Table 8. Count of cell towers (with percentages) per type that have a 2% probability of exceeding a particular level of shaking in the next 50 years.

PGA	MMI	LTE	CDMA	GSM	UMTS
0.092 < x <= 0.18	Strong	1755 (1.44%)	314 (2.41%)	175 (1.41%)	498 (0.76%)
0.18 < x <= 0.34	Very Strong	41414 (33.91%)	4034 (30.94%)	3343 (26.85%)	19989 (30.32%)
0.34 < x <= 0.65	Severe	75977 (62.2%)	8340 (63.96%)	8723 (70.06%)	44459 (67.44%)
0.65 < x <= 1.24	Violent	2995 (2.45%)	351 (2.69%)	209 (1.68%)	978 (1.48%)

As mentioned above, the cellular towers—compared to the other node infrastructures—are more broadly deployed across the PNW. Hence their deployment locations have a profound impact on how the risk groups look. Tables 7 and 8 show the raw counts and percentages of cell tower infrastructure risk categories for 10% and 2% probability of exceedance in the PNW area; the categories are shown for different technologies (i.e., LTE, CDMA, GSM, etc.). From Table 7, we note that over 97% of cellular infrastructures are in the *strong* to *severe* risk categories. With 2% probability of exceedance, the risk categories shift to *very strong* and *violent* in Table 8.

4.2 What are the Impacts of Infrastructure Outages on the Society?

Having looked into the infrastructure risk groups, we next assess the impacts of infrastructure outages on society. To this end, we combine the risk groups with MSAs (from [60]) using the overlap analysis capability in ShakeNet. Subsequently, for each return period (10% or 2%), we sort the MSAs by average PGA, then population density, then infrastructure concentration to obtain a combined risk ranking. Note that the values of PGA are uniformly higher in all areas for 2% in 50 years in comparison to 10% in 50 years, thus sorting either by 10% or 2% produces the same ranking.

Table 9. Top 5 MSAs with infrastructures ranked based on high earthquake risks.

Fiber cables	DCs/IXPs/Colos/POPs	Cell towers
Seattle-Tacoma-Bellevue	Seattle-Tacoma-Bellevue	Seattle-Tacoma-Bellevue
Portland-Vancouver-Hillsboro	Portland-Vancouver-Hillsboro	Portland-Vancouver-Hillsboro
Wenatchee	Eugene	Salem
Eugene	Olympia-Tumwater	Eugene
Klamath Falls	Bellingham	Olympia-Tumwater

Table 9 depicts the top 5 MSAs with the highest infrastructure risks due to shaking. It can be seen from the table that Seattle-Tacoma-Bellevue and Portland-Vancouver-Hillsboro MSAs are of the highest risk in all three infrastructure types. This is primarily due to two factors. First, these MSAs are densely populated and house the majority of fiber and node infrastructures in PNW. Second, since these two MSAs are connected together by fiber infrastructures running along the I-5 interstate and the area between Portland, OR and Seattle, WA has PGA values with predicted shaking ranging from *very strong* to *severe* shaking, the combined infrastructure risks are very high.

4.3   How to Minimize the Impacts of Earthquakes on Internet Infrastructures?

To answer this question, we apply ShakeNet's route planner capability for an "average" earthquake scenario that can potentially damage infrastructure deployments in and between Seattle-Tacoma-Bellevue and Portland-Vancouver-Hillsboro MSAs. These two MSAs, together, contain 43 colocation facilities, 399 POPs, and 31 data centers, all connected by 6,681 miles of fiber. This scenario is derived from the above probabilistic analyses, which consider a variety of possible earthquake sources in the region. To establish a baseline, we estimated the speed-of-light RTT based on the shortest path (i.e., via I-5) from the centers of MSAs as ∼3 ms. Further, we also noted the minimum, maximum, and average of the PGA in the contours that the fibers pass through for both 10% and 2% probability of exceedance. These statistics are shown in Table 10.

Table 10. PGA values and latencies for the shortest vs. other alternate paths from Seattle to Portland.

Routes	Latency	Avg 10%	Min 10%	Max 10%	Avg 2%	Min 2%	Max 2%
Baseline (along I-5)	∼3 ms	0.24	0.17	0.29	0.36	0.29	0.4
Yakima - Kennewick	∼6 ms	0.2	0.11	0.29	0.32	0.24	0.4
Spokane - Boise	∼18 ms	0.18	0.08	0.29	0.28	0.17	0.4

Using the route planner, we identified two alternate fiber paths with reduced PGAs. First is a path through eastern Washington to Oregon: that is, from Seattle to Spokane, then south to Lewiston, then west to Portland through Kennewick with ∼400 mile (i.e., ∼6 ms RTT) increase in fiber span and a PGA reduction of 0.06. The second alternate is through Spokane, WA, and Boise, ID. While this route is much longer (i.e., ~1200 miles or ~18 ms RTT) it has the benefit of being even further away from the CSZ and less adverse to risk (PGA reduction of 0.09). These alternate paths could be deployed in the long-term (via new deployments [61]) as well as short-term (via risk-aware routing [44]).

5 Summary and Future Work

To understand and mitigate (future) earthquake-related risks on Internet infrastructure in the PNW, we have devised a GIS-based framework called ShakeNet. ShakeNet uses a probabilistic approach to categorize the infrastructures into risk groups based on PGA and MMI, and estimate the potential extent of shaking-induced damages to infrastructures. Our analysis shows that ~65% of the fiber links and cell towers are susceptible to violent earthquake shaking. Further, infrastructures in Seattle-Tacoma-Bellevue and Portland-Vancouver-Hillsboro MSAs have a 10% chance to incur very strong to severe earthquake shaking. We design a route planner capability in ShakeNet and show that it is possible to mitigate the impacts of shaking risks by identifying longer albeit less-risky paths.

Further development of ShakeNet will use USGS ShakeAlert earthquake early warning messages to re-route traffic during the occurrence and growth of an earthquake to maintain critical Internet functionality for post-disaster responses. We also plan to extend ShakeNet and explore multi-hazard events (i.e., a cascading sequence of natural disasters such as aftershocks followed by a tsunami) which are expected to severely impact the Internet infrastructures. Similarly, earthquake-related permanent ground deformation (ground failure such as landslides and liquefaction) pose a significant threat to Internet infrastructures. For the former, we plan to consider Short-term Inundation Forecasting for Tsunamis (SIFT) [62] from NOAA tsunami forecasting [63] and do a multi-layer analysis of risks from shaking and tsunamis. For the latter, we will use probabilistic estimates of ground failure from models such as [41,64,64,65]. We will expand ShakeNet's route planner by considering individual provider networks: with this analysis, new routes can be produced with minimized risks for each provider.

Finally, ShakeNet can be extended to a performance-based earthquake engineering (PBEE) paradigm [66], which provides measurable assessments of the potential seismic performance of a system given decision-makers' determinations of its necessary functional level. This requires understanding the performance of various infrastructure components when exposed to a certain level of shaking. The resulting performance is convolved with 2% and 10% PGA estimates like we have shown here, to determine risk, and, finally, obtain a performance-based aspect of the infrastructure by defining various tolerance levels (e.g., partial functionality, increased latency but full functionality, etc.). This PBEE methodology can also be expanded with infrastructure vibration tolerances to reason about unique failure likelihoods for cables, cell towers, and buildings (data centers). This expansion is non-trivial and requires extensive research into tolerance thresholds for many types of infrastructures, potentially using numerical or physical modeling. Currently, no known solution exists.

Acknowledgments. We thank the anonymous reviewers and our shepherd, Zachary Bischof, for their insightful feedback. This work is supported by NSF CNS 1850297 award and Ripple faculty fellowship. The views and conclusions contained herein are those of the authors and should not be interpreted as necessarily representing the official policies or endorsements, either expressed or implied, of NSF or Ripple.

A   Appendices

A.1   Contour of Expected PGA Values

We use two sets of probabilistic PGA data which encompass the CSZ: expected PGA in the next 50 years at 10% (Fig. 5) and 2% (Fig. 6) for the PNW area. These data sets were computed using the USGS national seismic hazard map software for the 2014 map edition [53], obtained as raster information and converted to concentric polygons using *raster contouring* capabilities [54] in ArcGIS.

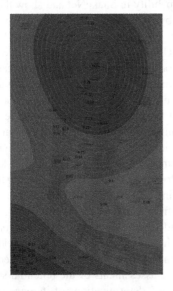

Fig. 5. Expected PGA with 10% chance in next 50 years.

Fig. 6. Expected PGA with 2% chance in next 50 years.

A.2   Miles of Fiber Affected Per Provider

Figures 7 and 8 show the fiber miles for individual providers for PGA values with 2% and 10% probability of exceedance within the next 50 years, respectively. From these figures, we see that Spectrum Business is at the highest risk as it has fiber assets in all higher PGA value bins, followed by Zayo and Integra.

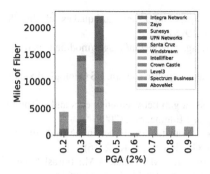

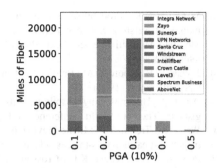

Fig. 7. Miles of fiber affected for expected PGA with 2% probability.

Fig. 8. Miles of fiber affected for expected PGA with 10% probability.

References

1. Given, D.D., et al.: Revised technical implementation plan for the shakealert system-an earthquake early warning system for the west coast of the united states. Technical report, US Geological Survey (2018)
2. Liu, S., Bischof, Z., Madan, I., Chan, P., Bustamante, F.: Out of sight, not out of mind - a user-view on the criticality of the submarine cable network. In: ACM IMC (2020)
3. Kumaran Mani, S., Hall, M., Durairajan, R., Barford, P.: Characteristics of metro fiber deployments in the us. In: 2020 Network Traffic Measurement and Analysis Conference (TMA). IEEE (2020)
4. Durairajan, R., Barford, C., Barford, P.: Lights out: climate change risk to internet infrastructure. In: Proceedings of Applied Networking Research Workshop (2018)
5. Durairajan, R., Barford, P., Sommers, J., Willinger, W.: InterTubes: a study of the US long-haul fiber-optic infrastructure. In: Proceedings of ACM SIGCOMM (2015)
6. Giovinazzi, S., et al.: Resilience and fragility of the telecommunication network to seismic events. Bull. N. Z. Soc. Earthq. Eng. **50**(2), 318–328 (2017)
7. Fukuda, K., et al.: Impact of tohoku earthquake on R&E network in Japan. In: Proceedings of the Special Workshop on Internet and Disasters, pp. 1–6 (2011)
8. The Kobe Earthquake: Telecommunications Survives at Kobe University. https://thejournal.com/Articles/1996/03/01/The-Kobe-Earthquake-Telecommunications-Survives-at-Kobe-University.aspx
9. Leelardcharoen, K.: Interdependent response of telecommunication and electric power systems to seismic hazard. Ph.D. dissertation, Georgia Institute of Technology (2011)
10. Esposito, S., Botta, A., De Falco, M., Iervolino, I., Pescape, A., Santo, A.: Seismic risk analysis of data communication networks: a feasibility study. In: 16th European Conference on Earthquake Engineering (2018)
11. Schulman, A., Spring, N.: Pingin' in the rain. In: ACM IMC, November 2011
12. Eriksson, B., Durairajan, R., Barford, P.: RiskRoute: a framework for mitigating network outage threats. In: ACM CoNEXT (2013)
13. Padmanabhan, R., Schulman, A., Levin, D., Spring, N.: Residential links under the weather. In: Proceedings of the ACM Special Interest Group on Data Communication, pp. 145–158 (2019)
14. ESRI ArcGIS. http://www.arcgis.com/features/
15. Baker, J.W.: An introduction to probabilistic seismic hazard analysis (PSHA). White paper, version, vol. 1, p. 72 (2008)

16. McGuire, R.K.: Probabilistic seismic hazard analysis and design earthquakes: closing the loop. Bull. Seismol. Soc. Am. **85**(5), 1275–1284 (1995)
17. Modified Mercalli Intensity Scale. https://www.usgs.gov/media/images/modified-mercalli-intensity-scale
18. Joyner, W.B., Boore, D.M.: Prediction of earthquake response spectra. US Geological Survey Open-file report (1982)
19. Wang, Z.: Understanding seismic hazard and risk: a gap between engineers and seismologists. In: The 14th World Conference on Earthquake Engineering (2008)
20. Wang, K., Tréhu, A.M.: Invited review paper: some outstanding issues in the study of great megathrust earthquakes-the cascadia example. J. Geodyn. **98**, 1–18 (2016)
21. Preston, L.A., Creager, K.C., Crosson, R.S., Brocher, T.M., Trehu, A.M.: Intraslab earthquakes: dehydration of the cascadia slab. Science **302**(5648), 1197–1200 (2003)
22. Wells, R.E., Blakely, R.J., Wech, A.G., McCrory, P.A., Michael, A.: Cascadia subduction tremor muted by crustal faults. Geology **45**(6), 515–518 (2017)
23. Willinger, W., Doyle, J.: Robustness and the internet: design and evolution. In: Robust-Design: A Repertoire of Biological, Ecological, and Engineering Case Studies (2002)
24. Doyle, J.C., et al.: The "robust yet fragile" nature of the internet. In: Proceedings of the National Academy of Sciences (2005)
25. Gorman, S.P., Schintler, L., Kulkarni, R., Stough, R.: The revenge of distance: vulnerability analysis of critical information infrastructure. J. Conting. Crisis Manag. **12**(2), 48–63 (2004)
26. Gorman, S.: Networks, Security And Complexity: The Role of Public Policy in Critical Infrastructure Protection. Edward Elgar (2005)
27. Zhou, L.: Vulnerability analysis of the physical part of the internet. Int. J. Crit. Infrastruct. **6**(4), 402–420 (2010)
28. Heegaard, P.E., Trivedi, K.S.: Network survivability modeling. Comput. Netw. **53**(8), 1215–1234 (2009)
29. Ho, P.-H., Tapolcai, J., Mouftah, H.: On achieving optimal survivable routing for shared protection in survivable next-generation internet. IEEE Trans. Reliab. **53**(2), 216–225 (2004)
30. Wu, J., Zhang, Y., Mao, Z.M., Shin, K.G.: Internet routing resilience to failures: analysis and implications. In: ACM CoNEXT Conference (2007)
31. Agarwal, P., Efrat, A., Ganjugunte, S., Hay, D., Sankararaman, S., Zussman, G.: The resilience of WDM networks to probabilistic geographical failures. In: IEEE INFOCOM (2011)
32. Eriksson, B., Durairajan, R., Barford, P.: RiskRoute: a framework for mitigating network outage threats. In: ACM CoNEXT, December 2013
33. Bush, R., Maennel, O., Roughan, M., Uhlig, S.: Internet optometry: assessing the broken glasses in internet reachability. In: ACM IMC (2009)
34. Katz-Bassett, E., Madhyastha, H.V., John, J.P., Krishnamurthy, A., Wetherall, D., Anderson, T.: Studying black holes in the internet with hubble. In: USENIX NSDI (2008)
35. Kant, K., Deccio, C.: Security and Robustness in the Internet Infrastructure (2012)
36. Katz-Bassett, E., et al.: LIFEGUARD: practical repair of persistent route failures. In: ACM SIGCOMM (2012)
37. Quan, L., Heidemann, J., Pradkin, Y.: Detecting internet outages with precise active probing (extended). USC Technical report (2012)
38. Glatz, E., Dimitropoulos, X.: Classifying internet one-way traffic. In: ACM IMC (2012)
39. Wang, H., Yang, Y.R., Liu, P.H., Wang, J., Gerber, A., Greenberg, A.: Reliability as an inter-domain service. In: ACM SIGCOMM (2007)
40. Andersen, D., Balakrishnan, H., Kaashoek, F., Morris, R.: Resilient overlay networks. In: ACM SOSP (2001)
41. Zhu, Y., Bavier, A., Feamster, N., Rangarajan, S., Rexford, J.: UFO: a resilient layered routing architecture. In: SIGCOMM CCR (2008)

42. Hansen, A.F., Kvalbein, A., Čičić, T., Gjessing, S.: Resilient routing layers for network disaster planning. In: Lorenz, P., Dini, P. (eds.) ICN 2005. LNCS, vol. 3421, pp. 1097–1105. Springer, Heidelberg (2005). https://doi.org/10.1007/978-3-540-31957-3_125

43. Gummadi, P.K., Madhyastha, H.V., Gribble, S.D., Levy, H.M., Wetherall, D.: Improving the reliability of internet paths with one-hop source routing. In: USENIX OSDI (2004)

44. Eriksson, B., Durairajan, R., Barford, P.: Riskroute: a framework for mitigating network outage threats. In: Proceedings of ACM CoNEXT (2013)

45. Madory, D.: Hurricane Sandy: Global Impacts — Dyn Blog. http://www.renesys.com/blog/2012/11/sandys-global-impacts.shtml

46. Cowie, J., Popescu, A., Underwood, T.: Impact of hurricane katrina on internet infrastructure. Report, Renesys (2005)

47. Anderson, S., Barford, C., Barford, P.: Five alarms: assessing the vulnerability of cellular communication infrastructure to wildfires. In: ACM IMC (2020)

48. Kaikoura quake produced strongest ground shaking in NZ, new research shows. https://www.gns.cri.nz/Home/News-and-Events/Media-Releases-and-News/strongest-ground-shaking-in-NZ

49. 2011 great tohoku earthquake, Japan. https://earthquake.usgs.gov/earthquakes/eventpage/official20110311054624120_30/executive

50. Evidence for Submarine cables terminating at nearby colocation facilities. http://cryptome.org/eyeball/cablew/cablew-eyeball.htm

51. Durairajan, R., Ghosh, S., Tang, X., Barford, P., Eriksson, B.: Internet atlas: a geographic database of the internet. In: ACM HotPlanet (2013)

52. OpenCelliD - The world's largest Open Database of Cell Towers. https://www.opencellid.org/

53. Petersen, M.D., et al.: The 2014 united states national seismic hazard model. Earthquake Spectra 31(S1), S1–S30 (2015)

54. ArcGIS Contour (3D Analyst). https://pro.arcgis.com/en/pro-app/tool-reference/3d-analyst/contour.htm

55. Arcgis intersect (analysis). https://pro.arcgis.com/en/pro-app/tool-reference/analysis/intersect.htm

56. Arcgis summarize within (analysis). https://pro.arcgis.com/en/pro-app/tool-reference/analysis/summarize-within.htm

57. Arcpy. https://pro.arcgis.com/en/pro-app/arcpy/get-started/what-is-arcpy-.htm

58. Quake shakes up the net, December 2006. http://www.thestar.com.my/story/?file=%2f2006%2f12%2f28%2fnation%2f16426778&sec=nation

59. Lindsey, N.J., et al.: Fiber-Optic Network Observations of Earthquake Wavefields. Geophys. Res. Lett. 44(23), 11792–11799 (2017)

60. USA Core Based Statistical Area. https://hub.arcgis.com/datasets/4d29eb6f07e94b669c0-b90c2aa267100_0

61. Durairajan, R., Barford, P.: A techno-economic approach for broadband deployment in underserved areas. In: Proceedings of ACM SIGCOMM CCR (2017)

62. NOAA Tsunami Forecasting System (SIFT). https://nctr.pmel.noaa.gov/Pdf/SIFT_3_2_2_Overview.pdf

63. NOAA Tsunami Forecasting. https://nctr.pmel.noaa.gov/tsunami-forecast.html

64. Nowicki, M.A., Wald, D.J., Hamburger, M.W., Hearne, M., Thompson, E.M.: Development of a globally applicable model for near real-time prediction of seismically induced landslides. Eng. Geol. 173, 54–65 (2014)

65. Allstadt, K.E., et al.: Usgs approach to real-time estimation of earthquake-triggered ground failure-results of 2015 workshop. Technical report, US Geological Survey (2016)

66. Naeim, F., Bhatia, H., Lobo, R.M.: Performance based seismic engineering. In: Naeim, F. (ed.) The Seismic Design Handbook, pp. 757–792. Springer, Boston (2001). https://doi.org/10.1007/978-1-4615-1693-4_15

DoS

New Kids on the DRDoS Block: Characterizing Multiprotocol and Carpet Bombing Attacks

Tiago Heinrich[1]($\boxtimes$) ⓘ, Rafael R. Obelheiro[2] ⓘ, and Carlos A. Maziero[1] ⓘ

[1] Federal University of Paraná, Curitiba, Brazil
{theinrich,maziero}@inf.ufpr.br
[2] Graduate Program in Applied Computing, UDESC, Joinville, Brazil
rafael.obelheiro@udesc.br

Abstract. Distributed reflection denial of service (DRDoS) attacks are widespread on the Internet. DRDoS attacks exploit mostly UDP-based protocols to achieve traffic amplification and provide an extra layer of indirection between attackers and their victims, and a single attack can reach hundreds of Gbps. Recent trends in DRDoS include multiprotocol amplification attacks, which exploit several protocols at the same time, and carpet bombing attacks, which target multiple IP addresses in the same subnet instead of a single address, in order to evade detection. Such attacks have been reported in the wild, but have not been discussed in the scientific literature so far. This paper describes the first research on the characterization of both multiprotocol and carpet bombing DRDoS attacks. We developed MP-H, a honeypot that implements nine different protocols commonly used in DRDoS attacks, and used it for data collection. Over a period of 731 days, our honeypot received 1.8 TB of traffic, containing nearly 20.7 billion requests, and was involved in more than 1.4 million DRDoS attacks, including over 13.7 thousand multiprotocol attacks. We describe several features of multiprotocol attacks and compare them to monoprotocol attacks that occurred in the same period, and characterize the carpet bombing attacks seen by our honeypot.

Keywords: Amplification attacks · Network characterization · Distributed reflection denial of service

1 Introduction

Distributed denial-of-service attacks (DDoS) have been seen on the Internet for nearly 25 years [13]. In these attacks, a set of machines sends traffic to a victim in a coordinated fashion. The volume of data leads to the exhaustion of system and/or network resources at the victim, causing service unavailability and hurting legitimate customers [17].

One kind of DDoS attack are Distributed Reflection Denial of Service (DRDoS) attacks (also known as amplification DDoS attacks), in which traffic is bounced off unsuspecting intermediate systems, known as reflectors [24].

© Springer Nature Switzerland AG 2021
O. Hohlfeld et al. (Eds.): PAM 2021, LNCS 12671, pp. 269–283, 2021.
https://doi.org/10.1007/978-3-030-72582-2_16

DRDoS attacks not only make attribution harder due to an extra layer of indirection, but they also provide traffic amplification, thus making it easier to generate enough traffic to disrupt the target, especially when multiple reflectors are used simultaneously. Moreover, DRDoS attacks can leverage several different protocols, notably UDP-based ones, and there is a large number of vulnerable and/or misconfigured Internet servers that can be used as reflectors [26]. All these benefits to attackers help to explain the prevalence of DRDoS traffic on the Internet. A study [19] has shown a 9% increase in DRDoS attacks between the second semester of 2017 and the same period of 2018, and statistics from April 2019 indicate that nearly 70% of DDoS attacks use reflection [6]. It has also been reported that attacks grew 15% from 2019 to 2020 (25% during the lockdown period due to the COVID-19 pandemic) [20].

Given the relevance of DRDoS attacks, researchers have worked on the analysis and characterization of the traffic associated with such attacks. However, there is a lack of research on multiprotocol DRDoS attacks, where a victim is attacked using multiple amplification protocols simultaneously, which is an emerging trend in the DDoS scene [21]. Most existing research considers either individual protocols [1,5,7,25,27], or multiple protocols in isolation from each other [9,10,22,26,29]. Another trend in DRDoS are carpet bombing attacks, which target multiple IP addresses in the same subnet (instead of a single IP address) in order to evade detection while still being able to cause disruption by flooding access links. Such attacks have not been discussed in the literature, although [9] presents some results when victims are aggregated by /16 CIDR blocks.

Our research aims to bridge these gaps in knowledge by characterizing multiprotocol and carpet bombing DRDoS attacks. We have designed and implemented MP-H, a honeypot that emulates reflectors for several protocols that are exploited in DRDoS attacks: Chargen, DNS, NTP, Memcached, QOTD, SSDP, CoAP, CLDAP, and Steam. Results from 731 days of data collected by our honeypot comprise nearly 20.7 billion requests and confirm that multiprotocol attacks are found in the wild: 2.9% of the victims of DRDoS attacks carried out using our honeypot as a reflector suffered a multiprotocol attack, with up to three protocols being used simultaneously. More than 3.7% of all attacks employed carpet bombing, affecting 21.8% of the victims observed.

In summary, this paper makes the following contributions: we propose a definition for what constitutes a multiprotocol DRDoS attack; we describe several characteristics of multiprotocol DRDoS attacks and compare them with monoprotocol attacks observed on the same honeypot; and we characterize carpet bombing attacks observed on our honeypot.

The remainder of this paper is organized as follows. Section 2 discusses related work. Section 3 describes our honeypot MP-H. Section 4 presents our data analysis. Finally, Sect. 5 concludes the paper.

2   Related Work

This section reviews related work on DRDoS traffic characterization, with an emphasis on the analysis of attacks in the wild rather than in controlled environments. Some studies are focused on a single protocol, such as DNS [1,7,25] and NTP [5,27]. Attack characteristics examined include temporal distribution, intensity and duration of attacks, victim locations, packet-level attributes (TTL, size), amplification factor, and payloads.

Rossow [26] explored how 14 different protocols could be used in amplification attacks, and estimated the amplification factor provided by each one. He also performed traffic analysis: flow data from an European ISP were used to identify victims and amplifiers within the network, UDP scans to darknet addresses were used to identify potential attackers, and honeypots were used mainly to confirm the occurrence of attacks, without deeper analysis.

Krämer et al. [9] introduced AmpPots, which are honeypots designed for observing and collecting DRDoS traffic using nine protocols (NTP, DNS, Chargen, SSDP, MS-SQL, NetBIOS, QOTD, SIP, and SNMP). They analyzed data collected from 21 AmpPots between February and May 2015, totaling more than 1.5 million attacks, and described characteristics such as attack duration, victim geolocation, and request entropy (payload diversity). They also performed an analysis of DDoS botnets.

Noroozian et al. [22] analyzed DRDoS traffic collected from eight AmpPots during 2014–2015, with a total of six network protocols (NTP, DNS, Chargen, SSDP, QOTD, and SNMP). The main thrust of their study is a characterization of DRDoS victims, including their network type (access, hosting, enterprise) and geolocation. They also discuss the duration of attacks per victim type.

Thomas et al. [29] analyzed DRDoS traffic collected from a large set of UDP honeypots for eight protocols (QOTD, Chargen, DNS, NTP, SSDP, MS-SQL, Portmap, and mDNS). They observed more than 5.8 million attacks over a period of 1010 days, and analyzed scanning behavior and several attack characteristics (duration, packet counts, number of attacks). NTP and DNS were the most popular protocols, but they also noticed significant amounts of SSDP traffic.

Jonkers et al. [8] analyzed DDoS traffic using both AmpPots and backscatter traffic from an Internet telescope. They observed more than 20 million attacks over two years (2015–2017), affecting more than 2.2 million /24 networks. They also describe joint attacks, which are attacks that employ both DRDoS and regular DDoS with spoofed source addresses (mostly TCP SYN floods).

While these studies investigated DRDoS attacks involving several protocols, they mostly ignore how these protocols are used together. In fact, Krämer et al. [9] acknowledge the existence of attacks using multiple protocols, but do not explore this further, while the joint attacks in [8] are combinations of DRDoS and regular DDoS. None of the studies consider carpet bombing attacks. In this paper we specifically address multiprotocol DRDoS and carpet bombing attacks, aiming to understand their characteristics and how they compare to monoprotocol ones.

3   MP-H, a Multiprotocol Honeypot

To observe and collect DRDoS traffic, we developed MP-H, a multiprotocol honeypot that supports nine different UDP-based protocols: Chargen, QOTD, DNS, NTP, SSDP, Memcached, CoAP, CLDAP, and Steam (used in online games). CoAP and CLDAP have been added in March and July 2020, respectively, while the other protocols have been supported from the beginning (September 2018). MP-H is designed to mimic a reflector: it receives requests and provides responses that look legitimate, logging all the received traffic. A list of ongoing attacks (with source IP address, number of requests, and the timestamps of the first and last seen requests) is updated in real-time and kept in memory, and periodically written to permanent storage when activity is low. Full packets are captured using Tcpdump [28] for off-line processing (e.g., payload analysis).

Since it does not host any publicly advertised service, an MP-H instance will become a reflector after it has been found through scanning. Once it has been uncovered, the honeypot address can be used in DRDoS attacks and will likely be shared among miscreants. Observing reflection attacks, however, does not require actually taking part in them. Therefore, the honeypot should respond correctly to scans (increasing the odds that it will be recruited for future attacks), but not contribute significantly to DRDoS attacks. To achieve this, MP-H responds to at most five responses per IP address per day; this should be enough to both provide positive feedback to a scanner and severely limits the amount of attack traffic it sends to a single victim. Every hour MP-H scans the list of banned IP addresses and removes offenders that have been there for 24 h or more.

There are several projects that scan the Internet for open reflectors, such as [4] and [23]. In order to avoid being reported as an open reflector, MP-H has a list of banned IP addresses for which no responses are sent. This list was compiled from several sources (e.g., [16], project web pages), and is updated manually whenever we discover new scanning addresses while analyzing logs.

MP-H is similar in design to AmpPot [9], with the main differences being in implementation specifics and in the set of supported protocols. In MP-H, DNS and Memcached requests are proxied to actual servers (thus eliciting truthful responses), while the other protocols are emulated by the honeypot, which synthesizes legitimate-looking responses with fabricated content. The honeypot is written in Python, and runs on Linux. The source code is not publicly available yet, but we are open to sharing the tool with interested researchers.

4   Data Analysis

An MP-H instance has been deployed in our university network since September 2018, collecting data 24/7. It has a public IP address and is exposed to the Internet (i.e., it is not behind a firewall or NAT box). In this section we analyze data collected using this instance over a period of 731 days, from September 2018 to September 2020. Section 4.1 gives overall traffic statistics. Section 4.2 explores attack intensity. Section 4.3 performs per-protocol analyses. Section 4.4 describes the victims. Finally, Sect. 4.5 dissects carpet bombing attacks.

4.1   Overview

Over a period of 731 days, our honeypot received 1.8 TB of traffic, containing nearly 20.7 billion (B) requests, an average of 28.3 million (M) requests per day. Only a tiny fraction (less than 7.2M, 0.034% of the total) of those requests received a response, showing the effectiveness of the response limiting mechanism.

In this work, we define a *monoprotocol attack* as a set of five or more requests with source IP addresses belonging to the same CIDR block (a *victim*) and the same destination UDP port, in which consecutive requests are at most 60 s apart. Victims are defined as IP addresses within a CIDR block instead of a single IP address due to carpet bombing attacks, as discussed in Sect. 4.5. The thresholds (5 requests and 60 s) were established empirically: we analyzed the traffic collected by the honeypot during the first three weeks manually, and observed distinct behaviors from the same source IP address:

1. "Slow": a small number (≤ 3) of requests, a few (1–2) seconds apart;
2. "Fast": many (≥ 10) nearly identical requests, in quick succession;
3. "Bursty": sequences of bursts of "fast" traffic, tens of seconds apart.

We classified the first as scan traffic and the others as attack traffic. We then experimented with distinct thresholds until we reached an automatic classification that closely matched our manual classification. We believe this approach is reasonable on a problem without ground truth, but acknowledge that future work may require different thresholds as we learn more about typical attacker behavior.

By analogy, we define a *multiprotocol attack* as a set of five or more requests with source IP addresses belonging to the same CIDR block and with two or more unique destination UDP ports, in which consecutive requests are at most 60 s apart. By this definition, two monoprotocol attacks against the same victim that use different protocols and are spaced by at most 60 s become a multiprotocol attack.

Table 1 shows the overall attack statistics. The honeypot observed nearly 1,4M DRDoS attacks, of which 99.05% were monoprotocol attacks and 0.95% were multiprotocol attacks. While monoprotocol attacks are much more prevalent, there were 13.8k multiprotocol attacks. Multiprotocol attacks account for 2.9% of the victims and 2.5% of the requests. The average number of requests per attack for multiprotocol attacks is 38.2k, almost twice the average for monoprotocol attacks, which is 19.8k requests per attack.

Our data collection period covered the Brazilian presidential elections (October 2018) and the lockdown period of COVID-19 (from March 2020 onwards), with some interesting results. Compared to the previous month, the packet rate doubled during the election month, and on the day of the second round (Oct 28th) the number of attacks had a 227% increase. We compared the four-month period with stricter lockdown (March–June) to the same period in 2019 and to the four months before it. We observed 4× growth of the packet rate during the lockdown period compared to the other two periods, and the emergence of new victims in health organizations, e-commerce, and academic institutions.

Table 1. Attack statistics

Type of attack	Requests	%	Victims	%	Attacks	%
Monoprotocol	20,203,393,971	97.50	1,079,210	97.08	1,432,775	99.05
Multiprotocol	518,684,765	2.50	32,369	2.91	13,798	0.95
Total	20,722,078,736	100	1,111,579	100	1,446,573	100

4.2   Attack Intensity

Figure 1 presents the empirical cumulative distribution function (CDF) for the number of requests per attack, and Table 2 (top) shows a statistical summary. Both types of attacks have right-skewed distributions. Multiprotocol attacks had more requests than monoprotocol attacks up to the 99.99th percentile. This means that a large majority of multiprotocol attacks had more requests than the corresponding fraction of monoprotocol attacks.

Table 2. Attack intensity statistics

	Monoprotocol	Multiprotocol
No. of attacks w/$\geq$ 1M requests	1,927 (0.1%)	60 (0.4%)
Attack w/most requests	221.9 M (1.0%)	7.8 M (1.5%)
Duration (median)	612.5 s	2673.9 s
No. of attacks lasting $\geq$ 1 h	39,886 (2.7%)	1,737 (12.5%)
Longest attack	178.6 h (7.4 days)	180.0 h (7.5 days)
Requests per day (avg/max)	27.6M/253.7M	1.3M/17.5M
Packets per second (avg)	31.7 pps	13.8 pps

Figure 2 shows the CDF for the duration of attacks. The duration is measured as the time difference between the first and last requests in an attack. The distribution is left-skewed for both mono and multiprotocol attacks. Multiprotocol attacks last longer than monoprotocol attacks up to the 99.99th percentile. Table 2 (middle) presents some statistics. In [9], 62% of the attacks were shorter that 15 min and 90% lasted up to 1 h; the corresponding fractions for MP-H were 87% and 95.9%, respectively, which means that the attacks we observed were shorter overall.

Figure 3 depicts the daily attacks observed by the honeypot. The number of attacks climbed quickly after the honeypot was deployed, and remained relatively steady until June 2020. The notable exception was a 15-day period bridging July (last 8 days) and August 2019 (first 7 days), when the average jumped from 1.9k to 18.4k attacks per day. This period saw predominantly small attacks (80% of attacks had up to 127 requests) that targeted unrelated victims, and we could not find an explanation for this spike. The rise starting in July 2020 is due to

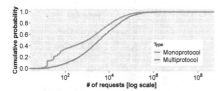
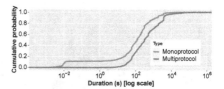

Fig. 1. ECDF for requests per attack   **Fig. 2.** ECDF for attack duration

the deployment of the CLDAP honeypot; the average for July–September was 6,621 attacks per day. Overall, the number of attacks per day was 1,449, and the maximum was 20.9k. Only 29 out of 731 days (4.0%) had 5,000 attacks or more, with 15 of these days in July-August 2019. There were 33 multiprotocol attacks per day on average, but they were observed on only 386 days (52.8%).

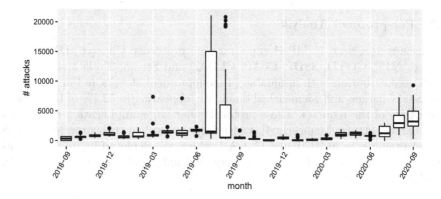

Fig. 3. Evolution of the number of attacks per day

Figure 4 depicts the number of requests per month, broken down by protocol. The number of requests varies each month, without discernible trend. The number of requests follows the number of attacks shown in Fig. 3, but imperfectly: in 2019, June had the most requests but not too many attacks, while July and August has the most attacks with a moderate number of requests (since most attacks were small). The protocol breakdown shows that Memcached and Chargen had the most monthly requests until July 2020, when we started collecting CLDAP traffic and this protocol became prevalent (this is further discussed in Sect. 4.3). Table 2 (bottom) shows statistics about requests per day/second. The number of requests per day for multiprotocol attacks is heavily skewed, and the average considers only days with attacks. The number of requests for other protocols fluctuated, but were mostly dwarfed by the leading protocols. Putting the two dimensions (attacks and requests) together, we find a rather low intensity of 30.6 pps for attack traffic (considering only busy periods).

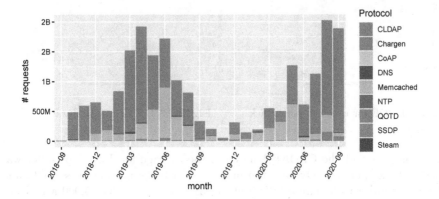

Fig. 4. Evolution of monthly requests (overall). We started observing CoAP and CLDAP traffic in 2020-03 and 2020-07, respectively.

4.3 Per-protocol Analyses

As discussed in Sect. 3, MP-H supports nine protocols: Chargen, DNS, Memcached, NTP, QOTD, SSDP, CoAP, CLDAP and Steam. Table 3 shows their relative contribution both in number of monoprotocol attacks and in number of requests. Chargen and Memcached dominate, appearing in 52.1% of the attacks and 84.2% of the requests. These protocols offer large amplification factors (60 for Chargen, 262 for Memcached), which helps to explain their prevalence. DNS gained prominence in 2020, and CLDAP, which was deployed in July 2020, has already climbed to number three in requests and number four in attacks (in absolute numbers).

Table 3. Protocol breakdown for monoprotocol attacks and requests

Protocol	Chargen	CLDAP	CoAP	DNS	Memcached	NTP	QOTD	SSDP	Steam
Attacks (%)	21.5	9.2	0.01	25.0	30.5	5.3	2.0	5.8	0.05
Requests (%)	60.9	12.6	0.0002	0.9	23.3	0.01	1.5	0.5	0.000004

Table 4 shows the average amplification factors observed for each protocol (Steam is omitted due to low traffic), along with factors previously reported in the literature. Memcached had the largest amplification factor, 262. Most protocols exhibited lower amplification factors than reported before; a possible explanation might be that our number is the average factor, while others may be the maximum factor rather than the average one. The exceptions were CLDAP and DNS, which remained within the reported range, and SSDP, which had a larger amplification factor than previously reported. The latter is due to the response synthesized by the honeypot being larger than the responses in [11,26].

Table 4. Amplification factors observed in MP-H and in the literature

Protocol	MP-H	Literature	Protocol	MP-H	Literature
Chargen	60	556.9 [26]	Memcached	262	51,200 [12]
CLDAP	62	46–70 [2,15]	NTP	42	556.9 [26]
CoAP	25	34–46 [3,18]	QOTD	78	140.3 [26]
DNS	50	28.7–64.1 [26]	SSDP	97	20–75.9 [11,26]

Table 5 presents the most popular combinations of protocols in multiprotocol attacks, ranked both by number of attacks and by number of requests. The most used protocols were Chargen, DNS, CLDAP, and SSDP; attacks with Chargen and one of the other three account for 82.2% of the attacks and 64.1% of the requests. Two noteworthy aspects are (i) Chargen being used in all top combinations, and (ii) CLDAP already being used in nearly two-thirds of the attacks. The Chargen:CLDAP attacks are less intense, however, than Chargen:DNS and Chargen:SSDP attacks, which account for a larger fraction of requests. There were just 230 attacks (1.66% of the multiprotocol attacks) with more than two protocols. We can conclude that monoprotocol attacks are exploiting a wider range of protocols, focusing on those with higher amplification factors. Multiprotocol attacks exploit a smaller set of protocols, with varying combinations, which explains the concentration in four protocols.

Table 5. Protocol combinations used in multiprotocol attacks (CG = Chargen)

Protocol	CG:DNS	CG:CLDAP	CG:SSDP	CG:Memcached	Others
Attacks (%)	8.2	65.4	8.6	5.6	12.2
Requests (%)	27.9	16.7	19.5	9.2	26.7

For protocols where responses do not depend on request contents, such as Chargen and QOTD, attackers can maximize the amplification factor by minimizing payload size. 100% of Chargen requests observed had just one byte of payload and 98.2% of QOTD requests had two bytes or less.

When amplification depends on message contents, not just size, we can identify some prevalent patterns. SSDP had 99.9% of M-SEARCH requests, used for service discovery, while NTP had 99.9% of MONLIST requests, used for listing recent peers. The protocols recently added to MP-H, CoAP and CLDAP, follow a similar pattern. 99.5% of the CoAP requests contained a null URI, while 99.1% of the CLDAP requests contained a searchRequest <ROOT> operation. In all cases, the aim is to maximize amplification.

DNS requests exploit a wide variety of resource records (RRs). 115.9k distinct RRs were observed, and the six most used, which account for 34.5% of the queries, are listed in Table 6 (size is not available for access-board.gov because its name servers no longer answer `ANY` queries). The top two queries were also reported in [9]. The most frequent query, `isc.org ANY`, yields an amplification factor of 71.1. While there are other names that provide larger responses, a possible reason for using this name is that ISC is responsible for the BIND name server, and thus at the forefront of DNS developments, which suggests the existence of many records in the zone apex and good name server availability. The query types observed are shown in Table 7. The vast majority (91.9%) of the queries were for `ANY`, which returns all records for a given name (regardless of type), usually resulting in larger responses.

Memcached is abused for amplification in two ways. One is requesting statistics from the server, which provides an amplification factor of 32 on average. The other is using `set` to store large values in the in-memory database and later repeatedly retrieving these values with `get` requests for the associated key. 99.99% of the requests observed in MP-H were of the second kind, mostly with random data. The amplification factor depends on the value size.

Table 6. DNS queries observed

Resource Record	%	Size
`isc.org ANY`	22.1	2701
`067.cz ANY`	4.0	388
`access-board.gov ANY`	3.6	N/A
`irs.gov ANY`	2.1	4302
`1x1.cz ANY`	1.6	1501
`pbgc.gov ANY`	1.1	4223
Others	65.5	–

Table 7. DNS query types observed

QTYPE	%
`ANY`	91.9
`TXT`	7.9
`A`	0.035
`CNAME`	0.014
`NS`	0.009
Others	0.14

4.4 Victims

Since DRDoS attacks employ IP spoofing, we consider the source IP addresses of attack traffic as victim addresses. They are grouped by CIDR block according to the GeoLite2 database [14], also the source for AS numbers and geolocation.

Monoprotocol attacks affected victims in 226 countries (country codes, actually), and 111 countries had victims of multiprotocol attacks. Table 8 shows the top countries in terms of monoprotocol and multiprotocol attacks. Victims in United States and China are targeted by 39.8% of the monoprotocol attacks and 63.6% of the multiprotocol attacks, with United Kingdom ranking third for both types of attacks. In spite of the top 3 countries being the same, the targets of monoprotocol and multiprotocol attacks are poorly correlated: the rank correlation for countries with at least one attack of each kind is weak (Spearman's coefficient $r_s = 0.36, p < 0.01$).

Table 9 shows the top six AS Numbers in terms of victims of both monoprotocol and multiprotocol attacks. Victims are widely distributed across ASNs,

Table 8. Top target countries in number of attacks

Mono	%	Multi	%
US	32.6	US	49.6
CN	7.2	CN	14.0
GB	3.6	GB	4.7
FR	2.6	CA	3.4
CA	2.2	BR	2.7
DE	2.1	AU	2.4
Others	49.7	Others	23.2

Table 9. Top target ASNs in number of victims

ASN	Country	Victims (%)
7922	US	7.1
7018	US	3.3
20115	US	1.8
37963	CN	1.6
701	US	1.5
16276	FR	1.3
Others	–	83.4

with the top ASNs accounting for just 16.6% of the victims. ASNs 7922 (COM-CAST), 7018 (AT&T INTERNET), 20115 (Charter Communications), and 701 (UUNET) belong to Internet service providers, while ASNs 37963 (Hangzhou Alibaba Advertising Co), and 16276 (OVH) belong to cloud providers.

Table 10 presents statistics about the number of attacks per victim. In general, there were more monoprotocol than multiprotocol attacks per victim, which was expected. Most victims received few attacks, which is similar to the findings in [9], where 79% of the victims were attacked just once and 0.8% suffered more than 10 attacks (our fraction of victims with more than 10 monoprotocol attacks is higher, though).

Table 10. Attacks per victim

	Monoprotocol	Multiprotocol
Attacks per victim (median)	2	1
Attacks per victim (max)	3,837	229
Fraction of victims w/only one attack	60.2%	83.8%
Fraction of victims w/≤10 attacks	97.7%	99.2%
Fraction of victims w/>10 attacks	2.3%	0.8%

4.5 Carpet Bombing Attacks

A recent trend in DRDoS attacks are carpet bombing attacks, which target multiple IP addresses within the same subnet or CIDR block in lieu of a single IP address [19]. The goal is to flood the access links of the intended victims while evading detection and hampering mitigation. Carpet bombing detection requires looking for anomalous traffic across entire subnets or CIDR blocks instead of anomalous flows involving a single IP address, while mitigation involves filtering traffic to the entire subnets/blocks, and/or diverting it to a scrubbing service.

A real example of carpet bombing observed on MP-H was an attack that lasted 14 min and used two protocols, Chargen and Memcached. This attack had 340k requests that were spread across 43 different IP addresses in the same CIDR block, averaging 7.9k requests per address.

Two variants of carpet bombing observed in MP-H are depicted in Figs. 5 and 6. Figure 5 shows the most prevalent case, where addresses in the same CIDR block are targeted in overlapping time intervals. The second case (Fig. 6) presents what we called an attack *with antecedents*. Here, the carpet bombing attack occurs after a few days where a single address is targeted each day. We have considered these individual attacks to be antecedents to the carpet bombing because they have similar characteristics – protocol (Chargen and Memcached), duration, number of requests –, even if the addresses are different.

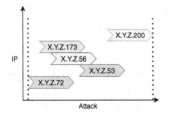

Fig. 5. Carpet bombing attack

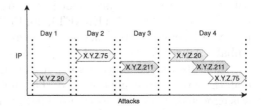

Fig. 6. Carpet bombing with antecedents

Table 11 presents statistics for carpet bombing attacks, with percentages relative to the totals in Table 1. We define a carpet bombing attack as an attack targeting multiple IP addresses from the same CIDR block. These attacks account for a small fraction of attacks and requests (3.7% of all attacks and 5.8% of the associated requests), but affect more than one-fifth of the victims (some victims suffered both mono- and multiprotocol carpet bombing).

Table 11. Carpet bombing statistics

Carpet bombing	Requests	%	Victims	%	Attacks	%
Monoprotocol	1,117,437,837	5.39	235,244	21.16	52,689	3.64
Multiprotocol	78,018,641	0.37	22,825	2.05	949	0.07
Total	1,195,456,478	5.76	242,030	21.77	53,638	3.71

We observed a total of 1.1M victims, of which 21.8% (242k) suffered carpet bombing attacks. Carpet bombing attacks averaged 31.2k requests overall, and 9.6k per host in a CIDR block. Considering only attacks that use more than 50% of a CIDR block, the average rises to 41.5k requests, albeit with an average of just 185 requests per host. This shows that, when attackers target a larger fraction of a CIDR block, the number of requests per host tends to be smaller. On average, each attack targeted 6.2% of the addresses in a CIDR block, but 1.7% of the attacks targeted 90% or more of a single CIDR block.

Table 12 shows the most popular protocols in carpet bombing attacks. Comparing to Tables 3 and 5, here we have a greater presence of SSDP, but there are still similarities with other choices of reflector protocols (90.8% of the multiprotocol attacks use just two protocols).

Table 12. Top protocols in carpet bombing attacks

Monoprotocol		Multiprotocol	
SSDP	29.3%	Chargen:DNS	20.8%
Chargen	15.2%	CLDAP:SSDP	14.8%
Memcached	12.9%	DNS:SSDP	14.6%
Others	42.6%	Others	49.8%

Table 13 presents statistics on the number of requests and duration of carpet bombing attacks, for both mono and multiprotocol attacks. Both distributions are heavily right-skewed. There were attacks with more than 1M requests (0.4% for mono, 1.6% for multi), a significant amount from the vantage point of a single reflector. Another notable finding is that almost 25% of multiprotocol carpet bombing attacks lasted 1 h or more.

Table 13. Carpet bombing attack statistics

	Monoprotocol	Multiprotocol
Requests (avg)	29.8k	86.4k
Requests (99th percentile)	431k	1.3M
Duration (avg)	20 min	4 h
No. of attacks lasting ≥ 1 h	1637 (3.1%)	221 (23.3%)
Longest attack	7 days	7.5 days

5   Conclusion

Distributed reflection denial of service (DRDoS) attacks still plague the Internet, and are constantly evolving to become more difficult to detect and mitigate. In this paper we present the first detailed study about multiprotocol DRDoS attacks. We used a honeypot that mimics a reflector to observe attack traffic. We found evidence that multiprotocol attacks are occurring but still in the minority; our belief is that they will increase in the future, due to the broader availability of reflectors and the increased difficulty of dealing with multiple protocols when defending. We also studied the recent phenomenon of carpet bombing attacks, describing several of their characteristics, including the potent combination of multiprotocol and carpet bombing. For the future we are working on a distributed honeypot platform so that we can deploy more data collection sensors, and on expanding the set of protocols supported by MP-H.

Acknowledgments. We thank the anonymous reviewers and our shepherd Bradley Reaves, for their helpful comments in reviewing this paper. This research was supported by FAPESC and UDESC, and financed in part by the Coordenação de Aperfeiçoamento de Pessoal de Nível Superior – Brasil (CAPES) – Finance Code 001.

References

1. Anagnostopoulos, M., Kambourakis, G., Kopanos, P., Louloudakis, G., Gritzalis, S.: DNS amplification attack revisited. Comput. Secur. **39**, 475–485 (2013)
2. Arteaga, J., Mejia, W.: CLDAP reflection DDoS, April 2017. https://bit.ly/3kqyIku
3. Cimpanu, C.: The CoAP protocol is the next big thing for DDoS attacks. ZDNet, December 2018. https://zd.net/333hymy
4. Cymru, T.: DNS research at Team Cymru (2020). http://dnsresearch.cymru.com/
5. Czyz, J., Kallitsis, M., Gharaibeh, M., Papadopoulos, C., Bailey, M., Karir, M.: Taming the 800 pound gorilla: the rise and decline of NTP DDoS attacks. In: Internet Measurement Conference, pp. 435–448. ACM (2014)
6. DDoSMon: Insight into global DDoS threat landscape, April 2019. https://ddosmon.net/insight/
7. Fachkha, C., Bou-Harb, E., Debbabi, M.: Inferring distributed reflection denial of service attacks from darknet. Comput. Commun. **62**, 59–71 (2015)
8. Jonker, M., King, A., Krupp, J., Rossow, C., Sperotto, A., Dainotti, A.: Millions of targets under attack: a macroscopic characterization of the DoS ecosystem. In: Internet Measurement Conference, pp. 100–113. ACM, New York (2017)
9. Krämer, L., et al.: AmpPot: monitoring and defending against amplification DDoS attacks. In: Bos, H., Monrose, F., Blanc, G. (eds.) RAID 2015. LNCS, vol. 9404, pp. 615–636. Springer, Cham (2015). https://doi.org/10.1007/978-3-319-26362-5_28
10. Kührer, M., Hupperich, T., Rossow, C., Holz, T.: Exit from hell? Reducing the impact of amplification DDoS attacks. In: USENIX Security Symposium (2014)
11. Majkowski, M.: Stupidly simple DDoS protocol (SSDP) generates 100 Gbps DDoS, June 2017. https://bit.ly/35lq2W0
12. Majkowski, M.: Memcrashed - major amplification attacks from UDP port 11211, February 2018. https://bit.ly/2HvD4Ix
13. Mansfield-Devine, S.: The growth and evolution of DDoS. Netw. Secur. **2015**(10), 13–20 (2015)
14. MaxMind: GeoLite2 database, October 2020. https://www.maxmind.com/
15. McAuley, C.: Following the crumbs: deconstructing the CLDAP DDoS reflection attack, November 2016. https://bit.ly/3mgR08h
16. Mertens, X.: Port scanners: the good and the bad, September 2015. https://bit.ly/3lQmFNF

17. Nazario, J.: DDoS attack evolution. Netw. Secur. **2008**(7), 7–10 (2008)
18. NETSCOUT: CoAP attacks in the wild, January 2019. aSERT blog. https://bit.ly/2HqNxou
19. NETSCOUT: Dawn of the terrorbit era. Threat intelligence report 2H 2018 (2019). https://www.netscout.com/
20. NETSCOUT: Netscout threat intelligence report for the first half of 2020 (2020). https://bit.ly/3mh3Tzb
21. NETSCOUT, Arbor: Insight into the global threat landscape, October 2017. Netscout Arbor's 13th Annual Worldwide Infrastructure Security Report
22. Noroozian, A., Korczyński, M., Gañan, C.H., Makita, D., Yoshioka, K., van Eeten, M.: Who gets the boot? Analyzing victimization by DDoS-as-a-service. In: Monrose, F., Dacier, M., Blanc, G., Garcia-Alfaro, J. (eds.) RAID 2016. LNCS, vol. 9854, pp. 368–389. Springer, Cham (2016). https://doi.org/10.1007/978-3-319-45719-2_17
23. OpenNTP: OpenNTPProject.org - NTP Scanning Project (2020). http://openntpproject.org/
24. Paxson, V.: An analysis of using reflectors for distributed denial-of-service attacks. ACM SIGCOMM Comput. Commun. Rev. **31**(3), 38–47 (2001)
25. van Rijswijk-Deij, R., Sperotto, A., Pras, A.: DNSSEC and its potential for DDoS attacks: a comprehensive measurement study. In: Proceedings of the 2014 Conference on Internet Measurement Conference, pp. 449–460. ACM (2014)
26. Rossow, C.: Amplification hell: revisiting network protocols for DDoS abuse. In: Network and Distributed System Security Symposium (NDSS) (2014)
27. Rudman, L., Irwin, B.: Characterization and analysis of NTP amplification-based DDoS attacks. In: Information Security for South Africa (ISSA). IEEE (2015)
28. TCPDUMP: TCPDUMP/LIBPCAP public repository (2020). https://www.tcpdump.org/
29. Thomas, D.R., Clayton, R., Beresford, A.R.: 1000 days of UDP amplification DDoS attacks. In: APWG Symposium on Electronic Crime Research (eCrime), pp. 79–84. IEEE (2017)

DDoS Never Dies? An IXP Perspective on DDoS Amplification Attacks

Daniel Kopp[1]([✉])(iD), Christoph Dietzel[1,2], and Oliver Hohlfeld[3](iD)

[1] DE-CIX, Cologne, Germany
{daniel.kopp,christoph.dietzel}@de-cix.net
[2] MPI for Informatics, Saarbrücken, Germany
[3] Brandenburg University of Technology, Cottbus, Germany
oliver.hohlfeld@b-tu.de

Abstract. DDoS attacks remain a major security threat to the continuous operation of Internet edge infrastructures, web services, and cloud platforms. While a large body of research focuses on DDoS detection and protection, to date we ultimately failed to eradicate DDoS altogether. Yet, the landscape of DDoS attack mechanisms is even evolving, demanding an updated perspective on DDoS attacks in the wild. In this paper, we identify up to 2608 DDoS amplification attacks at a single day by analyzing multiple Tbps of traffic flows at a major IXP with a rich ecosystem of different networks. We observe the prevalence of well-known amplification attack protocols (e.g., NTP, CLDAP), which should no longer exist given the established mitigation strategies. Nevertheless, they pose the largest fraction on DDoS amplification attacks within our observation and we witness the emergence of DDoS attacks using recently discovered amplification protocols (e.g., OpenVPN, ARMS, Ubiquity Discovery Protocol). By analyzing the impact of DDoS on core Internet infrastructure, we show that DDoS can overload backbone-capacity and that filtering approaches in prior work omit 97% of the attack traffic.

1 Introduction

With growing relevance for our society and in light of the commercial success of the Internet, naturally also misconduct is increasing. A popular security threat is to launch Distributed Denial-of-Service (DDoS) attacks [28,57,65] against application or service providers by consuming more critical resources than available, e.g., computing power or network bandwidth. The motivation to conduct in criminal activities are manifold and include financial gain [14,59], political motivation [6,40], and cyber warfare [27,61].

The main reason for the scale of current DDoS attacks [5,34,50,51] is the misuse of certain protocols to amplify attack traffic [28,57,65]. Responses to spoofed traffic [7,8,36,38,41], i.e., packets with modified source IP addresses, are reflected towards the DDoS target and not the original sender. The reflected traffic is not only sent to a different target but also *amplified* as small request can trigger significantly larger responses (up to $\times 50,000$) [53,54,62]. The so-called

© Springer Nature Switzerland AG 2021
O. Hohlfeld et al. (Eds.): PAM 2021, LNCS 12671, pp. 284–301, 2021.
https://doi.org/10.1007/978-3-030-72582-2_17

amplification factor depends on the misused protocol, e.g., NTP, DNS, or more recently Memcached [3,42,53].

To mitigate these attacks in practice, various reactive DDoS detection and defense techniques filter unwanted traffic of ongoing attacks, e.g., scrubbing services [2,23,29,43,63], blackholing [20,21,29,30], or ACLs and Flowspec [16,48]. In this arms race, spontaneously appearing new amplification vectors are quickly growing to cause substantial harm to even well positioned networks and applications [42,65]. To make matters worse for mitigation service providers and network operators, once exploited protocols for DDoS often remain a threat for decades, despite the joint effort of the research community, operators, and policy makers. While the impact on web services [55,64] or platform service providers [55] is well studied, only few works study DDoS attacks in the wild. These studies largely rely on measurements taken at the edge at *i)* honeypots [28,58], *ii)* a DDoS scrubbing service [43], or *iii)* by analyzing network backscatter [10,28]. Only one study analyzes DDoS attacks in Internet traffic captured at the Internet core [32] and solely focuses on NTP and Memcached as attack vectors. Thus, a more general study of DDoS attacks visible at the core of the Internet is still missing. Also, while the impact of DDoS attacks on their victims is known, their impact on core Internet infrastructure that forward attack traffic is unknown.

In this paper, we study properties of amplified DDoS attacks in Internet traffic captured at the core of the Internet—at a major Internet Exchange Point. We thereby provide an up-to-date perspective of the current threat landscape and their effects on the IXP itself. Our major contributions are:

- Well known amplification protocols persist to be the first choice for DDoS attacks and account for 89.9% of our observed DDoS attacks. Indeed, we find a high number of 14,083 DNS resolvers and 3,637 NTP servers used in attacks.
- We provide evidence for the emergence of recently discovered amplification vectors in the wild—with a staggering increase of 500% within our measurement period—with significant number of reflectors and observed attacks.
- We provide insight into the impact of DDoS on infrastructure at the core of the Internet. In general, the IXP and the connected customers were well equipped with sufficient spare capacity.
- From a view onto targets of DDoS attacks we find networks that received attacks to 28% of their address space and further find temporal attack patterns.
- Focusing on a single protocol is not enough: 24% of the observed victims received DDoS attack traffic using more than one amplification protocol.
- Port 0 with DDoS attacks can be an artifact of IP fragmentation in flow-traces.
- By comparing to a commercial world-wide honeypot network, we find largely diverging views: only 8.18% of the observed attacks (33% of the target IPs) were also observed by the honeypots. This provides the first comparison of a core-centric view (here at an IXP) to an edge-centric honeypot perspective that is often used in prior work. Our results indicate that both perspectives (core Internet and honyepot) have a partial and diverging view.

Structure. Section 2 describes our data set and DDoS detection approach. We study properties of DDoS attacks using new and legacy attack vectors in Sect. 3, their impact on IXP infrastructure in Sect. 4, and their targets in Sect. 5. Last, we correlate this new core (IXP) with the traditional edge (honeypot) perspective in Sect. 6.

2   Data Sets and DDoS Classification

Data Set. Anonymized and sampled IPv4 flow-based traffic traces (IPFIX) captured at a major European Internet Exchange Point (IXP) with >900 members between Sep. 23, 2019 and Apr. 20, 2020 with 1.3T flows were made available to us. They only contain DDoS amplification traffic filtered by our classification scheme and do not contain payload or any further protocol or header information. In addition, the IXP labeled when an attack was redirected to a connected scrubbing service or if blackholing was enabled for the attacked IP.

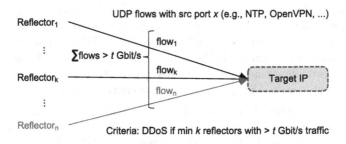

Fig. 1. We classify traffic as DDoS reflection attack if a target IP gets UDP traffic from at least k sources with an amplification source port and an aggregated rate $> t$ Gbps.

DDoS Classification. We use a flow-based classification approach to detect UDP-based DDoS reflection attacks in passive measurement traces as shown in Fig. 1. We classify traffic as DDoS reflection attack if a target IP receives traffic from at least $k = 10$ (total $n \geq k$) IPs with the *same* source port and an aggregate traffic rate of more than $t = 1$ Gbps. To restrict the filter to servers abused as amplifiers, we require the source port to be a well-known port of UDP-based protocols (e.g., NTP, OpenVPN, DNS) or additionally port 0. When these criteria match, we refer to the n source IPs as reflectors (i.e., servers sending to the target IP). We show that typical attacks have a much larger number of reflectors with n being in the order of hundreds or thousands. Here, the presence of at least k reflectors serves as detection threshold to differentiate DDoS traffic from traditional client-server traffic which could be induced due to legitimate use cases. In addition, we assume that it is unlikely for a *client* to receive traffic from k sources (*servers*) with the same source port (e.g., NTP time servers) with a high traffic rate t.

Validation. We validated our classification by manually inspecting 300 attack events including all amplification protocols. With the help of the Internet Exchange Point (IXP) we validate our samples to be plausible cases of DDoS attacks. The inspection process performed by the IXP included *i)* inspecting customer support cases *ii)* obtaining and examining the traffic levels towards the victim network before, after, and during the potential DDoS attack. All inspected cases where found to be plausible (e.g., victim port traffic levels are atypically high during the attack as compared to other times). While false positives are still possible, they are unlikely and we did not find cases. To systematically check for false positives, we examined two widely used protocols: DNS and QUIC. First, a false positive for DNS would require a target IP to receive more than 1 Gbps of traffic from at least 10 different DNS server IPs. We checked for false positives by high query volumes from authoritative DNS servers from/to a **root DNS server** collocated at our vantage point and didn't find any. Last, no **QUIC** flow—where clients contact a number of web servers—matches our filter criteria. We cross-check our classification approach for its proneness to false-positives by using QUIC (UDP/443) and alternatively including it into our filter. This approach did not produce any event that matched our classification. We therefore are convinced that our classification process is very well suited for our vantage point. We thus consider all matching flows as DDoS attacks.

No Impact of COVID-19. We remark that the start of the COVID-19 pandemic with global lockdowns and containments falls within our measurement period. While increasing Internet traffic levels were observed during COVID-19 in 2020 [22], we did not observe a noticeable increase in DDoS attacks due to COVID-19 within our measurement time frame.

The Mysterious Case of Port 0 as a Result of IP Fragmentation. While reserved [52] but never assigned and treated as request for a system-allocated port by socket APIs, port 0 should not be observed in Internet traffic. Prior work [11,12,21,35,37,39] observed low volumes of port 0 Internet traffic. Its origin can be multifold, e.g., as target port for DDoS attacks [37] or scanning [11] and system fingerprinting [37]. We also observe traffic carrying port 0, yet with a very different reason: IP fragmentation. In our case of analyzing IPFIX traces, packets that do not contain a transport protocol header due to fragmentation are assigned src and dst port 0 by the collecting switches. Similar behavior exists for Netflow V5, V9, and IPFIX export from routers from various vendors [60]. Such traces thus falsely suggest the existence of port 0 traffic in the presence of IP fragmentation and care must be taken in the analysis. When matching single protocol attacks by time and destination, 43% of our dataset contains port 0 traffic. Here, we see a strong correlation of port 0 traffic to DDoS attacks using DNS (in avg. +153% more traffic), CLDAP (avg. +140%), and Chargen (avg. +91%). Since we cannot reassemble port 0 fragments in the obtained IPFIX data to obtain the true port number, we decided to ignore port 0 and rather report clearly identifiable traffic. This impacts our results as we *under*estimate *i)* the number of attacks passing the threshold and *ii)* the absolute attack volume. We remark that this only impacts the reported absolute values (the previous figures

provide an approximation by what factor we underestimate attack volume of
DNS, CLDAP, and Chargen), not other results and conclusions.

3 DDoS in the Wild

We give a core Internet perspective on the current DDoS attack landscape,
beginning by first updating the current state of legacy amplification protocols
abused for DDoS attacks. We then study new protocols that recent DDoS attacks
leveraged. We present details of DDoS attacks we identified according to their
amplification protocols in Table 1 and the distribution of their attack volume
and frequency in Fig. 2. We observe 170,042 events of DDoS attacks which are
at least 1 Gbps with the largest one being 98 Gbps. Attacks that fall below the
1 *Gbps* threshold are counted as new event once they exceed 1 *Gbps* again. To
account for this, we group by day and protocol yielding 97,680 events. These
attacks targeted 58,180 individual IP addresses in 4,433 ASes. This is 6.5% of
all active ASes and 1.4% of all advertised prefixes of the Internet.

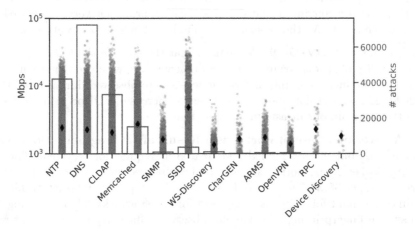

Fig. 2. Observed DDoS amplification attacks by protocol, with their attack size in
Mbps, the median shown as ♦ (left), and the number of attacks per protocol (right).

3.1 The State of Legacy DDoS Protocols

There exist a set of widely studied protocols—e.g., NTP [18,32,53]. Years have
passed since the disclosure of the vulnerability to abuse NTP as amplification
vector for DDoS attacks. The attack is well understood and workarounds or
solutions are known for years—in principle, this attack vector should no longer
exist. In 2014, an extensive measurement study [18] "chronicle[s] the rapid rise
and steady decline of the NTP DDoS attack phenomenon", concluding that the
operations communities' "efforts have had a visible impact in diminishing the
vulnerable amplifier population and reducing attack traffic". Yet, NTP is still a

Table 1. Details about the discovered attacks (size in Gbps and packet rate in Mpps, number of targets, attacks and duration) and observed amplification protocol features (number of reflectors, average packet size (pkt) and their standard deviation in byte).

		Gbps		Mpps				duration max	avg	reflectors		pkt size	
protocol	port	*max*	*avg*	*max*	*avg*	targets	attacks	*days*	*min*	*max*	*avg*	*avg*	*std*
CLDAP	389	**98**	2.1	64.84	1.36	12,086	**33,354**	3.85	6.4	2,040	328	1515	21
DNS	53	**66**	2.3	43.48	1.54	29,023	**72,679**	2.05	6.0	14,083	776	1474	59
SSDP	1900	**53**	4.8	**150.4**	13.9	1,036	3,618	7,49	**30**	11,102	1594	347	9.1
Memcached	11211	**37**	2.7	46.87	2.51	7,119	**15,151**	1,42	6.0	1,556	**35.6**	1285	207
NTP	123	**37**	2.4	77.22	5.03	21,853	**42,124**	3,04	6.5	3,637	164.7	481.1	10
RPC	111	**33**	2.3	36.27	3.5	37	73	0.02	4.7	12,217	1465	620.6	51
SNMP	161	9.9	**1.6**	9.32	1.21	577	885	5.52	9.0	3,541	506	1372	160
Chargen	19	7.6	**1.7**	6.05	1.35	105	168	0.04	7.4	577	247	1255	145
ARMS	3283	6.2	**1.7**	5.87	1.65	253	519	0.18	11	1,026	345	1053	1.3
WS-Dis.	3702	5.4	**1.4**	5.15	1.14	485	994	0.11	4.8	1,731	669	1216	199
Device Dis.	10001	5.2	**1.8**	24.33	8.7	10	13	0.01	6.5	**7,681**	2993	207.9	3.2
OpenVPN	1194	4.7	**1.4**	72.98	**21.5**	385	464	0.08	7.1	**8,987**	3736	64.5	0.3

popular vector for DDoS attacks [32] and by the rise of further protocols being abused for DDoS the attack landscape continues to increase. Well known other legacy protocols abused for amplification DDoS are DNS, Chargen, SNMP, and SSDP, whose vulnerability have been known since 2014 [53]. For some, e.g., DNS, no documented solution exists to generally prevent abuse for DDoS. We thus focus first on updating the current state of DDoS attacks using legacy protocols.

State of Legacy Amplification Protocol Attacks Today. We find CLDAP, NTP, and DNS-based DDoS attacks to still account for 89.9% of all our observed attacks (Table 1)—despite that the relevance of CLDAP and NTP should have declined long ago. Given the absence of a solution for DNS, we see most attacks using DNS followed by NTP and CLDAP. Legacy protocols account for the highest volume attacks from 33 Gbps (RPC) to 98 Gbps (CLDAP). Among these protocols we observe attacks with significantly higher rates of packets per second for SSDP, with a peak of 150.4 Mpps, which is 51% higher than the next protocol in the list (NTP). This makes SSDP-based DDoS attacks more dangerous to any packet processing device, compared to other attack vectors. Additionally, for SSDP we experience a very high average duration of 30 min from 3,618 attacks towards 1,036 targets, which leads to the assumption that this protocol is used in more sophisticated attacks. Moreover, although RPC is one of least frequent protocol that we observe, it can still generate large volumes of DDoS attacks, similar to the group of popular DDoS protocols. SNMP and Chargen are the least powerful of this group. Within our observation period they account for 1,053 attacks with sufficient attack traffic to impose a threat for most small to medium sized web services.

Despite the long time that has passed since the disclosure of these DDoS amplification vectors, they are still the dominant protocols abused for DDoS attacks today. We thus posit that better approaches for closing these attack vectors are indispensable.

3.2 New Kids on the Block

Besides the awareness of legacy protocols being exploited for DDoS attacks, new protocols are being abused additionally. We next focus on newly abused protocols that have received little (Memcached) to no attention in literature so far to be observed in Internet traffic ("Ubiquiti Device Discovery", "WS-Discovery", "ARMS", and "OpenVPN"). Among them we notice a steep rise for OpenVPN—first observed as reflection protocol end of 2019 [47]—growing by more than 500% in the last month of our observation.

Memcached: In 2018, the widely used database caching system Memcached was found to be vulnerable for amplification attacks with to this date unseen high amplification factors of up to 51,200. Research confirmed the existence of Memcached-based DDoS attacks in the wild [13,32,56], as well as white papers by the security industry [4,17], and tech news [66]. While the existence is known, their prevalence in Internet traffic hasn't been studied yet. Today, we still see 8.9% of all attacks using Memcached as amplification protocol.

Beyond Memcached, we report on the prevalence of DDoS attacks leveraging recently discovered attack vectors:

Ubiquiti Device Discovery: In early 2019, a network device discovery protocol was reported to be used as amplification protocol—with 486k potentially vulnerable devices [25]. While the reported amplification factors are inconsistent (between x4 and x35) [1,25] we observe an average packet size of 207.9 bytes, which supports the statement of an amplification factor of x4 [1]. The attacks consist of up to 7,681 reflectors which generate a volume of 5.2 Gbps.

WS-Discovery: In mid 2019, WS-Discovery—a protocol used by an increasing number of IoT devices to discover other UPnP devices within a local network—was reported as amplification protocols. Reports on the number of publicly exposed systems range from 65k [47] to 630k [15] and the amplification factor from x10 to x500. We see almost 1,000 cases which misuse the WS-Discovery service as amplification vector, with an average packet size of 1216 bytes. The largest attack we recorded was 5.4 Gbps combined from 1,700 reflectors, with the longest attack lasting for 2.64 h.

ARMS: In June 2019, a protocol used for remote desktop management was reported to be used within DDoS attacks. Around 54,000 potential amplification systems have been discovered at the time [9]. The amplification factor was reported to be x35.5 with two packets being send, the first 32 bytes, and the second packet with 1034 bytes. From our observation we can report an average packet size of 1052.9 bytes. We have seen 519 DDoS attacks towards 253 victims using the ARMS reflection vector during our measurement period.

OpenVPN: An industry report from 2020 considers OpenVPN as a new attack vector for DDoS attacks [47]. An article describes the attack in Sep. 2019 [49] with different vulnerability for reflection attacks allowing for x5 or x60 amplification by replying with multiple packets from one initial packet being send towards the reflector. We see this attack vector being used by 464 attacks towards 385 targets and up to 2993 reflectors. We observe an average packets size of 64.5 bytes, supporting the findings of the latest vulnerability report [49]. Figure 3 shows an uprise of DDoS attacks within the last month of our study by 500%.

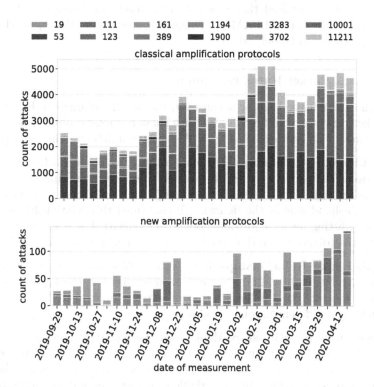

Fig. 3. Number of attacks using classical (upper) and new (bottom plot) amplification protocols over time. Bar colors indicate protocol ports and are shared with Fig. 4.

Takeaway. *Beyond anecdotal evidence, we confirm that recently discovered attack vectors in the form of new protocols are being actively abused for DDoS attacks. Our study quantifies their existence in the wild for the first time.*

We shared our findings with an international cyber security technology company with CERT services. The company is aware of most of the new amplification protocols, but didn't expect them to be already used in the wild. They acknowledged that Table 1 provides a good indication on which attack vectors to include in their mitigation and monitoring solution.

3.3 Multi-protocol Attacks

It is not enough to focus on just one of the most prominent or upcoming protocols. Within our dataset we observe 24% of victims received DDoS attacks by more than one amplification protocol, whereas 4.5% targets have been attacked with more than two amplification protocols over time. By investigating few booter services websites (i.e., DDoS as a service platforms see e.g., [32]) and their advertisement, we noticed that new attack methods are being added that are called "MIXAMP" or "ALLAMP"—suggesting the use of all supported amplification protocols to launch attacks.

3.4 Attack Packet Rates vs. Volume

When the amplification factor is constant, the attack volume can be scaled by the packet rate sent to reflectors. We thus show the relationship of packet rate and volume for all protocols in Fig. 4. We observe 3 different characteristics:

Single Linear Relationships. For most attacks, we observe a linear relationship between the packet rate and the attack volume size, hinting to a constant amplification factor. This is visible as straight lines in Fig. 4 (e.g., OpenVPN on the right-hand side of the figure). We confirmed this relationship for every protocol by fitting linear regression models (not shown). There are, however, two protocols that diverge from this simple linear relationship that we describe next.

Multiple Linear Relationships. In the case of WS-Discovery we observe multiple linear relationships. These are indicated in Fig. 4 in the lower plot at the right. This indicates that different protocol features are exploited for the attack, each yielding a different amplification factor.

No Observable Relationship. Memcached amplification is not linear in terms of packets to volume output, we observe a great variance of the packet rate to Mbps ratio. This effect can have two reasons, either Memcached behaves unpredictably for attackers due to variable response sizes and thus amplification factors, or the response of the Memcached server is controlled by the attacker to insert records retrieved for the attack.

Observed Volumes. DNS and CLDAP provide the highest volumetric DDoS attacks, OpenVPN on the other end is able to generate significant rates of packets while at the same time keeping the traffic volume low. This means that the highest volumetric attack we observed, with 98 Gbps, had a rate of 64.84 Mpps, whereas OpenVPN recorded a higher rate of packets with 72.98 Mpps and just 4.7 Gbps of volume. Nevertheless, the highest packet rate during our measurement period was due to a SSDP attack with 150.4 Mpps and 53 Gbps. Both ends of this scale (CLDAP and OpenVPN) can be favorable to attackers, as they either might want to maximize their invest on sent packets in terms of attack volume or they might want to be as stealth as possible regarding volume but maximizing the impact on packet processing devices.

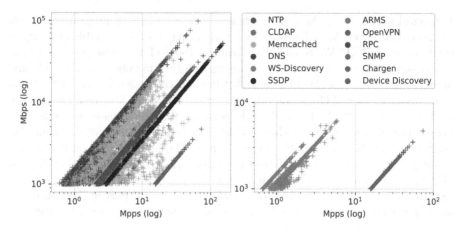

Fig. 4. Correlation of packet rate to volume (color set shared with Fig. 3)

Theoretical Maximum Volume. The results presented above raise the question on how large a combined DDoS attack can become. Assuming one could use all reflectors observed in one week of our measurements, we estimate a DDoS attack with at least 0.875 Tbps to be practical feasible. We use the average output Mbps per reflector, that we calculate from Table 1 and multiply with number of unique amplifiers that we can observe over the course of one week.

4 Infrastructure Perspective

We use the unique perspective of an IXP as infrastructure provider carrying traffic of more than 900 different ASes, and therefore also hundreds of substantial DDoS attacks. In particular, the challenge is to withstand the combined volume of many DDoS attacks simultaneously. In this section, we provide an infrastructure perspective on DDoS attacks.

IXP Infrastructure. At the measured IXP, the highest share of attack traffic forwarded due to multiple parallel DDoS events is 3.16% of the highest daily maximum traffic volume. The transported attack traffic is only a small share compared to the legitimate traffic and we find no evidence for DDoS traffic to impact the IXP's infrastructure. In theory, backbone capacity of infrastructures like IXPs cannot be overwhelmed by volumetric DDoS attacks due to the basic nature of their topology: the ingress equals the egress capacity. In reality, core Internet infrastructures are evolving and becoming more complex, conserving bandwidth over connections between locations and leased fibers is of growing economic interest [19].

IXP Ports. We study the DDoS volume in relation to the port capacity towards the victim's infrastructure (i.e., backbone links to other networks) for all 170k attacks and show it in Fig. 5. The maximum port capacity is indicated by a red horizontal line at 100%. Notably, we find 306 cases (0.18% of all attacks towards 48 individual networks) where DDoS attack surpassed the available capacity of the links at the IXP. We remark that traffic >100% of an egress port's capacity can traverse the peering platform from many other members at the IXP and arrive at the given port leading to packet loss. Of these 48 networks, 12% had a port capacity below 2 Gbps and 82% more than 10 Gbps. The average duration of this group of attacks is 21 min, which shows that these cases are not short bursts, but attacks that overwhelmed the port capacity for a notable time. We learn that our observed DDoS attacks are rarely larger than the size of the IXP member's egress port capacity. This view, however, ignores the typical utilization of the port. DDoS attack that require up to 50% of the network's egress link are seen for 26% of the attacked networks and this additional port utilization might already have led to packet loss and collateral damage at the target network.

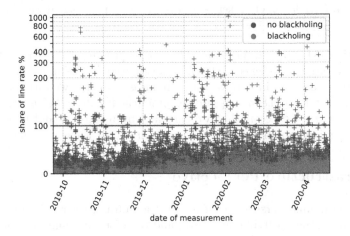

Fig. 5. Link capacity in relation to attack size.

DDoS Mitigation. To mitigate attacks, networks providers have two main tools available. One is to contract a DDOS mitigation services to scrub DDoS traffic and forward only legitimate traffic. Another option is to discard traffic for specific prefixes at the IXP before reaching their target network by using so-called blackholing (labeled in our data). The deployment of blackholing has been studied widely by previous work [20,21,24,44–46] which focuses on analyzing characteristics of the blackholed traffic and the activation of blackholing events. We observe that only 3.82% of the DDoS attacks in our dataset are *blackholed*, i.e., the victim asked the IXP to discard traffic to the attacked IP by a blackholing announcement in BGP (labeled by the IXP in our data set). In as few as 145 cases we saw a redirection of traffic towards to an external *scrubbing* service directly connected to the IXP. Thus, if blackholing is used as classifier to study attacks in prior work [45], the bulk of the DDoS traffic in our data set is omitted.

Next, we analyze DDoS amplification vectors that are mitigated by blackholing in comparison to all used DDoS amplification vectors. Whereas NTP attacks in the wild are only the second most prominent attack vector with 24.77%, they are mitigated the most with 58% of all blackholing events. The most prominent attack vector we observed, DNS with 42.74%, only has a share of 16.89% within mitigation. Memcached is mitigated with a share of 15.65% (in the wild 8.91%) and CLDAP with 8.31% (19.62% in the wild). This reveals a shift of NTP, and Memcached attacks being mitigated more frequently compared to DNS and CLDAP attacks relative to their occurrence. In Fig. 5, we see that 63% of the blackhole events correlate to DDoS traffic lower than 10% of the networks port capacity. In only 1.1% of the events the DDoS traffic was >50% of the capacity.

Looking at the delay from the start of the attack to the deployment of a mitigation, we see an average delay of 1.16 min for the blackholing. 70% of blackholing rules were installed prior to when we first detect the DDoS attack. In addition, we see a delay of <10 min for 98.7% and a delay of >4 min in 4.2% of all blackholing deployments. Only in 19 cases we record a delay greater than 30 min, with the highest delay being 5 h for an 8-h long attack. These findings are similar to prior work [30], that describes a delay of <10 min for 84.2% within their data set. The low attack volume in relation to the port capacity of blackholing events, in combination with the short delay, suggest an automation of the blackholing mitigation.

Takeaway. *While the share of DDoS traffic at the IXPs overall infrastructure is insignificant, it can exceed the port capacity of individual customers and thereby impact legitimate traffic. Blackholing as a DDoS defense technique was used in only 3% of the attacks we observed and therefor cannot be reliably be used as the sole criterion to report on the state of DDoS in the wild.*

5   View on Targets

Last, we analyze the victims of the observed DDoS attacks. We study how the DDoS attack landscape is distributed over different networks types and services.

Network Types. We aggregate victim networks by their infrastructure type according to PeeringDB. While the average attack volume is mostly the same for each class, some classes are attacked more frequently. While non-profit networks receive the least amount of attacks (0.06%), content hosting networks were attacked the most with 36.97% of all DDoS attacks. Enterprise and the remaining classes have a comparably low share on the attacks in our dataset. Beyond content, eyeball networks (cable/DSL/ISP and NSP) also receive a large number of attacks (34.51%) that we can attribute to residential users. This is in line with prior work showing that booter-based DDoS attacks are often launched by online-gamers against other players [31].

Share of Attacked Address Space. To understand if any targeted attacks against specific organizations exist, we study the share of attacked address space of individual networks. Most significantly, we observe a US based cloud payroll provider where DDoS attacks targeted 28% of the AS's IP space. With 16% a small network of a state bank in the south east Mediterranean region has been the victim of DDoS attacks. Furthermore, we see attacks that account for 15% address space of a south Korean cloud provider, and 10% of an US insurance with 19 h combined attack time.

DNS. To better understand the attacked infrastructure, we match the victim IPs to weekly DNS resolutions for www. labels, NS, and MX records of 200M+ domain names obtained from DNS zone files (including .com/net/org and new gTLDs) [26] during our measurement period. We can match 94.3% of the attacked IPs to DNS records. For 58.63% we find a matching www. label, suggesting the target to be a web server. For 27.23% we find a matching mail exchange (MX) and for 14.14% a matching authoritative DNS server (NS).

VPN. VPN service are a relevant service that enables remote work, e.g., during COVID-19 lockdowns. To find attacks against VPN services, we identify IPs labeled as *vpn* but not as www. in the DNS by searching for *vpn* in any domain label left of the public suffix (e.g., companyvpn3.example.com) in *i)* 2.7B domains from TLS in CT Logs from 2015—2020, *ii)* 1.9B domains from Rapid7 resolutions of reverse DNS, zonefiles, TLS certificates of March, and *iii)* 8M domains from the Cisco Umbrella top list in 2020. This gives us 1,2M unique VPN IPs. However, we only observed 101 attacks against 39 IPs in 30 ASes and no noticeable increase in the last months. This attack vector is (fortunately) not yet widely exploited. Despite, we posit that enterprises should consider protecting their VPNs from DDoS before widespread attacks emerge.

Temporal DDoS Attack Pattern. We report on two notably cases of DDoS attack. Figure 6 shows the longest consecutive attack within our study. The attack used the SSDP protocol and lasted for 7 1/2 days, with a peak at 8 Gbps and 23.5 Mpps. The attack was targeted against a Swedish Broadband network, whose backbone link never fully saturated. Second, we find a case of a DDoS attack against a Ukrainian ISP (Fig. 7) using DNS as attack vector, attacking one IP address every 1 min by consecutively traversing a /24 network range.

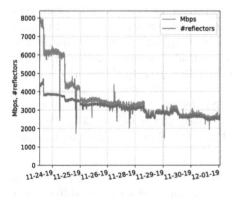

Fig. 6. SSDP attack over 7 days.

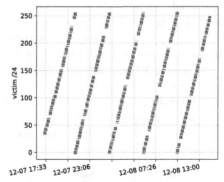

Fig. 7. DDoS onto /24 network.

We found other similar temporal attack patterns, where the attack changed between two IPs every minute within an attacked network address space.

Takeaway. *By focusing at the victims of amplification DDoS attacks, we find content and eyeball networks to be the most prominent targets. Due to the importance of being able to work from home during the COVID-19 outbreak, we take a look onto attacks towards VPN infrastructures, where we observe 101 attacks against 39 victims. Finally, we observe an interesting attack pattern, where an attacker changed the target IP within a victim's networks every minute, potentially to evade DDoS mitigation.*

6 Honeypot Perspective

Honeypots are a widely used tool to study DDoS attacks (see e.g., [28,33,58]), e.g., setup at universities as single vantage point. To put our measurements into perspective, we obtained DDoS attacks observed by the world-wide distributed honeypot network operated by CrowdStrike matching our measurement period. The dataset contains 3.3M events. We find largely diverging views: only 8.18% of the observed attacks (33% of the target IPs) were also observed by the honeypots. The missing 67% of targets in the honeypot dataset can be explained by the low likelihood of an attack choosing the honeypots as reflectors. In turn, our dataset only represents 0.95% of the targets visible in the honeypot dataset, this is likely due to our robust classification criterion of attacks being <1 Gbps, which misses any attack with a lower volume at the IXP. Other factors for the honeypot containing events and targets missing within our dataset are the limited view of the IXP onto Internet traffic and the different location within the Internet's topology. In contrast the honeypot dataset also consists of low volume and scanning events. Also the attack protocol popularity diverges, highlighted by 58% of the honyepot captured events to be Memcached.

Takeaway. *Our results put the use of honeypots (edge measurements, typically used in the literature) into a core Internet perspective and indicate that both perspectives (core Internet and honyepot) have a partial and diverging view. We thus posit that future research should take multiple perspectives to obtain a more complete view on the DDoS threat.*

7 Conclusions

This paper provides an updated perspective on the state of DDoS amplification attacks and protocols in the wild. Despite the prediction and hope that the relevance of long-known legacy amplification protocols (e.g., NTP) will decline, we show that opposite is true: CLDAP, NTP, and DNS-based DDoS attacks account for 89.9% of all observed attacks. In addition, we show that recently disclosed amplification protocols are already used to perform DDoS attacks and can generate effective attacks, e.g., for OpenVPN we even record a 500% rise within our measurement period. By taking a view onto the infrastructure at the core of the Internet, we see no severe impact due or degradation of network quality. We further show that honeypots—typically used to study DDoS—can provide a different picture than the one by traffic captures at the Internet core.

Acknowledgments. We thank the anonymous reviewers and our shepherd, Amogh Dhamdhere (Amazon Web Services), for their constructive comments. We further thank Mark Schloesser and CrowdStrike for their comments and for providing honeypot data. This work was supported by the German Federal Ministry of Education and Research (BMBF) project AIDOS (16KIS0975K, 16KIS0976).

References

1. Jim Troutman via Twitter. https://twitter.com/troutman/status/10902122431978-70081. Accessed 26 May 2020
2. Akamai: Prolexic Technologies by Akamai (2018). https://www.akamai.com/us/en/cloud-security.jsp
3. Akamai: State of the Internet Security Report (Attack Spotlight: Memcached) (2018). https://www.akamai.com/us/en/multimedia/documents/state-of-the-internet/soti-summer-2018-attack-spotlight.pdf
4. Alerts, A.S.: Memcached-fueled 1.3 tbps attacks (2018). https://blogs.akamai.com/2018/03/memcached-fueled-13-tbps-attacks.html
5. Antonakakis, M., et al.: Understanding the mirai botnet. In: USENIX Security Symposium (2017)
6. BBC: 'Hacking attacks' hit Russian political sites (2012). http://www.bbc.com/news/technology-16032402
7. Beverly, R., Berger, A., Hyun, Y., Claffy, K.: Understanding the efficacy of deployed internet source address validation filtering. In: ACM IMC (2009)
8. Beverly, R., Bauer, S.: The spoofer project: inferring the extent of internet source address filtering on the internet. In: Steps to Reducing Unwanted Traffic on the Internet Workshop (2005)
9. Bjarnason, S., Dobbins, R.: Netscout - A Call to ARMS: Apple Remote Management Service UDP Reflection/Amplification DDoS Attacks (2020). http://de.netscout.com/blog/asert/call-arms-apple-remote-management-service-udp
10. Blenn, N., Ghiëtte, V., Doerr, C.: Quantifying the spectrum of denial-of-service attacks through internet backscatter. In: International Conference on Availability, Reliability and Security (2017)
11. Bou-Harb, E., Lakhdari, N.E., Binsalleeh, H., Debbabi, M.: Multidimensional investigation of source port 0 probing. Digit. Investig. **11**, 114–123 (2014)
12. Brownlee, N., Claffy, K.C., Nemeth, E.: DNS measurements at a root server. In: IEEE GLOBECOM (2001)
13. Burke, I.D., Herbert, A., Mooi, R.: Using network flow data to analyse distributed reflection denial of service (DRDoS) attacks, as observed on the south african national research and education network (SANReN): a postmortem analysis of the memcached attack on the SANReN. In: Annual Conference of the South African Institute of Computer Scientists and Information Technologists (2018)
14. Büscher, A., Holz, T.: Tracking DDoS attacks: insights into the business of disrupting the web. In: USENIX Workshop on Large-Scale Exploits and Emergent Threats (2012)

15. Cimpanu, C.: ZDNet - Protocol used by 630,000 devices can be abused for devastating DDoS attacks. www.zdnet.com/article/protocol-used-by-630000-devices-can-be-abused-for-devastating-ddos-attacks/. Accessed 26 May 2020

16. Cisco: Implementing BGP Flowspec (2018). https://www.cisco.com/c/en/us/td/docs/routers/asr9000/software/asr9k_r5-2/routing/configuration/guide/b_routing_cg52xasr9k/b_routing_cg52xasr9k_chapter_011.html

17. Cloudflare: Memcached DDoS Attack. https://www.cloudflare.com/learning/ddos/memcached-ddos-attack/

18. Czyz, J., Kallitsis, M., Gharaibeh, M., Papadopoulos, C., Bailey, M., Karir, M.: Taming the 800 pound gorilla: the rise and decline of NTP DDoS attacks. In: ACM IMC (2014)

19. DE-CIX: DE-CIX GlobePEER Remote (2018). https://www.de-cix.net/de/de-cix-service-world/globepeer-remote

20. Dietzel, C., Feldmann, A., King, T.: Blackholing at IXPs: on the effectiveness of DDoS mitigation in the wild. In: Karagiannis, T., Dimitropoulos, X. (eds.) PAM 2016. LNCS, vol. 9631, pp. 319–332. Springer, Cham (2016). https://doi.org/10.1007/978-3-319-30505-9_24

21. Dietzel, C., Wichtlhuber, M., Smaragdakis, G., Feldmann, A.: Stellar: network attack mitigation using advanced blackholing. In: ACM CoNEXT (2018)

22. Feldmann, A., et al.: The lockdown effect: implications of the COVID-19 pandemic on internet traffic. In: ACM IMC (2020)

23. Gillman, D., Lin, Y., Maggs, B., Sitaraman, R.K.: Protecting websites from attack with secure delivery networks. IEEE Comput. Mag. **48**(4), 26–34 (2015)

24. Giotsas, V., Smaragdakis, G., Dietzel, C., Richter, P., Feldmann, A., Berger, A.: Inferring BGP blackholing activity in the internet. In: ACM IMC (2017)

25. Hart, J.: Rapid7 - Understanding Ubiquiti Discovery Service Exposures. http://blog.rapid7.com/2019/02/01/ubiquiti-discovery-service-exposures/. Accessed 26 May 2020

26. Hohlfeld, O.: Operating a DNS-based active internet observatory. In: ACM SIGCOMM Poster (2018)

27. Interfax-Ukraine: Poroshenko reports on DDoS-attacks on Ukrainian CEC from Russia on Feb. 24–25 (2019). https://www.kyivpost.com/ukraine-politics/poroshenko-reports-on-ddos-attacks-on-ukrainian-cec-from-russia-on-feb-24-25.html

28. Jonker, M., King, A., Krupp, J., Rossow, C., Sperotto, A., Dainotti, A.: Millions of targets under attack: a macroscopic characterization of the DoS ecosystem. In: ACM IMC (2017)

29. Jonker, M., Sperotto, A., van Rijswijk-Deij, R., Sadre, R., Pras, A.: Measuring the adoption of DDoS protection services. In: ACM IMC (2016)

30. Jonker, M., Pras, A., Dainotti, A., Sperotto, A.: A first joint look at DoS atacks and BGP blackholing in the wild. In: ACM IMC (2018)

31. Karami, M., McCoy, D.: Rent to pwn: analyzing commodity booter DDoS services. Usenix Login **38**(6), 20–23 (2013)

32. Kopp, D., Wichtlhuber, M., Poese, I., de Santanna, J.J.C., Hohlfeld, O., Dietzel, C.: DDoS hide & seek: on the effectiveness of a booter services takedown. In: ACM IMC (2019)

33. Krämer, L., et al.: AmpPot: monitoring and defending against amplification DDoS attacks. In: International Workshop on Recent Advances in Intrusion Detection (2015)

34. Krebs, B.: KrebsOnSecurity Hit With Record DDoS (2016). https://krebsonsecurity.com/2016/09/krebsonsecurity-hit-with-record-ddos

35. Lakhina, A., Crovella, M., Diot, C.: Characterization of network-wide anomaliesin traffic flows. In: ACM IMC (2004)
36. Lichtblau, F., Streibelt, F., Krüger, T., Richter, P., Feldmann, A.: Detection, classification, and analysis of inter-domain traffic with spoofed source IP addresses. In: ACM IMC (2017)
37. Luchs, M., Doerr, C.: The curious case of port 0. In: IFIP Networking (2019)
38. Luckie, M., Beverly, R., Koga, R., Keys, K., Kroll, J.A., Claffy, K.: Network hygiene, incentives, and regulation: deployment of source address validation in the internet. In: ACM SIGSAC Conference on Computer and Communications Security (2019)
39. Maghsoudlou, A., Gasser, O., Feldmann, A.: Zeroing in on port 0 traffic in the wild. In: PAM (2021)
40. Mohamed, J.: Daily Mirror: Hackers attack the Stock Exchange: Cyber criminals take down website for more than two hours as part of protest against world's banks (2016). http://www.dailymail.co.uk/news/article-3625656/Hackers-attack-Stock-Exchange-Cyber-criminals-website-two-hours-protest-against-world-s-banks.html
41. Moore, D., Voelker, G., Savage, S.: Inferring internet denial-of-service activity. In: USENIX Security Symposium (2001)
42. Morales, C.: NETSCOUT Arbor Confirms 1.7 Tbps DDoS Attack; The Terabit Attack Era Is Upon Us (2018). https://asert.arbornetworks.com/netscout-arbor-confirms-1-7-tbps-ddos-attack-terabit-attack-era-upon-us/
43. Moura, G.C.M., Hesselman, C., Schaapman, G., Boerman, N., de Weerdt, O.: Into the DDoS maelstrom: a longitudinal study of a scrubbing service. In: European Symposium on Security and Privacy Workshops (2020)
44. MSK-IX: Protection against DDoS-attacks by blackholing. www.msk-ix.ru/eng/routeserver.html#blackhole
45. Nawrocki, M., Blendin, J., Dietzel, C., Schmidt, T.C., Wählisch, M.: Down the black hole: dismantling operational practices of BGP blackholing at IXPs. In: ACM IMC (2019)
46. NETIX: Blackholing. www.netix.net/services/14/NetIX-Blackholing
47. Netscout: Netscout Threat Intelligence Report (2020–02) (2020). https://www.netscout.com/sites/default/files/2020-02/SECR_001_EN-2001_Web.pdf
48. NOKIA: Filter Policies (2020). https://documentation.nokia.com/html/0_add-h-f/93-0073-HTML/7750_SR_OS_Router_Configuration_Guide/filters.html. Accessed 24 May 2020
49. null001: OpenVPN service is used for UDP reflection amplification DDoS attack. http://13.58.107.157/archives/8190
50. Prince, M.: The DDoS That Knocked Spamhaus Offline (And How We Mitigated It) (2013). https://blog.cloudflare.com/the-ddos-that-knocked-spamhaus-offline-and-ho/
51. Prince, M.: Technical Details Behind a 400Gbps NTP Amplification DDoS Attack (2014). https://blog.cloudflare.com/technical-details-behind-a-400gbps-ntp-amplification-ddos-attack/
52. Reynolds, J., Postel, J.: Assigned numbers (1984). https://tools.ietf.org/html/rfc900
53. Rossow, C.: Amplification hell: revisiting network protocols for DDoS abuse. In: NDSS (2014)
54. Ryba, F.J., Orlinski, M., Wählisch, M., Rossow, C., Schmidt, T.C.: Amplification and DRDoS Attack Defense-A Survey and New Perspectives. arXiv preprint arXiv:1505.07892 (2015)

55. Sachdeva, M., Kumar, K., Singh, G., Singh, K.: Performance analysis of web service under DDoS attacks. In: IEEE International Advance Computing Conference (2009)
56. Singh, K., Singh, A.: Memcached DDoS exploits: operations, vulnerabilities, preventions and mitigations. In: International Conference on Computing, Communication and Security (2018)
57. Technologies, A.: 2018 State of the Internet/Security: A Year in Review (2018). https://www.akamai.com/us/en/multimedia/documents/state-of-the-internet/2018-state-of-the-internet-security-a-year-in-review.pdf
58. Thomas, D.R., Clayton, R., Beresford, A.R.: 1000 days of UDP amplification DDoS attacks. In: APWG Symposium on Electronic Crime Research (2017)
59. Times, N.Y.: Hackers Hit Dozens of Countries Exploiting Stolen N.S.A. Tool (2017). https://www.nytimes.com/2017/05/12/world/europe/uk-national-health-service-cyberattack.html
60. Trammel, B.: Private conversation (2021)
61. Traynor, I.: Russia accused of unleashing cyberwar to disable Estonia (2007). https://www.theguardian.com/world/2007/may/17/topstories3.russia
62. US-CERT: UDP-Based Amplification Attacks (2018). https://www.us-cert.gov/ncas/alerts/TA14-017A
63. Vissers, T., Goethem, T.V., Joosen, W., Nikiforakis, N.: Maneuvering around clouds: bypassing cloud-based security providers. In: ACM CCS (2015)
64. Vissers, T., Somasundaram, T.S., Pieters, L., Govindarajan, K., Hellinckx, P.: DDoS defense system for web services in a cloud environment. Futur. Gener. Comput. Syst. **37**, 37–45 (2014)
65. ZDNet: GitHub hit with the largest DDoS attack ever seen (2018). https://www.zdnet.com/article/github-was-hit-with-the-largest-ddos-attack-ever-seen/
66. ZDNet: Memcached ddos: The biggest, baddest denial of service attacker yet (2018). https://www.zdnet.com/article/memcached-ddos-the-biggest-baddest-denial-of-service-attacker-yet/

A Peek into the DNS Cookie Jar
An Analysis of DNS Cookie Use

Jacob Davis[1,2]([✉]) [iD] and Casey Deccio[2] [iD]

[1] Sandia National Laboratories, Livermore, CA 94551, USA
jacdavi@sandia.gov
[2] Brigham Young University, Provo, UT 84602, USA
{jacobdavis,casey}@byu.edu

Abstract. The Domain Name System (DNS) has been frequently abused for Distributed Denial of Service (DDoS) attacks and cache poisoning because it relies on the User Datagram Protocol (UDP). Since UDP is connection-less, it is trivial for an attacker to spoof the source of a DNS query or response. DNS Cookies, a protocol standardized in 2016, add pseudo-random values to DNS packets to provide identity management and prevent spoofing attacks. In this paper, we present the first study measuring the deployment of DNS Cookies in nearly all aspects of the DNS architecture. We also provide an analysis of the current benefits of DNS Cookies and the next steps for stricter deployment. Our findings show that cookie use is limited to less than 30% of servers and 10% of recursive clients. We also find several configuration issues that could lead to substantial problems if cookies were strictly required. Overall, DNS Cookies provide limited benefit in a majority of situations, and, given current deployment, do not prevent DDoS or cache poisoning attacks.

Keywords: Internet measurement · DNS · DNS Cookies · DNS security

1 Introduction

The Domain Name System (DNS) is an essential backbone of the internet used to translate domain names to Internet Protocol (IP) addresses. Since its inception in the 1980s, the DNS has been reliant on the User Datagram Protocol (UDP). While UDP has a major benefit of speed, its lack of identity management is easily exploitable. Off-path attackers can spoof UDP packets to pretend they, or a victim, are the source of the packet.

There are two major attacks utilizing spoofing. The first is cache poisoning, wherein an attacker sends malicious responses pretending to be a legitimate server. If successful, the victim is unknowingly directed towards a malicious IP address. The other attack is a DNS reflection attack. This attack is carried out by sending many DNS queries with the victim's IP address as the spoofed source and results in the victim being flooded with unsolicited response traffic—a form of distributed denial-of-service (DDoS).

© Springer Nature Switzerland AG 2021
O. Hohlfeld et al. (Eds.): PAM 2021, LNCS 12671, pp. 302–316, 2021.
https://doi.org/10.1007/978-3-030-72582-2_18

Both cache poisoning and reflection-based DDoS attacks exploit the lack of verification inherent with UDP. In an attempt to solve this issue, and provid.e identity management in the DNS, a new protocol, known as DNS Cookies, was standardized through the Request for Comments (RFC) process in 2016 [11]. With DNS Cookies, both client and server include a cryptographic identifier (the cookie) in their DNS messages which can then be verified in future messages. An off-path attacker is unable to learn the cookie values and thus cannot feasibly spoof them.

Since 2016, DNS Cookies have become increasingly common and are supported by many open-source DNS software vendors. However, to the best of our knowledge, no research has been done to quantify the level of support for cookies. The major contribution of this paper is a **study of client- and server-side support for DNS cookies**—the first such measurement of its kind. Additionally, we analyze DNS Cookie enforcement to see if any client or server rejects illegitimate DNS messages based on cookies. While clients and servers may be exchanging cookies, there is no benefit unless a missing or incorrect cookie affects the server's response.

In this paper, we make the following contributions:

- We measure support for DNS Cookies in high-demand authoritative DNS servers and open resolvers Internet-wide; we find that 30% of servers fully support cookies, and only 10% of recursive clients send cookies.
- We analyze the DNS Cookies we observed and discover several potential misconfigurations, such as inaccurate server clocks, some of which could break implementations.
- We examine the behavior of DNS clients and servers when encountering missing or illegitimate cookies and find that 80% of clients do not reject responses when they should and that 99% of servers handle these situations in the least restrictive manner by responding indifferently.
- We discuss the path forward for wider DNS Cookie adoption and possible solutions for enforcing the use of cookies.

Overall, our work, which is the first to measure DNS Cookies in the wild, reveals a low level of adoption and minimal enforcement of DNS Cookies. We believe that DNS Cookies have the potential to benefit the DNS, but greater adoption and strategies for enforcement are required.

Artifacts: The source code and datasets used to produce this paper can be found at the following link: https://imaal.byu.edu/papers/2021_pam_dns_cookies/.

2 Background

The Domain Name System (DNS) is primarily used to convert domain names (e.g. `example.com`) to Internet Protocol (IP) addresses (e.g. `192.0.2.1`) [18,19]. There are three components in the DNS: stub resolvers, recursive resolvers, and authoritative servers.

Stub resolvers are typically associated with end-devices such as a phone or desktop. To visit a given domain, a stub sends a DNS query to its configured recursive resolver. The recursive resolver can respond to the query immediately if the answer is cached. Otherwise, it queries several authoritative servers systematically until it obtains the answer.

The DNS continues to utilize the User Datagram Protocol (UDP) as its primary transport protocol. UDP does not provide identity management and therefore does not protect against spoofing attacks, wherein an attacker impersonates a client or server by using their IP address as the source.

One attack that utilizes spoofing to impersonate an authoritative server is DNS cache poisoning. With cache poisoning, an attacker can respond to a client with a malicious IP address, causing that client, and all who rely on its cache, to be redirected to the malicious IP.

Due to the severity of a successful cache poisoning attack, several measures have been encouraged to reduce the chance of a successful cache poisoning. These include source port randomization [15] and 0x20 encoding (randomized capitalization) [6]—both of which require only changes to client-side software. Another avenue would be for a client to use DNS-over-TCP [10], DNS-over-TLS (DoT) [14], or DNS-over-HTTPS (DoH) [13]. These three protocols all provide the identity management inherent in the TCP handshake, and DoT and DoH are showing increased adoption [9,17]. However, they result in increased latency [7]. A final approach, which avoids identity management altogether, is cryptographically authenticating DNS responses. This strategy is employed by DNSCurve [1] and the DNS Security Extensions (DNSSEC) [3–5]. Neither of these methods has seen widespread adoption.

Another attack that exploits the lack of identity management in UDP and the DNS is distributed denial-of-service (DDoS) attacks. Here the attacker impersonates the victim's client and sends many DNS queries. This results in traffic being reflected off of DNS servers and the victim being flooded with unsolicited response traffic. Past attacks have reached traffic volumes of 300 Gbps to 1.2 Tbps and are capable of affecting major services such as Amazon and Netflix [12,20]. Both of these attacks can have major effects but can be prevented with some form of identity management.

DNS Cookies [11] are designed as a lightweight mechanism that provides identity management at a strength similar to TCP, but without the latency burden. They are included in DNS messages as a COOKIE option inside the Extended DNS (EDNS) OPT resource record [8]. Both the client and server in a given communication can provide a plain-text cookie in their DNS messages. The client can then verify that the server includes the client cookie (i.e., provided by the client) in future communications—and vice-versa—to ensure that messages have not been spoofed by an off-path attacker. An example of this process is shown in Fig. 1. DNS Cookies do not provide protection against on-path attackers, but should still provide substantial benefit to securing the internet as a whole.

Client cookies are 8 bytes in length and are used to prevent cache poisoning by enabling the client to verify the server's identity. A stub or recursive resolver can

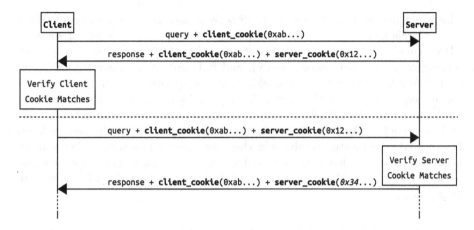

Fig. 1. An example communication using DNS Cookies. Here the client starts from a fresh state and reuses its cookie whereas the server generates a new cookie per query.

include a DNS client cookie in their queries and only accept a response containing the cookie. The suggested implementation for generating a client cookie is to use a cryptographic hash of the *(Client IP |Server IP |Client Secret)*. More recent suggestions remove the inclusion of the Client IP as it may not be known at the time of generation [21]. Regardless, a client should use a unique cookie per server and should not reuse a cookie across IP addresses as this would enable tracking the client.

A server cookie ranges in size from 8 to 32 bytes and is used to confirm a client's identity, in turn preventing reflection-based attacks. Authoritative and recursive servers may choose to send a server cookie when responding to a query with a client cookie in it. Clients should then include this cookie in future queries to verify their identity. If a server receives a query without a valid server cookie they may enforce cookie use by responding with the BADCOOKIE response code (rcode), a valid server cookie, and no DNS answers. The specification suggests that a server cookie consists of a 4-byte nonce, 4-byte timestamp, and an 8-byte cryptographic hash of the *(Server Secret |Client Cookie |Nonce |Time |Client IP)*. The time field results in a new cookie for every request and makes rejection of outdated cookies easy. Additionally, the server does not need to save any state to verify a cookie as the nonce and timestamp are provided in plain-text.

In 2019 an Internet draft was created to standardize the format for DNS Cookies to allow interoperability between different DNS software [21]. Of note, server cookies were visibly changed as the nonce was replaced with a version and reserved field.

3   Support for DNS Cookies

Here we establish a baseline measurement for DNS Cookie usage from the perspective of both clients and servers. We analyze DNS server-side cookie behavior, which includes both authoritative DNS servers and recursive resolvers in their "server" role to clients. For this analysis, we classify varying levels of support: EDNS capability (via the inclusion of an option (OPT) record in a response), echoing of a sent client cookie (only), and full support with a returned server cookie. While echoing a client cookie is not a specified option in the protocol, it does still protect the client. We also measure cookie usage of recursive resolvers in the "client" role in connection with queries to authoritative servers under our control. An analysis that included all perspectives would have included DNS Cookie use by stub resolvers in their communications with DNS recursive resolvers. However, that data is available only to recursive server operators, so we were unable to perform an analysis of stub resolver behavior with respect to DNS Cookies.

3.1   Server-Side Cookie Support

We queried a set of open recursive resolvers and two sets of authoritative servers to measure DNS Cookie support for "servers".

To generate a set of recursive resolvers to test, we issued a DNS query (for a domain we control) to every IPv4 address. We classified an IP address as a recursive resolver if it 1) queried our authoritative server or 2) responded to our query with the recursion available (RA) flag set and a response code of either NOERROR or NXDOMAIN. This data was collected from September 24–26, 2020. In total, we identified 1,908,397 open recursive resolvers.

For authoritative servers, we analyzed servers authoritative for the top 1 million Alexa domains [2] (actually 770,631 domains) and servers authoritative for the 1,509 top-level domains (TLDs) [16] (including the root servers). All data was collected on September 30, 2020, using the latest Alexa file and root zone available. The names and IP addresses (IPv4 and IPv6) for each domain in the collective lists were determined through 1) a lookup of type NS (name server) for the domain and 2) a lookup of type A and AAAA (IPv4 and IPv6 address, respectively) for each name returned in the NS query response. In total, we recorded 157,679 IP addresses for the Alexa sites and 6,615 for the TLDs.

To identify support for cookies, we issued up to 6 DNS queries to each server—stopping early if we received a response with a server cookie. We included the same client cookie in every query. During these queries, we experienced errors with 48% of resolvers, likely due to high churn. In particular, queries for 32% of resolvers timed out, and for 16% of resolvers, we received a response from a different IP address (often Cloudflare's 1.1.1.1) than we had queried. Removing these cases leaves us with 999,228 error-free resolvers. For authoritative servers, queries to 6,724 (4.3%) of Alexa IPs resulted in an error, as did queries to 58 (0.88%) TLD IPs. The errors associated with querying authoritative servers primarily consisted of time outs (98% of Alexa errors and 100% of TLD errors), though there were a handful of malformed packets or unexpected responses. We report all of our results as percentages of communications with error-free servers.

EDNS, which is a prerequisite for cookies, was supported (as evidenced by an OPT record in responses) by 699,402 (70%) of recursive resolvers, 147,878 (98%)

of Alexa IPs, and 6,557 (100%) of TLD IPs. The client cookie that we sent in our queries was returned by 208,526 (21%) of recursive resolvers, 48,262 (32%) of Alexa IPs, and only 1,249 (19%) of TLD IPs. The remaining servers returned a response that either did not include a COOKIE EDNS option or included a client cookie that did not match the one we sent. Servers that included a server cookie in their response (this implies the inclusion of a client cookie, by specification) include: 167,402 (17%) of open resolvers, 43,649 (29%) of Alexa IPs, and all 1,249 of the TLD IPs that returned the correct client cookie. However, 14 resolver IPs and 5 Alexa IPs returned a COOKIE option with a server cookie of all zeroes. The Alexa and TLD IPs that returned server cookies were collectively authoritative for 26,629 domains and 373 zones respectively.

Of note, 93 Alexa IPs and 41 resolvers IPs responded with a client cookie that did not match the one we sent. For 5 Alexa IPs and 22 resolvers IPs, the value of the client cookie returned was off by only one byte—the fourth most significant byte. An additional 5 Alexa and 14 resolver IPs replied with zeroed out client cookies. A single TLD IP, one of three servers authoritative for the gm TLD, returned a COOKIE option with all zeroes for both the client and server cookies. The remaining unexpected responses did not follow a discernible pattern.

Overall we observe high EDNS support (70% of resolvers and >98% of authoritative servers). However, cookie support is much lower. While nearly one-third of Alexa IPs fully supported cookies, less than 20% of TLD IPs and recursive resolvers did. As a result, there are still more than 100,000 authoritative servers and 800,000 recursive resolvers that can be used for reflection attacks because they lack a mechanism for validating client identity (Fig. 2).

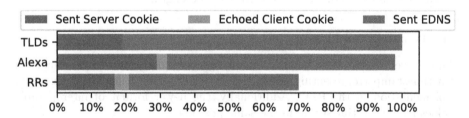

Fig. 2. Incremental support for DNS Cookies across the three datasets of recursive resolvers, TLD authoritative servers, and the top 1m Alexa authoritative servers. Servers in the leftmost group fully support DNS Cookies.

3.2 Client-Side Cookie Support in Recursive Resolvers

During our measurements of resolvers supporting the "server" role of cookies, we also measured their support for DNS Cookies while acting as a "client". Each query we issued consisted of a special domain name hosted at authoritative servers under our control. We recorded each incoming query for the domain name we were using and responded with NXDOMAIN and full DNS Cookie support. We observed queries to our authoritative servers from 93,395 unique IP addresses, of which 8,471 (9.1%) sent at least one response that contained a COOKIE option.

During this measurement, we encoded the IP address of the recursive resolver that we queried in the domain name. This reveals that 1,552,397 unique resolvers queried our backend through the 90,000 IP addresses. This discrepancy may be due to forwarding, as 56% of resolvers were represented by only 1000 IP addresses. In particular, Google and Cloudflare handled queries for 36% and 7.0% of resolvers respectively.

In our measurement for recursive resolvers sending cookies, we found client cookie support to be minimal. Of resolvers that queried our authoritative servers directly, only 9.1% of over 90,000 IPs sent a cookie. This is potentially alarming as these resolvers are not using cookies for cache poisoning protection. While they may employ other methods, DNS Cookies offer an extra layer of defense.

4   Server Cookie Analysis

For our measurement of DNS server cookies, we expand the datasets from Sect. 3.1. For each IP address we found to be sending server cookies, we sent an additional 60 queries. These queries were broken into 3 subsets: the first 20 queries never included a server cookie, the next 20 included the first server cookies received, and the final 20 included the latest server cookie we had received. Each subset had a 1-min pause after the first 10 queries, before issuing the final 10 queries.

Valid server cookies may be anywhere from 8 to 32 bytes in length. Of all of the cookies we received, >99% were 16 bytes in length.

4.1   Dynamic Cookies

Many server cookies are dynamic: changing consistently due to the inclusion of a timestamp (representing seconds since UTC). This follows the suggested implementation in the RFC. Additionally, the newer format of interoperable cookies includes a timestamp in the same position.

As a result, we classify a cookie as dynamic if bytes 5–8 represent a time within a window of 1 h in the past and 30 min in the future compared to the current time of our querying machine (NTP synchronized).[1]

Over 99% of authoritative servers and 83% of recursive resolvers that sent server cookies used at least one dynamic cookie.

Timestamps. We first consider the timestamps being used in dynamic cookies. We are primarily interested in three unusual patterns: timestamps consistently

---

[1] The chance of a non-dynamic cookie being classified as dynamic is extremely small. Our window size accepts only 5,400 values out of the 4.3 billion possible values in the 32 bit field.

off by more than a minute, cookies that are "sticky" for short periods, and slow-moving timestamps that update on a fixed interval of 10 or more seconds.

For each dynamic server cookie, we compared the timestamp with the current time of the querying machine (i.e., the client), which was NTP-synchronized: $ts_{diff} = ts_{cookie} - ts_{client}$. We consider a server cookie's timestamp to be *accurate* if $|ts_{diff}| \leq 5s$. This generous window accounts for any network delays. We consider a timestamp to be *significantly out-of-sync* if $|ts_{diff}| > 60s$. Finally, we classify "sticky" and slow-moving clock servers based upon the number of distinct values of ts_{diff} since this tells us that the ts_{cookie} remained static while ts_{client} advanced. "Sticky" servers are defined by having 8 or more distinct values in one of the 3 subsets of queries and less than 3 distinct values in another. Slow-moving clocks are defined by not being sticky and having 10 or more distinct values across all cookies.

Table 1 summarizes the major findings for each IP address. Over 95% of IPs consistently returned server cookies with accurate timestamps. For 2.8% of IPs, the timestamps were significantly out-of-sync, likely due to an incorrect clock. While an incorrect clock is unexpected, it is inconsequential for cookies since the cookie value only matters to the server itself.

A category that is perhaps more interesting is IPs for which we observed a mix of cookie timestamp behaviors—some accurate and some significantly out-of-sync. For example, one IP returned cookies resulting in the following values of ts_{diff}: $(1\ 1\ 1\ 1\ 75\ 1\ 2\ 1\ 75\ 1...)$. The timestamps for approximately one-fifth of the responses were consistently and significantly out-of-sync, while the remainder were accurate. This behavior is representative of a DNS server with five backend servers, one of which has a clock that is 75 s out of sync.

We additionally observe that some IPs use "sticky" cookies: cookies that remain static for short periods (typically 10 s) depending on the context. We observed two implementations of this. In the first implementation, cookies were sticky when our client was not querying with a server cookie. Once our client began sending server cookies, the server replied consistently with accurate timestamp cookies. We observed that 77 Alexa IPs and 775 resolver IPs followed this pattern. The second implementation acted in the opposite manner: the server replied with accurate timestamp cookies until our client sent one of the server cookies in a query. The server then made that valid cookie sticky and did not change it for a short period. We saw this pattern in only 12 Alexa IPs and 12 recursive IPs.

Our final category consists of slow-moving clocks: cookie timestamps that update on a fixed interval of 10 or more seconds. We classified 20 Alexa IPs and 4,413 recursive resolver IPs in this category. We observed that 3,296 recursive IPs had at least one timestamp off by more than 2 min and that 2,206 IPs displayed strictly increasing ts_{diff} values across every set of 10 queries. From this, we can gather that most recursive resolver IPs are using a slow-moving clock (possibly intentionally) with an update period of over 2 min.

The timestamps in DNS Cookies proved to be more interesting than originally expected. We found that most servers always return a cookie with a current timestamp; however, some implementations purposely hold onto a cookie for a short period. We also discovered potential configuration issues with some backends of an IP having an incorrect clock. If cookies were to be enforced, clients may be intermittently rejected if they present that backend's server cookie to another backend, and the cookie was too far out-of-sync to be considered valid.

Table 1. Summary of timestamps found in server cookies returned by IPs. ts_{diff} represents the difference between the timestamp in the cookie and the querying computer's current time.

	Alexa	TLDs	RRs
All Cookies Accurate ($|ts_{diff}| \leq 5s$)	41,639 (96%)	1,225 (98%)	131,520 (95%)
All Cookies Out-of-Sync ($|ts_{diff}| > 60s$)	1,615 (3.7%)	17 (1.4%)	3,544 (2.6%)
Mixed Accurate & Out-of-Sync	66 (0.15%)	0 (0.0%)	2,980 (2.2%)
"Sticky" Cookies	89 (0.21%)	0 (0.0%)	787 (0.67%)
Slow-Moving Clocks	20 (0.05%)	0 (0.0%)	4,413 (3.2%)
IPs Using Dynamic Cookies	**43,345**	**1,246**	**138,865**

Interoperable Cookie.s Interoperable Cookies are designed to standardize the generation of cookies across varying backend implementations. We classified a server cookie as interoperable if the cookie started with `0x01000000` as specified in the RFC draft (a one-byte version field and three bytes reserved) and the timestamp field met the criteria previously mentioned.

Of the 43,737 Alexa IPs that returned a server cookie, 1,778 (4.1%) used interoperable cookies consistently. For TLDs, 92 (7.4%) of 1,249 IPs used interoperable cookies. No IP in either dataset sent a mix of standard and interoperable cookies across all of our queries.

For the 167,402 recursive resolver IPs that sent a server cookie, we found that 30,078 (18%) sent at least one interoperable cookie. However, we also found that 10,948 (6.5%) of IPs sent a mix of interoperable and standard dynamic cookies[2]. This behavior was unexpected as the primary purpose of interoperable cookies is to standardize cookies across all backend servers behind a single IP address.

Overall adoption of interoperable cookies was low in authoritative servers (under 10%), but partial support in recursive resolvers was higher at 18%.

4.2 Static Cookies

While the majority of cookies can be classified as "dynamic", a number of servers reused the same cookie. We classified a server as using static cookies if only a

---

[2] It is possible that we misclassified a standard cookie with a nonce of `0x01000000` as being interoperable. 9,990 of these IPs sent at least two cookies that appeared interoperable in response to our 60 queries.

single cookie was used across our tests and the cookie did not contain a dynamic timestamp. We identified 38 recursive resolvers that used a unique 32-byte cookie for the entire duration of our test. Similarly, 33 Alexa servers always replied with a single, unique 8-byte cookie.

We further analyzed IPs for 4 Alexa domains that sent static cookies: `ibb.co`, `pantip.com`, `postimg.cc`, and `wikipedia.org`. For each IP address authoritative for these domains we sent queries every minute for four days and additional queries with varying client cookies and client IP addresses.

Our results show that all four domains used the client IP address and client cookie in the creation of their server cookie because changing either of these variables affected the cookie they returned. Each also changed their cookie at the start of every hour, implying that they either changed their secret or that an hourly timestamp was considered in the calculation. Of note, the authoritative servers for two domains—`wikipedia.org` and `pantip.com`—returned the same server cookie, regardless of which server was queried for the domain. However, the servers authoritative for `ibb.co` and `postimg.cc` acted independently, implying separate server secrets or some other unique value per server.

5   The State of Cookie Enforcement

In this section, we explore how clients and servers handle unexpected behavior. We begin by demonstrating to clients and servers that our infrastructure supports cookies. We then perform tests with missing cookies, missing EDNS, or fake cookies. With this, we can see whether clients and servers will enforce cookies if they know the other party supports them. If not, cookies provide little value as an attacker could simply exclude cookies in their spoofed packets.

5.1   Client Handling of Unexpected Server Behavior

For this experiment, we forced the 1.5 million resolvers (with or without cookie support) found in Sect. 3.2 to query our authoritative servers 6 times. We configured our authoritative server to respond differently depending on the query name it received. The response conditions we created are as follows (in order):

1. NORMAL: Respond with full cookie support: Correct client cookie and a server cookie—if the query included a client cookie.
2. NO-COOKIE: Respond with no `COOKIE` option.
3. BAD-ANSWER: Respond with the correct client cookie (if any), `BADCOOKIE` rcode, and an answer section.
4. BAD: Respond with the correct client cookie (if any), `BADCOOKIE` rcode, and *no* answer section.
5. NO-EDNS: Respond with no `OPT` record (i.e., no EDNS support).
6. FAKE: Respond with incorrect client cookie.

For each query, we made up to 3 attempts, as the stub resolver, to receive an answer. This experiment was run approximately one week after we discovered the 1.5 million IPs. As a result, we experienced a high churn and only saw 528,832 (34%) of IPs respond with both an answer and an rcode of NOERROR in our NORMAL condition.[3]

Responses with Missing/Invalid Client Cookies. Of those resolvers from which we still received responses, 28,605 (5.4%) included a cookie in the NORMAL condition (or the intermediate IP did). For these IPs in the NO-COOKIE scenario, we surprisingly got a normal response from 23,979 (84%) IPs. Of those with bad responses, 3,625 (13%) had a SERVFAIL rcode and an additional 909 (3.2%) timed out. For the NO-EDNS queries, we saw similar numbers compared to those who sent cookies: 24,798 (87%) responded to our stub resolver normally, 2,495 (8.7%) responded with SERVFAIL, and 1,236 (4.3%) timed out.

Finally, in the FAKE category, we began to see more rejection. This test was performed a day after NO-EDNS and as a result, there was more churn and some servers may have stopped sending EDNS since we appeared to not support it. We recorded 27,079 IPs which sent a cookie in a NORMAL query directly preceding this test. We saw a much lower percentage of acceptance here with only 5,115 (20%) responding to the stub resolver normally. Most failure is split between SERVFAIL with 10,059 (40%) of IPs and time outs with 9,564 (38%) of IPs.

The specification for DNS Cookies states that a client must discard a response with an invalid client cookie or a missing cookie when one is expected. However, we observed that 20% of recursive clients did not reject invalid cookies and that over 80% of clients did not discard responses that were missing a cookie when one should have been present (as demonstrated to the client in a previous query). This means that a majority of recursive clients may still be susceptible to cache poisoning attacks because a response without EDNS or a DNS COOKIE option is accepted as easily as a legitimate response with a valid client cookie.

Responses with BADCOOKIE Rcode. Two of our conditions tested how a recursive resolver responds to a BADCOOKIE rcode. In one condition we still included the answer, but in the other, we did not. This imitates an authoritative server strictly requiring cookies (though a correctly behaving serving would provide a valid server cookie and accept it in future queries). For these conditions, we consider all 528,832 servers who successfully answered the normal condition regardless of cookie use.

For the BAD queries, 301,929 (57%) of IPs timed out and 206,577 (39%) returned an rcode of SERVFAIL. We observed similar values for BAD-ANSWER: 272,041 (51%) timed out and 236,401 (45%) returned SERVFAIL. We did observe an extra effort by recursive resolvers receiving either a BAD or a BAD-ANSWER response to get a valid response. More than half of IP addresses issued at least 19 queries in connection with either of these responses—as opposed to a median

---

[3] We did not rerun the initial collection as the process is resource intensive and takes multiple days. We are also less interested in servers lost due to churn as they are unlikely to be true open resolvers as opposed to misconfigurations.

of 1 for NORMAL queries. Interestingly, 17,921 (3.4%) of recursive resolvers that responded to our BAD-ANSWER query returned to us the answer that our servers had given to them, despite the BADCOOKIE rcode in the response from our authoritative servers. Of those that returned an answer, 14,350 (80%) also set the rcode to SERVFAIL. The lack of enforcement is accompanied by a lack of consensus on how unexpected responses should be handled.

5.2 Server Handling of Unexpected Client Behavior

Here we performed a short test to determine how DNS servers would respond to unexpected client behavior, with regard to the server cookie sent by the client. Specifically, we had our client send 5 queries that included the most recently received server cookie, 5 queries without a server cookie, and 5 queries with a fake server cookie. In each of these conditions, the client cookie was sent as normal. In the latter two cases, the specification provides three options for a server [11]. They may silently discard the request, respond with the BADCOOKIE error code, or respond normally as if no cookie option was present. We sent these queries to all Alexa IPs, TLD IPs, and recursive resolver IPs identified in Sect. 3.1 that supported cookies.

For Alexa servers, we observed 41,083 IPs that responded to at least one normal query with a valid response and rcode of NOERROR. In our two other scenarios, nearly all of these IPs also had one or more standard responses: >99% for queries without cookies and with fake cookies. We observed 1 IP that used the BADCOOKIE rcode even when we sent the most recently received server cookie. We saw only 28 IPs use BADCOOKIE when we didn't send a cookie and 27 IPs when we sent a fake cookie.

For TLD servers, we initially observed 1,246 IPs that responded to at least one normal query with an rcode of NOERROR. All but 3 IPs returned an rcode of NOERROR in both the fake and missing cookie scenarios. These 3 IPs consistently returned an rcode of BADCOOKIE under these conditions, and all were authoritative for the il (Israel) TLD.

For recursive resolvers, we saw 137,896 IPs return an rcode of NXDOMAIN (we queried for a non-existent domain) for a normal query. Again we saw over 99% continue to behave normally when the server cookie was missing or fake. We measured 49 servers using BADCOOKIE for a missing cookie and 53 for a fake cookie (though 13 IPs sent BADCOOKIE incorrectly in the normal condition).

In summary, practically no server changes its behavior if it doesn't receive a server cookie or if it receives a fake one (even after the client previously sent valid cookies). While this behavior is consistent with the specification, it is the least restrictive approach. As a result, these servers can still potentially be used in reflection attacks because they will generate a full response regardless of the server cookie.

6   Discussion

We have now enumerated support for DNS Cookies and found that it is limited, both for clients and servers. We have also seen that few clients and servers supporting cookies enforce them. This begs the question of what contribution, if any, DNS Cookies currently make. DNS Cookies are also in a difficult situation because they require wide deployment for enforcement to be enabled, but there may be little value in adopting them today. We now discuss the perceived current benefits of cookies and the path forward to wider adoption and enforcement.

6.1   Cookie Benefits Today

DNS Cookies have minimal value in their current state. We found that cookies are used by less than 30% of servers and 10% of recursive clients. This alone means that 70% of servers can be abused for reflection attacks and 90% of clients are not strongly protected from cache poisoning attacks (though other measures exist). Also noteworthy is the fact that 90% of clients are not sending server cookies (as a client cookie is a prerequisite).

Due to relatively low adoption rates, those that do support cookies are unable to enforce them since doing so would break compatibility with the majority of infrastructure. In our testing, we demonstrated our support for cookies in preliminary queries but still observed that only 20% of clients and less than 1% of servers changed their behavior if a cookie was missing or fake.

The only benefit we see today is that receiving a valid cookie acts as a reassurance that the other party's identity is correct. In real-world applications, this reassurance provides little value since it does not change an implementation's behavior: it would accept the message regardless of a cookie.

In summary, we do not see any benefits from DNS cookies, as they are used today. Cookies exist mostly in a dormant state, but if adoption significantly improves such that they can be enforced, they can become effective.

6.2   Path Forward for Cookies

The obvious next step for cookies is to increase adoption among clients and servers. However, there is somewhat little benefit to doing so today due to the lack of enforcement. Additionally, servers may not be concerned with identification (as they're only a passive entity in reflection attacks) and clients may feel protected from cache poisoning through other measures.

To incentivize adoption, strategies for partial enforcement should be explored. For example, clients and servers could begin enforcing cookies use for parties they previously observe using cookies. In our testing, we saw that 80% of clients and 99% of servers did not do this. Another enforcement implementation could involve a mechanism to advertise cookie support. This would allow other parties to verify that an IP intends to use cookies and then apply strict enforcement on a case-by-case basis. Neither of these enforcement strategies will overcome the lack of cookie adoption because enforcement can only ever be applied to the small percentage of clients and servers supporting cookies.

As a result, the main step for cookies is to continue to grow adoption numbers. As adoption grows, opportunistic or learned enforcement will become more viable. Given the entrenchment of the DNS in internet infrastructure, it is unlikely that adoption will ever be universal, and as a result, strict enforcement may never be possible. Here we hope that strategic enforcement can be sufficient enough to deploy as a permanent strategy.

7   Ethical Considerations

All measurements and analyses performed in this paper were designed to be benign. Queries were sent at a low frequency, typically one per second, and never exceeded a volume of more than 20 queries per minute to a given IP address. Additionally, our probes were used solely to measure cookie usage and support. None of our probes were designed to exploit clients or servers.

8   Conclusion

In this paper, we present what is, to our knowledge, the first study of DNS Cookie usage. We find that cookie usage is limited, despite its standardization four years ago. We find that under 30% of IPs for the top 1 million Alexa domains and less than 20% of IPs for the TLDs supported cookies. We also observe that 17% of recursive resolvers support cookies as a "server", but only 9% do as a "client". We next analyzed a collection of server cookies and exposed potential issues, such as inconsistent clocks, which could potentially cause issues if cookies were enforced.

Finally, we experimented to see if any clients or servers enforced cookie usage. We observe that only 20% of clients and less than 1% of servers behave differently if an IP that previously supported cookies does not supply a cookie or replies with a fake cookie. This highlights that even those supporting cookies are not seeing any significant protection.

Overall, DNS Cookie adoption is limited, and there are few benefits for those using cookies. For cookies to leave their dormant state, higher adoption rates are necessary. From there, we believe that strategic enforcement may begin to produce real-world benefits.

Acknowledgments. We gratefully acknowledge the Comcast Innovation Fund for their support of the work that produced this material. We also thank the PAM 2021 reviewers and our shepherd for their helpful comments.

Sandia National Laboratories is a multimission laboratory managed and operated by National Technology and Engineering Solutions of Sandia, LLC., a wholly owned subsidiary of Honeywell International, Inc., for the U.S. Department of Energy's National Nuclear Security Administration under contract DE-NA-0003525.

References

1. dnscurve.org. (2009) https://dnscurve.org/
2. Amazon: Alexa top sites (2020). https://aws.amazon.com/alexa-top-sites/
3. Arends, R., Austein, R., Larson, M., Massey, D., Rose, S.: RFC 4033: DNS security introduction and requirements, March 2005
4. Arends, R., Austein, R., Larson, M., Massey, D., Rose, S.: RFC 4034: Resource records for the DNS security extensions, March 2005
5. Arends, R., Austein, R., Larson, M., Massey, D., Rose, S.: RFC 4035: protocol modifications for the DNS security extensions, March 2005
6. Bortzmeyer, S.: DNS query name minimisation to improve privacy, March 2016
7. Böttger, T., et al.: An empirical study of the cost of DNS-over-HTTPS. In: Proceedings of the ACM SIGCOMM Internet Measurement Conference, IMC pp. 15–21 (2019). https://doi.org/10.1145/3355369.3355575
8. Damas, J., Graff, M., Vixie, P.: Extension mechanisms for DNS (EDNS(0)), April 2013
9. Deccio, C., Davis, J.: DNS privacy in practice and preparation. In: CoNEXT 2019 - Proceedings of the 15th International Conference on Emerging Networking Experiments and Technologies (2019). https://doi.org/10.1145/3359989.3365435
10. Dickinson, J., Dickinson, S., Bellis, R., Mankin, A., Wessels, D.: Rfc 7766: DNS transport over TCP - implementation requirements, March 2016
11. Eastland, D., Andrews, M.: RFC 7873: Domain name system (DNS) cookies, May 2016
12. Hilton, S.: DYN analysis summary of Friday October 21 attack (2016). https://dyn.com/blog/dyn-analysis-summary-of-friday-october-21-attack/
13. Hoffman, P., McManus, P.: RFC 8484: DNS queries over https (DOH), October 2018
14. Hu, Z., Zhu, L., Heidemann, J., Mankin, A., Wessels, D., Hoffman, P.: RFC 7858: specification for DNS over transport layer security (tls), May 2016
15. Hubert, B., Mook, R.: RFC 5452: Measures for making DNS more resilient against forged answers, January 2009
16. Internet Assigned Numbers Authority: Root Files (2020). https://www.iana.org/domains/root/files
17. Lu, C., et al.: An end-to-end, large-scale measurement of DNS-over-encryption: how far have we come? In: Proceedings of the ACM SIGCOMM Internet Measurement Conference, IMC pp. 22–35 (2019)
18. Mockapetris, P.: RFC 1034: domain names - concepts and facilities, November 1987
19. Mockapetris, P.: RFC 1035: Domain names - implementation and specification, November 1987
20. Prince, M.: The DDoS that knocked spamhaus offline (and how we mitigated it). https://blog.cloudflare.com/the-ddos-that-knocked-spamhaus-offline-and-ho/ (2013)
21. Sury, O., Toorop, W., Eastland, D., Andrews, M.: Interoperable domain name system (DNS) server cookies, May 2020

Performance

What You Need to Know About (Smart) Network Interface Cards

Georgios P. Katsikas[ID], Tom Barbette[✉][ID], Marco Chiesa[ID], Dejan Kostić[ID], and Gerald Q. Maguire Jr.[ID]

KTH Royal Institute of Technology, Stockholm, Sweden
{katsikas,barbette,mchiesa,dmk,maguire}@kth.se

Abstract. Network interface cards (NICs) are fundamental components of modern high-speed networked systems, supporting multi-100 Gbps speeds and increasing programmability. Offloading computation from a server's CPU to a NIC frees a substantial amount of the server's CPU resources, making NICs key to offer competitive cloud services. Therefore, understanding the performance benefits and limitations of offloading a networking application to a NIC is of paramount importance.

In this paper, we measure the performance of four different NICs from one of the *largest NIC vendors worldwide*, supporting 100 Gbps and 200 Gbps. We show that while today's NICs can easily support multi-hundred-gigabit throughputs, performing frequent update operations of a NIC's packet classifier—as network address translators (NATs) and load balancers would do for each incoming connection—results in a dramatic *throughput reduction of up to 70 Gbps or complete denial of service*. Our conclusion is that all tested NICs cannot support *high-speed* networking applications that require keeping track of a large number of frequently arriving incoming connections. Furthermore, we show a variety of counter-intuitive performance artefacts including the performance impact of using multiple tables to classify flows of packets.

Keywords: Network interface cards · Hardware classifier · Offloading · Rule operations · Performance · Benchmarking · 100 GbE

1 Introduction

With the dramatic growth of Network Interface Card (NIC) speeds, optimizing I/O operations is essential for supporting modern-day applications. As evidenced by recent work, handling 40 Gbps of Transmission Control Protocol (TCP) traffic requires roughly 20%–60% of the CPU resources on a general-purpose server [10,31,48]. These communication overheads consume CPU cycles that could otherwise be used to run customers' applications, ultimately resulting in expensive deployments for network operators.

Offloading network operations to NICs is a pragmatic way to *partially* relieve CPUs from the burden of managing (some of the) network-related state.

© Springer Nature Switzerland AG 2021
O. Hohlfeld et al. (Eds.): PAM 2021, LNCS 12671, pp. 319–336, 2021.
https://doi.org/10.1007/978-3-030-72582-2_19

Examples of such offloading are TCP optimizations, such as Large Receive Offload (LRO) and TCP Segmentation Offload (TSO) [1]. Increasingly, NICs are equipped with built-in Field-Programmable Gate Arrays (FPGAs) or network processor cores that can be used to offload computation from a host's CPU directly into the NICs. Such NICs are referred to as SmartNICs. Several preliminary investigations of SmartNIC technologies have demonstrated potential benefits for offloading networking stacks [2,10,30–32], network functions [3,4,18,25,43], key-value stores[7,26,28], packet schedulers [44], neural networks [42], and beyond [21,38]. Despite the increasing relevance of (smart) NICs in today's systems, very few studies have focused on dissecting the performance of SmartNICs, comparing them with their predecessors, and providing guidelines for deploying NIC-offloaded applications, with a focus on packet classification.

Our Goal. In this work, we study the performance of (smart) NICs for widely deployed packet classification operations. A key challenge of *packet classification* is the ability of the classifier to both quickly (*i*) match incoming packets to their packet processing actions and (*ii*) adapt the state of the packet classifier, e.g., by inserting new rules or updating existing ones. For example, consider a cloud load balancer (LB) that keeps track of the mapping between incoming connections and the back-end servers handling these connections. The LB may utilize a NIC's packet classifier to map TCP/IP 5-tuples of incoming connection identifiers to their corresponding servers. As a single cluster in a large-scale datacenter may receive over 10 million new connections per second [29], it is critical to support fast updates for packet classifiers, thus achieving high throughput and low predictable latency. Our study of packet classifiers reveals unexpected performance bottlenecks in today's (smart) NICs and provides guidelines for researchers and practitioners, who wish to offload dynamic packet classifiers to (smart) NICs.

Findings. We analyzed the performance of four different NICs with speeds in the 100 Gbps to 200 Gbps range. Our key findings are summarized in Table 1. In short, we show that the forwarding throughput of the tested NICs sharply degrades when *i)* the forwarding plane is updated and *ii)* packets match multiple forwarding tables in the NIC. Moreover, we devise an efficient in-memory update mechanism that mitigates the impact of updating the rules on the forwarding throughput. The code to reproduce the experiments of this paper is publicly available along with supplementary graphs showing the experimental evaluation of all four NICs under test [17].

Paper Outline. This paper is organized as follows: Sect. 2 outlines the experimental methodology used in this work; Sect. 3 provides useful performance insights into modern NICs; Sect. 4 discusses related efforts in the area of programmable networking hardware beyond the work mentioned inline throughout the paper. Finally, Sect. 5 concludes this paper.

2 Measurement Methodology

This section outlines the testbed used to conduct the experiments as well as our methodology to extract results.

Table 1. Main findings of this paper.

Finding	Implication
There are parts of the NIC table hierarchy that do not yield the expected forwarding performance (Sect. 3.1)	Throughput degradation from 100 Gbps to 20 Mbps and multi-fold latency increase (Fig. 2a and Fig. 2c)
Uniformly spreading rules across a chain of NIC tables incurs performance penalty (Sect. 3.1)	Throughput degradation from 100 Gbps to 13 Gbps and 10x higher latency when using 16 tables (Fig. 2b and Fig. 2d)
A batch update of the NIC classifier, while processing traffic, makes the NIC temporarily unavailable (Sect. 3.1)	100% packet loss for up to several seconds with an increasing number of installed rules (Fig. 3)
Frequent updates of the NIC classifier, while processing traffic, causes substantial performance degradation (Sect. 3.1)	Throughput degradation from 100 Gbps to 30 Gbps and ~2x higher latency (Fig. 4)
Updating the NIC classifier from a separate core does not degrade the NIC performance (Sect. 3)	No performance impact when processing traffic on core 0 and updating rules from core 1 (Fig. 3 and Fig. 4)
The Internet protocol selection (i.e., IPv4 vs. IPv6) affects the NIC rule installation rate (Sect. 3.2.1)	IPv6 rule insertion rate is either 5–181 faster or 12% slower than the respective IPv4 rate, depending on the part of the NIC table hierarchy applied (Fig. 5a–5b)
The network slicing protocol selection affects the NIC rule installation rate (Sect. 3.2.1)	Installing VLAN-based rules is up to 50% faster than installing tunnel-based rules (Fig. 5c)
NIC rule update operations are non-atomic and rely on sequential addition and deletion (Sect. 3.2.2)	Too slow for applications that require heavy updates. Our dedicated update API performs up to 80% faster (Fig. 6)

2.1   Experimental Setup

Testbed. All of the experiments described in this paper used the testbed shown in Fig. 1. Two back-to-back interconnected servers, each with a dual-socket 16-core Intel® Xeon® Gold 6134 (SkyLake) CPU clocked at 3.2 GHz and 256 GiB of DDR4 Random Access Memory (RAM) clocked at 2666 MHz. Each core has 2 × 32 KiB L1 (instruction and data caches) and a 1 MiB L2 cache, while one 25 MiB Last Level Cache (LLC) is shared among the cores in each socket. Following today's best practices, hyper-threading is disabled on all servers [47] and the Operating System (OS) is the Ubuntu 18.04.5 distribution with Linux kernel v4.15. One server acts as a traffic generator and receiver while the other server is the Device Under Test (DUT).

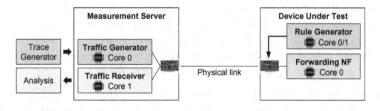

Fig. 1. Testbed setup and measurement methodology.

Tested NICs. We focus our study on one of the most widespread NICs available in Commercial off-the-shelf (COTS) hardware to date, as shown in Table 2. Such NICs, manufactured by NVIDIA Mellanox, operate at 100 Gbps link speeds (or beyond), while providing advanced processing capabilities. We also considered existing Intel NICs, such as the 10 GbE 82599 [12] and the 40 GbE XL710 [13], however these NICs operate at much lower link speeds and are limited to 8 K flow rules. The upcoming 100 GbE Intel E810 series network adapter [14] provides 16 K (masked) filters based on ternary content addressable memory (TCAM), which is still far from the range of several millions of flow rules tested with the NVIDIA Mellanox NICs. Moreover, the hardware limits of the Intel NICs are known, as Intel published relevant hardware datasheets [12–14]. NVIDIA Mellanox has not disclosed such information; thus our study sheds some light on unknown aspects of these popular NICs, while helping to understand how performance has evolved across the same family of NICs.

Table 2. The characteristics of the NICs used for the experiments in this paper.

Vendor	Model	Speed (Gbps)	# of Ports	Firmware Version	Driver	
					Name	Version
NVIDIA Mellanox	ConnectX-4 [35]	100	2	12.28.2006	mlx5_core	5.2–1.0.4
	ConnectX-5 [36]			16.29.1016		
	BlueField [34]			18.29.1016		
	ConnectX-6 [37]	200		20.29.1016		

All NICs except for the NVIDIA Mellanox ConnectX-6 use a PCIe 3.0 x16 bus to connect with a server's CPU. The ConnectX-6 adapter uses two PCIe 3.0 x16 slots. The BlueField NIC is a SmartNIC based on the ConnectX-5 adapter, also equipped with a 16-core ARM processor for additional in-NIC traffic processing. We briefly describe the general architecture and differences of the NVIDIA Mellanox NICs. All NICs have a first table, called *Table 0* or "root" table with space for 65 536 rule entries. All the NICs, except for the ConnectX-4, provide an additional sequence of high-performance exact-match tables (supporting a per-table mask) that can be used to massively offload packet classification from the CPUs to the NIC. Note that these NICs do not support Longest Prefix Match (LPM); instead the user should implement LPM with a combination of multiple tables with different masks. The capacity of these tables is only bounded by the host's available memory, thus they can accommodate a much larger number of rules, given the ample amount of RAM in modern servers. We refer to the first of those extra tables as Table 1 and note that any subsequent table (i.e., Table 2, 3, etc..) appears to have similar properties with Table 1.

Traffic Characteristics. A multi-core traffic generator and receiver, based on the Data Plane Development Kit (DPDK) v20.11 [46], is deployed on the measurement server as shown in Fig. 1. Four cores are allocated to the traffic generator, which inject a trace of 10K UDP flows at 100 Gbps. Each flow consists of MTU-sized (i.e., 1500-bytes) packets. This traffic first traverses the DUT and, if not dropped, then returns to the measurement server, this time reaching four different cores on the same CPU socket of the traffic generator.

Note that the measurement server injects traffic towards the DUT using the same 100 GbE ConnectX-5 NIC for all the experiments. This ensures that only the DUT's NIC hardware may vary across all of the experiments, thus potential differences among the experimental results solely depend on the performance of the underlying NIC in the DUT.

Measurements. Each experiment is executed 5 times; the collected measurements are plotted using either errorbars or boxplots, which visualize the 1st, 25th, 50th (i.e., median), 75th, and 99th values obtained across these 5 iterations, unless stated otherwise. The traffic receiver of the measurement server reports measurements related to end-to-end throughput, latency variance percentiles, per-queue packet & byte counters both at the measurement server and the DUT, packet loss, and the duration of each experiment. When reporting latency, we repeated experiments at 5Mpps ($\sim$60 Gbps), avoiding link speed to be a bottleneck on both the DUT and the traffic generator, thus ensuring latency changes are due to the NIC and not packets buffering in queues.

3   Analysis of Flow Tables

This section benchmarks the selected NICs focusing on three different aspects related to packet classifiers.

First, we quantify the performance impact of the NICs' hardware classifiers with (i) an increasing number of rules, (ii) an increasing number of tables hosting these rules, and (iii) increasingly larger or more frequent updates being installed by the control plane (see Sect. 3.1). Second, we analyse the performance of flow rule insertion/deletion operations in terms of latency for rule insertions and throughput (see Sect. 3.2.1). Finally, after discovering flow rule modifications are not supported by these NICs, we evaluate a different strategy to realize fast and atomic rule updates in the packet classifier of the analyzed NICs (see Sect. 3.2.2).

3.1   Hardware Classification Performance

Overview. In this section we measure packet classification performance of modern NICs under a variety of conditions. First, we show that the first table of these NICs drops almost all traffic when memory utilization exceeds $\sim$85%. We also show that the packet processing latency of the analyzed NICs exhibits a long tail in this situation (up to 120 ms). Moreover, spreading an increasing number of rules across four or more tables in these NICs results in substantial throughput degradation (23–88% when using 4–16 tables). Finally, we show that runtime modifications to the packet classifier's rules have a detrimental effect on the NIC's throughput: we observe a reduction of 70 Gbps of throughput (out of 100 Gbps).

Scenario. In the following experiments the DUT runs a single-core forwarding Network Function (NF) using the testbed described in Sect. 2.1. The NIC of the DUT dispatches input frames to this NF according to the flow rules installed in the NIC. These rules are stored either in the default "root" flow table of the NIC (i.e., Table 0) or in non-root tables (i.e., Tables 1–16). We differentiate between these two table categories as NVIDIA Mellanox explicitly mentions that Table 0 has a limited number of supported flow entries (i.e., 2^{16} rules) and the latter support a faster API based on shared memory between the NIC and the driver running in userlevel. We only show results for the ConnectX-5 NIC as we observe qualitatively similar trends for all the other NICs.

The rest of this section provides experimental evidence to address the following questions:

(Q1) **Does the number of rules and/or tables affect the performance of the NIC?**

Figure 2 shows the performance of the packet classifier with an increasing number of rules (x-axis) for all types of tables of the NVIDIA Mellanox ConnectX-5 NIC. We denote by Table 1-X the case where we uniformly install forwarding rules on the first X non-root tables, i.e., Table 1, ..., Table X. The rules installed in the NIC are simple exact matches and the generated traffic matches exactly one default rule installed in the NIC. We generate 8 Mpps of 1.5 KB packets towards the DUT, equivalent to 100 Gbps. Figure 2a and Fig. 2c show that the performance (i.e., throughput and packet processing latency) for Table 0 decreases

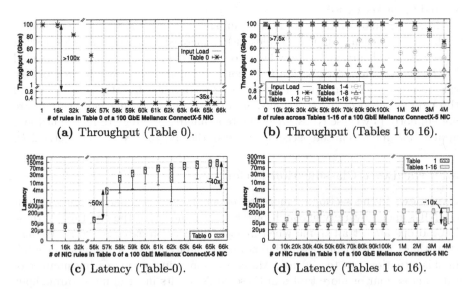

(a) Throughput (Table 0).   (b) Throughput (Tables 1 to 16).

(c) Latency (Table-0).   (d) Latency (Tables 1 to 16).

Fig. 2. Throughput and latency (on a logarithmic scale) of a hardware-based 100 GbE NVIDIA Mellanox ConnectX-5 NIC classifier with different number of pre-installed rules across Table 0 (left) and Tables 1–16 (right).

dramatically as soon as the occupancy of the table goes above 85%, hence the last 15% of memory is in practice unusable. Specifically, the throughput decreases from 100 Gbps down to 20 Mbps, while the latency increases by several orders of magnitude, from tens of μs to more than a hundred of ms. We observe a similar decrease in throughput for small packets (i.e., 64B), even when the input load is 3.5 Gbps, which is 30x lower than the maximum attainable throughput of the NIC under test. This confirms that the performance degradation issue is not a result of excessive input load, but rather a design artifact of the root table.

Figure 2b and Fig. 2d show that non-root tables (i.e., Tables 1–16) are much faster than the root table. Specifically, using a non-root table the NIC achieves line-rate throughput and low predictable latency even with $2M$ entries in Table 1. However, spreading rules across an increasing number of non-root tables results in substantial performance degradation. As shown in Fig. 2b, for most of the tested ruleset sizes, the NIC cannot achieve more than 20 Gbps throughput when using 16 tables, while the respective latency to access these tables exhibits a tenfold increase compared to the single-table case, as shown in Fig. 2d.

$\boxed{Q2}$ **Do updates to the classifier affect the performance of the NIC?**

The objective of this experiment is to understand how runtime modifications of the packet classifier's ruleset impact the throughput of the forwarded traffic. We envision two types of experiments motivated by two different use cases. In the first experiment, we generate a single *batch* of rule insertions to be installed into the NIC. This is reminiscent of scenarios in which a network suddenly reacts to a failure event that triggers many rule updates. For instance, Internet link failures may generate a burst of BGP updates for possibly 10 s of 100 s of thousands of IP prefixes received from a neighboring network [11]. In the second experiment, we generate periodic rule insertions in the packet classifier at a given frequency. This setting is reminiscent of cloud datacenter Layer 4 load balancers (LBs), where LBs insert a new rule into a packet classifier each time a new connection arrives. We note that, based on realistic connection size distributions taken from cloud datacenter workloads, the number of new rules to be installed ranges between 4K per second for "Hadoop' workloads to 36K and 338K per second for "cache follower" and "web server" workloads, respectively [41]. In both experiments, we generate a workload with packet sizes of 1.5 KB. To avoid external bias from the system's CPU, we measure two different cases for each experiment: In the first case (labeled as "Same Core" below), we use the same CPU core that performs traffic forwarding to install the rules in the NIC. In the second case (labeled as "Distinct Cores" below), we use one CPU core for traffic forwarding and another CPU core for rule installation. All the traffic matches a single rule in the classifier. As in the previous experiment, we obtain similar qualitative results for all the NICs and only show the NVIDIA ConnectX-5 ones.

Batch-Based Updates Have Detrimental Effects on Performance. Figure 3 shows the packet processing throughput (y-axis) achieved by the NIC's packet classifier over time (x-axis) for Tables 0 and 1, while the NIC simultaneously (i) receives a workload of 100 Gbps of 1500 B packets and (ii) inserts a number of new rules (see the legends) ranging between 1 and 100 K.

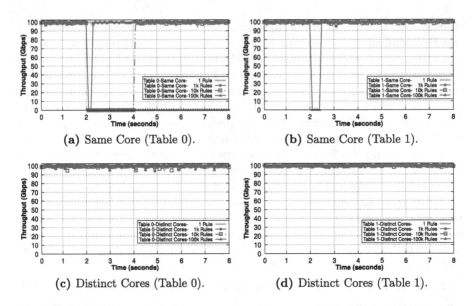

(a) Same Core (Table 0).   **(b)** Same Core (Table 1).

(c) Distinct Cores (Table 0).   **(d)** Distinct Cores (Table 1).

Fig. 3. Impact of <u>batch-based</u> updates on the performance of a 100 GbE NVIDIA Mellanox ConnectX-5 NIC classifier.

As shown in Fig. 3a even with a batch of 1K rules (see the green circles), the NIC fails to process any traffic for about 300 ms. For a 100 Gbps link with MTU-sized frames, this translates to a packet loss of around 2.5 M frames, while more than 40 M frames could have been lost from a 100 Gbps link with 64 B frames. Increasing the rules' batch size to 10K results in a longer failure of around 2 s (see the red squares), while in the case of 100K rules (blue triangles) the NIC does not recover even after 6 s. The down-time of Table 1 is 500 ms, but the problem manifests itself only in the case of 100 K rules as shown in Fig. 3b. On the other hand, installing the batch updates from a dedicated core does not affect the forwarding performance of the NF as shown in Fig. 3c and Fig. 3d.

We believe that these results have far-reaching implications on both (*i*) the security of the network functions, as batch-based updates could become a vector of denial-of-service attacks and (*ii*) the design of highly-reactive network controllers, e.g., to enable large data-plane updates for fast failover recovery [6].

Rate-Based Updates Reduce NIC Forwarding Capacities. Installing periodic batches of rules from the same core is a typical operation of NATs and Layer 4 load balancers, which need to reactively install rules matching new incoming connections. Installing rules from a different core allows us to dissect just the performance degradation due to interference in the NIC data-plane.

Figure 4a and 4b show the throughput of the forwarding NF when we simultaneously insert rules into the NIC classifier at a specific rate. The insertion rate ranges between 1 K to 10 K rules per second for Table 0 and 10 K to 500 K rules per second for Table 1. The inserted rules are not generated in response to a new incoming connection but pre-computed and inserted regardless of when new connections arrive. The results show that when inserting rules from a different

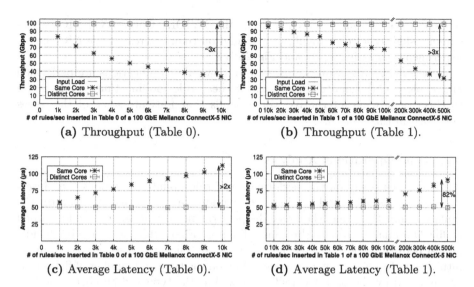

(a) Throughput (Table 0).   **(b)** Throughput (Table 1).

(c) Average Latency (Table 0).   **(d)** Average Latency (Table 1).

Fig. 4. Impact of <u>rate-based</u> updates on the performance of a 100 GbE NVIDIA Mellanox ConnectX-5 NIC classifier.

core, the throughput and average latencies (see also Fig. 4c and 4d) are mostly unaffected by the parallel insertion. However, when the insertions are generated from the same core running the forwarding NF, we observe a significant performance drop. Specifically, Fig. 4a and 4b show that the throughput decreases by roughly 70 Gbps for 10K and 500K rule insertions per second in Table 0 and Table 1, respectively. As shown in Fig. 4c and 4d, the respective latency increase is up to more than 2x for Table 0 and 82% for Table 1. This result demonstrates that the bottleneck of the update operation is the standard API provided by the NIC vendor for updating the forwarding table (which requires long time and interrupts the normal forwarding for prolonged period of times).

We note that installing rules from a different core is not a panacea. One would need expensive inter-core communication to install a rule as well as reserve extra CPU resources to handle the rule installation. For instance, to install i.e., 500K rules consumes 100% of a CPU core for several hundreds of milliseconds.

Summary. Our results show that it is possible to introduce a denial of service attack to the packet classifier of the NICs under test or dramatically reduce its throughput *by up to* 70 Gbps, by updating the classifier's rules using the same CPU core that performs traffic processing. This technique is commonly used by sharded high-speed data planes [4], as it would be the case for per-connection NFs. We note that realistic datacenter workloads generate new connections in the range of 4K-400K new connections per second. Our results indicate that one would *not* gain any benefit from offloading applications, such as cloud NATs and load balancers, with highly dynamic tables, to the analyzed NICs. Moreover, all NICs under test achieve similar performance across all the experiments in this section; with the only difference being the NVIDIA ConnectX-6 NIC, which exhibits slightly lower throughput degradation than the rest of the NICs in the experiment shown in Fig. 2a and Fig. 2b [17].

In the next subsection, we investigate how rule modifications are performed and explore performance limitations of these rule modifications. In response to this, we provide alternative workarounds that mitigate some of the issues described in this section.

3.2   Rule Operations Analysis

We now focus solely on the performance of rule update operations (i.e., insertions, deletions, and modifications' completion times). Clearly, the shorter the update completion time, the lower the performance disruption on the forwarded traffic. Our analysis reveals three main findings. First, while modern NICs handle almost 500K insertions per second, there is a significant and sometimes counter-intuitive performance difference depending on the type and number of fields that are matched by the packet classifier, as well as the type and number of actions that are applied by a rule. Surprisingly, installing rules matching IPv4 in Table 0 is a much slower process than installing IPv6 rules. Our second finding is that the cost of installing VLAN-based rules for network slicing is substantially lower than the respective cost of installing GRE/VXLAN/GENEVE-based rules. Our third and final finding relates to the fact that rule modification operations are not atomically supported by the analyzed NICs: one has to delete the old rule and insert a new one. Our analysis shows that rule modification time can be decreased by 80% compared to the insertion/deletion operations supported by the standard API of the vendors, by directly modifying the content of the exact match tables in the NIC memory.

3.2.1   Insertion/Deletion of Rules

We now compute the rule insertion rate supported by an NVIDIA Mellanox ConnectX-5 NIC in Tables 0 and 1. We use a single CPU core to insert a number of rules in the range between 1 and 65536 and measure the time that it takes to insert them. From this value, we compute the rule insertion rate.

Figure 5a shows that the rules insertion rate for Table 0 for five types of rules matching different combinations of fields, such as Ethernet, IPv4, IPv6, and TCP. A single action is applied to a packet matching any of these rules. Surprisingly, our measurements show a striking difference between IPv4 and IPv6. Specifically, inserting rules matching IPv4 results in a sharp slow-down in the insertion rate compared to IPv6 rules, which is already 5x slower with just $16K$ entries. We profiled both operations to unveil the reasons of this performance diversity and found that IPv4 rules are directly installed by the kernel in hardware, using the firmware API, while the IPv6 rules are managed by the userlevel DPDK driver similarly to the rules of non-root tables. On the contrary, Fig. 5b shows the same experiment for Table 1. We note that in this case matching on IPv4 results in a 12% higher insertion rate compared to IPv6, the opposite of

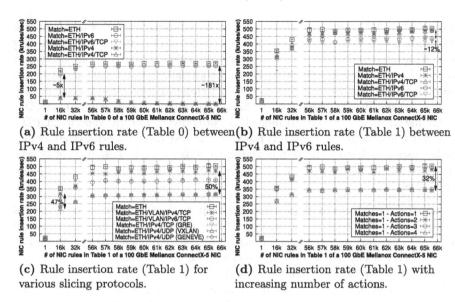

(a) Rule insertion rate (Table 0) between IPv4 and IPv6 rules.

(b) Rule insertion rate (Table 1) between IPv4 and IPv6 rules.

(c) Rule insertion rate (Table 1) for various slicing protocols.

(d) Rule insertion rate (Table 1) with increasing number of actions.

Fig. 5. Rule insertion performance (in kRules/sec) of a hardware-based 100 GbE NVIDIA Mellanox ConnectX-5 NIC classifier with various rule sets in [1, 65536] stored in two different tables.

what we observed for Table 0. This is because Table 1 is managed in software, thus both IPv4 and IPv6 are managed by the respective DPDK driver.

We then investigate how different extensively adopted network slicing protocols affect the insertion rate into the NIC's most performant Table 1. We consider VLAN, GRE, VXLAN, and GENEVE virtualization headers, which are widely used in datacenter and wide-area network deployments. Figure 5c shows that rules matching VLAN tags can be installed up to 50% more rapidly than those relying on the other virtualization schemes.

We now verify whether the extent to which the actions associated to the rules impact the rules' insertion rate. Figure 5d shows that increasing the number of actions performed on a packet may result in 32% slower insertion rate. We believe these results are inline with the natural intuition of slower insertions for more complex actions.

We finally repeat all the previous experiments but in this case we remove entries from the NIC's packet classifier. To our biggest surprise, when we add a TCP match on a set of rules in Table 0, the deletion becomes faster than without having the TCP header. This counter-intuitive result demonstrates once more that any deployment on Table 0 should be accompanied by a comprehensive testing of the classifier's structure to avoid unexpected performance slowdown.

3.2.2 Modification of Rules

We now investigate the problem of *updating* a set of rules on the analyzed NICs. We first observe that **none** of the evaluated NICs support direct flow modifications through their APIs. One has to first delete and then insert an entry, which results in two major issues: (i) there are periods when the network configuration is incorrect and (ii) as observed in the previous subsection, rule modifications are extremely slow for the needs of real platforms. We therefore show how one can carefully engineer flow modifications for simple 5-tuple matching rules to speed up rule modifications in the NIC. We refer to our technique as *enhanced in-memory update*. Our technique does not rely on the standard API provided by the NIC vendor in DPDK and the rdma-core library to modify rules, but instead directly accesses the memory of the exact-match stages in the pipeline and modifies them in a less disruptive way. We defer the reader later in this section for more details on our improved update technique.

Enhanced In-Memory Updates Are Up to 80% Faster. We employed DPDK's *flow-perf* tool to measure the NICs update rate, using the standard sequential deletion and insertion process. Then, we modified this tool to update all installed rules by using our in-memory update. Figure 6 shows the update rate (y-axis) in krules/sec achieved by both (i) the standard API deletion/insertion (black squares) and (ii) our enhanced in-memory update scheme (blue stars) with an increasing number of rules (x-axis) in the NIC classifier.

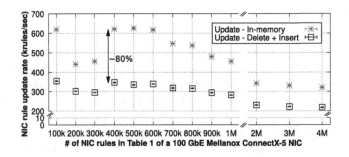

Fig. 6. Evaluation of the enhanced in-memory update mechanism.

We note that the standard API achieves 300K TCP/IP flow updates per second[1] on average, possibly disrupting all the forwarded traffic as shown in Sect. 3.1 in Q2. Our enhanced in-memory updates of the NIC classifier increases the insertion rate for TCP/IP rules by up to 80%. We observe the CPU stalls during the experiment, waiting for the NIC to complete memory synchronization commands, hence reaching the limit of the NIC Direct Memory Access (DMA) engine. We leave the problem of making the update mechanism more generic, possibly in collaboration with NVIDIA Mellanox, as future work.

Enhanced In-Memory Updates Explained. We now explain more in detail how one can realize faster rule insertions/deletions/modifications on the analyzed

---

[1] The employed DPDK v20.11 flow API is single-threaded. Higher performance could be achieved using multi-threaded rule insertion/deletion added in DPDK v21.02 [15].

NICs. While NIC vendors provide their own standard API for rule modifications, we added our own API for rule updates in DPDK and implemented support for the API in the `mlx5` driver (supporting ConnectX-4 and higher NVIDIA Mellanox NICs), and the backing `rdma-core` library that handles messaging between the NIC driver and the NIC itself. Instead of inserting and then removing a rule, our new API is based on efficient in-memory updates to avoid as many memory allocations in the driver as possible, while reusing the data-structure and only changing the match/action field values. In the ConnectX-5 and above NICs, a rule in a non-root table is implemented using a series of exact match hash-tables. Each hash-table only supports a unique mask, i.e., it is left to the user to implement techniques, such as tuple-space search, to implement an efficient LPM strategy by using a series of various exact-match masked prefixes.

In the case of standard TCP 5-tuple, one needs *two* hash tables. The first table matches the IP version, and the second one matches the 5-tuple itself. As far as our reverse-engineering of this undocumented mechanism can tell, this separation of the header fields into multiple hash-tables is dictated by the firmware, which supports a certain set of groups of fields per hash-table. Each of these two hash-tables work on one of those group of fields, eventually masked. Adding more fields from the application layer, or diverse tunnel types (VXLAN, GRE, etc.) will add more hash-tables in the chain. We note that the NIC handles hash-table collisions using a per-bucket linked-list of colliding entries. When inserting a new TCP/IP 5-tuple, the standard API would take an atomic reference on the entry for the IP-version and insert an entry into the 5-tuple hash-tables, and then remove the old rule from both hash-tables. Our update mechanism tries to minimize the number of modifications by following the existing rule, leaving it in the same place when the bucket does not change, not changing atomic reference (as it is the case for the IP-version hash-table), and then we either rewrite in-place the bucket of the hash-table if the bucket index (i.e., a CRC32 hash of the masked fields value) did not change (it is probable as all hash-tables start with a very small size and grow as needed), or move the entry in the pointed bucket to a new bucket if the index changes. This also avoids multiple calls to the DMA engine to insert and remove the rule, by only selectively updating the memory zone of the field that changed, as well as limiting the number of memory accesses. As far as consistency matters, our approach tries to guarantee atomicity of the update in the NIC. There exists a small amount of time during which, when the bucket entry is moved, the old and the new entries co-exist before the old entry is marked as invalid. We believe this co-existence does not open a security vulnerability since both entries are valid. Operators should fall back to the standard API if this is a concern.

For now, we only support updates on match operations' values; to implement action operations' value updates, such as redirecting packets to a different queue, would be fairly similar. This is particularly suitable for connection tracking, such as NAT and load balancers. Updating the masks of a rule is another complex operation that we currently do not support. This is challenging because different hash-tables implement different masked elements, possibly defeating the benefits of re-using some pre-installed elements.

4 Related Work

Measuring the performance of emerging network technologies has brought enormous benefits in our understanding of where the critical bottlenecks reside in today's deployed network systems. Neugebauer et al. [33] have investigated the performance of the PCIe device interconnecting modern NICs to the CPUs and memories showing surprisingly low performance with small packets. Farshin et al. (i) quantified the impact of direct cache access in Intel processors [9] and (ii) proposed software stack optimizations to achieve per-core hundred-gigabit networking [8]. Kuzniar et al. [23,24] have unveiled a variety of issues with the initial OpenFlow-based switches, such as the lack of consistency during updates. In contrast, we focus on NIC performance. Liu et al. [28] analyzed the memory characteristics, number of cores required to forward a certain amount of traffic, and Remote Direct Memory Access (RDMA) capabilities of five different Smart-NICs. In our work, we focus on the packet classifier component of a NIC and the impact of memory occupancy and runtime modifications on its performance.

A variety of efforts have been devoted to the orthogonal problem of scheduling updates in a network [16,19,20,22,27,39,40] or designing faster data structures at the data-plane level that are amenable to quick modifications [5,6,45].

5 Conclusions

Motivated by the ever-growing increase of networking speeds and offloading trends, this paper investigates the performance bottlenecks of today's NIC packet classifiers. We focused on several evolving models of one of the largest NIC vendors worldwide, showing a variety of critical performance limitations depending of the memory occupancy, the pipeline length, runtime rule modifications, and rule modification speed. We explored the idea of performing gradual updates directly in the NIC, improving the unveiled bottlenecks as well as many obstacles towards building a more efficient and generic API.

Acknowledgments. We would like to thank our shepherd Dr. Diego Perino and the anonymous reviewers for their insightful comments on this paper. This work has received funding from the European Research Council (ERC) under the European Union's Horizon 2020 research and innovation programme (grant agreement No. 770889). This work was also funded by the Swedish Foundation for Strategic Research (SSF) and KTH Digital Futures.

References

1. Antichi, G., Callegari, C., Giordano, S.: Implementation of TCP large receive offload on open hardware platform. In: Proceedings of the 2013 ACM Workshop on High Performance and Programmable Networking, pp. 15–22 (2013). https://doi.org/10.1145/2465839.2465842
2. Arashloo, M.T., Lavrov, A., Ghobadi, M., Rexford, J., Walker, D., Wentzlaff, D.: Enabling programmable transport protocols in high-speed NICs. In: 17th USENIX Symposium on Networked Systems Design and Implementation (NSDI 20), pp. 93–109. USENIX Association, Santa Clara, CA, February 2020. https://www.usenix.org/conference/nsdi20/presentation/arashloo
3. Ballani, H., et al.: Enabling end-host network functions. In: Proceedings of the 2015 ACM Conference on Special Interest Group on Data Communication. SIGCOMM 2015, pp. 493–507, New York, NY, USA. Association for Computing Machinery (2015). https://doi.org/10.1145/2785956.2787493
4. Barbette, T., Katsikas, G.P., Maguire, Jr., G.Q., Kostić, D.: RSS++: load and state-aware receive side scaling. In: Proceedings of the 15th International Conference on Emerging Networking Experiments and Technologies. CoNEXT 2019, New York, NY, USA, pp. 318–333. ACM (2019). https://doi.org/10.1145/3359989.3365412
5. Bonaventure, O., Filsfils, C., Francois, P.: Achieving sub-50 milliseconds recovery upon BGP peering link failures. IEEE/ACM Trans. Netw. **15**(5), 1123–1135 (2007). https://doi.org/10.1109/TNET.2007.906045
6. Chiesa, M., et al.: PURR: a primitive for reconfigurable fast reroute: hope for the best and program for the worst. In: Proceedings of the 15th International Conference on Emerging Networking Experiments And Technologies. CoNEXT 2019, pp. 1–14, New York, NY, USA. Association for Computing Machinery (2019). https://doi.org/10.1145/3359989.3365410
7. Eran, H., Zeno, L., Tork, M., Malka, G., Silberstein, M.: NICA: an infrastructure for inline acceleration of network applications. In: Proceedings of the 2019 USENIX Conference on Usenix Annual Technical Conference. USENIX ATC 2019, pp. 345–361, USA. USENIX Association (2019). https://www.usenix.org/system/files/atc19-eran.pdf
8. Farshin, A., Barbette, T., Roozbeh, A., Maguire Jr., G.Q., Kostić, D.: Packet-Mill: Toward per-core 100-GBPS Networking. In: Proceedings of the Twenty-Sixth International Conference on Architectural Support for Programming Languages and Operating Systems. ASPLOS 2021, New York, NY, USA. Association for Computing Machinery (2021). https://doi.org/10.1145/3445814.3446724
9. Farshin, A., Roozbeh, A., Maguire Jr., G.Q., Kostić, D.: Reexamining direct cache access to optimize I/O intensive applications for multi-hundred-gigabit networks. In: 2020 USENIX Annual Technical Conference (USENIX ATC 20), pp. 673–689, New York, NY, USA. USENIX Association, July 2020. https://www.usenix.org/conference/atc20/presentation/farshin
10. Firestone, D., et al.: Azure accelerated networking: SmartNICs in the public cloud. In: 15th USENIX Symposium on Networked Systems Design and Implementation (NSDI 2018), Renton, WA, pp. 51–66. USENIX Association (2018). https://www.usenix.org/system/files/conference/nsdi18/nsdi18-firestone.pdf
11. Holterbach, T., Vissicchio, S., Dainotti, A., Vanbever, L.: SWIFT: predictive fast reroute. In: Proceedings of the Conference of the ACM Special Interest Group on Data Communication, pp. 460–473 (2017). https://doi.org/10.1145/3098822.3098856

12. Intel: 82599 10 GbE Controller Datasheet (2016). http://www.intel.com/content/www/us/en/embedded/products/networking/82599-10-gbe-controller-datasheet.html

13. Intel: Ethernet Converged Network Adapter XL710 10/40 GbE (2016). https://www.intel.com/content/dam/www/public/us/en/documents/product-briefs/ethernet-xl710-brief.pdf

14. Intel: Ethernet Controller E810 (2021). https://www.intel.com/content/www/us/en/design/products-and-solutions/networking-and-io/ethernet-controller-e810/technical-library.html

15. Wisam, J.: app/flow-perf: add multi-core rule insertion and deletion, January 2021. https://inbox.dpdk.org/dev/20201126111543.16928-4-wisamm@nvidia.com/T/

16. Jin, X., et al.: Dynamic Scheduling of Network Updates. In: Proceedings of the 2014 ACM Conference on SIGCOMM. SIGCOMM 20114, New York, NY, USA, pp. 539–550. ACM (2014). https://doi.org/10.1145/2619239.2626307

17. Katsikas, G.P., Barbette, T.: GitHub repository hosting the NIC benchmarks and collected data. https://github.com/nic-bench

18. Katsikas, G.P., Barbette, T., Kostić, D., Steinert, R., Maguire Jr., G.Q.: Metron: NFV service chains at the true speed of the underlying hardware. In: 15th USENIX Conference on Networked Systems Design and Implementation. NSDI 2018, Renton, WA, pp. 171–186. USENIX Association (2018). https://www.usenix.org/system/files/conference/nsdi18/nsdi18-katsikas.pdf

19. Katta, N., Hira, M., Kim, C., Sivaraman, A., Rexford, J.: HULA: scalable load balancing using programmable data planes. In: Proceedings of the Symposium on SDN Research, SOSR 2016, New York, NY, USA, pp. 10:1–10:12. ACM (2016). https://doi.org/10.1145/2890955.2890968

20. Katta, N.P., Rexford, J., Walker, D.: Incremental Consistent Updates. In: Proceedings of the 2nd ACM SIGCOMM Workshop on Hot Topics in Software Defined Networking. pp. 49–54. HotSDN '13, ACM, New York, NY, USA (2013). https://doi.org/10.1145/2491185.2491191

21. Kim, D., et al.: Hyperloop: group-based NIC-offloading to accelerate replicated transactions in multi-tenant storage systems. In: Proceedings of the 2018 Conference of the ACM Special Interest Group on Data Communication, pp. 297–312 (2018). https://doi.org/10.1145/3230543.3230572

22. Kuźniar, M., Perešíni, P., Kostić, D.: Providing reliable FIB Update Acknowledgments in SDN, In: Proceedings of the 10th International Conference on Emerging Networking Experiments and Technologies. CoNEXT 2014, New York, NY, USA, pp. 415–422., ACM (2014). https://doi.org/10.1145/2674005.2675006

23. Kuźniar, M., Perešíni, P., Kostić, D.: What You Need to Know About SDN Flow Tables. In: Passive and Active Measurement (PAM). Lecture Notes in Computer Science, vol. 8995, pp. 347–359 (2015). https://doi.org/10.1007/978-3-319-15509-8_26

24. Kuźniar, M., Perešíni, P., Kostić, D., Canini, M.: Methodology, measurement and analysis of flow table update characteristics in hardware OpenFlow switches. In: Computer Networks: The International Journal of Computer and Telecommunications Networking, Elsevier, vol. 26 (2018). https://doi.org/10.1016/j.comnet.2018.02.014

25. Le, Y., et al.: Uno: uniflying host and smart NIC offload for flexible packet processing. In: Proceedings of the 2017 Symposium on Cloud Computing, pp. 506–519 (2017). https://doi.org/10.1145/3127479.3132252

26. Li, B., Ruan, Z., Xiao, W., Lu, Y., Xiong, Y., Putnam, A., Chen, E., Zhang, L.: KV-direct: high-performance in-memory key-value store with programmable MIC. In: Proceedings of the 26th Symposium on Operating Systems Principles, pp. 137–152 (2017). https://doi.org/10.1145/3132747.3132756

27. Liu, H.H., Wu, X., Zhang, M., Yuan, L., Wattenhofer, R., Maltz, D.: zUpdate: updating data center networks with zero loss. In: Proceedings of the ACM SIG-COMM 2013 Conference on SIGCOMM. SIGCOMM 2013, New York, NY, USA, pp. 411–422. ACM (2013). https://doi.org/10.1145/2486001.2486005

28. Liu, M., Cui, T., Schuh, H., Krishnamurthy, A., Peter, S., Gupta, K.: Offloading distributed applications onto smartNICs using iPipe. In: Proceedings of the ACM Special Interest Group on Data Communication, pp. 318–333. Association for Computing Machinery (2019). https://doi.org/10.1145/3341302.3342079

29. Miao, R., Zeng, H., Kim, C., Lee, J., Yu, M.: Silkroad: making stateful layer-4 load balancing fast and cheap using switching ASICs. In: Proceedings of the Conference of the ACM Special Interest Group on Data Communication, pp. 15–28 (2017). https://doi.org/10.1145/3098822.3098824

30. Mittal, R., et al.: Revisiting network support for RDMA. In: Proceedings of the 2018 Conference of the ACM Special Interest Group on Data Communication, pp. 313–326 (2018). https://doi.org/10.1145/3230543.3230557

31. Moon, Y., Lee, S., Jamshed, M.A., Park, K.: AccelTCP: accelerating network applications with stateful TCP offloading. In: 17th USENIX Symposium on Networked Systems Design and Implementation (NSDI 2020), Santa Clara, CA, pp. 77–92. USENIX Association, February 2020. https://www.usenix.org/conference/nsdi20/presentation/moon

32. Narayan, A., et al.: Restructuring endpoint congestion control. In: Proceedings of the 2018 Conference of the ACM Special Interest Group on Data Communication, pp. 30–43 (2018). https://doi.org/10.1145/3230543.3230553

33. Neugebauer, R., Antichi, G., Zazo, J.F., Audzevich, Y., López-Buedo, S., Moore, A.W.: Understanding PCIe performance for end host networking. In: Proceedings of the 2018 Conference of the ACM Special Interest Group on Data Communication, SIGCOMM 2018, Budapest, Hungary, August 20–25, 2018, pp. 327–341. ACM (2018). https://doi.org/10.1145/3230543.3230560

34. NVIDIA Mellanox: BlueField®SmartNIC for Ethernet (2019). https://www.mellanox.com/related-docs/prod_adapter_cards/PB_BlueField_Smart_NIC.pdf

35. NVIDIA Mellanox: ConnectX®-4 EN Card 100Gb/s Ethernet Adapter Card (2020). http://www.mellanox.com/related-docs/prod_adapter_cards/PB_ConnectX-4_EN_Card.pdf

36. NVIDIA Mellanox: ConnectX®-5 EN Card 100Gb/s Ethernet Adapter Card (2020). http://www.mellanox.com/related-docs/prod_adapter_cards/PB_ConnectX-5_EN_Card.pdf

37. NVIDIA Mellanox: ConnectX®-6 EN IC 200GbE Ethernet Adapter IC (2020). https://www.mellanox.com/related-docs/prod_silicon/PB_ConnectX-6_EN_IC.pdf

38. Palkar, S., Abuzaid, F., Bailis, P., Zaharia, M.: Filter before you parse: faster analytics on raw data with sparser. Proc. VLDB Endowment 11(11), 1576–1589 (2018). https://doi.org/10.14778/3236187.3236207

39. Perešíni, P., Kuźniar, M., Canini, M., Kostić, D.: ESPRES: transparent SDN update scheduling. In: Proceedings of the 3rd Workshop on Hot Topics in Software Defined Networking. HotSDN 2014, New York, NY, USA, pp. 73–78. ACM (2014). https://doi.org/10.1145/2620728.2620747

40. Reitblatt, M., Foster, N., Rexford, J., Schlesinger, C., Walker, D.: Abstractions for network update. In: Proceedings of the ACM SIGCOMM 2012 Conference on Applications, Technologies, Architectures, and Protocols for Computer Communication. SIGCOMM 2012, New York, NY, USA, pp. 323–334. ACM (2012). https://doi.org/10.1145/2342356.2342427

41. Roy, A., Zeng, H., Bagga, J., Porter, G., Snoeren, A.C.: Inside the social network's (datacenter) network. In: Proceedings of the 2015 ACM Conference on Special Interest Group on Data Communication, pp. 123–137 (2015). https://doi.org/10.1145/2785956.2787472

42. Siracusano, G., et al.: Running neural networks on the NIC (2020). https://arxiv.org/abs/2009.0235

43. Spaziani Brunella, M., et al.: hXDP: efficient software packet processing on FPGA NICs. In: 14th USENIX Symposium on Operating Systems Design and Implementation (OSDI 2020), Banff, Alberta. USENIX Association, November 2020. https://www.usenix.org/conference/osdi20/presentation/brunella

44. Stephens, B., Akella, A., Swift, M.: Loom: flexible and efficient NIC packet scheduling. In: 16th USENIX Symposium on Networked Systems Design and Implementation (NSDI 2019), Boston, MA, pp. 33–46. USENIX Association, February 2019. https://www.usenix.org/conference/nsdi19/presentation/stephens

45. Stephens, B., Cox, A.L., Rixner, S.: Scalable multi-failure fast failover via forwarding table compression. In: Proceedings of the Symposium on SDN Research, SOSR 2016, Santa Clara, CA, USA, March 14–15, 2016, p. 9. ACM (2016). https://doi.org/10.1145/2890955.2890957

46. The Linux Foundation: Data Plane Development Kit (DPDK). http://dpdk.org

47. Zhang, T., Linguaglossa, L., Gallo, M., Giaccone, P., Iannone, L., Roberts, J.: Comparing the performance of state-of-the-art software switches for NFV. In: Proceedings of the 15th International Conference on Emerging Networking Experiments And Technologies, pp. 68–81 (2019). https://doi.org/10.1145/3359989.3365415

48. Zhu, Y., et al.: Congestion control for large-scale RDMA deployments. ACM SIGCOMM Comput. Commun. Rev. **45**(4), 523–536 (2015). https://doi.org/10.1145/2785956.2787484

Scouting the Path to a Million-Client Server

Yimeng Zhao[1]([✉]), Ahmed Saeed[2], Mostafa Ammar[1], and Ellen Zegura[1]

[1] Georgia Institute of Technology, Atlanta, USA
[2] Massachusetts Institute of Technology, Cambridge, USA

Abstract. To keep up with demand, servers will scale up to handle hundreds of thousands of clients simultaneously. Much of the focus of the community has been on scaling servers in terms of aggregate traffic intensity (packets transmitted per second). However, bottlenecks caused by the increasing number of concurrent clients, resulting in a large number of concurrent flows, have received little attention. In this work, we focus on identifying such bottlenecks. In particular, we define two broad categories of problems; namely, admitting more packets into the network stack than can be handled efficiently, and increasing per-packet overhead within the stack. We show that these problems contribute to high CPU usage and network performance degradation in terms of aggregate throughput and RTT. Our measurement and analysis are performed in the context of the Linux networking stack, the most widely used publicly available networking stack. Further, we discuss the relevance of our findings to other network stacks. The goal of our work is to highlight considerations required in the design of future networking stacks to enable efficient handling of large numbers of clients and flows.

1 Introduction

Modern servers at large scale operators handle tens of thousands of clients simultaneously [33,38,45]. This scale will only grow as NIC speeds increase [1,3,5] and servers get more CPU cores [4,23]. For example, a server with a 400 Gbps NIC [3] can serve around 80k HD video clients and 133k SD video clients.[1] This scale is critical not only for video on demand but also for teleconferencing and AR/VR applications. The focus of the community has been on scaling servers in terms of packets transmitted per second [13,25,27,28,34,36], with little attention paid to developing complete stacks that can handle large numbers of flows well [26,29].

We envisage servers delivering large volumes of data to millions of clients simultaneously. Our goal is to identify bottlenecks that arise when servers reach that scale. In particular, we take a close look at network stack components that become the bottleneck as the number of flows increases. We find that competition between flows can lead to overall performance degradation, requiring fine-grain scheduling. Further, the increase in flow numbers leads to higher overhead of

---

[1] HD and SD videos consume up to 5 Mbps and 3 Mbps, respectively [9].

© Springer Nature Switzerland AG 2021
O. Hohlfeld et al. (Eds.): PAM 2021, LNCS 12671, pp. 337–354, 2021.
https://doi.org/10.1007/978-3-030-72582-2_20

Table 1. Summary of findings with results reported at 100k flows compared to more efficient baselines for admission control or performance with lower number of flows for per-packet overhead.

Category	Identified Issue	Impact	Existing systems mitigating it
Admission Control	Overpacing	5% increase in CPU utilization	–
	Inefficient backpressure	Throughput unfairness and hundreds of milliseconds in latency	Per-flow scheduling [31,46]
	Oblivious hardware offloads	2× increase in interrupts	–
Per-packet Overhead	Data structure inefficiency	2× increase in CPU utilization and 2× increase in latency	Low-overhead data structures [38,39]
	Lock contention	2× increase in latency	Distributed scheduling [24,38,42]
	Cache pressure	1.8× increase in latency	–

per-flow bookkeeping and flow coordination. Thus, we categorize problems that arise due to an increase in the number of concurrent flows into two categories:

1) Admission Control to the Stack: The admission policy determines the frequency at which a flow can access the stack and how many packets it can send per access. The frequency of a flow accessing network resources and the duration of each access determine the throughput it can achieve. As the number of flows increases, admission control becomes critical for the efficiency of the stack. For example, admitting and alternating between flows at a high frequency can reduce Head-of-Line (HoL) blocking and improve fairness but at the expense of CPU overhead, which can become a bottleneck, leading to throughput loss. We consider backpressure mechanism as a critical part of the admission control as it determines how a flow is paused (e.g., denied admission) and resumed (i.e., granted admission).

2) Per-packet Overhead within the Stack: The overhead of most per-packet operations is almost constant or a function of packet size (e.g., checksum, routing, and copying). However, the overhead of some operations depends entirely on the number of flows serviced by the system. For example, the overhead of matching an incoming packet to its flow (i.e., demultiplexing), and the overhead of scheduling, for some scheduling policies (e.g., fair queueing), are tied to the number of flows in the system.

We focus our attention on Linux servers. Despite its well documented inefficiencies (e.g., the overhead of system calls, interrupts, and per-packet memory allocation [15,26]), the Linux networking stack remains the most widely used publicly available networking stack. Further, even when new userspace stacks are deployed, they still rely, at least partially, on the Linux stack to make use of its comprehensive Linux functionality and wide use [31]. Hence, our focus on Linux is critical for two reasons: 1) our results are immediately useful to a wide range of server operators, and 2) we are able to identify all possible bottlenecks that might not appear in other stacks because they lack the functionality.

We focus on the overhead of long-lived flows. Long-lived flows help expose problems related to scaling a stack in terms of the number of flows. Scheduling long-lived flows requires the scheduler to keep track of all active flows, exposing inefficient data structures whose overhead increases with the number of tracked flows and highlighting issues that arise because of the interactions between the transport layer and the scheduler. It also exposes cache inefficiencies as information about a flow has to be retained and edited over a long period of time. Applications with long-lived flows include video on demand and remote storage. The inefficiency of short-lived flows is rooted in creation and destruction of states, and has been studied in earlier work [33]

The contribution of this work is in evaluating the scalability of the network stack as a whole, at hundreds of thousands of clients, leading to the definition of broader categories of scalability concerns. Table 1 summarizes our findings and existing systems that mitigating the problems. It should be noted that inefficient backpressure and data structure problems are only partially addressed by the existing solutions and we'll discuss the remaining challenges in Sect. 4 and 5. In earlier work there have been several proposals to improve the scalability of different components of the network stack (e.g., transport layer [26,29,33] and scheduling [18,38,39]). These proposals consider specific issues with little attempt to generalize or categorize such scalability concerns. Further, the notion of scalability considered in earlier work is still limited to tens of thousands of flows, with a general focus on short flows.

2 Measurement Setup

Testbed: We conduct experiments on two dual-socket servers. Each server is equipped with two Intel E5-2680 v4 @ 2.40 GHz processors. Each server has an Intel XL710 Dual Port 40G NIC Card with multi-queue enabled. The machines belong to the same rack. Both machines use Ubuntu Server 18.04 with Linux kernel 5.3.0.

Testbed Tuning: The affinity of the interrupts and application to CPU cores significantly affects the network performance on a multi-core and multi-socket machine. To reduce cache synchronization between different cores and improve interrupt affinity, we pin each transmit/receive queue pair to the same core. We enable Receiver Packet Steering (RPS), which sends the packet to a CPU core based on the hash of source and destination IPs and ports. We limit all network processing to exclusively use the local socket because we observe that the interconnection between different sockets leads to performance degradation at 200k or more flows. We enabled different hardware offload functions including GSO, GRO, and LRO to lower CPU utilization. We also enabled interrupt moderation to generate interrupts per batch, rather than per packet. We use TCP CUBIC as the default transport protocol, providing it with maximum buffer size, to avoid memory bottlenecks. The entire set of parameters is shown in Appendix B.

Traffic Generation: We generate up to 300k concurrent flows with neper [8]. We bind multiple IP addresses to each server so the number of flows that can be generated is not limited by the number of ports available for a single IP address.

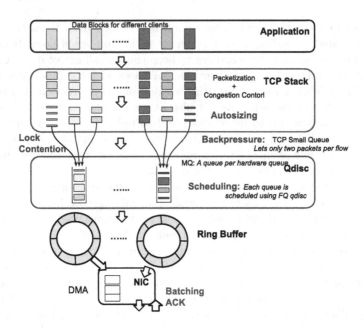

Fig. 1. Schematic of the packet transmission path with identified pain points marked in red.

With 40 Gbps aggregate throughput, the per-flow rate can range from 133 Kbps, which is a typical flow rate for web service [17], to 400 Mbps, which might be large data transfer [19]. We ran experiments with different numbers of threads ranging from 200 to 2000. In particular, we spawn N threads, create M flows that last for 100 s, and multiplex the M flows evenly over the N threads. We observed that using more threads causes higher overhead in book-keeping and context switch, leading to degraded throughput when the server needs to support hundreds of thousands of flows. The results shown in this paper are with 200 threads if not specified otherwise. We use long-lived flows for experiments because our focus is on the scaling problem in terms of the number of concurrent flows. The scaling problem of short-lived flows is more related to the number of connecting requests per second rather than the number of concurrent flows. With fixed number of flows, the short-lived flows should not have higher overhead than long-lived flows. For the rest of the paper, we use flows and clients interchangeably.

Figure 1 visualizes our assumed stack architecture. Our focus is on the overhead of the transport and scheduling components of the stack. We experiment with different scheduling algorithms by installing different Queuing Disciplines (qdiscs). We use multiqueue qdisc (mq) to avoid having a single lock for all hardware queues. All scheduling algorithms are implemented by per-queue within mq. By default, mq handles packets FIFO in its queues. However, we use Fair Queue (fq) [21] as the default qdisc combined with mq. Compared to pfifo_fast, fq achieves better performance in terms of latency and CPU usage when handling a large number of flows [46]. In some experiments, we limit the total flow rate to 90% of the link speed to avoid queueing in Qdiscs and show that the performance degradation cannot be avoided by simply lowering the total rate. We also use `fq_codel` [7] to reduce latency within the qdisc in some cases.

Measurement Collection: In all experiments, machines are running only the applications mentioned here making any CPU performance measurements correspond with packet processing. We track overall CPU utilization using `dstat` [6] and track average flow RTT using `ss` [12]. We track the TCP statistics using `netstat` [10]. Performance statistics of specific functions in the kernel is obtained using `perf` [11].

3   Overall Stack Performance

We start by measuring the overall performance of the stack with the objective of observing how bottlenecks arise as we increase the number of flows. In particular, we look at aggregate throughput, CPU utilization, average RTT, and retransmissions. Figure 2 shows a summary of our results. Our setup can maintain line rate up to around 200k flows (Fig. 2a). Thus, we limit our reporting to 300k flows.

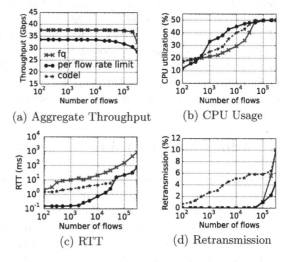

(a) Aggregate Throughput

(b) CPU Usage

(c) RTT

(d) Retransmission

Fig. 2. Overall performance of the network stack as a function of the number of flows

As the number of flows increases, the CPU utilization steadily increases until it becomes the bottleneck. Recall that we are only using a single socket, which means that 50% utilization means full utilization in our case (Fig. 2b). The aggregate throughput shows that the number of bytes per second remains constant. Thus, the increase in CPU utilization is primarily due to the increase in the number of flows handled by the systems.

The most surprising observation is that the average delay introduced by the stack can reach *one second* when the stack handles 300k flows, a five orders of magnitude increase from the minimum RTT. There are several problems that can lead to such large delays. The Linux stack is notorious for its inefficiencies due to relying on interrupts, especially on the ingress path [2,15,26,32]. Further, head-of-line blocking in hardware can add significant delays [42]. Our focus in this paper is to identify problems that are caused by inefficiencies that arise due to the growth in the number of flows. Such problems are likely to occur in the transport and scheduling layers, the layers aware of the number of flows in the system. Our first step is to try to understand which part of the stack is causing these delays, to better understand the impact of the number of flows on the performance of the stack.

Our baseline performance, denoted in the Fig. 2 by `fq`, is for the case when flows are not rate limited and scheduled following a fair queuing policy, requiring packets to be queued for some flows so that other flows can achieve their fair share. To quantify that delay, we compare the performance of the baseline to a scenario in which each flow is rate limited such that the aggregate rate that is 90% of NIC capacity, denoted in Fig. 2 by `per flow rate limit`. Under this scenario, no queuing should happen in the Qdisc as demand is always smaller than the network capacity. Latency drops by an order of magnitude in that scenario at 300k flows and by more at smaller numbers of flows, leading to the conclusion that hundreds of milliseconds of delay are added because of queuing delays at the Qdisc. We further validate this conclusion by employing a Qdisc that implements the CoDel AQM algorithm, configured with a target latency of 100 μs. CoDel drops packets if their queueing delay exceeds the target delay. At 300k flows, the delay of `codel` is lower than the baseline by an order of magnitude, validating our conclusion. Note that CoDel comes at a price of higher CPU utilization due to packet drop and retransmission (Fig. 2d). For the rest of the paper, we attempt to better understand the causes of the observed large delays and high CPU utilization at large numbers of flows.

4   Admission Control to the Stack

Network stacks are typically optimized to maximize the number of packets per second they can handle, allowing applications unrestricted access to the stack in many cases, especially in Linux. However, as the number of flows increases, applications can overwhelm the stack by generating packets at a larger rate than the network stack can process and transmit them. This congestion, left unchecked, can lead to hundreds of milliseconds of added delay. Admission control of packets to the stack can avoid this problem by regulating the access of applications to stack resources. Linux already has several such mechanisms, which work well with a relatively small number of flows (e.g., tens of thousands of flows), but fail at large numbers of flows (e.g., hundreds of thousands). We examine admission control mechanisms based on the knob they control. In particular, admission control mechanisms decide three values: 1) the size of each individual packet (the larger the packets the smaller the packet rate for the same byte rate), 2) the total number of admitted packets (i.e., limiting the number of packets through backpressure), and 3) the size of a new batch of admitted packets.

4.1   Packet Sizing

The Linux stack implements packet autosizing, an operation that helps improve the pacing function for low throughput flows. Pacing is an integral function for several modern congestion control algorithms including BBR [16,21]. In particular, pacing spreads out packets over time to avoid sending them in bursts. The autosizing algorithm is triggered if a flow is sending at a rate lower than 512 Mbps (i.e., a thousand Maximum Segment Sized (MSS) segments every second, assuming an MSS of 64KB). When triggered, it reduces the size of the segments transmitted every 1ms, where inter-packet gap is enforced through a pacer (e.g., fq [21]) and packet

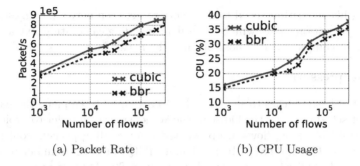

(a) Packet Rate   (b) CPU Usage

Fig. 3. CUBIC v.s. BBR with 5% drop rate. The relationship between number of flows and packet rate is similar at 0% drop but there is no difference between BBR and CUBIC at 0% drop rate (Appendix E).

segmentation to MTU size is done in hardware. Automatic packet sizing can also be beneficial for ensuring fairness between flows [42].

Autosizing infers the rate of a flow by dividing the number of bytes sent during an RTT (i.e., the cwnd) over the measured RTT. This allows for maintaining the same average sending rate while spreading packet transmission over time. The technique provides a tradeoff between CPU utilization and network performance by increasing the number of packets per second handled by the server while lowering the size of bursts the network deals with. The CPU cost of autosizing is affected by the number of flows handled by the server. In particular, the same aggregate rate of 512 Mbps can result in a packet rate of 1k packets per second for one flow or 1M packets per second for 1k flows in the worst case.[2]

This **overpacing** can overwhelm the stack, leading to an increase in delay (Fig. 2c). This leads the autosizing algorithm to misbehave. In particular, the RTT increases when the stack is overloaded, leading to underestimation of the rates of all flows handled by the stack. This causes the autosizing mechanism to reduce the size of bursts unnecessarily, creating more packets, increasing the congestion at the server [46]. Another side effect of autosizing is causing different congestion control algorithms to have different CPU costs. In particular, algorithms that react more severely to congestion (e.g., CUBIC which halves its window on a packet drop) send at lower rates, forcing autosizing to create more packets. However, algorithms that react mildly to congestion (e.g., BBR), maintain high rates and send lower number of packets. Figure 3 shows the difference between CUBIC and BBR at 5% drop rate induced by a netem Qdisc at the receiver. We set MTU size to 7000 to eliminate the CPU bottleneck.

Reducing delay introduced in the stack can help autosizing infer the rates of flows more accurately. However, as we will show later, scheduling flows, including delaying packets, is essential to scaling the end host. This means that

---

[2] The number of packets is typically much smaller than the worst case scenario due to imperfect pacing. Delays in dispatching packets, resulting from imperfect pacing, require sending larger packets to maintain the correct average rate, leading to a lower packet rate. However, the CPU cost of autosizing increases with the number of flows even with imperfect pacing.

autosizing-like algorithms need to differentiate between network congestion and end-host congestion. This will be useful in avoiding generating extra packets which might congest the end host but not the network.

4.2 Backpressure

When a flow has a packet to send, its thread attempts to enqueue the packet to the packet scheduler (i.e., the Qdisc in the kernel stack). In order to avoid Head-of-Line (HoL) blocking, flows are prevented from sending packets continuously by TCP Small Queue (TSQ). In particular, TSQ limits the number of packets enqueued to the Qdisc to only two packets per flow [20]. TSQ offers a rudimentary form of admission control that is based on a per-flow threshold to control the total number of packets in the stack.

As the number of flows increases, TSQ becomes ineffective because the number of packets admitted to the stack grows with the number of flows. Consequently, the length of the queue in the Qdisc will grow as the number of flows grows, leading to long delays due to bufferbloat. If we limit the queue length of the Qdisc, packets will be dropped at the Qdisc after they are admitted by TSQ. The current approach in Linux is to immediately retry to enqueue the dropped packets, leading to poor CPU utilization as threads keep retrying to enqueue packets. Figure 4 shows the CPU usage for transmitting packets from the TCP layer to the qdisc with different values of maximum queue length at the qdisc. The CPU usage includes only the operation before enqueuing the packet onto the qdisc. The shorter the queue length, the higher the drop rate, leading to higher CPU utilization.

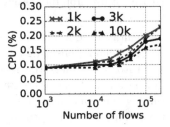

Fig. 4. CPU usage as a function of Qdisc queue length

Another down side of the lack of backpressure is that packet scheduling becomes reliant on thread scheduling. In particular, when a packet is dropped, it is the responsibility of its thread to try to enqueue it again immediately. The frequency at which a thread can "requeue" packets depends on the frequency at which it is scheduled. This is problematic because the thread scheduler has no notion of per-flow fairness, leading to severe unfairness between flows. As explained in the previous section, starvation at the Qdisc leads to hundreds of milliseconds of delay on average. We further investigate the effects of this unfairness on per-flow throughput. Figure 5 compares the CDF of rates achieved when fq is used with a small number of 300 and 30k flows. The two scenarios are contrasted with

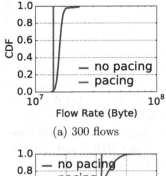

(a) 300 flows

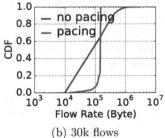

(b) 30k flows

Fig. 5. CDF of flow rate

the per-flow pacing scenario which achieves best possible fairness by rate limiting all flows to the same rate, with aggregate rate below NIC capacity, thus avoiding creating a bottleneck at the scheduler. In the 30k flows scenario, the largest rate is two orders of magnitude greater than the smallest rate. This is caused by the batching on the NIC queue. The `net_tx_action` function calls into the Qdisc layer and starts to dequeue skb through the `dequeue_skb` function. Multiple packets can be returned by some queues, and a list of skb may be sent to NIC, blocking packets from other queues. We observe that there are many more requeue operations in Qdisc when pacing is not used than when pacing is used, indicating that pacing prevents the NIC from being overwhelmed by a subset of queues.

Some previous works address the problem partially by enforcing per-flow scheduling instead of per-packet scheduling and only allowing a flow to enqueue a packet when there is room for it in the scheduler, avoiding unnecessary drops and retries [31,46], however, these works do not consider the interaction between layers that may lead to unfairness when fairness is enforced separately on each layer as we show in this section.

4.3   Batching Ingress Packets

The two previous sections discuss controlling the packet rate on the egress path. In this section, we consider controlling the packet rate on the ingress path. It should be noted that although we focus on egress path on server side, ingress path efficiency may also affect the egress path efficiency because delayed ACK caused by CPU saturation can lead to performance degradation in traffic transmission.

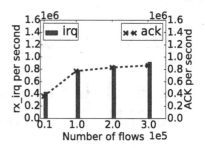

Fig. 6. Rates of RX Interrupts and ACKs per second

A receiver has little control on the number of incoming packets, aside from flow control. By coalescing packets belonging to the same flow on the ingress path using techniques like LRO, the receiver can improve the CPU efficiency of the receive path by generating less interrupts. Batching algorithms deliver packets to the software stack once the number of outstanding packets in the NIC reach a certain maximum batch size or some timer expires. As the number of flows increases, the chances of such coalescing decrease as the likelihood of two incoming packets belong to the same flow decreases (Fig. 6). In the Linux setting, this is especially bad as increasing the number of incoming packets results in an increase in the number of interrupts, leading to severe degradation in CPU efficiency.

Better batching techniques that prioritize short flows, and give LRO more time with long flows, can significantly help improve the performance of the ingress path. Some coarse grain adaptive batching techniques have been proposed [30,43]. However, we believe that better performance can be achieved with fine-grain per-flow adaptive batching, **requiring coordination between the hardware and software components of the stack.**

5   Per-Packet Overhead

To identify the operations whose overhead increases as the number of flows increases, we use `perf` [11] and observe the CPU utilization and latency of different kernel functions as we change the number of flows. The CPU utilization results show the aggregated CPU usage by all flows. We keep the aggregate data rate the same and only change the number of flows. Our goal is to find the operations whose computational complexity is a function of the number of flows. Operations that are bottlenecked on a different type of resource will have higher latency as we increase the number of flows. Figures 7a and 7b show the top four functions in each category. There is an overlap between functions with high latency and functions with high CPU utilization; this is typical because high CPU utilization can lead to high latency (e.g., `fq_dequeue` and `inet_lookup`). However, there are functions with high latency but low CPU utilization (e.g., `tcp_ack` and `dev_queue_xmit`). Through further profiling of the code of these functions, we find that there are two types of bottlenecks that arise: cache pressure and lock contention. Note that the overhead of the `tg3_poll_work` function is part of inefficiency of the Linux reception path [14] and is not the focus of our work.

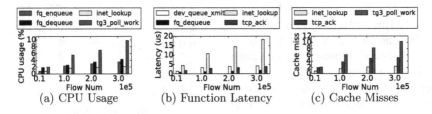

(a) CPU Usage   (b) Function Latency   (c) Cache Misses

Fig. 7. Function profiling

Data Structures: There are two operations whose complexity is a function of the number of flows: packet scheduling and packet demultiplexing. The overhead of packet scheduling is captured by the CPU utilization of `fq_enqueue` and `fq_dequeue`. The two functions handle adding and removing packets to the `fq` Qdisc, which sorts flows in a red-black tree based on the soonest transmission time of their packets. The overhead of enqueue and dequeue operations in $O(\log(n))$, where n is the number of flows. The overhead of packet demultiplexing is captured by the CPU utilization of `inet_lookup` which matches incoming packets to their flows using a hashmap. In the case of collision, finding a match requires processing information of flows whose hash collide. This increases the cache miss ratio of the function (Fig. 7c), further increasing the latency of the function.

Some approximation scheduling algorithms have been proposed to reduce the data structure overhead [18,38,39], but their main focus is to improve FQ. Data structure overhead requires reexamining all complex data structures used in the stack, taking into account that the stack can process millions of packets per second coming from millions of flows.

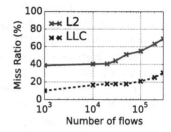

Fig. 8. Aggregate cache misses

Cache Pressure: One of the functions with the highest cache miss ratio is `tcp_ack`, which clears the TCP window based on received acknowledgements. The function does not use any complex data structures or wait on locks so the high cache miss stems from the overhead of fetching flow information and modifying it. As shown in Fig. 8, the cache miss ratio in both L2 cache and Last Level Cache (LLC) increases as the number of flows increases. While cache misses are not a huge bottleneck in our setting, we believe that as the number of flows increases, with tighter requirements on latency, cache miss ratio will have to be minimized.

Lock Contention: Another source of increased latency is lock contention when accessing shared resources. Our experiment confirms that the biggest critical section in the networking stack is the one used to protect access to the qdisc, done in `dev_queue_xmit`. The overhead of acquiring the qdisc lock is well documented [35,38], and increasing the number of flows exacerbates the problem, even with constant packet rate. Figure 9 shows that as the time to acquire lock increases by 4 times as the number of flow increases from 1k to 300k. Another

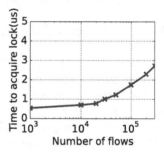

Fig. 9. Time to acquire qdisc lock

factor contributing to the increase in lock acquisition time is the increase in packet rate which we have shown to increase as the number of flows increases (Fig. 3a). Distributed and lazy coordination between independent queues can help alleviate the problem by reducing the need for locking [24,38].

6   Related Work

As we present throughout the paper, there has been significant work improving different components of the stack including scheduling [18,24,38,39] and backpressure [46]. However, they fail to consider the interactions between different components, and none of the existing optimized components was tested with a load larger than 50k flows. Our work defines a broader category of limitations and looks at the complicated interaction between different components.

Much of the focus of the previous work has been on scaling servers in terms of aggregate traffic intensity in terms of packets transmitted per second, while maintaining low latency [2,13,28,34,36]. Some recent proposals address scaling the whole stack to handle a large number of flows [26,29,33,37]. mTcp [26] is a scalable user-space TCP/IP stack built over kernel-bypass packet I/O engines, but the evaluation was only performed at a maximum of 16k flows. Further, it focuses on improving connection locality and reducing system overhead without paying much attention to scheduling and backpressure. Other systems are evaluated at a few thousands flows [29] and up to twenty thousand flows [33,36,37,44]. These systems improve specific functionality (e.g., RPC performance or transport layer performance) by dedicating network interfaces to individual application or by optimizing the kernel TCP/IP stack, with typical emphasis on short lived flows. In this paper, we are more concerned with scaling to hundreds of thousands of long-lived flows where transport and scheduling are implemented. To the best of our knowledge, this is the first such study.

Another observation is that hardware offload solutions [22,40,41] alone cannot completely solve the problem. Careful hardware design can help reduce the latency of complex operations [40]. However, data structure issues do not disappear when implemented in hardware. In addition, admission control requires careful coordination between the software part of the stack, including the application, and the hardware part of the stack.

7   Relevance of Findings to Other Stacks

In this paper, we focus on the Linux stack because of its ubiquitous usage in both industry and academia. However, most of our findings focus on abstract functions that are needed in a stack in order to efficiently handle a large number of flows. For example, admission control can avoid overwhelming the stack resources by relying on per-flow scheduling and accurate batching sizing. The lack of similar functions in any stack can lead to performance degradation as the number of flows grows. Further, the need for better data structures for scheduling and demultiplexing can lead to significant CPU savings. Contrarily, some of the problems we define are Linux specific, arising from components developed by companies to handle their specific workloads. For example, autosizing was developed by Google, making problems like overpacing a Linux-specific problem.

Some stacks inherently solve some of the problems we have identified. For instance, Snap [31] provides per-flow scheduling providing efficient backpressure. Further, stacks that rely on lightweight threading and asynchronous messages like Snap and Shenango might not suffer significant performance degradation due to lock contention. However, none of them handles all problems The goal of our work is to identify abstract functions that stacks will have to implement in order to scale.

Some of the problems we have identified are only exposed at a very large number of flows. To the best of our knowledge, these problems are yet to be handled by any stack. For instance, delays introduced due to cache misses will require innovation in speculative pre-fetching based on network behavior. Further, network accelerators and programmable hardware components will require new techniques to coordinate their behavior with changes in the load generated by the software component of the stack.

8   Conclusion

In this paper, we identify the different bottlenecks that arise when we scale the number of flows to hundreds of thousands in a fully implemented stack. As we present throughout the paper, there have been efforts to address some of the individual problems in isolation. However, integrating and testing such solutions at the scale of hundreds of thousands to millions of long-lived simultaneously-active flows remains an open problem. We hope that this paper sheds some light on the pain points that stack designers should pay attention to when building next generation stacks that scale to terabits per second and millions of flows.

A   Linux Stack Overview

Packet transmission in an end-host refers to the process of a packet traversing from user space, to kernel space, and finally to NIC in packet transmission process. The application generates a packet and copies it into the kernel space TCP buffer. Packets from the TCP buffer are then queued into Qdisc. Then there are two ways to a dequeue packet from the Qdisc to the driver buffer: 1)dequeue a packet immediately, and 2) schedule a packet to be dequeued later through softriq, which calls net_tx_action to retrieve packet from qdisc (Fig. 10).

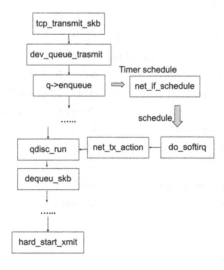

Fig. 10. Packet Transmission

(a) Throughput (b) CPU Usage (c) RTT (d) Retransmission

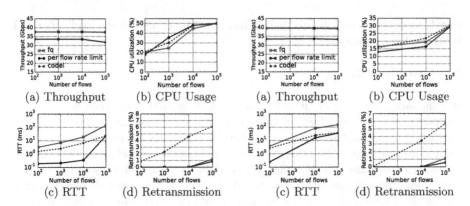

Fig. 11. Overall performance of the network stack as a function of the number of flows with fixed TSO disabled and 1500 MTU size

(a) Throughput (b) CPU Usage (c) RTT (d) Retransmission

Fig. 12. Overall performance of the network stack as a function of the number of flows with TSO enabled and 9000 MTU size

B Parameter Configuration

Table 2 shows all the parameters we have used in our setup.

Table 2. Tuning parameters

Parameter	Tuned
RX-Ring	MAX [4096]
net.core.netdev_max_backlog	65536
net.core.tcp_max_syn_backlog	65536
net.ipv4.tcp_rmem	8192 65536 16777216
net.ipv4.tcp_wmem	8192 87380 16777216
net.ipv4.tcp_mem	768849 1025133 1537698
net.core.somaxconn	65535
net.netfilter.nf_conntrack_max	600000
TSO,GSO	enabled
interrupt moderation	enabled
irqbalance	disabled

C Overall Stack Performance

We find that the trends shown in Fig. 2 remain the same regardless of packet rate. In particular, we disable TSO, forcing the software stack to generate MTU packets. This ensures that the packet rate remains relatively constant across experiments. Note that we perform experiments with a maximum number of 100k flows. We try two values for the MTU: 1500 Bytes and 9000 Bytes. As expected, the performance of the server saturates at a much lower number of flows when generating packets of 1500 Bytes (Fig. 11). This is because the packet rate increases compared to the experiments discussed in Sect. 3. One the other hand, the performance of the server when using 9000 Byte packets is similar to that discussed in Sect. 3 (Fig. 12).

D   FQ v.s. PFIFO

We compare the `fq` with `pfifo_fast` qdiscs in terms of enqueueing latency (Fig. 13). The time to enqueue a packet into `pfifo_fast` queue is almost constant while the enqueue time for `fq` increases with the number of flows. This is because the FQ uses a tree structure to keep track of every flow and the complexity of insertion operation is $O(\log(n))$. The cache miss when fetching flow information from the tree also contributes to the latency with large number of flows.

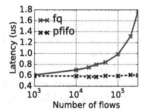

Fig. 13. Enqueue time

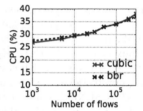

Fig. 14. BBR v.s. CUBIC

E   Packet Rate with Zero Drops

We verified that BBR and CUBIC has similar CPU usage when PPS is fixed (Fig. 14). We disable TSO and GSO to fix the packet size and set MTU size to 7000 to eliminate CPU bottleneck. We also observe that with more than 200k flows, CUBIC consumes slightly more CUBIC than BBR because CUBIC reacts to packet drop by reducing packet size, thus generating more packets.

References

1. High-performance, feature-rich netxtreme® e-series dual-port 100g pcie ethernet nic. https://www.broadcom.com/products/ethernet-connectivity/network-adapters/100gb-nic-ocp/p2100g
2. Intel DPDK: Data plane development kit (2014). https://www.dpdk.org/
3. IEEE standard for ethernet - amendment 10: Media access control parameters, physical layers, and management parameters for 200 gb/s and 400 gb/s operation. IEEE Std 802.3bs-2017 (Amendment to IEEE 802.3-2015 as amended by IEEE's 802.3bw-2015, 802.3by-2016, 802.3bq-2016, 802.3bp-2016, 802.3br-2016, 802.3bn-2016, 802.3bz-2016, 802.3bu-2016, 802.3bv-2017, and IEEE 802.3-2015/Cor1-2017), pp. 1–372 (2017)
4. Microprocessor trend data (2018). https://github.com/karlrupp/microprocessor-trend-data
5. IEEE 802.3 Industry Connections Ethernet Bandwidth Assessment Part II (2020)
6. dstat-Linux man page (2020). https://linux.die.net/man/1/dstat
7. FlowQueue-Codel (2020). https://tools.ietf.org/id/draft-ietf-aqm-fq-codel-02.html
8. neper: a Linux networking performance tool (2020). https://github.com/google/neper
9. Netflix Help Center: Internet Connection Speed Recommendations (2020). https://help.netflix.com/en/node/306
10. netstat-Linux man page (2020). https://linux.die.net/man/8/netstat
11. Perf Manual (2020). https://www.man7.org/linux/man-pages/man1/perf.1.html
12. ss-Linux man page (2020). https://linux.die.net/man/8/ss
13. Belay, A., Prekas, G., Klimovic, A., Grossman, S., Kozyrakis, C., Bugnion, E.: {IX}: a protected dataplane operating system for high throughput and low latency. In: 11th {USENIX} Symposium on Operating Systems Design and Implementation ({OSDI} 14), pp. 49–65 (2014)
14. Benvenuti, C.: Understanding Linux Network Internals. O'Reilly Media, Inc. (2006)
15. Brouer, J.D.: Network stack challenges at increasing speeds. In: Proceedings of the Linux Conference, pp. 12–16 (2015)
16. Cardwell, N., Cheng, Y., Gunn, C.S., Yeganeh, S.H., Jacobson, V.: BBR: congestion-based congestion control. Queue **14**(5), 20–53 (2016)
17. Cavalcanti, F.R.P., Andersson, S.: Optimizing Wireless Communication Systems, vol. 386. Springer, Cham (2009). https://doi.org/10.1007/978-1-4419-0155-2
18. Checconi, F., Rizzo, L., Valente, P.: Qfq: Efficient packet scheduling with tight guarantees. IEEE/ACM Trans. Networking **21**(3)(2013)
19. Chen, Q.C., Yang, X.H., Wang, X.L.: A peer-to-peer based passive web crawling system. In: 2011 International Conference on Machine Learning and Cybernetics, vol. 4, pp. 1878–1883. IEEE (2011)
20. Dumazet, E., Corbet, J.: TCP small queues (2012). https://lwn.net/Articles/507065/
21. Dumazet, E., Corbet, J.: Tso sizing and the FQ scheduler (2013). https://lwn.net/Articles/564978/
22. Firestone, D., et al.: Azure accelerated networking: Smartnics in the public cloud. In: 15th {USENIX} Symposium on Networked Systems Design and Implementation ({NSDI} 2018), pp. 51–66 (2018)
23. Geer, D.: Chip makers turn to multicore processors. IEEE Computer **38**(2005)

24. Hedayati, M., Shen, K., Scott, M.L., Marty, M.: Multi-queue fair queuing. In: 2019 USENIX Annual Technical Conference (USENIX ATC 2019) (2019)
25. Hock, M., Veit, M., Neumeister, F., Bless, R., Zitterbart, M.: TCP at 100 gbit/s-tuning, limitations, congestion control. In: 2019 IEEE 44th Conference on Local Computer Networks (LCN), pp. 1–9. IEEE (2019)
26. Jeong, E., et al.: MTCP: a highly scalable user-level {TCP} stack for multicore systems. In: 11th {USENIX} Symposium on Networked Systems Design and Implementation ({NSDI} 2014), pp. 489–502 (2014)
27. Kalia, A., Kaminsky, M., Andersen, D.: Datacenter RPCs can be general and fast. In: 16th {USENIX} Symposium on Networked Systems Design and Implementation ({NSDI} 2019), pp. 1–16 (2019)
28. Kaufmann, A., Peter, S., Sharma, N.K., Anderson, T., Krishnamurthy, A.: High performance packet processing with flexnic. In: Proceedings of the Twenty-First International Conference on Architectural Support for Programming Languages and Operating Systems, pp. 67–81 (2016)
29. Kaufmann, A., Stamler, T., Peter, S., Sharma, N.K., Krishnamurthy, A., Anderson, T.: TAS: TCP acceleration as an OS service. In: Proceedings of the Fourteenth EuroSys Conference, 2019, pp. 1–16 (2019)
30. Li, Y., Cornett, L., Deval, M., Vasudevan, A., Sarangam, P.: Adaptive interrupt moderation (Apr 14 2015), uS Patent 9,009,367
31. Marty, M., et al.: Snap: a microkernel approach to host networking. In: Proceedings of the 27th ACM Symposium on Operating Systems Principles. SOSP 2019, pp. 399–413 (2019)
32. Mogul, J.C., Ramakrishnan, K.: Eliminating receive livelock in an interrupt-driven kernel. ACM Trans. Comput. Syst. **15**(3), 217–252 (1997)
33. Moon, Y., Lee, S., Jamshed, M.A., Park, K.: Acceltcp: accelerating network applications with stateful TCP offloading. In: 17th USENIX Symposium on Networked Systems Design and Implementation (NSDI 2020), pp. 77–92 (2020)
34. Ousterhout, A., Fried, J., Behrens, J., Belay, A., Balakrishnan, H.: Shenango: Achieving high CPU efficiency for latency-sensitive datacenter workloads. In: Proceedings of USENIX NSDI 2019 (2019)
35. Radhakrishnan, S., .: {SENIC}: Scalable {NIC} for end-host rate limiting. In: 11th {USENIX} Symposium on Networked Systems Design and Implementation ({NSDI} 2014), pp. 475–488 (2014)
36. Rizzo, L.: Netmap: a novel framework for fast packet i/o. In: 21st USENIX Security Symposium (USENIX Security 2012), pp. 101–112 (2012)
37. Rotaru, M., Olariu, F., Onica, E., Rivière, E.: Reliable messaging to millions of users with migratorydata. In: Proceedings of the 18th ACM/IFIP/USENIX Middleware Conference: Industrial Track, pp. 1–7 (2017)
38. Saeed, A., Dukkipati, N., Valancius, V., Lam, T., Contavalli, C., Vahdat, A.: Carousel: scalable traffic shaping at end-hosts. In: Proceedings of ACM SIGCOMM 2017 (2017)
39. Saeed, A., et al.: Eiffel: Efficient and flexible software packet scheduling. In: Proceedings of USENIX NSDI 2019 (2019)
40. Shrivastav, V.: Fast, scalable, and programmable packet scheduler in hardware. In: Proceedings of the ACM Special Interest Group on Data Communication. SIGCOMM 2019 (2019)
41. Stephens, B., Akella, A., Swift, M.: Loom: flexible and efficient {NIC} packet scheduling. In: 16th {USENIX} Symposium on Networked Systems Design and Implementation ({NSDI} 19), pp. 33–46 (2019)

42. Stephens, B., Singhvi, A., Akella, A., Swift, M.: Titan: Fair packet scheduling for commodity multiqueue nics. In: 2017 {USENIX} Annual Technical Conference (USENIX ATC 2017), pp. 431–444 (2017)
43. Sun, L., Kostic, P.: Adaptive hardware interrupt moderation, January 2 2014. uS Patent App. 13/534,607
44. Yasukata, K., Honda, M., Santry, D., Eggert, L.: Stackmap: low-latency networking with the {OS} stack and dedicated nics. In: 2016 {USENIX} Annual Technical Conference ({USENIX}{ATC} 2016), pp. 43–56 (2016)
45. Zhang, T., Wang, J., Huang, J., Chen, J., Pan, Y., Min, G.: Tuning the aggressive TCP behavior for highly concurrent http connections in intra-datacenter. IEEE/ACM Trans. Networking **25**(6), 3808–3822 (2017)
46. Zhao, Y., Saeed, A., Zegura, E., Ammar, M.: ZD: a scalable zero-drop network stack at end hosts. In: Proceedings of the 15th International Conference on Emerging Networking Experiments and Technologies, pp. 220–232 (2019)

Building Out the Basics with Hoplets

Prathy Raman$^{(\boxtimes)}$ and Marcel Flores

Verizon Media Platform, Los Angeles, USA
William.Pressly@verizondigitalmedia.com

Abstract. Maintaining a performant Internet service is simplified when operators are able to develop an understanding of the path between the service and its end users. A key piece of operational knowledge comes from understanding when i) segments of a path contribute to a significant portion of the path's delay ii) when these segments occur across end users. We propose *hoplets*, an abstraction for describing delay increases between an end-user and a content provider built on traceroutes. We present a mechanism for measuring and comparing hoplets to determine when they describe the same underlying network features. Using this mechanism, we construct a methodology to enable wide scale measurement that requires only limited contextual data.

We demonstrate the efficacy of hoplets, showing their ability to effectively describe round-trip-time increases observed from a global content delivery network. Additionally, we perform an Internet-scale measurement and analysis of the hoplets observed from this infrastructure, exploring their nature and topological features where we find that nearly 20% of bottlenecks occurred along paths with no visible alternative. Finally, we demonstrate the generality of the system by detecting a likely network misconfiguration using data from RIPE Atlas.

1 Introduction

Measuring the path between an Internet service and its users is one of the mechanisms in which operators are able to improve end-user performance. Locating performance bottlenecks along these paths can be used to ensure accurate replica selection for content delivery [8,18] and improve DNS performance [26].

When assessing these paths, it is frequently important to understand which components of a path are contributing large portions of the path's latency. For many large-scale providers, these may be shared across many users, as the same large transit providers, IXPs, and other shared infrastructure make up a set of common upstream providers. However, recognizing the presence of such segments, *i.e.* that the communication with multiple end hosts may encounter these common bottlenecks, can be difficult.

We propose a path measurement and analysis approach built around traceroutes. We present a methodology for detecting RTT-contribution outliers along the path called *hoplets*. Hoplets comprise of a subset of a traceroute, *i.e.* a subsequence of hops and RTT values, that exhibits notable increases in RTT,

© Springer Nature Switzerland AG 2021
O. Hohlfeld et al. (Eds.): PAM 2021, LNCS 12671, pp. 355–370, 2021.
https://doi.org/10.1007/978-3-030-72582-2_21

including those cause by non-optimal routing, congestion, and long-haul links (*e.g.* trans-oceanic links). With this information, operators are able to determine appropriate remediations (*e.g.* routing configurations) or if the presence of such anomalies is expected. In the case of services focused on local delivery, such as CDNs, such increases are likely to represent unwanted performance anomalies.

Hoplets are built to detect the occurrence of poor round trip time (RTT) performance. While not the only important factor in performance optimization, for many user-facing services it represents the opportunity for the greatest improvements. We further provide an approach for detecting, combining, and prioritizing hoplets, called the *aggregator* which builds on the foundations of hoplets, and is designed to compare and combine hoplets across measurements. In this way, consistent increases observed across many individual measurements can be combined. This system is designed to be flexible to the types of inputs it receives, and avoids sensitivity to both the breadth and number of input measurements.

Using a set of nearly 130,000 traceroutes taken from a commercial CDN network beginning in early 2020, we demonstrate the hoplet system's ability to detect a variety of frequent network bottlenecks that represent long-term performance challenges. We use the measurements to conduct a large scale study of the frequency and magnitude of hoplets seen across the Internet. Here we find regional differences in the frequency and impact of measured hoplets, with South American hoplets contributing the largest RTT increases. Next, we explore the topological features of hoplets, demonstrating that nearly 20% of RTT increase events occur on a path with no clearly visible alternative in public BGP data. The geographic spread of these cases further demonstrates the challenges of optimizing network performance in certain regions. Finally, we demonstrate the generality of hoplets by extracting and aggregating a set of hoplets from traceroutes taken from the RIPE Atlas platform. Here, hoplets enable us to quickly discover a likely misconfiguration in the anycast configuration of one of the root letters in April of 2020.

The remainder of this paper is organized as follows. Section 2, provides details on the definition, extraction, and comparison of hoplets. In Sect. 3 we provide a look at some of the examples visible in the context of a CDN. Then, in Sect. 4 we take a broader look at the global patterns we observe in hoplet occurrence. In Sect. 5 we extract hoplets from traceroutes taken from RIPE atlas. We compare to existing systems in Sect. 6, and conclude in Sect. 7.

2   System Design

The goal of the hoplets system is to transform a collection of traceroutes and provide a framework for extracting interesting behaviors and combining measurements which describe similar underlying experiences. Once these combinations are complete, the resulting hoplet abstractions can be sorted and assessed by operators to provide new contextual insight into client delay experiences on the Internet. However, before we begin, it is important to ensure that we are extracting meaningful and accurate information from the traceroutes.

2.1   Using Traceroute Data

Suppose that a traceroute begins at content provider point of presence P, then passes through hops A, B, C before reaching a destination user U. A traceroute from P to U would reveal the hops along the forward path from P to U, as well as RTTs from P to each hop along the way. We consider the decomposition of the RTT from P to the first hop A as:

$$RTT_{PA} = \overline{PA} + \overline{AP},$$

where $\overline{PA}$ denotes the one-way delay from P to A, and vice versa.

When examining a traceroute in this fashion, we may consider the difference between the RTT of two subsequent hops, known as the *differential RTT* [12]. It is tempting to assume that this differential RTT reveals the delay between the subsequent hops. However, traceroute timings provide a round trip time and the response origins only reveal portions of the forward path. In the context of our example, we know that $\overline{PB} = \overline{PA} + \overline{AB}$, but the same cannot be said for the return path $\overline{BP}$: indeed the packets may skip A entirely.

Therefore, these differential RTTs do not necessarily represent the cost of particular hops along the paths. Instead we interpret them as a reflection of the ultimate fate of packets travelling between B and P. In other words, hop-over-hop increases in the differential RTT between A and B indicate that for some reason, routing between B and P comes with increased RTT, compared to A, on either the forward path $\overline{AB}$ or the return path $\overline{BP}$. This may be due to sub-optimal routing, long back-haul links, trans-oceanic links or other configurations with cause longer trip times. Regardless of the root cause, they represent performance realities for traffic flowing along this path.

However, from the context of the performance of our user U, we must consider additional factors. Such increases may not *carry through*: *i.e.* the differential RTT may not be positive for the remainder of the hops in the traceroute. A negative differential RTT would indicate that subsequent hop C has an alternative route to P, which avoids the bottleneck encountered by B. Therefore, users U avoid such penalty. It's further possible that a subsequent hop C with a *positive* differential RTT *also* does not traverse through B, and is instead capturing a path with a return path with comparable delay. In such cases, we still note B as the first occurrence, and therefore the most meaningful source of focus.

We therefore consider all occurrences of positive differential RTT that feature carry-through. We define a *hoplet* to be an adjacent subsequence of responses in a traceroute that appear to be associated with a significant increase in RTT (we provide a rigorous definition in the next section). While a hoplet is described by its point of first detection, as seen in the above discussion of differential RTT, this does not necessarily reveal the underlying location of this increase.

2.2   Hoplet Extraction

Alerting. The hoplet detection process begins by examining the differential RTTs measured in the traceroute. Consider a traceroute consisting of a sequence of responses $r_1, \ldots, r_n$, where each r_i contains both a responding address R_i and a RTT, RTT_i. We annotate this list using BGP data from RouteViews [2], in particular adding the origin AS of the prefix each R_i.

Let the differential RTT between each pair of hops i and $i + 1$ be $\Delta_i = RTT_{i+1} - RTT_i$. Given a traceroute, we compute each of the Δ_i. To determine the significant points of RTT increase, we use the *median absolute deviation* (MAD) of all the Δ_i, and say that Δ_i has triggered our alert condition if $\Delta_i -$ median(Δ_i) > (1.4826 * MAD), *i.e.* that Δ_i varies from the median by more than an estimate of the standard deviation [12, 35]. We further require that the Δ_i be greater than 10 ms, focusing our alert scenarios to cases most likely to be perceived by users.

The above detection mechanism is not intended to be canonical, and is instead intended only as a straightforward way of assessing RTT outliers within a traceroute. Indeed, other mechanism for detecting outliers may also prove effective. Critical to our formulation, however, is the relative nature of outliers: a significant contributor in one traceroute may be within normal for another. As a result, the system do not detect high end-to-end delays from many marginal outliers, resulting in no single large increases.

For a hoplet to be detected, we also require that the traceroute reached the destination AS of the target, therefore that the last responsive r_i came from the same AS as the target address. Hops which provided no response, we store as placeholders, maintaining the order and placement within the original traceroute. We further require that any alerting differential RTT also satisfy the carry-through condition described in the previous subsection. However, the simple condition that all subsequent deltas must be non-negative fails to account for much of the variations seen in Internet measurement. We therefore set a threshold of not allowing a decrease in RTT of more than 12%, *i.e.* for Δ_i to satisfy the alert condition $RTT_{i+2} > .88 * RTT_i$.[1]

This approach naturally enables the aggregation of additional data. If multiple traceroutes are available, or traceroutes are performed with multiple probes for each TTL, the median of all values from the same hop can be computed before performing the above procedure. Furthermore, as hoplet detection only depends on a single traceroute, it can be scaled simply by doing additional traceroutes from more vantage points to a broader set of destinations.

Extraction. Next, we build a representation that captures not only the response where delay increase is observed, but the nearby context. Once complete, this will include information from 3 ASes: the alerting network, as well as the previous and next ASes. Assume that Δ_i has triggered the above condition. We then store the corresponding r_{i+1}, which we take to be the *center* of our hoplet, as it is the first hop exhibiting the detected RTT increase. Next, we add all adjacent responses where the response AS matches that of r_{i+1}, This gives us a set $r_{i+1-k}, \ldots r_{i+1}, \ldots r_{i+1+l}$ where k, l are the number of responses before and after the center within the same AS and may be 0. We further add a single response on either end, *i.e.* one additional response from the prior AS and the

---

[1] We explore the selection of this value in the Appendix.

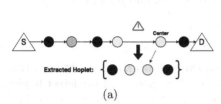

Delay (ms)	IP (Anon)	Network
0.15 ms	104.63.27.182	CDN
0.318	71.76.114.146	AS A
33.383	211.113.96.188*	AS B
37.795	39.180.191.248	AS B
58.996	55.216.72.215	AS C

(a)   (b)

Fig. 1. (a) The extraction process. Each node along the path represents a hop in the traceroute, and the pattern shows its AS. (b) A hoplet extracted from a traceroute. The * denotes the hoplet center.

subsequent AS, if they exist. If multiple hops trigger the alert condition within the same AS, they are combined into a single hoplet. Figure 1a shows a diagram of this process and Fig. 1b shows a real world example of a hoplet.

Our resulting structure is a sequence of response and AS tuples from a traceroute which are centered on an increase in RTT along the path. Our structure also contains the route-contextual information on where that increase was observed, *i.e.* the previous and next ASes. The key notion is that the hoplet describes the general conditions in which the increase occurred, for example when passing through a particular transit provider, crossing a physically distant link, or passing into a persistently congested edge network. We refer to the differential RTT of the hoplet center as the *penalty*, *i.e.* how much the RTT increased at that point. Note a single traceroute may result in multiple hoplets.

2.3 Hoplet Comparison

Next, we provide a mechanism by which to compare two extracted hoplets. In particular we would like a way to describe when two hoplets, potentially extracted from traceroutes with different sources and destinations, describe the same underlying topological features. We therefore require our comparisons to be permissive – allowing matches on similar, but not exact, responses, such as paths with load balancing across routers or router aliases causing non-matching traceroute responses [20,24]. However, we must further avoid the need for extensive additional measurements. Therefore instead of performing any explicit interface matching we instead consider the following formulation.

Given two hoplets extracted in the above fashion, call them h_1 and h_2, we define a similarity function $S(h_1, h_2)$ based on the edit distance between our two hoplets [25]. We consider each input hoplet as a sequence of its constituent response addresses. The edit distance then considers the hop-by-hop similarity, where additions and deletions have an edit cost of 1. We however modify the cost of a replacement: instead of a uniform cost, replacement costs proportional to the longest-prefix match of the addresses being replaced. In particular, for an address length of M (32 for IPv4 and 128 for IPv6), and prefix match of P:

$$C_{\text{swap}} = \frac{M - P}{M}.$$

The intuition is that many paths may pass through nearly identical infrastructure, ultimately seeing similar, but not identical, responses. If we detect hoplets at such locations, we would like to be able to identify that those may be functionally the same. Therefore, the above cost function allows us to bias towards matching similar addresses, hinting at similar underlying infrastructure. Once we have computed the edit distance, we normalize by the length of the longer sequence, providing a value between 0 and 1. We then take the complement, subtracting from 1, thereby converting the distance to similarity with 0 being entirely dissimilar and 1 being identical.

2.4   Hoplet Aggregator

Using this similarity function and matching criteria we are able to define a larger collection known as *hoplet sets*. Specifically, given a group of hoplets, we perform hierarchical clustering using single-linkage clustering [30], combining hoplets into clusters as long as their similarity remains above a threshold t.

This clustering is performed in two phases: first we cluster hoplets detected between the same source and destination in separate measurements. We consider any addresses in the same smallest-announced prefix to represent the same destination, as visible from RouteViews [2] at time of collection. This first phase allows us to compute how frequently a hoplet was observed between a particular source and destination. In the second phase, we cluster hoplets from the same source to many destinations.

Once the extraction is complete, we have transformed a collection of traceroutes to a potentially large variety of sources to a list of hoplet sets that describe similar underlying features. This list can be sorted and managed, for example by the frequency and severity of the described hoplets. Additionally, as we explore in the next section, these hoplets can be further considered on their geographic and topological locations.

By design, the aggregator has no knowledge of time: all traceroute samples are treated equally, even of samples between the same source and destination. Doing so enables operators to treat a collection of traceroutes as a snapshot in time. Alternatively, traceroutes can be bucketed by time, and hoplets extracted and aggregated separately, allowing for usual time series analysis.

3   Hoplets at a CDN

We examine a 24 h sample of traceroutes taken in mid-April of 2020 from a commercial CDN. These are taken from over 150 globally distributed points of presence towards the most popular client prefixes. In particular, we sample clients from the 50 most popular prefixes at each site each hour. To accommodate the needs of the production network, the resource consumption of these traceroutes is strictly limited: each consists of only a single probe at each TTL. Traceroutes further face a hard limit of 10 s, potentially resulting in timeouts for the worst performing settings. We note, however, that the following analysis is generic, and can be performed on a variety of traceroutes implementations.

This scan includes $127,812$ traceroutes taken between $28,844$ aggregated source and destination pairs. From these traceroutes $16,694$ pairs encountered at least one hoplet, for a total $133,256$ individual hoplets, though in Sect. 4 we will show that this number reduces significantly after aggregation and filtering. These detected hoplets were found in $1,107$ ASes en route to $1,859$ destination ASNs. We found these numbers to be stable over the course of the scan, and use this output for the studies in the remainder of this section. Processing this set can be completed in 10s of minutes on a modern laptop, making real time processing for smaller data-sets feasible.

Parameter Trade-Offs. Next, we measure the impacts of our aggregation threshold t. We perform the aggregation process described in Sect. 2.4 on our extracted hoplets for a range of t values. For each t, we consider two metrics: the relative median deviation in RTT penalty among hoplets in a set, and the resulting number of hoplet sets. Since we aim for hoplets to describe common path performance, we expect that among a set, hoplets experience similar delay. Therefore an overly-aggressive combination will result in high RTT deviation. On the other hand, overly strict combination requirements will result in too many individual hoplet sets, making the resulting data difficult to interpret.

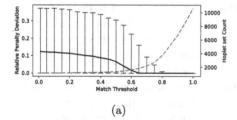

Region	S, D Pairs	Hoplet Sets
Asia	4604	261
EMEA	7381	427
North America	12123	766
South America	3583	133

(a)   (b)

Fig. 2. (a) Threshold impacts: the solid line shows median penalty deviation, error bars show the interquartile range, and the dashed line shows the total number of hoplet sets. (b) Regional breakdown of aggregated and measured source and destination pairs and the corresponding counts of hoplet sets.

Figure 2a shows the impacts on these features in response to the changing threshold. Generally, decreasing the threshold introduces significant RTT variation in each group, with the median variation quickly reaching .1 below a threshold of .5 As expected, stricter thresholds result in very low deviation, but a much higher number of groups, suggesting little combination is occurring. This experiment further provides information about two potential heuristic alternatives to our edit distance: the furthest left point of the plot, where threshold is 0, the only criteria for combination is that the center AS matches. On the far right, with a threshold 1 shows the impact of requiring exact matches. In order to strike a balance between these two extremes, we select a threshold of 0.6, requiring slightly more than half a hoplet to match to be considered the same.

4   Global Hoplet Behaviors

Next, we group each hoplet by the region of the world it's source PoP is located: Asia, EMEA (Europe, Middle East, and Africa), North America, and South America. As the CDN serves content to geographically local clients, these likely correspond with the geographic location of the hoplet and target networks.

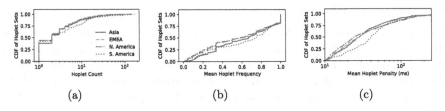

(a)   (b)   (c)

Fig. 3. (a) The number of destinations found in each hoplet set by region. (b) The frequency distribution for hoplet sets in each region. (c) The mean RTT penalty for hoplet sets in each region.

Figure 2b shows the breakdown of the measurements and hoplets after performing extraction and aggregation. The biases of the underlying infrastructure are clear in the measured pairs, with North America and EMEA providing the bulk of the measurements. Despite this bias, these measurements still provide a view into the behaviors of networks in a broad set of regions.

Figure 3a shows the distribution of the number of destination prefixes found in each hoplet set by region, *i.e.* the number of distinct clients that experienced the same bottlenecks. First, we note that a significant fraction of sets contain only a single destination: 43% in North America, South America, and EMEA and 38% in Asia. These represent hoplets which only occurred en route to a single destination. We further observe slightly larger sets in South America, with a 75th percentile of 7 vs 4 in the remaining regions, suggesting the same underlying infrastructure contributes to many South American bottlenecks. Finally, we note that in all regions, there is a small percentage of very large sets, that contain more than 10 and as many as 100 individual hoplets, showing the same infrastructure likely contributing to the RTT observed by many clients.

It's possible that a hoplet is not detected on every measurement to a destination. This is particularly likely if a hoplet is caused by ephemeral behavior, for example congestion. In order to understand the different regional behaviors, we examine the fraction of measurements to a destination which observed the hoplet. We refer to this value as the hoplet *frequency*.

Figure 3b shows the frequency distribution for each region. Low frequencies are relatively rare: the lowest median frequency is .58 in North America. South American on the other hand has a median of .74, suggesting a greater number of bottlenecks are long-lived features. Inspection of the underlying hoplets suggests that this is due to greater occurrences of routing and replica selection challenges in Asia and South America, compared to less consistent congestion observed in EMEA and North America. Furthermore, in all regions at least 18% of sets had a frequency of 1, indicating that a hoplet was detected on every measurement, an outcome most likely with long-lived bottlenecks, such as long-distance links.

Next, we examine the performance impact from the hoplets seen in each region by examining the distribution of the mean RTT penalty observed in each hoplet set. Figure 3c shows the distributions by region. North America presents the most moderate case, with a median of just under 25 ms. South America provides the highest penalties, with a median of over 40 ms, suggesting that more clients must cross high-delay infrastructure. Notably, all regions encounter a full range of increases, with each seeing a handful of outliers above with extremely high values. Manual inspection revealed these to be extreme scenarios, generally resulting from taking extremely long paths to reach clients, *e.g.* cross continent.

4.1   Topological Analysis

Table 1. Location of Hoplets. 'meas' indicates the fraction with measurable hegemony. Borderline is the percent of middle networks that may be misclassified.

Region	Total	Origin	Middle (meas.)	Borderline	Destination
Asia	1339	2.32	48.92 (46.87%)	26.18%	48.77
EMEA	1999	2.75	48.77 (81.33)	28.05	48.47
N. America	4381	0.46	40.81 (73.60)	17.43	58.73
S. America	1037	1.35	46.77 (63.09)	9.52	51.88

Here, we examine our detected hoplet sets from the perspective of *where* they occur in each path. As noted in [15], we can consider three areas where bottlenecks occur: the origin network (*i.e.* the CDN), the middle, or destination networks where the hosts are located. We recall that hoplets do not provide guarantees that a bottleneck is caused by a network. Instead, we measure where we observe delays increase: actual root-causes may reside in other networks. This analysis would not be possible with only end-to-end performance information, such as RTT measurements, as it requires information on the intermediate hops.

We perform our analysis here on the *per destination* level, allowing us retain all information about the context of the original measurements. This enables us to answer topological questions about their placement in a path. Once these are combined into potentially multi-destination hoplet sets, this information is lost, as a hoplet set may describe a feature observed en route to many destinations.

Table 1 shows the regional breakdown for where each hoplet occurs. The column labeled "Borderline" shows the percentage of middle hoplets which landed directly on the border and, as a result of interface aliasing, may represent routers which lie in the destination network [24]. We include these in our below analysis of middle hoplets, but note that they may complicate the classification. Consistent with related findings in [15], we find that the vast majority of Hoplets occur in the middle and destination networks. Due to space constraints, we consider a detailed analysis of only the middle networks below.

To understand the importance of each network, we consider the *AS Hegemony* of each middle network that contains a hoplet to the destination networks. AS Hegemony provides a value between 0 and 1 which indicates the weighted fraction of paths that must pass through that network en route to a destination [13], as measured via a number of public datasets. A higher hegemony value indicates that more paths pass through that network, and a lower value suggests fewer. For purposes of our measurement, we only include middle and target network pairs for which there was detectable hegemony (the fraction of middle-hoplets that satisfy this condition are shown in parenthesis in the middle column of Table 1), as we are unable to distinguish between no hegemony and low visibility. While its dependence on public data means there may be links not included in the hegemony calculations, it provides insight into network connectivity.

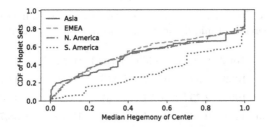

Fig. 4. The hegemony distribution for hoplet sets in each region.

Figure 4 shows the distribution of measurable hegemony for each region. Here, we see that the South American networks that contain hoplets appear to stand out as having particular high hegemony, with a median of 0.7, compared to 0.37 in North America. This suggests that the hoplets frequently occur in upstream networks with no alternative path, potentially making them difficult to resolve by simply routing around troubled paths.

We further note that all regions exhibit a significant mode at 1.0, accounting for nearly 18% of hoplet sets in North America, and nearly 27% in South America. In these cases, every path to the destination must cross through the AS where the hoplet was detected. These networks are largely unavoidable. Such information can be critical for content providers when assessing where and how to deploy new infrastructure: any new deployment which fails to get closer to the destination networks than the hegemonic upstream providers may not provide improved performance. Such knowledge can influence the architecture and design of future deployments and site selections, as seen in [7,36].

5   Other Data Sources

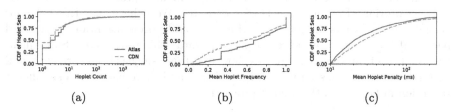

Fig. 5. The (a) count, (b) frequency, and (c) penalty distributions for the Atlas measurements. The dashed line shows CDN hoplets with source aggregation.

Here, we examine hoplets extracted and aggregated from traceroutes performed by the RIPE Atlas platform [1]. We consider hoplets extracted from a sample of the built-in measurements that RIPE probes perform to the DNS root letters over both IPv4 and IPv6. We take a sample of 90 minutes (*i.e.* three traceroutes from each probe) in Mid April 2020 from all available probes, resulting in a total of 290, 236 traceroutes. After performing our aggregation, we have a total of 8, 731 sources, for a total of 58, 835 source and destination pairs.

Unlike the CDN context, where we generally expect the replica selection process will result in destinations being unique across measurement sources, it's possible that many probes may traverse the same path to reach a common destination. We therefore consider an additional aggregation step, in which we compare all hoplet sets, regardless of the measurement source. This creates the opportunity to combine hoplets that may occur on such shared paths.

Figure 5 presents the counts, frequency, and the mean RTT penalty for the observed hoplet sets compared with the source-aggregated data from the CDN. We note in (*a*) that a smaller fraction of hoplet sets impact only a single network than in the CDN case, likely due to the increased likelihood that the probes are crossing similar RTT constraints towards the root letters. The frequency and impact distributions generally follow the patterns of the North American and EMEA measurements from the CDN, though we note a slight decrease in the median of the penalties to 20 ms, suggesting differences in the paths used by Atlas probes and CDN users.

Unexpected Behaviors. As further analysis, we rank the hoplets by the product of the number of destinations in a set and the frequency, balancing the impact and breadth. The notable contributors are eyeball networks, as well as the destination networks, *i.e.* root letter operators. Such hoplets are expected, and in line with our findings from the CDN data. However, there was a significant contribution from a European transit provider. Hoplets in this provider frequently occurred as a pair with a hoplet in a regional ISP from Bahrain.

In the transit provider, we observed a hoplet set with frequency of .88 and over 66 ms of penalty. The second hoplet, which appears after passing through the ISP network has a frequency of 0.85 and a penalty of 18 ms en route to another local ISP in the region. Inspection of the hoplets revealed that the majority of the sources were probes in Europe, making providers in Bahrain an unlikely portion of a path to a DNS root letter. We believe that this behavior is the result of a misconfiguration. Hoplets readily drew attention to the odd path and its frequent presence on paths towards this root server. Subsequent examinations from these traceroutes show that this issue has been corrected, and no further hoplets are seen in the regional ISP, and there has been a significant reduction in hoplets in the transit provider.

6   Related Work

Traceroute has long been a popular tool for discovering the behavior of networks. Significant work has gone into developing improvements on the original technique [5,23]. Others have examined how to improve measurement and scanning, learning from global routing behaviors [6,19]. The hoplets system learns from these findings, and incorporates many of their principles into its inferences.

Many systems measure networks based on probes from end systems. These include systems for detecting network outages [29], routing failure [17], and performance anomalies [21,27,39]. Many of these focus on large scale changes in network behavior, including shifting paths or changes in performance compared to a baseline. Hoplets are focused on extracting value from a collection of measurements and determining bottlenecks that appear within a single traceroute and comparing the resulting structures. In [34], the authors examined international detours. Hoplets are designed to perform a similar qualitative assessment of paths, but focus on the context of the traceroute itself and avoid geolocation. In [12] the authors use existing traceroute measurements to detect when performance degrades. In contrast, hoplets can be used on both large collections of measurements and standalone snapshots. Hoplets do not directly detect changes over time, but instead focus on outliers within a single measurement.

Other systems have used direct measurements to construct large and comprehensive systems. These have been used for latency prediction [20], CDN Performance [8,15,18,32], general wide-area analysis [10,16,38], and in more specific settings such as data centers and IPTV networks [3,4,22,31]. Others still build large controllers, designed to take many inputs and make decisions accordingly [28,33,37]. Hoplets are complementary to such systems: taking a single, easy to obtain input, and providing a meaningful signal about the nature of the path as a result. This primitive can likely be incorporated into many of these, and similar, systems, making use of relevant context.

Notable for their focus on grouping service end-users and providing shared root cause analysis are WhyHigh [18] and BlameIt [15]. BlameIt employs a budgeted active measurement system that provides granularity and specificity by comparing to baseline measurements. Hoplets are designed for direct detection of standout behavior in measurements, requiring less input data, but providing no guarantees regarding root cause.

The field of network tomography seeks to develop an understanding of the characteristics of a network based on end to end measurements [9,11,14]. In contrast to such work, hoplets avoid many of the underlying topological questions, instead assessing the ultimate impacts of a path, acknowledging that the underlying processes may be more complex.

7   Conclusions

In this paper, we presented a system which uses a single set of input traceroutes to detect significant RTT contributors along the path to a destination we all hoplets. We further presented an aggregation system which allows for the comparison of hoplets across many measurements, allowing for the easy detection of common performance bottlenecks. We conducted a large scale measurement study, examining the frequency and magnitude of detected hoplets in CDN paths. Finally, we demonstrated the generality of the system, exploring the hoplets extracted from traceroutes on the RIPE Atlas platform, demonstrating comparable patterns to those seen on the CDN and detecting a potential misconfiguration in a Root letter. Given their flexibility and ease of implementation, hoplets are able to provide helpful insights on network behavior, both as a standalone system and as a component in a larger scale measurement and analysis platform.

Acknowledgments. We would like to thank our shepherd, Romain Fontugne, and reviewers for their helpful feedback. We also thank the Verizon Media Platform Traffic Management team for their support.

8   Appendix

8.1   Parameter Selection

Here, we provide a brief examination of the parameter selection process used in our development of the hoplets system. These parameters are ultimately a reflection of the underlying data and the desired sensitivity to processing that data. Alternative sources of data may find it necessary to repeat these experiments.

Alert Threshold. Recall that the alert threshold determines the deviation necessary for a differential RTT to trigger the creation of a hoplet. Here we consider our thresholds as a multiple of the standard deviation, as estimated using the MAD. Here we consider a range of values, from .2 to 10. Recall, that our

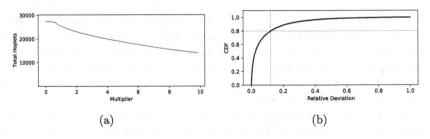

(a)   (b)

Fig. 6. (a) Increasing the alert threshold reduces the total number of hoplets found in the data. (b) For our ping measurements, 80% of measurements see variation under 12%.

minimum criteria also requires a differential RTT of at least 10 ms, a requirement we retain here.

Figure 6a shows the number of extracted hoplets for each multiplier. Indeed, increasing the multiplier reduces the total number of hoplets detected, nearly linearly. Recall that hoplets do not represent a discrete event, *i.e.* a degradation, but instead are a description of the observed behavior. Lower sensitivity means the system will produce information only about the largest source of RTT, and higher sensitivity means it will provide information on more segments with a rider range of RTT deviations.

In order to manage this balance, we use a single standard deviation (*i.e.* a multiplier of 1), building hoplets only around hops which demonstrate large increases, but not requiring that they represent egregious outliers. Other alerting functions, for example based on the deviation percentile, may also perform well. An important constraint, however, is that the threshold be relative to the traceroute itself, though absolute criteria may prove valuable for operators in certain condition with tight constraints.

Carry-Through Tolerance. Next, we examine the selection of the 12% variation which is permitted in the *carry-through* requirement. Here, we consider all traceroute measurements taken over a day as a series of independent ping measurements. We take all destinations (*i.e.* intermediate hops in the traceroute) for which we had at least 3 measurements, which leaves us with a total of 24,916 measurements. We then compute the median measured RTT and the median deviation observed over those measurements.

Figure 6b shows a CDF of these deviations. Here we see that 80% of our measurements had variation under .12. This suggests that while we see some differences over the course of our measurements, the true measurement noise is relatively small. Therefore an allowance of 12% allows such measurements to still be used, while still maintaining our carry-through condition.

References

1. RIPE Atlas. https://atlas.ripe.net
2. RouteViews. http://www.routeviews.org
3. Arzani, B., et al.: 007: democratically finding the cause of packet drops. In: Proceedings of NSDI 2018 (2018)
4. Arzani, B., Ciraci, S., Loo, B.T., Schuster, A., Outhred, G.: Taking the blame game out of data centers operations with netpoirot. In: Proceedings of SIGCOMM 2016 (2016)
5. Augustin, B., et al.: Avoiding traceroute anomalies with Paris traceroute. In: Proceedings of IMC 2006 (2006)
6. Broido, A., Claffy, K.: Analysis of RouteViews BGP data: policy atoms. In: Network Resource Data Management Workshop (2001)
7. Calder, M., Fan, X., Hu, Z., Katz-Bassett, E., Heidemann, J., Govindan, R.: Mapping the expansion of Google's serving infrastructure. In: Proceedings of IMC 2013 (2013)
8. Calder, M., et al.: Odin: Microsoft's scalable fault-tolerant CDN measurement system. In: Proceedings of NSDI 2018 (2018)
9. Castro, R., Coates, M., Liang, G., Nowak, R., Yu, B.: Network tomography: recent developments. Stat. Sci. **19**, 499–517 (2004)
10. Dhamdhere, A., et al.: Inferring persistent interdomain congestion. In: Proceedings of SIGCOMM 2018 (2018)
11. Duffield, N.: Network tomography of binary network performance characteristics. IEEE Trans. Inf. Theory **52**(12), 5373–5388 (2006)
12. Fontugne, R., Pelsser, C., Aben, E., Bush, R.: Pinpointing delay and forwarding anomalies using large-scale traceroute measurements. In: Proceedings of IMC 2017 (2017)
13. Fontugne, R., Shah, A., Aben, E.: The (thin) bridges of as connectivity: measuring dependency using as hegemony. In: Proceedings of PAM 2018 (2018)
14. Ghita, D., Karakus, C., Argyraki, K., Thiran, P.: Shifting network tomography toward a practical goal. In: Proceedings of CoNEXT 2011 (2011)
15. Jin, Y., et al.: Zooming in on wide-area latencies to a global cloud provider. In: Proceedings of SIGCOMM 2019 (2019)
16. Kanuparthy, P., Dovrolis, C.: Pythia: diagnosing performance problems in wide area providers. In: Proceedings of USENIX ATC 2014 (2014)
17. Katz-Bassett, E., Madhyastha, H.V., John, J.P., Krishnamurthy, A., Wetherall, D.: Studying black holes in the Internet with hubble. In: Proceedings of NSDI 2008 (2008)
18. Krishnan, R., et al.: Moving beyond end-to-end path information to optimize CDN performance. In: Proceedings of IMC 2009 (2009)
19. Lee, Y., Spring, N.: Identifying and aggregating homogeneous ipv4/24 blocks with hobbit. In: Proceedings of IMC 2016 (2016)
20. Madhyastha, H.V., et al.: Iplane: an information plane for distributed services. In: Proceedings of OSDI 2006 (2006)
21. Mahajan, R., Zhang, M., Poole, L., Pai, V.: Uncovering performance differences among backbone ISPS with Netdiff. In: Proceedings of NSDI 2008 (2008)
22. Mahimkar, A.A., et al.: Towards automated performance diagnosis in a large IPTV network. In: Proceedings of SIGCOMM 2009 (2009)
23. Mao, Z.M., Rexford, J., Wang, J., Katz, R.H.: Towards an accurate as-level traceroute tool. In: Proceedings of SIGCOMM 2003 (2003)

24. Marder, A., Luckie, M., Dhamdhere, A., Huffaker, B., Claffy, K.C., Smith, J.M.: Pushing the boundaries with bdrmapIT: mapping router ownership at Internet scale. In: Proceedings of IMC 2018 (2018)
25. Morandi, I., Bronzino, F., Teixeira, R., Sundaresan, S.: Service traceroute: tracing paths of application flows. In: Choffnes, D., Barcellos, M. (eds.) PAM 2019. LNCS, vol. 11419, pp. 116–128. Springer, Cham (2019). https://doi.org/10.1007/978-3-030-15986-3_8
26. Müller, M., Moura, G.C.M., de O. Schmidt, R., Heidemann, J.: Recursives in the wild: engineering authoritative DNS servers. In: Proceedings of IMC 2017 (2017)
27. Padmanabhan, V.N., Ramabhadran, S., Padhye, J.: NetProfiler: profiling wide-area networks using peer cooperation. In: Castro, M., van Renesse, R. (eds.) IPTPS 2005. LNCS, vol. 3640, pp. 80–92. Springer, Heidelberg (2005). https://doi.org/10.1007/11558989_8
28. Pujol, E., Poese, I., Zerwas, J., Smaragdakis, G., Feldmann, A.: Steering hyper-giants' traffic at scale. In: Proceedings of CoNEXT 2019 (2019)
29. Quan, L., Heidemann, J., Pradkin, Y.: Trinocular: understanding Internet reliability through adaptive probing. In: Proceedings of SIGCOMM 2013 (2013)
30. Rokach, L., Maimon, O.: Clustering methods. In: Maimon, O., Rokach, L. (eds.) Data Mining and Knowledge Discovery Handbook. Springer, Boston (2005). https://doi.org/10.1007/0-387-25465-X_15
31. Roy, A., Zeng, H., Bagga, J., Snoeren, A.C.: Passive realtime datacenter fault detection and localization. In: Proceedings of NSDI 2017 (2017)
32. Schlinker, B., Cunha, I., Chiu, Y.-C., Sundaresan, S., Katz-Bassett, E.: Internet performance from Facebook's edge. In: Proceedings of IMC 2019 (2019)
33. Schlinker, B., et al.: Engineering egress with edge fabric: steering oceans of content to the world. In: Proceedings of SIGCOMM 2017 (2017)
34. Shah, A., Fontugne, R., Papadopoulos, C.: Towards characterizing international routing detours. In: Proceedings of AINTEC 2016 (2016)
35. Wei, L., Flores, M., Bedi, H., Heidemann, J.: Bidirectional anycast/unicast probing (BAUP): optimizing CDN anycast. In: Proceedings of TMA 2020 (2020)
36. Wohlfart, F., Chatzis, N., Dabanoglu, C., Carle, G., Willinger, W.: Leveraging interconnections for performance: the serving infrastructure of a large CDN. In: Proceedings of SIGCOMM 2018 (2018)
37. Yap, K.-K., et al.: Taking the edge off with espresso: scale, reliability and programmability for global Internet peering. In: Proceedings of SIGCOMM 2017 (2017)
38. Zhang, M., Zhang, C., Pai, V., Peterson, L., Wang, R.: Planetseer: Internet path failure monitoring and characterization in wide-area services. In: Proceedings of OSDI 2004 (2004)
39. Zhang, Y., Mao, Z.M., Zhang, M.: Effective diagnosis of routing disruptions from end systems. In: Proceedings of NSDI 2008 (2008)

Network Security

NATting Else Matters: Evaluating IPv6 Access Control Policies in Residential Networks

Karl Olson[✉], Jack Wampler[✉], Fan Shen[✉], and Nolen Scaife[✉]

University of Colorado Boulder, Boulder, USA
{karl.olson,jack.wampler,fan.shen,scaife}@colorado.edu

Abstract. Customer edge routers are the primary mode of connection to the Internet for a large portion of non-commercial users. As these consumer networks migrate from IPv4 to IPv6, stateful firewalls are needed to protect devices in the home. However, policy details crucial to the implementation of these inbound access controls are left to the discretion of the device manufacturers. In this paper, we survey ten customer edge routers to evaluate how manufacturers implement firewalls and user controls in IPv6. The result is a systemic, demonstrable failure among all parties to agree upon, implement, and communicate consistent security policies. We conclude with future research directions and recommendations for all parties to address these systemic failures and provide a consistent model for home security.

Keywords: IPv6 · Consumer gateway · Network address translation · Security

1 Introduction

For over twenty years, IPv4 network address translation (NAT) dictated a common operational template for customer edge (CE) routers across a diverse set of hardware manufacturers. Fueled by Internet growth and address scarcity rather than intended design, the ubiquitous usage of NAT, combined with RFC 1918 addressing, provides consumers and developers with a common behavioral standard [20, 21]. While unintentional, NAT meaningfully isolates devices inside the network from those outside it. This allows device manufacturers, and consumers by proxy, to benefit from automatic and default attack surface reduction.

In contrast, IPv6 provides enough address space that individual devices receive their own public, globally-routable addresses. This model eliminates the need for NAT and allows other devices on the Internet to communicate directly with devices in the home. The IETF provides little guidance or standard for firewall configurations [3, 16], allowing router manufacturers to implement filtering policies at their own discretion. With approximately two-thirds of consumer devices maintaining default settings [6] or failing to keep up with system or security updates [17], internal devices' exposure to external threats becomes dependent on the router's design. Without a default security perimeter in place, once "secured" devices within a home network now rely on the consumer to

© Springer Nature Switzerland AG 2021
O. Hohlfeld et al. (Eds.): PAM 2021, LNCS 12671, pp. 373–389, 2021.
https://doi.org/10.1007/978-3-030-72582-2_22

either individually maintain each device or to implement a technical solution, such as detailed firewall rules, on their own.

In this work, we perform the first study of IPv6 CE routers to examine how manufacturers are implementing filtering and access control for IPv6 residential networks. We assess ten popular CE routers to evaluate their default firewall policies and the ability for consumers to implement custom rules. Our findings show inconsistency in the implementation of default configurations, overexposure of services, and an overall lack of messaging to consumers about the baseline policy of a device. As a result, in cases where no default firewall is enabled, consumers may be unaware of the exposure of their devices and developers may have incorrectly assumed that a device's services are not exposed to the Internet.

The remainder of this paper is structured as follows: In Sect. 2, we provide a short overview of IPv6 features, operation considerations and competing security paradigms. We then present our methodology for assessing IPv6 implementation in CE routers across a spectrum of features and configurations in Sect. 3 before presenting our results in Sect. 4. We discuss the necessity for a single device baseline standard and recommend consistent messaging in Sect. 5. Finally, we conclude in Sect. 6.

2   Background

Although functionally similar to IPv4, IPv6 provides a few small but impactful changes to the typical consumer network. In this section, we give a brief history of the transition from IPv4 to IPv6 before covering some key differences between the two protocols and their potential impact on consumers.

2.1   IPv4 NAT

NAT shaped the CE routing environment for two primary reasons: First, the scalability of NAT delayed the eventual address exhaustion of IPv4 in a period of explosive Internet growth and provided a simple path to connect significantly more devices to the Internet. Internet Service Providers (ISPs), who manage public address distribution in their networks, effectively required CE routers to support NAT by allocating exactly one public IP to each household gateway [8].

Second, the simplicity of NAT lowered the barrier for non-technical users to operate their own network. Home networks are often unmanaged or rely heavily on default configurations to meet the needs of non-technical users [3,4,20]. By adopting NAT, CE routers were able to provide simple or automatic initialization that required minimal configuration beyond Service Set Identifier (SSID), Wi-Fi Protected Access (WPA) password, and any ISP-specific settings (such as a PPPoE username/password) [4]. Once established, a suite of protocols (UPnP, STUN, etc.) provide an interface for connected devices to negotiate with the router directly such that the user would rarely need to interact with the network [7,16,19]. NAT also removed the need to define and manage an ingress filtering policy, as the one public address is multiplexed for use by all internal hosts. The prevalence and ubiquity of NAT are now synonymous with the default-deny ingress policy that has become the de facto security model of CE networks, a policy that *is often the only ingress access control deployed.*

However, the motivation for the adoption of NAT in IPv4 is negated by a core feature in the design of IPv6: there is no longer an addressing shortage meaning we again have the ability to assign one or more addresses to each device. With this transition, inbound access controls are now discretionary; IPv6 allows CE networks to operate without the network perimeters and default access control necessitated by NAT.

While the IETF explicitly acknowledges that care should be taken in designing the baseline operation of CE routers, they avoid proposing default configurations due to a constructive tension between the desires for transparent end-to-end connectivity on the one hand, and the need to detect and prevent intrusion by unauthorized public Internet users on the other [20]. The strongest recommendation provided by the IETF is for manufactures to include a toggle to allow customers to choose between an open, unfiltered gateway where security is left to endpoint devices, or a closed perimeter approach, similar to NAT, where traffic is filtered and only allowed through careful exception [3,20]. In the absence of efforts by manufacturers to provide standardization or documentation of the defaults that they implement, consumers are left to assess whether the security model that their network implements is sufficient.

2.2   IPv6 Reachability

A significant consideration in the adoption of IPv6 is the ability to uniquely address each device that joins the Internet. No longer defined by NAT architectures and private subnets, this addressing allows for every device to be globally *reachable.* Devices designed for the home environment often pose a serious risk when exposed to the open Internet [2,9,10]. However, globally reachable does not automatically imply a device is globally *accessible.*

The IETF's RFCs give router manufacturers discretion for handling unsolicited inbound traffic in IPv6. The two basic options for default policies are:

- **Default Deny**: drop all unsolicited WAN-to-LAN inbound traffic. To permit inbound traffic, users can either manually add firewall exceptions or rely on protocols that allow exceptions to be negotiated directly with the router. This policy resembles the existing model of IPv4 networks instrumented with NAT and UPnP.
- **Default Permit**: allow unsolicited inbound WAN-to-LAN traffic. Devices are globally accessible, offloading the responsibility for filtering unwanted traffic to each individual device. The advantage of this model is that developers can easily design and deploy their Internet-capable devices without consideration for including and maintaining additional security mechanisms such as firewalls, hole punching mechanisms, or their associated user interface controls.

Whichever default policy is used, the mental model that a user employs must change from that of IPv4. If a user wishes to manually configure an exception

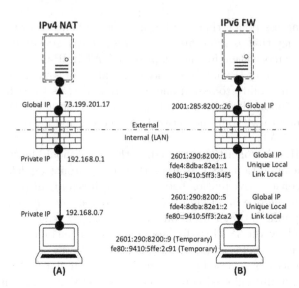

Fig. 1. IPv6 network layout – IPv6 represents a fundamental shift in the addressing of local networks. In (A) NAT, computers follow a one-to-one mapping of local network private IP with a single globally-routable IP shared by many internal devices. In (B) IPv6, devices can have many addresses depending on operational scope. Additionally, IP addresses are unique and can be routed globally if it has the correct scope – a direct contrast to IPv4 NAT.

to the ingress policy that their router implements, the subtle difference between NAT and individually globally-addressed devices is significant. For example, individual devices in IPv6 can have more than one address assigned concurrently, and those addresses may be link-local or transient as demonstrated in Fig. 1. In order to administer their IPv6 network in a manner equivalent to IPv4, users must understand technical details about IPv6 operation and firewall behavior. This is further complicated by the fact that the control interfaces provided by manufacturers and across devices have no common nomenclature or abstractions for configuration tasks. A study of enterprise IPv6 networks found that enterprise operators likewise have difficulty implementing appropriate controls in these networks [5]. These challenges should not imply that there is anything inherently wrong with IPv6 - the same model provided by IPv4 NAT can similarly be implemented in IPv6 [18] - but further demonstrate the need to provide a common expectation for baseline operation.

The flexibility of implementation among CE routing devices combined with globally reachable addressing creates a potential issue: unlike IPv4 networks where the de facto model is effectively required, in IPv6 CE routers are free to expose all internal endpoints. Furthermore, as devices transition from IPv4 to IPv6, this exposure could occur without any communication to the end user as they attempt to administrate their network. Because inbound access control implementation is left to the discretion of manufacturers, we suspect that there is variance among implementations. In the next section, we describe our methodology for evaluating a set of off-the-shelf CE routers to assess how IPv6 access control is implemented in practice.

3   Methodology

Our study aims to measure the security implementation of consumer grade gateways and the configuration options that they provide for IPv6. In this section, we describe our methodology for selecting and evaluating these routers.

3.1   Router Selection and Network Configuration

In order to choose routers that are representative of those deployed in real networks, we rely on the work of Kumar *et al.*, who provide insight into the most commonly used global gateways by manufacturer and region [10]. Out of 4.8K router vendors globally, we selected 12 routers which covered 25.2% of the most commonly deployed global brands. Only routers that specifically mention compatibility with IPv6 were chosen for our comparison. We were unable to find any routers that advertise or provide messaging about filtering policies. To evaluate the potential differences within a manufacturer we include multiple Linksys (EA3500, and EA6350) routers. Two of the selected routers (the Tenda AC18 and the Wavlink Aerial G2) were excluded because they did not actually support IPv6 upon arrival. The remaining ten devices used in our assessment are shown in Sect. 4, Table 1.

Our architecture consists of four key elements marked with letters in Fig. 2. Two vantages were established to assess traffic flows: an external host located on a public cloud provider (A) scanning across a public ISP toward the firewall (B) or internal host (C), and an internal vantage (D) which conducted the same scans focused outbound (with the exception of targeting an external host due to the ubiquitous outbound permit policy of the firewalls). All devices sending and receiving probes associated with scans were under our control at all times and at no time did we perform any scanning or analysis of public or private systems outside of our controlled scope. This architecture allowed us to pass traffic across the public internet via local consumer grade ISPs and through the assessed routers from different vantages to analyze real-world operational modes.

3.2   Evaluation Methodology

In order to allow unsolicited inbound connections (e.g., peer-to-peer connections), IPv4 routers must provide the ability to *port forward*; the router establishes a list of port numbers and destination (internal) addresses. When a packet is received on the public interface at a port in the list, the router bypasses any NAT lookup and immediately rewrites the destination address and forwards the packet internally. Forwarding is common in IPv4; devices rely on the UPnP and NAT-PMP protocols to automate the setup of forwarding rules. Without these protocols, users would need to manually create such rules, a technical task requiring knowledge of IP addresses and TCP/UDP ports.

Forwarding is effectively meaningless in IPv6 without NAT as devices can be addressed directly. Instead, routers must provide a mechanism to create firewall exceptions if a firewall is implemented. While these rules can be as simple as port forwarding rules (e.g., a destination IP and a port number), how they are implemented and the options available to users may vary. We evaluate the following basic characteristics of each router:

- **Default IPv6.** We first check if each router supports IPv6 and whether it enables that support by default. When IPv6 is enabled by default, IPv6-capable devices on the internal network automatically request addresses. Default IPv6 support requires that the upstream ISP also supports IPv6. It is notable that router support for IPv6 and default enable state can be changed in a firmware update pushed remotely by the manufacturer, and ISPs can (and do) add support for IPv6 without notifying consumers. Therefore, *devices in the home environment can transition to IPv6 overnight without the user's knowledge.*
- **Firewall Present.** Next, we evaluate whether or not the device implements a firewall. In cases where a firewall is not present, the device will pass all traffic to internal hosts.
- **Firewall Enabled.** If a firewall is present, we evaluate whether or not it is enabled (i.e., filtering) by default.
- **One-Click Open.** While RFC 7084 refrains from proposing a default IPv6 ingress filter policy for consumer gateways, it advises that gateways implement a single button to toggle all firewall ingress filtering [16]. We evaluate whether or not the device includes this functionality.
- **Security Warning.** When the One-Click Open option is used, we evaluate if there is any warning or communication to the user about the danger of disabling the firewall.
- **Rule Generation.** We evaluate whether each device includes the ability to create exceptions to the default firewall policy. Such rules may be necessary for allowing specific services or applications to function in the presence of a firewall. Because we are comparing to existing functionality in IPv4 networks, we specifically exclude examining more expressive firewall capabilities than IP/device/port tuples.
- **IP Specification.** We evaluate whether or not rule creation specifies an individual IP as the destination.
- **Device Specification.** As IPv6 devices are often assigned multiple addresses (in some cases, one per application), creating a rule may be complicated by device/address identification. We evaluate whether rules can be created by specifying a device (e.g., by MAC address or another identifier) rather than a specific IP address.
- **IPv6 UPnP Support.** Finally, we evaluate the router's capability to offer *automatic* rule generation. Devices on the local network can use UPnP to create firewall rules programmatically if the router offers this capability.

Since routers do not explicitly advertise their firewall policies, we conduct a series of black-box scans in order to establish the default filtering model, firewall filtering policies, and hosted router services. We designed and built a custom traffic monitor on the internal host to ensure accurate collection of packets arriving through the firewall. During a scan, this monitor would listen for and record inbound IPv6 traffic with a timestamp, arrival port, protocol and scanning source IP. We reconciled the packets received with packets sent from the scanner to filter unwanted traffic and verify correct operation.

Scans were conducted using Nmap against the most common 1,000 TCP and UDP ports (as defined by the scanner). This scope was chosen due to interest in exposure of the most common ports and scan duration considerations. A complete assessment of each CE router involved nine total scans from two sources, each conducted with the firewall on and off as shown in Fig. 2: First, scan (1) is conducted from the external vantage to the internal host establishing the inbound filtering strategy of the firewall. Scan (2) probes the external router interface from the external vantage to identify open ports and exposed services; (3) repeats this scan on the internal interface to determine if this traditionally concealed interface is exposed under IPv6. For each interface, we conduct a banner scan against exposed ports (4 and 5). This process is repeated from the internal vantage first targeting the exposed services on each router interface (6 and 7) before conducting the same banner grab on exposed services (8 and 9).

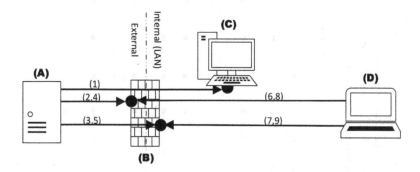

Fig. 2. Scanning protocol – To fully evaluate the security policy of each router we scan from two vantage points (A) and (D) against three targets: (C) an internal host, and (B) the firewall internal and external interfaces. In total, we conducted 9 unique scans for each router.

The combination of sources and targets allowed complete measurement of IPv6 filtering policies, exposure, and default operational model of the CE router. These results were then compared with our evaluation of basic router characteristics to complete a holistic router assessment, presented in Sect. 4: Results.

Table 1. Routers – This table displays the heterogeneous nature of management options and default configurations among the devices evaluated. Bolded device names indicate that the router implements a default-permit firewall policy and IPv6 is enabled by default. Configuration options for unsupported features are marked with dashes. No device used IPv6 NAT.

Device	Brand	Firmware version	Default IPv6	Firewall present	Firewall enabled	One-click open	Security warning	Rule generation	IP specification	Device specification	IPv6 UPnP support
Amazon Eero	Amazon	Eero OS 3.15.2-1	○	●	●	○	○	●	○	●	○
AmpliFi Gamer's Edition	Ubiquiti	v3.3.0	○	●	●	●	●	○	–	–	●
Cisco DPC3941T XB3	Cisco	2.3.10.13.5.5.0.5	●	●	●	●	○	○	–	–	○
Google Nest (2nd Gen)	Google	12371.71.11	○	●	●	○	○	●	○	●	○
Linksys EA3500	Linksys	1.1.40.162464	●	●	●	●	○	●	●	○	○
Linksys EA6350 AC1200	Linksys	3.1.10.191322	●	●	●	●	○	●	●	○	○
Motorola MR2600	Motorola	1.0.10	●	●	○	○	○	●	●	○	○
Nighthawk X4 R7000	Linksys	1.0.0.124	○	●	●	●	○	○	–	–	○
Surfboard SBG10 DOCSIS 3.0	Arris	9.1.103AA72	●	●	●	●	○	●	●	●	○
TP-Link AC1750 v2	TP-Link	180114	●	○	–	–	○	○	–	–	○

4   Results

In this section, we present the results of our experiments for each of the CE routers. In general, we find CE routers with IPv6 capability have little commonality of security implementation across manufacturers.

4.1   Operational Defaults

Table 1 presents an overview of our findings showing a wide variance in default operation, security, and user control. Eight of the ten routers assessed have an enabled default firewall policy (i.e., default-deny) for IPv6 while the remaining two devices (TP-Link AC1750 and Motorola MR2600[1]) do not have a default firewall (i.e., default-permit). Neither of these two devices communicates this design decision to the consumer. At the time of writing, the TP-Link AC1750 is Amazon US's top-selling router [1] and TP-link is the top global provider, accounting for 15.9% of all deployed devices [10], suggesting that the default permit model may be commonly deployed.

Five of these eight default deny devices further provide a "One-Click Open" option for opening the network to inbound connections. This option immediately transitions the network to a default permit model allowing all ingress traffic through to the internal hosts. The effect that this has on ingress filtering can be seen in Fig. 3 in the Appendix. Only one of the ten devices evaluated provides an explicit warning to the user before allowing the firewall to be disabled using this feature. Users with minimal technical knowledge who are accustomed to a default closed model from IPv4 NAT may be unaware of the additional exposure this option creates.

Two routers, the Motorola MR2600 and TP-Link AC1750, enable IPv6 routing by default with a default permit firewall. This combination of configuration settings exposes all IPv6-capable devices to the wider Internet by default. While the Motorola MR2600 allows consumers to *optionally* enable the firewall, the user must be aware of the current state and possess the technical capability to do so. Worse, the TP-Link router only provides the ability to disable IPv6 and has no capability to enable any filtering.

4.2   Firewall Policies and Pinholing

We find a spectrum of firewall management options offered to the consumers ranging from subscription model services for packet inspection and filtering, to singular on/off toggles, to complete lack of firewall configuration for IPv6. Depending on the router, modifying the configuration can be accomplished through a smartphone application or a locally hosted web portal, with a few devices supporting both.

---

[1] *Responsible Disclosure* Given the severity of enabling IPv6 support by default and a default-permit posture, we disclosed our findings to both Motorola and TP-Link in August 2020. In November 2020, Motorola issued a public patch to correct the issue. TP-Link did not respond to our disclosure.

For routers that provide an interface to create exceptions to the default firewall filtering policy (pinholes), we found that two out of six connect those rules to the device MAC address. We verified that in these cases, traffic destined for *any* associated address for the device is forwarded. The other four out of six routers allow users to provide a single, static address that the rule applies to; the rules are not updated if the device migrates or is assigned additional IPv6 addresses over time.

Of the routers that do not support IPv6 pinholing, only the TP-Link AC1750 provides no ability to configure the firewall aside from disabling IPv6 (because it does not have such a firewall). For the remaining three routers, Cisco DPC3941T XB3 also provides several options of choosing what kind of traffic is blocked besides the "One-Click Open" option, while for Ubiquiti AmpliFi and Netgear Nighthawk, *One-Click Open is the only method available for users to control the firewall.* As an example, the Ubiquiti AmpliFi provides users with minimal control over IPv4 policies through port-forwarding controls, but the management interface lacks an equivalent ability to create pinholes in IPv6. Ubiquiti notes this on their official FAQ: "AmpliFi does not support editing firewall configurations, and cannot be disabled unless you place the router in bridge mode" [15]. Contrary to this statement, they do allow automated modification of firewall rules through the embedded UPnP WANIPv6FirewallControl:1 device template. For manual control, the web interface instead offers an "Allow all incoming IPv6 connections" as the only actionable solution for non-technical users.

4.3   Router Scanning

We find that when CE routers are globally accessible a majority of them expose open services to the Internet as shown by Table 2. Whether the firewalls are disabled manually or by default, six routers do not employ rules to restrict access to local network services from the global Internet. We found that services (e.g., SMTP, HTTP, and SMB) available on internal router interfaces were also offered on the external interfaces as well as the link local address on these devices. Interestingly, this indicates that the manufacturers are configuring their internal services to listen on all interfaces; when the firewall is off, these services are no longer protected. It is unclear if this is an oversight or expected operation.

We discovered two exceptional implementations: First, the Motorola MR2600 maintains a small subset of exposed open ports on its external interface even with the firewall enabled. Second, the TP-Link AC1750 maintains an outdated version of Dropbear SSH despite the public availability of a CVE describing a remote code execution vulnerability [13]. It is notable that, of the routers that expose ports in any firewall configuration, there appear to be a common set of ports that are open, but provide no banner. We hypothesize that these ports are associated with common services that each router provides but does not enable by default, though the ports remain open. For example, multiple routers advertise the ability to set up local storage sharing, likely using SMB on port 445. Though we did not exercise this functionality, the exposure of these ports suggests that if a client were to enable these features they would also be accessible to the wider Internet over IPv6. The default states and mix of services available provide enough unique scan data to individually identify the device manufacturer; six of the ten routers we obtain have uniquely identifying features. As a result, we believe it may be possible to fingerprint routers through probing open IPv6 ports and services, though we leave this to future work.

Table 2. Externally Exposed Services – This table lists the IPv6 services and open TCP ports that are exposed by each device with the firewall either enabled or disabled for the routers that support such an option. Ports in bold indicate that a service responded with a banner. We document the services associated with the address from the router's external interface. Most routers have a separate address assigned to their internal interface from their allocated subnet, though we find that the exposed services are typically the same between the two.

Device	Default FW	FW enabled	FW disabled
Amazon Eero	●	–	No disable option
AmpliFi Gamer's Edition	●	–	–
Cisco DPC3941T XB3	●	–	–
Google Nest (2nd Gen)	●	–	No disable option
Linksys EA3500	●	–	25, 53, **80**, 135, 139, 443, 445, **2601**, 1080, **10000**
Linksys EA6350 AC1200	●	–	25, 53, **80**, 135, 139, **443**, 445, **2601**, 1080, **10000**
Motorola MR2600	○	25, 135, 139, 445, 1080	25, 135, 139, 445, 1080
Nighthawk X4 R7000	●	–	25, 43, 80, 135, 139, 443, 445, 548, 1080, **2601**
Surfboard SBG10 DOCSIS 3.0	●	–	25, 80, 135, 139, 443, 445, 1080
TP-Link AC1750 v2	○	No enable option	**22**, 25, 135, 139, 445,1080

To summarize, our work shows that there is little standardization among the routers evaluated in this work around the security or operational functionality provided for IPv6 CE networks. This is in direct contrast to IPv4 where devices and services are not exposed. While NAT was not designed as a security framework, the deny-all, permit by exception ingress policy serves as an invariant for consumer routing devices and is noted as such within RFCs when debating the default recommendations of CE routers [3,16,20]. We see this argument manifest in the inconsistency between device implementations; the default policies maintained by devices put real users and systems at risk.

5 Discussion

The CE environment provides a unique challenge in balancing device capability against user ability and need. This work demonstrates that the shift to IPv6 removes the consistency of one of its most crucial layers of defense: homogeneity in router operation. Without a safe default policy, consumers must rely on the security of each of their endpoint devices, which can be difficult to ensure, especially in CE environments where device maintenance is not guaranteed. We recognize that many of these problems are not caused by or unique to IPv6 consumer networks, but we note that unclear IPv6 implementation strategies exacerbate these issues by offloading responsibility for securing and configuring the network to consumers.

We see in our assessment a struggle to shape and define what exactly is the right amount of control without under-offering or overwhelming targeted consumer demographics. This has left router manufacturers to determine what are the correct abstractions and implementations, and how to communicate these clearly to a wide demographic of users. Accordingly, we believe that addressing the general inconsistency is the most direct path to securing CE networks in IPv6.

5.1 Recommendations

There are multiple parties involved in CE environments each of which have different motivations and risk factors, but it is important that the design of CE networks prioritizes the wholesale security of consumer data and devices. We structure our recommendations around the following principles:

- The default operation mode should be secure, and the bulk of network configuration should be moved from consumers to developers.
- Configuration options should be consistent and only as permissive as necessary.
- Configuration pitfalls should have confirmation warnings that ensure users understand the risks associated with the changes they are making (*e.g.* making devices globally accessible).
- Documentation should share abstractions and language across manufacturers and be as minimally complex as feasible.

It is important to present a clear, consistent threat model to consumers whose ability and understanding often lags that of developers, to avoid oversight on responsibility for securing devices connected to home networks. This is the responsibility of both standardization bodies and the CE router industry as a whole. We strongly recommend the following defaults:

Standardization. We recommend that CE routers universally standardize around a default ingress filtering policy that denies incoming traffic. We further recommend manufacturers remove or restrict the "one-click open" option on CE routers as home users are likely to unknowingly expose their whole network, violating the security principle of least privilege. If this is a required functionality, routers should warn users (and/or suggest to use IPv6 pinholing) before allowing them to use this option.

For manual exceptions we recommend that manufacturers implement both device and IP based rules and develop a consistent vocabulary for describing them. Providing users with the resources to understand when each option is preferable will require that the language used to describe IPv6 configuration options is consistent across manufacturers.

Documentation. It is irrelevant what standards require if manufacturers ignore them or if parties involved fail to understand their importance or the importance of their abstractions. Fostering consumer and developer understanding of IPv6 security can create pressure on manufacturers to adhere to standards and promote transparency ahead of purchase. Establishing consistent language and abstractions for describing the security mechanisms of IPv6 networks is the first step.

Currently manufacturers of customer edge routers highlight IPv6 as an enhanced feature in their product marketing, though we found no instance of educating users about IPv6 or describing its security implications. Instead, phrases such as "provides infinite addresses for more devices", "best possible experience", and "simplifies the router's tasks" are offered as slogans to encourage user commitment [11,12]. These approaches are problematic. This hides a transparent shift in the security model of home networks that consumers cannot be expected to inherently understand on their own.

Morgner *et al.*present one possible solution of offering device label standards similar to nutrition labels on food [14]. Here, the authors focused on manufacturer guarantees for duration of product support and timeliness of updates in a standardized label. We argue to take this concept further with a holistic approach to additional aspects of security such as default configuration, control mechanisms, and 3rd party certifications. Requirements for labelling standards incentivize manufacturers to provide and document security features necessary for consumers to have a functional understanding of their network posture at purchase.

5.2 Future Work

While this work discusses at length the "One-Click Open" option, we have not conducted a formal user experience study to confirm that users will rely on this option to achieve simple routing changes in their IPv6 networks as a first choice. A proper study of the UX/UI design involved in home network security would be informative and could provide developers with a better understanding of consumer needs and approaches to IPv6 security.

While we use this work to gauge the scope of current security policies of IPv6 CE routers, a large scale examination of router IPv6 firewall behavior is required to better understand the breadth of the impact that the transition from IPv4 to IPv6 has on CE routing. Specifically, a tool assisting clients to better understand the defaults that their network implements could prove a strong contribution towards this result. Similar large scale studies of IoT and smart devices operating in IPv6 environments are reserved for future efforts as well.

6 Conclusion

In IPv4 networks, the use of NAT afforded a ubiquitous, de facto default-deny security posture. The growing deployment of IPv6, which eliminates address scarcity, no longer requires NAT. In the absence of strong guidance for how router manufacturers should implement filtering, we examined a diverse set of routers to measure real-world implementations. We find that the access control models and controls implemented to manage these networks are coarse and contain unsafe defaults that likely expose devices on the network – often without warning to the consumer. The result is a systemic, demonstrable failure among all parties to agree upon, implement and communicate consistent security policies. While IPv6 brings important advances to the Internet, significant effort by academia and industry is needed to help address and solve access control issues in the home, including adequately communicating information about these postures to consumers.

7 Appendix

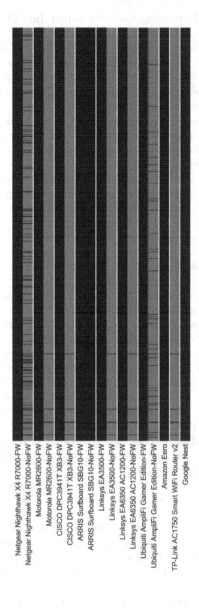

Fig. 3. Firewall ingress policies (TCP) – We use Nmap to scan the most common 1000 TCP ports on an internal host from an external vantage point. For each packet the host receives we mark the associated port GREY. Conversely, if the firewall drops the packet or the packet fails to reach the host due to network failure the associated port is marked BLACK. For routers that have an optional firewall we include a scan in both states indicated by FW or NoFW.

References

1. Amazon.com. Amazon Sales Popularity - Computer Routers (2020). https://web.archive.org/web/20201023233343/www.amazon.com/gp/bestsellers/pc/300189/ref=zg_b_bs_300189_1. Accessed 23 Oct 2020
2. Antonakakis, M., et al.: Understanding the Mirai botnet. In: USENIX - 26th Security Symposium, pp. 1093–1110 (2017)
3. Chown, T., Arkko, J., Brandt, A., Troan, O., Weil, J.: IPv6 home networking architecture principles. RFC 7368, Internet Engineering Task Force (October 2014)
4. Frontier Communications: Frontier home Internet setup guide (2020). https://frontier.com/~/media/HelpCenter/Documents/internet/installation-setup/hsi-self-install-guide.ashx?la=en. Accessed 18 Oct 2020
5. Czyz, J., Luckie, M., Allman, M., Bailey, M.: Don't forget to lock the back door! A characterization of IPv6 network security policy. In: Proceedings of the 23rd Annual Network and Distributed System Security Symposium (NDSS 2016), San Diego, California, USA (February 2016)
6. De Leon, N.: Many wireless routers lack basic security protections, consumer reports' testing finds (2019). https://www.consumerreports.org/wireless-routers/wireless-routers-lack-basic-security-protections. Accessed 20 Oct 2020
7. Open Connectivity Foundation: UPnP+ Specification (2020). https://openconnectivity.org/developer/specifications/upnp-resources/upnp/#upnp-plus. Accessed 18 Oct 2020
8. Hain, T.: Architectural implications of NAT. RFC 2993, Internet Engineering Task Force (November 2000)
9. Kolias, C., Kambourakis, G., Stavrou, A., Voas, J.: DDoS in the IoT: Mirai and other botnets. IEEE Comput. **50**(7), 80–84 (2017)
10. Kumar, D., et al.: All things considered: an analysis of IoT devices on home networks. In: USENIX - 28th Security Symposium, pp. 1169–1185 (2019)
11. Linksys: Differences between IPv4 and IPv6 (2020). https://www.linksys.com/us/support-article/?articleNum=139604. Accessed 18 June 2020
12. Microsoft. Support: IPv6 on Xbox one (2020). https://support.xbox.com/help/Hardware-Network/connect-network/ipv6-on-xbox-one. Accessed 18 June 2020
13. MITRE: CVE-2016-7406 (September 2016). https://cve.mitre.org/cgi-bin/cvename.cgi?name=CVE-2016-7406. Accessed 20 Oct 2020
14. Morgner, P., Mai, C., Koschate-Fischer, N., Freiling, F., Benenson, Z.: Security update labels: establishing economic incentives for security patching of IoT consumer products. arXiv:1906.11094 (2019)
15. Ubiquiti Networks. FAQ: does AmpliFi have a firewall? (2020). https://help.amplifi.com/hc/en-us/articles/115009611867-Does-AmpliFi-have-a-firewall-. Accessed 18 Oct 2020
16. Singh, H., Beebee, W., Donley, C., Stark, B.: Basic requirements for IPv6 customer edge routers. RFC 7084, Internet Engineering Task Force (November 2013)
17. Tripwire: SOHO wireless router (In)Security (2014). http://www.properaccess.com/docs/Tripwire_SOHO_Router_Insecurity_white_paper.pdf. Accessed 20 Oct 2020
18. Van de Velde, G., Hain, T., Droms, R., Carpenter, B., Klein, E.: Local network protection for IPv6. RFC 4864, Internet Engineering Task Force (May 2007)
19. Wing, D., Cheshire, S., Boucadair, M., Penno, R., Selkirk, P.: Port control protocol (PCP). RFC 6887, Internet Engineering Task Force (April 2013)

20. Woodyatt, J. (ed.): Recommended Simple Security Capabilities in Customer Premises Equipment (CPE) for Providing Residential IPv6 Internet Service. RFC 6092, Internet Engineering Task Force (January 2011)
21. Zhang, L.: A retrospective view of network address translation. IEEE Netw. **22**(5), 8–12 (2008)

Plight at the End of the Tunnel

Legacy IPv6 Transition Mechanisms in the Wild

John Kristoff[(✉)], Mohammad Ghasemisharif, Chris Kanich, and Jason Polakis

University of Illinois at Chicago, Chicago, USA
{jkrist3,mghas2,ckanich,polakis}@uic.edu

Abstract. IPv6 automatic transition mechanisms such as 6to4 and ISA-TAP endure on a surprising number of Internet hosts. These mechanisms lie in hibernation awaiting someone or something to rouse them awake. In this paper we measure the prevalence and persistence of legacy IPv6 automatic transition mechanisms, together with an evaluation of the potential threat they pose. We begin with a series of DNS-based experiments and analyses including the registration of available domain names, and demonstrate how attackers can conduct man-in-the-middle attacks against all IPv6 traffic for a significant number of end systems. To validate another form of traffic hijacking we then announce a control set of special-purpose IPv6 prefixes that cannot be protected by the RPKI to see these routes go undetected, accepted, and installed in the BGP tables of over 30 other upstream networks. Finally, we survey the Internet IPv4 address space to discover over 1.5 million addresses are open IPv6 tunnel relays in the wild that can be abused to facilitate a variety of unwanted activity such as IPv6 address spoofing attacks. We demonstrate how many attacks can be conducted remotely, anonymously, and without warning by adversaries. Behind the scenes our responsible disclosure has spearheaded network vendor software updates, ISP remediation efforts, and the deployment of new security threat monitoring services.

1 Introduction

The meteoric rise of the Internet motivated the proposal of IPv6 over two decades ago. However, rather than decree an instantaneous conversion and face the unavoidable disruption that would ensue, a slow migration started around the turn of the century and is still underway [33]. Around 25 years later, reports from Akamai [7] and Google [26] suggest that over 25% of client systems are using IPv6 in 2020. While IPv6 adoption has been substantial, a significant majority of users lack IPv6 connectivity. The slow migration necessitated the design, implementation, and deployment of transition mechanisms in order to maintain reachability between communicating hosts that lack direct connectivity to each other using their chosen version of IP.

A handful of security-related concerns about transition mechanisms were documented in IETF RFCs after the technology first arose [34,39]. These early concerns mentioned the lack of authentication on endpoints, and how they can be

© Springer Nature Switzerland AG 2021
O. Hohlfeld et al. (Eds.): PAM 2021, LNCS 12671, pp. 390–405, 2021.
https://doi.org/10.1007/978-3-030-72582-2_23

used for launching distributed denial-of-service attacks or IPv4 policy avoidance. The referenced RFCs summarize certain potential security threats, but do not provide specific guidance on how to mitigate them. Despite the concerns, these mechanisms were still added to commodity operating systems. More importantly, reports had not envisioned the DNS-based attacks and the extent of implementation weaknesses we uncover in this work. Based on reports [42,44] that provide statistics on the versions of users' Windows operating system, ~33% *of all Windows machines in the wild* currently have these automatic transition mechanisms *enabled by default.* Transition mechanisms are also supported by almost all other major operating systems.

Since transition mechanisms are intended to work around the shortcomings of a local IPv4-only network connection, many of them were designed as host-initiated tunneling protocols. Tunnels are the most straightforward solution to the network protocol transition problem, but as we will show, the implementation of the IPv6 automatic transition mechanisms were designed with little consideration for long term effects of on-by-default settings or the ease at which man-in-the-middle (MitM) attacks can be conducted.

We present several techniques that allow a remote attacker to meet the preconditions for activating the transition mechanism implementations undetected. Activation enables attackers to perpetrate stealthy traffic hijacking on a significant population of Windows hosts where these mechanisms currently lie dormant. Furthermore, with IPv6 being the generally preferred network layer protocol when given the choice between IPv6 and IPv4 [41], transition mechanism tunnels will handle a large portion of the network traffic for hosts without native IPv6 connectivity. The attack's impact may be further amplified by manipulating unauthenticated DNS responses that traverse a malicious tunnel by adding or including AAAA answers, thus "guiding" the client towards more IPv6 destinations.

In this paper, we investigate the persistence of *legacy* transition mechanisms by conducting a series of measurements, including a longitudinal study over the course of 13 months using data from multiple network vantage points, detailing the severity and feasibility of different attacks.

We consider two different attack vectors that capture adversaries with vastly different capabilities and resources. First, we demonstrate how an attack that requires only a domain name registration allows an adversary to hijack the IPv6 traffic for a substantial number of hosts having a domain suffix in a zone we control or can register a name for. We can directly observe 32,156 hosts susceptible to IPv6 traffic hijacking using this technique. The only additional requirement for this attack is the absence of network address translation (NAT). While these vulnerabilities can be directly exploited through the registration of specific domain names, we also explore a more sophisticated attack, where an adversary can announce BGP routes into the Internet routing tables.

Lastly, we conduct an Internet survey of open relay tunnels in the wild and how they can be used as a springboard for attacks, such as traffic reflection, spoofing, or the discovery of private network infrastructure. Our Internet-wide scans reveal over 1.5 million IPv4 addresses that can be exploited for such attacks, with further investigation revealing a portion of those relays consist of a widely deployed backbone router that allows IPv6 tunneling for anyone on the Internet by natively forwarding encapsulated IPv6 traffic arriving on an IPv4 interface. To the best of our knowledge, we are the first to report on these IPv4 hosts functioning as open IPv6 tunnel relays and the potential for misuse. Overall, our study sheds light on new attack vectors that pose a significant threat to the Internet, and highlights the importance of mobilizing the networking and operational security communities for deploying appropriate countermeasures.

In summary, our research contributions are as follows:

- We conduct a measurement of the contemporary use of legacy IPv6 automatic transition mechanisms within end hosts, transition mechanism-providing servers, and network infrastructure. We find multiple MitM attack vectors which are enabled by default on millions of Internet-connected hosts including DNS-based vectors unanticipated by the original designers or earlier reports.
- We further explore the practical implications of these MitM attacks, both in scope and severity. Our experimental analysis, driven by data collected from academic institutions, ISPs, and other organizations reveals the magnitude of the threat.
- Due to the severity of these vulnerabilities, we have reported them and coordinated with various trusted communities of network administrators of vulnerable networks, router vendors, and multiple incident response and threat intelligence reporting organizations. We also discuss countermeasures and mitigation strategies.

2   Background

A full accounting of all IPv6 transition mechanisms is beyond the scope of this paper. For example, newer mechanisms such as 6rd [45], DS-Lite [21], and 464XLAT [36] are not considered here. Instead, we focus on a subset of *legacy* automatic transition mechanisms. Three of the earliest and most popular are 6to4, ISATAP, and Teredo. Their peculiar use of specific address prefixes, the DNS, or tunnel bootstrapping allows us to conduct extensive measurements and experiments demonstrating their susceptibility to various forms of attack.

6to4. IETF RFC 3056 [9] describes one of the earliest automatic transition mechanisms for IPv6 in IPv4 tunneling. The Internet Assigned Numbers Authority (IANA) designated the 2002::/16 prefix to be used by 6to4 systems [30]. Bits 17 to 48 of a 6to4 address correspond to the globally unique 32-bit IPv4 address of the 6to4 host or site network. Systems behind a network address translator (NAT) or using private addresses cannot use 6to4. A 6to4 system can communicate with IPv6 over an intermediate IPv4 subpath by encapsulating IPv6 packets in IPv4 towards a well-known destination address from the IANA-designated special-use anycast prefix 192.88.99.0/24. Any network announcing this prefix must be willing to accept a 6to4 system's encapsulated packet, remove the outer

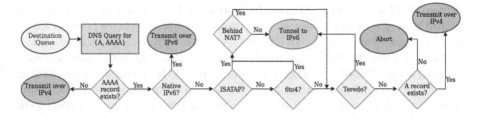

Fig. 1. Conceptual flowchart outlining the conditions for an IPv6 transition mechanism to be used.

IPv4 layer, and relay the enclosed IPv6 packet towards the IPv6 destination directly. Conversely, traffic back to a 6to4 system needs a relay that can add the IPv4 encapsulation onto an IPv6 datagram so that it may continue on the subpath that is IPv4-only. Like the IPv4 anycast prefix, a network advertising 2002::/16 must be willing to perform this relay service in the opposite direction.

ISATAP. Where 6to4 relies on the global routing infrastructure with well known prefixes and addressing for host configuration and packet forwarding, the Intra-Site Automatic Tunnel Addressing Protocol (ISATAP) is widely implemented with the help of the DNS to automatically construct an IPv6 over IPv4 tunnel [25]. A typical ISATAP client issues a DNS A query for a name with the suffix of the locally defined zone and a label prefix of *isatap* (e.g., isatap.myzone.example.net). If an address is indeed returned for this name, an ICMPv6 router solicitation and ICMPv6 router advertisement are exchanged over an IPv4 tunnel. The ISATAP client uses the source of the router advertisement response as the default IPv6 tunnel relay router. As with 6to4, ISATAP only works on hosts that are not behind a NAT.

Teredo. IETF RFC 4380 [29], describes an IPv6 over UDP-based automatic transition mechanism intended for clients behind a NAT device. Teredo clients communicate with a configured or discovered tunnel relay like ISATAP, except they do not need a public IPv4 address. Teredo client IPv6 addresses are derived from a combination of server and client attributes appended to the well-known Teredo prefix (2001::/32).

Interface and Mechanism Selection. It is possible for a system to have multiple active IPv6 interfaces and addresses. When such an IPv6 host has traffic to deliver, it must select an interface and source address from which to send traffic. IETF RFC 6724 [43] outlines the default address selection algorithms that should be used. If multiple transition mechanisms are active and available on a host without native IPv6 connectivity, traffic delivery and reception will tend to use only one available transition mechanism at a time. To illustrate interface selection, Fig. 1 depicts how a Microsoft Windows system will make it's choice. As shown in the top left, a client commonly starts communication with a DNS query. If an IPv6 address answer is provided, the most preferred interface type that is available will be used, falling back to IPv4 as a last resort.

Network Connectivity Status Indicator. When joining new networks or activating a new network interface, Microsoft Windows machines perform a connectivity test with a HTTP GET request for www.msftncsi.com/ncsi.txt. If this test succeeds the interface is assumed functional for as long as the interface state remains active. In order to more accurately measure IPv6 transition mechanism usage in our tunnel relay experiments, we want to ensure this test is successful. Microsoft systems will always attempt to use an IPv6 interface that passed the "ncsi" test, but will fall back to IPv4 with little to no perceived interruption of service if IPv6 communications fail.

3   Methodology and Data

In this section we provide a high-level overview of our experimental setup, methodology, limitations and network vantage points for measuring transition mechanism behavior, security threats, and privacy risks.

Domain Registrations. We registered dozens of *isatap* names in EDU-A, EDU-B, top-level domains (TLDs) and shared domain providers. Where possible we ran our own authoritative name servers for these names with the EDNS0 client subnet option [13] and extensive logging configured. These vantage points provide a diverse, but limited view of the global DNS name space and client population for our experiments.

EDU-A Functional ISATAP Relay. We setup a fully functional ISATAP relay that handed out public IPv6/64 prefixes and relayed tunneled traffic received from any of the institution's client population that had ISATAP enabled by default.

EDU-B Dysfunctional ISATAP Relay. This relay was configured to receive tunnel requests for all clients within the institution's primary DNS domain and the computer science domain. It was also the relay for a sample of ISATAP domains we registered in a number of TLDs and dynamic DNS providers. This tunnel relay system operated in the "dysfunctional" state, which would appear as a valid IPv6 path, but would ultimately reject traffic not associated with tunnel establishment and control.

DNS Query Logs. From EDU-A we received anonymized client query logs from their local resolvers. A large U.S. cable modem operator also provided us with anonymized DNS query log data for a large city service area containing any IPv6 transition mechanism label in the query name. We also leverage the DNS query data collected by the DNS-OARC DITL project for the two prior two years available [20].

BGP Route Announcements. We coordinated with the EDU-A upstream research and education network (REN) to announce five distinct IPv6 subprefixes in the 2002::/16 6to4 block corresponding to three EDU-A IPv4 prefixes (a/16, /18, and /20). This allowed us to measure the potential to launch a global IPv6 transition mechanism hijack without altering the path of any actual traffic.

Internet-Wide Scans. We survey the entire Internet IPv4 address space for open and accessible IPv6 tunnel relay services. We first issue a single ICMPv6 router solicitation encapsulated in IPv4 to discover any open ISATAP relays. We then issue an ICMPv6 echo request encapsulated in IPv4. These ICMPv6 messages uncover either 6to4 or raw protocol 41 processing nodes if we receive a corresponding ICMPv6 echo response at our control IPv6 destination.

Ethical and Privacy Considerations. Our experiments required careful planning and review to steer clear of compromising user privacy and to avoid adversely altering Internet application functionality. We performed several internal experiments to ensure that global experiments would not negatively impact users' connectivity or privacy. In all but the experiments being led and controlled by EDU-A, our experiments are limited to tunnel discovery and bootstrapping traffic. To ensure that there is no violation of the privacy of users, all data collection scripts aggregated and anonymized the results (raw data was not retained) without human intervention and the data collection was operated by computing support staff who verified the code's operation and only provided the anonymized, aggregated results to the research team. EDU-A deployed a local, production ISATAP relay, to which we had no direct access, in order to establish ground truth and ensure our attack scenarios could be carried out on real application traffic in practice without user intervention. We submitted a detailed description of our experimental protocol to our university's IRB prior to any experiments, and they determined that this research does not qualify as incorporating human subjects.

4   Analysis

The various legacy automatic transition mechanisms we examine are architecturally similar. They each consist of two fundamental types of systems, tunnel clients and tunnel relays. We present our analysis by examining the threats from the perspective of each system type. The primary vulnerability tunnel clients face is the threat of stealthy man-in-the-middle attacks on all traffic bound for IPv6 hosts. Tunnel relays on the other hand can be impersonated and abused. Impersonation attacks against relays can be enable MitM attacks against tunnel clients. Moreover, tunnel relay abuse can enable various kinds of unwanted activities such as service theft or origination spoofing attacks.

4.1   Attacks Against Tunnel Clients

DNS Capture. Since ISATAP clients typically perform a look up based on the client's default zone, we focus our attention on this mechanism where an attacker could most easily gain access to a number of zones without raising suspicion. Other types of DNS capture attacks, such as cache poisoning could also be used.

Our registered ISATAP domain names received approximately three million queries per month between April 2018 and May 2019. Recall that a DNS query

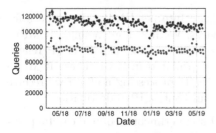
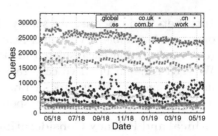
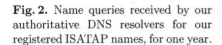

Fig. 2. Name queries received by our authoritative DNS resolvers for our registered ISATAP names, for one year.

Fig. 3. Most popular ISATAP name queries received by our authoritative DNS resolvers, for one year.

is the first step in bootstrapping an ISATAP tunnel client. Until we registered these names, the queries likely went unanswered and the client's ISATAP bootstrapping process ceased until a change in interface state restarted the process. The daily volume shown in Fig. 2 exhibits a noticeable work week oscillation, suggesting that many of these queries originate from end user systems that tend to go offline during the weekend. We observe a slow decline towards the end of the monitoring period, which may correspond with the roll out of new systems that have ISATAP disabled by default.

We also break down the queries for the six most popular domain names we registered in Fig. 3. The fact that these domains receive thousands of ISATAP queries per day suggests the relative frequency for more popular domains (e.g., ending in .comcast.net) will likely be orders-of-magnitude higher. We believe that our top level names are a relatively small sample of the coverage that attacks leveraging IPv6 automatic transition mechanisms can reach. When we examined the DNS-OARC DITL data we see relatively few ISATAP queries for existing zones, but tens of millions of queries for vendor, special-use, or names in private domain over the course of just two days.

In our experiments almost 3K out of 163K resolvers supply EDNS0 client subnet option data. While that is a small fraction of the total number of resolvers observed, over 30% of all queries contain client subnet data. This is due to the disproportionate query volume Google contributes, as their resolvers supply the client subnet data by default if they detect it is supported at the authoritative server. The distinct number of client subnets we see over the course of one year's worth of queries is 96,061. We geo-locate these client subnets to their country of origin and find that they are located all over the world. The extensive use of third-party DNS resolvers (e.g., Google) highlights that these entities are well positioned to impose protections.

We also examine transition mechanism queries seen at EDU-A and a cable modem ISP's resolvers by Microsoft Windows clients for one day in Fig. 4. This includes type A (IPv4 address mapping) queries for any name with the *isatap* prefix label, and the fully qualified domain names *6to4.ipv6.microsoft.com* or *teredo.ipv6.microsoft.com*. The cable modem ISP client population is largely

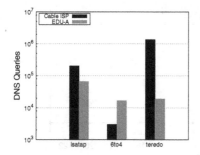 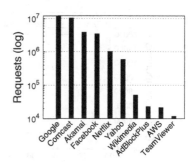

Fig. 4. Comparison of DNS queries for two networks.

Fig. 5. Top 10 destination domain requests seen at EDU-A.

behind consumer-grade NAT devices. This is reflected in the proportionally higher number of Teredo queries seen at the ISP than EDU-A. Nevertheless, ISATAP queries still make up a large amount of the transition mechanism activity observed in both environments.

Relay Capture. We extend our analysis of threats against clients with the operation of the EDU-A Functional and EDU-B Dysfunctional ISATAP tunnel relays. Figure 5 summarizes the most popular network destinations EDU-A ISA-TAP tunnel client users were destined for over the course of one 24-h period. The EDU-A network operations team reviewed these traffic patterns and they believed them to be expected client system traffic behavior that was running over IPv6 instead of IPv4. The traffic includes various forms of email communications, social networking, e-commerce activity, and scientific research.

Client connections to the EDU-B ISATAP relay came primarily, but not entirely, from the EDU-B user population. The ISATAP names registered in co.uk and net.br were also a popular source of ISATAP clients. The most popular IPv6 destinations from clients were concentrated at popular web hosting properties such as Google, Cloudflare, Microsoft, and a handful of content distribution providers. While most attempted traffic through the relay can be classified as HTTP(S), we also observed DNS, FTP, NTP, SMTP, SNMP, SSH, and VPN tunnel attempts. Figure 6 shows the eight destination ports that received the highest number of client connections from a random representative weekday, and that a significant amount of unencrypted HTTP and DNS traffic would be visible to a hypothetical attacker. Since most DNS stub resolvers do not perform DNSSEC-based authentication of answers, attackers could filter out A responses and leave only the valid AAAA answers, forcing all victim traffic to IPv6 capable hosts to transit the malicious tunnel.

Route Hijacking. In April 2019 we began originating five more-specific BGP routes within the 6to4 2002::/16 prefix from EDU-A. We wanted to evaluate whether we could successfully conduct a targeted attack against 6to4 traffic. The upstream REN agreed to allow these prefixes into their backbone, but they limited the propagation to a subset of regional REN participants for safety

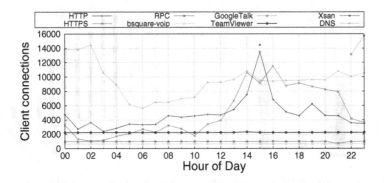

Fig. 6. Top destination services based on port numbers.

reasons; they were not relayed to commercial or international peering partners. Nonetheless, at least twelve REN participant networks installed these routes into their routing tables, and RouteViews [3] observed the route from over 30 networks, including multiple tier 1 ISPs. This experiment demonstrates that while customer route filtering may be common practice for ISPs, route filtering between large ISPs and RENs is typically less strict and often inconsistent. Since the IPv6 transition prefixes are not currently protected by the RPKI [35] and may be announced by any origin network, the feasibility of traffic capture is even easier than traditional unicast route hijacking. This experiment ran for many months and to the best of our knowledge there were no public reports or inquiries about the nature of these spurious announcements.

4.2   Attacks Against Tunnel Relays

Theft of Service. In November 2018 and April 2019 we surveyed the entire IPv4 address space for ISATAP-compatible open tunnel relays on the public Internet. The 2018 survey recorded 765 ICMPv6 router advertisement (RA) responses while the 2019 survey recorded 628 responses, totaling 841 unique addresses. Further examination suggests that these hosts are mostly Microsoft IIS web servers with firewalls disabled and forwarding capability for remote hosts activated. Their router advertisement responses typically include a number of available routes, most commonly 6to4 prefixes, but also some Teredo and unique local IPv6 unicast prefixes [27]. We did not find any probed hosts offering unique global IPv6 addresses. We classify these as ISATAP-capable since our client was able to successfully self-configure using the ISATAP address acquisition process.

Upon seeing how most open ISATAP tunnel relays would provide 6to4 addresses by default, in April 2019 we issued ICMPv6 echo request messages, encapsulated in IPv4 protocol 41 packets, to the entire IPv4 address space. Much to our chagrin we discovered 1,546,843 IPv4 addresses around the globe would relay the enclosed IPv6 message to the intended destination. We were surprised that such a large number of system configurations not only had the 6to4 mechanism enabled, but were left unprotected on the public Internet, allowing anyone

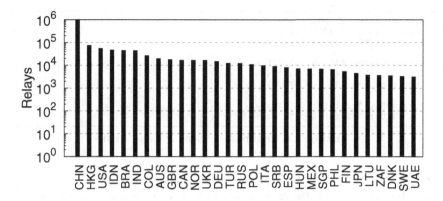

Fig. 7. Open 6to4 relays' country of origin.

to relay traffic through them. We break down those relays according to their geographic distribution and find that China, Hong Kong, USA, Indonesia and Brazil have the most relays. We provide a list of the top 30 countries in Fig. 7.

We ran an *nmap* [24] survey on a sample of these open IPv6 tunnel relays and discovered an alarming number of fingerprints matched backbone routers from one of the world's largest networking vendors, which we confirmed through two different network operators. We estimated that approximately 7% of the addresses discovered were from this particular vendor. This particular brand of equipment exhibited particularly curious behavior. They process IPv4 protocol 41 datagrams by first removing the IPv4 header. Then the IPv6 destination address is consulted and the IPv6 datagram is forwarded along its way. In other words, this particular class of equipment acts as an IPv6 default router for any IPv6 traffic it receives, even if encapsulated in IPv4 first. This led to additional interesting observations, two of which we briefly describe below.

Infrastructure Abuse. These vendor backbone routers had a noteworthy peculiarity. They were rarely configured to support the 6to4 mechanism. Therefore, if the embedded IPv6 destination is the 6to4 equivalent destination of the backbone router's own IPv4 address, the packet will attempt to follow whatever path the router has to the 2002::/16 prefix. A 6to4 network service provider upon receiving this packet will examine the IPv6 destination, put the IPv6 message into an IPv4 packet and send it back towards the router's IPv4 address where the process repeats until the enclosed IPv6 hop limit field eventually expires, but not before the packet iterates through this loop. This leads to a potential DoS attack where sending one tunnel packet can expand to multiple packets cycling in a loop between the 6to4 gateway and the backbone router.

Infrastructure Disclosure. Another observation from those backbone routers appeared when we attempted to evaluate the IPv6 path of the aforementioned loops. Output from traceroute often showed our relayed packets were able to traverse IPv6 paths not accessible via the native public IPv6 Internet. Listing 1.1

```
$ traceroute -n -q1 2002:c000:0201::1
traceroute to 2002:c000:0201::1,
30 hops max, 80 byte packets
1  *
2  2001:4958:300:449::b  63.779 ms
3  2001:4958:300:449::a  63.764 ms
4  ::ffff:64.230.193.173  70.472 ms
5  *
6  2001:4958:300:d::1b  64.748 ms
7  2001:470:1:802::1  64.122 ms
```

Listing 1.1. Traceroute traversing hidden paths.

shows the partial path through an IPv6 open relay on a North American ISP network (the target destination address has been anonymized). In this example, traceroute should have terminated at the first hop. However, this class of equipment blindly forwards this packet along a path towards a route advertised for the 2002::/16 prefix. The fourth hop shows an IPv4-mapped address, which should not appear on the public Internet. Access to addresses and paths intended for internal-only use may facilitate network reconnaissance or attacks that bypass security policies.

Origination Spoofing. Open tunnel relay systems not only allowed us to obtain an IPv6 address and relay traffic through them, they facilitated source IP address spoofing. Most operators of networks, where directly attached hosts emit packets, perform a form of source address validation (SAV) on IP datagrams at the first hop ingress router [5]. However, routers only perform this validation on the outer IP layer, not on the IPv6 source address of encapsulated packets. We were able to set the IPv6 source address to most any value of our choosing. The tunnel relays re-encapsulate our original IPv6 datagrams inside a new outer IPv4 header using the tunnel's IPv4 source address before relaying further. By the time a 6to4 gateway finally receives the packet, all SAV of the IPv6 address has been bypassed. If coupled with a reflection and amplification style attack, this behavior can significantly complicate denial-of-service attack mitigation.

5 Discussion

Susceptible Population. According to online reports, over 30% of Microsoft Windows machines in the wild [42] run OS versions up to Windows 8.1, which have these mechanisms enabled *by default*. While more recent versions of Windows have begun to disable all legacy IPv6 transition mechanisms, the functionality still remains in the operating system. Judging by the significant volume of DNS queries we see for ISATAP names and the vast number of open tunnel relays on many other types of systems, we can safely conclude these mechanisms stubbornly persist, posing risks not only to the systems and users, but to the entire Internet.

Countermeasures. Effective mitigation strategies require significant global coordination as we outline below. We summarize various mitigations that can be implemented to prevent exploitation of these transition mechanisms.

Protocol 41 is used to identify whether an IPv6 datagram is encapsulated within an IP payload, and is at the epicenter of these transition mechanisms. Limiting the transmission of protocol 41 packets would mitigate most attacks we uncover. Some part of transition mechanism bootstrapping, such as DNS queries, may continue unfettered, but would be rendered largely ineffective if protocol 41 packets cannot be relayed.

DNS. As we have shown, the most popular laptop and desktop operating system has made extensive use of DNS to locate and prepare IPv6 links. This feature is susceptible to attacks from off-path attackers. However, the DNS infrastructure is also a place to apply control and policies. Operators of resolvers can exert control over these well known transition mechanism names, either by configuring a local authoritative zone for the names or using response policy zones (RPZ) [47], to render them inactive. Domain name registries, registrars, and ICANN could institute policies to declare certain special-use names as off-limits for registration.

Routing. Legacy IPv6 automatic transition mechanisms such as 6to4 and Teredo utilize well known address prefixes. The routing system provides an operationally centralized means of control to monitor and limit the dissemination of route announcements covering the well known transition address space.

OS and Network Configurations. It is a positive step that Microsoft has disabled these mechanisms in recent versions of their OS. However, reports of older Windows hosts in the wild and our measurements indicate that millions of systems still have these mechanisms turned on. Furthermore, the vast number of open tunnel relays we identified are rarely Windows systems, highlighting the fact that automatic transition threats span a variety of operating systems and device types. These automatic mechanisms can be disabled (or removed) from individual systems by default.

Responsible Disclosure. We have proactively engaged the vendor and operational community for mitigating the attacks we described that can target publicly vulnerable systems. After months of verification, software refactoring, and testing the routing operating system code, a router vendor issued a "high" alert encouraging customers to upgrade or apply configuration work-arounds to avoid the vulnerability. Another hardware vendor verified an issue with their equipment and sent us one to further evaluate in our lab. We also leveraged our personal contacts in the incident response and network security community [1,2,23,31] to coordinate the responsible disclosure of our findings to other vendors and operators affected by the suite of threats we uncovered. Our findings have also renewed discussions in the IPv6 community to officially deprecate these transition mechanisms, encouraging their removal not only from service, but from being made available in systems even when not enabled by default. One of the largest 6to4 service providers has also informed us they are considering a complete shut down of their relay service. Finally, with the help of threat intelligence reporting organizations [4,6,14], notifications for systems identified to be at risk can be disseminated to administrative contacts before these findings enter the public sphere. These organizations can also use our findings to build automated scanning and alerting reports for the Internet community at large.

6   Related Work

IPv6 Concerns. Ullrich et al. [46] provide a broad overview of security and privacy concerns related to IPv6, and while they mention tunneling between IP protocols, they do not mention the lack of authentication on tunnel creation that enables the attacks we describe.

IPv6 as an Evasion Technique. Carter [11] warned of attackers setting up proxy interfaces to relay traffic between IPv4 and IPv6 hosts. US-Cert [18] drew attention to malware that enables IPv6 transport, including automatic transition mechanisms, to evade IPv4-only defenses. Blumbergs et al. [8] discussed the limitations intrusion detection systems have when IPv6 transition mechanism tunnels are used for data exfiltration. Czyz et al. [17] highlighted the discrepancies in the access to specific ports. Hong et al. [28] found several vulnerabilities in cellular networks.

Measuring of Transition Mechanisms. While IPv6 deployment has increased in recent years [12,15,19], the underlying factors influencing its adoption [38] indicate that it's unlikely that IPv4 will disappear anytime soon. Czyz et al. [16] deployed an IPv6 sensor on unused address space to observe unsolicited activity. In a similar study, Karis et al. [32] conducted active measurements of IPv6-enabled web clients. Elrich et al. [22] explored the behavior and traffic patterns seen by active Teredo and 6to4 clients on a large academic network and compared them to automatic tunneling mechanisms and native IPv4 communications. Savola compiled a number of observations in the operation of a large, public 6to4 relay service [40] and characterized client system behavior and traffic patterns.

Traffic Hijacking Attacks. Very similar to the MitM attacks we describe are the Chen et al. [10] hijacking attacks enabled by the Web Proxy Auto-Discovery (WPAD) protocol. Nakibly and Arov discussed a class of routing loop attacks using IPv6 tunnels [37], which took advantage of inconsistency between different transition technologies.

7   Conclusion

We presented a comprehensive exploration of legacy IPv6 transition mechanisms on the Internet along with a series of experiments demonstrating the security and privacy risks they continue to pose. We conducted a study using data collected from multiple network vantage points and found a significant number of hosts run operating systems with IPv6 automatic transition mechanisms enabled by default. These mechanisms often lie dormant, idling by until the right set of circumstances triggers their use. If an attacker provisions the necessary resources or successfully positions themselves in the network path, they can covertly intercept all IPv6 traffic, including traffic towards critical and high-value services like Google and Facebook. Our DNS registration and route announcement experiments explored the practicality and feasibility of different attack vectors that capture adversaries of varying sophistication and resourcefulness. Furthermore, we found a significant number of open tunnel relays, including many on high-cost specialized ISP backbone routers that can facilitate a wide range of attacks such as IPv4 address spoofing and policy bypass. While we have set things in motion by disclosing our findings to certain network administrators, hardware vendors, ISPs, and incident reporting organizations, we hope to bring more attention to the prevalence and risk of legacy IPv6 automatic transition mechanisms in order to accelerate their extinction and countermeasures.

Acknowledgments. We would like to thank our shepherd Ioana Alexandrina Livadariu and the anonymous reviewers for their valuable feedback. We are grateful and indebted to a number groups and individuals that helped make this work possible. The ACCC at UIC, IS at DePaul University, DNS-OARC, Randy Bush, Brian Carpenter, Geoff Huston, Alex Latzko, and the anonymous network operators and vendors who helped validate our findings, or worked to mitigate potential problems. This work was partially supported by the National Science Foundation under contract CNS-1934597. Any opinions, findings, conclusions, or recommendations expressed herein are those of the authors, and do not necessarily reflect those of the US Government.

References

1. NSP Security Forum. https://puck.nether.net/mailman/listinfo/nsp-security
2. Ops-Trust. https://portal.ops-trust.net
3. RouteViews. https://www.routeviews.org
4. Shadowserver. https://www.shadowserver.org/
5. Spoofer: Protect your network and the global Internet. https://spoofer.caida.org
6. Team Cymru. https://www.team-cymru.com/
7. Akamai: Akamai State of the Internet IPv6 Visual Adoption. https://www.akamai.com/us/en/resources/our-thinking/state-of-the-internet-report/state-of-the-internet-ipv6-adoption-visualization.jsp
8. Blumbergs, B., Pihelgas, M., Kont, M., Maennel, O., Vaarandi, R.: Creating and detecting IPv6 transition mechanism-based information exfiltration covert channels. In: Brumley, B.B., Röning, J. (eds.) NordSec 2016. LNCS, vol. 10014, pp. 85–100. Springer, Cham (2016). https://doi.org/10.1007/978-3-319-47560-8_6
9. Carpenter, B.E., Moore, K.: Connection of IPv6 domains via IPv4 clouds. RFC 3056, RFC Editor (February 2001). https://rfc-editor.org/rfc/rfc3056.txt
10. Chen, Q.A., Osterweil, E., Thomas, M., Mao, Z.M.: MitM attack by name collision: cause analysis and vulnerability assessment in the new gTLD era. In: Proceedings of the 2016 IEEE Symposium on Security and Privacy, S&P 2016, pp. 675–690 (2016)
11. Cisco: Securing IPv6 transition technologies (2011). https://web.archive.org/web/blogs.cisco.com/security/securing-ipv6-transition-technologies

12. Colitti, L., Gunderson, S.H., Kline, E., Refice, T.: Evaluating IPv6 adoption in the Internet. In: Krishnamurthy, A., Plattner, B. (eds.) PAM 2010. LNCS, vol. 6032, pp. 141–150. Springer, Heidelberg (2010). https://doi.org/10.1007/978-3-642-12334-4_15
13. Contavalli, C., Gaast, W.V.D., Lawrence, D.C., Kumari, W.: Client subnet in DNS queries. RFC 7871, RFC Editor (May 2016). https://rfc-editor.org/rfc/rfc7871.txt
14. CyberGreen: Cybergreen. https://www.cybergreen.net
15. Czyz, J., Allman, M., Zhang, J., Iekel-Johnson, S., Osterweil, E., Bailey, M.: Measuring IPv6 adoption. In: Proceedings of the SIGCOMM Conference, SIGCOMM 2014, pp. 87–98 (2014)
16. Czyz, J., Lady, K., Miller, S.G., Bailey, M., Kallitsis, M., Karir, M.: Understanding IPv6 Internet background radiation. In: Proceedings of the 2013 Internet Measurement Conference, IMC 2013, pp. 105–118 (2013)
17. Czyz, J., Luckie, M., Allman, M., Bailey, M.: Don't forget to lock the back door! A characterization of IPv6 network security policy. In: Proceedings of the Network and Distributed System Security Symposium, NDSS 2016 (2016)
18. Department of Homeland Security: Malware Tunneling in IPv6 (2012). https://www.us-cert.gov/security-publications/malware-tunneling-ipv6
19. Dhamdhere, A., Luckie, M., Huffaker, B., Claffy, K., Elmokashfi, A., Aben, E.: Measuring the deployment of IPv6: topology, routing and performance. In: Proceedings of the 2012 Internet Measurement Conference, IMC 2012, pp. 537–550 (2012)
20. DNS-OARC: DITL traces and analysis. https://www.dns-oarc.net/oarc/data/ditl
21. Durand, A., Droms, R., Woodyatt, J., Lee, Y.L.: Dual-stack lite broadband deployments following IPv4 exhaustion. RFC 6333, RFC Editor (August 2011). https://rfc-editor.org/rfc/rfc6333.txt
22. Elich, M., Velan, P., Jirsik, T., Celeda, P.: An investigation into Teredo and 6to4 transition mechanisms: traffic analysis. In: Proceedings of the 7th IEEE Workshop on Network Measurements, WLN 2013, pp. 1018–1024 (2013)
23. FIRST.org: Forum of incident response security teams. https://www.first.org
24. Fyodor: Nmap - network mapper. https://nmap.org
25. Gleeson, T., Thaler, D., Templin, F.: Intra-site automatic tunnel addressing protocol (ISATAP). RFC 5214, RFC Editor (March 2008). https://rfc-editor.org/rfc/rfc5214.txt
26. Google: Google IPv6 statistics. https://www.google.com/intl/en/ipv6/statistics.html
27. Hinden, R.M., Haberman, B.: Unique local IPv6 unicast addresses. RFC 4193, RFC Editor (October 2005). https://rfc-editor.org/rfc/rfc4193.txt
28. Hong, H., Cet al.: When cellular networks met IPv6: security problems of middleboxes in IPv6 cellular networks. In: Proceedings of the IEEE European Symposium on Security and Privacy, Euro S&P 2017, pp. 595–609 (2017)
29. Huitema, C.: Teredo: tunneling IPv6 over UDP through network address translations (NATs). RFC 4380, RFC Editor (February 2006). https://rfc-editor.org/rfc/rfc4380.txt
30. IANA: IPv6 global unicast address assignments. https://www.iana.org/assignments/ipv6-unicast-address-assignments/ipv6-unicast-address-assignments.xhtml
31. Internet2: Internet2. https://www.internet2.edu

32. Karir, M., Huston, G., Michaelson, G., Bailey, M.: Understanding IPv6 populations in the wild. In: Roughan, M., Chang, R. (eds.) PAM 2013. LNCS, vol. 7799, pp. 256–259. Springer, Heidelberg (2013). https://doi.org/10.1007/978-3-642-36516-4_27

33. Kastenholz, F., Partridge, D.C.: Technical criteria for choosing IP the next generation (IPng). RFC 1726, RFC Editor (December 1994). https://rfc-editor.org/rfc/rfc1726.txt

34. Krishnan, S., Davies, E.B., Savola, P.: IPv6 transition/co-existence security considerations. RFC 4942, RFC Editor (September 2007). https://doi.org/10.17487/RFC4942, https://rfc-editor.org/rfc/rfc4942.txt

35. Lepinski, M., Kent, S.: An infrastructure to support secure Internet routing. RFC 6480, RFC Editor (February 2012). https://rfc-editor.org/rfc/rfc6480.txt

36. Mawatari, M., Kawashim, M., Bryne, C.: 464XLAT: combination of stateful and stateless translation. RFC 6877, RFC Editor (April 2013). https://rfc-editor.org/rfc/rfc6877.txt

37. Nakibly, G., Arov, M.: Routing loop attacks using IPv6 tunnels. In: Proceedings of the 3rd USENIX Workshop on Offensive Technologies, WOOT 2009, pp. 1–7 (2009)

38. Nikkhah, M., Guerin, R.: Migrating the Internet to IPv6: an exploration of the when and why. IEEE/ACM Trans. Netw. 24(4), 2291–2304 (2016)

39. Patel, C., Savola, P.: Security considerations for 6to4. RFC 3964, RFC Editor (December 2004). https://rfc-editor.org/rfc/rfc3964.txt

40. Savola, P.: Observations of IPv6 traffic on a 6to4 relay. ACM SIGCOMM Comput. Commun. Rev. 35(1), 23–28 (2005)

41. Schinazi, D., Pauly, T.: Happy eyeballs version 2: better connectivity using concurrency. RFC 8305, RFC Editor (December 2017). https://rfc-editor.org/rfc/rfc8305.txt

42. StatCounter: Desktop windows version market share worldwide. http://gs.statcounter.com/windows-version-market-share/desktop/worldwide

43. Thaler, D., Draves, R., Matsumoto, A., Chown, T.: Default address selection for internet protocol version 6 (IPv6). RFC 6724, RFC Editor (September 2012). https://rfc-editor.org/rfc/rfc6724.txt

44. Thurrott, P.: Windows 10 version 1803 surges to 90 percent usage share (2018). https://www.thurrott.com/windows/windows-10/176435/windows-10-version-1803-surges-to-90-percent-usage-share

45. Townsley, M., Troan, O.: Pv6 rapid deployment on IPv4 infrastructures (6rd) - protocol specification. RFC 5969, RFC Editor (August 2010). https://rfc-editor.org/rfc/rfc5969.txt

46. Ullrich, J., Krombholz, K., Hobel, H., Dabrowski, A., Weippl, E.: IPv6 security: attacks and countermeasures in a nutshell. In: Proceedings of the 8th USENIX Workshop on Offensive Technologies, WOOT 2014, p. 5 (2014)

47. Vixie, P., Schryver, V.: DNS response policy zones. https://dnsrpz.info

An Online Method for Estimating the Wireless Device Count via Privacy-Preserving Wi-Fi Fingerprinting

Pegah Torkamandi[(⊠)], Ljubica Kärkkäinen, and Jörg Ott

Chair of Connected Mobility, Technical University of Munich, Munich, Germany
{torkaman,kaerkkal,ott}@in.tum.de

Abstract. Initially envisioned to accelerate association of mobile devices in wireless networks, broadcasting of Wi-Fi probe requests has opened avenues for researchers and network practitioners to exploit information sent out in this type of frames for observing devices' digital footprints and for their tracking. One of the applications for this is crowd estimation. Noticing the privacy risks that this default mode of operation poses, device vendors have introduced MAC address randomization—a privacy preserving technique by which mobile devices periodically generate random hardware addresses contained in probe requests. In this paper, we propose a method for estimating the number of wireless devices in the environment by means of analyzing Wi-Fi probe requests sent by those devices and in spite of MAC address randomization. Our solution extends previous work that uses Wi-Fi fingerprinting based on the timing information of probe requests. The only additional information we extract from probe requests is the MAC address, making our method minimally privacy-invasive. Our estimation method is also nearly real-time. We conduct several experiments to collect wireless measurements in different static environments and we use these measurements to validate our method. Through an extensive analysis and parameter tuning, we show the robustness of our method.

Keywords: Wi-Fi fingerprinting · Wi-Fi probe requests · MAC address randomization · Wireless measurements · Crowd estimation

1 Introduction

Crowd (density) estimation refers to a set of techniques used to estimate the number of people at a given location. Traditionally used for security purposes such as assessing occupancy levels and people flows in public areas for evacuation systems planning, crowd estimation today has found application in various domains: from monitoring and management of large public events [22] to infrastructure design (e.g., of smart spaces [25]) to surveillance [15], as well as in business domain [24]. Providing an accurate estimation of the crowd size, also its real-time dynamics, is therefore of high importance for the said applications.

Owing to the widespread adoption of mobile devices (e.g., smartphones), the detection of a device presence can be used as a proxy indicator for a person's presence. One of the ways to achieve this is through tracking Wi-Fi and Bluetooth activity of the device [10], for instance, by capturing and analyzing Wi-Fi probe requests sent by the

© Springer Nature Switzerland AG 2021
O. Hohlfeld et al. (Eds.): PAM 2021, LNCS 12671, pp. 406–423, 2021.
https://doi.org/10.1007/978-3-030-72582-2_24

device in an unassociated state. However, the possibility to track individuals by this type of device tracking raised serious privacy concerns and resulted in countermeasures that device vendors are increasingly employing. One such measure is *MAC address randomization*—a privacy technique whereby devices do not use their real hardware addresses during active scanning, but instead generate and broadcast random MAC addresses. It has been shown, however, that using randomization cannot fully obfuscate the device activity and is therefore still susceptible to attacks and other sorts of exploitation [11, 13, 19]. This is because devices exhibit certain (probing) patterns which can be used for their identification and tracking.

In this paper, we seek to answer the question whether it is possible to count devices that use randomization—in a privacy-preserving way and based on the observed characteristics of their probing behavior—and furthermore, if this can be done with high accuracy such that it can be employed in applications to accurately estimate the number of devices in the environment. To answer these questions, we develop a method for mapping randomized MAC addresses to the same physical device (Sect. 3). We conduct several experiments and collect wireless measurements in different static environments, i.e., when the number of people remains constant (Sect. 4), which we use to validate our method and verify that it can achieve reasonable accuracy (Sect. 5). Section 6 surveys related work. As we conclude this study, we also note that our approach has several limitations, which we will address in our future work (Sect. 7).

2   Preliminaries

Let us first briefly provide background and assumptions used in our work.

Device Fingerprinting via Probe Requests. A probe request is a type of a management frame in wireless communication sent by stations during active scanning. Early fingerprinting techniques used the time difference between consecutive request frames, *inter frame arrival time* (IFAT) [5] to characterize the device's unique probing pattern. First, all frames containing the device's unique MAC address are grouped together, to calculate IFATs between captured frames. Then, by using the binning method, IFATs are assigned to the equal size discrete bins, and the frequency of IFATs in each bin is used to determine the device's unique identifier. However, this approach was developed before vendors started implementing randomization in devices.

MAC Address Randomization. Wi-Fi enabled devices continuously send frames for wireless communication which can be captured by a passive observer. These frames contain a unique identifier—the device's MAC address. For privacy protection, device vendors and operating system developers are currently deploying a countermeasure on new devices: MAC address randomization, where the idea is to use, instead of the device's MAC address, a new, frequently changed random identifier [13]. MAC address randomization is deployed in most operating systems, i.e., Android since version 6 [1], iOS since version 8 [17], and Windows version 10 and later [21].

Assumptions on the Consistency of the Device's Probing Behavior. Extending the approach from [5], recent works [11, 13] showed that the device behavior is relatively consistent, and can be tracked even when randomization is in place. This forms the base for our approach, detailed in the next section.

3 Methods

In this section we describe our proposed method for mapping randomized MAC addresses to the corresponding physical devices. The mapping method utilizes solely the MAC addresses extracted from probe requests and the timing information from time stamps when these probe requests were captured by our measurement kit. We first introduce some terms that we will use throughout the paper, and then describe initial data pre-processing steps.

3.1 Terminology and Definitions

We distinguish between *randomized* and *globally unique (non-randomized)* MAC addresses by examining the second least significant bit of Organizationally Unique Identifier (OUI) part of the MAC address: the MAC address is randomized if this bit is set to 1 and globally unique otherwise [7].

A *counting time window* (CTW) is the time interval on which our counting algorithm operates. This is the smallest time interval that allows for accurate wireless behavior fingerprinting, while still performing counting in an online manner.

A *burst* is a set of probe requests sent within a short time interval (not longer than 100 ms) [12]. During a burst, the device sends a number of probe requests, actively searching for previously accessed Wi-Fi networks. Our key assumption—also used in [13]—is that even when a device uses randomization, the randomized address remains constant for all probe requests over at least two (entire) bursts. To assess how the timing information of intra-burst probing activity can be used for fingerprinting, we group all the probe request frames sent by the same randomized MAC address and calculate the time difference between time stamps for each two consecutive frames. The distribution of these time differences across all randomized MAC addresses is skewed and shows that more than 50% of them are lower than or equal to 10 ms. This property does not aid characterization of unique devices, thus in the following we use inter-burst time differences, specifically the time difference between the timestamps of the first frame in a burst and the last frame in the previous burst. With this choice, we are trading off abundant low-resolution data points for the few more characteristic ones, since we only observe a few bursts per MAC address (the average number is 3.7 while 93% MAC addresses appear in less than 10 bursts).

To characterize the behavior of a wireless device that uses randomization, we look at the *MAC address signature*. A signature is a vector that contains information about the number of bursts captured within a CTW, and time differences between them. To generate a signature, we first group all the frames with the same MAC address and calculate the time difference between each two consecutive bursts, *delta*, then discretize these continuous delta values using the equal-width binning method (as described in [5]), and finally obtain the vector of delta frequencies by normalizing the count of deltas in each bin. For instance, one vector of delta frequencies obtained with the bin size of 0.2 s can include 20% of deltas mapped to the bin 0s (that is, shorter than 0.2 s), 30% mapped to the bin 0.2 s (deltas are between 0.2 s and 0.4 s), 40% falling into the 0.4 s bin and 10% into the 1.2 s bin. The average number of bursts containing randomized MAC addresses in the datasets (Sect. 4.2) is about four, thus the average number of deltas in a vector is three. Each signature corresponds to a MAC address, and is assigned the attributes *lastSeen* and *validation*. *lastSeen* is the time stamp of the last probe included to make the signature, and *validation* attribute is a boolean parameter that indicates whether the signature is still valid (being used by a device).

Wireless devices that use randomization occasionally generate new randomized MAC addresses. By a *device cluster* we consider a set of randomized MAC address signatures which are assumed to belong to the same physical device. Each cluster is assigned the following attributes: a *set* of signatures, *count*, *lastSeen*, and *validation*. The *count* attribute is the number of valid signatures in the cluster, *lastSeen* is the latest time when a signature was mapped to the cluster, and *validation* is a boolean flag for the device cluster's validity. We will use the term *database* to refer to the set of all observed clusters. In Sect. 3.2 we explain how MAC addresses are mapped to a device cluster.

A *signature time window* (STW), of length $sigTime$, is the time interval during which the device uses a single randomized MAC address. In our datasets, we observed that the distribution of time lengths during which one MAC address appears in probe bursts, the MAC address *lifetime*, is long-tailed with the average value of about two minutes. Specifically, in one of the datasets 91% of MAC address lifetimes are shorter than this, while the average is 92 s. Thus, to make a signature, we need to track each randomized MAC address for at least two minutes. To ensure correct characterization of the MAC address signature the chosen CTW duration, denoted as $countTime$, should be larger than the STW length, $countTime > sigTime$.

3.2 Mapping Randomized MAC Addresses to a Device Cluster

The mapping of different signatures that correspond to different randomized MAC addresses, to the same device cluster is based on the similarity between signatures. In order to map a new signature to a cluster, we calculate the distance between a newly observed signature and other valid clusters already present in the database.

Let DB be the database, C be a cluster in DB, D the distance threshold, $\mathcal{B}$ the set of bin values, and S a signature in C ($S \in C$). Let p_b^S and q_b be the percentage of burst deltas for the bin attribute b of the signature S and the new signature, respectively. We use the method from [5] and Eqs. (1), (2) to calculate the distance between the new signature and all signatures already assigned to the cluster C. If all distances between the new signature and other signatures in the cluster are lower than the distance threshold, then the new signature can be mapped to the cluster (Eq. (1)). If more than one cluster satisfies the distance threshold for the new signature, then we assign the new signature to a cluster which has the lowest total distance (D_C), computed as the sum of all distances between the new signature and other signatures in the cluster (Eq. (2)).

$$F = \min(\forall S \in C(D - \sum_{b=1}^{|\mathcal{B}|} |p_b^S - q_b|)) \tag{1}$$

$$D_C = \begin{cases} \infty, & \text{if } F < 0 \\ \sum_{S=1}^{|C|} \sum_{b=1}^{|\mathcal{B}|} |p_b^S - q_b|), & \text{if } F \geq 0 \end{cases} \tag{2}$$

Now we can proceed with the details of our device-counting algorithm.

3.3 Device Counting

We now turn to our proposed online method for estimating the number of wireless devices present in the environment, which is based on the MAC addresses extracted from captured probe requests. Since a globally unique MAC address corresponds to a single device, the focus of our method is on mapping of randomized MAC addresses.

Our method starts by creating the initial database of device clusters (Algorithm 1). First, it creates signatures for all randomized MAC addresses observed in the first *boot-strapTime* minutes of the experiment (Algorithm 2). Next, we use k-means clustering to map similar signatures to a device cluster (Algorithm 3). To assess the optimal number of clusters k, we apply *silhouette coefficient analysis*. This method uses the silhouette coefficient metric, which measures how similar an object is to other objects in the same cluster. The optimal number of clusters is chosen such that the silhouette coefficient averaged over all samples is maximized. After the clustering step, the initial database of device clusters contains k clusters; each cluster is assigned three attributes: *lastSeen, validation*, and *count* (Sect. 3).

Generating signatures for online estimation requires a certain degree of caution. Recall from Sect. 3.1 that our algorithm proceeds in time increments defined by the CTW. Also recall that to accurately estimate a signature, we need to observe probe requests for a time interval no shorter than the signature time window. Since devices send bursts of probe requests in a non-deterministic manner, it can happen that one burst is split across two consecutive CTWs, as depicted in Fig. 1. In this figure, *startTime* and *endTime* are the limits of the CTW, and *MAC1* and *MAC2* are two observed MAC addresses. The last burst sent by the device with *MAC1* covers two CTWs. Splitting this burst into two and generating two signatures would lead to incorrect characterization of the device's probing behavior. To avoid this, we delay making the complete signature until the second CTW and ignore the burst's appearance in the first window, or more precisely in the interval $[startTime, endTime - sigTime]$. Note that this can also occur when generating the initial cluster database, and the same principle applies.

After *bootstrapTime* has elapsed, the method proceeds by consuming captured probes from the dataset in the next CTW, as well as those probe frames passed from the previous CTW, and by generating the corresponding signatures (Algorithm 2). Then,

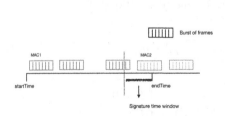

Fig. 1. The effect of the CTW and STW on the device counting.

Fig. 2. Raspberry Pi equipped with four Wi-Fi adapters and external battery.

in order to map a new input signature to the appropriate cluster, we calculate the distance between the new signature and all the valid clusters in the database as described in Sect. 3.2. If none of the clusters satisfies the distance threshold condition, a new cluster containing the new signature is created. Next, we check if the MAC address of the input signature is in the database and was seen in the previous CTW. If this is the case, we compare the cluster of the old signature, C_1 with that of the new signature, C_2, and if $C_1 = C_2$ we increase the cluster's count and update its *lastSeen* value to the *lastSeen* of the new signature. Otherwise, if $C_1 \neq C_2$, either the new signature belongs to the new device with the same randomized MAC address, or the device remained present but changed its probing behavior. As the goal of our work is to count the number of present devices, these reasons do not impact the counting part. Thus, in this case we map the new signature to C_2, decrement the C_1's count, and invalidate the old signature. Finally, we map the new signature to its cluster and update the database, the cluster's *count* and *lastSeen*. The number of unique valid clusters, each representing a device, in a given CTW corresponds to the number of detected devices during this time.

We have observed that some clusters in the database do not get updated for a long time (about 30 min), which implies that neither new nor old signatures have been observed. The reasons for this could be that the device has moved out of the range of our testing kit or stopped probing—hence no probes have been captured recently, or that the device changed its signature, that is, its probing behavior. The exact reason, however, cannot be easily determined. We proceed by excluding this cluster from further consideration. We assume that a cluster is valid for $clusterValidTime = 1$ h after the parameter *lastSeen* has been updated, and invalidate clusters that do not satisfy this condition. A few words about the choice of $clusterValidTime$ are in order: One hour is a rather conservative bound which ensures re-identification of the device that has been silent for a long time, after it becomes active again. On the other hand, if we needed to choose a tighter bound (e.g., to reduce the space complexity of our algorithm) we could set $clusterValidTime$ to a value not shorter than *countTime* (a fixed lower bound). In either case, the method produces correct results since we are only interested in the total count of devices (not in tracking of individual ones), and simultaneously reducing and increasing the number of clusters by one (for each invalidate cluster) does not change the total count.

To summarize, having generated a database of collected signatures we can map randomized MAC addresses to corresponding devices and subsequently, estimate the number of devices observed in the experiment environment.

4   Experiments and Datasets

This section details the setup of the experiments where our data was collected, and the acquired datasets used for evaluation.

4.1   Data Collection

We use a wireless sniffing kit inspired by [18]. The kit consists of a battery-powered Raspberry Pi 3 (Model B) and four external Wi-Fi adapters (Fig. 2). We opt for a multi-adapter setup for increased spectrum coverage, allowing the system to passively listen to four different Wi-Fi channels in the 2.4 and 5 GHz bands.[1] The channels are chosen from a preselected set in a round-robin fashion. We choose channels 1 and 11 in the 2.4 GHz band and channels 36 and 44 in the 5 Ghz band), thus avoiding channel switching, relying on the mobile devices to perform scanning across all channels. We use `airodump-ng` [2] for channel management and `tshark`(1) for packet capturing, with the appropriate kernel filtering to only collect control frames but no data traffic.

4.2 Datasets

We seek to capture Wi-Fi probe packet traces in an environment with a static user (and device) population and hence choose international flights of at least two hours flight time. The aircraft were equipped with onboard Wi-Fi so that running Wi-Fi devices throughout the flight was permissible. The three specific flights (from 2020) during which we collected the datasets used in this paper were between European countries, their durations being 3, 3, and 2.5 h, respectively. We denote the datasets $DatasetN, N = 1, 2, 3$. We trim the recorded datasets to ensure that only packets captured during flight time are considered, resulting in 2.5 h of data ($Dataset1, Dataset2$) and 2 h for $Dataset3$. The total number of passengers and crew on the two 3 h flights were 148 and 157, respectively.

Ethics Considerations. Device fingerprinting and counting methods, such as those we propose, may raise privacy concerns. As noted above, only Wi-Fi management frames were collected and, of those, we only evaluated the (randomized) source MAC address and frame timing. No SSIDs were inspected and no attempt is made to identify individuals. By its very intent and design, our method focuses on group size estimation with minimal information. Therefore, we believe that our method does not pose any threat to the privacy of the individuals.

5 Evaluation

We first conduct the analysis of our method's robustness, carried out in order to tune the parameters used in the method's algorithms. We then validate the proposed method, by evaluating its performance on three datasets representing static environments.

5.1 Parameter Tuning

Wi-Fi fingerprinting techniques that use timing information of the probe requests are based on the assumption that the device behavior is relatively stable and can be characterized by a unique signature [5, 11, 12, 19]. Therefore, an accurate representation of the MAC address signature is essential for capturing probing behavior and mapping multiple randomized MAC addresses to a single device. This work utilizes the same approach and extends these earlier techniques, using the observations obtained through our exploratory analysis. Based on the datasets we collected, our initial analysis revealed that the choice of parameters used for making and comparing signatures is fundamental, since it affects the method's robustness and applicability across different datasets.

---

[1] While, with just four adapters, we do not obtain full channel coverage and thus may miss frames, this leaner design makes the system portable, e.g., to be carried in a backpack.

Specifically, two key parameters with the greatest impact on the signature creation are *bin size B* and *distance threshold D*. However, the parameter values suggested in [5, 13] ($B = 0.8$ s, $D = 0.4$) could not be employed in our setup since they would render signature generation inaccurate, especially the large bin size (Sect. 3.1). First, the majority of the inter-burst deltas in our datasets are smaller than the suggested bin size, with about half of them shorter than 40 ms. Second, device distributions across the examined datasets differ: Notice that our datasets are fairly recent and therefore more likely to contain higher proportion of devices that deploy randomization, which were less represented in the older datasets used for parametrization. Therefore, the first step towards adjusting our method was parameter tunning. We performed grid search to find optimal values for bin size and distance threshold. In the following we introduce the evaluation metric we used for parameter tuning, and we elaborate on the impact of the two examined parameters.

Evaluation Metric. Our algorithm creates a database of clusters, each cluster holding similar signatures of different randomized MAC addresses. For the MAC addresses belonging to the same cluster, our assumption is that there can be no time overlap between the times when these addresses are in use, i.e., the device uses one randomized MAC address for one or several bursts, after which it discards the address and generates a new one. We introduce the metric *MAC pair with time overlap* defined as follows: two different randomized MAC addresses, *MAC1* and *MAC2*, which were mapped to the same cluster and sent probe requests in time intervals T_1 and T_2, respectively, have a time overlap if T_1 and T_2 have an overlap. We consider all clusters in the database and count the number of these MAC pairs, labeling them with *overlap-MAC*.

Impact of the Bin Size. First we investigate the impact of the bin size on the proposed metric, *overlap-MAC*. Note, however, that we cannot completely isolate the impact of this parameter from the impact of the second parameter, distance threshold. This is because large bin sizes decrease the difference between burst deltas and large distance thresholds decrease the difference between signatures of different devices. On the one hand, choosing larger values for both parameters can result in mapping signatures of different devices to the same cluster, and subsequently in increasing the time overlap. On the other hand, small distance thresholds may be too restrictive, making a distinction between signatures of the same device and wrongly mapping them to different clusters. Thus, to tune the two parameters, we perform an extensive search in the (B, D) space. For this part, we use only probe frames containing randomized MAC addresses.

We assess the evaluation metric using our algorithm for mapping randomized MAC addresses for a range of bin sizes and distance thresholds, labeled B $-$ 0.1, ..., B $-$ 1 and D $-$ 0.1, ..., D $-$ 1. The results for two datasets are plotted in Fig. 3. As we can see, the *overlap-MAC* mostly decreases with decreasing the bin size and distance threshold. For instance, in *Dataset1* (Fig. 3a) the number of MAC pairs with overlap for bin size $B = 0.1$ s with distance threshold $D = 0.1$ and $D = 0.2$ is zero, for $D = 0.4$ it is one, for $D = 0.6$ four, for $D = 0.8$ eight, and for $D = 1$ the number is 149. Notice, however, that the reduction of the bin size does not entirely eliminate overlaps in *Dataset2*, (Fig. 3b): *overlap-MAC* for the smallest bin size is 44. Nevertheless, this means that at most 5% of all observed MAC addresses experience overlaps. Further, for each bin size the overlap mostly increases for larger distance thresholds because

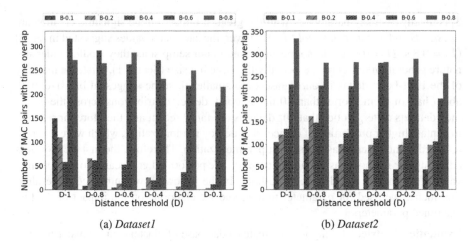

(a) *Dataset1*   (b) *Dataset2*

Fig. 3. The impact of different bin sizes and distance thresholds on *overlap-MAC*.

it leads to mapping the signatures with large distances, which may belong to different devices, to one cluster as well as to increasing the time overlap. Also, for a specific distance threshold it is expected that the *overlap-MAC* mostly increases for larger bin sizes, that decrease the difference between the signatures of different devices. Further, the *overlap-MAC* for the bin size 0.1 and the distance threshold lower than or equal to 0.4 does not change much. Therefore, the bin size of $B = 0.1$ s and distance threshold in the range $D \in [0.1, 0.4]$ appear to be good values for our method.

Impact of the Distance Threshold. For fine-tuning of this parameter, we analyze signatures of the devices that use only global MAC addresses. Since those signature are expected to be relatively stable, calculating the distance between two signatures of the same device can give us a good estimation of the distance threshold.

For each global MAC address and each CTW in which the address was observed, we create signatures using the same algorithm as for randomized MAC addresses,

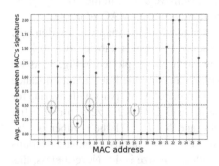

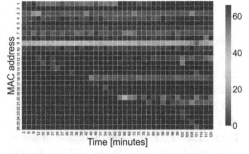

Fig. 4. The average distance between global MAC's signatures for *Dataset1*.

Fig. 5. The number of bursts sent by global MAC addresses, in each CTW for *Dataset1*.

Algorithm 2 with bin size $B = 0.1$ s. Then, we calculate the distances for each pair of signatures (of the same global MAC address), and find the average of these distances. These average distances are shown in Fig. 4 (the distance for the MAC addresses with one signature is zero). For each address, we also count the number of bursts in which they are included, in each CTW and plot the results in Fig. 5. We observe that the average distances for the signatures of global MAC addresses correlate with the frequency of the corresponding devices sending bursts—for frequently observed devices the distances are smaller than 0.5. The distances are usually larger for the addresses for which we do not have enough observations. We also calculated distances between the signatures of different devices (from the same or different vendors). Similarly to the distances between signatures of infrequently observed devices, distances between signatures of devices from different vendors are mostly larger than 1, which implies that the chosen distance threshold should be in the range $[0.1, 1]$. According to the data analysis of randomized MAC address datasets, a smaller distance threshold decreases the number of pairs with time overlap.

To conclude, the previous analysis of probe requests with global and randomized MAC addresses showed that choosing bin size $B = 0.1$ s and distance threshold $D = 0.4$ minimizes the number of MAC pairs with overlap, hence we decide to use these values in the remainder of this evaluation.

5.2 Method Validation

The last parameter whose impact on the method we need to investigate is *bootstrapTime*. A sensible choice of this parameter is important because it determines the minimum time necessary to capture probe requests before actually starting to count devices in an online manner. We analyze several experiment setups, in which we set the bin size to 0.1 s, distance threshold to 0.4, *countTime* to 10 min, *sigTime* to 2 min, and by varying the length of *bootstrapTime* we assess its impact on the method's robustness.

In Fig. 6 we plot the number of detected devices for different values of the bootstrap time: 10, 20, and 30 min. The top line (*All MACs*) gives the total number of observed randomized MAC addresses in each CTW. The other three lines represent the number of detected devices using our method (Sect. 3) for different *bootstrapTime* values. The figure shows there are no significant differences among the estimated device counts, thus confirming that our method performs well in static environments, and, moreover, that a relatively short *bootstrapTime*= 10 min suffices to make the initial cluster database. However, we have observed that increasing the bootstrap time indeed helps the correct cluster initialization, but only up to a certain point—in our datasets this threshold is 30 min, and we use this value in our remaining analysis. Appendix A.1 provides a more detailed discussion and justification for this choice of the threshold.

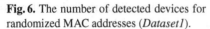
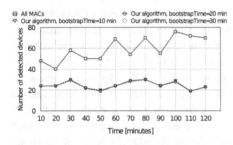
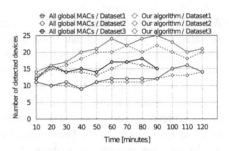

Fig. 6. The number of detected devices for randomized MAC addresses (*Dataset1*).

Fig. 7. The number of detected devices for global MAC addresses (all datasets).

Next, we validate our method for mapping different signatures to the same device by looking at signatures of global MAC addresses. Since the devices with global MAC addresses are uniquely identifiable, we can use the count of these devices as the ground truth to assess how well our method performs in distinguishing different devices and their signatures. Using the same setup as in the previous analysis, we compare the count estimate obtained by our method with the device count obtained from the datasets.

In Fig. 7 lines denoted *All global MACs* represent the number of devices according to the number of captured global MAC addresses (ground truth), and the lines labeled with *Our algorithm* represent the number of detected devices using our algorithm. The number of detected devices is close to the ground truth, differing in 1 to 4 devices (the highest error is 17%), for the three datasets. However, it can be noticed that our method underestimates device counts in some CTWs. This is because we do not include in the count fragmented signatures for the MAC addresses split across two CTWs. The other cause of this discrepancy is the limitation of our testing kit, which may be unable to capture all probe requests from the device in its vicinity, either due to frequency hopping or the distance and signal attenuation. Even with these limitations, our analysis suggests that our method indeed is able to provide a good approximation of the device count.

5.3 Device Counting Evaluation

Finally, we show the results for the count of all devices with global and randomized MAC addresses for the three datasets in Fig. 8. The figure depicts the number of all captured MAC addresses ignoring the MAC randomization technique (*All MACs*), the total number of devices, including those with global and randomized MAC addresses, where the former is computed from the dataset and the latter is estimated with our algorithm (*Our algorithm (randomized)*), and the total count of devices where both numbers of devices with randomized and global MAC addresses are computed by using our algorithm (*Our algorithm*). The estimated numbers are in good agreement, and moreover, they seem to exhibit oscillations in the same CTWs. According to Fig. 5, many devices do not send probes in every CTW, thus it is expected to see oscillations

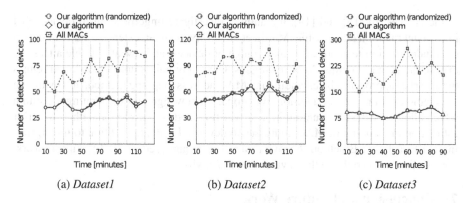

Fig. 8. The total number of detected devices for the three datasets.

in the number of detected devices. These oscillations happen due to periods of device inactivity, during which the device's presence cannot be detected, which is also another limitation of our device counting approach.

The available data about the passenger count does not easily lend itself to comparison with our results since we cannot determine the ground truth for the number of devices that remained in the normal working mode during the flight. Recall that the total number of passengers for *Dataset1* and *Dataset2* is 148 and 157, respectively; we do not have the exact count for *Dataset3*. However, the number of all detected devices using our algorithm varies in the ranges: [32, 47] (*Dataset1*), [47, 70] (*Dataset2*), and [75, 108] (*Dataset3*), which may be a good indicator that our results are reasonable.

6 Related Work

This paper addresses two topics: crowd estimation and analysis of Wi-Fi probing behavior. Therefore, we position our work along these two axes and compare it with related studies. Techniques for crowd estimation have received a considerable amount of interest both in academia and industry. We refer the interested reader to recent surveys [8,9] for an extensive overview, while we focus mainly on techniques that exploit wireless activity of mobile devices carried by users. Similarly to our approach, [14,20] utilize information extracted from Wi-Fi probes for estimating the occupancy and dynamics of people in commercial buildings and public transportation. Our work differs from these in that we utilize timing information of the probe requests captures. Other approaches demonstrate how the radio signal characteristics can be exploited for similar crowd measurements, namely by analyzing Received Signal Strength (RSS) [4,18] and Channel State Information (CSI) [23].

MAC address randomization and its implications on user privacy have been investigated in [6,11,13,19]. Freudiger [6] examined how the sequence numbers and timing information can be used to map randomized MAC addresses (generated by iOS) to the devices. In [13] and [19], the authors investigate fingerprinting of devices that implement randomization, while Martin et al. [11] perform an extensive study of different randomization techniques across a range of devices, and reveal possible attacks to expose the globally unique MAC addresses. Our study builds upon [5,13], and refines these earlier approaches by extending the MAC address mapping method, and by tuning the method parameters. In addition, we propose a new signature-generating algorithm which allows for device counting in near real-time and we develop a method for error estimation in mapping of MAC addresses to devices. Lastly, in addition to fingerprinting Wi-Fi activity, Bluetooth behavior can also be analyzed [3,10,16]. In this work, however, we focus only on the device's Wi-Fi activity.

7   Conclusion and Future Work

In this study we proposed and validated a method for estimating the number of devices in the given environment based on the devices' Wi-Fi probing behavior. To that end, we extended previously established methods for Wi-Fi fingerprinting and for mapping randomized MAC addresses to their corresponding devices. Specifically, we introduced a new step for clustering randomized MAC addresses, and we fine-tuned parameters used in our method, through an extensive analysis of the Wi-Fi probe request captures, which we obtained from three experiments. The end result is that our method is able to accurately estimate device count in static environments, in spite of MAC randomization.

Our approach has several limitations: First, it can only detect devices that are actively scanning the environment for nearby Wi-Fi networks, which can vary based on the device's usage, mode of operation, battery status and so on. Second, the method may suffer from large packet losses—i.e., when the measurement system fails to capture probes of distant or quickly moving devices—since it relies on good characterization of the device's probing behavior. Our analysis also showed that the probing behavior can change between bursts of probe requests. Thus, in our future work, we will further explore the limits of our approach, in attempt to address some of the previous questions and to provide a more detailed analysis of the method's robustness. Furthermore, our goal is to explore the feasibility of a robust crowd estimation system for dynamic environments, i.e., the environments where the crowd size is subjected to frequent fluctuations. In that respect, we will work on collecting representative experimental data and on the further customization of our estimation method.

Finally, our algorithm, like the others characterizing mobile devices based upon their (probing) behavior, is subject to this behavior exhibiting repetitive characteristics across a certain period of time, which may change at any time with operating system versions appearing. Given how well MAC address randomization has been picked up and improved in recent years, such mechanisms—even if not designed for tracking but just for counting—may function less well in the future than they did in the past. While we have 10 data sets from European flights from 2019 and early 2020 (but most of them are shorter), to be explored further, more recent real-world data samples are missing because of lack of travel due to COVID-19.

To assess recent trends, we carried out a small-scale experiment in an RF-shielded environment, using the same Raspberry Pi kit as on the flight and 10 mobile phones, running recent Android and iOS versions. The set of devices includes five LG Nexus phones (running Android 8.1) and one of each: iPhone 6 (iOS 12.5), iPhone 7 (iOS 14.2), Google Pixel (Android 10), Samsung Galaxy S7 (Android 8), and LG G4 (Android 7). We find that MAC address randomization improved and 95% of the MAC addresses were only seen in a single burst. At the same time, the number of probe frames per burst grew, shifting the emphasis again back to single burst analysis. Since this is only a small snapshot of available devices, we stipulate that future work will need to look at a combination of intra- and inter-burst characteristics. This will also fit more dynamic environments, when not many consecutive bursts, from numerous devices, may be easy to capture. As our interest is in crowd size estimation in the environment and not in individual device tracking, even approximate estimations will be beneficial for real-life applications.

Appendix A   Data Exploration for Parameter Tuning

A.1   Analysis of the Algorithm Bootstrap Time

Table A.1 lists *overlap-MAC* and the number of all valid created clusters, *cluster-DB*, for different *bootstrapTime* values used when initializing the cluster database with Algorithm 3 for two datasets. The results in the table show that *overlap-MAC* decreases or remains the same whereas *cluster-DB* decreases as we extend *bootstrapTime*. Thus, creating the initial cluster database using a larger subset of data (longer *bootstrapTime*) ensures fewer errors in signature clustering. In addition, as shown in Fig. 6, the estimated number of devices is almost the same for different *bootstrapTime*. This suggests that smaller *bootstrapTime* leads to creating extra clusters. However, since our device counting method is able to cope with "stale" clusters the end result is that the estimates for the number of detected devices do not differ by more than 1, as already explained in Sect. 3.3. As our trimmed flight datasets contain approximately 2.5 h of measurements, we set *bootstrapTime* to 30 min.

Table A.1. Cluster databases statistics for different boostrap times.

BootstrapTime DB Properties		10 min	20 min	30 min
Dataset1	Overlap-MAC	8	1	1
	cluster-DB	115	95	82
Dataset2	Overlap-MAC	44	44	44
	cluster-DB	141	133	117

Appendix B   Algorithms

Algorithm 1. MAPRANDOMIZEDMACADRESSES

1: **Input:**
2: inp :   Input dataset
3: B :   Bin size
4: D :   Distance threshold
5: $bootstrapTime$:   Time to initialize DB (bootstrap time)
6: $countTime$:   Counting time window (CTW)
7: $sigTime$:   Signature time window (STW)
8: $clusterValidTime$:   Duration of the cluster validity
9: **Algorithm:**
10:    $macListCurrentCTW \leftarrow \emptyset$ // List of MAC addresses in the current CTW
11:    $macListNextCTW \leftarrow \emptyset$ // List of MACs which pass to the next CTW
12:    $macListPrevCTW \leftarrow \emptyset$ // List of MACs from previous CTW
13:    $timeInp \leftarrow 0$ // The index of CTW
14:    $numDevices \leftarrow \emptyset$ //An array of the numbers of detected devices in each CTW
15:    $DB, macListNextCTW \leftarrow$ INITIALIZECLUSTERDATABASE$(inp, B,$
16:                    $bootstrapTime, countTime, sigTime)$
17: **while** $startTime <$ LASTTIMESTAMP(inp) **do**
18:        $timeInp \leftarrow timeInp + 1$
19:        $deviceList \leftarrow \emptyset$ // The list of present devices
20:        $startTime \leftarrow bootstrapTime+(timeInp - 1) \cdot countTime$ // CTW start time
21:        $endTime \leftarrow startTime + countTime$ // CTW end time
22:        $macListCurrentCTW, macListNextCTW \leftarrow$ GETMACS$(inp, startTime,$
23:                    $endTime, macListPrevCTW)$
24:        $macList \leftarrow$ MERGELISTS$(macListCurrentCTW, macListPrevCTW)$
25:        **for** $mac : macList$ **do**
26:            $inpSig \leftarrow$ MAKESIGNATURE$(inp, mac, startTime, endTime,$
27:                        $B, countTime, sigTime)$
28:            $C \leftarrow$ FINDNEARESTCLUSTER$(inpSig, D, DB)$
29:            **if** $inpSig \in DB$ **then**
30:                $DB \leftarrow UpdateCluster(inpSig, C)$
31:            **end if**
32:            $DB \leftarrow UpdateDB(DB, InpSig, C)$
33:            $deviceList.$APPEND(C)
34:        **end for**
35:        $NumDev[timeInp] \leftarrow deviceList.$GETSIZE$()$
36:        **if** $timeInp \cdot countTime \geq clusterValidTime$ **then**
37:            $DB \leftarrow$ UPDATECLUSTERSVALIDATION$(DB, timeInp, countTime)$
38:        **end if**
39:        $macListPrevCTW \leftarrow macListNextCTW$ // Update for the next CTW
40: **end while**

Algorithm 2. MAKESIGNATURE

1: **Input**:
2:     $inp, mac, startTime, endTime, B, countTime, sigTime$
3: **Output**:
4:     sig // Return the signature object
5: **Algorithm**:
6:     $deltas \leftarrow$ CALCBURSTDELTA$(inp, mac, startTime, endTime, countTime, sigTime)$
7:     $sig.vector \leftarrow$ BINNINGMETHOD $(deltas, B)$
8:     $sig.lastSeen \leftarrow$ FINDLASTSEEN$(sig, startTime, endTime)$
9:     $sig.validation \leftarrow$ ISVALID(sig)
10: **return** sig

Algorithm 3. INITIALIZECLUSTERDATABASE

1: **Input**:
2:     $inp, B, bootstrapTime, countTime, sigTime$
3: **Output**:
4:     $DB, macListNextCTW$ // The database of clusters; list of MACs for the next CTW
5: **Algorithm**:
6:     $sig \leftarrow \emptyset$
7:     $startTime \leftarrow 0$
8:     $endTime \leftarrow bootstrapTime$
9:     $macListCurrentCTW \leftarrow \emptyset$
10:     $macListNextCTW \leftarrow \emptyset$
11:     $macListPrevCTW \leftarrow \emptyset$
12:     $macListCurrentCTW, macListNextCTW \leftarrow$ GETMACS$(inp, startTime,$
13:                                    $endTime, macListPrevCTW)$
14:     $signatures \leftarrow \emptyset$
15: **for** $mac : macList$ **do**
16:         $sig \leftarrow$ MAKESIGNATURE $(inp, mac, startTime, endTime, countTime, sigTime)$
17:         $signatures.$APPEND(sig)
18: **end for**
19:     $K \leftarrow SilhouetteCoefficient(timeSig)$
20:     $DB \leftarrow KMeansMethod(timeSig, K)$
21: **for** $cluster : DB.clusters$ **do**
22:         $cluster.lastSeen \leftarrow$ FINDLASTSEEN $(cluster, startTime, endTime, countTime)$
23:         $cluster.validation \leftarrow$ ISVALID $(cluster, endTime)$
24:         $DB.macs \leftarrow cluster.macs$
25: **end for**
26: **return** $DB, macListNextCTW$

References

1. Android Documentation (API Level 23). https://developer.android.com/about/versions/marshmallow/android-6.0-changes
2. d'Otreppe de Bouvette, T.: Aircrack-ng. https://www.aircrack-ng.org/doku.php?id=main. Accessed Oct 2016
3. Celosia, G., Cunche, M.: Fingerprinting bluetooth-low-energy devices based on the generic attribute profile. In: Proceedings of the 2nd International ACM Workshop on Security and Privacy for the Internet-of-Things (2019)
4. Depatla, S., Mostofi, Y.: Crowd counting through walls using WiFi. In: 2018 IEEE International Conference on Pervasive Computing and Communications (PerCom) (2018)

5. Franklin, J., McCoy, D., Tabriz, P., Neagoe, V., van Randwyk, J., Sicker, D.: Passive data link layer 802.11 wireless device driver fingerprinting. In: 15th USENIX Security Symposium (2006)
6. Freudiger, J.: How talkative is your mobile device? An experimental study of Wi-Fi probe requests. In: Proceedings of the 8th ACM Conference on Security and Privacy in Wireless and Mobile Networks (WiSec) (2015)
7. IEEE Standards Association: Guidelines for Use of Extended Unique Identifier (EUI), Organizationally Unique Identifier (OUI), and Company ID (CID) (2017). https://standards.ieee.org/content/dam/ieee-standards/standards/web/documents/tutorials/eui.pdf
8. Irfan, M., Marcenaro, L., Tokarchuk, L.: Crowd analysis using visual and non-visual sensors, a survey. In: IEEE Global Conference on Signal and Information Processing (GlobalSIP) (2016)
9. Kouyoumdjieva, S.T., Danielis, P., Karlsson, G.: Survey of non-image-based approaches for counting people. IEEE Commun. Surv. Tutor. **22**(2), 1305–1336 (2020)
10. Longo, E., Redondi, A.E., Cesana, M.: Accurate occupancy estimation with WiFi and bluetooth/BLE packet capture. Comput. Netw. **163**, 106876 (2019)
11. Martin, J., et al.: A study of MAC address randomization in mobile devices and when it fails. In: Proceedings on Privacy Enhancing Technologies (2017)
12. Matte, C.: Wi-Fi tracking: fingerprinting attacks and counter-measures. Ph.D. thesis, Université de Lyon, INSA Lyon, France (2017)
13. Matte, C., Cunche, M., Rousseau, F., Vanhoef, M.: Defeating MAC address randomization through timing attacks. In: Proceedings of the 9th ACM Conference on Security and Privacy in Wireless and Mobile Networks (WiSec) (2016)
14. Myrvoll, T.A., Hakegard, J.E., Matsui, T., Septier, F.: Counting public transport passenger using WiFi signatures of mobile devices. In: 2017 IEEE 20th International Conference on Intelligent Transportation Systems (ITSC) (2017)
15. Saleh, S.A.M., Suandi, S.A., Ibrahim, H.: Recent survey on crowd density estimation and counting for visual surveillance. Eng. Appl. Artif. Intell. **41**, 103–114 (2015)
16. Schauer, L., Werner, M., Marcus, P.: Estimating crowd densities and pedestrian flows using Wi-Fi and Bluetooth. In: Proceedings of the 11th International Conference on Mobile and Ubiquitous Systems: Computing, Networking and Services (MOBIQUITOUS) (2014)
17. Skinner, K., Novak, J.: Privacy and your app. In: Apple Worldwide Development Conference (WWDC) (2015)
18. Tonetto, L., Untersperger, M., Ott, J.: Towards exploiting Wi-Fi signals from low density infrastructure for crowd estimation. In: Proceedings of the 14th Workshop on Challenged Networks (CHANTS) (2019)
19. Vanhoef, M., Matte, C., Cunche, M., Cardoso, L.S., Piessens, F.: Why MAC address randomization is not enough: an analysis of Wi-Fi network discovery mechanisms. In: Proceedings of the 11th ACM on Asia Conference on Computer and Communications Security (2016)
20. Vattapparamban, E., Ciftler, B.S., Güvenc, I., Akkaya, K., Kadri, A.: Indoor occupancy tracking in smart buildings using passive sniffing of probe requests. In: 2016 IEEE International Conference on Communications Workshops (ICC) (2016)
21. Wang, W.: Wireless networking in Windows 10. In: Windows Hardware Engineering Community conference (WinHEC) (2015)
22. Wirz, M., Franke, T., Roggen, D., Mitleton-Kelly, E., Lukowicz, P., Tröster, G.: Inferring crowd conditions from pedestrians' location traces for real-time crowd monitoring during city-scale mass gatherings. In: 2012 IEEE 21st International Workshop on Enabling Technologies: Infrastructure for Collaborative Enterprises (2012)

23. Xi, W., Zhao, J., Li, X., Zhao, K., Tang, S., Liu, X., Jiang, Z.: Electronic frog eye: counting crowd using WiFi. In: Proceedings IEEE Inofocom (2014)
24. Zeng, Y., Pathak, P.H., Mohapatra, P.: Analyzing shopper's behavior through WiFi signals. In: Proceedings of the 2nd Workshop on Workshop on Physical Analytics (WPA) (2015)
25. Zou, H., Zhou, Y., Yang, J., Spanos, C.J.: Device-free occupancy detection and crowd counting in smart buildings with WiFi-enabled IoT. Energy Build. **174**, 309–322 (2018)

DNS

Cache Me Outside: A New Look at DNS Cache Probing

Arian Akhavan Niaki[1]([✉]), William Marczak[2,3], Sahand Farhoodi[4],
Andrew McGregor[1], Phillipa Gill[1], and Nicholas Weaver[3,5]

[1] University of Massachusetts Amherst, Amherst, MA, USA
{arian,mcgregor,phillipa}@cs.umass.edu
[2] Citizen Lab, Toronto, Ontario, Canada
[3] University of California Berkeley, Berkeley, CA, USA
wrm@cs.berkeley.edu
[4] Boston University, Boston, MA, USA
sahand@bu.edu
[5] International Computer Science Institute, Berkeley, CA, USA
nweaver@icsi.berkeley.edu

Abstract. DNS cache probing infers whether users of a DNS resolver
have recently issued a query for a domain name, by determining whether
the corresponding resource record (RR) is present in the resolver's cache.
The most common method involves performing DNS queries with the
"recursion desired" (RD) flag set to zero, which resolvers typically answer
from their caches alone. The answer's TTL value is then used to infer
when the resolver cached the RR, and thus when the domain was last
queried. Previous work in this space assumes that DNS resolvers will
respond to researchers' queries. However, an increasingly common policy for resolvers is to ignore queries from outside their networks. In
this paper, we demonstrate that many of these DNS resolvers can still
be queried indirectly through open DNS forwarders in their network.
We apply our technique to localize website filtering appliances sold by
Netsweeper, Inc and, tracking the global proliferation of stalkerware. We
are able to discover Netsweeper devices in ASNs where OONI and Censys fail to detect them and we observe a regionality effect in the usage
of stalkerware apps across the world.

Keywords: DNS · Internet measurement · Censorship.

1 Introduction

Many connections on the Internet rely on the DNS protocol to resolve a domain
name into a set of IP addresses. For performance reasons, DNS resolvers typically have a *cache* of recently resolved domain names that is shared amongst all
of the resolver's users [21,22]. Unsurprisingly, this shared state exposes a side-
channel by which a user of a resolver can figure out if some other user has issued
a query for a specific domain name. This process is called DNS cache snooping

© Springer Nature Switzerland AG 2021
O. Hohlfeld et al. (Eds.): PAM 2021, LNCS 12671, pp. 427–443, 2021.
https://doi.org/10.1007/978-3-030-72582-2_25

(or probing) [18]. Prior work has presented various applications of this technique, including measuring the size of botnets and proliferation of malware [29], inferring web usage patterns [37] and providing a lower-bound estimate of the popularity of rare applications [30]. These prior studies assume that researchers can elicit answers by directly issuing queries to resolvers. However, most DNS resolvers nowadays do not respond to queries from outside their network. This is partly as a countermeasure to DNS amplification attacks [28], where an attacker can trick a resolver into sending a large response to a target of the attacker's choosing by spoofing the query source address.

In this paper, we instead probe the caches of ISP DNS resolvers through *DNS forwarders* on ISP networks, devices that may be misconfigured customer-premises equipment. Prior to our work, accessing these ISP DNS resolvers has been a challenge for Internet measurement researchers. We develop and validate a tool, *dmap*, that can probe resolvers through these forwarders. We demonstrate the applicability of our technique via two case studies, (1) Netsweeper device localization, and (2) tracking the global proliferation of stalkerware.

Case Study: Netsweeper Appliance Localization. Netsweeper, Inc., is a company that provides Internet filtering devices that has received considerable recent attention, because their appliances appear to be used for Internet censorship of political and LGBTQ content in a number of repressive countries [12,13]. Measuring the proliferation and use of these tools can help hold companies to account for uses of their technology that may violate the right to free expression, and can sometimes expose cases where technology is resold or transferred to third parties [20]. Previous work on localizing Netsweeper devices [12] typically focuses on fingerprinting *block pages* that the appliances inject, and globally accessible *admin pages* used to configure the system. We show that DNS cache probing can be a complementary measurement strategy, because it indicates Netsweeper activity that these other techniques miss.

Case Study: Tracking the Global Proliferation of Stalkerware. Stalkerware are a type of spyware that have powerful surveillance capabilities and are marketed as monitoring software used for stalking [27]. Previous work has investigated the technical aspects of stalkerware and the protections that antivirus and app stores can offer [27]. However, there has been little quantification of their prevalence across the world. Only a recent work has studied the popularity of stalkerware apps in the United States by cache probing public DNS services [30]. Since these spyware can be fingerprinted by the unique domain names they resolve [34], we measure the global proliferation of stalkerware by leveraging DNS cache probing.

Through our case studies, we make the following key observations:

1. Expanding our view of Netsweepr globally. We identify Netsweeper devices in 18 ASNs which were not identified by related efforts [1,14]. We are also able to confirm Netsweeper activity in 42% of the ASNs identified by related efforts [1,14].

2. Shedding light on stalkerware. We perform one of the first global characterizations of stalkerware using DNS cache probing. Through this analysis, we find 22 stalkerware apps active in 79 countries. The top countries are the United States, Brazil, and Germany. We observe a regionality effect in the prevalence of stalkerware apps, where apps in the Russian language are more prevalent in Russia and Ukraine.

In ongoing work, we are examining how our method can be applied to other devices and applications that perform DNS queries.

2   Background

In this section, we provide background on the operation of DNS caches, as well as prior investigation of DNS cache probing.

2.1   DNS Caching and Recursion

The mapping between a domain name and some other information (such as an IP address) is called a Resource Record (RR). The TTL field of a DNS RR is set by its authoritative nameserver and indicates how long resolvers should cache the RR [22]. If an RR for a DNS query is not cached, the resolver will try to "recursively" resolve the domain name. Once the resolver obtains the RR(s), it will send the answer to the user, and add the RR(s) to its cache for the number of seconds specified by the TTL.

A DNS query may set the Recursion Desired (RD) bit to indicate that the DNS server should attempt recursive resolution [21]. If the bit is unset (RD = 0), the DNS server answers the query using local information alone. In practice, some resolvers ignore this flag and always perform recursive resolution on every query. We discuss these "ill-behaved" resolvers in Sect. 3.1. If the resolver answers an RD=0 query from its cache, we can use the TTL value it returns to infer the arrival time of the query that caused the answer to be cached. This process is known as DNS cache probing (or snooping) [18].

2.2   DNS Cache Probing

The original treatment of DNS cache probing [18] discusses various alternate ways to infer DNS caching beyond the RD = 0 technique, including measuring the DNS resolver's response time. Further, they propose a set of recommendations to mitigate DNS cache snooping, such as restricting cache access to local users, an approach that is popular today.

A popular application of DNS cache probing has been understanding the usage and popularity of networked services. Rajab et al. [29] apply DNS cache probing to estimate the density of clients accessing a network service. They measure the relative popularity of websites using this approach, but do not mathematically validate their approach. Similarly, Wills et al. [37] characterize the relative popularity of Internet applications using cache probing of 20 Local DNS servers. Akcan et al. [4] takes a similar approach, but leverages geographically distributed open DNS resolvers to extract web usage patterns.

A second popular application of DNS cache probing has been to understand the prevalence of bots and malware that often query distinct domains via DNS. Rajab et al. [3] perform DNS cache probing on 800K DNS resolvers to infer the footprint of a botnet. Their study is based on the fact that the botnet in question issued DNS queries to resolve the Internet Relay Chat (IRC) servers used for command-and-control. They considered their result to be a lower bound on the botnet population. Randall et al. [30] perform DNS cache probing on four large public DNS resolvers (Google, Cloudflare Quad1, OpenDNS, and Quad9) and infer their caching architecture. Finally, they use their tool to estimate the number of filled caches for each resolver with a relative error of 10%–50% and present a lower-bound estimate of 22 stalkerware apps in the U.S.

These prior approaches assume direct access to the DNS server or use open DNS resolvers. Nowadays, these resolvers appear to be overwhelmingly configured to respond to queries from only clients on their network (Sect. 3.1). Thus, the techniques from these prior approaches are becoming increasingly less applicable to today's Internet. Our leveraging of *DNS forwarders* for probing resolver (DNS backend) caches unlocks a vast trove of data missed by directly probing resolvers alone.

Furthermore, to the extent that previous work have performed DNS cache probing, there is no indication that they have distinguished between DNS forwarders and DNS backends. DNS forwarders are included in consumer NAT/gateway devices in order to respond to DNS queries within the LAN, while DNS backends are recursive DNS resolvers. This distinction is necessary for having a reliable measurement and preventing double counting.

3   Revisiting DNS Cache Probing

In this section, we describe how we leverage DNS forwarders to enable DNS cache probing. DNS forwarders are necessary to probe DNS resolvers that only respond to local clients. We first quantify the prevalence of resolvers that only respond to local clients where we find that 75% of resolvers likely respond to only their local clients (Sect. 3.1). Using DNS forwarders, local to the resolver of interest, we are able to get around this limitation. DNS forwarders are hosts that forward a DNS query to their ISP's recursive DNS resolver [31]. This is usually the consequence of poorly engineered or misconfigured consumer NAT/gateway devices. We describe how we identify these DNS forwarders (Sect. 3.1) and how we use them to perform measurements (Sect. 3.2). We validate the set of forwarders in Sect. 3.3 and discuss the potential ethical implications of our method in Sect. 3.4.

3.1   Locating DNS Forwarders

Consumer NAT/gateway devices include a DNS forwarder so they can provide a DHCP lease (which requires specifying the DNS resolver's IP address) to clients before the gateway itself obtains a DHCP lease. These DNS forwarders are intended to only respond to DNS queries from within the LAN but many are improperly firewalled, and will also forward external DNS requests to the ISP's recursive resolver.

The steps we take to identify DNS forwarders are as follows:

Step 1: Scanning the Internet's IPv4 Space for DNS Resolvers. We begin by extracting the results of the October 5 to 11, 2020 Censys [14] DNS scans from the Censys dataset on Google's BigQuery platform. Censys' DNS scans send an RD=1 DNS query to the entire IPv4 address space. The nameserver of the *scan domain* name included in the Censys scan's DNS question will always return two answers: a fixed IP address (the *control answer*) used to establish that the host correctly resolves DNS queries, and the source IP address from which the nameserver received the DNS query packet (we call this the *resolver address* or the *backend address*).

We process the Censys results as follows. First, we filter out any IPs from the Censys results that did not respond correctly. An IP responded correctly if it answered Censys' DNS question with exactly two answers, where one answer is the control answer. Second, we attempt to exclude *shared DNS services*, such as Google's 8.8.8.8 or OpenDNS, by including only those IPs that are in an AS categorized as "Access/Transit" by CAIDA's *AS Classification* dataset [6], and who responded with a *resolver address* that is also in an "Access/Transit" AS. We exclude shared DNS services because their users may be globally distributed, making location inference challenging. In other words, since users from different geographical locations can send queries to shared DNS services, the fidelity of the information we get from shared DNS services will not indicate specific countries or ISPs. Furthermore, previous work have shown that the majority of end-user ISPs continue to operate their own LDNS services [7].

Step 2: Determining which Resolvers are Suited to Cache Probing. We are only interested in DNS forwarders that forward to DNS resolvers that respect the RD=0 flag, i.e., they will not perform resolution on a DNS query containing an RD=0 flag. We are also only interested in *caching* DNS resolvers that are likely to have interesting things in their caches. To find the set of DNS forwarders that exclusively forward to *caching* well-behaved DNS resolvers, we perform our own scanning to filter the list of IPs from Step 1. We run some experiments from a single vantage point in the United States using our own scan domain, whose nameserver is configured identically to the Censys scan domain and is hosted from the West Coast of the United States. We use a timeout of 20 s throughout the process of our measurement. In particular, our nameserver will return exactly two answers: a control answer, and the resolver address. We filter the list of IPs from Step 1 to include only those IPs that:

– Respond four times to RD = 0 requests to unique subdomains of our scan domain with zero answers.
– Respond four times to RD = 1 requests to unique subdomains of our scan domain with a resolver address in a single "Access/transit" AS, and the resolver address returned with *approximately full TTL*.

– Respond to at least one of ten RD = 0 requests for google.com with an IP in Google's AS (AS15169)[1].

We consider DNS forwarders that meet the criteria set out in Step 1 and Step 2 to be "well-behaved". Table 1 shows how many forwarders passed each phase of our filtering process on seven consecutive days in October 2020.

Table 1. Number of DNS forwarders passing each stage of our filtering process during the week of October 5–11, 2020.

Forwarders filtered	10/5	10/6	10/7	10/8	10/9	10/10	10/11
Filtered Censys Scan	811,914	814,863	817,935	823,345	790,313	793,807	811,783
RD = 0 check	468,882	450,421	434,773	426,936	461,981	444,785	426,350
Forward check	311,140	295,560	282,458	277,183	307,889	293,075	276,150
Google check	246,710	233,441	223,014	218,417	244,032	230,042	216,049

Since google.com is regularly the number one domain name on the Alexa Top Sites list [5], and the Cisco Umbrella 1 Million list [11], we would expect a correct answer for this domain to typically be present in most caching DNS servers with a significant number of users (with the notable exception of countries that inject fake answers for google.com, such as Iran and China [24,36]). We also would not expect our scan subdomains to be present in any caches, since we freshly generate a unique subdomain for each measurement, thus we expect them to be returned with *approximately full TTL* when queried with RD = 1. As we have configured our scan domain's DNS server to return answers with TTL=60, we define approximately full TTL as either TTL=59 or TTL=60. We believe our results are not impacted by EDNS client subnet prefix per-prefix caching, since previous work have shown [7] that there is little adoption outside of Google's Public DNS and OpenDNS, which we have excluded.

We repeat the measurements to get a sense of the behavior of the *universe* of resolvers that a forwarder may use for DNS resolution. During our DNS cache probing, we continually validate the behaviors of respecting the RD=0 flag, and forwarding to only a single "Access/transit" AS, as forwarder behavior may change over time. We also take privacy precautions about these DNS forwarders, as some of them might be pointing to caches of home routers. In this case, when querying our scan domain from the DNS forwarders, the answer returned by our nameserver will include the control answer and the DNS forwarder's address instead of the resolver's address. This indicates that the request is not being forwarded. Thus, we remove these DNS forwarders from the set of "well-behaved" forwarders. The output of our process is a set of (forwarder, resolver) pairs.

Population of Forwarders/Resolvers. Table 2 presents the breakdown of DNS forwarders that responded correctly to a query for our control domain and

---

[1] We analyze Farsight Security's Passive DNS Project data [2], and the responses they observed for google.com since March 2, 2018, all belong to AS15169.

Table 2. Number of DNS forwarders and the number of countries and ASes on each continent where we have access to DNS resolvers (aggregated over a week). AF = Africa, AS = Asia, EU = Europe, NA = North America, OC = Oceania/Australia, SA = South America.

	AF	AS	EU	NA	SA	OC
All Forwarders	66,626	531,867	392,148	263,730	120,505	14,988
After filtering	7,890	63,411	87,826	137,341	17,337	4,883
Resolvers	419	2,609	7,545	5,671	2,238	475
Resolver countries	42	40	48	32	12	14
Resolver ASes	152	550	2,347	1,095	624	137

the set of DNS forwarders after our filtering process, across continents. After obtaining the set of resolvers each forwarder talks to, we present the population of DNS resolvers we have access to in Table 2. As shown, we have more coverage in Europe and North America in comparison to other continents. Our dataset allows us to access at least 3 DNS backends in 84% of the countries (188) and at least 2 ASNs in 74% of the countries (188).

Availability of DNS Resolvers. A relevant question is to what extent the use of DNS forwarders provides any appreciable benefit over just directly querying DNS resolvers that answer external queries. We measured this by taking our list of (forwarder, resolver) pairs, and measuring what proportion of resolvers answered queries from our measurement machine located in the US. In the measurement we ran, there were 25,665 distinct resolvers. 75% of the resolvers were not responsive to a query for our scan domain when asked directly, but did respond when we queried them via a forwarder.

3.2 Probing DNS Forwarders

We use Google's *gopacket* library [17] to develop our DNS cache probing tool, *dmap*. As input, *dmap* takes a list of (forwarder, resolver) pairs from our filtering process, a list of domains to probe, an *exclude-list* of IP ranges of owners who have complained and chosen to be excluded from such probing, and an *interval* (which should be chosen less than the smallest authoritative TTL for any of the domain names being probed). Alternatively, a *dmap* user can specify a different TTL for each domain name, such as in the case where domain names have vastly different TTLs.

From the (forwarder, resolver) pairs, *dmap* maintains a subset of *active forwarders* that may change over time. At any given time, *dmap* tries to have two active forwarders for each resolver. If a forwarder goes offline, or is detected misbehaving (resolving an RD = 0 query for a random subdomain of our control domain, returning resolver addresses in two different ASes, or returning a resolver address with a TTL that is not approximately full), then *dmap* removes it from the active forwarders list. For each resolver associated with this forwarder, *dmap* activates an additional forwarder in its list that talks to the same resolver.

dmap sends a DNS query packet for each domain name to each *active forwarder* every *interval* seconds. *dmap* probes at a constant rate and iterates over the space of (forwarder, domain) pairs in a random order using the method of *zmap* [15]: generating a cyclic multiplicative group ($\mathbb{Z}/p$ for a prime p larger than twice the product of the number of forwarders and domains). It is unlikely, but should the size of the set of active forwarders increase beyond this prime, a new random order will be chosen. At the same interval, *dmap* continues probing our scan domain on each forwarder (as in **Step 2** in Sect. 3.1) to determine whether each forwarder continues to respect the RD = 0 flag, and continues to forward only to resolvers in a single ("Access/transit") AS. *dmap* remembers any new resolvers discovered for a forwarder, and uses this information when maintaining the set of active forwarders.

At the same time as *dmap* is sending DNS query packets, it is listening for DNS responses. DNS responses are filtered to ensure their relevance. DNS responses containing no answers, or no answers for the exact domain name in the question are discarded. DNS responses containing error codes are discarded. All other DNS responses are recorded in a JSON format consistent with that generated by *zmap*'s DNS module, except responses to the RD=0 and forwarding behavior validation queries. The TTL values in the DNS responses allow us to infer the date and time when the domain name was added to the DNS cache, by subtracting the response TTL from the record's authoritative TTL (measured by a direct query to the domain's authoritative nameserver).

To ensure that new forwarders to probe are discovered in a timely fashion, we re-process the latest Censys scan results and re-load these into *dmap* every 24 h. When these new (forwarder, resolver) pairs are loaded, *dmap* may begin probing new forwarders as necessary to ensure that at least two forwarders are being probed for each resolver.

3.3   Ground Truth Validation

To validate that our methodology can detect and infer timestamps for a nontrivial amount of DNS lookups, we performed a two-part ground truth experiment on March 23, 2019. We used ∼1,000 RIPE Atlas nodes across 106 countries to send recursive queries to a single subdomain of our scan domain once per hour with random start times (using RIPE Atlas' random function) for 72 h. At the same time, we used *dmap* to probe for the same subdomain (across approximately 16,000 DNS forwarders in 187 countries) for a period of 26 h.

In our experiment, only 1,473 unique forwarders ever returned an answer (*i.e.*, they contacted a resolver that had received a query for our scan subdomain). These forwarders used 1,247 unique resolvers in 64 countries.

Multiple Caches are Common. If a forwarder only ever uses a single resolver, we would expect to observe our domain cached for a total of TTL seconds per hour in a given resolver. However, we observed this in only 60 of the resolvers we study, with DNS forwarders using four DNS resolvers on average, with a median value of 2 resolvers.

Because our scan domain is specially configured to return the resolver address, we can see which resolver's cache answered a given probe. However, when probing a domain with a standard nameserver, we cannot see which resolver's cache answered a given probe. Since many forwarders use multiple caching resolvers (all in a single AS), we must be careful when making cache inferences.

Timestamp Validation. We cross-checked the timestamps inferred from our DNS cache probing results with *ground truth* timestamps from our DNS nameserver logs that show when a resolver actually contacted our nameserver, and timestamps from our RIPE Atlas measurement logs.

The forwarders showing cache hits in our experiment queried 1,247 unique resolvers, including resolvers that never handled our queries. We found 1,198 of these resolver IP addresses in our nameserver logs, and compared their log timestamps with the timestamps inferred from DNS cache probing. We found that our timestamp inference was accurate to 5 s for 97% of the resolvers we probed (1,166).

RIPE Atlas Requests. The data from our RIPE Atlas measurement includes: (1) The RIPE node's IP address and (2) The base64 encoded DNS question and answers; recall that a correct answer for our scan subdomain always includes the resolver address. Thus, the RIPE Atlas data effectively tells us which resolver contacted our nameserver at which time.

The RIPE Atlas data reflects that queries sent by the 1,000 RIPE nodes over our 72 h experiment caused 5,451 distinct resolvers to query our DNS server. Of these DNS resolvers, the *dmap* output reflects that we received responses from forwarders talking to 1,142 of these resolvers. Again, our inferred timestamps are accurate (per the RIPE Atlas data) to 5 s for 97% (1,100) of the resolvers.

3.4   Ethics

Since our study uses hosts on the Internet that accept queries from arbitrary sources, care must be taken to avoid overloading (or otherwise causing trouble for) the hosts. This is especially true because many DNS forwarders are in residential networks [31].

Sending Queries at a Low Rate. In our experiments, we probe each forwarder once per DNS TTL period for the set of domains we measure, which results in a maximum probing of 28 times per minute.

This is less than one query per second. We estimate that this results in less than 1 KB/sec of bandwidth usage on the forwarder, including the forwarder receiving our query, the forwarder sending our query to the resolver, the forwarder receiving the resolver's response, and the forwarder sending the resolver's response to us.

Because of the low rate, we do not expect our queries to cause a notable loss in performance for the host we are probing, or use a significant portion of the host's bandwidth allotment, or trigger any unwanted attention from ISPs or network administrators. We note that normal user activity, such as visiting a website, can sometimes result in multiple DNS queries in a short period, far in excess of our one query per second scanning rate.

Avoiding Illegal or Controversial Domains. Since we could be using residential networks to forward our queries, there is a concern over the types of domains we query. Querying a domain name containing controversial or illegal content may invite unwanted attention from authorities who erroneously interpret our query as evidence of the forwarder's intent to participate in illegal activity. Thus, we are careful to exclude any domains that may include objectionable or censored content, or any domains associated with products or software that might be illegal in a given jurisdiction.

Privacy Issues. Although we are leveraging end-user systems, our probes are typically answered from the caches of ISP resolvers. We are thus unable to determine whether a particular end-user has looked up a particular domain.

4 Case Studies

4.1 Case Study: Netsweeper Device Localization

We applied our DNS cache probing to identify the location of Internet filtering devices sold by Netsweeper. While these devices are marketed for use in schools, libraries, and enterprise settings, previous technical work has established that these devices are also used to block political and human rights content on major consumer-facing ISPs in several repressive countries, including Bahrain, the UAE, Somalia, and Sudan [12]. The previous work used strategies including scanning the Internet for administrator login pages associated with Netsweeper deployments, and looking for Netsweeper blockpages in data collected by OONI [1] to localize these devices.

While these techniques produce useful results, they may fail to detect devices configured to *drop* Internet traffic rather than inject a blockpage attributable to Netsweeper, and may not detect installations configured without a globally accessible administrator login page. This may be especially true going forward, given increasing security concerns about exposing these login pages: an April 2020 unauthenticated remote code execution vulnerability in Netsweeper's administrator login page would have allowed an attacker to hijack a Netsweeper installation and redirect users to malicious websites [26].

Measuring the proliferation of commercial censorship tools like Netsweeper's product can help hold companies to account for selling these tools to abusive customers, and can sometimes expose cases where technology is resold or transferred to third parties [20]. Finding additional strategies to localize these devices is thus highly desirable.

In addition to blocking websites specified by operators, Netsweeper devices can communicate with Netsweeper's servers to download and block lists of "objectionable" content, such as pornography and gambling sites. Netsweeper's system documentation [23] mentions that Netsweeper installations run a daemon called *freshnsd* that attempts to download updated versions of these URL categorization lists from update.netsweeper.com (the *Netsweeper update domain*). We performed a one-week measurement looking for cache hits on the Netsweeper update domain. We considered a backend to have a *Netsweeper activity* if there were cache hits for the Netsweeper update domain on at least six of the seven days of our scan.

Results. We compared our cache probing results to results from Censys [14] during our scan period. We queried Censys using Netsweeper fingerprints from a previous Citizen Lab study [12]. The Netsweeper activity was matched by IP addresses in 70 ASNs. Of these 70 ASNs, our DNS cache probing was able to probe at least one backend in 24 of the ASNs. We found Netsweeper activity in 10 of these ASNs (roughly 42%). Our cache probing also found Netsweeper activity on backends in 18 ASNs that did not show up in the Censys results. We show our results in Table 3, locations are inferred (where possible) from PTR records of DNS resolver addresses.

Table 3. DNS resolvers with Netsweeper activity.

Country	ASN	Censys?	Organization	Location(s)	Country	ASN	Censys?	Organization	Location(s)
Australia	1221		Telstra			209		CenturyLink	
	4739		iiNet	Adelaide, SA Hobart, TAS		2572	×	MOREnet	MO
Austria	8447		A1 Telekom			2914		NTT America	
Bahrain	5416		Batelco		USA	7018		AT&T	TX
	35457	×	Etisalcom						Beaverton, OR
Canada	852		TELUS	Edmonton, AL					Boston, MA
Colombia	19429		ETB			7022		Comcast	Denver, CO
	17426	×	Primenet						Wilmington, DE
India	17753		Data Ingenious Global						Newark, NJ
	54410	×	Vodafone Idea						Lancaster, PA
Ireland	25441	×	Imagine			702		UUNET	
Kuwait	9155		QualityNet			2856	×	British Telecom	
New Zealand	23655	×	2degrees		UK	5089		Virgin Media	
Sudan	15706	×	Sudatel			44611	×	Wavenet	Manchester
UAE	15802		Du			206747		NCSC	
Vietnam	45543		Saigontourist Cable		Yemen	30873	×	Yemennet	

One of the puzzling ASNs in which we found Netsweeper activity was ASN 206747, listed as "UK Ministry of Defence," where we found 64 backends with Netsweeper activity. On closer inspection, the IP addresses were in a range belonging to the UK's National Cyber Security Center (NCSC), which offers a "Protective DNS" service [8] for national and local government agencies in the UK. An NCSC blog post explains that the service is designed to detect and block malware, and that as of 2017, 44 organizations were using the service [9]. Some UK government agencies use Netsweeper, according to Censys scanning, including the Lancashire and Essex local councils. We suspect that these councils (or other government Netsweeper users in the UK) are using the NSCS's Protective DNS service.

Discussion. Of the ASNs showing Netsweeper activity in our DNS cache probing, but not matching any Netsweeper fingerprints on Censys, some are known to be using Netsweeper based on data from OONI. For example, OONI data shows evidence of Netsweeper use on Bahraini ISP Batelco and UAE ISP Du, though no Batelco or Du IPs were seen matching Netsweeper fingerprints in a previous Citizen Lab study [12]. In Kuwait, two ISPs (FASTtelco and Zain) are known to use Netsweeper per OONI data and previous Censys scans [12], though there appears to be relatively little OONI testing on QualityNet, per OONI's explorer tool [25]. There appears to be limited (or no) OONI data for some other ISPs, such as Saigontourist, and Data Ingenious Global Limited [25].

Of course, similar to OONI and Censys data, it is hard to conclude based on DNS data alone whether Netsweeper installations are deployed ISP-wide, or within an institutional or enterprise setting using the ISP's DNS servers. Nevertheless, the fact that DNS cache probing can detect Netsweeper activity that is not connected to known Censys or OONI results shows that it can be useful as an additional measurement tool for studying Internet filtering and censorship. In future work, we plan to examine the update infrastructure associated with several additional censorship and DPI products.

4.2 Case Study: Tracking the Global Proliferation of Stalkerware

We also applied our DNS cache probing to track the global proliferation of *stalkerware*, a type of generally available spyware that allows an operator to covertly monitor a target's devices [19]. While stalkerware applications are often marketed as "employee monitoring" or "child safety monitoring" tools, they also enable Intimate Partner Surveillance or Violence (IPS or IPV) [10,19,27]. In the case of IPS, an abuser first installs the stalkerware on the victim's mobile phone. The installation of the app may cause data from the phone to be sent to the stalkerware company's servers, where the abuser can log in to access it. Stalkerware applications are generally able to gather data including text messages, location, and logs of phone calls.

Statista reported that around 3.5 billion people have smartphones in 2020 [33]. Mobile devices are generally acknowledged to contain a vast treasure trove of information about their owners. Identifying widely used stalkerware tools can help focus advocacy efforts on specific companies and specific geographic areas, and highlight the scale of the stalkerware problem.

Previous work have studied how stalkerware is used in IPS [16,32,35] and highlighted that while these apps often are marketed for ostensibly legal purposes, they can be easily employed for abusive ones [10]. One recent work estimated the prevalence of stalkerware apps on four shared DNS resolver services in the US, though none have done so globally.

We first obtained a set of domain names associated with the network activity of 46 stalkerware apps [34]. We filtered out domain names that appear to host the stalkerware company's website, as these are likely to experience DNS lookups unrelated to stalkerware activity, and obtained a final list of domains representing 22 apps. We used *dmap* to perform a one-week measurement looking for cache hits on these stalkerware domain names. Similar to the Netsweeper study in Sect. 4.1, if there were cache hits at a backend resolver for a stalkerware domain during at least six out of the seven days of our measurement, we hypothesize that a user behind that backend resolver has the stalkerware app installed.

Global Proliferation. Our cache probing found stalkerware activity on backends in 432 ASNs and in 79 countries. The top-five stalkerware apps are shown in Table 4 based on their activity in the most number of countries. The complete results can be found in Appendix A. The Cocospy app is the most prevalent stalkerware app found in 71 countries, 239 ASNs, and 889 backend resolvers. We have also listed the top-three countries for each of the apps that had the most number of backends showing stalkerware activity. For instance, the Cocospy app is observed from 200 backend resolvers in the US. We can observe that the United States and Brazil are always among the top-three countries. Figure 1 presents the number of stalkerware applications we see across the world. The United States (21), Brazil (19) and Germany (18), Great Britain (17), and Russia (16) are the top-five countries with the most number of active stalkerware apps.

Table 4. The top-five stalkerware apps prevalent in the most number of countries.

Apps	Countries	ASNs	Backend resolvers	Top countries
Cocospy	71	239	889	BR (207), US (20), GB (84)
XNSpy	60	207	981	BR (255), US (176), GB (85)
Hoverwatch	59	187	789	US (154), BR (136), GB (69)
Spyzie	57	222	757	BR (250), US (109), DE (70)
Snoopza	53	174	673	BR (106), US (88), GB (73)

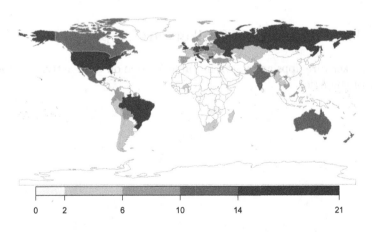

0   2   6   10   14   21

Fig. 1. Heatmap of the number of stalkerware applications observed over the world.

Regionality of the Apps. We observe a direct relationship between the language of these stalkerware apps and the region where we see the app being most active according to our measurements. For instance, two stalkerware apps, "Repticulus" and "Talklog" are both Russian products and are mostly seen in backends in Russia and Ukraine. Further, "Espiao Android" and "Meuspy" which are mostly active in Brazil, are primarily available in the Portuguese language. Although a public ground truth dataset about stalkerware prevalence does not exist, this finding validates our measurements to some extent.

5   Conclusion

In this paper, we revisit DNS cache probing and show that DNS forwarders can enable DNS cache probing, even in light of resolvers only responding to local clients. We leverage these DNS forwarders to probe DNS resolver caches that were otherwise not feasible. We then develop a formulation that allows us to infer the number of network devices behind a given DNS serve and validate this technique via controlled experiments. Further, we present two case studies, (1) we localize Netsweeper devices based on a daemon available on these devices that attempts to download updated versions of URL categorization list from Netsweeper's update domain, and (2) we study the global proliferation of stalkerware using their known indicators. In ongoing work, we are examining how our method can be applied to other applications that perform DNS queries.

Acknowledgments. We would like to thank our shepherd, Matt Calder, and all of the anonymous reviewers for their feedback on this paper. We also thank Amin Nejatbakhsh, Armin Niaki, Ilia Shumailov, Milad Nasr, Mohammad Motiei, and Negar Ghorbani for helpful comments and suggestions.

This research was financially supported by the National Science Foundation, United States, under awards CNS-1740895 and CNS-1719386. The opinions in this paper are those of the authors and do not necessarily reflect the opinions of the sponsors.

A   Global Tracking of Stalkerware Apps

The 22 stalkerware apps are shown in Table 5 based on their activity in the most number of countries.

Table 5. The 22 stalkerware apps prevalent in the most number of countries.

Apps	Countries	ASNs	Backend resolvers	Top countries
Cocospy	71	239	889	BR (207), US (20), GB (84)
XNSpy	60	207	981	BR (255), US (176), GB (85)
Hoverwatch	59	187	789	US (154), BR (136), GB (69)
Spyzie	57	222	757	BR (250), US (109), DE (70)
Snoopza	53	174	673	BR (106), US (88), GB (73)
Free Android Spy	47	136	493	US (129), GB (59), BR (57)
HighsterMobile	34	95	417	US (161), GB (57), DE (44)
GuestSpy	28	50	144	GB (25), US (21), IT (18)
Easy Logger	29	87	290	US (118), GB (64), BR (12)
AndroidMonitor	27	96	328	US (87), DE (40), RU (31)
FoneTracker	19	44	127	BR (33), GB (30), US (16)
Catwatchful	18	32	88	MX (22), US (16), GB (14)
mobispy	17	19	35	DE (8), RU (4), US (3)
TheTruthSpy	16	25	49	IT (9), DE (8), US (7)
Repticulus	16	62	132	RU (62), UA (32), BY (13)
TalkLog	15	83	209	RU (92), DE (35), UA (32)
Copy9	15	20	43	UA (10), NL (10), CA(7)
iSpyoo	7	12	19	US (5), CH (4), BR (3)
Espiao Android	6	54	355	BR (336), US (11), DE (3)
mxspy	5	6	13	DE (6), GB (3), RU (2)
HelloSpy	4	4	6	PL (2), US (2), BR (1)
Meuspy	2	27	256	BR (249), US (3)

References

1. Open observatory of network interference. https://ooni.torproject.org/
2. Farsight security (2020). https://www.farsightsecurity.com/solutions/dnsdb/
3. Abu Rajab, M., Zarfoss, J., Monrose, F., Terzis, A.: A multifaceted approach to understanding the botnet phenomenon. In: Proceedings of the 6th ACM SIG-COMM Conference on Internet Measurement, New York, NY, USA, pp. 41–52. IMC 2006, ACM (2006). https://doi.org/10.1145/1177080.1177086. http://doi.acm.org/10.1145/1177080.1177086
4. Akcan, H., Suel, T., Brönnimann, H.: Geographic web usage estimation by monitoring dns caches. In: Proceedings of the First International Workshop on Location and the Web, LOCWEB 2008, New York, NY, USA, pp. 85–92. ACM (2008). https://doi.org/10.1145/1367798.1367813. http://doi.acm.org/10.1145/1367798.1367813
5. Alexa: The top 500 sites on the web. https://www.alexa.com/topsites
6. CAIDA: As classification (2017). http://www.caida.org/data/as-classification/. Accessed April 2019
7. Calder, M., Fan, X., Zhu, L.: A cloud provider's view of EDNs client-subnet adoption. In: 2019 Network Traffic Measurement and Analysis Conference (TMA), pp. 129–136. IEEE (2019)
8. Centre UNCS. Protective DNS (PDNS). https://www.ncsc.gov.uk/information/pdns

9. Centre UNCS. Protective DNS service for the public sector is now live. https://www.ncsc.gov.uk/blog-post/protective-dns-service-public-sector-now-live
10. Chatterjee, R., et al.: The spyware used in intimate partner violence. In: 2018 IEEE Symposium on Security and Privacy (SP), pp. 441–458. IEEE (2018)
11. Cisco: Cisco umbrella 1 million. https://umbrella.cisco.com/blog/cisco-umbrella-1-million
12. Dalek, J., et al.: Planet netsweeper (2018). https://citizenlab.ca/2018/04/planet-netsweeper/
13. Dalek, J., et al.: A method for identifying and confirming the use of URL filtering products for censorship. In: ACM Internet Measurement Conference (2013)
14. Durumeric, Z., Adrian, D., Mirian, A., Bailey, M., Halderman, J.A.: A search engine backed by internet-wide scanning. In: Proceedings of the 22nd ACM SIGSAC Conference on Computer and Communications Security, CCS 2015, New York, NY, USA, pp. 542–553. ACM (2015). https://doi.org/10.1145/2810103.2813703. http://doi.acm.org/10.1145/2810103.2813703
15. Durumeric, Z., Wustrow, E., Halderman, J.: Zmap: fast internet-wide scanning and its security applications, pp. 605–620 (2013)
16. Freed, D., Palmer, J., Minchala, D.E., Levy, K., Ristenpart, T., Dell, N.: Digital technologies and intimate partner violence: a qualitative analysis with multiple stakeholders. In: Proceedings of the ACM on Human-Computer Interaction 1(CSCW), pp. 1–22 (2017)
17. Google: gopacket: Provides packet processing capabilities for Go. https://github.com/google/gopacket
18. Grangeia, L.: DNS cache snooping. Technical report, Securi Team-Beyond Security (2004)
19. Heasley, C.: Watching The Watchers: The Stalkerware Surveillance Ecosystem (2020). https://github.com/diskurse/android-stalkerware. Accessed Oct 2020
20. Marquis-Boire, M., et al.: Planet blue coat: Mapping global censorship and surveillance tools (2013). https://citizenlab.ca/2013/01/planet-blue-coat-mapping-global-censorship-and-surveillance-tools/
21. Mockapetris, P.: Domain names - concepts and facilities. RFC 1034, RFC Editor, November 1987. http://www.rfc-editor.org/rfc/rfc1034.txt
22. Mockapetris, P.: Domain names - implementation and specification. RFC 1035, RFC Editor, November 1987. http://www.rfc-editor.org/rfc/rfc1035.txt
23. Netsweeper: Netsweeper 6.3 Documentation: List Management - Freshnsd. https://helpdesk.netsweeper.com/docs/6.3/#t=List_Management_Docs%2FFreshnsd%2FFreshnsd.htm
24. Niaki, A.A., Hoang, N.P., Gill, P., Houmansadr, A., et al.: Triplet censors: demystifying great firewall's DNS censorship behavior. In: 10th USENIX Workshop on Free and Open Communications on the Internet (FOCI 2020) (2020)
25. OONI: OONI Explorer. https://explorer.ooni.org/
26. Osborne, C.: Severe Netsweeper zero-day leaves gaping hole in users networks. https://portswigger.net/daily-swig/severe-netsweeper-zero-day-leaves-gaping-hole-in-users-networks
27. Parsons, C., et al.: The predator in your pocket: A multidisciplinary assessment of the stalkerware application industry
28. Paxson, V.: An analysis of using reflectors for distributed denial-of-service attacks. SIGCOMM Comput. Commun. Rev. 31(3), 38–47 (2001). https://doi.org/10.1145/505659.505664. http://doi.acm.org/10.1145/505659.505664

29. Rajab, M.A., Monrose, F., Provos, N.: Peeking through the cloud: client density estimation via DNS cache probing. ACM Trans. Internet Technol. **10**(3), 9:1–9:21 (2010). https://doi.org/10.1145/1852096.1852097. http://doi.acm.org/10.1145/1852096.1852097

30. Randall, A., et al.: Trufflehunter: Cache snooping rare domains at large public DNS resolvers. In: Proceedings of the ACM Internet Measurement Conference, pp. 50–64 (2020)

31. Schomp, K., Callahan, T., Rabinovich, M., Allman, M.: On measuring the client-side DNS infrastructure. In: Proceedings of the 2013 Conference on Internet Measurement Conference, IMC 2013, New York, NY, USA, pp. 77–90. ACM (2013). https://doi.org/10.1145/2504730.2504734. http://doi.acm.org/10.1145/2504730.2504734

32. Southworth, C., Finn, J., Dawson, S., Fraser, C., Tucker, S.: Intimate partner violence, technology, and stalking. Violence Against Women **13**(8), 842–856 (2007)

33. Statista: Number of smartphone users worldwide from 2016 to 2021. https://www.statista.com/statistics/330695/number-of-smartphone-users-worldwide/

34. Te-k: Indicators on Stalkerware (2019). https://github.com/Te-k/stalkerware-indicators. Accessed Oct 2020

35. Tseng, E., et al.: The tools and tactics used in intimate partner surveillance: an analysis of online infidelity forums. In: 29th USENIX Security Symposium (USENIX Security 2020), pp. 1893–1909. USENIX Association (2020). https://www.usenix.org/conference/usenixsecurity20/presentation/tseng

36. Wander, M., Boelmann, C., Schwittmann, L., Weis, T.: Measurement of globally visible DNS injection. IEEE Access **2**, 526–536 (2014)

37. Wills, C.E., Mikhailov, M., Shang, H.: Inferring relative popularity of internet applications by actively querying DNS caches. In: Proceedings of the 3rd ACM SIGCOMM Conference on Internet Measurement, IMC 2003, New York, NY, USA, pp. 78–90. ACM (2003). https://doi.org/10.1145/948205.948216. http://doi.acm.org/10.1145/948205.948216

Can Encrypted DNS Be Fast?

Austin Hounsel[1]([⊠]), Paul Schmitt[1], Kevin Borgolte[2], and Nick Feamster[3]

[1] Princeton University, Princeton, NJ 08544, USA
{ahounsel,pschmitt}@cs.princeton.edu
[2] TU Delft, 2628 BX Delft, The Netherlands
k.borgolte@tudelft.nl
[3] University of Chicago, Chicago, IL 60637, USA
feamster@uchicago.edu

Abstract. In this paper, we study the performance of encrypted DNS protocols and conventional DNS from thousands of home networks in the United States, over one month in 2020. We perform these measurements from the homes of 2,693 participating panelists in the Federal Communications Commission's (FCC) Measuring Broadband America program. We found that clients do not have to trade DNS performance for privacy. For certain resolvers, DoT was able to perform *faster* than DNS in median response times, even as latency increased. We also found significant variation in DoH performance across recursive resolvers. Based on these results, we recommend that DNS clients (*e.g.*, web browsers) should periodically conduct simple latency and response time measurements to determine which protocol and resolver a client should use. No single DNS protocol nor resolver performed the best for all clients.

Keywords: DNS · Privacy · Security · Performance

1 Introduction

The Domain Name System (DNS) is responsible for translating human-readable domain names (*e.g.*, nytimes.com) to IP addresses. It is a critical part of the Internet's infrastructure that users must interact with before almost any communication can occur. For example, web browsers may require tens to hundreds of DNS requests to be issued before a web page can be loaded. As such, many design decisions for DNS have focused on minimizing the response times for requests. These decisions have in turn improved the performance of almost every application on the Internet.

In recent years, privacy has become a significant design consideration for the DNS. Research has shown that conventional DNS traffic can be passively observed by network eavesdroppers to infer which websites a user is visiting [2, 25]. This attack can be carried out by anyone that sits between a user and their recursive resolver. As a result, various protocols have been developed to send DNS queries over encrypted channels. Two prominent examples are DNS-over-TLS (DoT) and DNS-over-HTTPS (DoH) [8,10]. DoT establishes a TLS session

O. Hohlfeld et al. (Eds.): PAM 2021, LNCS 12671, pp. 444–459, 2021.
https://doi.org/10.1007/978-3-030-72582-2_26

over port 853 between a client and a recursive resolver. DoH also establishes a TLS session, but unlike DoT, all requests and responses are encoded in HTTP packets, and port 443 is used. In both cases, a client sends DNS queries to a recursive resolver over an encrypted transport protocol (TLS), which in turn relies on the Transmission Control Protocol (TCP). Encrypted DNS protocols prevent eavesdroppers from passively observing DNS traffic sent between users and their recursive resolvers. From a privacy perspective, DoT and DoH are attractive protocols, providing confidentiality guarantees that DNS lacked.

Past work has shown that typical DoT and DoH query response times are typically marginally slower than DNS [3,9,14]. However, these measurements were performed from university networks, proxy networks, and cloud data centers, rather than directly from homes. It is crucial to measure DNS performance from home networks in situ, as they may be differently connected than other networks. An early study on encrypted DNS performance was conducted by Mozilla at-scale with real browser users, but they did not study DoT, and they did not explore the effects of latency to resolvers, throughput, or Internet service provider (ISP) choice on performance [15]. Thus, the lack of controlled measurements prevents the networking community from fully understanding how encrypted DNS protocols perform for real users.

In this work, we provide a large-scale performance study of DNS, DoT, and DoH from thousands of home networks dispersed across the United States. We perform measurements from the homes of 2,693 participating panelists in the Federal Communications Commission's (FCC) Measuring Broadband America program from April 7th, 2020 through May 8th, 2020. We measure query response times and connection setup times using popular, open recursive resolvers, as well as resolvers provided by local networks. We also study the effects of latency to resolvers, throughput, and ISP choice on query response times.

2 Method

In this section, we describe the measurement platform we used to study DNS, DoT, and DoH performance and outline our analyses. We then describe the experiments we conduct and their limitations.

2.1 Measurement Platform

The FCC contracts with SamKnows [20] to implement the operational and logistical aspects of the Measuring Broadband America (MBA) program [6]. SamKnows is a company that specializes in developing custom software and hardware (also known as "Whiteboxes") to evaluate the performance of broadband access networks. Whiteboxes act as Ethernet bridges that connect directly to existing modems/routers, which enables us to control for poor Wi-Fi signals and cross-traffic. In accordance with MBA program objectives, SamKnows has deployed Whiteboxes to thousands of volunteers' homes across the United States.

We were granted access to the MBA platform through the FCC's MBA-Assisted Research Studies program (MARS) [5], which enables researchers (generally from the United States) to run measurements from the Whiteboxes. We utilize the platform to evaluate how DNS, DoT, and DoH perform from home networks.

We perform measurements from each Whitebox using SamKnows' DNS query tool. For each query, the tool reports a success/failure status (and failure reason, if applicable), the DNS resolution time excluding connection establishment (if the query was successful), and the resolved record [19]. For DoT and DoH, the tool separately reports the TCP connection setup time, the TLS session establishment time, and the DoH resolver lookup time. For this study, we only study queries for 'A' and 'AAAA' records. We note that queries for DNS and DoT are sent synchronously, *i.e.*, they must each receive a response before the next query can be sent. On the other hand, DoH queries are sent asynchronously, functionality that is enabled by the underlying HTTP protocol.

The query tool handles failures in several ways. First, if a response with an error code is returned from a recursive resolver (*e.g.*, NXDOMAIN or SERV-FAIL), then the matching query is marked as a failure. Second, if the tool fails to establish a DoT or DoH connection, then all queries in the current batch (explained in Sect. 2.3) are marked as failures. Third, the query tool times out conventional DNS queries after three seconds, at which point it re-sends them. If three timeouts occur for a given query, the tool marks the query as a failure. Finally, the query tool marks DoT/DoH queries as failures if either five seconds have passed or if TCP hits the maximum number of re-transmissions allowed by the operating system's kernel (Linux 4.4.79). The Whiteboxes we measure use the default TCP settings configured by the kernel (*e.g.*, $net.ipv4.tcp\_frto = 2$, $net.ipv4.tcp\_retries1 = 3$, and $net.ipv4.tcp\_retries2 = 15$).

In total, we collected measurements from 2,804 Whiteboxes, each of which use the latest generation of hardware and software (8.0) [21]. Our measurements were performed continuously from April 7th, 2020 through May 8th, 2020 in collaboration with SamKnows and the FCC. We filtered out certain Whiteboxes from our analysis in several ways. First, we filtered out 56 Whiteboxes that we did not have *any* network configuration information about (*e.g.*, ISP speed tier, ISP name, and access technology). Second, we filtered out 25 Whiteboxes that were connected by satellite. Third, we filtered out 30 Whiteboxes for which we did not know the access technology or ISP speed tier. This left us with 2,693 Whiteboxes to analyze, with 96% of queries marked as successful. The Whiteboxes were connected to 14 ISPs over cable, DSL, and fiber.

2.2 Analyses

We studied DNS, DoT, and DoH performance across several dimensions: connection setup times, query response times for each resolver and protocol, and query response times relative to latency to resolvers, throughput, and ISPs. Our analyses are driven by choices that DNS clients are able to make (*e.g.*, which protocol and resolver to use) and how these choices affect DNS performance.

Connection Setup Times. Before any query can be issued for DoT or DoH, the client must establish a TCP connection and a TLS session. As such, we measure the time to complete a 3-way TCP handshake and a TLS handshake. Additionally, for DoH, we measure the time to resolve the domain name of the resolver itself. The costs associated with connection establishment are amortized over many DoT or DoH queries as the connections are kept alive and used repeatedly once they are open. We study connection setup times in Sect. 3.1.

DNS Response Times. Query response times are crucial for determining the performance of various applications. Before any resource can be downloaded from a server, a DNS query often must be performed to learn the server's IP address (assuming a response is not cached). As such, we study query response times for each resolver and protocol in Sect. 3.2. We remove TCP and TLS connection establishment time from DoT and DoH query response times. The DNS query tool we use closes and re-establishes connections after ten queries (detailed in Sect. 2.3). As this behavior is unlikely to mimic that of stub resolvers and web browsers [7,16,17], we remove connection establishment times to avoid negatively biasing the performance of DoT and DoH.

DNS Response Times Relative to Latency and Throughput. Conventional DNS performance depends on latency, as the protocol is relatively lightweight; therefore, latency to the DNS resolver can have a significant effect on overall performance. Furthermore, encrypted DNS protocols may perform differently than conventional DNS in response to higher latency, as they are connection-oriented protocols. We study the effect of latency on query response times for each open resolver and protocol in Sect. 3.3. SamKnows also provides us with the subscribed downstream and upstream throughput for each Whitebox. We use this information to study the effect of downstream throughput on query response times in Sect. 3.3.

DNS Response Times Relative to ISP Choice. Lastly, SamKnows provides us with the ISP for each Whitebox. We study query response times for a selection of ISPs in Sect. 3.4.

2.3 Experiment Design

We describe below which recursive resolvers and domain names we perform measurements with and how we arrived at these choices.

DNS Resolvers. For each Whitebox, we perform measurements using three popular open recursive DNS resolvers (anonymized as X, Y, and Z, respectively[1]), as well as the recursive resolver automatically configured on each Whitebox (the "default" resolver). Typically, the default resolver is set by the ISP that

---

[1] We anonymize the resolvers as per our agreement with the FCC.

Table 1. Recursive resolver latency characteristics.

Resolver	Observations	Latency (ms)			
		Minimum	Median	Maximum	Std dev
X DNS and DoT	1,593,506	0.94	20.38	5,935.80	43.61
X DoH	1,567,337	0.14	22.75	8,929.88	43.25
Y DNS and DoT	1,596,964	2.00	20.90	9,701.82	46.79
Y DoH	1,552,595	0.14	20.50	10,516.31	40.68
Z DNS and DoT	1,579,605	2.35	31.41	516,844.73	414.26
Z DoH	1,533,380	0.14	33.00	9,537.42	41.11
Default DNS	2,009,086	0.13	0.85	8,602.39	22.93

the Whitebox is connected to. Resolvers X, Y, and Z all offer public name resolution for DNS, DoT, and DoH. However, the default resolver typically only supports DNS. As such, for the default resolver, we only perform measurements with conventional DNS. If a Whitebox has configured Resolver X, Y, or Z as its default resolver, then we leave its default resolver measurements out of our analysis.

In Table 1, we include the latency to each resolver across all Whiteboxes. We measure latency by running five ICMP ping tests for each resolver at the top of each hour and computing the average. We separate latency to DoH resolvers from latency to DNS and DoT resolvers because the domain names of DoH resolvers must be resolved in advance. As such, the IP addresses for the DoH resolvers are not always the same as DNS and DoT resolvers. We note that the latencies for the default resolvers are particularly low because these resolvers are often DNS forwarders configured on home routers. We exclude measurements with five failures or with an average latency of zero (0.7% of the total measurements).

We identified 41 Whiteboxes with median latencies to Resolvers X, Y, and Z DNS of up to 100 ms, despite median query response times of less than 1 ms. We consulted with SamKnows, and based on their experience, they believed this behavior could be attributed to DNS interception by middleboxes between Whiteboxes and recursive resolvers. For example, customer-premises equipment (CPE) can run DNS proxies (*e.g.*, dnsmasq) that can cache DNS responses to achieve such low query response times. Furthermore, previous reports from the United Kingdom indicate that ISPs can provide customer-premises equipment that is capable of passively observing and interfering with DNS queries [11]. We found that 29 of these 41 Whiteboxes are connected to the same ISP. We also identified two Whiteboxes with median latencies to X, Y, and Z DoH of less than 1 ms. Lastly, we identified one Whitebox with median latencies to X, Y, and Z DoT of up to 100 ms, despite median query response times of less than 1 ms. We analyze the data for these Whiteboxes for completeness.

Domain Names. Our goal was to collect DNS query response times for domain names found in websites that users are likely to visit. We first selected the top 100 websites in the Tranco top-list, which averages the rankings of websites in the

Alexa top-list over time [13]. For each website selected, we extracted the domain names of all included resources found on the page. We obtained this data from HTTP Archive Objects (or "HARs") that we collected from a previous study [9].

Importantly, we needed to ensure that the domain names were not sensitive in nature (*e.g.*, `pornhub.com`) so as to not trigger DNS-based parental controls. As such, after we created our initial list of domain names, we used the Webshrinker API to filter out domains associated with adult content, illegal content, gambling, and uncategorized content [24]. We then manually reviewed the resulting list. In total, our list included 1,711 unique domain names.[2]

Measurement Protocol. The steps we take to measure query response times from each Whitebox are as follows:

1. We randomize the input list of 1,711 domain names at the start of each hour.
2. We compute the latency to each resolver with a set of five ICMP ping tests.
3. We begin iterating over the randomized list by selecting a batch containing ten domain names.
4. We issue queries for all 10 domain names in the batch to each resolver/protocol combination. For DoT and DoH, we re-use the TLS connection for each query in the batch, and then close the connection. If a batch of queries has not completed within 30 s, we pause, check for cross-traffic, and retry if cross-traffic is present. If there is no cross traffic, we move to the next resolver/protocol combination.
5. We select the next batch of 10 domain names. If five minutes have passed, we stop for the hour. Otherwise, we return to step four.

Limitations. Due to bandwidth usage concerns and limited computational capabilities on the Whiteboxes, we do not collect web page load times while varying the underlying DNS protocol and resolver. Additionally, while we conducted our measurements, the COVID-19 pandemic caused many people to work from home. We did not want to perturb other measurements being run with the Measuring Broadband America platform or introduce excessive strain on the volunteers' home networks. Due to these factors, we focus on DNS response times.

3 Results

This section presents the results of our measurements. We organize our results around the following questions: (1) How much connection overhead does encrypted DNS incur, in terms of resolver lookup (in the case of DoH), TCP connect time, and TLS setup time; (2) How does encrypted DNS perform versus conventional DNS?; (3) How does network performance affect encrypted DNS

---

[2] Our list of domain names that we measured is available at https://github.com/noise-lab/dns-mba-public.git.

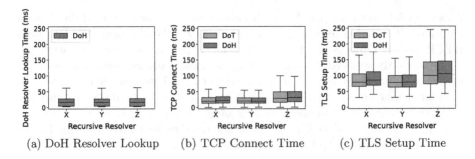

Fig. 1. Connection setup times for DoT and DoH.

performance?; and (4) How does encrypted DNS resolver performance depend on broadband access ISP? Our results show that in the case of certain resolvers—to our surprise—DoT had *lower* median response times than conventional DNS, even as latency to the resolver increased. We also found significant variation in DoH performance across resolvers.

3.1 How Much Connection Overhead Does Encrypted DNS Incur?

We first study the overhead incurred by encrypted DNS protocols, due to their requirements for TCP connection setup and TLS handshakes. Before any batch of DoT queries can be issued with the SamKnows query tool, a TCP connection and TLS session must be established with a recursive resolver. In the case of DoH, the resolver's domain name is also resolved (*e.g.*, `resolverX.com`). In Fig. 1, we show timings for different aspects of connection establishment for DoT and DoH. The results show that lookup times were similar for all three resolvers (Fig. 1(a)). This result is expected because the same default, conventional DNS resolver is used to look up the DoH resolvers' domain names; the largest median DoH resolver lookup time was X with 17.1 ms. Depending on the DNS time to live (TTL) of the DoH resolver lookup, resolution of the DoH resolver may occur frequently or infrequently.

Next, we study the TCP connection establishment time for DoT and DoH for each of the three recursive resolvers (Fig. 1(b)). For each of the three individual resolvers, TCP establishment time for DoT and DoH are similar. Resolvers X and Y are similar; Z experienced longer TCP connection times. The largest median TCP connection establishment time across all resolvers and protocols (Resolver Z DoH) was 30.8 ms.

Because DoT and DoH rely on TLS for encryption, a TLS session must be established before use. Figure 1(c) shows the TLS establishment time for the three resolvers. Again, Resolver Z experienced higher TLS setup times compared to X and Y. Furthermore, DoT and DoH performed similarly for each resolver. The largest median TLS connection establishment time across all recursive resolvers and protocols (Resolver Z DoH) was 105.2 ms. As with resolver lookup overhead, the cost of establishing a TCP and TLS connection to the recursive resolver for a system would ideally occur infrequently, and should be amortized over many queries by keeping the connection alive and reusing it for multiple DNS queries.

Connection-oriented, secure DNS protocols will incur additional latency, but these costs can be (and are) typically amortized by caching the DNS name of the DoH resolver, as well as multiplexing many DNS queries over a single TLS session to a DoH resolver. Many browser implementations of DoH implement these practices. For example, Firefox establishes a DoH connection when the browser launches, and it leaves the connection open [16,17]. Thus, the overhead for DoH connection establishment in Firefox is amortized over time.

In the remainder of this paper we do not include connection establishment overhead when studying DNS query response times. We omit connection establishment time for the rest of our analysis because the DNS query tool closes and re-opens connections for each batch of queries. Thus, inclusion of TCP and TLS connection overheads may negatively skew query response times.

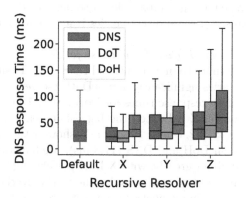

Fig. 2. Aggregate query response times.

3.2   How Does Encrypted DNS Perform Compared with Conventional DNS?

We next compare query response times across each protocol and recursive resolver. Figure 2 shows box plots for DNS response times across all Whiteboxes for each resolver and protocol. "Default" refers to the resolver that is configured by default on each Whitebox (which is typically the DNS resolver operated by the Whitebox's upstream ISP).

DNS Performance Varies Across Resolvers. First of all, conventional DNS performance varies across recursive resolvers. For the default resolvers configured on Whiteboxes, the median query response time using conventional DNS is 24.8 ms. For Resolvers X, Y, and Z, the median query response times using DNS are

23.2 ms, 34.8 ms, and 38.3 ms, respectively. Although X performs better than the default resolvers, Y and Z perform at least 10 ms slower. This variability could be attributed to differences in deployments between open resolvers.

DoT Performance Nearly Matches Conventional DNS. Interestingly DoT lookup times are close to those of conventional DNS. For Resolvers X, Y, and Z, the median query response times for DoT are 20.9 ms, 32.2 ms, and 45.3 ms, respectively. Interestingly, for X and Y, we find that DoT performs 2.3 ms and 2.6 ms *faster* than conventional DNS, respectively. For both of these resolvers, the best median DNS query performance could be attained using DoT. Z's median response time was 7 ms slower. The performance improvement of DoT over conventional DNS in some cases is interesting because conventional wisdom suggests that the connection overhead of TCP and TLS would be prohibitive. On the other hand, various factors, including transport-layer optimizations in TCP, as well as differences in infrastructure deployments, could explain these discrepancies. It may also be the case that DoT resolvers have lower query loads than conventional DNS resolvers, enabling comparable (or sometimes faster) response times. Investigating the causes of these discrepancies is an avenue for future work.

DoH Response Times were Higher Than Those for DNS and DoT. DoH experienced higher response times than conventional DNS or DoT, although this difference in performance varies significantly across DoH resolvers. For Resolvers X, Y, and Z, the median query response times for DoH are 37.7 ms, 46.6 ms, and 60.7 ms, respectively. Resolver Z exhibited the biggest increase in response latency between DoH and DNS (22.4 ms). Resolver Y showed the smallest difference in performance between DoH and DNS (11.8 ms). Median DoH response times between resolvers can differ greatly, with X DoH performing 23 ms faster than Z DoH. The performance cost of DoH may be due to the overhead of HTTPS, as well as the fact that DoH implementations are still relatively nascent, and thus may not be optimized. For example, an experimental DoH recursive resolver implementation by Facebook engineers terminates DoH connections to a reverse web proxy before forwarding the query to a DNS resolver [4].

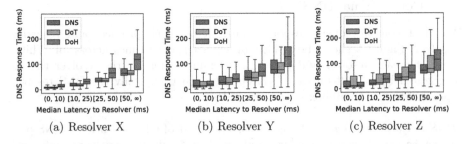

(a) Resolver X   (b) Resolver Y   (c) Resolver Z

Fig. 3. DNS response times based on median latency to resolvers.

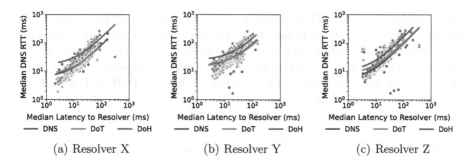

(a) Resolver X   (b) Resolver Y   (c) Resolver Z

Fig. 4. Ridge regression models comparing median latency to resolvers to median DNS response times (alpha = 1).

Table 2. Coefficients, intercepts, and errors for ridge regression models.

Resolver	Coefficient	Intercept	Mean absolute error	Mean squared error
X DNS	0.79	6.01	3.70	62.06
X DoT	0.74	7.48	4.23	33.89
X DoH	1.41	16.39	11.82	551.74
Y DNS	0.79	15.57	8.35	109.25
Y DoT	0.71	16.67	9.20	126.43
Y DoH	1.26	25.17	12.36	289.20
Z DNS	0.93	4.82	4.46	221.03
Z DoT	0.95	8.07	5.58	221.91
Z DoH	1.59	9.75	14.29	482.44

3.3   How Does Network Performance Affect Encrypted DNS Performance?

We next study how network latency and throughput characteristics affect the performance of encrypted DNS.

DoT Can Meet or Beat Conventional DNS Despite High Latencies to Resolvers, Offering Privacy Benefits for no Performance Cost. Figure 3 shows that DoT can perform better than DNS as latency increases for Resolvers X and Y; in the case of Resolver Z, DoT nearly matches the performance of conventional DNS. We observe similar behavior with the linear ridge regression models shown in Fig. 4. As discussed in Sect. 3.2, these results could be explained by transport-layer optimizations in TCP, differences in infrastructure deployments, and lower query loads on DoT resolvers compared to conventional DNS resolvers.

DoH Performs Worse Than Conventional DNS and DoT as Latencies To Resolvers Increase. Figure 3 shows that DoH performs substantially worse when latency between the client and recursive resolver is high; Fig. 4 shows a similar result with a ridge regression model. As discussed in Sect. 3.2, this result could be explained by either HTTPS overhead, nascent DoH implementations and deployments, or both.

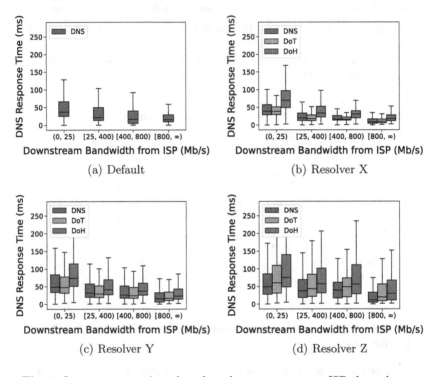

Fig. 5. Query response times based on downstream access ISP throughput.

Subscribed Throughput Affects DNS Performance. Figure 5 shows DNS response times across each of the open resolvers as well as the default resolver. We bin the downstream throughput into four groups using clustering based on kernel density estimation. The performance for all protocols tends to improve as throughput increases, with DoH experiencing the most relative improvement. For example, for users with throughput that is less than 25 Mbps, the median query response times for Resolver Y DoH and Y DNS are 73.4 ms and 48.7 ms, respectively. As throughput increases from 25 Mbs to 400 Mbps, the median query response times for Y DoH and Y DNS are 41.2 ms and 31.4 ms, respectively. DoT performs similarly to conventional DNS regardless of downstream throughput. Across all groups, the absolute performance difference between Resolver X DoT and X DNS by 0.2 ms, 1.9 ms, 0.1 ms, and 1.4 ms, respectively. For Resolver Y, DoT again performs faster than DNS in median query response times when throughput is less than 800 Mbps. For the three lower throughput groups, Y DoT performs faster than Y DNS by 1.4 ms, 2.5 ms, and 1.7 ms, respectively.

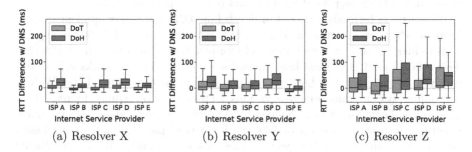

(a) Resolver X   (b) Resolver Y   (c) Resolver Z

Fig. 6. Per-ISP query response times.

3.4 Does Encrypted DNS Resolver Performance Vary Across ISPs?

Figure 6 shows how encrypted DNS response times vary across different resolvers and ISPs. In short, the choice of resolver matters, and the "best" encrypted DNS resolver also may depend on the user's ISP. For instance, while ISP C is comparable to the other ISPs for queries sent to Resolver X, ISP C has significantly lower query response times to Resolver Y, and is one of the poorest performing ISPs on Resolver Z. The difference in median query response times between Resolver X DoH and X DNS was 20.9 ms for Whiteboxes on ISP D, and 8.9 ms for Whiteboxes on ISP E; for Z DoH, the difference in median times was 34.5 ms for Whiteboxes on ISP D, and 47.9 ms for Whiteboxes on ISP E.

Resolver performance can also differ across ISPs. For ISP B, the median query response time for Z DoT is 11.1 ms faster than Z DNS. However, for ISP C, Z DoT is significantly slower than DNS, with a difference in median query response times of 30.6 ms. We attribute this difference in performance to higher latency to Resolver Z via ISP C. The median latency to Z DNS and DoT across Whiteboxes on ISP C was 50 ms, compared to 18.5 ms on ISP B.

4 Related Work

Researchers have compared the performance of DNS, DoT, and DoH in various ways. Zhu et al. proposed DoT to encrypt DNS traffic between clients and recursive resolvers [25]. They modeled its performance and found that DoT's overhead can be largely eliminated with connection re-use. Böttger et al. measured the effect of DoT and DoH on query response times and page load times from a university network [3]. They find that DNS generally outperforms DoT in response times, and DoT outperforms DoH. Hounsel et al. also measure response times and page load times for DNS, DoT, and DoH using Amazon EC2 instances [9].

They find that despite higher response times, page load times for DoT and DoH can be *faster* than DNS on lossy networks. Lu et al. utilized residential TCP SOCKS networks to measure response times from 166 countries and found that, in the median case with connection re-use, DoT and DoH were slower than conventional DNS over TCP by 9 ms and 6 ms, respectively [14].

Researchers have also studied in depth how DNS influences application performance. Sundaresan et al. used an early MBA deployment of 4,200 home gateways to identify performance bottlenecks for residential broadband networks [22]. This study found that page load times for users in home networks are significantly influenced by slow DNS response times. Wang et al. introduced WProf, a profiling system that analyzes various factors that contribute to page load times [23]. They found that queries for uncached domain names at recursive resolvers can account for up to 13% of the critical path delay for page loads. Otto et al. found that CDN performance was significantly affected by clients choosing recursive resolvers that are far away from CDN caches [18]. As a result of these findings. Otto et al. proposed *namehelp*, a DNS proxy that sends queries for CDN-hosted content to directly to authoritative servers. Allman studied conventional DNS performance from 100 residences in a neighborhood and found that only 3.6% of connections were blocked on DNS with lookup times greater than either 20 ms or 1% of the application's total transaction time [1].

Past work studied the performance impact of "last mile" connections to home networks in various ways. Kreibich et al. proposed Netalyzr as a Java applet that users run from devices in their home networks to test debug their Internet connectivity. Netalyzr probes test servers outside of the home network to measure latency, IPv6 support, DNS manipulation, and more. Their system was run from over 99,000 public IP addresses, which enabled them to study network connectivity at scale [12]. Dischinger et al. measured bandwidth, latency, and packet loss from 1,894 hosts and 11 major commercial cable and DSL providers in North America and Europe. This work found that the "last mile" connection between an ISP and a home network is often a performance bottleneck, which they could not have captured by performing measurements outside of the home network. However, their measurements were performed from hosts located within homes, rather than the home gateway. This introduces confounding factors between hosts and the home gateway, such as poor Wi-Fi performance.

5   Conclusion

In this paper, we studied the performance of encrypted DNS protocols and DNS from 2,693 Whiteboxes in the United States, between April 7th, 2020 and May 8th, 2020. We found that clients do not have to trade DNS performance for privacy. For certain resolvers, DoT was able to perform *faster* than DNS in median response times, even as latency increased. We also found significant variation in DoH performance across recursive resolvers. Based on these results, we recommend that DNS clients (*e.g.*, web browsers) measure latency to resolvers and DNS response times determine which protocol and resolver a client should use. No single DNS protocol nor resolver performed the best for all clients.

There were some limitations to our work that point to future research. First, due to bandwidth restrictions, we were unable to perform page loads from White-boxes. Future work could utilize platforms of similar scale to SamKnows to measure page loads, such as browser telemetry systems. Second, future work should perform measurements from mobile devices. DoT was implemented in Android 10, but to our knowledge, its performance has not been studied "in the wild." Finally, future work could study how encrypted DNS protocols perform from networks that are far away from popular resolvers. This is particularly important for browser vendors that seek to deploy DoH outside of the United States.

Acknowledgements. We thank the Federal Communications Commission's Measuring Broadband America (MBA) program and the associated MBA-Assisted Research (MARS) Program for assistance in conducting this study, Jason Livingood and Al Morton for initial study design suggestions, the MBA collaborative for experiment input, and Sam Crawford from SamKnows with assistance in measurement implementation and deployment. This research was funded in part by National Science Foundation Award CNS-1704077 and a Comcast Innovation Fund.

References

1. Allman, M.: Putting DNS in context. In: Chritin, N., Pelechrinis, K., Sekar, V. (eds.) Proceedings of the 2020 Internet Measurement Conference (IMC). Association for Computing Machinery (ACM) (2020)
2. Bortzmeyer, S.: DNS Privacy Considerations. RFC 7626, RFC Editor (2015). http://www.ietf.org/rfc/rfc7626.txt. (Informational)
3. Böttger, T., et al.: An empirical study of the cost of DNS-over-https. In: Sperotto, A., van Rijswijk-Deij, R., Hesselman, C. (eds.) Proceedings of the 2019 Internet Measurement Conference, Amsterdam, Netherlands, pp. 15–21. Association for Computing Machinery (ACM) (2019). https://doi.org/10.1145/3355369.3355575. https://dl.acm.org/doi/pdf/10.1145/3355369.3355575
4. Facebook Experimental: Doh proxy (2020). https://facebookexperimental.github.io/doh-proxy/
5. Federal Communications Commission: MBA Assisted Research Studies (2020). https://www.fcc.gov/general/mba-assisted-research-studies
6. Federal Communications Commission: Measuring Broadband America (2020). https://www.fcc.gov/general/measuring-broadband-america
7. getdns Team: getdns/stubby (2019). https://github.com/getdnsapi/stubby
8. Hoffman, P., McManus, P.: DNS Queries over HTTPS (DoH). RFC 8484, RFC Editor (2018). http://www.ietf.org/rfc/rfc8484.txt. (Proposed Standard)
9. Hounsel, A., Borgolte, K., Schmitt, P., Holland, J., Feamster, N.: Comparing the effects of DNS, dot, and DOH on web performance. In: Huang, Y., King, I., Liu, T.Y., van Steen, M. (eds.) Proceedings of the 28th The Web Conference (WWW), Taipei, Taiwan, pp. 562–572. Association for Computing Machinery (ACM) (2020). https://doi.org/10.1145/3366423.3380139. https://dl.acm.org/doi/pdf/10.1145/3366423.3380139
10. Hu, Z., Zhu, L., Heidemann, J., Mankin, A., Wessel, D., Hoffman, P.: Specification for DNS over Transport Layer Security (TLS). RFC 7858, RFC Editor (2016). http://www.ietf.org/rfc/rfc7858.txt. (Proposed Standard)

11. Jackson, M.: Firmware update for UK sky broadband ISP routers botches DNS update (2019). https://www.ispreview.co.uk/index.php/2019/04/firmware-update-for-uk-sky-broadband-isp-routers-botches-dns.html

12. Kreibich, C., Weaver, N., Nechaev, B., Paxson, V.: Netalyzr: illuminating the edge network. In: Allman, M. (ed.) Proceedings of the 10th ACM SIGCOMM Conference on Internet Measurement (IMC), Melbourne, Australia, pp. 246–259. Association for Computing Machinery (ACM) (2010). https://doi.org/10.1145/1879141. 1879173. https://dl.acm.org/doi/pdf/10.1145/1879141.1879173

13. L. Pochat, V., V. Goethem, T., Tajalizadehkhoob, S., Korczyński, M., Joosen, W.: Tranco: a research-oriented top sites ranking hardened against manipulation. In: Oprea, A., Xu, D. (eds.) Proceedings of the 26th Network and Distributed System Security Symposium (NDSS), San Diego, CA, USA, pp. 1–15. Internet Society (ISOC) (2019). https://doi.org/10.14722/ndss.2019.23386. https://www.ndss-symposium. org/wp-content/uploads/2019/02/ndss2019_01B-3_LePochat_paper.pdf

14. Lu, C., et al.: An end-to-end, large-scale measurement of DNS-over-encryption: how far have we come? In: Sperotto, A., van Rijswijk-Deij, R., Hesselman, C. (eds.) Proceedings of the 2019 Internet Measurement Conference, Amsterdam, Netherlands, pp. 22–35. Association for Computing Machinery (ACM) (2019). https://doi.org/ 10.1145/3355369.3355580. https://dl.acm.org/doi/pdf/10.1145/3355369.3355580

15. McManus, P.: Firefox Nightly Secure DNS Experimental Results (2018). https:// blog.nightly.mozilla.org/2018/08/28/firefox-nightly-secure-dns-experimental-results/

16. Mozilla: All.js (2020). https://searchfox.org/mozilla-central/source/modules/ libpref/init/all.js#1425

17. Mozilla: TRRServiceChannel.cpp (2020). https://searchfox.org/mozilla-central/ source/netwerk/protocol/http/TRRServiceChannel.cpp#512

18. Otto, J.S., Sánchez, M.A., Rula, J.P., Bustamante, F.E.: Content delivery and the natural evolution of DNS: remote DNS trends, performance issues and alternative solutions. In: Mahajan, R., Snoeren, A. (eds.) Proceedings of the 2012 Internet Measurement Conference (IMC), Boston, MA, USA, pp. 523–536. Association for Computing Machinery (ACM) (2012). https://doi.org/10.1145/2398776.2398831. https://dl.acm.org/doi/pdf/10.1145/2398776.2398831

19. SamKnows: DNS resolution (2020). https://samknows.com/technology/tests/dns-resolution

20. SamKnows: SamKnows (2020). https://www.samknows.com/

21. SamKnows: SamKnows Whitebox (2020). https://samknows.com/technology/ agents/samknows-whitebox#specifications

22. Sundaresan, S., Feamster, N., Teixeira, R., Magharei, N.: Measuring and mitigating web performance bottlenecks in broadband access networks. In: Gummadi, K., Partidge, C. (eds.) Proceedings of the 2013 Internet Measurement Conference (IMC), Barcelona, Spain, pp. 213–226. Association for Computing Machinery (ACM) (2013). https://doi.org/10.1145/2504730.2504741. https://dl.acm.org/doi/ 10.1145/2504730.2504741

23. Wang, X.S., Balasubramanian, A., Krishnamurthy, A., Wetherall, D.: Demystifying page load performance with WProf. In: Feamster, N., Mogul, J. (eds.) Proceedings of the 10th USENIX Symposium on Networked Systems Design and Implementation (NSDI), Lombard, IL, USA, pp. 473–487. USENIX Association (2013). https://www.usenix.org/conference/nsdi13/ technical-sessions/presentation/wang_xiao

24. Webshrinker: APIs - Webshrinker (2020). https://www.webshrinker.com/apis/
25. Zhu, L., Hu, Z., Heidemann, J., Wessels, D., Mankin, A., Somaiya, N.: Connection-oriented DNS to improve privacy and security. In: Shmatikov, V., Bauer, L. (eds.) Proceedings of the 36th IEEE Symposium on Security & Privacy (S&P), San Jose, CA, USA, pp. 171–186. Institute of Electrical and Electronics Engineers (IEEE) (2015). https://doi.org/10.1109/sp.2015.18. https://ieeexplore.ieee.org/stamp/stamp.jsp?arnumber=7163025

Fragmentation, Truncation, and Timeouts: Are Large DNS Messages Falling to Bits?

Giovane C. M. Moura[1]($\boxtimes$), Moritz Müller[1,2], Marco Davids[1],
Maarten Wullink[1], and Cristian Hesselman[1,2]

[1] SIDN Labs, Arnhem, The Netherlands
{giovane.moura,moritz.muller,marco.davids,maarten.wullink,
cristian.hesselman}@sidn.nl
[2] University of Twente, Enschede, The Netherlands

Abstract. The DNS provides one of the core services of the Internet, mapping applications and services to hosts. DNS employs both UDP and TCP as a transport protocol, and currently most DNS queries are sent over UDP. The problem with UDP is that large responses run the risk of not arriving at their destinations – which can ultimately lead to *unreachability*. However, it remains unclear how much of a problem these large DNS responses over UDP are in the wild. This is the focus on this paper: we analyze 164 billion queries/response pairs from more than 46k autonomous systems, covering three months (July 2019 and 2020, and Oct. 2020), collected at the authoritative servers of the .nl, the country-code top-level domain of the Netherlands. We show that fragmentation, and the problems that can follow fragmentation, rarely occur at such authoritative servers. Further, we demonstrate that DNS built-in defenses – use of truncation, EDNS0 buffer sizes, reduced responses and TCP fall back – are effective to reduce fragmentation. Last, we measure the uptake of the DNS flag day in 2020.

1 Introduction

The Domain Name System (DNS) [31] provides one of the core Internet services, by mapping hosts, services and applications to IP addresses. DNS specifications states that both UDP and TCP should be supported [4,31] as transport protocols, and nowadays most queries are UDP [48,54]. Performance wise, UDP's main advantage is that it can deliver faster responses, within one round-trip time (RTT), while TCP requires an additional RTT due to its session establishment handshake.

Rather common, small DNS responses fit into the 512-byte limit that the original DNS over UDP (DNS/UDP hereafter) has, but larger responses – such as the ones protected with DNSSEC [3,4,27] – may not fit. To overcome this 512-byte size limit, the Extension Mechanisms for DNS 0 (EDNS0) [7,52] standard was proposed. EDNS0 allows a DNS client to advertise its UDP buffer size, and an EDNS0-compatible authoritative server "may send UDP packets up to that client's announced buffer size without truncation" [52] – up to 65,536 bytes.

© Springer Nature Switzerland AG 2021
O. Hohlfeld et al. (Eds.): PAM 2021, LNCS 12671, pp. 460–477, 2021.
https://doi.org/10.1007/978-3-030-72582-2_27

If, however, a DNS response is larger than the client's advertised EDNS0 limit (or 512 bytes in the absence of EDNS0), the authoritative server should then *truncate* the response to a size that fits within the limit and *flag* with the TC bit [32]. Upon receiving a truncated response, the client should, in turn, resend the query over TCP [4,10] (DNS/TCP hereafter), and leverage TCP's design to handle large messages with multiple segments.

However, the EDNS0 announced buffer size is agnostic to the path between client and authoritative server's maximum transmission unit (MTU), which is the largest packet size that can be forwarded by all routers in the path. The most common MTU on the core Internet is 1500 bytes [4], and EDNS0 buffer sizes can easily exceed that – we show in Sect. 4 that 4096 bytes is the most common value. If it does *exceed* the entire path MTU, then the packet will *not* be able to be forwarded by the routers along the way, which will to packets being either discarded or *fragmented* [11,39] at the IP layer.

IP fragmentation, in turn, comes with a series of problems [5] – fragmented IP packets may be blocked by firewalls [4,5,8], leading to *unreachability* [51,53]. Moreover, IP fragmentation has been exploited in cache poisoning attacks on DNS [17,50], and DNS cache poisoning can be further exploited to compromise the trust in certificate authorities (CAs) [6]. As as result of these problems, there is currently a consensus in the IP and DNS communities that IP fragmentation should be avoided in DNS [5,12,58].

In this paper, we scrutinize the issue of large DNS responses using as vantage point the .nl zone, the country-code top-level domain (ccTLD) of the Netherlands. Our datasets cover 3 months of data, from 2019 and 2020, with more than 164 billion queries/responses pairs from more than 3 million resolvers from more than 46,000 Autonomous Systems (ASes). We investigate responses sizes, truncation, and server-side fragmentation in Sect. 3, as well as determining if resolvers fall back to TCP. Then, in Sect. 4, we characterize resolver's EDNS0 buffer sizes and the uptake of the DNS Flag day 2020.

2   Datasets

There are two main types of DNS server software: *authoritative servers* and *recursive resolvers*. Authoritative servers "know the content of a DNS zone from local knowledge" [19] (such as the Root DNS servers [46] for the Root zone [23]), while DNS resolvers (such as the Quad{1,8,9} public resolver services [1,16,36, 40]), resolve domain names by querying authoritative servers on behalf of users.

We analyze DNS queries and responses to/from authoritative servers of .nl. We collect data from two of the three authoritative server of .nl (NS1 and NS3, the remaining authoritative services did not support traffic collection at the time). The .nl zone has several million domain names in its zone, with the majority of the domains being signed using DNSSEC [48].

The analyzed authoritative servers are run by different third-party DNS providers (one from Europe, the other from North America). Both services are replicated using IP anycast [29,37] – which allows the same IP address to be announced using BGP [41] from multiple locations across the globe, over both IPv4 and IPv6. In total, NS1 and NS3 are announced from 61 global locations (sites). We employ ENTRADA [47,56], an open-source DNS analysis platform to analyze this data.

Table 1 shows the datasets we analyze in this paper. In total, we study more than 164 billion DNS queries and responses – 157.77 billion over UDP and 6.25 billion over TCP, covering two full months (July 2019 and 2020) and October 2020 (the first month *after* the DNS 2020 flag day [58]).

Table 1. Evaluated datasets of `.nl` zone.

	July 2019		July 2020		October 2020	
	IPv4	IPv6	IPv4	IPv6	IPv4	IPv6
Queries/responses	29.79B	7.80B	45.38B	15.87B	48.58B	16.62B
UDP	28.68B	7.54 B	43.75B	15.01B	46.94B	15.87B
UDP TC off	27.80B	7.24B	42.06B	13.88B	45.49B	14.93B
UDP TC on	0.87B	0.31B	1.69B	1.14B	1.44B	0.93B
Ratio (%)	2.93%	3.91%	3.72%	7.15%	2.96%	5.59%
TCP	1.11B	0.25B	1.63B	0.85B	0.36B	0.20B
Ratio (%)	3.72%	3.32%	3.59%	5.37%	3.17%	5.09%
Resolvers						
UDP TC off	3.09M	0.35M	2.99M	0.67M	3.12M	0.62M
UDP TC on	0.61M	0.08M	0.85M	0.12M	0.87M	0.13M
TCP	0.61M	0.08M	0.83M	0.12M	0.87M	0.13M
ASes						
UDP TC off	44.8k	8.3k	45.6k	8.5k	46.4k	8.8k
UDP TC on.	23.3k	4.5k	27.6k	5.4k	28.2k	5.6k
TCP	23.5k	4.3k	27.3k	5.2k	27.9k	5.4k

We see that a small fraction of all responses are truncated – 2.93% to 7.15% – depending on the month/year and IP version. Our datasets cover more than 3 million resolvers (defined by distinct IP addresses) from more than 46k ASes, which is far larger than previous studies on DNS issues with fragmentation [51,53] and from active measurements platforms such as Ripe Atlas [45], which has ~11k active vantage points and cover 8670 /24 IPv4 network prefixes [44] (May 2020).

3 Dissecting Responses from a ccTLD

3.1 How Common Are Large Responses?

Before addressing problems related to large DNS/UDP responses, we need first to understand how often do they really occur in the wild, from our datasets.

Figure 1 shows the CDF of the response sizes (DNS payload only) per anycast server, transport protocol, and IP version, for both July 2019 and July 2020. We see that most responses are smaller than 1232 bytes (right vertical line) – more than 99.99% for all responses, for both servers, protocols/IP version.

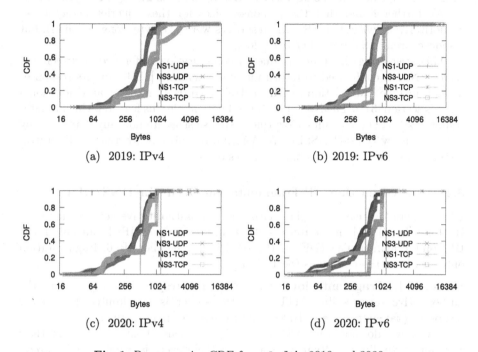

Fig. 1. Response size CDF for `.nl`: July 2019 and 2020

This value is similar to what is reported by Google Public DNS [16], a public DNS resolver service, also reports that 99.7% of responses are smaller than 1232 bytes [28]. Differently from ours, they run a *resolver* service, that queries *multiple* TLDs and their delegations, while ours covers only one ccTLD. Still, similar figures holds for both vantage points.

The exception for `.nl` was in 2019, where NS3-TCP over IPv4 had 78.6%, and NS1-TCP over IPv6 had 94.9% of the responses smaller than 1232 bytes. Altogether, for July 2019 and 2020, these large responses account for 95M queries, out of the more than 98B queries (Table 1).

What Queries Generate Large Responses? We then proceed to determine what queries led to large responses. DNSSEC is often blamed for causing large responses. At `.nl`, DNSSEC we see that DNSSEC increases response size, but rarely beyond 1232 bytes.

Resolvers set the DO-flag in their queries if they want to receive DNSSEC related resource records for each signed response (e.g. DS and RRSIG). Responses to these queries have a median response size of 594 bytes, whereas responses that do not contain DNSSEC records only have a median response size of 153 bytes. Responses that stand out are A [32] and AAAA [49] queries (asking for IPv4 and IPv6 records, respectively) for `ns*.dns.nl` – the authoritative servers of the `.nl` zone, accounting for 99% of all responses larger than 1232 bytes. Without DNSSEC records, this response is merely 221 bytes long.

We further found that the responses sizes for these queries *changed* per authoritative service. For NS1, the responses were 217 bytes long (median), but responses from NS3 were 1117 bytes long.

This staggering difference is due to configuration differences between the servers. NS1 is configured to return minimal responses [2,24], and its responses do not include two sections with "extra" records (authority and additional records section [31]). The NS3 operator did not enable this feature, which inflates response sizes. These results show that response sizes are not only determine by the DNS query types (DNSSEC, A, AAAA), but also by whether authoritative servers configured with minimal responses or not.

3.2   How Often Does IP Fragmentation Occur for DNS/UDP?

IP fragmentation can take place either at the authoritative servers (for both IPv4 and IPv6) and on the routers along the way only for IPv4, but only if the IP Don't Fragment flag (DF) in the IPv4 is not set. For IPv6, fragmentation only occurs on the end hosts (Sect. 5 in [9]).

Server-Side Fragmentation: If a DNS/UDP response is *larger* than the authoritative server's link MTU (and the server is not limited from large responses (`max-udp-size` in BIND9 [24]) the server may fragment it.

Given we do not run NS1 and NS3, we cannot know what is their `max-udp-size` limits. What we can know, however, is what is the *largest* DNS/UDP response they have sent and that was not fragmented. This value provides a lower bound for their `max-udp-size` of the authoritative servers. Table 2 shows the results. We see that in NS3 send far larger responses than NS1 in 2020[1].

Table 2. Maximum DNS/UDP response size (bytes) per authoritative server and IP version.

	NS1		NS3	
Year	IPv4	IPv6	IPv4	IPv6
July 2019	1451	1470	1484	1494
July 2020	1391	1391	2866	2866

Table 3. NS3 - ICMP error messages caused by large packets.

	IPv4	IPv6
	ICMP Type3, Code4	ICMPv6 Type 2
July 2019	73	16
July 2020	641	599

Then, we proceed to analyze the number of DNS/UDP fragmented responses per authoritative server and IP version. Figure 2 shows a timeseries of these

---

[1] We also see that the response sizes almost doubled for NS3 from 2019 to 2020, although the NS3 operator confirmed they have not changed minimal response sizes or ENDS buffer sizes in the period.

responses. We see very few occur: fewer than 10k/day, compared to a total of 2.2B/day. Notice that NS1 has no fragmented responses in 2020, which is probably due to the reduction on the response sizes in 2020 (Table 2).

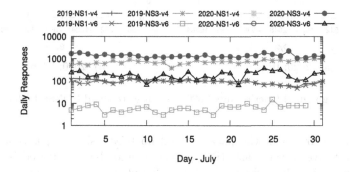

Fig. 2. UDP fragmented queries for `.nl` authoritative servers.

Still, even if there are few fragmented queries, why do they occur? First, we see most fragmented queries are from NS3 (Fig. 2), given NS3 does not return minimal responses (Sect. 3.1), which inflates responses[2].

But the resolvers have their own share of responsibility. We single out these DNS/UDP fragmented responses, and analyzed the announced EDNS0 buffer sizes. Figure 3 shows the results for July 2020, for both IPv4 and IPv6. We see that most fragmented queries are smaller than 2048 bytes, but we see that most of these resolvers announced a large EDNS0 buffer size – most equal to 4096 bytes, which is the default value on BIND (up to version 9.16.6)[3,4] [24]. So while our vantage point does not allow to tell if clients experience fragmentation on their side, it shows that authoritative servers very rarely fragment responses.

Packets Larger Than Path MTU: Since we collect traffic only at the authoritative servers, we cannot directly know if there was IPv4 fragmentation along the path. However, we can still use the ICMP protocol to determine if *some* of the DNS responses exceed the path MTU.

The routers along the path have a standard way of handling IP packets larger than their MTU, both using ICMP. If it is an IPv4 packet, and the fragmented flag (DF) is set, then the router should discard the packet and send a ICMP Type 3, code 4 packet as a response ("Fragmentation Needed and Don't Fragment was Set" [38]) back to the authoritative server. If the DF flag is off, then

---

[2] The advantage of having minimal responses disabled is that it can reduce the total number of queries, given resolvers already receive extra information.

[3] BIND9 uses a *dynamic* EDNS value: when it first contacts a server, it uses 512 bytes. From that point on, it uses the configured value – 4096 by default. If it receives no responses, it will lower it to 1432, 1232 and 512 bytes. See `edns-udp-size` in [24].

[4] Unbound changed the default buffer size to 1232 on 29 sept. 2020 [55], and so did BIND on version 9.16.8.

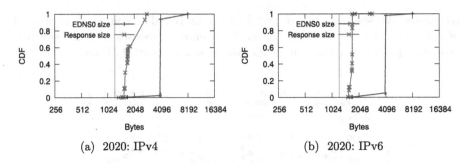

(a) 2020: IPv4   (b) 2020: IPv6

Fig. 3. Fragmented Queries July 2020: response sizes and EDNS0 buffer sizes.

the router can fragment the packet – and no ICMP signaling is sent back to the authoritative server. Last, IPv6 packets cannot be fragmented by routers, and routers facing them should send an ICMPv6 Type 2 message ("packet too big" [26]) back to the authoritative server.

In our setup, only the DNS provider of NS3 provides us with ICMP traffic. We analyze the ICMP traffic and show in Table 3 distribution of ICMP error messages associated with large packets, and see there are only few ICMP packets.

In the worst case scenario, these large DNS/UDP would be discarded by routers and both client and servers would not know about it, which could, in theory lead to unreachability. However, previous research has shown that, in the wild, DNS resolvers have built-in a series of fail-tolerance features, and will retry *multiple times* the same server and or switch from server/IP version, to the point of "hammering" the authoritative severs, in order to obtain responses [33,35]. In this scenario, even if one authoritative server becomes "unresponsive" – from the point-of-view of the resolver – having multiple authoritative servers (defined by distinct NS records), running on *dissimilar* networks, should minimize the probabilities of unreachability.

Network Issues with Large Responses: Our vantage point does not allow to know if clients received their large DNS/UDP responses. To determine if clients indeed receive large responses, we resort to Ripe Atlas probes and NS3, and evaluate 1M queries from roughly 8500 probes, over a period of one day. We show in Sect. A.1 that 2.5% of small (221 bytes) DNS/UDP responses *time-out*. For large responses (1744 bytes), this value is 6.9% – only considering a single DNS/UDP query without TCP fallback. Comparing to server-side fragmentation, we show that it is far more likely to happen on the network. Similar numbers were reported by Huston [22], who measured 7% drop with a similar response size on IPv6 and Van den Broek et al. [51] have shown that even up to 10% of all resolvers might be unable to handle fragments.

3.3   DNS Truncation: How and When?

Table 1 shows that 2.93–7.15% of all evaluated queries were truncated. Next we investigate why this happens. For each truncated response, we fetch its response size and its respective query' EDNS0 buffer size. Figure 4 shows the CDF for these values for July 2020, for NS1 (Sect. A shows NS3 for 2020 and the 2019 results for NS1 and NS3). We see that most DNS/UDP responses are truncated to values under 512 bytes, independently IP version (Response line).

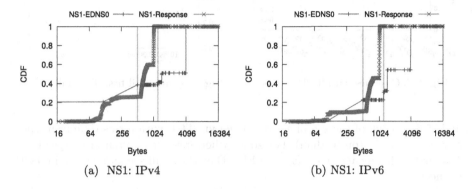

(a) NS1: IPv4   (b) NS1: IPv6

Fig. 4. NS1: CDF of DNS/UDP TC responses for `.nl`: July 2020

Small or no EDNS0 values lead to truncation: we see that most EDNS buffer sizes are equal to 512, which is rather too small for many queries (but the initial value by BIND when it first contact a server [24]). As such, if resolvers would advertise larger buffers, that would probably reduce truncated responses.

Oddly, we also see that only NS1 receives 13% of queries that are truncated with no EDNS0 extension, but not the other servers or IP version (shown as EDNS0=1 in Fig. 4). We found that this is due to an anomaly from two ASes (AS2637 – Georgia Tech and AS61207 – Ilait AB). Resolvers from these ASes have a "sticky" behavior [35], sending queries only to NS1 over IPv4. Both ASes send most queries without EDNS0 UDP buffer value (1 in the graph), and that is why Fig. 4a is skewed.

Large EDNS0 values are no insurance against truncation: We also see that even if clients announce large EDNS0 buffers, they still receive truncated responses. Even though 4096 bytes is enough to fit most responses (§3.1), the authoritative server can truncate responses based on its local MTU or `max-udp-size`.

3.4   Do Resolvers Fall Back to TCP?

Upon receiving a DNS/UDP truncated response, DNS resolvers *should* resend the query over TCP – what is know as *TCP fall back* [10]. In July 2020 (Table 1), we see 7.15% DNS/UDP TC queries over IPv6. However, we see only 5.37% of TCP queries over IPv6 – suggesting 1.78% were not followed by DNS/TCP queries. We next investigate this behavior.

Figure 5 shows how many UDP responses with TC flag are followed by a TCP query, within 60 s from the same IP address. The majority, 80% in IPv4

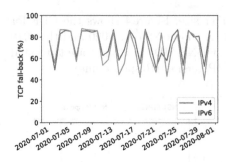

Fig. 5. TC replies with TCP retries

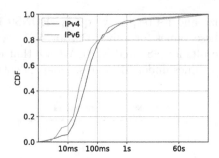

Fig. 6. Time until first TCP fall back

and 75% in IPv6 of these replies are retried via TCP within this time frame per day in July 2020 (on median). For zones where responses often are larger than 1232 bytes this means that after the Flag Day, they will see an increase in TCP connections.

If a resolver retries a query via TCP, then this query is sent usually within less than 100 ms. Figure 6 shows the time between the name server received the initial UDP query and the TCP retry on July 1 2020. 80% of all retries are sent within 100 ms and 90% within one 1 s. Retries from IPv6 addresses reach our authoritative servers slightly faster.

Missing TCP Queries: there are multiple reasons why truncated queries may not be followed by TCP ones. For example, queries from non-resolvers, such as crawlers, or malware. Also, as we discuss in Sect. 2, our datasets do not include data from NS2, the other anycast authoritative server for .nl. Given resolvers may switch from server to server [35], our dataset misses those[5]. Resolver farms may be partially to blame – the TCP query may be sent from adjacent IP addresses[6]. Dual-stacked resolvers may only send a TCP query over one (the first) IP version response arriving[7]. Altogether, we estimate that we miss up to 4.8% of retries in our initial measurement.

This still leaves 15–21% of TC replies without a TCP retry. We found that, for July 1st 2020, 47% of these queries without TCP retries were from Google (AS15169), a well-known large public resolver operator [16] that employs a complex, multi-layered resolver architecture spread across different IP ranges [34].

---

[5] We see 1.9% of TC IPv4 queries switching between NS1 and NS3 on July 1st, 2020, and 3.2% of IPv6 TC queries.

[6] For July 1 2020, we measure, how many TCP retries are first issued from a different resolver than the resolver of the original UDP query, but located in the same subnet (/24 subnet for IPv4 and /48 subnet for IPv6). There, 1.6% of retries via IPv4 and 0.1% via IPv6 are sent from a different resolver, likely belonging to the same farm.

[7] Of a sample of 3M queries that trigger a TC response, 4% were likely issued by those kind of resolvers. 58% then sent their TCP retry via both interfaces, leaving 42% of the TC replies without a TCP retry. Extrapolating these numbers to our measurements we can assume that around 1.3% of TC replies are not retried via TCP because of dual stacked resolvers.

Given their large infrastructure, one could hypothesize that Google could use a different resolver to send the TCP fallback query. To evaluate if that is the case, we extend our query matching criteria for TCP fallback: for each DNS/UDP TC reply, we evaluate if *any* IP address from Google (AS15169) sent a TCP query within 60 s after the sending of the TC reply. By doing this, we find that, in fact, Google resolvers almost *always* fallback to TCP, by having 99% of UDP TC queries being followed up by a TCP query. This shows how dynamic and complex a large DNS service can be.

4   Resolver EDNS0 Buffer Sizes

Next we analyze the EDNS0 buffer sizes for all resolvers we seen in our datasets (Table 1). For 2020, we see in Fig. 7a that roughly 30% of all resolvers announce 512 bytes EDNS0 buffer sizes or less, and 48.86% announce 1232 or less. The majority announce 4096 bytes: 33%. For ASes, we have a more even distribution: 20% announce 512 bytes or less, and 71% announce up to 1232 or less. Taking altogether, we can conclude that most resolvers announce a 4096 ENDS0 buffer size value (which is BIND9 default value up to version 9.16.7) are to blame partially for DNS/UDP fragmentation.

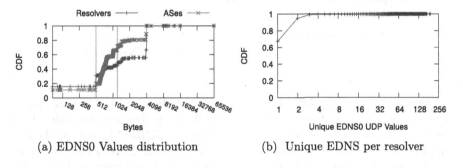

(a) EDNS0 Values distribution   (b) Unique EDNS per resolver

Fig. 7. EDNS0 per resolver and values: July 2020

Figure 7b shows he number of unique EDNS0 buffer sizes announced per resolver for the month of July 2020. We can see that more than 60% of resolvers announce only one EDNS0 value over the period. Only 5% of the resolvers showed 3 or more EDNS0 values in the period – maybe due to dynamic ENDS values [24] or configuration changes. Finally, 7% of resolvers (not shown in the figure), have no EDNS0 support – likely from old, non compliant clients.

4.1   DNS Flag Day 2020: What Was the Uptake?

The DNS Flag Day 2020 was proposed by members of the DNS community in order to avoid IP fragmentation on DNS/UDP, by not allowing UDP queries larger than 1232 bytes. This value was chosen based on a MTU of 1280 bytes – the minimum required by IPv6 [9] – minus 48 bytes of IPv6/UDP headers. The chosen date (2020-10-01) was a suggestion for operators to change their authoritative DNS servers and DNS resolvers.

To determine the Flag Day uptake, we compare the EDNS0 values from resolvers from July 2020 to October 2020, from Table 1, for UDP queries. The former we used it as a baseline, and the observed differences in the latter determine the uptake. Table 4a summarizes this data. We see in total 1.85M resolvers active on both datasets, and they sent 117.5B queries in the period.

Table 4. DNS Flag day datasets and changing resolvers

	July 2020	October 2020
Resolvers	3.78M	3.84M
∩	1.85 M	
UDP Queries	60.3B	62.81B
∩	117.54 B	

(a) Before and After Datasets

Resolvers	11338
from 4096 bytes	7881
from 1680 bytes	1807
from 512 bytes	1252
rest	398
ASes	958
Queries	3.01B

(b) EDNS0 1232 resolvers

Figure 8 shows the CDF of resolvers' EDNS0 buffer sizes. We see hardly any changes in the resolver EDNS behavior (if the resolver had multiple EDNS values, we picked the most frequent, also to remove BIND9 512 byte at the first try). On July 2020, we see 14.6% of the resolvers using EDNS0 buffers smaller or equal to 1232 bytes, and on October 2020, this value went to 16.0%. For both months, however, the most popular EDNS0 buffer value is 4096 bytes, with roughly 53% of the resolvers using it.

Resolvers that Adopted the DNS Flag Day Value: We identified 11338 resolvers that changed their EDNS0 value to 1232 bytes, as can be seen in Table 4. There resolvers were responsible for 3.01B queries, out of the 117.54B. They belonged to 958 different ASes, but most of them (6240) belonged to only two ASes – one in Taiwan and the other in Poland.

Looking Back to 1.5 Years: The Flag Day 2020 was originally proposed in Oct. 2019. Given some operators may deploy it *before* the Flag Day chosen date (Oct. 1 2020), we analyze the proportion resolvers we see over more than 1.5 years (May 2019-December 2020). Figure 9 shows the percentage of unique IP addresses announcing different buffer sizes per day. From May 2019 to Oct. 2020, we see that despite the increase of resolvers using EDNS0 1232, they winded up

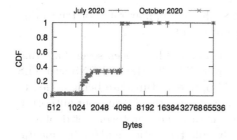

Fig. 8. CDF EDNS0 resolvers

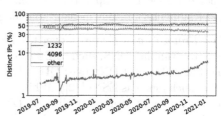

Fig. 9. Daily EDNS buffer distribution by resolvers (y axis in log-2 scale).

accounting for only 4.4% of the total resolvers. 4096 byte resolvers reduced from 50% to 40%. Since November 2020 the number of resolvers announcing 1232 bytes is growing faster and has reached 6.5% by the end of December 2020. Despite the latest increase, these results show that a large population of resolvers still needs to be reconfigured to use EDNS0 1232 bytes.

5 Related Work

IP Fragmentation: the problems related with IP fragmentation are well known [5]: it has problems with "middleboxes" (such as network address translation (NAT) devices, with stateless firewalls), by being expensive and error prone and may lead to unreachability [4,5,8,14]. It has also security vulnerabilities – it has been used DNS for cache poisoning attacks on DNS [17,50], and to compromise CAs based on it. Besides, there are several well-know attacks that exploit fragmentation [13,25,30,57]. Given these series of problems, IP fragmentation is considered fragile and should be avoided, also in DNS [5,12,58].

DNS and Large Responses: Large DNS/UDP responses have been previously shown to cause unreachability [51,53]. In 2011, using active measurements, Weaver *et al.* [53] have shown that 9% of clients could not receive fragmented DNS/UDP packets. Given our vantage point are not clients, we cannot determine this rate. We showed, however, the number of ICMP messages showing that DNS messages exceed the path MTU (Sect. 3.2). In a 2012 study [51], the authors analyzed DNSSEC messages (8.4M) from 230k resolvers to authoritative servers hosted SURFnet, the Dutch NREN. for 4k+ zones. They showed how 58% of resolvers received fragmented responses for DNSSEC queries.

Our results show a contrast to both of these studies: by analyzing 164B queries from more than 3M resolvers, for one zone (.nl), we show a tiny fraction of fragmented queries (10k/day, Sect. 3.2), but our VP allows only to measure the *server-side*. Besides, we also analyze truncation, responses sizes distribution, resolver behavior, EDNS0 distribution, from two distinct large DNS anycast operators that provide DNS service to .nl. Another (non-academic) study from

Google Public DNS operators in 2020 [28] showed similar rates of truncation and fragmentation, but measure on the resolver side.

New Protocols and Features. over the last years there have been several alternatives to "vanilla" DNS, such as DoH (DNS over HTTPS) [18] and DNS over TLS (DoTLS) [20], and DNS over QUIC [21]. Also, new features are being added to DNS, such (such as ESNI [42]). While we do not cover them here – our authoritative servers only support traditional DNS – as these new protocols get deployed, it will be necessary to evaluate how they handle truncation and/or fragmentation. For example, Google *rarely* truncate responses for its public DoTLS and DoH service [15], even if both run on TCP.

6   Conclusions

DNS/UDP large messages that lead to fragmentation have been long feared and blamed for causing unreachability. Drawing from 164B queries/responses, we asses state of affairs of large messages on DNS. We show that large responses are rare (for `.nl`), and that server-side IP fragmentation is minimal. In case of clients experience query timeouts on DNS/UDP, we show that 75% of resolvers do fall back to TCP – and by this way are able to retrieve large responses. Previous research has shown that "hammering" and server switching – behaviors shown by resolvers in the wild – are expected to be useful in avoiding unreachability.

Still, our evaluation of more than 3M resolvers show that they still have a long way to go: many of them announce either small (512 bytes) or large (4096 bytes) EDNS0 buffer sizes, both leading to more truncation, and increasing the chances of fragmentation/packets being lost on the network.

We also show that the initial uptake of the DNS Flag Day 2020 suggested EDNS0 buffer size has not been very wide, however, similar to DNSSEC algorithms adoption, it would be interesting to evaluate this adoption over time, especially now that major resolver vendors have adopted this value.

Acknowledgments. We thank Klaus Darillion, the anonymous PAM reviewers and our shepherd, Balakrishnan Chandrasekaran, for feedback and reviewing paper drafts. This work is partially funded by the European Union's Horizon 2020 CONCORDIA project (Grant Agreement # 830927).

A   Extra graphs

Fig. 10 shows the truncated queries for NS3 in 2020. Figure 11 shows the time-series of truncated queries for `.nl` on July 2019. We see in the same figures a close match between UDP truncated queries and TCP ones – however not quite the same. Figure 11 shows the CDF of DNS/UDP truncated queries for 2019, per server.

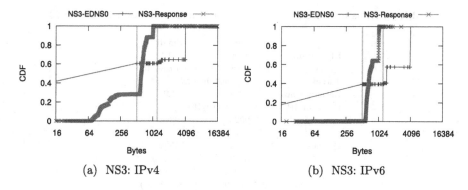

Fig. 10. NS3: CDF of DNS/UDP TC responses for `.nl`: July 2020

A.1 Clients and Large DNS/UDP Responses

We evaluate if DNS messages are being lost along the way from authoritative servers to clients. To do that, we setup two measurements using RIpe Atlas (∼10k probes), as shown in Table 5. We configure each probe to send a query directly to NS3, the server that returns additional records. As such, probes *bypass* local resolvers, so they cannot fallback to TCP: they simply send one UDP query. We setup two measurements: one that retrieves *large* DNS/UDP responses (1744 bytes, Large column) and one that retrieves *small* ones (221 bytes).

In total, we see 8576 probes being active on both measurements – sending more than 1M queries (512k on the Large, 510k on the Small). For each probe, we

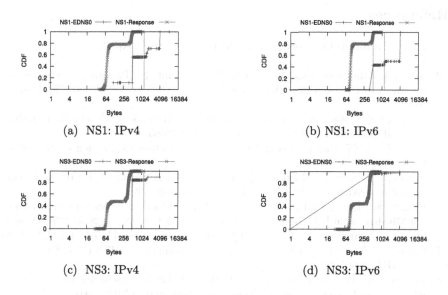

Fig. 11. CDF of DNS/UDP TC answers for `.nl`: July 2019

Table 5. Atlas measurements for large and small responses. Datasets:[43]

	Large	Small
EDNS0 buffer	4096	512
Query	ANY NS .nl	A ns1.dns.nl
Target	ns3.dns.nl	
Response Size	1744	221
Protocol/IP	UDP/IPv4	
Active Probes	9323	9322
∩	8576	
Queries	557047	555007
∩	512351	510575
OK	473606	497792
timeout	38745(6.9%)	12783 (2.5%)

look then into the number of failed responses (timeout), for the small and large measurements. We see that 6.9% of queries timeout for the large measurement, however, 2.5% of them also timeout for short responses.

Next we investigate each probe and compute the percentage of timeout queries per dataset. We then compute the difference between the rate of failed queries for the large and the small datasets. Out of the 8576 probes on both datasets, 6191 have no error difference for both large and small queries (72%). 10% in fact have more errors for the small dataset query, and only 17% have more errors for the longer answers. 325 have 100% of errors for the large datasets, but no errors for the small datasets. Overall, this measurement show the fragmentation is still an issue on the client side –which justifies the flag day.

References

1. 1.1.1: The Internet's fastest, privacy-first DNS resolver, AprIL 2018. https://1.1.1.1/
2. Abley, J., Gudmundsson, O., Majkowski, M., Hunt, E.: Providing minimal-sized responses to DNS Queries That Have QTYPE=ANY. RFC 8482, IETF, January 2019
3. Arends, R., Austein, R., Larson, M., Massey, D., Rose, S.: DNS security introduction and requirements. RFC 4033, IETF, March 2005
4. Bellis, R.: DNS Transport over TCP - implementation requirements. RFC 5966, IETF, August 2010
5. Bonica, R., Baker, F., Huston, G., Hinden, R., Troan, O., Gont, F.: IP fragmentation considered fragile. RFC 8900, IETF, September 2020
6. Brandt, M., Dai, T., Klein, A., Shulman, H., Waidner, M.: Domain validation++ For MitM-resilient PKI. In: CCS 2018, New York, NY, USA, pp. 2060–2076. Association for Computing Machinery (2018). https://doi.org/10.1145/3243734.3243790
7. Damas, J., Graff, M., Vixie, P.: Extension mechanisms for DNS (EDNS(0)). RFC 6891, IET, April 2013
8. De Boer, M., Bosma, J.: Discovering Path MTU black holes on the Internet using RIPE Atlas. Master's thesis, University of Amsterdam (2012). https://nlnetlabs.nl/downloads/publications/pmtu-black-holes-msc-thesis.pdf

9. Deering, S., Hinden, R.: Internet Protocol, Version 6 (IPv6) Specification. RFC 2460, IETF, December 1998

10. Dickinson, J., Dickinson, S., Bellis, R., Mankin, A., Wessels, D.: DNS transport over TCP - implementation requirements. RFC 7766, IETF, March 2016

11. Elvy, M., Nedved, R.: Network mail path service. RFC 915, IETF, December 1984

12. Fujiwara, K., Vixie, P.: Serving stale data to improve DNS resiliency (work in progress). Internet Draft, April 2020. https://tools.ietf.org/html/draft-fujiwara-dnsop-avoid-fragmentation-03

13. Gont, F.: Security implications of predictable fragment identification values. RFC 7739, IETF, February 2016

14. Gont, F., Linkova, J., Chown, T., Liu, W.: Observations on the dropping of packets with IPv6 extension headers in the real world. RFC 7872, IETF, June 2016

15. Google: secure transports for DNS: DNS response truncation, January. https://developers.google.com/speed/public-dns/docs/secure-transports#tls-sni

16. Google: Public DN, January 2020. https://developers.google.com/speed/public-dns/

17. Herzberg, A., Shulman, H.: Fragmentation considered poisonous, or: one-domain-to-rule-them-all. In: 2013 IEEE Conference on Communications and Network Security (CNS), pp. 224–232. IEEE (2013)

18. Hoffman, P., McManus, P.: DNS queries over HTTPS (DoH). RFC 8484, IETF, October 2018

19. Hoffman, P., Sullivan, A., Fujiwara, K.: DNS Terminology. RFC 8499, IETF, January 2019

20. Hu, Z., Zhu, L., Heidemann, J., Mankin, A., Wessels, D., Hoffman, P.: Specification for DNS over transport layer security (TLS). RFC 7858, IETF, May 2016

21. Huitema, K., Mankin, A., Dickinson, S.: Specification of DNS over dedicated QUIC connections (work in progress). Internet Draft, October 2020. https://datatracker.ietf.org/doc/draft-ietf-dprive-dnsoquic/

22. Huston, G.: Dealing with IPv6 fragmentation in the DNS, August 2017. https://blog.apnic.net/2017/08/22/dealing-ipv6-fragmentation-dns/

23. Internet Assigned Numbers Authority (IANA): Root Files (2020). https://www.iana.org/domains/root/files

24. ISC: 4. bind 9 configuration reference (2020). https://bind9.readthedocs.io/en/v9_16_6/reference.html

25. Krishnan, S.: Handling of overlapping IPv6 fragments. RFC 5722, IETF, December 2009

26. Kulkarni, M., Patel, A., Leung, K.: Mobile IPv4 dynamic home agent (HA) assignment. RFC 4433, IETF, March 2006

27. Laurie, B., Sisson, G., Arends, R., Blacka, D.: DNS Security (DNSSEC) Hashed authenticated denial of existence. RFC 5155, IETF, March 2008

28. Lieuallen, A.: DNS Flag Day 2020 and Google Public DNS, October 2020. https://www.youtube.com/watch?v=CHprGFJv_WE

29. McPherson, D., Oran, D., Thaler, D., Osterweil, E.: Architectural considerations of IP anycast. RFC 7094, IET, January 2014

30. Miller, I.: Protection against a variant of the tiny fragment attack (RFC 1858). RFC 3128, IETF, June 2001

31. Mockapetris, P.: Domain names - concepts and facilities. RFC 1034, IETF, November 1987

32. Mockapetris, P.: Domain names - implementation and specification. RFC 1035, IETF, November 1987

33. Moura, G.C.M., Heidemann, J., Müller, M., de O. Schmidt, R., Davids, M.: When the dike breaks: dissecting dns defenses during DDoS. In: Proceedings of the ACM Internet Measurement Conference, Boston, MA, USA, pp. 8–21, October 2018

34. Moura, G.C.M., Heidemann, J., de O. Schmidt, R., Hardaker, W.: Cache me if you can: effects of DNS Time-to-Live. In: Proceedings of the ACM Internet Measurement Conference, Amsterdam, The Netherlands, pp. 101–115. ACM, October 2019

35. Müller, M., Moura, G.C.M., de O. Schmidt, R., Heidemann, J.: Recursives in the wild: engineering authoritative DNS servers. In: Proceedings of the ACM Internet Measurement Conference, London, UK, pp. 489–495. ACM (2017)

36. OpenDNS: setup guide: OpenDNS. https://www.opendns.com/setupguide/, January 2019. https://www.opendns.com/setupguide

37. Partridge, C., Mendez, T., Milliken, W.: Host Anycasting Service. RFC 1546, IETF, November 1993

38. Postel, J.: Internet control message protocol. RFC 792, IETF, September 1981

39. Postel, J.: Internet Protocol. RFC 791, IETF, September 1981

40. Quad9: Internet security & privacy in a few easy steps. https://quad9.net, January 2021

41. Rekhter, Y., Li, T., Hares, S.: A border gateway protocol 4 (BGP-4). RFC 4271, IETF, January 2006

42. Rescorla, E., Oku, K., Sullivan, N., Wood, C.: TLS encrypted client hello (work in progress). Internet Draft, December 2020. https://tools.ietf.org/html/draft-ietf-tls-esni-09

43. RIPE NCC: RIPE Atlas measurement IDS, October 2020. https://atlas.ripe.net/measurements/ID. where ID is the experiment ID: large:27759950, small:27760294

44. RIPE NCC: RIPE Atlas Probes, May 2020. https://ftp.ripe.net/ripe/atlas/probes/archive/2020/05/

45. RIPE Ncc Staff: RIPE atlas: a global internet measurement network. Internet Protocol Journal (IPJ) **18**(3), 2–26 (2015)

46. Root Server Operators: Root DNS, May 2020. http://root-servers.org/

47. SIDN Labs: ENTRADA - DNS big data analytics, January 2020 https://entrada.sidnlabs.nl/

48. SIDN Labs: nl stats and data (2020). http://stats.sidnlabs.nl. https://stats.sidnlabs.nl/en/dnssec.html

49. Thomson, S., Huitema, C., Ksinant, V., Souissi, M.: DNS extensions to support IP version 6. RFC 3596, IETF, October 2003

50. Tomas, H.: IP fragmentation attack on DNS. In: RIPE 67, - Athens, Greece, October 2016. https://ripe67.ripe.net/presentations/240-ipfragattack.pdf

51. Van Den Broek, G., Van Rijswijk-Deij, R., Sperotto, A., Pras, A.: DNSSEC meets real world: dealing with unreachability caused by fragmentation. IEEE Commun. Mag. **52**(4), 154–160 (2014)

52. Vixie, P.: Extension Mechanisms for DNS (EDNS0). RFC 2671, IETF, August 1999

53. Weaver, N., Kreibich, C., Nechaev, B., Paxson, V.: Implications of Netalyzr's DNS measurements. In: Proceedings of the First Workshop on Securing and Trusting Internet Names (SATIN), Teddington, United Kingdom. Citeseer (2011)

54. Wessels, D.: RSSAC002-data, May 2020. https://github.com/rssac-caucus/RSSAC002-data/

55. Wijngaards, W.: release-1.12.0: Unbound 1.12.0 (2020). https://github.com/NLnetLabs/unbound/releases/tag/release-1.12.0

56. Wullink, M., Moura, G.C., Müller, M., Hesselman, C.: Entrada: A high-performance network traffic data streaming warehouse. In: Network Operations and Management Symposium (NOMS), 2016 IEEE/IFIP, pp. 913–918. IEEE, April 2016
57. Ziemba, G., Reed, D., Traina, P.: Security considerations for IP fragment filtering. RFC 1858, IETF, October 1995
58. Špaček, P., Surý, O.: DNS flag day 2020, October 2020. https://dnsflagday.net/2020/

Capacity

On the Accuracy of Tor Bandwidth Estimation

Rob Jansen[✉] and Aaron Johnson

U.S. Naval Research Laboratory, Washington, D.C., USA
{rob.g.jansen,aaron.m.johnson}@nrl.navy.mil

Abstract. The Tor network estimates its relays' bandwidths using relay self-measurements of client traffic speeds. These estimates largely determine how existing traffic load is balanced across relays, and they are used to evaluate the network's capacity to handle future traffic load increases. Thus, their accuracy is important to optimize Tor's performance and strategize for growth. However, their accuracy has never been measured. We investigate the accuracy of Tor's capacity estimation with an analysis of public network data and an active experiment run over the entire live network. Our results suggest that the bandwidth estimates underestimate the total network capacity by at least 50% and that the errors are larger for high-bandwidth and low-uptime relays. Our work suggests that improving Tor's bandwidth measurement system could improve the network's performance and better inform plans to handle future growth.

1 Introduction

Tor [12] is an anonymous communication overlay network with thousands of *relays* that forward over 200 Gbit/s of traffic for millions of daily *clients* [3,25] in order to provide unlinkability between the source and destination of traffic flows.

In order to balance client traffic across the relays, Tor relies on TorFlow to estimate of the speed at which relays can forward traffic through the network [30], and these *forwarding capacity* estimates are essential to both the performance and security of the network [5,21,22,31]. A relay's capacity estimate is derived from a self-measurement called the *observed bandwidth*: the highest throughput it has sustained over any ten second period over the last five days (see Sect. 2). This measure is imprecise and may be inaccurate in many realistic cases: (i) a *new* relay will not have forwarded any traffic and thus will be estimated to have a low capacity regardless of its available resources; (ii) a relay that is used *inconsistently* may not sustain a high throughput long enough to result in an accurate capacity estimate; and (iii) a relay that is *underutilized* will underestimate its capacity. TorFlow uses relays' capacity estimates as the basis for its relay selection algorithm that drives more user traffic load to higher-capacity relays [30]. Therefore, inaccurate capacity estimates could result in sub-optimal load balancing which would degrade user-perceived network performance and security [21].

Inaccurate capacity estimates also make it more difficult to understand how to prioritize research and development effort in order to plan future network

© Springer Nature Switzerland AG 2021
O. Hohlfeld et al. (Eds.): PAM 2021, LNCS 12671, pp. 481–498, 2021.
https://doi.org/10.1007/978-3-030-72582-2_28

improvements [32]. For example, obtaining funding to improve Tor scalability is more challenging without understanding the current limits of the network [27]. Improper network management also complicates relay recruitment and retention, and may dissuade the development of incentive schemes [13,14,17–19,26,28].

In this paper, we explore the inconsistency in Tor's estimated relay capacities using: (i) passive measurements collected by relays and published by Tor metrics [3]; and (ii) an active relay speed test measurement experiment. In Sect. 3 we study variability in relay capacity estimates, which we use as an indication of inaccurate estimation. We find significant variation in relays' advertised bandwidths: the capacity estimates of 25% of relays vary by more than 41%, the capacity estimates of 10% of relays vary by 71% or more, and some relays' capacity estimates vary by more than 200%. We find that higher variation is associated with lower capacity relays and with relays that are online less frequently. In Sect. 4 we present an active speed test experiment, through which we find that: (i) Tor underestimates its total capacity by about 50%; (ii) most relays increased their capacity estimate following our experiment (some by a $10\times$ or greater factor); and (iii) larger error is associated with high-capacity relays, exit relays, and relays with lower uptimes than with other types of relays. Our results suggest that indeed relay underutilization is a cause of significant error in capacity estimates.

Our work provides the first systematic exploration of the error in Tor's capacity estimation technique, and our results suggest that improvements to capacity estimates could significantly improve load balancing and network performance. Our research artifacts are available at https://torbwest-pam2021.github.io.

2   Background and Related Work

The Tor Network: The Tor network consists of thousands of *relays* forwarding traffic for millions of *clients* [3,25]. To assist in balancing client traffic load across relays, Tor assigns a *weight* to each relay according to an estimate of the relay's available bandwidth and publishes relay information (including addresses, weights, and various other *flags*) in a *network consensus* document [2, Sect. 3.4.1]. To use the network, a Tor client downloads the consensus and computes *selection probabilities* from the weights. The client builds a *circuit* through a series of typically three relays, using the selection probabilities to choose a relay for each *position*; relays with the Exit flag typically serve in the *exit* position, relays with the Guard flag (but not the Exit flag) typically serve in the *entry* position, and relays with neither flag serve in the *middle* position [11]. The client tunnels application data (e.g., web requests) through the constructed circuit, rotating to new circuits every 10 min (or when they browse to new websites). Although circuits rotate frequently, clients generally use long-term entry Guard relays [9] to help prevent predecessor attacks [34]. To be a Guard, Tor requires that a relay maintain high *uptime*: the percentage of hours during which it is online.

Relay Bandwidth: A relay's *forwarding capacity* is the maximum sustainable rate at which it can forward traffic through the network and is useful for balancing traffic load across relays. Relay operators do not directly report the true forwarding capacity of their relays, so Tor uses a heuristic to estimate it. Each relay calculates its *observed bandwidth* by tracking the highest throughput that it was able to sustain for any 10 s period during each of the last 5 days [10, Sect. 2.1.1]. To bootstrap the observed bandwidth calculation, a relay conducts a bandwidth self-test when it starts by creating four circuits through Tor and sending 125 KiB over each circuit; if this process completes within 10 ss, the relay will start with an observed bandwidth of $4 \cdot 125/10 = 50$ KiB/s ($\approx$410 Kbits/s) [8]. Additional remote measurements are conducted by TorFlow [30] (discussed below), and the observed bandwidth is updated over time as a relay forwards client traffic. Relay operators may limit the amount of bandwidth a relay consumes by configuring *average bandwidth* and *burst bandwidth* options, which control the refill rate and size of an internal token bucket rate limiter. Every 18 h, relays publish a *server descriptor* file [10, Sect. 2.1.1] which contains their latest observed, average, and burst bandwidth values. A relay's *advertised bandwidth* is the minimum of the observed and average bandwidths published by the relay, and is used as a basis for load balancing.

Load Balancing: Tor uses a measurement tool called TorFlow [30] to assist in balancing client traffic across relays. TorFlow measures relay performance by creating two-hop circuits through each relay and downloading files ranging in size from 16 KiB to 64 MiB from a known server through the circuit. TorFlow produces relay weights by: (i) computing the ratio of the measurement speed of each relay to the mean measurement speed of all relays; and (ii) multiplying each relay's ratio by its advertised bandwidth. The relay weights are published in the consensus and used to compute relay selection probabilities as described above.

Related Work: Previous work has established that TorFlow is insecure and vulnerable to manipulation, in part because a relay can detect when it is being measured [5,21,22,33]. Several alternative bandwidth measurement systems that produce relay weights have been proposed. SmarTor [4] and Simple Bandwidth Scanner [24] are similar in measurement design to TorFlow and suffer from similar limitations. EigenSpeed proposes that relays conduct peer measurement, and produces per-flow throughput estimates rather than estimates of relay forwarding capacity [31]. PeerFlow is a passive peer measurement system that proposes a secure aggregation inference technique to produce relay capacity estimates from multiple peers observations [22]. TightRope proposes a centralized approach for optimally balancing load given a set of accurate capacity weights [7], and Ting focuses on measuring latencies between relays [6].

Dingledine outlines the lifecycle of a new relay and explains that it can take three days for a relay to be measured by TorFlow, several weeks for a relay to obtain the Guard flag, and even longer to reach steady state [8]. Dingledine motivates the need for further analysis of Tor metrics data to better understand relay operations in the real world. Using both passive and active measurements, our work provides the first systematic exploration of the error in Tor's capacity estimation technique. More recently, Greubel et al. analyze load distribution in Tor and find that relays with more forwarding capacity are associated with larger relay weights [15]. Although we are focused on measuring the accuracy of forwarding capacity estimates rather than relay weights, the association established by Greubel et al. will aid in explaining some of our results.

3   Analysis of Tor Metrics Data

To better understand the accuracy of Tor's capacity-estimation heuristic, we analyze publicly available Tor metrics data [3]. Relays passively measure throughput over time and publish bandwidth information in their server descriptors [10, Sect. 2.1.1], while the load-balancing weights that TorFlow derives from the bandwidth information are published in network consensus files [2, Sect. 3.4.1]. The Tor Project has collected these documents for over a decade [3], and we analyze the data published throughout the 52 week period starting on 2018-08-01.

Relay Capacity Variation: A relay with a perfect capacity estimation algorithm would consistently report the same advertised bandwidth; thus, *variation* in advertised bandwidths indicates *inaccurate* capacity estimation. Let $A(r, w)$ be the sequence of advertised bandwidths published by relay r during week w. We quantify the variability in $A(r, w)$ by computing the *relative standard deviation* (RSD) as

$$\mathrm{RSD}(A(r, w)) = \mathrm{stdev}(A(r, w))/\mathrm{mean}(A(r, w)) \qquad (1)$$

where stdev() and mean() compute the standard deviation and mean, respectively. Higher RSDs are associated with more fluctuation of the capacity estimate around the expected capacity and indicate error in the estimation.

We summarize the variability in the estimated relay capacity for relay r by computing the mean of $\mathrm{RSD}(A(r, w))$ over all $1 \leq w \leq n$ weeks in which r published at least one *valid* server descriptor. We remove potential sources of bias by considering a server descriptor for r valid unless: (i) it was published before r was measured (i.e., before r appeared in a consensus without the unmeasured flag); or (ii) it was published during a week in which a change in r's average or burst bandwidth options caused a reduction in the advertised bandwidth. We call $\mathrm{mean}(\mathrm{RSD}(A(r, 1)), \ldots, \mathrm{RSD}(A(r, n)))$ the *mean weekly RSD* for relay r. We compute mean weekly RSDs for only those relays that were not flagged as unmeasured in at least one consensus (to avoid potential bias from bootstrapping new relays). Although we suppose that the true forwarding capacity of each relay does not often change (i.e., relays do not often upgrade to faster network access links), computing the RSD on a weekly basis ensures that any upgrades that do occur during one of the weeks in our analysis period are likely to only affect a small fraction of the n total weeks that we consider (and thus have a small effect on the mean weekly RSD summary statistic).

Analysis Results: We compute mean weekly RSDs for relays over $n = 52$ weeks, where $w = 1$ includes the seven days starting on 2018-08-01 and $w = 52$ includes the seven days starting on 2019-07-24. During this analysis period, 34,850 unique relays appeared across 8,736 consensus files (many more than are

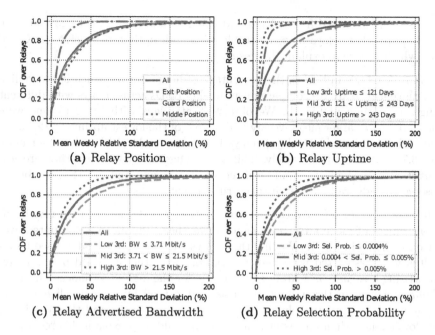

Fig. 1. The distribution of the mean weekly RSD over all valid relays. For each valid relay r, we compute the RSD for each week that r published a valid server descriptor, and then compute the mean over all such weeks to get the mean weekly RSD for r.

online at any given time due to churn). Of these, 11,296 (32%) were never measured (i.e., never appeared in any consensus without the unmeasured flag), and an additional 1,503 (4.3%) were measured but did not publish a valid descriptor (as explained above). We consider the remaining 22,051 relays (63%) as valid in our analysis, and we compute the mean weekly RSDs for these valid relays.

Figure 1 compares the distribution of the mean weekly RSD over all such valid relays and over distinct subsets that are separated by common relay characteristics (position, uptime, advertised bandwidth, and selection probability). Over all relays (the solid line in each subfigure), we find that the reported advertised bandwidths exhibit significant variation. The mean over all relays of the mean weekly RSD is 27%, while 25% and 10% of the relays have a mean weekly RSD of 35% and 66% or more, respectively (and a non-trivial fraction of relays have RSDs of 100% or greater). Such variation is larger than expected when the true capacity does not change. We also find that the largest RSDs are associated with lower capacity relays and relays that are online less frequently, as we explain next.

Position: A relay's position is that in which it serves most frequently throughout the year. We compare mean weekly RSDs across relays of different positions in Fig. 1a. We observe that guard relays exhibited significantly lower variation in their advertised bandwidths than did exits and middles: compared to exits, guards' RSDs dropped from 16% to 7.0% at P50 and from 71% to 23% at P90. Tor requires that relays must be stable with high uptime to receive the Guard flag, which may help explain this result.

Uptime. A relay's uptime is the percentage of hours during which it was online over the entire year. We compare mean weekly RSDs across relays with different ranges of uptime in Fig. 1b. We observe that relays with lower uptime were correlated with larger mean weekly RSDs: 25% of the lowest uptime (≤121 days) and highest uptime (>243 days) relays had mean weekly RSDs of 46% or more and 6.7% or more, respectively. This result suggests that relays that are less consistently available are underutilized by Tor clients and are thus unable to observe enough traffic to reach their true capacity.

Advertised Bandwidth. We compare mean weekly RSDs across relays with different ranges of mean advertised bandwidths (here, the mean is computed over the entire year) in Fig. 1c. We find that relays with lower mean advertised bandwidths were associated with higher variation, with the one-third of the relays advertising less than 3.71 Mbit/s accounting for the highest variance. The same *absolute* change in throughput (such as that caused by a single client) could result in a larger *relative* change in advertised bandwidth (and thus the RSD) for slower relays than for faster relays, which could help explain this result.

Selection Probability. We compare weekly RSDs across relays with different ranges of selection probabilities (the mean normalized weight from all consensuses in which it appeared throughout the year) in Fig. 1d. Relays with the lowest one-third of selection probability were correlated with higher mean weekly RSDs, while relays with the highest one-third of selection probability were correlated with lower variation. Since selection probability is directly associated with the amount of traffic a relay will observe, it follows that relays that are chosen most consistently report advertised bandwidths with the least variation.

Overall, we find significant variation in relays' advertised bandwidth, and that lower capacity and lower uptime relays are correlated with higher variation. However, we are unable to deduce the *true* causes of the observed associations because *correlation does not imply causation*. Next we conduct an active measurement experiment to help us further understand error in capacity estimates.

4 Tor Relay Speed Test Experiment

Our analysis of variation in advertised bandwidths suggests that there is significant error in Tor's system for determining relay capacities. However, without more information, it seems difficult to tell why and to what extent these errors are made. Based on our understanding of the TorFlow system, though, we can hypothesize that the predominant error is to *underestimate* the true capacity of Tor relays. This hypothesis seems plausible because the observed bandwidth is a self-measurement that mostly is limited by how much client traffic is sent through a relay, and it has been observed that there is a slow feedback process in which some client traffic is attracted, the observed bandwidth increases and causes the relay weight to increase, and then more client traffic is attracted [8].

To test this hypothesis, we perform a speed test on the live Tor network by actively attempting to send 1 Gbit/s of Tor traffic through each relay. If a relay is not already receiving sufficient client traffic to reach its true capacity (at least for 10 ss every 5 days), the extra traffic we add should increase its observed bandwidth, as reported in its server descriptors. The resulting observed bandwidths should increase our overall estimate of Tor's capacity and give us a more accurate estimate of how much total client traffic it could forward.

Moreover, as suggested by our capacity variation analysis, we may be able to identify differences in the amount of underestimation depending on the relays' positional flags (e.g. Guard and Exit), advertised bandwidth, and uptime. For example, our previous results may lead us to hypothesize that relays with lower uptime will have a larger increase in observed bandwidth due to the speed test (i.e., their current observed bandwidths are larger underestimates of their forwarding capacity). Such non-uniform errors would imply that Tor's load balancing is suboptimal, where relays with higher degrees of capacity underestimation receive too little traffic and relays with lower degrees receive too much.

Setup: We added 487 lines of code to Tor v0.3.5.7 in support of our speed test experiment. Our changes include the addition of a new SPEEDTEST cell; when a SPEEDTEST cell that was sent by a client running our version of Tor is received by a relay running our version of Tor, the relay will simply return the cell back to the client over the same circuit. When creating a circuit that starts and ends with a client and relay running our version of Tor, the SPEEDTEST cell allows us to send a burst of traffic in both directions through the circuit. We also added Tor client controller commands to enable us to instruct a client (through the control port) to build speed test measurement circuits through a path of relays, to start and stop sending SPEEDTEST cells through a measurement circuit, and to extract information about each measurement result.

We conduct our speed test experiment from a single dedicated machine with 32 GiB of RAM, 8 CPU cores, and a 1 Gbit/s symmetric network link. We set up 10 Tor clients $(C_1, \ldots, C_{10})$ and 10 Tor relays $(R_1, \ldots, R_{10})$ on this machine that each run our enhanced version of Tor. We connect our relays to the Tor network so they function as regular Tor relays; we set the MaxAdvertisedBandwidth Tor option to the minimum allowed value (300 Kbits/s) to ensure that our relays do not receive a large weight and are seldom used by Tor clients that we do not control. The speed test experiment proceeds sequentially as follows:

1. We download the latest list of relays from a Tor directory mirror;
2. We randomly choose an *untested* target relay T from the list;
3. For $i \in [1, 10]$, we command C_i to build a circuit $C_i \rightleftarrows T \rightleftarrows R_i$;
4. For $i \in [1, 10]$, we command C_i to send SPEEDTEST cells to R_i through the circuit with T for 20 s as fast as Tor (and TCP) will allow;
5. Upon receiving the SPEEDTEST cells from T, R_i sends them back to T;
6. T simply forwards the cells in each direction as it would on any other circuit;
7. When the 20 s measurement is complete, we close the measurement circuits, mark T as *tested*, and continue from 1.

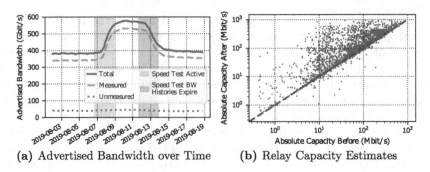

(a) Advertised Bandwidth over Time   **(b)** Relay Capacity Estimates

Fig. 2. The effects of the speed test on Tor relays (≈200 Gbit/s of capacity discovered).

By using 10 circuits in parallel (20 sockets in parallel on T), we increase the traffic rate through T while mitigating any potential rate limits imposed by Tor's stream and circuit flow control or by TCP congestion control. Our measurement has the potential to send a burst of traffic at an aggregate rate of 1 Gbit/s through each target T. The measurement effect will be reflected in the following server descriptor that T publishes, in which it will report its observed bandwidth (the highest throughput that it was able to sustain for any 10 s period).

Our experiment is designed to minimize Tor network relay overhead. We add load to only one remote target relay at a time and only for a short period. We submitted our experimental design and plans to the Tor Research Safety Board [1] for feedback. We received encouraging feedback and a "no objections" decision. We also explained our plans to the Tor community through a post to the public *tor-relays* mailing list [16]. We gave instructions on how to opt out and allowed one week to collect feedback. Finally, we served a web page containing a link to the mailing list post on the IP addresses used in the experiment.

Results: Our speed test experiment ran for just over 2 days (51 h) starting on 2019-08-06. We plot in Fig. 2a the sum of the most-recently published advertised bandwidths of all online relays over time. The first green region shows the period during which the speed test was active, and the second gray region shows the period during which the effects of the speed test expired. Note that the delay in the increase and decrease in advertised bandwidth relative to our experiment is caused by: (i) the 18 h server descriptor publishing interval; and (ii) the observed bandwidth algorithm which stores history for each of the last 5 days. We successfully *tested* 4,867 relays, while 2,132 relays were *untested* due to circuit building timeouts. On average, the tested relays represent 341/382 Gbit/s (89%) and 525/570 Gbit/s (92%) of the total advertised bandwidth before and after the speed test took effect, respectively, whereas the untested relays represent 41/382 Gbit/s (11%) and 45/570 Gbit/s (8%).

In the remainder of our analysis, we consider only those 4,867 relays that we successfully tested. We take the relay capacity before the test to be the maximum advertised bandwidth over the period from 2019-08-01 until the speed test starts on 2019-08-06, and we take the relay capacity afterwards to be the maximum advertised bandwidth from the speed test start until 2019-08-12.

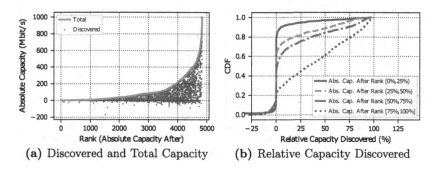

(a) Discovered and Total Capacity   **(b)** Relative Capacity Discovered

Fig. 3. Rank is by the capacity after the speed test. Discovered capacity is after−before, whereas relative discovered is (after − before)/after. Summary of relay capacities after the speed test (in Mbit/s): min=0.262, Q1=12.4, med=53.6, Q3=135, max=998.

Relay Results. Fig. 2b shows the per-relay capacities before and after the speed test: we observe that many relays increased their capacity estimates, some by a 10× or greater factor. We do see some relays with slightly reduced capacity estimates, which could be due to reasons such as reduced bandwidth rates (i.e., average bandwidths) or increased background traffic from other applications.

Network Results. We find that the estimated network capacity (the sum of relay capacities) increases by about 50% after our speed tests push relays into reporting higher observed bandwidths. Specifically, the network increases from 360 Gbit/s before the experiment to 550 Gbit/s afterwards, which gives a 52.9% increase in estimated total capacity. The capacity increase among exit relays (i.e., with the Exit flag) is 30.0 Gbit/s (32.6%), the increase among guard relays (i.e., with the Guard flag but not the Exit flag) is 91.2 Gbit/s (40.1%), and the increase among the middle relays (i.e., those remaining) is 61.3 Gbit/s (157%). Because exit bandwidth limits Tor's overall throughput, we therefore could expect that Tor could handle 30.0 Gbit/s (32.6%) more traffic than previously expected. We emphasize that these results may still underestimate the true capacity of the network: our test setup was limited by a 1 Gbit/s network link and we were unable to test many relays, so our results should be taken as a lower bound on both Tor's true capacity and on the degree of error in its current capacity estimates.

Effects of Capacity. There are at least a couple of reasons to expect that the capacity of a relay may affect the amount by which its capacity is currently underestimated. First, the variance of client traffic is likely lower on higher-capacity relays, as the number of clients they attract is larger, and so by the law of large numbers we expect the variance in the sum of client traffic to decrease. Because observed bandwidths take the maximum bandwidth over several days, small relays are more likely by chance to attract a large amount of traffic relative to their size. Second, large relays have fewer peers that they can be paired with during TorFlow measurements without the other relay acting as a bottleneck during the measurement. We therefore investigate how the capacity of a relay affects the amount of capacity "discovered" during the speed test, that is, the change in the advertised bandwidth after the speed test.

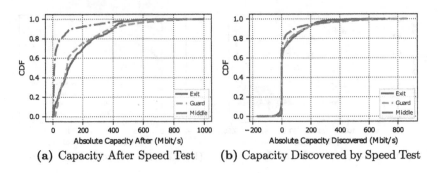

(a) Capacity After Speed Test   (b) Capacity Discovered by Speed Test

Fig. 4. Capacity after and discovered by speed test by relay position.

Figure 3a shows the capacity discovered per relay ranked by the capacity after the speed test. The capacity after the speed test should be closer to the true capacity. We notice that at all capacity ranks, the discovered capacity ranges from none to all of the post-speed-test capacity. To better understand the quantitative relationship between relay capacity and discovered capacity, Fig. 3b plots CDFs for relative discovered capacity after ranking relays by capacity afterwards and dividing that list into quartiles. Note that the discovered capacity is calculated relative to the capacity after the speed test, and thus is almost always a value between 0% and 100%.

We observe that higher-capacity relays have higher discovered capacity, *even relative to their capacity*. The median increase is 0.0% for the quartile with the lowest-capacity relays, 0.0% for the second quartile, 0.9% for the third quartile, and 32.5% for the highest quartile. This result shows that the largest Tor relays have the most inaccurate capacity estimates, on both an absolute and relative basis. It also suggests that the Tor weights may be too low for such relays, reducing load-balancing and thus Tor performance overall. We do notice that for all but the smallest relays, there is a high degree of capacity underestimation: at P90 the relative discovered capacity is 4.74% for the first quartile, 53.8% for the second, 72.7% for the third, and 89.4% for the fourth.

Effects of Position. We might also expect that relays in different positions have different degrees of capacity underestimation. An exit relay, for example, carries more traffic relative to its capacity than other relays because the exit position has the least total bandwidth, and so we may expect that it has a better estimate of its true capacity. Figure 4a shows the distribution of advertised bandwidths after the speed test. We again (and throughout the paper) consider relays with the Exit flag to be exits, relays with the Guard but not Exit flag to be guards, and the remaining relays to be middles. There were 764 exits, 2,049 guards, and 1,943 middles. We see that exit and guard relays have similar distributions, with medians of 109 Mbit/s and 92.3 Mbit/s, respectively. The middle relays have significantly smaller capacities, with a median of 10.0 Mbit/s. Figure 4b shows the amount of discovered capacity by position. While the median values are all at or near zero, we discovered a relatively large amount of bandwidth for

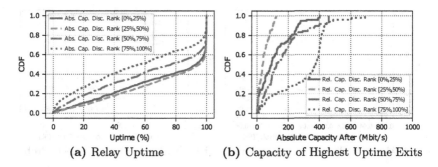

Fig. 5. The effects of uptime on discovered capacity. (a) Relay uptime, where relays are ranked by absolute discovered capacity (after − before). Absolute discovered capacities summary (in Mbit/s): min = −169, Q1 = 0.00, med = 0.01, Q3 = 20.8, max = 881. (b) Relay capacity after the speed test of exits with ≥ 75% uptime (379 such exits). Relays are ranked by relative discovered capacity ((after − before)/after). Relative discovered capacities summary: min = −96.6%, Q1 = 0.00%, med = 0.00%, Q3 = 10.2%, max = 91.0%.

a significant fraction of relays in each position, with third quartile (P75) values of 39.1 Mbit/s for exits, 31.1 Mbit/s for guards, and 5.35 Mbit/s for middles. These results show surprisingly that exit relays generally had the most discovered capacity, despite their relatively high traffic load.

Effects of Uptime. To investigate the capacity estimation errors, we next consider how a relay's uptime affects its discovered capacity. We expect that increased uptime will lead to lower discovered capacity because of the slow feedback between increasing the observed bandwidth, which attracts additional client traffic, which then further increases the observed bandwidth [8].

We compute uptime as the fraction of consensuses (i.e., hours) in which the relay was present during the year preceding our speed test (2018-08-01 to 2019-07-30). Figure 5a shows that increased uptime is correlated with decreased discovered capacity. The median annual uptime of the top quartile of relays (i.e., those with the largest discovered capacities) is 56.6%, while the median uptime of the bottom quartile is 93.2%. We note that the bottom two quartiles each have nearly zero discovered capacity, explaining their similar uptime distributions. If we consider the uptimes by position, we observe the same general pattern: guards generally have higher uptime and middles generally have lower. These results support the observed phenomenom that relays' observed capacities increase over time towards the true amounts [8].

We have shown that position, capacity, and uptime separately lead to different amounts of error in the advertised bandwidth. To somewhat disentangle these effects, we consider now the discovered capacity for the exit position (other positions are similar and appear in the Appendix), and we only consider relays with an uptime of at least 75% during the year preceding our experiment. By considering only the relays that were online for many months, we expect to largely remove the slow-increase phase of Tor's measurement system. Moreover, by considering just

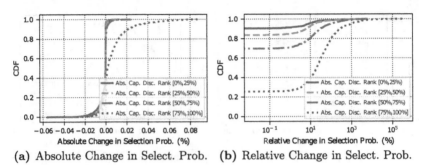

(a) Absolute Change in Select. Prob.   (b) Relative Change in Select. Prob.

Fig. 6. Change in selection probabilities before and after the speed test. Discovered capacities summary (in Mbit/s): min $= -169$, Q1 $= 0.00$, med $= 0.01$, Q3 $= 20.8$, max $= 881$.

the exit position, we focus on the position for which the capacity is most limited and the effects of poor load balancing thus most impactful.

We show the results in Fig. 5b. Among the high-uptime exits (for which we might have expected little undiscovered bandwidth), there are large relative discovered capacities among the largest quarter by capacity after the speed test, ranging from 10.2% in the third quartile to 91.0% at maximum. Moreover, larger amounts of capacity are clearly still discovered among the largest exits, with a median of 375 Mbit/s capacity among the relays in the highest quartile of relative discovered capacity, compared to 124 Mbit/s, 34.6 Mbit/s, and 94.8 Mbit/s in the median for the third to first quartiles, respectively. This is despite the fact that relays are ranked by *relative* discovered capacity, which means that not only do the largest exits have the largest total error in capacity measurement, they have the largest *fraction* of capacity error. This is consistent with a hypothesis that the largest Tor relays are unable to attract enough traffic to recognize their true capacity. It shows a consistent *bias* in the Tor bandwidth measurement system against large relays, which consequently is likely to cause the Tor weights to be too low for such relays, reducing Tor performance overall. Note that these results are shown by absolute discovered capacity in the Appendix.

Effects on Load Balancing. To understand how Tor load balancing is affected by its biased capacity estimation, we analyze the relay selection probabilities before and after the speed test. Our speed test is designed to investigate the advertised bandwidths, and the resulting effects on the weights are complicated both by any changes in the relay population and by the somewhat complex effects of the TorFlow load balancing system. However, Greubel et al. [15] find high correlation between the advertised bandwidths and the Tor weights that determine the selection probabilities, and Tor's load-balancing goal is indeed to choose each relay proportional to its capacity. Therefore, we expect biases in the advertised bandwidths to result in suboptimal selection probabilities.

Figure 6 shows the change in selection probabilities caused by the speed test. Relays are divided into quartiles by the total amount of discovered capacity. We can clearly see that, as expected, the relays with the largest discovered capacity experienced the largest increases in their selection probabilities. For relays ranked in the top quartile, the change in the median selection probability is 0.002% (a 20.3% relative increase), while at P90 we observe an even more extreme weight change of 0.021% (a 267% relative increase).

5 Discussion

Throughout the paper, we have highlighted the performance implications of Tor's capacity estimation errors. We note further that the bandwidth estimation errors we have observed have security implications. A primary security mechanism Tor uses is to make it expensive to run a large fraction of the network by requiring a large amount of bandwidth to observe a large fraction of client traffic. It accomplishes this by making the selection weights highly correlated with (i.e., roughly proportional to) the advertised bandwidths [15]. The errors we have discovered allow an adversary to more cheaply attract and attack client connections (e.g., traffic correlation [23] or website fingerprinting [29]). Our results imply that an adversary can gain an advantage by maintaining many high-uptime relays each with low capacity. Moreover, we show that the sensitive exit and guard positions are vulnerable to this exploitation.

Thus, an adversary could run a large number of low-bandwidth relays for many weeks as both exits and (eventual) guards. Simply due to the bias of Tor's measurement system, those relays would obtain higher total weight than the relative cost of running them. Running additional relays simply requires additional IP addresses, due to Tor's limit of two relays per IP address. Therefore, assuming bandwidth is the dominant cost, the adversary would spend less to observe and attack a given amount of client traffic than if the network bandwidth were accurately measured. The adversary could use its relays to deanonymize clients via known attacks.

We further observe that our speed test could be executed by a malicious party to direct more client traffic to *any* subset of the Tor network, by raising the advertised bandwidths of relays in that subset and thus their weights. Easier attacks to inflate malicious relay bandwidth are already known [5,20–22,33]. However, in this attack the adversary need not control the relays to which it directs traffic. For example, a malicious network adversary (e.g., an ISP or nation-state) is able to direct more client traffic to relays on networks it can observe, without running any of those relays. Such an ability again would enable deanonymization attacks on the connections thus directed. This ability also enables denial-of-service by allowing the adversary to artificially increase the weights of a subset of the network, overloading those relays and degrading network performance.

6   Conclusion

Estimates of Tor relays' forwarding capacity are used to balance client traffic load across relays and therefore accurate estimates are vital to the performance and security of the Tor network. We analyzed the accuracy of Tor relay capacity estimation using passive measurements of relay bandwidth that are published by Tor metrics [3]. We found significant variation in relays' advertised bandwidths which indicates inaccurate estimation; higher variation was associated with lower capacity relays and relays that were online less frequently. We further explore the accuracy of Tor capacity estimation techniques through an active speed test experiment on the live Tor network. Through this experiment, we find that Tor underestimates its total capacity by about 50%, and that most relays increased their capacity estimate following our experiment (some by a 10× or greater factor). We also found that higher capacity relays and exit relays discovered more capacity than lower capacity and non-exit relays, respectively, and that relays with lower uptimes were correlated with higher discovered capacity. Our results suggest that improvements to capacity estimates could significantly improve load balancing, which could lead to better network performance and security.

Acknowledgments. This work has been partially supported by the Office of Naval Research (ONR), the Defense Advanced Research Projects Agency (DARPA), and the National Science Foundation (NSF) under award number CNS-1925497.

Appendix

Figure 7 shows for each relay position the uptime by absolute discovered capacity quartiles. We observe that for all positions relays with higher discovered capacity have higher uptime, although we notice that guard relays have higher overall uptime (due to the additional uptime and stability requirements to get the Guard flag), and middles have a larger number of relays with low uptime.

Figure 8 shows the capacity of guard and middle relays after the speed test by quartiles of relative discovered capacity. It includes only relays with at least 75% uptime. It shows that for high-uptime relays in both positions, most of the discovered capacity is among the largest relays. We can especially see that for middle relays, the low amount of discovered capacity is due to the large number of relays with very little total or discovered capacity.

Figure 9 shows the effect of relay capacity on the discovered capacity by position when only relays with at least 75% uptime are considered.

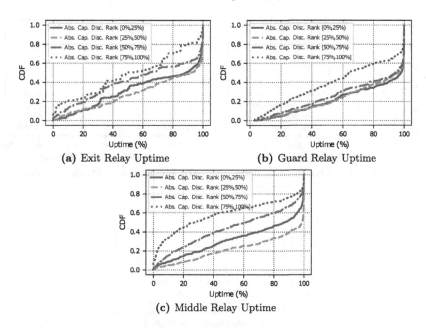

Fig. 7. The effect of relay uptime, where relays are ranked by their absolute discovered capacity. (a) Shows exit relays split into 4 sets by rank. Summary of the absolute discovered capacities (in Mbit/s): min $= -88.0$, Q1 0.00, med $= 0.0$, Q3 $= 39.1$, max $= 707$. (b) Shows guard relays split into 4 sets by rank. Summary of the absolute discovered capacities (in Mbit/s): min $= -90.3$, Q1 $= 0.00$, med $= 0.428$, Q3 $= 31.1$, max $= 881$. (c) Shows middle relays split into 4 sets by rank. Summary of the absolute discovered capacities (in Mbit/s): min $= -169$, Q1 $= 0.00$, med $= 0.00$, Q3 $= 5.13$, max $= 774$.

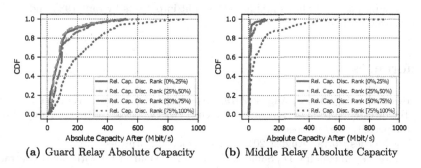

Fig. 8. Absolute capacity of relays after the speed test, where relays are ranked by their relative discovered capacity. Relative discovered capacity is computed as (after $-$ before)/after. Includes only relays with uptime of 75% (273 days) or more during the year preceding the speed test. (a) Shows guard relays split into 4 sets by rank (1,238 guards had at least 75% uptime). (b) Shows middle relays split into 4 sets by rank (983 middles had at least 75% uptime).

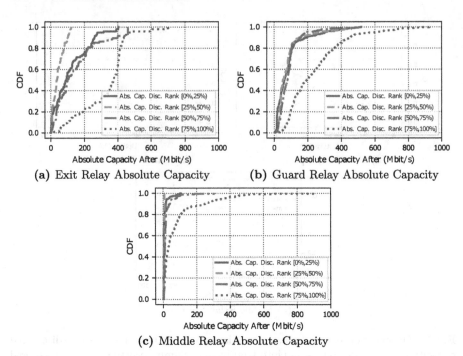

(a) Exit Relay Absolute Capacity   **(b)** Guard Relay Absolute Capacity

(c) Middle Relay Absolute Capacity

Fig. 9. Absolute capacity of relays after the speed test, where relays are ranked by their absolute discovered capacity. Absolute discovered capacity is computed as after − before Includes only relays with uptime of 75% (273 days) or more during the year preceding the speed test. (a) Shows exit relays split into 4 sets by rank (379 exits had at least 75% uptime). (b) Shows guard relays split into 4 sets by rank (1,238 guards had at least 75% uptime). (c) Shows middle relays split into 4 sets by rank (983 middles had at least 75% uptime).

References

1. Research safety board, August 2019. https://research.torproject.org/safetyboard
2. Tor directory protocol, version 3, September 2019. https://gitweb.torproject.org/torspec.git/tree/dir-spec.txt
3. Tor Metrics Portal, August 2019. https://metrics.torproject.org
4. Andre, G., Alexandra, D., Samuel, K.: SmarTor: smarter tor with smart contracts: improving resilience of topology distribution in the Tor network. In: Annual Computer Security Applications Conference (ACSAC) (2018)
5. Bauer, K., McCoy, D., Grunwald, D., Kohno, T., Sicker, D.: Low-resource routing attacks against Tor. In: Workshop on Privacy in the Electronic Society (WPES) (2007)
6. Cangialosi, F., Levin, D., Spring, N.: Ting: measuring and exploiting latencies between all Tor nodes. In: Conference on Internet Measurement (IMC) (2015)
7. Darir, H., Sibai, H., Borisov, N., Dullerud, G., Mitra, S.: TightRope: towards optimal load-balancing of paths in anonymous networks. In: Workshop on Privacy in the Electronic Society (WPES) (2018)

8. Dingledine, R.: The lifecycle of a new relay. Tor Blog Post, September 2013. https://blog.torproject.org/lifecycle-new-relay
9. Dingledine, R., Hopper, N., Kadianakis, G., Mathewson, N.: One fast guard for life (or 9 months). In: Workshop on Hot Topics in Privacy Enhancing Technologies (HotPETs) (2014)
10. Dingledine, R., Mathewson, N.: Tor protocol specification, November 2018. https://gitweb.torproject.org/torspec.git/tree/tor-spec.txt
11. Dingledine, R., Mathewson, N.: Tor path specification, September 2019. https://gitweb.torproject.org/torspec.git/tree/path-spec.txt
12. Dingledine, R., Mathewson, N., Syverson, P.: Tor: the second-generation onion router. In: USENIX Security Symposium (2004)
13. Dinh, T.N., Rochet, F., Pereira, O., Wallach, D.S.: Scaling up anonymous communication with efficient nanopayment channels. Proc. Priv. Enhanc. Technol. (PoPETs) **2020**(3), 175-203 (2020)
14. Ghosh, M., Richardson, M., Ford, B., Jansen, R.: A TorPath to TorCoin: proof-of-bandwidth altcoins for compensating relays. In: Workshop on Hot Topics in Privacy Enhancing Technologies (HotPETs) (2014)
15. Greubel, A., Pohl, S., Kounev, S.: Quantifying measurement quality and load distribution in Tor. In: Annual Computer Security Applications Conference (ACSAC) (2020)
16. Jansen, R.: Measuring the accuracy of tor relays' advertised bandwidths, July 2019. https://lists.torproject.org/pipermail/tor-relays/2019-July/017535.html
17. Jansen, R., Hopper, N., Kim, Y.: Recruiting new tor relays with BRAIDS. In: Conference on Computer and Communications Security (CCS) (2010)
18. Jansen, R., Johnson, A., Syverson, P.: LIRA: lightweight incentivized routing for anonymity. In: Network and Distributed System Security Symposium (NDSS) (2013)
19. Jansen, R., Miller, A., Syverson, P., Ford, B.: From onions to shallots: rewarding tor relays with TEARS. In: Workshop on Hot Topics in Privacy Enhancing Technologies (HotPETs) (2014)
20. Jansen, R., Tschorsch, F., Johnson, A., Scheuermann, B.: The sniper attack: anonymously deanonymizing and disabling the Tor network. In: Network and Distributed System Security Symposium (NDSS) (2014)
21. Jansen, R., Vaidya, T., Sherr, M.: Point break: a study of bandwidth denial-of-service attacks against Tor. In: USENIX Security Symposium (2019)
22. Johnson, A., Jansen, R., Hopper, N., Segal, A., Syverson, P.: PeerFlow: secure load balancing in Tor. Proceedings on Privacy Enhancing Technologies (PoPETs) **2017**(2), 74-94 (2017)
23. Johnson, A., Wacek, C., Jansen, R., Sherr, M., Syverson, P.: Users get routed: traffic correlation on tor by realistic adversaries. In: Conference on Computer and Communications Security (CCS) (2013)
24. Juga: How bandwidth scanners monitor the tor network. tor blog post, April 2019. https://blog.torproject.org/how-bandwidth-scanners-monitor-tor-network
25. Mani, A., Brown, T.W., Jansen, R., Johnson, A., Sherr, M.: Understanding Tor usage with privacy-preserving measurement. In: Internet Measurement Conference (IMC) (2018)
26. Moore, W.B., Wacek, C., Sherr, M.: Exploring the potential benefits of expanded rate limiting in Tor: slow and steady wins the race with tortoise. In: Annual Computer Security Applications Conference (ACSAC) (2011)
27. Mozilla: Mozilla research grants 2019H1 (2019). https://mozilla-research.forms.fm/mozilla-research-grants-2019h1/forms/6510. call for Proposals

28. "Johnny" Ngan, T.-W., Dingledine, R., Wallach, D.S.: Building incentives into Tor. In: Sion, R. (ed.) FC 2010. LNCS, vol. 6052, pp. 238–256. Springer, Heidelberg (2010). https://doi.org/10.1007/978-3-642-14577-3_19

29. Panchenko, A., et al.: Website fingerprinting at Internet scale. In: Network and Distributed System Security Symposium (NDSS) (2016)

30. Perry, M.: TorFlow: Tor network analysis. In: Workshop on Hot Topics in Privacy Enhancing Technologies (HotPETs) (2009)

31. Snader, R., Borisov, N.: EigenSpeed: secure peer-to-peer bandwidth evaluation. In: International Workshop on Peer-to-Peer Systems (IPTPS) (2009)

32. Mozilla research call: tune up tor for integration and scale, May 2019. https://blog.torproject.org/mozilla-research-call-tune-tor-integration-and-scale

33. Thill, F.: Hidden service tracking detection and bandwidth cheating in Tor anonymity network. Master's thesis, University of Luxembourg (2014)

34. Wright, M., Adler, M., Levine, B.N., Shields, C.: The predecessor attack: an analysis of a threat to anonymous communications systems. ACM Trans. Inf. Syst. Secur. (TISSEC) 4(7), 489–522 (2004)

Comparison of TCP Congestion Control Performance over a Satellite Network

Saahil Claypool[1], Jae Chung[2], and Mark Claypool[1(✉)]

[1] Worcester Polytechnic Institute, Worcester, MA, USA
{smclaypool,claypool}@wpi.edu
[2] Viasat, Marlborough, MA, USA
jaewon.chung@viasat.com

Abstract. While satellite Internet bitrates have increased, latency can still degrade TCP performance. Realistic assessment of TCP over satellites is lacking, typically done by simulation or emulation, if at all. This paper presents experiments comparing four TCP congestion control algorithms – BBR, Cubic, Hybla and PCC – on a commercial satellite network. Analysis shows similar steady state bitrates for all, but with significant differences in start-up throughputs and round-trip times caused by queuing of packets in flight. Power analysis combining throughput and latency shows during steady state, PCC is the most powerful, due to relatively high throughputs and consistent, relatively low round-trip times, while for small downloads Hybla is the most powerful, due to fast throughput ramp-ups. BBR generally fares similarly to Cubic in both cases.

1 Introduction

Satellites are an essential part of modern networking, providing ubiquitous connectivity even in times of disaster. There are 2100+ satellites in orbit, a 67% increase from 2014 to 2019 [2]. Improvements in satellite technology have increased transmission capacities more than 20x with the total capacity of planned Geosynchronous orbit satellites over 5 Tb/s.

Geosynchronous orbit satellites have about 300 milliseconds of latency to bounce a signal up and down [8], a hurdle for TCP protocols that use round-trip time communication to advance their data windows. TCP congestion control algorithms play a critical role determining throughput in the presence of network latency and loss. A better understanding of TCP congestion control algorithm performance over satellite networks is needed in order to assess challenges and opportunities that satellites have to better support TCP moving forward.

However, there are few published studies measuring network performance over actual satellite networks [17], with most studies either using just simulations [3] or emulations with satellite parameters [1,11,18,19].

This paper presents results from experiments that measure the performance of TCP over a commercial satellite Internet network. We compare four TCP congestion control algorithms, chosen based on their representative approaches to

© Springer Nature Switzerland AG 2021
O. Hohlfeld et al. (Eds.): PAM 2021, LNCS 12671, pp. 499–512, 2021.
https://doi.org/10.1007/978-3-030-72582-2_29

congestion control: default loss-based Cubic [15], bandwidth-delay product-based BBR [16], utility function-based PCC [11], and satellite-optimized Hybla [4]. Our network testbed and experiments are done on the Internet, but are designed to be comparable by interlacing runs of each protocol serially to minimize temporal differences and by doing 80 bulk downloads for each protocol to provide for a large sample. In addition, a custom ping application provides several days worth of round-trip time and lost packet data for a baseline satellite network with no other traffic.

Analysis of our "quiet" network gives baseline satellite loss and round-trip time characteristics. Analysis comparing the four algorithms show differences in throughput, round-trip times and retransmissions during steady state and start-up phases, with power providing a combined measure of throughput and delay.

The rest of this report is organized as follows: Sect. 2 presents related work, Sect. 3 describes our methodology, Sect. 4 analyzes the data, and Sect. 5 summarizes our conclusions and future work.

2   Related Work

Caini and Firrinielli [4] propose TCP Hybla to overcome the limitations TCP NewReno flows have when running over high-latency links (e.g., a Satellite). TCP Hybla modifies the standard congestion window increase with an extension based on the round-trip time. In Hybla slow-start, $cwnd = cwnd + 2^\rho - 1$ and in congestion avoidance $cwnd = cwnd + \frac{\rho^2}{cwnd}$, where $\rho = RTT/RTT_0$. RTT_0 is fixed at a "wired" round-trip time of 0.025 s. Hybla is available for Linux as of kernel 2.6.11 (in 2005).

Ha et al. [15] develop TCP Cubic as an incremental improvement to earlier congestion control algorithms. Cubic is less aggressive than previous algorithms in most steady-state cases, but can probe for more bandwidth quickly when needed. TCP Cubic has been the default in Linux as of kernel 2.6.19 (in 2007), Windows 10.1709 Fall Creators Update (in 2017), and Windows Server 2016 1709 update (in 2017).

Cardwell et al. [16] provide TCP Bottleneck Bandwidth and Round-trip time (BBR) as an alternative to Cubic's (and Hybla's) loss-based congestion control. BBR uses the maximum bandwidth and minimum round-trip time observed to set the congestion window size (up to twice the bandwidth-delay product). BBR has been deployed by Google servers since at least 2017 and is available for Linux as of kernel 4.9 (end of 2016).

Dong et al. [11] propose TCP PCC that observes performance based on small measurement "experiments". The experiments assess throughput, loss, and round-trip times with a utility function, adopting the rate that has the best utility. PCC is not generally available for Linux, but Compira Labs[1] provided us with a Linux-based implementation.

---

[1] https://www.compiralabs.com/.

Cao et al. [5] analyze measurement results of BBR and Cubic over a range of different network conditions, showing that the relative difference between the bottleneck buffer size and bandwidth-delay product dictates when BBR performs well. Our work extends this work by providing evaluation of Cubic and BBR in a satellite configuration, with round-trip times significantly beyond those tested by Cao et al.

Obata et al. [17] evaluate TCP performance over actual (not emulated, as is typical) satellite networks. They compare a satellite-oriented TCP congestion control algorithm (STAR) with NewReno and Hybla. Experiments with the Wideband InterNetworking Engineering test and Demonstration Satellite (WINDS) network show throughputs around 26 Mb/s and round-trip times around 860 milliseconds. Both TCP STAR and TCP Hybla have better throughputs over the satellite link than TCP NewReno – we evaluate TCP Hybla, but there is no public Linux implementation of TCP STAR available.

Wang et al. [19] provide preliminary performance evaluation of QUIC with BBR on an emulated a satellite network (capacities 1 Mb/s and 10 Mb/s, RTTs 200, 400 and 1000 ms, and packet loss up to 20%). Their results confirm QUIC with BBR has throughput improvements compared with TCP Cubic for their emulated satellite network.

Utsumi et al. [18] develop an analytic model for TCP Hybla for steady state throughput and round-trip time over satellite links. They verify the accuracy of their model with simulated and emulated satellite links (capacity 8 Mb/s, RTT 550 ms, and packet loss rates up to 2%). Their analysis shows substantial improvements to throughput over that of TCP Reno for loss rates above 0.0001%

Our work extends the above with comparative performance for four TCP congestion control algorithms on an actual, commercial satellite network.

3 Methodology

We setup a testbed, measure network baseline loss and round-trip times, serially bulk-download data using each algorithm, and analyze the results.

3.1 Testbed

We setup a Viasat satellite Internet link so as to represent a client with a "last mile" satellite connection. Our servers are configured to allow for repeated tests and comparative performance by consecutive serial runs with all conditions the same, except for the change in TCP congestion control algorithm.

Our testbed is depicted in Fig. 1. The client is a Linux PC with an Intel i7-1065G7 CPU @ 1.30 GHz and 32 GB RAM. There are four servers, each with a different TCP congestion control algorithm: BBR, Cubic, Hybla and PCC. Each server has an Intel Ken E312xx CPU @ 2.5 GHz and 32 GB RAM. The servers and client all run Ubuntu 18.04.4 LTS, Linux kernel version 4.15.0.

The servers connect to our University LAN via Gb/s Ethernet. The campus network is connected to the Internet via several 10 Gb/s links, all throttled to 1

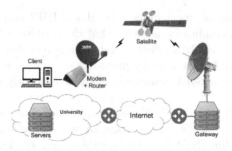

Fig. 1. Satellite measurement testbed.

Gb/s. Wireshark captures all packet header data on each server and the client. The client connects to a Viasat satellite terminal (with a modem and router) via a Gb/s Ethernet connection. The client's downstream Viasat service plan provides a peak data rate of 144 Mb/s.

The terminal communicates through a Ka-band outdoor antenna (RF amplifier, up/down converter, reflector and feed) through the Viasat 2 satellite[2] to the larger Ka-band gateway antenna. The terminal supports adaptive coding and modulation using 16-APK, 8 PSK, and QPSK (forward) at 10 to 52 MSym/s and 8PSK, QPSK and BPSK (return) at 0.625 to 20 MSym/s.

The Viasat gateway performs per-client queue management, where the queue can grow up to 36 MBytes, allowing a maximum queuing delay of about 2 s at the peak data rate. Queue lengths are controlled at the gateway by Active Queue Management (AQM) that randomly drops 25% of incoming packets when the queue is over a half of the limit (i.e., 18 MBytes).

The performance enhancing proxy (PEP) that Viasat deploys by default is disabled for all experiments in order to assess congestion control performance independent of the PEP implementation, and to represent cases where a PEP could not be used (e.g., for encrypted flows).

3.2 Baseline

For the network baseline, we run UDP Ping[3] from a server to the client continuously for 1 week. This sends one 20-byte UDP packet every 200 ms (5 packets/s) from the server to the client and back, recording the round-trip time for each packet returned and the number of packets lost. Doing round-trip time measurements via UDP avoids any special treatments routers may have for ICMP packets.

3.3 Downloads

We compare the performance of four congestion control algorithms, chosen as representatives of different congestion control approaches: loss-based Cubic,

---

[2] https://en.wikipedia.org/wiki/ViaSat-2.
[3] http://perform.wpi.edu/downloads/#udp.

bandwidth-delay product-based BBR (version 1), satellite-optimized loss-based Hybla and utility function-based PCC. The four servers are configured to provide for bulk-downloads via `iperf3`[4] (v3.3.1), each server hosting one of our four congestion control algorithms. Cubic, BBR and Hybla are used without further configuration. PCC is configured to use the Vivace-Latency utility function [12], with throughput, loss, and round-trip time coefficients set to 1, 10, and 2, respectively.

For all hosts, the default TCP buffer settings are changed on both the server and client – setting `tcp_mem`, `tcp_wmem` and `tcp_rmem` to 60 MBytes – so that flows are not flow-controlled and instead are governed by TCP's congestion window.

The client initiates a connection to one server via iperf, downloading 1 GByte, then immediately proceeding to the next server. After cycling through each server, the client pauses for 1 min. The process repeats a total of 80 times – thus, providing 80 network traces of a 1 GByte download for each protocol over the satellite link. Since each cycle takes about 15 min, the throughput tests run for about a day total. We analyze results from a weekday in July 2020.

4 Analysis

4.1 Network Baseline

We start by analyzing the network baseline loss and round-trip times, obtained on a "quiet" satellite link to our client – i.e., without any of our active bulk-downloads. Table 3 provides summary statistics.

The vast majority (99%) of round-trip times are between 560 and 625 ms (median 597 ms, mean 597.5 ms, std dev 16.9 ms). However, the round-trip times have a heavy-tailed tendency, with 0.1% from 625 ms to 1500 ms and 0.001% from 1700 to 2200 ms. These high values show multi-second round-trip times can be observed on a satellite network even without any self-induced queuing. There are no visual time of day patterns to the round-trip times.

In the same time period, only 604 packets are lost, or about 0.05%. Most of these (77%) are single-packet losses, with 44 multi-packet loss events, the largest 11 packets (about 2.2 s). There is no apparent correlation between these losses and the round-trip times (i.e., the losses do not seem to occur during the highest round-trip times observed). Note, these loss rates are about 15x lower than the reported WINDS satellite loss of 0.7% [17].

4.2 Representative Behavior

We begin by examining the TCP congestion control performance over time for a single download representative of typical behavior for each algorithm for our satellite connection. Figure 2 depicts the throughput, round-trip time and retransmission rate where each value is computed per second from Wireshark traces on the server.

---

[4] https://software.es.net/iperf/.

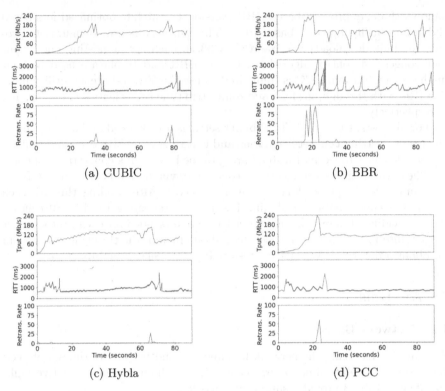

Fig. 2. Stacked graph comparison. From top to bottom, the graphs are: through-put (Mb/s), round-trip time (milliseconds), and retransmission rate (percent). For all graphs, the x-axis is time (in seconds) since the flow started.

TCP Cubic illustrates typical exponential growth in throughput during start-up, but exits slow start relatively early, about 15 s in where throughput is far lower than the link capacity. Thus, it takes Cubic about 30 s to reach the expected steady state throughput of about 100 Mb/s. During steady state (post 45 s) the AQM drops enough packets to keep Cubic from persistently saturating the queue, resulting in round-trip times of about 1 s. However, several spikes in transmission rates yield corresponding spikes in round-trip times above 3 s and retransmission rates above 20%.

TCP BBR ramps up to higher throughput more quickly than Cubic, but this also causes high round-trip times and loss rates around 20 s as BBR over-saturates the bottleneck queue. At steady state, BBR operates at a fairly steady 140 Mb/s, with relatively low loss and round-trip times about 750 ms since the 2x bandwidth-delay product BBR keeps in flight is below the AQM queue limit. However, there are noticeable dips in throughput every 10 s when BBR enters its PROBE_RTT state. In addition, there are intermittent round-trip time spikes and retransmissions from loss which occur when BBR enters PROBE_BW and increases its transmission rate for 1 round-trip time.

TCP Hybla ramps up quickly, faster than does Cubic since it adjusts congestion window growth based on latency, causing queuing at the bottleneck, evidenced by the high early round-trip times. However, there are few retransmissions. At steady state Hybla achieves consistently high throughput, with a slight growth in the round-trip time upon reaching about 140 Mb/s. Thereupon, there is a slight upward trend to the round-trip time until the queue limit is reached accompanied by some retransmissions.

TCP PCC ramps up somewhat slower than Hybla but faster than Cubic, causing some queuing and some retransmissions, albeit fewer than BBR. At steady state, throughput and round-trip times are consistent, near the minimum round-trip time (around 600 ms), and the expected maximum throughput (about 140 Mb/s). The lower round-trip times are expected since round-trip time is used by the PCC utility function.

4.3 Steady State

TCP's overall performance includes both start-up and congestion avoidance phases – the latter we call "steady state" in this paper. We analyze steady state behavior based on the last half (in terms of bytes) of each trace.

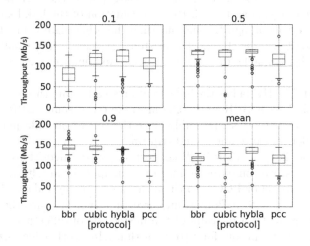

Fig. 3. Steady state throughput distributions for 10%, 50%, 90% and mean.

For each algorithm, we compute steady state throughput in 1 s intervals, extracting the 10th, 50th and 90th percentiles (and means) across all flows. Figure 3 shows the boxplot distributions. The top left is the distribution for the 10th percentiles, the top right the 50th (or median), the bottom left the 90th percentile and the bottom right the mean. Each box depicts quartiles and median for the distribution. Points higher or lower than 1.4 × the inter-quartile range are outliers, depicted by the circles. The whiskers span from the minimum to maximum non-outlier. Table 1 shows the corresponding summary statistics.

Table 1. Steady state throughput summary statistics.

Algorithm	Mean (Mb/s)	Std Dev
BBR	112.9	12.2
Cubic	123.3	17.0
Hybla	130.1	17.2
PCC	112.6	17.9

Table 2. Steady state throughput effect size (versus Cubic).

	t(158)	p	Effect Size
BBR	4.44	<.0001	0.7
Hybla	2.51	**0.0129**	0.4
PCC	3.88	**0.0002**	0.6

From the graphs, at the 10th percentile BBR has lowest distribution of steady state throughput. This is attributed to its reduced throughput during the round-trip time probing phase, which, if there is no change to the minimum round-trip time, triggers every 10 s and lasts for about 1 s. PCC's throughput at the 10th percentile is also a bit lower than Cubic's or Hybla's, possibly because PCC's reward for a low round-trip time can result in occasional under-utilization.

BBR, Cubic and Hybla all have similar median steady state throughputs, while PCC's is a bit lower.

BBR has the highest distribution of throughput at the 90th percentile, followed by Cubic, Hybla and PCC. BBR's estimation of the link bandwidth may yield more intervals of high throughput than the other algorithms. Hybla's 90th percentile distribution is the most consistent (as seen by the small box), while PCC's is the least, maybe due to fuller queues and emptier queues, respectively (see Table 4).

From the table, Hybla has the highest mean steady state throughput, followed by CUBIC, and then BBR and PCC are about the same. BBR steady state throughput varies the least, probably since the consistent link quality provides for a steady delivery rate and round-trip time.

Since Cubic is the default TCP congestion control algorithm for Linux and Windows servers, we compare the mean throughput for an alternate algorithm choice – BBR, Hybla or PCC – to the mean for Cubic by independent, 2-tailed t tests ($\alpha = 0.05$) with a Bonferroni correction and compute the effect sizes. An effect size provides a measure of the magnitude of difference – in our case, the difference of the means for two algorithms. In short, effect size quantifies how much the difference in congestion control algorithm matters. The Cohen's d effect size assesses the differences in means in relation to the pooled standard deviation. Generally small effect sizes are anything under 0.2, medium is 0.2 to 0.5, large 0.5 to 0.8, and very large above 0.8. The t test and effect size results are shown in Table 2. Statistical significance is highlighted in bold.

From the table, the mean steady state throughput differences compared to Cubic are all statistically significant. BBR and PCC have lower steady state throughputs than Cubic with large effect sizes. Hybla has a higher throughput than Cubic with a moderate effect size.

Figure 4 shows the round-trip times during steady state. The x-axis is the round-trip time in seconds computed from the TCP acknowledgments in the Wireshark traces, and the y-axis is the cumulative distribution. There is one trendline for each algorithm. Table 4 shows the summary statistics.

Table 3. Baseline round-trip time summary statistics.

Mean	597.5 ms
Std dev	16.9 ms
Median	597 ms
Min	564 ms
Max	2174 ms

Table 4. Steady state round-trip time summary statistics.

Algorithm	Mean (ms)	Std Dev
BBR	780	125.1
Cubic	821	206.4
Hybla	958	142.1
PCC	685	73.1

During steady state, Hybla typically has round-trip times about 200 ms higher than any other algorithm, likely because its aggressive congestion window growth with high round-trip time yields more queuing delay. PCC has the lowest and steadiest round-trip times, near the link minimum, likely because its utility function rewards low round-trip times. BBR and Cubic are in-between, with BBR being somewhat lower than Cubic and a bit steadier. Cubic, in particular, has a few cases with extremely high round-trip times. Across all flows, about 5% of the round trip times are 2 s or higher.

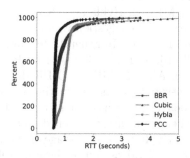

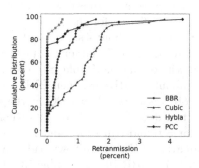

Fig. 4. Steady state round-trip time distributions.

Fig. 5. Steady state retransmission distributions.

Figure 5 shows the retransmissions during steady state. The axes and data groups are as for Fig. 4, but the y-axis is the percentage of retransmitted packets computed over the second half of each flow.

From the figure, Cubic has the highest retransmission distribution and Hybla the lowest. BBR and PCC are in-between, with BBR moderately higher but PCC having a much heavier tail. Hybla and PCC are consistently low (0%) for about 75% of all runs, compared to only about 20% for BBR and Cubic.

While higher round-trip times generally mean larger router queues and more drops and retransmissions, the Viasat AQM does not drop packets until the queue is above about 1 s of delay. This means if a flow's round-trip times remain under about 1.6 s, it can avoid retransmissions.

4.4   Start-Up

We compare the start-up behavior for each algorithm by analyzing the first 30 s of each trace, approximately long enough to download 50 MBytes on our satellite link. This is indicative of algorithm performance for some short-lived flows and is about when we observed throughput growth over time "flattening" for most flows.

The average Web page size for the top 1000 sites was around 2 MBytes as of 2018 [10], including HTML payloads and all linked resources (e.g., CSS files and images). The Web page size distribution's 95th percentile was about 6 MBytes and the maximum was about 29 MBytes. Today's average total Web page size is probably about 5 MBytes [13], dominated by images and video.

Many TCP flows stream video content and these may be capped by the video rate, which itself depends upon the video encoding. However, assuming videos are downloaded completely, about 90% of YouTube videos are less than 30 MBytes [7].

Figure 6 depicts the time on the y-axis (in seconds) to download an object for the given size on the x-axis (in MBytes). The object size increment is 1 MByte. Each point is the average time required by a algorithm to download an object of the indicated size, shown with a 95% confidence interval.

From the figure, for the smallest objects (1 MByte), Hybla and PCC download the fastest, about 4 s, owning to the larger initial congestion windows they both have (2.5x to 5x larger than either BBR or Cubic). In general, this larger initial window means Hybla downloads small objects fastest followed by PCC up to about 20 MBytes, then BBR and Cubic. After 20 MBytes, BBR downloads objects faster than PCC, perhaps because BBR exits its starting phase later than does PCC – BBR exits when the delivery rate has not increased by 25% for 3 round-trip times and PCC exits when its utility function decreases. For an average Web page download (5 MBytes), Hybla takes an average of about 4 s, PCC 7 s, BBR 10 s and Cubic 13 s. For 90% of all videos and the largest Web pages (30 MBytes), Hybla takes about 8 s, BBR and PCC about twice that and Cubic about thrice.

Table 5 presents the summary statistics for the first 30 s of each flow for each algorithm. During start-up, Cubic has a low round-trip time, mostly because it takes a long time to ramp up throughput. BBR has the highest round-trip time despite not having the highest throughput – that is had by Hybla, despite having a lower round-trip time than BBR. The relatively higher average round-trip time for BBR may be because it keeps up to a bandwidth-delay product of packets in queue. PCC has average throughputs and round-trip times, but the steadiest

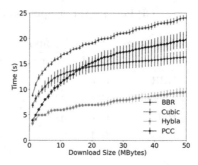

Fig. 6. Download time versus download object size.

round-trip times, possibly stabilized by the utility function rather than probing for increased data rates (and causing variable amounts of queuing) as do the other algorithms.

Table 5. Start-up summary statistics.

Algorithm	Tput (Mb/s)		RTT (ms)	
	Mean	Std Dev	Mean	Std Dev
BBR	23.1	1.8	917	42.9
Cubic	16.6	0.3	757	22.3
Hybla	40.8	2.9	799	130.8
PCC	20.3	1.6	806	15.1

Table 6. Startup throughput effect size (versus Cubic).

	t(158)	p	Effect Size
BBR	31.9	<.0001	5
Hybla	74.2	<.0001	12
PCC	20.3	<.0001	3.2

Table 6 is like Table 2, but for start-up (the first 30 s). From the table, the start-up throughput differences compared to Cubic are all statistically significant. The effect sizes for comparing Cubic throughput to PCC, BBR and Hybla throughputs are all very large.

4.5 Power

In addition to examining throughput and round-trip time separately, it has been suggested that throughput and delay can be combined into a single "power" metric by dividing throughput by delay [14] – the idea is that the utility of higher throughput is offset by higher delay and vice-versa. Doing power analysis using the mean throughput (in Mb/s) and delay (in seconds) for each algorithm for start-up and steady state yields the numbers in Table 7 (units are MBits). The algorithm with the most power in each phase is indicated in bold.

Table 7. TCP Power – throughput ÷ delay

Algorithm	Power (MBits)	
	Steady	Start-up
BBR	145	25
Cubic	150	22
Hybla	136	**51**
PCC	**164**	25

During steady state, PCC is the most powerful based on high throughput with the lowest round-trip times. Cubic is more powerful than BBR or Hybla since it has good throughput and round-trip times, whereas BBR is deficient in throughput and Hybla in round-trip times.

At start-up, Hybla has the most power by far, primarily due to its high throughput. BBR, Cubic and PCC are similar at about half the power of Hybla.

5   Conclusion

Satellite Internet connections are important for providing reliable connectivity, but to date, there are few published research papers detailing TCP congestion control performance over actual satellite networks.

This paper presents results from experiments on a commercial satellite network, comparing four TCP congestion control algorithms – the two dominant algorithms, Cubic and BBR, a commercial implementation of PCC, and the satellite-tuned Hybla. These algorithms have different approaches to congestion control: loss-based (Cubic), bandwidth estimation-based (BBR), utility function-based (PCC), and satellite-optimized (Hybla). Results from 80 downloads for each protocol, interlaced so as to minimize temporal differences, provide for steady state and start-up performance. Baseline satellite network results are obtained by long-term round-trip analysis in the absence of our other traffic.

Overall, the production satellite link has consistent baseline round-trip times near the theoretical minimum (about 600 ms) and very low (about 0.2%) loss rates. For TCP downloads, during steady state, the four algorithms evaluated – Cubic, BBR, Hybla and PCC – have similar median throughputs, but Hybla and Cubic have slightly higher mean throughputs owing to BBR's bitrate reduction when probing for minimal round-trip times (probing ~10 s, each lasting for ~1.5 s). During start-up, Hybla's higher throughputs allow it to complete small downloads (e.g., Web pages) about twice as fast as BBR (~5 s versus ~10), while BBR is about 50% faster (~10 s versus ~15 s) than Cubic. Hybla is able to avoid some of the high retransmission rates for Cubic and BBR, and to a lesser extent PCC, caused by saturating the bottleneck queue. However, Hybla does have consistently higher round-trip times, an artifact of continually having more packets in the bottleneck queue, while PCC has the lowest. Combining throughput and round-trip into one "power" metric shows PCC the most powerful at steady state, owing to high throughput and steady, low round-trip times, and Hybla the most powerful during start-up owing to fast throughput ramp-ups.

Future work includes evaluating settings for TCP, such as the initial congestion window, and algorithm-specific settings such as RTT_0 for Hybla. Since BBR does not always share equitably with Cubic [9], future work is to run multiple flows over the satellite link. When BBR v2 is out of alpha/preview, we plan to evaluate it, and QUIC [6], too. Other future work is to compare the algorithms with a performance enhancing proxy (PEP), designed to mitigate the high-latencies on the satellite link.

Acknowledgments. Thanks to Amit Cohen, Lev Gloukhenki and Michael Schapira of Compira Labs for providing the implementation of PCC. Also, thanks to the anonymous reviewers and shepherd Srikanth Sundaresan for their thoughtful feedback on improving our paper.

References

1. Arun, V., Balakrishnan, H.: Copa: practical delay-based congestion control for the Internet. In: Proceedings of the Applied Networking Research Workshop, Montreal, QC, Canada, July 2018
2. Association, S.I.: Introduction to the satellite industry (2020). https://tinyurl.com/y5m7z77e
3. Barakat, C., Chaher, N., Dabbous, W., Altman, E.: Improving TCP/IP over geostationary satellite links. In: Proceedings of GLOBECOM. Rio de Janeireo, Brazil, December 1999
4. Caini, C., Firrincieli, R.: TCP Hybla: a TCP enhancement for heterogeneous networks. Int. J. Satell. Commun. Netw. **22**(5), 547–566 (2004)
5. Cao, Y., Jain, A., Sharma, K., Balasubramanian, A., Gandhi, A.: When to use and when not to use BBR: an empirical analysis and evaluation study. In: Proceedings of the Internet Measurement Conference (IMC), Amsterdam, NL, October 2019
6. Cardwell, N., Cheng, Y., Yeganeh, S.H., Jacobson, V.: BBR congestion control. IETF Draft draft-cardwell-iccrg-bbr-congestion-control-00, July 2017
7. Che, X., Ip, B., Lin, L.: A survey of current Youtube video characteristics. IEEE Multimedia **22**(2), 56–63 (2015)
8. Cisco: Interface and Hardware Component Configuration Guide, Cisco IOS Release 15M&T. Cisco Systems, Inc. (2015). chapter: Rate Based Satellite Control Protocol
9. Claypool, S., Claypool, M., Chung, J., Li, F.: Sharing but not caring - performance of TCP BBR and TCP CUBIC at the network bottleneck. In: Proceedings of the 15th IARIA Advanced International Conference on Telecommunications (AICT), Nice, France, August 2019
10. Data and analysis: webpages are getting larger every year, and here's why it matters. Solar Winds Pingdom, 15 November 2018. https://tinyurl.com/y4pjrvhl,
11. Dong, M., Li, Q., Zarchy, D., Godfrey, P.B., Schapira, M.: PCC: re-architecting congestion control for consistent high performance. In: Proceedings of the 12th USENIX Symposium on Networked Systems Design and Implementation (NSDI), Oakland, CA, USA (2015)
12. Dong, M., et al.: PCC Vivace: online-learning congestion control. In: Proceedings of the 15th USENIX Symposium on Networked Systems Design and Implementation (NSDI), Renton, WA, USA, April 2018

13. Everts, T.: The average web page is 3 MB. how much should we care? Speed Matters Blog, 9th August 2017. https://speedcurve.com/blog/web-performance-page-bloat/
14. Floyd, S.: Metrics for the evaluation of congestion control mechanisms. RFC 5166, March 2008
15. Ha, S., Rhee, I., Xu, L.: CUBIC: a new TCP-friendly high-speed TCP variant. ACM SIGOPS Oper. Syst. Rev. **42**(5), 64–74 (2008)
16. Cardwell, N., Cheng, Y., Gunn, C.S., Yeganeh, S.H., Jacobson, V.: BBR: congestion-based congestion control. Commun. ACM **60**(2), 58–66 (2017)
17. Obata, H., Tamehiro, K., Ishida, K.: Experimental evaluation of TCP-STAR for satellite Internet over WINDS. In: Proceedings of the International Symposium on Autonomous Decentralized Systems. Tokyo, Japan, March 2011
18. Utsumi, S., et al.: A new analytical model of TCP Hybla for satellite IP networks. J. Netw. Comput. Appl. **124**, 137–147 (2018)
19. Wang, Y., Zhao, K., Li, W., Fraire, J., Sun, Z., Fang, Y.: Performance Evaluation of QUIC with BBR in Satellite Internet. In: Proceedings of the 6th IEEE International Conference on Wireless for Space and Extreme Environments (WiSEE), Huntsville, AL, USA, December 2018

Throughput Prediction on 60 GHz Mobile Devices for High-Bandwidth, Latency-Sensitive Applications

Shivang Aggarwal[1]([✉]), Zhaoning Kong[2], Moinak Ghoshal[1], Y. Charlie Hu[2], and Dimitrios Koutsonikolas[1]

[1] Northeastern University, Boston, USA
aggarwal.sh@northeastern.edu
[2] Purdue University, West Lafayette, USA

Abstract. In the near future, high quality VR and video streaming at 4K/8K resolutions will require Gigabit throughput to maintain a high user quality of experience (QoE). IEEE 802.11ad, which standardizes the 14 GHz of unlicensed spectrum around 60 GHz, is a prime candidate to fulfil these demands wirelessly. To maintain QoE, applications need to adapt to the ever changing network conditions by performing quality adaptation. A key component of quality adaptation is throughput prediction. At 60 GHz, due to the much higher frequency, the throughput can vary sharply due to blockage and mobility. Hence, the problem of predicting throughput becomes quite challenging.

In this paper, we perform an extensive measurement study of the predictability of the network throughput of an 802.11ad WLAN in downloading data to an 802.11ad-enabled mobile device under varying mobility patterns and orientations of the mobile device. We show that, with carefully designed neural networks, we can predict the throughput of the 60 GHz link with good accuracy at varying timescales, from 10 ms (suitable for VR) up to 2 s (suitable for ABR streaming). We further identify the most important features that affect the neural network prediction accuracy to be past throughput and MCS.

1 Introduction

The past few years have witnessed the rise of a number of high-bandwidth, latency-sensitive applications including virtual reality (VR), high-resolution video streaming, live video streaming, and connected autonomous vehicles. Such applications are characterized by stringent user-perceived quality of experience (QoE) requirements, which in turn dictate high demand for the network performance in terms of ultra high throughput and low latency. Further, such applications typically run on mobile devices, which require high network performance to be supported wirelessly. For example, 8K resolution VR demands 1.2 Gbps [28] in order to satisfy the 20 ms photon-to-motion latency, while live 4K video streaming at 30 FPS demands 1.8 Gbps [16] for good user QoE.

© Springer Nature Switzerland AG 2021
O. Hohlfeld et al. (Eds.): PAM 2021, LNCS 12671, pp. 513–528, 2021.
https://doi.org/10.1007/978-3-030-72582-2_30

Such stringent demand for network performance could not be supported in the past decade. However, the advent of mmWave technologies in recent years has made such network performance within reach and holds the promise to enable these demanding applications. For example, the IEEE 802.11ad WLAN standard [20] governs the use of the unlicensed spectrum around 60 GHz and supports 2 GHz wide channel to provide PHY data rates of up to 6.7 Gbps.

However, 60 GHz networks also come with higher dynamics due to their vastly different propagation characteristics compared to sub-6 GHz networks. In particular, due to the high attenuation loss at 60 GHz, directional communication is needed, making the wireless link highly susceptible to human blockage and mobility [42,43]. Due to these challenges, a user watching a 360° video or playing a VR game over a 60 GHz network may experience long periods of rebuffering/stalls due to intervals of low to no connectivity [16,44,48]. For example, the user may be moving around in such a way so as to face completely away from the AP and thus self-block the link. For this reason, a 60 GHz WLAN often cannot be used as a standalone technology to enable these high resolution applications, and the legacy sub-6 GHz WiFi, which does not suffer from blockage and mobility, may be required as a backup [16,42].

Fortunately, most of the network-demanding applications already have some type of quality adaptation built-in, to deal with the network dynamics. For example, adaptive bitrate (ABR) streaming has become a de facto mechanism implemented in modern video streaming systems such as YouTube, backed by a number of adaptive streaming standards introduced over the years [3,11,33,40]. In a nutshell, ABR streaming continuously monitors the network conditions and adapts the content quality to optimize the QoE, which typically is a function of the frame resolution, frame continuity, and rebuffering time. ABR streaming has been applied in all the recent proposals for high-resolution 360° video streaming [18,34,37] as well as live video streaming [16]. Similar adaptation techniques have also been proposed for state-of-the-art mobile VR systems [26].

The very first task of network adaptation in such network-demanding applications is the estimation of network conditions for the next time interval. For example, in video streaming, most ABR systems estimate the throughput in the next time interval and choose a video quality level based on the throughput estimate and playback buffer occupancy [39,41], as both can affect the QoE. More recently, the use of deep learning (DL) to select the most appropriate quality level has gained popularity [29,46] and ML-based ABR algorithms have been shown to outperform traditional algorithms.

The unique characteristics of the 60 GHz links, however, make throughput prediction in 60 GHz WLANs a much more challenging problem than in legacy WLANs. Although throughput estimation/prediction has been studied in the past in the context of sub-6 GHz WLANs [22,23,38] and cellular networks [27], no previous work, to our best knowledge, has studied throughput prediction at 60 GHz networks. In this work, we carry out the first measurement study of the throughput predictability in 60 GHz WLANs using ML.

There are two main challenges to conduct this measurement study. First, in order to reliably train and test any ML model, we need to collect a significant amount of data. Since 60 GHz WLANs are not widely deployed (the first 802.11ad-enabled smartphone model was only launched in 2019), we cannot collect data from real networks, as in previous ABR studies [29,46]. Further, the only two phones that support 802.11ad, the ASUS ROG Phone [5] and the ASUS ROG Phone II [6], are not VR Ready; hence, we cannot perform real VR experiments with volunteers, as in previous VR studies [26,45]. Thus, we need to develop a methodology to collect traces in a controlled environment efficiently and in an automated way, in order to obtain a large amount of data while covering a wide variety of realistic mobility patterns. To meet these conflicting requirements, we mounted the 802.11ad phone on a programmable 3-axis motion controller typically used by professional photographers. Using this setup, we collected more than 100 h of traces while running different applications under random mobility patterns. Second, unlike in previous works, which make predictions only on coarse-grained timescales, e.g., in the order of a few seconds for ABR video streaming [46,47], we study throughput prediction at timescales as fine as 10 ms, which are needed by some of the demanding applications such as VR. To support throughput prediction at such fine timescales, we need ML models that strike a good balance between being accurate as well as being lightweight enough to run on mobile devices within such short timescales. To overcome this challenge, we started with a neural network model previously shown to work well at the 2-s timescale [46], and performed multiple iterations of grid search on the two configuration dimensions (number of layers and number of nodes) to find the smallest configuration, beyond which the performance increase is marginal, to derive a model configuration that balances accuracy and inference latency. We also considered a recurrent neural network (RNN) model, Long Short Term Memory (LSTM), which is suitable for processing time series data, as is the case with throughput prediction. We again went through configuration search to arrive at a cost-effective LSTM model for our throughput prediction problem. We then experimentally compared both models throughout our measurement study.

In summary, our work makes the following contributions.

- We conducted the first measurement study of the throughput predictability of a 60 GHz WLAN to a mobile device. The dataset is publicly available [1].
- We tuned the parameters of state-of-the-art throughput-prediction DNNs to strike a balance between prediction accuracy and lightweightness usable for online throughput prediction. Our two models run in 0.41 ms and 4.02 ms on the ASUS ROG Phone II and require less than 4 MB of memory.
- We found that TCP throughput prediction in static scenarios is highly accurate for 40 to 2000 ms, with 95th percentile error ranging between 10.6% for 40 ms and 5.7% for 2 s. For 10–20 ms, the accuracy drops but still remains at satisfactory levels.

- However, the accuracy drops in random mobility scenarios, typical of real applications. The 95th percentile error increases to 38.1% for 10 ms and 19.4% for 2 s timescales.
- We performed a feature selection study and found that only a few features are important to make accurate throughput predictions. At timescales smaller than 100 ms, past throughput is the most important, but for larger timescales, MCS becomes more useful.
- Our study suggests that VR apps should be conservative in the use of throughput prediction. In particular, at the 10 ms timescale the prediction error is above 10% for 40% of the time, and the 95th percentile prediction error is 38%.

2   Experimental Methodology

Devices. We used a Netgear Nighthawk X10 Smart WiFi router [12] and an ASUS ROG Phone II [6] for our measurements. The Netgear router has a 10-Gigabit SFP+ Ethernet port, which we use to connect to a powerful desktop acting as the server in our experiments. The ASUS ROG Phone II has an octa-core Snapdragon 855 Plus processor with a maximum CPU frequency of 2.96 GHz, a 6000 mAh battery, and an 8 GB RAM, and runs the Android OS 10. Both devices support all 12 802.11ad single carrier MCSs, yielding theoretical data rates up from 385 Mbps to 4.6 Gbps. However, similar to previous studies using laptops as 802.11ad clients [16,35,36], the maximum TCP throughput is limited to 1.65 Gbps in practical scenarios.

Experimental Setup and Trace Collection. In all our experiments, except for those with real applications in Sect. 3.4, we used nuttcp [13] with the default CUBIC congestion control to generate backlogged TCP traffic from the server to the phone and logged throughput every 10 ms. We developed an Android app that runs on the phone and logs sensor and link state information. This information is used as input in the ML models, described in Sect. 2. Specifically, the app uses the Android Sensor API [4] to log information from the

Fig. 1. Mobility experiments setup

TYPE_ROTATION_VECTOR/TYPE_GAME_ROTATION_VECTOR sensors, which report the phone's rotation angle in the azimuth and pitch dimensions (Fig. 1), and from the accelerometer (TYPE_ACCELEROMETER) sensor, which gives the acceleration of the phone (in m/s^2) on the x-, y-, and z-axis. Sensor data are logged every 10 ms. The app also logs 60 GHz link information reported by the wil6210 driver on the phone every 20 ms. This includes the MCS used by the AP for data transmission, link quality estimators (SQI, RSSI), the link status (OK, RETRYING, FAILED), and the selected beamforming sectors.

Since 60 GHz WLANs are not widely deployed, we cannot collect data from real networks, as in previous ABR studies over the Internet [29,46]. In addition, our phone is not VR Ready and we cannot perform real VR experiments with volunteers, as in previous VR studies [26,45]. Hence, we used the following methodology to collect a large amount of data, while covering a wide variety of realistic mobility patterns in a controlled environment efficiently and in an automated way. For all our experiments, we kept the phone in a Google Cardboard [9] headset at a distance of 4 m from the AP, to emulate a realistic signal propagation environment. For the experiments involving mobility, we mounted the headset on a Cinetics Lynx 3-Axis Slider [7], used by professional photographers (Fig. 1). This setup enabled us to perform full 360° rotation in the azimuth and pitch dimensions at a speed of up to 48°/s and translational motion of up to 1 m. We used the Dragonframe software [8] to program custom mobility patterns (e.g., emulating a user playing a VR game or watching a 360° video). Using this methodology, we collected over 100 h of traces.

Trace Processing. Applications have diverse requirements on the timescale of throughput prediction. For example, VR applications need to predict the throughput in the window of the next tens of milliseconds. On the other end of the spectrum, video streaming applications usually fetch video chunks of several seconds in length and therefore need to predict the average throughput in the window of the next few seconds. As such, we study the throughput predictability over 802.11ad covering the full range of practical timescales, including timescales of 10 ms, 20 ms, 40 ms, 100 ms, 400 ms, 1000 ms, and 2000 ms.

To support the above study of multiple timescales, we always log throughput samples at the finest timescale, i.e., every 10 ms, and then offline convert the logged throughput into multiple coarser timescales, by combining consecutive samples using their mean value. For example, to obtain 20 ms traces, every 2 adjacent data points are combined. For all other features, which consist of categorical values, and are not meaningful when averaged, we consider the last data point in each window. In addition, the last value in the window can more accurately reflect the up-to-date state of the feature. To make a consistent comparison of throughput predictability across different timescales, we always use the first 15,000 data points for training, and the following 3,000 for testing.

Machine Learning-Based Prediction. Recent work has shown that simple DNN can predict throughput well at the 2-s timescale [46]. We therefore focus on a number of DNNs for making throughput predictions. In addition to prediction accuracy, we also need the DNN to be lightweight so that it can be used in even the most-latency sensitive applications, such as VR, when running on mobile devices. We experimented with three neural networks. For each network, we performed multiple iterations of grid search on the two configuration dimensions (number of layers and number of nodes) to find the smallest configuration, beyond which the performance increase is marginal, to derive a model configuration that balances accuracy and inference latency.

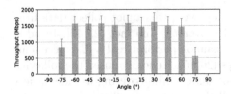
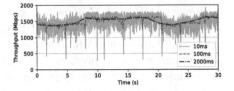

Fig. 2. Throughput at different azimuth angles.

Fig. 3. Throughput timeline within the FoV (0°) at different timescales.

BP8: a fully-connected neural network with 3 hidden layers, each of 40 neurons. It takes as input the actual throughput in the past 8 windows, pose information (azimuth and pitch) in the past 1 window, and link layer information (MCS, transmit beamforming sector, link status, SQI, and RSSI) in the past 1 window.

RNN8: a recurrent neural network with 3 hidden layers, each with 20 neurons. It takes as input the actual throughput, pose information, and link layer information in the past 8 windows.

RNN20: same as RNN8, but takes information in the past 20 windows as input.

We also experimented with the BP8 model to take as input all information in the past 8 windows like RNN8, but the results were very similar.

The neural network outputs the probability distribution (PD) of the throughput in the current window T_t. The PD $P_1, ..., P_{21}$ is over 21 bins of throughput in Mbps: $B_1 = [0, 50), ..., B_{21} = [1950, 2000]$. We calculate the expected throughput based on the PD as the prediction output:

$$Throughput = 0 \times P_1 + \sum_{i=2}^{20} median(B_i) \times P_i + 2000 \times P_{21} \tag{1}$$

Accuracy Metrics. We evaluate the performance of the throughput prediction models in terms of 3 metrics: (i) *RMSE*: The root mean squared error between the prediction and the actual throughput; (ii) *ARE95*: The absolute relative error of the prediction at the 95% percentile; and (iii) *PARE10*: The percentage of predictions with absolute relative error below 10%. To gain insight into which input features are the most useful for a high prediction accuracy, we also run a feature pruning algorithm which ranks the importance of the features.

3   Results and Analysis

In this section, we present the results using our neural network models. We consider three scenarios: (i) static scenarios, where the phone is fixed at a given azimuth and pitch at a distance of 4 m in front of the AP, (ii) random mobility scenarios, where the phone simultaneously moves along all three dimensions (azimuth, pitch, slide) at different speeds, and (iii) real application scenarios, where we use real application traces – VR and ABR video streaming – instead of backlogged TCP traffic generate by nuttcp, under random mobility.

3.1   Impact of the Phased Array Field of View

Practical phased arrays used by COTS devices have a limited angular coverage area on the receiving end, called field-of-view (FoV) in [44], outside of which throughput drops sharply. Previous studies using 802.11ad APs and laptops [35, 44] showed that the FoV is around 170°. We begin our study by measuring the throughput when the AP stays within/outside the phone's FoV. We place the phone facing the AP from a distance of 4 m, and rotate it to change its azimuth with respect to the AP. Our results in Fig. 2 show that, when the azimuth is within (−60°, 60°), the average throughput is always ∼1.5 Gbps. Once the azimuth moves outside this region, the throughput drops below 1 Gbps and becomes 0 for angles greater than ±90°. Hence, the FoV is even smaller in the case of these first generation 802.11ad smartphones. In the rest of the paper we focus on predicting throughput when the AP is within the phone's FoV.

Interestingly, Fig. 3 shows that throughput can vary significantly over time even within the FoV, especially at fine timescales. At the 10 ms timescale, the throughput varies between 1 Gbps and 1.8 Gbps and sometimes drops even below 500 Mbps. Such large variations are caused by the 802.11ad MAC layer mechanisms, including the periodic beaconing by the AP every 100 ms, beam-forming between the phone and the AP (triggered periodically, every 3 s, as well as in case of missing ACKs), and the interplay between beamforming and rate adaptation [35], all of which make make throughput prediction quite challenging at fine timescales. At the coarser timescales of 100 ms and 2000 ms though, the variations are averaged out and throughput appears much smoother.

3.2   Static Scenarios

We first explore the throughput predictability when the phone is stationary. In this section, we aim to understand how well we can predict throughput changes caused by channel variations and MAC layer mechanisms only.

We collected 5 static traces, listed in Table 1, by placing the phone at various azimuth and pitch angles with respect to the AP. We trained and evaluated a separate model on each trace. Since the phone is static for the duration of each trace, we do not use the azimuth, pitch, and link status data in training and testing our models as these features remain constant. The results shown in Figs. 4a–4c are averaged over the 5 traces.

Table 1. Static traces collected

Trace #	Azimuth	Pitch	Length	Average Throughput
Static 1	0°	0°	10 hr	1588 Mbps
Static 2	30°	0°	10 hr	1575 Mbps
Static 3	60°	0°	10 hr	1568 Mbps
Static 4	0°	40°	10 hr	1566 Mbps
Static 5	0°	−40°	10 hr	1585 Mbps

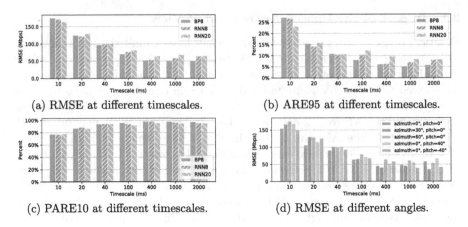

(a) RMSE at different timescales.   (b) ARE95 at different timescales.

(c) PARE10 at different timescales.   (d) RMSE at different angles.

Fig. 4. Model performance for static traces. The input for timescales above 100 ms does not include throughput, see Feature Selection in this section.

Figures 4a, 4b, 4c show that the accuracy with all three models and for all three metrics generally improves as we move from finer to coarser timescales. Overall, the accuracy is very high at timescales coarser than 40 ms, where there are no significant throughput variations, as we saw in Fig. 3. The RMSE remains below 100 Mbps, the ARE95 metric remains below 12%, and the PARE10 metric above 92% at those timescales. For the fine timescales (10–20 ms) required for VR applications, the 95th percentile of the error is higher, 14–16% at 20 ms and 23–27% at 10 ms, due to the the large throughput variations at such short timescales, which we observed in Fig. 3. Nonetheless, the RMSE remains at satisfactory levels (122–175 Mbps) and 78–88% of the prediction errors are still lower than 10%. Overall, *DNN models can make accurate throughput predictions at all timescales in static conditions.*

When we compare the three DNN models, we observe that there are no significant differences among them. The RNN models perform slightly better in terms of the RMSE and ARE95 metrics at 10 ms, but the BP model becomes slightly more accurate at coarser timescales. All three models perform similarly in terms of the PARE10 metric. Between the two RNN models, RNN8 outperforms RNN20 at all timescales except for 10 ms.

To study the impact of the different angles that the phone is kept at within the FoV, we picked the best model for each angle at each timescale and plotted the RMSE in Fig. 4d. For timescales up to 100 ms, the prediction is most accurate when the phone is facing exactly towards the AP (0° azimuth, 0° pitch). At coarser timescales, there is no clear trend. In most cases, the 60° azimuth trace has the worst RMSE, which is most likely due to the fact that at 60° azimuth the AP is very close to the edge of the phone's FoV (Sect. 3.1) and hence experiences higher throughput variations. In terms of the pitch, +40° has lower RMSE for some timescales but −40° for other timescales. Overall, *in static conditions, the model performance is not affected significantly by the azimuth or pitch angles.*

Feature Selection. To understand which of these features are more useful in the prediction, we perform the following iterative feature removal exercise.

We start with all N features. For each feature, we temporarily remove it from the input, and train a model using the remaining $N-1$ features. We then compare the resulting models and identify the least useful feature among the N features as the one removing which results in the model with the least prediction accuracy reduction. We permanently remove this feature from the input, and iteratively perform the same procedure on the remaining $N - 1$, $N - 2$, $N - 3$... features, until all but one features have been removed. Effectively, this algorithm ranks the features by their importance to the model's accuracy. We run this algorithm for all the timescales. The results, averaged over all 5 datasets in Table 1, are shown in Table 2 only for the BP8 model and 3 representative timescales (10 ms, 100 ms, and 2000 ms) due to the page limit.

At the 10 ms timescale, we observe that removing SQI, MCS, and Tx Sector marginally improves the RMSE. However, when we remove RSSI (and hence we only use the past throughput), the RMSE increases by ∼5 Mbps. Thus, *at the 10 ms timescale, the past throughput is the most important feature that contributes to the model's accuracy* followed by RSSI.

Surprisingly, *at the coarser timescales of 100 ms and 2000 ms, we observe that throughput actually is the least important feature*. In particular, at 2000 ms, excluding throughput from the input features improves the RMSE by 6 Mbps. On the other hand, MCS, which was not very important at the 10 ms timescale, now becomes the most important feature. In fact, we observed that for all timescales less than 100 ms, throughput is the most important feature while for all coarser timescales MCS becomes the most important feature.

Table 2. Features selection for static traces

Removal step	10 ms		100 ms		2000 ms	
	Removed	RMSE	Removed	RMSE	Removed	RMSE
	–	175.01	–	71.75	–	57.38
1	SQI	174.33	Throughput	70.26	Throughput	51.56
2	MCS	174.34	Tx Sector	69.47	RSSI	51.85
3	Tx Sector	173.79	SQI	70.46	Tx Sector	52.80
4	RSSI	178.17	RSSI	70.17	SQI	52.28
Last feature	Throughput		MCS		MCS	

3.3 Mobile Scenarios

In this section, we explore the impact of realistic smartphone motion patterns (typical with applications like VR and 360° video streaming) on throughput prediction. We collected a 10 h long trace, where the phone simultaneously moved in the azimuth, pitch, and slide dimensions at different speeds. In the azimuth dimension, the phone moved in the $[-60°, 60°]$ range at various speeds between $10°/s$ and $40°/s$. In the pitch dimension, the phone moved in $[-40°, 40°]$ range at speeds between $6°/s$ and $20°/s$. These speeds were picked as they represent typical VR motion speeds [26,48]. In the slide dimension, the phone moved at a speed of $0.05\,m/s$ (the maximum speed supported by the Cinetics slider). We found that, at such low speeds, translational motion along the $1\,m$ slider has no impact on throughput. Hence, we do not include the y-coordinate or the acceleration along the y-axis in our feature set.

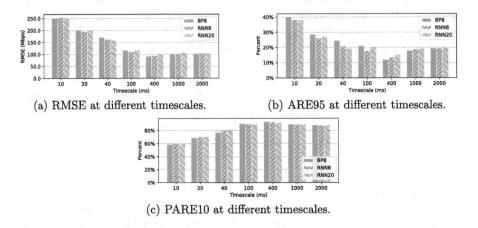

(a) RMSE at different timescales.   (b) ARE95 at different timescales.

(c) PARE10 at different timescales.

Fig. 5. Model performance for random motion traces. The input for timescales above 100 ms does not include throughput.

As expected, the prediction accuracy under mobility worsens (Fig. 5) with all three models and for all three metrics compared to the static scenarios (Figs. 4a, 4b, 4c). The RMSE ranges from 92–258 Mbps (vs. 50–175 Mbps in Fig. 4a), the ARE95 metric ranges from 12–40% (vs. 5–27% in Fig. 4b), and the PARE10 metric from 59–94% (vs. 78–98% in Fig. 4c). Nonetheless, prediction at timescales of 100 ms or higher retains high accuracy. Interestingly, we observe a "sweet spot" at 400 ms with respect to all three metrics, which was not present in the static scenarios. This suggests that motion introduces an interesting trade-off between the length of history as input, and the prediction window in the future.

We now look at the results at the two ends of the spectrum. *At timescales of 1 and 2 s, corresponding to video streaming applications, the accuracy remains at satisfactory levels*; the 95th percentile of the error is below 20% and about 89% of the errors are lower than 10%. On the other hand, *the accuracy drops significantly at VR timescales, 10 and 20 ms*. In particular, the ARE95 metric ranages between 38–40% and 26–29%, and the PARE10 metric is below 60% and 70%, respectively.

Finally, when we compare the accuracy of the three models, we observe that the RNN models perform slightly better for up to 40 ms and the BP model performs better at coarser timescales. However, the difference in the performance among the three models is even smaller compared to the results in Fig. 4.

Feature Selection. Table 3 shows the feature selection results in random mobility scenarios. Similar to the results in Table 2, we observe that throughput is the most important feature for only the 10 ms and 20 ms timescales, while for all coarser timescales, MCS becomes the most important feature. At 10 ms, RSSI remains the second most important feature, same as in Table 2, while the phone's pitch and azimuth interestingly do not contribute much to the accuracy. In contrast, at 2000 ms, azimuth and pitch are the most important features after MCS. At 100 ms, the contribution of all features other than throughput and MCS is marginal.

Table 3. Features selection for random motion traces

Removal step	10 ms		100 ms		2000 ms	
	Removed	RMSE	Removed	RMSE	Removed	RMSE
	–	250.98	–	117.30	–	110.39
1	MCS	258.18	Throughput	110.34	Throughput	98.56
2	Pitch	252.39	RSSI	108.50	RSSI	97.57
3	Azimuth	254.36	SQI	107.62	Link Status	97.87
4	SQI	255.01	Azimuth	108.01	Tx Sector	99.69
5	Link Status	256.10	Link Status	109.12	SQI	101.69
6	Tx Sector	261.69	Tx Sector	109.95	Pitch	105.32
7	RSSI	270.20	Pitch	112.67	Azimuth	112.81
Last feature	Throughput		MCS		MCS	

3.4 Applications

To further understand the throughput predictability using real applications, which may not always be sending backlogged traffic, we collected throughput traces for 2 applications: VR and video streaming. Both applications stream video frames encoded with H.264 compression over TCP. For both traces, the phone moved along all 3 dimensions at various speeds as described in Sect. 3.3. In the case of VR, we pre-encoded a 60 FPS Viking Village scene at 8K and we wrote a client app that requests frames from a local server. Assuming that the VR application wants to make quality adaptation decisions on a per-frame basis, it would require a throughput prediction every 16 ms at a frame rate of 60 FPS. We considered 8K VR, because 4K VR does not demand throughput more than 300 Mbps, which can be supported even by legacy WiFi [24,30]. In the case of streaming, we used a 4K, 50 FPS video from the Derf's collection under Xiph [2], encoded at a bitrate of 1.3 Gbps, and used the same app to request video chunks of 2 s from the local server, in order to emulate ABR video streaming applications, which generally download chunks of 2 s and would need throughput predictions at that timescale.

The performance of the three models is shown in Table 4. For VR, in terms of the ARE95 and the PARE10 metrics, the performance is similar to what was shown in Sect. 3.3 at a 20 ms timescale, while the RMSE is ~156–164 Mbps. We conclude that 60 FPS VR applications can benefit from throughput prediction only if they use it conservatively and can tolerate a certain margin of error.

Table 4. Model performance for real applications

	VR			ABR		
	BP8	RNN8	RNN20	BP8	RNN8	RNN20
RMSE	156.78	163.65	163.66	114.54	115.77	113.87
ARE95	29.08%	28.82%	27.92%	18.15%	17.72%	17.58%
PARE10	72.79%	70.52%	69.24%	86.93%	86.10%	87.03%

For ABR video streaming, as expected, the models perform better due to the much coarser timescale. With ~86–87% of the errors being within 10% of the actual throughput and having a prediction error of ~17–18% at the 95th percentile, ABR video streaming applications can use these predictions with much more confidence to ensure a high user QoE.

3.5 Prediction Time (NN Inference Delay)

We wrote an Android application that uses the jpmml-evaluator [10] and tensor-flow [14] modules to make predictions for BP8 and RNN(s), respectively, and ran it on the phone's GPU to measure the inference delay and memory consumption for each model. We ran each model 100 times and the averaged inference delay and memory consumption results are shown in Table 5. We observe that BP8 runs in less than 0.5 ms and thus can be used by both VR and streaming applications. In contrast, the RNN models run in 2–4 ms and can only be used for streaming applications. The memory consumption is negligible for all 3 models.

Table 5. Inference time and memory consumption of the 3 NN models

Model	Inference delay (ms)	Memory consumption (MB)
BP8	0.41	3.71
RNN8	1.94	0.20
RNN20	4.02	0.29

4 Related Work

Throughput Prediction Over the Internet. Traditional ABR algorithms were classified into two categories: rate-based [21,25,31] and buffer-based

[19,39]. Recently, control-theoretic, data-driven approaches, using Model Predictive Control (MPC), e.g., [15,41,47], became the state-of-the-art approach to ABR, as they combine the use of both throughput prediction and playback buffer occupancy. More recent studies [29,46] have shown that DNN-based algorithms outperform all previous approaches. Our work differs from [29,46] in two key ways. First, we focus on 60 GHz throughput prediction, thus making predictions at the Gbps scale compared to the Mbps scale in those works. Second, while those works make predictions at timescales of a few s, we also look at timescales as low as a few ms, for low latency applications such as VR.

Throughput Prediction Over Wireless Networks. Past works focused on throughput prediction for sub-6 GHz mobile networks at much coarser timescales [17,27]. Lumos5G [32] is a recent work that explores using ML to predict mmWave 5G throughput. However, since cellular networks have very different characteristics from WLANs, the ML models developed in [32] have completely different input features (e.g., geographic coordinates, cellular tower-related features, handoffs, etc.) compared to our models and, similar to previous works, target much longer timescales, from a few seconds up to a few days. Recent works on mobile 360° video streaming [18,34] consider timescales of a few seconds, similar to their Internet counterparts. Firefly [26] is a recently proposed approach for mobile VR that performs adaptation at the frame level (a few ms). However, Firefly modifies the AP firmware to obtain accurate available bandwidth statistics. In contrast, we consider client-side adaptation and our prediction models only use features readily available in the user space.

High-Bandwidth, Latency-Sensitive Applications Over 60 GHz. The work in [44] was the first to show that performance drops drastically when the AP falls outside the client's FoV. Based on this observation, the authors proposed a binary predictor to predict whether the AP will fall inside the client's FoV in the next 500 ms. Our work showed that throughput variations are non-negligible at fine timescales, even for static clients. The work in [48] argues that typical VR/Miracast motion is highly unpredictable and can lead to large and sudden drops in signal quality. The work in [16] used the average throughput of the previous 40 ms window to predict the average throughput of the next 30 ms window and showed that it leads to prediction errors of up to 500 Mbps even in static conditions. Based on this result, the authors concluded that throughput cannot be predicted in 60 GHz WLANs. In contrast, our study shows that it is feasible to use 60 GHz throughput prediction for quality adaptation, especially for video streaming applications (the target application of [16]).

Viewport Prediction. Several recent works have looked at viewport prediction for 360° video streaming, e.g., [18, 34, 37]. Those works are orthogonal to our work, as we show from our feature selection study that the user's angular position with respect to the AP has little to no correlation with the resulting throughput when the AP falls within the client's FoV.

5   Conclusion and Future Directions

We presented the first measurement study of the throughput predictability on 802.11ad-enabled mobile devices. Our study shows the throughput in general can be predicted well in real time using carefully designed small neural network models, and further has several implications to the predictor design. First, our feature selection study shows that using scaled throughput history (keeping the ratio of the history window and the prediction window constant) helps prediction accuracy at the 10 ms timescale but hurts at the 2000 ms timescale. This suggests that a new design that limits the length of history as the model input can potentially achieve good accuracy for all timescales. Second, our feature selection study further shows that, for different timescales, using different sets of features gives the best prediction accuracy. This suggests that a single neural network for use in different applications can potentially improve its prediction accuracy by adapting the set of features according to application latency requirements. Further, in this work we performed all our experiments in a single environment. An interesting avenue for future work is to study the impact of different environments on throughput predictability.

Acknowledgements. We thank our shepherd, Prof. Özgü Alay, and the anonymous reviewers for their valuable comments. This work was supported in part by the NSF grant CNS-1553447.

References

1. GHz Throughput Prediction Dataset. https://github.com/NUWiNS/pam2021-60ghz-throughput-prediction-data
2. Xiph.org Video Test Media [derf's collection]. https://media.xiph.org/video/derf/
3. Adobe HTTP Dynamic Streaming. https://www.adobe.com/products/hds-dynamic-streaming.html
4. Android Sensors Overview. https://developer.android.com/guide/topics/sensors/sensors_overview
5. ASUS Republic of Gamers (ROG) Phone. https://www.asus.com/us/Phone/ROG-Phone/
6. ASUS Republic of Gamers (ROG) Phone II. https://www.asus.com/us/Phone/ROG-Phone-II/
7. Cinetics Lynx 3 Axis Slider. https://cinetics.com/lynx-3-axis-slider/
8. Dragonframe Stop Motion Software. https://www.dragonframe.com
9. Google Cardboard. https://arvr.google.com/cardboard/
10. JPMML-Evaluator - Java Evaluator API for Predictive Model Markup Language (PMML). https://github.com/jpmml/jpmml-evaluator

11. Microsoft Smooth Streaming. https://www.microsoft.com/silverlight/smooth-streaming/
12. Netgear Nighthawk® X10. https://www.netgear.com/landings/ad7200
13. nuttcp - Network Performance Measurement Tool. https://www.nuttcp.net
14. Tensorflow for android. https://www.tensorflow.org/lite/guide/android
15. Akhtar, Z., et al.: Oboe: auto-tuning video abr algorithms to network conditions. In: Proceedings of ACM SIGCOMM (2018)
16. Baig, G., et al.: Jigsaw: robust live 4K video streaming. In: Proceedings of ACM MobiCom (2019)
17. Bui, N., Michelinakis, F., Widmer, J.: A model for throughput prediction for mobile users. In: Proceedings of IEEE EWC (2014)
18. He, J., Qureshi, M., Qiu, L., Li, J., Li, F., Han, L.: Rubiks: practical 360-degree streaming for smartphones. In: Proceedings of ACM MobiSys (2018)
19. Huang, T.Y., Johari, R., McKeown, N., Trunnell, M., Watson, M.: A buffer-based approach to rate adaptation: evidence from a large video streaming service. In: Proceedings of ACM SIGCOMM (2014)
20. IEEE 802.11 Working Group: IEEE 802.11ad, Amendment 3: Enhancements for Very High Throughput in the 60 GHz Band (2012)
21. Jiang, J., Sekar, V., Zhang, H.: Improving fairness, efficiency, and stability in http-based adaptive video streaming with festive. In: Proceedings of ACM CoNEXT (2012)
22. Kajita, S., Yamaguchi, H., Higashino, T., Urayama, H., Yamada, M., Takai, M.: Throughput and delay estimator for 2.4GHz WiFi APs: a machine learning-based approach. In: Proceedings of IFIP WMNC (2015)
23. Khan, M.O., Qiu, L.: Accurate WiFi packet delivery rate estimation and applications. In: Proceedings of IEEE INFOCOM (2016)
24. Lai, Z., Hu, Y.C., Cui, Y., Sun, L., Dai, N.: Furion: engineering high-quality immersive virtual reality on today's mobile devices. In: Proceedings of ACM MobiCom (2017)
25. Li, Z., et al.: Probe and adapt: rate adaptation for http video streaming at scale. IEEE J. Sel. Areas Commun. **32**(4), 719–733 (2014)
26. Liu, X., Vlachou, C., Qian, F., Wang, C., Kim, K.H.: Firefly: untethered multi-user VR for commodity mobile devices. In: Proceedings of USENIX ATC (2020)
27. Liu, Y., Lee, J.Y.B.: An empirical study of throughput prediction in mobile data networks. In: Proceedings of IEEE GLOBECOM (2015)
28. Mangiante, S., Klas, G., Navon, A., GuanHua, Z., Ran, J., Silva, M.D.: VR is on the edge: how to deliver 360° videos in mobile networks. In: Proceedings of VR/AR Network (2017)
29. Mao, H., Netravali, R., Alizadeh, M.: Neural adaptive video streaming with pensieve. In: Proceedings of ACM SIGCOMM (2017)
30. Meng, J., Paul, S., Hu, Y.C.: Coterie: exploiting frame similarity to enable high-quality multiplayer VR on commodity mobile devices. In: Proceedings of ACM ASPLOS (2020)
31. Mok, R.K.P., Luo, X., Chan, E.W.W., Chang, R.K.C.: QDASH: a QoE-aware dash system. In: Proceedings of ACM MMSys (2012)
32. Narayanan, A., et al.: Lumos5G: mapping and predicting commercial mmwave 5g throughput (2020)
33. Pantos, R.: Apple HTTP Live Streaming 2nd Edition. Internet-Draft draft-pantos-hls-rfc8216bis-07, Internet Engineering Task Force (2020). https://datatracker.ietf.org/doc/html/draft-pantos-hls-rfc8216bis-07

34. Qian, F., Han, B., Xiao, Q., Gopalakrishnan, V.: Flare: practical viewport-adaptive 360-degree video streaming for mobile devices. In: Proceedings of ACM MobiCom (2018)
35. Saha, S.K., et al.: Fast and infuriating: performance and pitfalls of 60 GHz WLANs based on consumer-grade hardware. In: Proceedings of IEEE SECON (2018)
36. Saha, S.K., Aggarwal, S., Pathak, R., Koutsonikolas, D., Widmer, J.: MuSher: an agile multipath-TCP scheduler for dual-band 802.11ad/ac wireless LANs. In: Proceedings of ACM MobiCom (2019)
37. Shi, S., Gupta, V., Jana, R.: Freedom: fast recovery enhanced VR delivery over mobile networks. In: Proceedings of ACM MobiSys (2019)
38. Song, L., Striegel, A.: Leveraging frame aggregation for estimating WiFi available bandwidth. In: Proceedings of IEEE SECON (2017)
39. Spiteri, K., Urgaonkar, R., Sitaraman, R.K.: BOLA: near-optimal bitrate adaptation for online videos. In: Proceedings of IEEE INFOCOM (2016)
40. Stockhammer, T.: Dynamic adaptive streaming over HTTP: standards and design principles. In: Proceedings of ACM MMSys (2011)
41. Sun, Y., et al.: CS2P: improving video bitrate selection and adaptation with data-driven throughput prediction. In: Proceedings of ACM SIGCOMM (2016)
42. Sur, S., Pefkianakis, I., Zhang, X., Kim, K.H.: WiFi-assisted 60 GHz wireless networks. In: Proceedings of ACM MobiCom (2017)
43. Sur, S., Venkateswaran, V., Zhang, X., Ramanathan, P.: 60 GHz indoor networking through flexible beams: a link-level profiling. In: Proceedings of ACM SIGMETRICS (2015)
44. Wei, T., Zhang, X.: Pose information assisted 60 GHz networks: towards seamless coverage and mobility support. In: Proceedings of ACM MobiCom (2017)
45. Xu, T., Han, B., Qian, F.: Analyzing viewport prediction under different VR interactions. In: Proceedings of ACM CoNEXT (2019)
46. Yan, F.Y., et al.: Learning in situ: a randomized experiment in video streaming. In: Proceedings of USENIX NSDI (2020)
47. Yin, X., Jindal, A., Sekara, V., Sinopoli, B.: A control-theoretic approach for dynamic adaptive video streaming over HTTP. In: Proceedings of ACM SIGCOMM (2015)
48. Zhou, A., Wu, L., Xu, S., Ma, H., Wei, T., Zhang, X.: Following the shadow: agile 3-D beam-steering for 60 GHz wireless networks. In: Proceedings of IEEE INFOCOM (2018)

Exposing Hidden Behaviors

Characterizing the Security of Endogenous and Exogenous Desktop Application Network Flows

Matthew R. McNiece[1,2], Ruidan Li[2], and Bradley Reaves[1(✉)]

1 North Carolina State University, Raleigh, NC, USA
{mrmcniec,bgreaves}@ncsu.edu
2 Cisco Systems, Inc., Raleigh, NC, USA
ruidali@cisco.com

Abstract. Most desktop applications use the network, and insecure communications can have a significant impact on the application, the system, the user, and the enterprise. Understanding *at scale* whether desktop application use the network securely is a challenge because the application provenance of a given network packet is rarely available at centralized collection points. In this paper, we collect flow data from 39,758 MacOS devices on an enterprise network to study the network behaviors of individual applications. We collect flows *locally* on-device and can definitively identify the application responsible for every flow. We also develop techniques to distinguish "endogenous" flows common to most executions of a program from "exogenous" flows likely caused by unique inputs. We find that popular MacOS applications are in fact using the network securely, with 95.62% of the applications we study using HTTPS. Notably, we observe security sensitive-services (including certificate management and mobile device management) do not use ports associated with secure communications. Our study provides important insights for users, device and network administrators, and researchers interested in secure communication.

1 Introduction

Most desktop applications make connections over the network to pull content, check for a license, or save a resource. While encrypted communications were once rare, Google recently reported that 95% of Chrome connection on Mac platforms use HTTPS [1]. However, studies on TLS adoption have not accounted for non-browser applications—the vast majority of networked software. Measuring per-application network use requires a vantage point that can map network traffic to the originating application. At a small scale, tools such as personal firewalls can let an individual determine what sorts of connections applications on their device are making, but are limited to a single device. Network-layer telemetry tools like middleboxes can provide a higher-level view of desktop flows but lose definitive context of the application responsible for the flow.

In this paper, we bridge these two viewpoints, bringing the local context of observing an application making a connection but providing visibility across

© Springer Nature Switzerland AG 2021
O. Hohlfeld et al. (Eds.): PAM 2021, LNCS 12671, pp. 531–546, 2021.
https://doi.org/10.1007/978-3-030-72582-2_31

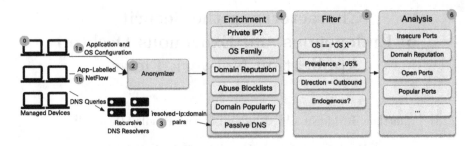

Fig. 1. Telemetry collected from a population of 39,758 MacOS devices contains application-labelled netflow that is anonymized and enriched for further analysis.

39,758 MacOS devices in an enterprise setting. At scale, we run into challenges when examining the traffic from even a single application across many hosts, as some connections are made on behalf of the user, while others are part of what an application does natively. For example, a word processor may check for updates while simultaneously loading embedded content in a particular document. The software developer is only responsible for one of these network uses, so differentiating these two classes of behaviors is critical to properly evaluate the security behavior of the application. Our perspective is interesting because we are able to study a large population of hosts, with a vantage point into each host in the population that can attribute traffic back to a specific process. Studying this as a population of hosts allows us to reasonably and confidently make claims about an application's behavior, while in individual studies we could observe point data but would be limited to describing an instance of an application. These measurements and insights can provide valuable context for administrators and incident responders to understand expected behaviors of applications on managed devices and for application developers to better understand the holistic connections their applications are making. Our work makes the following contributions:

- We perform the first large scale study of application network behavior on desktop applications
- We demonstrate and evaluate a technique to differentiate user-triggered and application-endogenous behavior
- We examine listening ports, reputation of over 282,000 domains, and over *three billion* connections to evaluate the attack surface of 143 desktop applications
- We investigate popular applications such as Microsoft Office and MacOS daemons that do not entirely use secure communication channels.

2   Methods

Figure 1 shows a high-level view of our phased methodology and analysis pipeline. Our goal is to combine our data sources while maintaining the anonymity of any users, use accurate matching techniques, and deal with the challenges of combining billion-row datasets. We begin in **Phase 0** with a population of around 39,000 IT-managed devices, all of which are desktops or laptops. These devices belong to a Fortune 500 company and we consider these to be representative of a typical enterprise managed device. We are interested in two types of collected telemetry: application and OS configuration (**1a**) and application-labelled flow data (**1b**). Application and OS configuration contains information about currently installed processes on the system, OS version information, and more. Application-labelled flow data contains metadata about connections made on behalf of some application on the device. In their raw form, both of these data sources contain fields that include potential human-identifying information such as usernames, machine names, and MAC addresses. **Phase 2** removes or encrypts all human identifiers. **Phase 3** consists of a data source that has passively collected DNS queries generated by all devices on the network. **Phase 4** transforms and enriches the now anonymized data feeds from **1a** and **1b**. Flow data is first enriched with fields indicating the OS family of the device that generated the traffic, and if the source and destination IPs are each private or public. Then, the flow data is joined with the (`domain,resolved_ip`) pairs observed from the passive DNS data, recovering the domains associated with each flow. Finally, using the recovered domain we check against blocklists, popularity, and reputation sources and look for any matches at the second-level domain.

In **Phase 5** we apply filters to the enriched flow data and configuration data. We restrict both datasets to only MacOS devices and only consider traffic from applications installed on more than 5% of the device population. We further restrict flows to outbound connections (i.e., a device talking to some remote server). Finally, we make a determination if a particular connection for an application is common across installs of that application, and restrict analysis to those that we believe to be common. We performed the data processing and analysis on a large Spark [2] cluster. In total, our pipeline and analysis took approximately 4,200 CPU hours and 37,000 GB memory hours.

2.1 Data Collection and Characterization

Application Labelled Flows (Phase 1b): Our primary dataset is telemetry from Cisco AnyConnect VPN's Network Visibility Module (NVM) [3]. This tool records all network traffic from a host and critically, the process associated with the traffic. The records generated by NVM include the source and destination IP address, source and destination port, flow size and duration, as well as the name and SHA256 hash of the process binary associated with the flow. We use one day's telemetry collected from NVM on a large enterprise network in September 2020, which is about 320 GB of compressed JSON. This contains records from 39,758 hosts, 143 unique applications, and 3,211,451,385 total flows. This dataset contains only network telemetry, so an application that generates no network traffic is not represented. There were two challenges with using this data. First, flows are bidirectional but do not indicate if the flow originated on the laptop or a remote server. We address this in Subsect. 2.3. Second, flows frequently do not have a domain name associated with the destination, so we use the observed passive DNS data to recover domains from IP addresses.

Application and OS Configuration (Phase 1a): We use OSQuery [4] to learn about the state of a device, its installed applications, and recent network activity. Our dataset contains the query results from 35,678 managed endpoints from a single day in September 2020.[1]

Passive DNS (Phase 3): At each recursive DNS resolver on the network, there is a passive collector that records logs of DNS queries and responses. Because these collectors are internal to the network, observing a query/response means that a device inside the network made a query for some specific domain that had a specific IP in the response. All devices in our population are configured to use these DNS resolvers. We use logs collected from the same 24 h window as the application-labelled flows. This consists of 9.5 billion query/response pairs, approximately 115 Gb of compressed Parquet [5]. We use this data to perform reverse DNS lookups to recover the domains of an observed IP in the flow metadata.

Additional Sources of Enrichment (Phase 4): We use the Snort IP Block-list [6] and a paid commercial feed of domains associated with spam campaigns as sources of maliciousness. We use the Umbrella Top 1 Million domains list [7] as a proxy for goodness and the Umbrella Investigate Risk Score [8] as a source of domain reputation.

2.2 Data Preparation and Preprocessing

Anonymization (Phase 2): In raw form, the flow data, configuration data contain human-identifying information. The datasets that the research team had access to have had all human-identifying fields (e.g., usernames, MAC addresses) removed with the exception of the machine name. The machine name was encrypted with a key the research team did not have access to; this field was pseudo anonymized so there remained a way to track flows associated with the same device and calculate the number of unique devices in the population that share some trait. Appendix A contains a full discussion of our data ethics.

Passive DNS (Phase 3): We used passively observed DNS data to generate "lookups" that we could use to recover a domain name from an IP address. We use A,AAAA records and collected pairs of rdata,rrname observed responses, these two fields contain no human identifiable data and thus bypasses the anonymization step. From this key-value pair, we can enrich observed IP addresses from the flow data with all observed domains that resolved to that IP.

Application and OS Configuration (Phase 1a): We used a single query [9] to obtain a snapshot of all active listening ports on the system and the process that owns them.

---

[1] This is fewer hosts than are in the flows dataset, but certainly large enough to be a representative sample. OSQuery data was not available for every host that NVM was installed on.

Application Labelled Flows (Phase 1b): We perform three lightweight operations on the data before it proceeds to the fusing step: remove any records that are NULL, add a label with the OS family (Windows or MacOS), and use RFC 1918 [10] to label each source and destination address as "Private" or "Public".

2.3   Enrichment (Phase 4)

We fuse together application-labeled flows with the observed ip:domain pairs from pDNS to recover domains from the flow metadata. While we were not able to match exact pDNS queries to hosts due to a lack of consistent identifiers, the pDNS data was collected from the same network in the same 24-h period. When we observe the same IP on the same network within a time window we have high confidence that it resolved to that domain. In cases where a single IP resolves to multiple domains, we report all matched domains.[2] Enriching the flow data with the DNS lookups requires a join between 3.2 billion flows and 2.9 billion ip:domain pairs. Some IPs resolve to orders of magnitude more domains (e.g., AWS, CloudFlare) which causes a skewed join. Skewed joins are painful for many distributed compute systems, including ours, it took us multiple iterations and about 1,000 CPU hours to make this single join work.

Traffic Direction: NVM records symmetrical flow metadata, but does not indicate if the origin of the connection was remote or local, so it is unclear if the source IP was the local device or the remote server. We did not use ports as an indication of which end was the remote (e.g., if destination port was HTTP/80) because if we assumed well-known or registered ports were always the remote, that would bias any research questions involving port usage. We did not have access to an authoritative record of the IP address allocated to a given device, which could have helped bypass this challenge.

We used RFC 1918 to build a simple heuristic to determine traffic direction. We then label each flow as Internal, Outbound, Inbound or NAT, for more information see Appendix B. We hypothesize that most traffic should be Outbound as most applications follow a client-server pattern where an application initiates connections to some Internet-facing service. We then looked at the distribution of traffic and found that 81.9% of traffic was Outbound, which supports that hypothesis. Internal consisted of 2.86% of traffic, Inbound 15.19% and NAT 0.05%. Outbound represents more than 80% of the traffic and we can best reason about it, so we restrict our analysis to this type only. We revisit inbound traffic using OSQuery in Subsect. 3.5.

2.4   Filtering (Phase 5)

We restricted our dataset in three ways. First, we restricted our analysis to only MacOS applications, as we had more devices running MacOS in the population.

---

[2] This overapproximates possible domains, risking misclassifying an IP as disreputable in our analysis. Because our results do not identify any endogenous domain as disreputable, this concern is moot.

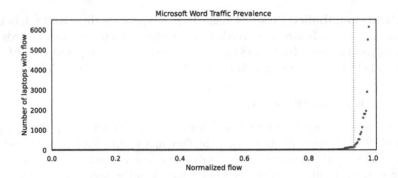

Fig. 2. Each dot represents a unique connection (`port,2LD`) made by an Microsoft Word. Most connections (239 of 323 total) appear on a single device, however a small number appear on many more. We apply our endogenous heuristic to draw a line at a prevalence of 159 devices, which includes the most prevalent 6% flows.

Second, we only consider applications with observed traffic from more than 5% 1,987 of devices. This excludes rare applications (e.g., Steam) as they would not be indicative of the applications installed on a typical enterprise device. Finally, we removed traffic associated with `*.acme.TLD`, the domain of the enterprise where data was collected. In addition to this being a non-negotiable requirement from the data provider, this allows our results to be more generalizable. `*.acme.TLD` is likely to appear endogenous when using our techniques and we would like to isolate this from actual endogenous traffic. Many users visiting the ACME homepage would make that domain appear to be part of endogenous traffic for a browser. This lets us focus on application behavior in general and less on behavior within a specific domain or IT configuration. In practice, this removed 3.2% of flows overall, or 1.2% of flows at the 2LD.

Application Endogenous Traffic: Throughout this work, we considered that a user can cause an application to make connections to destinations that the developer had no knowledge of. For example, consider two connections from Microsoft Word, the first to `mastercard.com` on port 443 across 97 unique devices, and the second to `office.com` on port 443 across 5,498 unique devices. Intuitively, these are two different types of connections. It is likely that Word connects to `office.com` because of code that the application developer wrote, while it's also more likely that a user action triggered the network connection to `mastercard.com`.

More generically, consider an application installed and used by thousands of independent users and the popularity of individual network connections made by that application. If the same connections are made by many different users, either these users are all using the application in the same way or the application itself has a common behavior using the network. As these connections become more and more popular it is more likely that it is application behavior. Alternatively, if an extremely common user behavior triggers a network request, if it is popular enough it may as well be owned by the application. For example, if hitting "save" in Word triggers a network connection, that may as well be considered application behavior because it is ubiquitous across users.

We distinguish these types of traffic into two categories, *application endogenous* versus user triggered, or *exogenous*. Endogenous is a term borrowed from biology that indicates that something grows or originates from within an organism. This differs from something exogenous that grows or originates from outside an organism. The tie here is that such endogenous traffic originates from within an application's native behavior, not external influences.

Given the collected metadata, we observe that *application endogenous* traffic will appear on more devices than user triggered traffic. Second, we observe that if, for each application, we plot each flow against the number of unique hosts it appeared on, a fairly regular pattern occurs, as seen in Fig. 2. Our intuition is that this is following a Pareto distribution. However, different applications will have different distribution parameters, complicating a simple decision criteria. To solve this, we identify the point on the observed distribution where the curve grows steeply, i.e., the "elbow" of the plot [11]. We then consider any types of flows that fall at or higher than the elbow to be endogenous to the application and flows that fall below to be user triggered. We acknowledge that there are some confounds with this approach, namely if there is some extremely popular destination, e.g. google.com, it may be indistinguishable from an endogenous behavior due to its ubiquity. We restrict most of our analysis to these endogenous connections, and while there are almost certainly interesting things happening in the exogenous flows, our focus is on application native behavior which endogenous traffic better represents. We further explore this approach and cases where it succeeds and fails in Subsect. 3.1.

3 Analysis

We observed traffic from 39,758 unique MacOS hosts over a 24-h period in September 2020. Each host in this population is a user-facing endpoint, such as a desktop or laptop. We observed 143 unique applications installed on more than 5% of the population ($\geq$1,987 hosts). These applications generated 3,211,451,385 total connections. After recovering domains with pDNS, we observed 282,715 unique domains, 61,607 (21.8%) of which were unique second-level domains, e.g., google.com. The typical endpoint in our population produces a large number of unique flows with a median 23,642 connections, where a unique flow is defined by tuple (application,destinationport,domain).

3.1 How Many of an Application's Connections Are Endogenous?

We applied the "elbow" filtering techniques described in Subsect. 2.4 and examined how traffic changed before and after this filtering. First, when considering the number of flows per application, defined by tuple (application, destinationport,domainat2LD), before filtering there were median 17.50 unique

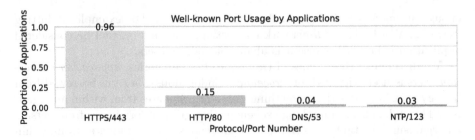

Fig. 3. Well-known ports used as part of application's endogenous traffic. 96% of applications use HTTPS in endogenous connections.

flows, after there were median 3.0. This reduction in types of traffic suggests that many applications have few types of endogenous traffic. The maximum number of unique flows before filtering was 70,175 and after 2,309. When considering the maximum case, the application here is Google Chrome, and our elbow approach struggles to reduce the endogenous traffic to a manageable set, although it does reduce by 96.7%. Chrome and other browsers have orders of magnitude more apparent endogenous connections than other applications. We explore browsers' behavior with elbow filtering in Subsect. 3.6. We see similar trends between number of flows and number of second-level domains. The median number of second-level domains connected to per application was 15.00, after filtering it was 3.0. In the maximum case for Google Chrome, before there were 50,691 unique 2LDs, after 2,288. Lastly, we consider the destination ports used per application. In the median case an application used 2 ports before filtering, after there was 1. In the maximum case, there were 9,427 ports connected to by an application, afterwards there were 9. In this case, Google Chrome was the maximum before, but after it filtered down to 4 ports; VMware-Nat was the maximum after filtering.

By considering only traffic that is endogenous to an application, we have a tractable dataset to consider within each applications as most applications do not have many types of endogenous traffic. This is not a tautologically true statement by construction. There are cases (namely browsers) that do have many types of endogenous traffic. Within browsers, there are types of traffic (e.g., email) that are common but are not endogenous behavior. This technique does separate those types of connections from those less common, such as checking niche websites.

Takeaway: There are few connections made by applications that are common across hosts, so differentiating endogenous versus exogenous connections can drastically reduce the dataset size.

3.2 What Ports Do Applications Use to Communicate?

Building on results from Subsect. 3.1, we know that in the median case, an application uses few ports, both before and after looking only at endogenous traffic. We find that most applications only use well-known ports (below 1024);

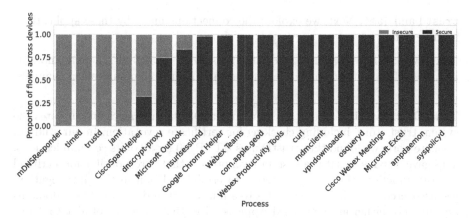

Fig. 4. Distribution between secure and insecure ports for 20 most popular applications. Insecure connections made by applications are further explored in Subsect. 3.3

in endogenous traffic, there are only 4 ports used by more than 2 applications: HTTPS, HTTP, DNS, and NTP. Figure 3 shows that 95.62% of all applications we consider use HTTPS in their endogenous traffic, while 15.33% use HTTP. These are not mutually exclusive; an application that uses both HTTP and HTTPS is counted in both categories. Some common ports (SMTP) are not included here as they only had connections to *.acme.TLD which were excluded. We acknowledge that having a connection on a port does not guarantee the intended protocol is used, we assume that this is the case but did not have access to PCAPs to validate this assumption.

Takeaway: Our unique perspective reinforces the common wisdom that HTTP/S has become the main communication protocol for virtually all traffic.

3.3 What Applications Are Not Using Secure Ports?

We are looking only at "well known" (<1,024) ports. We assume that if there is traffic on a well known port, that traffic is using the protocol expected on that port, but we do not have ground truth for this. While there is not an authoritative list of "secure" ports, we define the following ports as secure: SSH/22,HTTPS/443,NTTPS/563,LDAPS/636,IEEE-MMS-SSL/695,SILC/706,FTPS/989,FTPS/990,TELNET-SSL/992,IMAPS/993,POP3S/995. We then define an insecure port as a port not being in that set. Some exceptions here that we did not account for are ports designed to be secure over plaintext, such as Kerberos, or ports where the secure component is >1,024. In Fig. 4 we consider all traffic for an application across all devices and plot the distribution between insecure and secure ports. There are applications that appear to transmit sensitive data or contain some security feature that communicate over insecure channels, such as trustd and jamf. Next, we explore the connections made by these applications in more detail.

Takeaway: While most endogenous traffic is secure by default, there are notable instances of prominent applications featuring insecure communication channels.

TrustD: trustd is a system daemon on MacOS that manages and updates the system trust store, including checking for certificate revocation. In our study of insecure ports we found that trustD uses HTTP/80 for all of its communications. This gave us pause, as it is a system-level process that is responsible for a critical security function, thus we expected it to use TLS. Upon further investigation, we discovered that this process talks to a limited set of domains. These domains appear to be either authenticated Apple services that we were not able to determine their exact use and purpose (pancake.apple.com and mesu.apple.com) or OCSP checks from major CAs (ocsp.digicert.com,ocsp.apple.com, etc.). OCSP is a certificate revocation protocol that uses a signed request and response. Although the data is authenticated, the sender is not, which exposes a potentially exploitable attack surface if an attacker could craft a malicious OCSP or certificate that the service attempts to load. **Takeaway**: trustd gained some attention in the news and our findings align with what other researchers [12] found and further explains why OCSP must happen over HTTP.

Microsoft Office: Microsoft Excel and Outlook are the only office applications that break the "top 20" to appear on Fig. 4, but we will examine all the Office products (Excel, Outlook, Powerpoint, Word, OneNote, AutoUpdate). Of those, Outlook is the only product to have any endogenous traffic on an insecure port. Outlook's has connections to 164 unique 2LD with port HTTP/80. Marketo, a marketing automation company, appears to own 153 of these domains. These Marketo domains appeared on the same number of hosts, we suspect this is because they are all hosted on the same IP and the pDNS domain recovery matched all of them. These domains appeared on <2% of hosts that were running Outlook so we suspect the elbow heuristic failed for this case. Of the remaining 11 domains, 3 are additional marketing services e.g. sendgrid.net, 5 are CDNs or IaaS providers including amazonaws.com,akamaiedge.net, 1 is office.com, and the remaining 2 are HR service providers. office.com appears both with connections on HTTP/80 and on HTTPS/443 suggesting that not all the connections Outlook makes back to Microsoft use TLS.

Device Management (jamf): jamf is a tool used for IT device and policy management for MacOS and typically runs with root or sub-root privilege. jamf has a single insecure connection, on HTTP/80 to akamaiedge.net, which largely means that it could be connecting and pulling down anything hosted by Akamai, a large CDN.

CiscoSparkHelper: CiscoSparkHelper has 7 endogenous flows and uses 3 ports, 444, 5004, 33434. On both port 5004 and 33434, there are 3 connections each, two to (`wbx2.com` and `webex.com`) which appear to be domains owned by Cisco WebEx; the third connection is to `amazonaws.com`. For port 444 we see a single connection to `wbx2.com`. Port 444 official use is for SNPP, while 5004 and 33434 are used for VoIP audio/video calls. 5004 and 33434 were not included in our "secure" ports as they are not $<1,024$.

3.4   Are Applications Communicating with Reputable Domains?

Next, we are interested evaluating the reputation of domains that applications connect to using proxies for danger and safeness. We focus on 2LDs, and only those that are part of the endogenous set of traffic for an application. We use four proxies for danger: if a domain resolved to an IT-managed DNS blackhole, if a domain appeared in a Snort IP blocklist [6], if a domain appeared in a commercial domain abuse feed, or if a domain appeared as part of DGA for a handful of well known campaigns (Mirai, Zeus, Cryptolocker). We use two proxies for safeness, the reputation score of a domain from OpenDNS Umbrella [8], and the position of a domain on the Umbrella Top 1M [7]. We found no domains that matched any of our proxies for danger, and no domains that flagged as malicious in OpenDNS Umbrella. In all 143 applications, we found that at least 50% of 2LDs per application are in the Umbrella Top 1M Popular Domains, and 15 applications had 100% of their 2LDs in the Top 1M.

Takeaway: Domain reputation services are correctly evaluating endogenous traffic as benign, which is not surprising and would have been interesting if they were not. "Popular" sites lists from Alexa, OpenDNS, etc. can be used by incident responders and network administrators to help determine if a particular site is worth further investigation. However, there's a large portion of endogenous traffic in popular enterprise application that do not appear on these lists. This could be a limitation of these popularity lists where a more focused list of common traffic for a specific application would be useful.

3.5   What Is the Attack Surface that Applications Expose Through Open Ports?

In this experiment, instead of using the application-labelled flow data, we use configuration information generated through OSQuery. The query-pack for "listening-ports" provides information about all listening ports assigned to a process. This is a better way of identifying listening ports than using the flow data since we have an authoritative snapshot of the ports used, and can avoid using heuristics to determine traffic direction. We find on average an application exposes 11.1 listening ports per host, with a median of 1. A few outliers cause this skew, these applications are listening on many different ports: Docker (254 unique ports), dnscrypt-proxy (67), mDNSResponder (28) CiscoSparkHelper (28), Safari (16), vmware-natd (14), Microsoft Teams Helper (11), Spotify (9) zoom.us (4) and Dropbox (3). Docker is, by far, the application that exposes the most listening ports, which in retrospect is logical. Developers can run containers on their laptop using Docker, and can configure the ports that the container listens to on the host OS. Interestingly there are also applications that are exposing more ports than the median that we did not expect to have such a network presence, such as: BetterTouchTool (2), HP Device Monitor (3), [VisualStudio] Code Helper (Renderer) (4). We were unable to confidently attribute these connections back to the domains where they originated because a lack of consistent identifiers between OsQuery and NVM.

Takeaway: Applications that expose listening ports add exposed attack surface that deserves further investigation. There have been cases of applications running webservers that they use to communicate with their web-clients that lead to vulnerabilities [13–15]. We leave determining what applications are doing with these listening ports for future work.

3.6   How Is Endogenous Traffic Represented in Browsers?

As mentioned in Subsect. 3.1, our approach for determining what traffic is endogenous for an application struggles to narrow down traffic observed from browsers. We suspect that this is because browsers are entirely user-triggered applications and there are likely large similarities in browsing destinations between users. In our dataset, we observed traffic for three browsers: Google Chrome, Mozilla Firefox, and Apple Safari. Browsing behavior for users between browsers is fairly similar as common tasks (email, social media, news) are not functions exclusive to any one browser. Across all three browsers, there are 2,671 unique connections (domain at 2LD, port), 1,720 (64%) of those are common across at least two browsers, and 1,335 (50%) are common across all three. Looking at endogenous connections exclusive to a single browser, Chrome has 593 unique connections, Firefox has 187 connections, and Safari has 171. This mimics the rough pattern of popularity of each of these browsers within our device population, so we do not make any conclusions about one of these browsers having a smaller set of endogenous behavior. **Takeaway**: Browsers have fundamentally different types of traffic from other desktop applications, but their traffic is similar to each other.

4   Related Work

Host-based anomaly detection has been a staple of security research since the early 2000s [26] and numerous works have explored addressing anomalous activity on a host [22,40,41]. Anomaly detection has been well explored at the network level with tools like Snort [36] and NetFlow based techniques [29,43]. Identifying applications and operating systems through observing network traffic and reconnaissance has also been well explored [25,34,42], including single packet fingerprints of operating systems [37,38]. There are also enterprise software offerings that can identify the application generating network traffic and measure aspects of flows [16,20,21,31]. Researchers have also used TLS fingerprints as a method of identifying software [17], provided techniques to impersonate common software to circumvent censorship [27], and shown how parrot-based circumvention can fail [30]. By contrast, we act as an omniscient passive observer of traffic and study the connections made by applications focusing on the common connections rather than the anomalous.

Internet-scale measurement has been conducted to look at HTTPS and TLS implementation and weakness [24,39], building features to measure DNS [19,32], or scraping the internet to measure the use of cryptographic libraries [35]. With regard to work in desktop application security, in 2006 Bellissimo et al. studied the updated mechanisms of popular desktop applications [18]. In 2012, Georgiev et al. found that the implementation of SSL certification validation was fundamentally broken in many widely used libraries [28]. In contrast, our work does not examine TLS implementation but instead measures apparent TLS usage. In 2017 Dormann published a blog about the consequences of insecure software updates [23], and a year later, Microsoft was still distributing software over HTTP [33]. To the best of our knowledge, there has not been a prior large-scale, extensive study of the security posture of desktop applications communication channels.

A   Data Ethics

While working on this project, we followed all institutional procedures from all affiliated institutions. Our IRB reviewed our proposal and datasets and determined that this was not human subjects research. All human and machine identifiers in our dataset have been removed and replaced with encrypted versions that are encrypted with a key that the research team does not have access to. All telemetry was collected through existing monitoring infrastructure that has strict ACLs. Furthermore, all telemetry was collected from corporate managed and owned devices where users are made aware that the devices are monitored for security and compliance. Throughout our analysis we focus on the network behavior of applications not individual users. Any individual user's data could be excluded from our dataset without impact to our findings. We made no attempt to find evidence of sensitive actions or non-work-related activity (video games, streaming video, social media, etc.) The focus of our research is on the network behavior of applications, not of the individuals using the applications.

B   RFC 1918

RFC 1918 [10] describes and reserves 3 IP ranges for private use only, we used this to label each source IP and destination IP as "private" or "public". If an IP is "private" then it is not on the Internet, and is instead on some internal/private network. After labeling each flow, there are four possible combinations:

- Private Source to Private Destination (Internal) - Neither end is an Internet facing IP, communication to internal services

- Private Source to Public Destination (Outbound) - Destination is an Internet facing IP, likely an outbound connection
- Public Source to Private Destination (Inbound) - Destination is not an Internet facing IP, so is either a connection from a NAT device to an internal service, or an inbound connection from a public service to a device
- Public Source to Private Destination (NAT) - Both ends have an Internet facing IP, but one must be local device with a NAT IP though we can't tell which.

References

1. https://transparencyreport.google.com/https/overview
2. https://spark.apache.org/
3. https://www.cisco.com/c/en/us/td/docs/security/vpn_client/anyconnect/anyconnect47/administration/guide/b_AnyConnect_Administrator_Guide_4-7/nvm.html
4. https://osquery.io/
5. https://parquet.apache.org/
6. https://snort.org/downloads/ip-block-list
7. https://umbrella.cisco.com/blog/cisco-umbrella-1-million
8. https://docs.umbrella.com/investigate-api/docs/security-information-for-a-domain-1
9. https://github.com/osquery/osquery/blob/master/packs/incident-response.conf#L211
10. https://tools.ietf.org/html/rfc1918
11. https://github.com/georg-un/kneebow
12. https://blog.jacopo.io/en/post/apple-ocsp/
13. https://nvd.nist.gov/vuln/detail/CVE-2019-13450
14. https://nvd.nist.gov/vuln/detail/CVE-2019-13449
15. https://nvd.nist.gov/vuln/detail/CVE-2019-15006
16. Anderson, B., McGrew, D.: Identifying encrypted malware traffic with contextual flow data. In: Proceedings of the 2016 ACM Workshop on Artificial Intelligence and Security, AISec 2016, pp. 35–46. ACM, New York (2016)
17. Anderson, B., McGrew, D.: TLS beyond the browser: combining end host and network data to understand application behavior. In: Proceedings of the Internet Measurement Conference, IMC 2019, pp. 379–392. Association for Computing Machinery, New York (2019)
18. Bellissimo, A., Burgess, J., Fu, K.: Secure Software Updates: Disappointments and New Challenges. HotSec, pp. 37–43 (2006)
19. Chen, Y., Antonakakis, M., Perdisci, R., Nadji, Y., Dagon, D., Lee, W.: DNS Noise: Measuring the pervasiveness of disposable domains in modern DNS traffic. In: Proceedings - 44th Annual IEEE/IFIP International Conference on Dependable Systems and Networks, DSN 2014, pp. 598–609 (2014)
20. Cisco Systems Inc: Cisco Security Analytics White Paper (2018). https://www.cisco.com/c/dam/en/us/products/collateral/security/stealthwatch/white-paper-c11-740605.pdf
21. Cisco Systems Inc: Cisco Encrypted Traffic Analytics - White Paper (2019). https://www.cisco.com/c/dam/en/us/solutions/collateral/enterprise-networks/enterprise-network-security/nb-09-encrytd-traf-anlytcs-wp-cte-en.pdf

22. Denning, D.E.: An intrusion-detection model. In: 1986 IEEE Symposium on Security and Privacy, pp. 118–118 (1986)
23. Dormann, W.: The Consequences of Insecure Software Updates (2017). https://insights.sei.cmu.edu/cert/2017/06/the-consequences-of-insecure-software-updates.html
24. Durumeric, Z., et al.: The Security Impact of HTTPS Interception (2017)
25. Durumeric, Z., Wustrow, E., Halderman, J.A.: ZMap: fast internet-wide scanning and its security applications. In: 22nd USENIX Security Symposium (USENIX Security 2013), pp. 605–620. USENIX Association, Washington, D.C., August 2013
26. Forrest, S., Hofmeyr, S., Somayaji, A., Longstaff, T.: A sense of self for Unix processes, pp. 120–128. Institute of Electrical and Electronics Engineers (IEEE), December 2002
27. Frolov, S., Wustrow, E.: The use of TLS in censorship circumvention. In: Proceedings of The Network and Distributed System Security Symposium (2019)
28. Georgiev, M., Iyengar, S., Jana, S., Anubhai, R., Boneh, D., Shmatikov, V.: The most dangerous code in the world: validating SSL certificates in non-browser software. In: ACM Conference on Computer and Communications Security, pp. 38–49 (2012)
29. Hofstede, R., Bartoš, V., Sperotto, A., Pras, A.: Towards real-time intrusion detection for NetFlow and IPFIX. In: 2013 9th International Conference on Network and Service Management, pp. 227–234 (2013)
30. Houmansadr, A., Brubaker, C., Shmatikov, V.: The parrot is dead: observing unobservable network communications. In: Proceedings - IEEE Symposium on Security and Privacy, pp. 65–79 (2013)
31. Kleopa, C., Judge, C.: Snort - OpenAppID (2015) https://www.snort.org/documents/openappid-detection-webinar
32. Kountouras, A., et al.: Enabling network security through active DNS datasets. In: Monrose, F., Dacier, M., Blanc, G., Garcia-Alfaro, J. (eds.) RAID 2016. LNCS, vol. 9854, pp. 188–208. Springer, Cham (2016). https://doi.org/10.1007/978-3-319-45719-2_9
33. Leonhard, W.: Microsoft is distributing security patches through insecure HTTP links — Computerworld (2018). https://www.computerworld.com/article/3256304/microsoft-is-distributing-security-patches-through-insecure-http-links.html
34. Lyon, G.F.: Nmap Network Scanning: The Official Nmap Project Guide to Network Discovery and Security Scanning. Insecure, USA (2009)
35. Nemec, M., Klinec, D., Svenda, P., Sekan, P., Matyas, V.: Measuring popularity of cryptographic libraries in internet-wide scans, pp. 162–175 (2017)
36. Roesch, M.: Snort - lightweight intrusion detection for networks. In: Proceedings of the 13th USENIX Conference on System Administration, LISA 1999, pp. 229–238. USENIX Association, USA (1999)
37. Shamsi, Z., Cline, D.B.H., Loguinov, D.: Faulds: a non-parametric iterative classifier for internet-wide OS fingerprinting. In: ACM Conference on Computer and Communications Security, pp. 971–982 (2017)
38. Shamsi, Z., Nandwani, A., Leonard, D., Loguinov, D.: Hershel: single-Packet OS Fingerprinting. IEEE/ACM Trans. Netw. **24**(4), 2196–2209 (2016)
39. Springall, D., Durumeric, Z., Halderman, J.A.: Measuring the Security Harm of TLS Crypto Shortcuts, pp. 33–47 (2016)
40. Wagner, D., Soto, P.: Mimicry attacks on host-based intrusion detection systems. In: Proceedings of the 9th ACM Conference on Computer and Communications

Security, CCS 2002, pp. 255–264. Association for Computing Machinery, New York (2002)

41. Yeung, D.Y., Ding, Y.: Host-based intrusion detection using dynamic and static behavioral models. Pattern Recogn. **36**(1), 229–243 (2003)

42. Zalewski, M.: P0F V3: Passive Fingerprinter (2012). http://lcamtuf.coredump.cx/p0f3/README

43. Zhenqi, W., Xinyu, W.: NetFlow based intrusion detection system. In: Proceedings - 2008 International Conference on MultiMedia and Information Technology, MMIT 2008, pp. 825–828 (2008)

Zeroing in on Port 0 Traffic in the Wild

Aniss Maghsoudlou$^{(\boxtimes)}$, Oliver Gasser, and Anja Feldmann

Max Planck Institute for Informatics, Saarbrücken, Germany
{aniss,oliver.gasser,anja}@mpi-inf.mpg.de

Abstract. Internet services leverage transport protocol port numbers to specify the source and destination application layer protocols. While using port 0 is not allowed in most transport protocols, we see a non-negligible share of traffic using port 0 in the Internet.

In this study, we dissect port 0 traffic to infer its possible origins and causes using five complementing flow-level and packet-level datasets. We observe 73 GB of port 0 traffic in one week of IXP traffic, most of which we identify as an artifact of packet fragmentation. In our packet-level datasets, most traffic is originated from a small number of hosts and while most of the packets have no payload, a major fraction of packets containing payload belong to the BitTorrent protocol. Moreover, we find unique traffic patterns commonly seen in scanning. In addition to analyzing passive traces, we also conduct an active measurement campaign to study how different networks react to port 0 traffic. We find an unexpectedly high response rate for TCP port 0 probes in IPv4, with very low response rates with other protocol types. Finally, we will be running continuous port 0 measurements and providing the results to the measurement community.

1 Introduction

Transport protocols use port numbers to identify different Internet services. Common port numbers are TCP/80 and TCP/443 for the Web, TCP/25 for SMTP, or UDP/443 for QUIC. There are different categories of port numbers: Officially registered ports at IANA [23], unofficially but well-known ports, and dynamic ports, which cannot be registered and are free to use by anyone. In contrast, there are also some ports which are reserved and should not be used. One of these reserved port numbers is port 0. It is reserved in most common transport layer protocols, i.e., TCP [37], UDP [37], UDP-Lite [27], and SCTP [39]. When providing a port number 0 to the `bind()` system call to establish a connection, operating systems generally choose a free port from the dynamic range [28,33]. Therefore, one needs to create a raw socket in order to send port 0 packets. However, previous work has shown that there is a non-negligible share of traffic using port number 0 both in darknets and the Internet [9,29,30].

In this work, we shed light on port 0 traffic in the Internet, by analyzing the traffic from real networks, rather than darknets as is done in most related work, and by performing active measurements to survey the real-world reaction of hosts and routers to port 0 traffic.

© Springer Nature Switzerland AG 2021
O. Hohlfeld et al. (Eds.): PAM 2021, LNCS 12671, pp. 547–563, 2021.
https://doi.org/10.1007/978-3-030-72582-2_32

To the best of our knowledge, this is the first work which conducts both active and passive measurements on port 0 in the Internet, to better understand port 0 traffic characteristics and origins. Specifically, this work has the following three main contributions:

- We leverage a flow-level dataset from a large European IXP to inspect the origins of port 0 traffic (cf. Sect. 4). We find that out of the top 10 ASes originating port 0 traffic, the majority does not follow typical diurnal patterns of common protocols such as TCP/80.
- We inspect four packet-level datasets to discover the actual contents and detailed characteristics of port 0 packets (cf. Sect. 5). We show that the majority of non-empty packets in UDP are related to BitTorrent. We find that most TCP packets do not contain any payload and are one-way. However, most of the two-way TCP streams are scanning artifacts.
- We perform active measurements both in IPv4 and IPv6 to gain a tangible perspective over port 0 responsive IP addresses (cf. Sect. 6). We find that IPv4 traffic using TCP uncovers a substantial number of responsive hosts in a small number of ASes. We also perform traceroute-style active measurements to better understand port 0 traffic filtering in wild, and find discrepancies between IPv4 and IPv6. Finally, we will run periodic port 0 measurements and make the results available to the research community.

2   Related Work

Already in 1983, Reynolds and Postel specified that port number 0 is reserved in TCP and UDP [37]. Over the course of several years, similar provisions have been introduced for other transport protocols as well [27,39]. Traffic sent from or to port 0 thus violates these specifications. Fittingly, most reports on port 0 traffic are associated with DDoS attacks [25,31,41] and malformed packets [10].

Even though there is traffic on port 0 in the Internet, there is little research on its root causes. Motivated by port 0 traffic spikes observed in November 2013 at the Internet Storm Center and reports from security researchers at Cisco Systems, Bou-Harb et al. [9] study port 0 traffic on 30 GB of darknet data. They filter out any misconfigured traffic and packets with non-conforming TCP flags common in backscatter traffic [43]. Using fingerprinting techniques [8], they argued that more than 97% of their identified port 0 traffic was related to probing activities, some orchestrated by malware.

In 2019, Luchs and Doerr [29] revisit the case of port 0 traffic, by studying data obtained from a /15 darknet over a period of three years. They find that out of about 33,000 source IP addresses involved in port 0 traffic, 10% can be attributed to DDoS attacks, 6% to OS fingerprinting, and less than 1% to scanning activities. When aggregating by the number of packets instead, scanning traffic dominates with 48% of all port 0 packets.

More recently, Maghsoudlou et al. [30] analyze port 0 traffic for a single passive measurement source. Similarly to our results, they find that a small number of ASes are responsible for about half of all port 0 traffic.

In contrast to the related work [9,29,30], which all focus their efforts on the analysis of a single passive data source, in this paper we analyze four complementing passive datasets in addition to conducting an active measurement campaign to better understand port 0 traffic in the wild.

3   Datasets Overview

We leverage two different kinds of passive datasets to study port 0 traffic characteristics: Flow-level and packet-level data. Throughout the paper, port 0 traffic refers to the subset of the traffic which has either source port or destination port or both set to zero. Flow-level data gives us a high-level overview of Internet traffic and can be used to analyze the aggregate flow of traffic. In our case, we use one week of IPFIX flow data from a large European IXP. On the other hand, to be able to dissect detailed traffic characteristics like fragmentation, header flags, and different payloads, we need to inspect every single packet. Therefore, we use four different packet-level datasets, namely long-term and short-term MAWI, CAIDA, and Waikato. Different packet-level datasets are used to cover different geographical and temporal vantage points.

As shown in Table 1, we use the following datasets:

IXP One week of sampled IPFIX data from the end of January 2020 captured at a large European IXP.

MAWI These datasets [32] contain packet traces from the transit link of the WIDE backbone [42] to the upstream ISP captured at samplepoint-F. They include partial packet payload. To obtain a more comprehensive view, we use two variants of MAWI datasets:

   – **MAWI-long** This dataset captures 15-minute snapshots each month from January 2007 to July 2020.

   – **MAWI-short** We also use the most recent MAWI dataset being part of the Day in the Life of the Internet project [12], which is April 8–9, 2020.

CAIDA This dataset [11] contains anonymized packet traces without payload from CAIDA's passive monitors. For our analysis we use the most recent dataset available at the time of writing, which is the one-hour period from 14:00–15:00 UTC recorded on January 17, 2019.

Waikato This dataset [40] contains packet header traces including the first few bytes of payload and is captured at the border of the University of Waikato network in New Zealand.

We analyze port 0 traffic seen in passive data in detail in Sect. 4 and 5. In addition to passive flow and packet data, we also conduct active measurements. More specifically, we run two types of measurements to analyze responsiveness on port 0 and filtering of port 0 traffic in the Internet:

Port scan. We use ZMap [16,46] and ZMapv6 [47] to find responsive addresses on port 0. In IPv4 we conduct Internet-wide measurements, in IPv6 we leverage an IPv6 hitlist [19–21].

Table 1. Overview of passive port 0 datasets.

Dataset	IXP	MAWI-long	MAWI-short	Waikato	CAIDA
Timespan	Jan. 25–31, 2020	2006–2020	Apr. 8–9, 2020	Apr.–Nov., 2011	Jan. 17, 2019
Duration	1 week	14 years	2 days	86 days	2 hours
Format	Flows	Packets	Packets	Packets	Packets
%IPv4,IPv6 (Port0)	99.8%,0.2%	100%,0%	100%,0%	100%,0%	99.7%,0.3%
%UDP,TCP (Port0)	96.8%,3.2%	22.4%,77.6%	30.2%,69.8%	15.5%,84.5%	43.8%,56.2%
Payload	No	Yes	Yes	Yes	No
Sampled	Packet-based	Time-based	No	No	No
# Packets	34.3×10^9	23×10^9	15.9×10^9	27.822×10^9	8.2×10^9
% Port 0 packets	0.25%	0.0008%	0.0001%	0.002%	0.0002%
# Bytes	25.5 TB	14.6 TB	6.7 TB	16.9 TB	4.3 TB
% Port 0 bytes	0.28%	0.00012%	0.0002%	0.001%	0.00002%

Traceroute. We use Yarrp [7,45] to traceroute addresses in IPv4 and IPv6 prefixes in order to analyze port 0 traffic filtering in the Internet.

We present results from our active measurement campaign in Sect. 6. By leveraging both passive and active measurements we can analyze different aspects of port 0 traffic in the wild.

3.1 Ethical Considerations

Before conducting active measurements, we follow an internal multi-party approval process which incorporates proposals by Partridge and Allman [36] and Dittrich et al. [15]. We follow scanning best practices [16] by limiting our probing rate, maintaining a blocklist, and using dedicated servers with informing rDNS names, websites, and abuse contacts. During our active measurements, we received one email asking to be blocked, to which we immediately complied.

When analyzing passive flow and packet data, we fully comply with the respective NDAs and do not share any personally identifiable information. Contrary to the active measurements, we will not publish any passive measurement data.

3.2 Reproducible Research

To foster reproducibility in measurement research [1,38], we make data, source code, and analysis tools of our active measurements publicly available [18]. Due to privacy reasons we will not publish data from the passive datasets.

3.3 Continuous Port 0 Measurements

To allow further analysis of port 0 responsiveness and filtering over time, we periodically run active port 0 measurements. The raw results of these measurements are publicly available for fellow researchers at:

inet-port0.mpi-inf.mpg.de

4   Flow-Level Analysis

Analyzing the traffic flowing between different Autonomous Systems is helpful to detect high-level patterns. To investigate port 0 traffic patterns, we use the IXP dataset and inspect the ASes originating or being targeted by port 0 traffic. In one week of IXP flow data, we find 23,000 ASes contributing to port 0 traffic. We observe that the source AS with highest number of packets in sends port 0 traffic to 4357 distinct destination ASes. Also, the destination AS with highest number of port 0 packets being destined to, is targeted by 1245 distinct source ASes.

We also observe that in 9 out of 10 top source ASes involved in port 0 traffic, port number 0 is among the top-5 source and destination port numbers along with TCP/80 (HTTP) and TCP/443 (HTTPS). We find that more than 99% of port 0 traffic has both source and destination port set to zero. Interestingly, more than 99% of all TCP traffic contains no TCP flags. This leads us to believe that this is not actual port 0 traffic and is most likely an artifact of packet fragmentation [26], which is incorrectly classified as TCP/0 traffic by the flow exporter [35]. We also analyze the 1% of the TCP traffic with non-zero TCP flags, composed of 867 packets. We find that 30% of this traffic sets their TCP flags to CWR/URG/ACK, 27% to ACK only, and 25% to URG/ACK/PSH/SYN. 62% of this traffic has an average packet size of less than 100 bytes, while 18% has an average packet size of more than 1480 bytes. To investigate more in-depth on how different networks react to port 0 traffic, we perform active measurements (cf. Sect. 6).

To further investigate origins and causes of port 0 traffic, we analyze the diurnal patterns of traffic originated by the top 10 source ASes and compare them with the more common Web traffic on TCP/80. Figure 1 shows a heatmap of the Spearman correlation of the diurnal patterns of these ASes and TCP/80 traffic. We see that while AS2 is the most correlated to TCP/80 traffic, AS4 and AS7 show highly similar patterns to each other and moderate correlation to TCP/80 traffic. Moreover, AS3 shows a unique pattern with no correlation to either other ASes or TCP/80.

AS3 is a cloud computing provider while other ASes are web hosting providers, ISPs, or telecommunication companies. The unique traffic pattern originated by AS3 implies irregular usage such as scanning or reset attack. For the interested reader we provide a time series plot for the aforementioned ASes in Appendix B.

To better understand the causes of port 0 traffic, we analyze average payload sizes observed in the IXP dataset. For easier comparison with the packet-level datasets (cf. Sect. 5), we choose to analyze the payload size instead of the average packet size reported directly in the flow data. We estimate the payload size by subtracting the IP and TCP/UDP headers without options. As shown in Fig. 2, for TCP, we observe that nearly 88% of packets are smaller than 100 bytes, while in UDP, more than 75% of packets are larger than 100 bytes. Having roughly 20% full-sized packets in UDP, along with many mid-sized packets, indicates possible fragmentation. Unfortunately, our IPFIX dataset does not include fragmentation

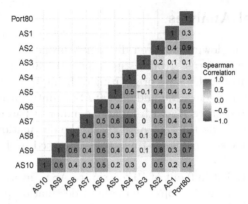

Fig. 1. Correlation coefficients between port 80 traffic and the top 10 source ASes involved in port 0 traffic in the IXP.

information for IPv4 flows. It does, however, include information about the IPv6 next header value. We find no IPv6 flows with the next header value set to fragmentation (i.e., 44). To investigate further on the exact fragmentation header flag, we inspect the IPFIX field containing a list of all IPv6 extension headers in a flow. We find, however, that the content of this IPFIX field does not conform to the IPFIX specifications as defined by the RFC. This is possibly due to an erroneous early version of the RFC, which has since been corrected [2]. As IPFIX datasets usually depend heavily on how their exporter is implemented, researchers who would like to work on them should be extra cautious to make sure that their data is flawless.

To summarize, multiple indicators lead us to believe that most of port 0 traffic seen at the IXP is an artifact of packet fragmentation. Nevertheless, we find that the IXP data gives valuable information on diurnal patterns. By analyzing the correlation between diurnal patterns of different ASes and port 80 traffic, we find one AS deviating heavily from the common diurnal patterns. This indicates possible scanning or other irregular activities which requires a more in-depth analysis which can only be performed on packet-level data. Therefore, we analyze the four packet-level datasets in the upcoming section.

5 Packet-Level Analysis

Although using a flow-level dataset provides us with useful information about the origin and targets of port 0 traffic, it cannot provide information on what the packets actually contain. Knowing the packet content, we can infer the cause of port 0 usage more precisely. To this end, we use the MAWI-long, MAWI-short, CAIDA, and Waikato datasets. CAIDA contains no payload, while others provide partial payload data. We begin our packet-level analysis by investigating packet payload sizes, for which we use the packet length field found in UDP and TCP headers. As Fig. 2 shows, nearly all packets in MAWI-short, MAWI-long and Waikato have a payload size of less than 100 bytes. In both the MAWI-short and the CAIDA dataset, more than 99% of the TCP port 0 traffic does not have any payload, while UDP traffic always contains payload. Note that Fig. 2 only shows those TCP packets with payload, i.e., for CAIDA and MAWI-short, it shows less than 1% of all TCP packets. In the CAIDA dataset, while UDP traffic includes payload sizes smaller than 104 bytes in 99% of the packets, TCP traffic shows more mid-sized payload sizes. Investigating further into the CAIDA dataset shows that all packets contain zero as fragment offset and all the fragmentation flags are set to *Don't Fragment*. This suggests that port 0 traffic in the CAIDA dataset is likely not a fragmentation artifact. However, we find some bogus packets, e.g. with zero header length among these mid-sized TCP packets.

Similar to our analysis in Sect. 4, we investigate port 0 traffic origins and destinations in the MAWI dataset. We find that most of the traffic, namely more than 60%, is destined to only 2 ASes, as shown in Fig. 3. Figure 4 shows the cumulative distribution of IP addresses in port 0 traffic in different datasets. We exclude the MAWI-long dataset since aggregating through 14 years would not give us useful information. We observe that more than 75% of port 0 traffic is originated by less than 10 IP addresses in CAIDA, IXP, and MAWI-short. Also in all the datasets, more than 87% of port 0 traffic is destined to less than 10 IP addresses.

In Fig. 5, we show the payload distribution classified with libprotoident [3] for each year in the MAWI-long dataset. The red line along with the right Y-axis show total number of packets throughout different years. The stacked bar plots show different categories of payloads excluding *No Payload* and *Unknown UDP*. We find that BitTorrent traffic is a constant contributor to port 0 traffic in Waikato, MAWI-short, and in different years in MAWI-long.

In MAWI-short, we find that 70% of the payloads belong to the BitTorrent UDP protocol. Additionally, a payload pattern covering 16% of the traffic, probably belonging to a custom application-layer protocol, DNS, OpenVPN, and NTP, contributes to other payloads in MAWI-short port 0 traffic in our dataset. In Waikato, BitTorrent-UDP and Skype are among the top payloads.

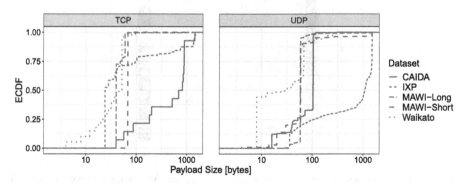

Fig. 2. Cumulative distribution of payload size in port 0 traffic. Note that the X-axis is log-scaled.

In MAWI-short, MAWI-long, and CAIDA, Malformed packets contribute less than 2% to port 0 packets, e.g., with wrong checksums, having UDP length of higher than IP length, etc. However, in Waikato, we find that 16.2% of the traffic is malformed. This shows that port 0 traffic can also be caused by misconfiguration, programming errors, or people sending malformed traffic on purpose.

Next, we analyze different TCP flags in packet-level datasets to better understand possible causes of port 0 traffic. Attackers and scanners usually use specific TCP control bits in their packets to achieve their goals. For instance, attackers sending spoofed traffic set the SYN bit to try to initiate TCP connections with their targets, which in backscatter traffic we see as SYN/ACK, RST, RST/ACK, or ACK packets [43]. Therefore, we investigate TCP control flags in the datasets. We observe that most of the TCP flags are only SYNs: More than 66% in MAWI-short, and 92% in CAIDA, which might indicate that most of the TCP port 0 traffic in these two datasets is caused by scanning. We analyze TCP flags in MAWI-long dataset per year, as shown in Fig. 6. First, we check whether all packets in a TCP stream are one-way or two-way. We find that a large fraction of the TCP streams are one-way. This also holds for all other packet-level datasets. Then, we categorize two-way TCP streams as follows:

– Scan to closed port: Client sends SYN, receives RST or RST/ACK.
– Scan to open port: Client sends SYN, receives SYN/ACK, client then sends RST or RST/ACK.
– No SYN: No SYN is ever sent. The stream begins with other flags, mostly SYN/ACKs followed by RSTs from the other side.
– Not scan: None of the above, i.e., client sends SYN but receives no RST.

We find that a major fraction of two-way TCP streams are scans to closed ports for most of the years. Among the streams in the *Not scan* category, we find two long streams of ACK/PSH followed by multiple ACKs in 2015 or ACK/PSH/FIN

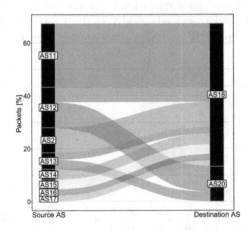

Fig. 3. Traffic between top 10 (source AS, destination AS) pairs involved in port 0 traffic in the MAWI-short dataset.

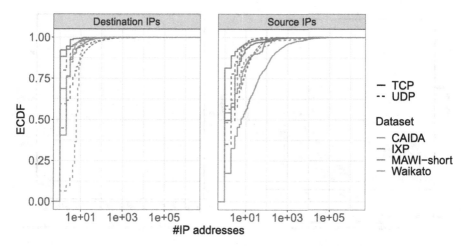

Fig. 4. Cumulative distribution of IP addresses in port 0 traffic. Note that the X-axis is log-scaled.

in 2019, respectively. We believe that these streams are related to an ACK/PSH flood attack [22] considering the relatively high number of packets sent in these streams. Next, we analyze specific years of the MAWI-long dataset with very characteristic spikes more in-depth. In 2009, we see the largest number of total packets of any year, with a TCP:UDP ratio of about 2:1. The majority of UDP traffic is originating with source port UDP/8000 from many different IP addresses within a Chinese ISP AS which are mostly destined to UDP/0 towards a single IP address belonging to a Japanese university inside WIDE. For TCP, the majority of traffic is sourced from a single IP address within a Canadian ISP and destined to many different IP addresses. Almost all sources are TCP/0 and the destinations are TCP/22 (SSH). As is shown in Fig. 6, these are very likely scanning activities.

In 2012 we see the largest number of TCP streams as shown in Fig. 6. We find a factor of 54 times more TCP traffic this year than UDP traffic. Almost 80% of all TCP/0 traffic is from a single IP address within a hosting company, the destination addresses and ports are evenly distributed. The TCP flags of all packets are set to RST/ACK. These indicators lead us to believe that this is backscatter traffic from attack traffic using spoofed IP addresses [43].

Finally, we investigate the current year 2020, from January to July. During this period we see 26 times as much TCP traffic compared to UDP. The majority of TCP traffic originates from a single IP address at a hosting company, which uses TCP/43573 as a source port. For the IP address in question we find many different reports on abuse DB websites, which hint at scanning and vulnerability probing.

To summarize, we find that a large fraction of TCP streams in port 0 traffic is one-way. However, we still see some two-way streams related to scanning

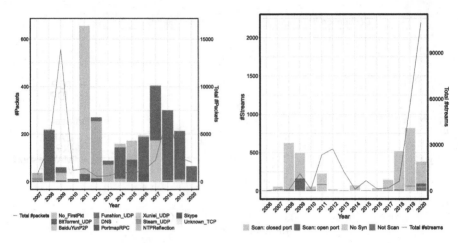

Fig. 5. Payload distribution (bar plots) and total packet count (red line) for MAWI-long. (Color figure online)

Fig. 6. TCP stream categorization (bar plots) and total streams (red line) for MAWI-long. (Color figure online)

activities. Analyzing packet payloads throughout all our datasets, we observe that BitTorrent UDP traffic is a constant contributor to port 0 traffic.

6   Active Measurements

As discussed in the previous sections, we observed a significant number of RST/ACKs and even some SYN/ACKs which indicate scanning activities. To better understand how the network reacts to port 0 traffic, we stage an active measurement campaign. We run two types of measurements: (1) Port scan measurements allow us to analyze responsiveness of IP addresses to port 0 probes and (2) traceroute measurements provide information on where port 0 packets are being filtered.

6.1   Responsive Addresses

We run four types of port scan measurements, for each possible combination of IPv4/IPv6 and TCP/UDP. The IPv4 measurements are run on the complete address space minus a blocklist, the IPv6 measurements use an IPv6 hitlist [20]. For the TCP measurements we send regular SYN packets, for UDP we send the most prominent payload found in our passive packet traces.

For the four protocol combinations, we get vastly differing results. With 2.3 M, the largest number of addresses responds to our IPv4 TCP port 0 probes. Only 2222 unique addresses respond to IPv4 UDP probes and 120 respond to IPv6 TCP probes. We find not a single responsive address for IPv6 UDP probes.

When mapping responsive addresses to ASes [4,13], we find that a small number of ASes makes up the majority of responses. Figure 7 shows the AS

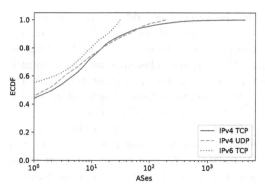

Fig. 7. Cumulative distribution of responsive IP addresses per AS. Note that the X-axis is log-scaled.

Table 2. Top 10 ASes of non-reachable target addresses when comparing TCP/0 and TCP/80.

	ASN	AS Name	Count
1	6830	Liberty Global	4822
2	6327	Shaw	3257
3	812	Rogers	2297
4	33915	Vodafone	2152
5	11492	Cable One	1095
6	30036	Mediacom	688
7	12389	Rostelecom	643
8	4134	Chinanet	575
9	3320	Deutsche Telekom	552
10	4766	Korea Telecom	498

distribution of responses for the different protocols. The top ten ASes make up 72%, 73%, and 79% of all responses for IPv4 TCP, IPv4 UDP, and IPv6 TCP, respectively. When we look at the overlap of responding addresses in TCP and UDP for IPv4, we find that 61% of IPv4 UDP addresses are present in IPv4 TCP results. In IPv4 TCP, where we see the most responses by far, most of the top 10 ASes belong to ISPs. This leads us to believe that faulty or misconfigured ISP equipment is to blame for responses to port 0 probes.

Next, we analyze the initial TTL (iTTL) value [6,24,34], UDP reply payload, and combine these with the responding AS. For IPv4 TCP we find that the most common iTTL values are 64 (57%), which is the default for Linux and macOS, 255 (36%), the default for many Unix devices, and 128 (7%) the default for Windows. When combining these iTTL values with the responding AS we find no clear patterns. In contrast, for IPv4 UDP we find a clear correlation between iTTL, payload, and AS. The most common response payload (32%) is sent from six different ASes with an iTTL value of 32 or 64. The second most common response payload (14%) is identical to our request payload, i.e., the probed hosts simply mirror the payload that they receive. Packets with this payload originate from a single AS (AS7922, Comcast) and all of them have an iTTL of 255. The third most common payload (8%) is made up of 16 zero bytes and originates from AS14745 (Internap Corporation) with an iTTL of 32.

These findings suggest that only a small number of networks contain misconfigured devices erroneously responding to port 0 probes.

6.2 Port 0 Traceroutes

To better understand how port 0 traffic is handled inside the network, we conduct traceroute-style measurements using Yarrp [45]. This allows us to see if port 0 traffic is treated differently by routers compared to standard TCP/80 or TCP/443 traffic.[1] In IPv4, we split the announced address space into 11 M /24 prefixes and send a trace to a random address within each of these prefixes. In IPv6, the equivalent would be sending traces to every /48 prefix. This is, however, not feasible due to the vast address space. Therefore we decide to pick one random address per announced IPv6 prefix, no matter the prefix length. We ensure that random addresses for less specific prefixes do not fall into more specific prefixes. In total, we send probes to about 88 k IPv6 prefixes.

When analyzing the reached target addresses depending on the used port numbers, we find that in IPv4 there is a significant difference between port 0 and other ports. 91 k of IPv4 port 0 traces reach their target, whereas 118 k traces on TCP/80 and TCP/443 reach their target IPv4 address, an increase of almost 30%.

In IPv6, however, almost no targets are reached for either port number, as the likelihood of a randomly generated address in a prefix actually being assigned is quite low. Therefore, we perform additional analyses based on the reachability of the target BGP-announced prefix.

The general picture in IPv4 does not change drastically when analyzing the reachability of the target prefix: Port 0 probes reach fewer target prefixes compared to port 80 and port 443 probes, although the difference is reduced to 14.2% and 9.5%, respectively.

When we analyze the reached target prefixes for IPv6, however, we see a slight difference of 3%.

As the difference of reachable addresses is most apparent in IPv4, we investigate this phenomenon in more detail. We identify on a per-target basis the addresses which see no responses in TCP/0, but do see responses in TCP/80. These non-responsive port 0 addresses are mapped to 4102 distinct ASes, exhibiting a long-tailed distribution. Next, we check whether we find other addresses in these 4102 ASes to be responsive to port 0 traceroutes, to exclude the possibility of missing responses due to ICMP rate limiting. We find responses to port 0 traceroutes for only 15 of these ASes, making up only 0.4% of the total 4102 ASes. This underlines the fact that these ASes are indeed handling port 0 traceroutes differently compared to other ports. Furthermore, as is shown in Table 2, 9 out of the top 10 ASes belong to ISPs, further indicating that these might be ASes blocking port 0 traffic to their clients [5,17,44]. We analyzed many additional aspects of traceroute responses, by checking for differences in the last responsive hop, comparing the number of responsive hops per trace, evaluating ICMP types and codes, but finding no additional differences between traceroutes using port 0 compared to other ports. We provide these results for the interested reader in Appendix A.

To summarize, our findings show that packets are handled differently based on the destination port number. Port 0 is more likely to be filtered on the path

---

[1] Note that due to the nature of traceroute measurements, missing traceroute responses could stem either from filtered packets on the forward path, rate-limiting of ICMP packets at the routers, as well as dropping of ICMP responses on the return path.

as well as at the target hosts. Interestingly, the phenomenon of fewer responses for TCP/0 seems to be much more common in IPv4 compared to IPv6, which could be due to inconsistent firewall rules [14].

7   Conclusion

In this work, we dissected port 0 traffic by analyzing five complementing passive datasets and by conducting active measurements. We showed that the majority of port 0 traffic in the wild flows between a small number of source and destination ASes/IP addresses. Moreover, for some ASes we identified similar diurnal patterns in port 0 traffic as with regular traffic, along with many TCP packets with no TCP flags, hinting at a prevalence of fragmented traffic in the IXP dataset. Additionally, we found that a major fraction of UDP port 0 traffic contains payload, with BitTorrent being a common contributor. Moreover, we showed that TCP port 0 traffic usually does not contain any payload and is mostly one-way. Two-way streams were identified as mostly scanning traffic. Finally, by staging an active measurement campaign, we showed unusually high response rates to TCP port 0 probes in IPv4, in addition to uncovering the presence of port 0 packet filtering.

Acknowledgments. We are thankful to the anonymous reviewers as well as our shepherd Ramakrishna Padmanabhan for their constructive feedback. We also thank the large European IXP, MAWI, the University of Waikato, and CAIDA for providing the data used in our analysis.

A   Additional Traceroute Analyses

We perform additional analyses for the active traceroute measurements, which we provide in the following.

A.1   Last Responsive Hops

We analyze the last responsive hop of each trace specifically. More concretely, we are interested in the distance, i.e., the largest TTL value of traceroutes, where we get an ICMP response to. This allows us to determine whether TCP/0 traceroutes are e.g., dropped earlier in the network and therefore are terminated earlier in the Internet.

Therefore, we compare the distribution of the last responsive hop. The left part of Fig. 8 shows the distribution of the last responsive hop for IPv4 and IPv6, respectively. The only visible difference we see for IPv4 are the lower whiskers for TCP/0, stemming from the fact that TCP/80 and TCP/443 has slightly more outliers with high TTLs when it comes to the last responsive hops. For IPv6 we see that TCP/0 has a median of 13 and TCP/80 as well as TCP/443 have a median last responsive hop TTL of 14. Since the median is almost identical, this is due to the median only being able to represent integer values if all elements (namely path lengths) are integers. TCP/0's median is therefore "just below" 14 and the others' median is "just above" 14. All in all, the box plots show that there is no significant difference when analyzing last responsive hops depending on the transport port.

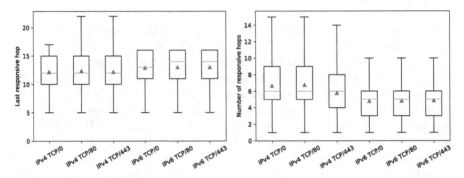

Fig. 8. Box plot of last responsive hop (left) and the number of responsive hops (right) aggregated by transport port protocol for IPv4 and IPv6 showing the median, first and third quantiles, mean (▲), and 1.5 times IQR as whiskers.

A.2   Number of Responsive Hops

Next, we try to answer the question whether fewer routers on the path send ICMP messages for port 0 traceroute traffic or not.

In the right part of Fig. 8 we show the box plot of the number of responsive hops. Again, we see no evidence of router sending fewer ICMP responses for port 0 traffic. We see a slight reduction of TCP/443 ICMP responses per trace in IPv4.

A.3   ICMP Types and Codes

Finally, we evaluate the different ICMP types and codes sent by routers.

Figure 9 shows the distribution of type and code combinations for ICMP and ICMPv6, respectively. As expected, the vast majority are of type "Time to Live exceeded in Transit" for IPv4 and 'hop limit exceeded in transit" for IPv6. We see almost identical distributions for the port 0 and other ports.

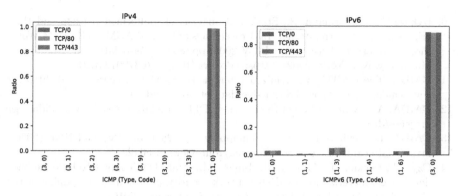

Fig. 9. Distribution of ICMP(v6) type and code combinations for all responses split by transport protocol for IPv4 (left) and IPv6 (right).

B   Additional Passive Analysis

We analyze hourly patterns of port 0 traffic grouped by source AS, compared with the total port 80 traffic as a reference for regular traffic. Due to space limitations we publish the figure on our website:

inet-port0.mpi-inf.mpg.de

References

1. ACM: Artifact Review and Badging (2020). https://www.acm.org/publications/policies/artifact-review-badging
2. Aitken, P.: RFC Erratum 1738 (2009). http://www.rfc-editor.org/errata_search.php?eid=1738
3. Alcock, S., Nelson, R.: Libprotoident: traffic classification using lightweight packet inspection. WAND Network Research Group, Technical report (2012)
4. Asghari, H.: pyasn on Github (2018). https://github.com/hadiasghari/pyasn
5. AT&T: Broadband Information - Network Practices (2020). https://about.att.com/sites/broadband/network
6. Backes, M., Holz, T., Rossow, C., Rytilahti, T., Simeonovski, M., Stock, B.: On the feasibility of TTL-based filtering for DRDoS mitigation. In: Monrose, F., Dacier, M., Blanc, G., Garcia-Alfaro, J. (eds.) RAID 2016. LNCS, vol. 9854, pp. 303–322. Springer, Cham (2016). https://doi.org/10.1007/978-3-319-45719-2_14
7. Beverly, R.: Yarrp'ing the internet: randomized high-speed active topology discovery. In: Proceedings of the Internet Measurement Conference, pp. 413–420 (2016)
8. Bou-Harb, E., Debbabi, M., Assi, C.: On fingerprinting probing activities. Comput. Secur. **43**, 35–48 (2014). https://doi.org/10.1016/j.cose.2014.02.005. http://www.sciencedirect.com/science/article/pii/S0167404814000248
9. Bou-Harb, E., Lakhdari, N.E., Binsalleeh, H., Debbabi, M.: Multidimensional investigation of source port 0 probing. Digit. Investig. **11**, S114–S123 (2014)

10. Bykova, M., Ostermann, S.: Statistical analysis of malformed packets and their origins in the modern internet. In: Proceedings of the 2nd ACM SIGCOMM Workshop on Internet Measurment, IMW 2002, pp. 83–88. Association for Computing Machinery, New York (2002). https://doi.org/10.1145/637201.637211

11. CAIDA: The CAIDA Anonymized Internet Traces Data Access (2019). https://www.caida.org/data/passive/passive_dataset_download.xml

12. CAIDA: A Day in the Life of the Internet (DITL) (2020). https://www.caida.org/projects/ditl/

13. CAIDA: Routeviews Prefix-to-AS mappings (pfx2as) for IPv4 and IPv6 (2020). http://data.caida.org/datasets/routing/routeviews-prefix2as/

14. Czyz, J., Luckie, M., Allman, M., Bailey, M., et al.: Don't forget to lock the back door! A characterization of IPv6 network security policy. In: Proceedings of the Network and Distributed Systems Security Symposium (2016)

15. Dittrich, D., et al.: The Menlo Report: Ethical Principles Guiding Information and Communication Technology Research. US DHS (2012)

16. Durumeric, Z., Wustrow, E., Halderman, J.A.: ZMap: fast internet-wide scanning and its security applications. In: Proceedings of the 22nd USENIX Security Symposium, pp. 605–620 (2013)

17. Fischer, D.: nanog mailing list: TCP and UDP Port 0 - Should an ISP or ITP Block it? (2020). https://mailman.nanog.org/pipermail/nanog/2020-August/209228.html

18. Gasser, O.: Analysis scripts and raw data for active port 0 measurements (2021). https://doi.org/10.17617/3.5f

19. Gasser, O., et al.: Clusters in the expanse: understanding and unbiasing IPv6 hitlists. In: Proceedings of the Internet Measurement Conference, pp. 364–378 (2018)

20. Gasser, O., et al.: IPv6 Hitlist Service (2018). https://ipv6hitlist.github.io/

21. Gasser, O., Scheitle, Q., Gebhard, S., Carle, G.: Scanning the IPv6 internet: towards a comprehensive hitlist. In: Proceedings of the Traffic Monitoring and Analysis Workshop (2016)

22. Hallman, R., Bryan, J., Palavicini, G., Divita, J., Romero-Mariona, J.: Ioddos-the internet of distributed denial of service attacks. In: 2nd International Conference on Internet of Things, Big Data and Security, pp. 47–58. SCITEPRESS (2017)

23. IANA: Service Name and Transport Protocol Port Number Registry (2020). https://www.iana.org/assignments/service-names-port-numbers/service-names-port-numbers.xhtml

24. Jin, C., Wang, H., Shin, K.G.: Hop-count filtering: an effective defense against spoofed DDoS traffic. In: Proceedings of the ACM Computer and Communications Security Conference (2003)

25. Jones, T.: DDoS Attacks on Port 0 - Does it mean what you think it does? (2013). https://blog.endace.com/2013/08/27/ddos-attacks-on-port-0-does-it-mean-what-you-think-it-does/

26. Kopp, D., Dietzel, C., Hohlfeld, O.: DDoS never dies? An IXP perspective on DDoS amplification attacks. In: Proceedings of the Passive and Active Measurement Conference (2021)

27. Larzon, L.-A., Degermark, M., Pink, S., Jonsson, L.-E., Ericsson, Ed., Fairhurst, G.: The Lightweight User Datagram Protocol (UDP-Lite). RFC 3828, RFC Editor, July 2004. https://tools.ietf.org/html/rfc3828#section-3.1

28. Linux man-pages project: bind(2) – Linux manual page (2020). https://man7.org/linux/man-pages/man2/bind.2.html

29. Luchs, M., Doerr, C.: The curious case of port 0. In: Proceedings of the IFIP Networking Conference, pp. 1–9 (2019)
30. Maghsoudlou, A., Gasser, O., Feldmann, A.: Reserved: Dissecting Internet Traffic on Port 0 (2020)
31. Majkowski, M.: Reflections on reflection (attacks) (2017). https://blog.cloudflare.com/reflections-on-reflections/
32. MAWI project: MAWI Working Group Traffic Archive (2020). http://mawi.wide.ad.jp/mawi/
33. Microsoft: Windows bind function (2018). https://docs.microsoft.com/en-us/windows/win32/api/winsock/nf-winsock-bind
34. Mukaddam, A., Elhajj, I., Kayssi, A., Chehab, A.: IP spoofing detection using modified hop count. In: Proceedings of the Advanced Information Networking and Applications Conference (2014)
35. Nokia: Router Configuration Guide Release 16.0.R4 (2018). https://infoproducts.nokia.com/cgi-bin/dbaccessfilename.cgi/3HE14136AAABTQZZA01_V1_7450%20ESS%207750%20SR%207950%20XRS%20and%20VSR%20Router%20Configuration%20Guide%2016.0.R4.pdf
36. Partridge, C., Allman, M.: Ethical considerations in network measurement papers. Commun. ACM **59**(10), 58–64 (2016)
37. Reynolds, J., Postel, J.: Assigned numbers. RFC 870, RFC Editor, Fremont, CA, USA, October 1983. 10.17487/RFC0870. https://www.rfc-editor.org/rfc/rfc870.txt. obsoleted by RFC 900
38. Scheitle, Q., Wählisch, M., Gasser, O., Schmidt, T.C., Carle, G.: Towards an ecosystem for reproducible research in computer networking. In: Proceedings of the ACM SIGCOMM Reproducibility Workshop (2017)
39. Stewart, R.: Stream Control Transmission Protocol. RFC 4960, RFC Editor, September 2007. https://tools.ietf.org/html/rfc4960
40. WAND Network Research Group: WITS: Waikato VIII (2020). https://wand.net.nz/wits/waikato/8/
41. Wanner, R.: Port 0 DDOS (2013). https://isc.sans.edu/forums/diary/Port+0+DDOS/17081/
42. WIDE project: WIDE project website (2020). http://www.wide.ad.jp/index_e.html
43. Wustrow, E., Karir, M., Bailey, M., Jahanian, F., Huston, G.: Internet background radiation revisited. In: Proceedings of the 10th ACM SIGCOMM Conference on Internet Measurement, IMC 2010, pp. 62–74. Association for Computing Machinery, New York (2010). https://doi.org/10.1145/1879141.1879149
44. Xfinity: Blocked Internet Ports List (2020). https://www.xfinity.com/support/articles/list-of-blocked-ports
45. Yarrp authors: Yarrp on Github (2020). https://github.com/cmand/yarrp/
46. ZMap authors: ZMap on Github (2020). https://github.com/zmap/zmap/
47. ZMapv6 authors: ZMapv6 on Github (2020). https://github.com/tumi8/zmap/

A Study of the Partnership Between Advertisers and Publishers

Wenrui Ma[1] and Haitao Xu[2]([envelope]) [ORCID]

[1] Shantou University, Shantou, China
mawenrui@stu.edu.cn
[2] Zhejiang University, Hangzhou, China
haitaoxu@zju.edu.cn

Abstract. Ad networks (e.g., Google Ads and Facebook Ads), advertisers, publishers (websites and mobile apps), and users are the main participants in the online advertising ecosystem. Ad networks dominate the advertising landscape in terms of determining how to pair advertisers with publishers and what ads are shown to a user. Previous works have studied the issues surrounding how ad networks tailor ads to a user (i.e., the ad targeting mechanisms) extensively and mainly from the perspective of users. However, it is largely unknown regarding the practices of how ad networks match between advertisers and publishers.

In this paper, we present a measurement study of the practices of how ad networks pair advertisers with publishers as well as advertisers' preference on ad networks from the perspective of advertisers. To do this, we manage to harvest a unique advertising-related dataset from a leading digital market intelligence platform. We conducted paired comparison analysis, i.e., analyzing advertisers and publishers in pairs, to examine whether they are significantly similar or dissimilar to each other. We also investigate if advertisers in different categories have different preferences on ad networks, whether an advertiser partners with only one ad network for its ad campaign, and how much traffic that its ad campaign could bring about to its site. Specifically, we found that about a third of advertisers have their ads mostly displayed on publishers with the same category as themselves. In addition, most advertisers partner with multiple ad networks at the same time for their ad campaigns. We also found that the `Adult`, `Romance & Relationships`, and `Gambling` websites rely on advertising to attract visitors more than other advertiser categories. Our study produces insightful findings which provide advertisers more visibility into the complex advertising ecosystem so that they could make better decisions when launching ad campaigns.

Keywords: Online advertising · Advertising practice · Measurement

1 Introduction

Online advertising is the primary revenue source for millions of web sites and mobile apps, and is thus crucial to the whole Internet ecosystem. Ad networks,

© Springer Nature Switzerland AG 2021
O. Hohlfeld et al. (Eds.): PAM 2021, LNCS 12671, pp. 564–580, 2021.
https://doi.org/10.1007/978-3-030-72582-2_33

advertisers, publishers, and users are the main parties in the online advertising ecosystem. Ad networks oversee the whole advertising business in terms of connecting advertisers to publishers and determining what ads are displayed to a user. An ad network is involved in every workflow step, including helping an advertiser create an ad, partnering with millions of publishers to reserve ad placement spots, profiling users based on user behavior tracking, and finally tailoring ads to a user visiting a partnered publisher. To some extent, ad networks know all other three parties better than the parties know themselves.

However, ad networks fail to provide sufficiently informative feedback reports for other parties, especially advertisers which are ad networks' revenue source, to independently evaluate what could be a better advertising practice for them. For example, ad networks usually provide ad campaign reports to inform advertisers of post-click performance metrics about users who clicked on the ads and then came through to the advertiser's site. However, for an advertiser, such reports typically fail to provide information about publishers where their own ads are displayed and publishers where their peer advertisers operating similar business get their ads delivered. Such information is certainly important for advertisers to evaluate the effectiveness of their ad campaigns through a horizontal comparison.

Previous works have studied the online advertising ecosystem mainly from the perspective of users. Some works investigate the effectiveness and transparency of the ad targeting mechanisms leveraged by ad networks to match ads and users [8–10,12,13,15,19,21,28,29]. Some propose mechanisms to promote user privacy and social equality in online advertising [14,16,17,23,24,30,35,36,39]. A few studies research on security issues caused by malicious usage of online advertising [20,26,27,34,37,38,40,42]. However, there is still a lack of literature regarding the advertiser-publisher pairings (i.e., what publishers display an advertiser's ads) and advertiser-ad network pairings (i.e., what ad networks are responsible for distributing an advertiser's ads) from an advertiser's perspective.

In this paper, we present a measurement study of the practice of advertiser-publisher pairings and advertiser-ad network pairings, for advertisers to gain a better understanding of their own and peer advertisers' ad campaigns. By complementing feedback reports from ad networks, our study could offer advertisers additional insights into the advertising ecosystem.

A real-world dataset containing information about both advertisers and their paired publishers and ad networks is central to the objective of our study. With a list of top Alexa domains, we queried each of them against a popular web analytics service provider and managed to gather ample advertising-related information regarding the domain, such as leading publishers where the domain's ads are displayed, leading ad networks responsible for the domain's ad campaigns, and the proportion of incoming traffic contributed by advertising.

With the dataset, we are able to conduct paired comparison analysis, i.e., analyzing advertisers and publishers in pairs, to examine whether they are significantly similar or dissimilar to each other, so that we may understand the rationale why ad networks deliver an advertiser's ads to one publisher rather than another. We are well aware of the three primary ad targeting mechanisms, i.e., contextual-based, behavioral-based, and remarketing-based [28], but in this work, we are trying to explore *objectively* whether the similarity/dissimilarity between advertisers and publishers could also be a possible factor for ad networks to associate advertisers and publishers together by ad delivering, besides the ad targeting mechanisms.

In addition, our dataset also allows us to investigate if advertisers in different categories have different preferences on ad networks, whether an advertiser only partners with one ad network for its ad campaign, and how much traffic that its ad campaign could bring about to its site. Specifically, we found that about 60% advertisers have their ads mostly delivered to the publishers which attract a large volume of visitor traffic, such as news websites, social networks, and video streaming services. And typically an advertiser's site is usually not so popular as its associative publisher in attracting visitor traffic. In addition, most advertisers are found to partner with multiple ad networks at the same time for their ad campaigns. Finally, we found that the `Adult`, `Romance & Relationships`, and `Gambling` websites rely on advertising to attract visitors more than other advertiser categories. We report our data collection and the findings in detail in the rest sections.

2 Our Dataset

Ad networks, advertisers, publishers, and users are the main participants in the online advertising ecosystem. Ad networks connect advertisers to publishers and determine what ads are displayed to a user. When a user visits a publisher, views or clicks on an ad, the corresponding advertiser would pay to the associative ad network, which in turn pays a share to the publisher [1,7].

A representative real-world dataset, containing information about advertisers, their paired publishers, and their partnered ad networks, is essential for our study. In this section, we describe our data collection methodology and the dataset we obtained.

Data Collection. Starting from a list of top 30K Alexa domains [3] (the reason for the relatively small data is explained below), we queried each domain (or site, used exchangeably in this paper) against `SimilarWeb` [4], a leading website categorization and analytics service. The reason we chose SimilarWeb over Alexa [2] is that SimilarWeb provides us ample advertising-related information regarding a domain, which is crucial to our study, such as ad networks partnered with the domain, top publishers where its ads are displayed, as well as the proportion of incoming traffic contributed by advertising.

Out of consideration of budget, in our study, we use the SimilarWeb service with a free user account, which allows individual query only and limits 5 results per metric if the metric has a list of values. For instance, given a domain, only the top 5 ad networks responsible for its ad distribution are available. However, the top 5 results of a metric usually contribute a significant proportion together, close to 100% sometimes, and thus the data is adequate for our statistical study.

Within a time period of two weeks, we conducted data collection in a semi-automated manner. That is, given a top Alexa domain, we manually[1] launched a query against SimilarWeb, saved the result webpage locally as an HTML file, and later on automatically parsed the HTML file with Python scripts. We have made our dataset publicly available[2].

Data Explained. For each domain, SimilarWeb provides us the following information.

- *Leading ad networks* that the domain partners with to launch ad campaigns
  - Denoted as $\{<AdNetwork_i, Share_i>|\ i = 1..5\}$, i.e., the top 5 ad networks adopted by the domain, and the percentage of ads each ad network is responsible for.
- *Leading publishers* where most of the domain's ads are displayed
  - Denoted as $\{Publisher_i|\ i = 1..5\}$.
- *Advertising traffic* to the domain's website
  - Specifically, the percentage of incoming traffic due to advertising is provided, as well as the share of other traffic sources, including direct access, referrals from other sites, search on search engines, social networks, and emails.
- *Traffic statistics* of the domain, including the following information:
  - *Category*: the site's category, determined based upon the web content.
  - *Country*: the country where the most visitors to the site are from, usually consistent with the origin country of the site.
  - *Global rank*: traffic rank of the site, as compared to all other sites in the world.
  - *Visits*: total number of visits in the recent 6 months.
- *Audience interests* of the site
  - Denoted as $\{<AudienceInterest_i, Share_i>|\ i = 1..5\}$, i.e., the top 5 online interests of the users visiting this site, and the percentage of audience in each interest category.

SimilarWeb Approach of Data Harvesting. SimilarWeb is an Israeli digital market intelligence company and is readying for an IPO on Nasdaq as of this writing[3]. According to its own introduction about their data [5], SimilarWeb leverages hundreds of diverse data sources, calibrates data with real feedback, e.g., Google Analytics, and aggregates those mixed data sources through machine learning algorithms into a single data set available to users. The hundreds of data sources can be categorized into four groups: (i) public data points easily obtained using crawling techniques, (ii) first-party data directly shared by website and mobile apps owners, (iii) external partners, e.g., Internet service providers, who usually have millions of subscribers, and (iv) panel-based behavioral data obtained through add-ons, extensions, apps and plugins.

---

[1] We cannot utilize the browser automation tool `Selenium` to crawl SimilarWeb pages due to the latter's web scraping prevention measures.

[2] https://www.jianguoyun.com/p/Da1yvg4QuKftCBjMpNsD.

[3] Online traffic intelligence co SimilarWeb eyes Nasdaq: https://bit.ly/3iAegxl.

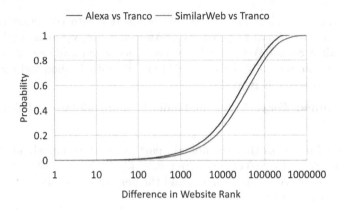

Fig. 1. Deviation of SimilarWeb and Alexa from Tranco ranking.

Data Validity. In this study, we heavily rely on the dataset obtained by querying a domain against SimilarWeb. Since how SimilarWeb collects and processes data is still largely unknown to the public, we validated the dataset as follows. First, we compare SimilarWeb to other website ranking systems. Tranco is a research-oriented ranking system, which is claimed to create robust rankings transparently and reproducibly [6,33]. Hence we use Tranco as a benchmark and then examine whether SimilarWeb ranking has a significantly larger deviation from Tranco ranking than the deviation of Alexa ranking from Tranco ranking. We randomly selected 20,000 website domains and then obtained their rankings in Tranco, SimilarWeb, and Alexa. We then calculated the deviation of SimilarWeb from Tranco ranking and the deviation of Alexa from Tranco ranking for each domain, respectively. We plotted the cumulative distribution function (CDF) curves in Fig. 1. It shows that (1) both SimilarWeb and Alexa rankings could have a large deviation from Tranco ranking. Specifically, for about 70%-75% domains, the difference of their website ranking value in SimilarWeb and Alexa from that in Tranco could be larger than 10,000; (2) As for the deviation from Tranco ranking, Alexa did not perform better than SimilarWeb, and the ranking values provided by SimilarWeb are as trustworthy as those provided by Alexa. Moreover, we compared SimilarWeb and Alexa in terms of other traffic metrics and did not find statistically significant difference either. For example, Table 1 lists the traffic data returned by SimilarWeb and Alexa for espn.com. As for the advertising-related data about a domain, unfortunately, we did not find any other web analytics services including Alexa that provide such data, and thus we cannot perform a comparison as we do in Table 1. We assume SimilarWeb provides trustworthy web analytics data.

Our Data Processing. Our research approach is to conduct paired comparison analysis, i.e., analyzing advertisers and publishers in pairs, to examine whether they are significantly similar or dissimilar to each other. Thus, starting with the raw data $\{Publisher_i|\ i = 1..5\}$, i.e., the top 5 publishers directing advertising

Table 1. SimilarWeb versus Alexa in traffic statistics about espn.com.

Web analytics	Global rank	Pages/Visit	Traffic source			
			Direct	Referral	Search	Social
SimilarWeb	83	3.40	73.99%	1.01%	18.24%	3.80%
Alexa	88	3.96	78%	7.47%	13.76%	0.77%

traffic to an advertiser, we parse it into five pairs $< Advertiser, Publisher_i >$, $i = 1..5$. In this way, we managed to extract 34,229 distinct pairs of advertiser and publisher. There are 26,456 distinct domains in total in those 2-tuples, including 16,870 distinct advertisers[4] and 12,142 distinct publishers. Note that a domain could advertise itself in other websites with the help of ad networks as an advertiser and meanwhile host the ads from other websites as a publisher. And 9.7% (2,556 out of 26,456 sites) are found to be an advertiser and a publisher at the same time. We choose not to exclude those domains or treat them differently, since it is very common in the practice that a domain could take both the roles.

Data Representativeness. We examined the representativeness of our dataset in terms of domain category distribution and domain country distribution.

Dataset Distribution by Domain Category. Figure 9 (placed in Appendix due to page limit) depicts the distribution of the domains in the dataset by category[5]. It shows that all those domains in our study fall into 30 categories. The top 5 categories, including Computers and Technology, News and Media, Arts and Entertainment, Science and Education, and Games, account for 44.0% of all domains. None of the domains in the rest categories occupy more than 5%. Thus, the domains in our study are quite diverse in category.

Dataset Distribution by Domain Country. The country which contributes the most traffic to a domain is deemed as its primary country. All the domains are found to be from 119 countries, and those primary countries contribute 57.8% traffic to a domain on average. The top 20 countries shown in Fig. 10 (in Appendix) account for 88.5% of all domains. Nearly a half (47.7%) of domains are from the United States. Our dataset seems biased in this metric, but actually it makes sense, given that United States owns about 41.0% of know registered domains based on the domain name registration's statistics[6].

---

[4] Several hundreds of domains in our original domain list were removed, since SimilarWeb did not manage to obtain their corresponding publisher information. Actually, it is common and normal that SimilarWeb may not return complete data for each data field we described before.

[5] As explained before, the category information is provided by SimilarWeb.

[6] Domain name registration's statistics: https://domainnamestat.com/statistics/overview.

3   Paired Comparison Analysis

In this section, we conduct paired comparison analysis, i.e., analyzing advertisers and publishers in pairs, to examine whether they are significantly similar or dissimilar to each other. We also check how much traffic that advertisers' ad campaigns with ad networks could bring to their sites as well as which ad networks are popular with advertisers. We report our analysis results on 34,229 pairs of advertisers and publishers in below.

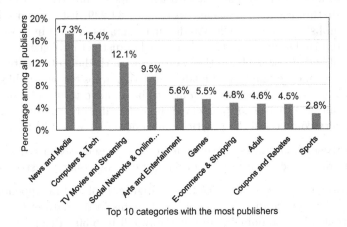

Fig. 2. Top 10 categories of publishers that are associated with the most advertisers. Y axis denotes the percentage of all advertisers.

3.1   Similarity or Dissimilarity Between Publishers and Advertisers

What Categories of Publishers are Paired with the Most Advertisers? Data analysis reveals that no matter what category of advertiser websites, 59.9% advertisers have their ads displayed on publisher websites falling under the 5 categories, including News and Media, Computers and Technology, TV Movies and Streaming, Social Networks & Online Communities, and Arts and Entertainment, as shown in Fig. 2. And the publishers under the other 5 categories, including Games, E-commerce & Shopping, Adult, Coupons and Rebates, and Sports, are also popular ad placement choices, which account for 22.2% combined.

We further examined why publishers in these 10 categories are delivered with the most ads (assuming that the more advertisers associated with a publisher, the more ads delivered to it), by looking into the number of visits to those publishers in the last 6 months. We found that 7 out of the top 10 most popular publisher categories are among the top 10 categories with the most visitors, shown in Fig. 3. Although the rest 3 categories – Games, Coupons and Rebates,

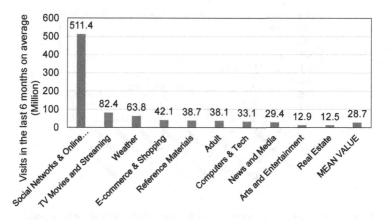

Fig. 3. Top 10 categories of publishers with the most visits in the last 6 months.

and **Sports** – did not appear in Fig. 3, actually the publishers in those three categories also attract huge volume of user traffic. Thus, the results indicate that *visitor traffic does positively affect the number of ads that are delivered to a publisher website.*

Do Ad Networks Deliver an Advertiser's Ads to Publishers with the Same Category as the Advertiser? We analyzed the leading publishers that are associated with each of advertisers in all 30 categories, and found that a third of advertisers end up with their ads mostly shown on publishers with the same category as them. Figure 4 shows the top 10 categories of advertisers with their ads mostly shown on publishers with the same category. We can see that up to 66.9% **Adult** advertisers have their ads mostly shown on **Adult** publishers, 35.6% **Games** advertisers mainly showing ads on **Games** publishers, and 17.5% **Gambling** advertisers showing ads on **Gambling** publishers[7]. The results are reasonable, since the visitors to a publisher would highly likely show interest in the advertised products or services from advertisers of the same category as the publisher.

For the rest 20 advertiser categories, 13 categories of advertisers display ads mostly on **News and Media** publishers; advertisers in the other 7 categories mainly have their ads delivered by ad networks to publishers in categories: **Computers and Technology**, **Social Networks and Online Communities**, and **Adult**. As depicted in Fig. 3, all those four publisher categories, i.e., **News and Media**, **Computers and Technology**, **Social Networks and Online Communities**, and **Adult**, are among the top 10 categories with the most visits in the last 6 months, so the ads on them could get more exposure.

---

[7] Note that 17.5% is already a very large ratio, given the quite small ratio of **Gambling** publishers among all publishers on the Internet. In our dataset, only 1.4% domains fall into the **Gambling** category.

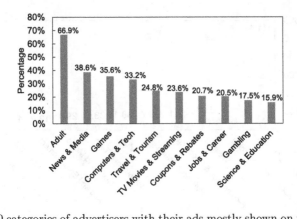

Fig. 4. Top 10 categories of advertisers with their ads mostly shown on publishers with the same category. Y axis denotes the percentage of advertisers in one category.

So, we conclude that *ad networks deliver an advertiser's ads either to publishers with the same category as the advertiser or to publishers with a large volume of visitor traffic.*

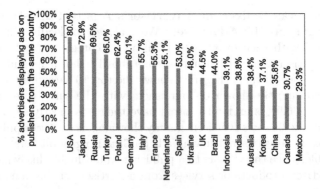

Fig. 5. Percentage of advertisers in the top 20 countries whose ads are displayed mostly on publishers from the same country.

Do Ad Networks Deliver an Advertiser's Ads to Publishers in the Same Country as the Advertiser? As shown in Fig. 10, the top 20 countries account for 88.5% of all websites in our dataset, and we focus on those 20 countries. For each country, we compute the proportion of advertisers which have their ads mainly shown on publishers from the same country. The results are illustrated in Fig. 5. It shows that in all 20 countries, a significant proportion of advertisers (from 29.3% to 80.0%, 50.7% on average) have most of their ads delivered to publishers from their own country. In the top 6 countries, including United States, Japan, Russia, Turkey, and Poland, more than 60%

advertisers and their corresponding leading publishers are from the same country. One may argue that the conclusion is quite obvious and expected, but we believe that it is still worth a quantitative measurement.

The 6 rightmost countries in Fig. 5 are the only exceptions, since in those countries, advertisers have their ads delivered to the United States publishers more often than to publishers in their own country. Specifically, 58.1% advertisers from Canada, 48.6% from Korea, 45.5% from Australia, 43.2% from India, 48% from Mexico, and 37.9% from China are scheduled by ad networks to show ads mainly on the United States publishers. Publishers from the United States seem very popular with worldwide advertisers. In all other 12 out of the top 20 countries (also excluding United States itself and Ukraine), United States publishers come second in hosting their ads. This probably reflects the preference of advertisers, since ad networks do allow advertisers to decide their target countries.

Do Ad Networks Pair an Advertiser with Publishers with Higher-Volume Traffic than the Advertiser? We compared between publishers and advertisers in our dataset in traffic volume. As illustrated in Fig. 6, the boxplot chart shows that advertisers have much fewer visits than publishers in terms of the total visits in the recent 6 months. Specifically, on average, within a 6-month time period, an advertiser website receives 45.3 million visits, and a publisher website receives 3.59 billion visits, about 79 times of the traffic to advertisers. The median visits to them are 5.18 million and 27 million, respectively. Hence, *statistically, advertisers' ads are more likely to be displayed on publishers with higher user traffic than that of advertisers.* The result makes sense considering that ads displayed on a publisher with high-volume traffic could get more attention of potential customers and thus bring a great return on investment (ROI) for advertisers.

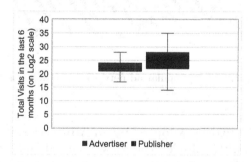

Fig. 6. Comparison between advertisers and publishers in terms of visitor traffic.

Do Ad Networks Pair Advertisers with the Right Publishers? We explored this question by checking whether an advertiser's audiences will highly likely visit its leading publishers. We match an advertiser's top audience interests against the categories of its top 5 publishers. A matching would indicate an advertiser's ads are indeed delivered to the right publishers. Among 11,961 advertisers with both top audience interests and leading publishers information available, 79.6% advertisers have their audience interests matching with the corresponding publishers. *The result suggests that ad networks may do a good job in pairing advertisers and publisher but still have much room for improvement.*

3.2   Advertisers' Preference on Ad Networks

Ad networks play a crucial role in online advertising ecosystem. Next, we would like to examine which ad networks are popular with advertisers when they consider launching an ad campaign.

Top 20 Most Popular Ad Networks. A total number of 199 unique ad networks are identified in our dataset. Figure 7 shows the top 20 most popular ad networks and the percentage of advertisers choosing them. `Google Display Network` is clearly the dominant ad network, and accounts for 23.6% of advertisers' ad network choices. `Skimlinks` comes second and is chosen by 9.5% advertisers. All other 197 ad networks, including those not shown in the figure, only attract a share of less than 5% advertisers.

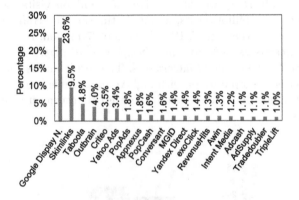

Fig. 7. Top 20 popular ad networks with advertisers.

Number of Ad Networks Adopted by an Advertiser. It is possible that an advertiser partners with multiple ad networks for its ad campaigns. Data analysis reveals that (1) 41.8% advertisers only adopt one ad network, and 52.2% of those advertisers adopt `Google Display Network` only and 10.2% choose `Skimlinks` only, (2) 19.5% advertisers partner with two ad networks, and one of the two ad networks takes the largest share, accounting for 81.1% ads on average, (3) 10.8% advertisers with 3 ad networks, and one of those ad networks account for 73.0% ads on average, (4) 6.8% with 4 ad networks, and one of them accounts for 68.1% ads on average, and (5) 21.1% with at least 5 ad networks (since we can only see the top 5 leading ad networks), and one ad network accounts for 61% ads on average. So, *only 41.8% advertisers stick to only one advertiser, which has a 52.2% chance to be* Google Display Network. *For those advertisers partnering with more than one ad network, one of the ad networks take the largest share, often responsible for more than 60% ads.*

Most Popular Ad Networks for Advertisers with Different Categories.
We then checked if the advertisers under different categories have different preferences on ad networks. We found that Google Display Network is the number one choice for advertisers in 29 out of the total 30 categories, with the category Adult as the only exception. We use a pie chart[8] in Fig. 8 to show the major ad networks preferred by Adult advertisers. It shows that exoClick, PopCash, and AdSupply are the 3 most popular ad networks with Adult advertisers, accounting for 15.5%, 9%, and 9%, respectively. Note that although these 3 ad networks are among the top 20 popular ad networks with all categories of advertisers in Fig. 7, none of them get a share of more than 2%, which implies that these ad networks focus their business on Adult advertisers.

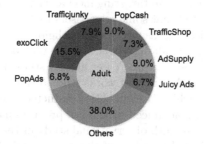

Fig. 8. Ad networks preferred by Adult advertisers.

How Much Traffic is Driven by Advertising to Advertisers' Websites?
Lastly, we check how large proportion of traffic that advertising could bring about to an advertiser's site. Our dataset contains the traffic source information for all 26,456 unique websites under all 30 categories. Figure 11 (in Appendix due to page limit) shows the average proportion of the incoming traffic that arises from advertising by category. We can see that statistically, for advertisers in any category, the traffic due to advertising occupies less than 10%, which is quite normal because a website could have quite diverse traffic sources, including but not limited to search (Google, Bing, etc.), direct (bookmark, type-in), and social (Twitter, Facebook, etc.), and also even 8.7% traffic from advertising (i.e., for Adult advertisers) would cost advertisers a big amount of money. Specifically, advertisers in the three categories: Adult, Romance & Relationships, and Gambling rely on advertising to attract visitors more than website in any other categories. On average, about 5.6% to 8.7% visitors navigate to those websites

---

[8] In here, Fig. 8 is not used to illustrate numerical proportion. We just borrow the form of pie chart for better illustration.

through advertising. It makes sense since after all those websites cannot attract as much traffic as `News` and `Media` websites in the normal way.

Limitations. This study is based on a small dataset with potential bias.

4   Related Work

Our work represents a new effort towards increasing transparency into the complex online advertising ecosystem. There is a large body of work studying the other aspects of the online advertising ecosystem. Gill et al. [22] investigated the relationship between personal information collected and its economic value for advertising. Papadopoulos et al. [32] implemented a system to allow end users to compute in real time the value advertisers pay to reach them. Some works [8–10,28] studied the ad targeting mechanisms. Liu et al. [28] investigated the prevalence of three primary ad targeting mechanisms and found that behavioral-based targeting was the most popular one. Barford et al. [10] characterized a large corpus of ads and studied the ad targeting mechanisms from various perspectives. Andreou et al. [8] reported that some advertisers target users with ads of potentially sensitive categories such as politics and religion. Some other works studied new forms of advertising. Chalermsook et al. [18] studied a new form of advertising, i.e., sponsored viral marketing. Yu et al. [41] studied in-vehicle advertising and its economic impact. A couple of works studied the newly introduced mechanisms or standards. Pachilakis et al. [31] conducted a measurement study of Header Bidding (HB), an advanced method of programmatic ad buying. Bashir et al. [11] presented a 15-month observational study of the `ads.txt` standard. A few works [24,25] studied the impact of the usage of ad-block and anti-adblock tools on the advertising ecosystem. Compared to the above-mentioned works, we study the online advertising ecosystem with a unique dataset and from the perspective of advertisers.

5   Conclusion

In this paper, we study the practice of pairing between advertisers and publishers as well as advertisers' preference on ad networks from the perspective of advertisers, with a unique dataset collected from a leading website analytics service. Our study produces ample findings which offer advertisers additional insights into the complex advertising ecosystem and help guide their ad campaigns.

Acknowledgment. We would like to thank our shepherd **Patricia Callejo** and anonymous reviewers for their insightful and detailed comments. The co-author **Haitao Xu** is the contact author of this paper.

6 Appendix

Figure 9 depicts the distribution of the domains in the dataset by category. Figure 10 shows the top 20 origin countries of the domains. Figure 11 shows the average proportion of the incoming traffic that arises from advertising by category.

Fig. 9. Distribution of 26,456 domains by category.

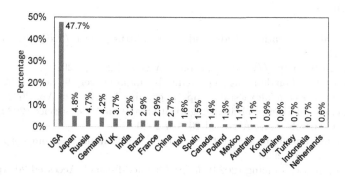

Fig. 10. Distribution of 26,456 domains by country.

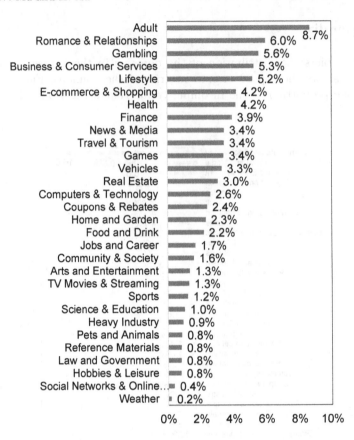

Fig. 11. The average proportion of the incoming traffic that arises from advertising, for advertisers under each category.

References

1. Iab digital ad operations study guide (2017). https://bit.ly/2NQclJQ. Accessed 29 Jan 2021
2. Alexa (2020). https://www.alexa.com/. Accessed 20 Apr 2020
3. Alexa top 1 million domains (reported to be updated every 90 days) (2020). http:// s3.amazonaws.com/alexa-static/top-1m.csv.zip. Accessed 20 Apr 2020
4. Similarweb, a leading website categorization and analytics service (2020). https:// www.similarweb.com/. Accessed 20 Apr 2020
5. The similarweb approach (2020). https://www.similarweb.com/corp/ourdata/. Accessed 20 Apr 2020
6. Tranco top sites ranking (2020). https://tranco-list.eu/. Accessed 20 Apr 2020
7. Iab: Interactive advertising bureau (2021). https://www.iab.com/. Accessed 29 Jan 2021
8. Andreou, A., Silva, M., Benevenuto, F., Goga, O., Loiseau, P., Mislove, A.: Measuring the facebook advertising ecosystem (2019)

9. Andreou, A., Venkatadri, G., Goga, O., Gummadi, K., Loiseau, P., Mislove, A.: Investigating ad transparency mechanisms in social media: a case study of Facebook's explanations (2018)
10. Barford, P., Canadi, I., Krushevskaja, D., Ma, Q., Muthukrishnan, S.: Adscape: harvesting and analyzing online display ads. In: Proceedings of the 23rd International Conference on World Wide Web, pp. 597–608. ACM (2014)
11. Bashir, M.A., Arshad, S., Kirda, E., Robertson, W., Wilson, C.: A longitudinal analysis of the ads. txt standard. In: Proceedings of the Internet Measurement Conference, pp. 294–307 (2019)
12. Bashir, M.A., Arshad, S., Robertson, W., Wilson, C.: Tracing information flows between ad exchanges using retargeted ads. In: 25th USENIX Security Symposium (USENIX Security 2016), pp. 481–496 (2016)
13. Bashir, M.A., Wilson, C.: Diffusion of user tracking data in the online advertising ecosystem. Proc. Privacy Enhancing Technol. **2018**(4), 85–103 (2018)
14. Bilenko, M., Richardson, M., Tsai, J.: Targeted, not tracked: client-side solutions for privacy-friendly behavioral advertising. In: TPRC (2011)
15. Bleier, A., Eisenbeiss, M.: Personalized online advertising effectiveness: the interplay of what, when, and where. Mark. Sci. **34**(5), 669–688 (2015)
16. Cabañas, J.G., Cuevas, Á., Cuevas, R.: Unveiling and quantifying Facebook exploitation of sensitive personal data for advertising purposes. In: 27th USENIX Security Symposium (USENIX Security 2018), pp. 479–495 (2018)
17. Castelluccia, C., Olejnik, L., Minh-Dung, T.: Selling off privacy at auction (2014)
18. Chalermsook, P., Das Sarma, A., Lall, A., Nanongkai, D.: Social network monetization via sponsored viral marketing. ACM SIGMETRICS Perform. Eval. Rev. **43**(1), 259–270 (2015)
19. Cook, J., Nithyanand, R., Shafiq, Z.: Inferring tracker-advertiser relationships in the online advertising ecosystem using header bidding. Proc. Privacy Enhancing Technol. **2020**(1), 65–82 (2020)
20. DeBlasio, J., Guha, S., Voelker, G.M., Snoeren, A.C.: Exploring the dynamics of search advertiser fraud. In: Proceedings of the 2017 Internet Measurement Conference, pp. 157–170 (2017)
21. Farahat, A., Bailey, M.C.: How effective is targeted advertising? In: Proceedings of the 21st International Conference on World Wide Web, pp. 111–120. ACM (2012)
22. Gill, P., Erramilli, V., Chaintreau, A., Krishnamurthy, B., Papagiannaki, K., Rodriguez, P.: Best paper-follow the money: understanding economics of online aggregation and advertising. In: Proceedings of the 2013 Conference on Internet Measurement Conference, pp. 141–148 (2013)
23. Guha, S., Cheng, B., Francis, P.: Privad: practical privacy in online advertising. In: USENIX Conference on Networked Systems Design and Implementation, pp. 169–182 (2011)
24. Guha, S., Reznichenko, A., Tang, K., Haddadi, H., Francis, P.: Serving ads from localhost for performance, privacy, and profit. In: HotNets, pp. 1–6 (2009)
25. Iqbal, U., Shafiq, Z., Qian, Z.: The ad wars: retrospective measurement and analysis of anti-adblock filter lists. In: Proceedings of the 2017 Internet Measurement Conference, pp. 171–183 (2017)
26. Kanich, C., et al.: Show me the money: characterizing spam-advertised revenue. In: USENIX Security Symposium, vol. 35 (2011)
27. Li, Z., Zhang, K., Xie, Y., Yu, F., Wang, X.: Knowing your enemy: understanding and detecting malicious web advertising. In: Proceedings of the 2012 ACM Conference on Computer and Communications Security, pp. 674–686 (2012)

28. Liu, B., Sheth, A., Weinsberg, U., Chandrashekar, J., Govindan, R.: Adreveal: improving transparency into online targeted advertising. In: Proceedings of the Twelfth ACM Workshop on Hot Topics in Networks, p. 12. ACM (2013)

29. Malheiros, M., Jennett, C., Patel, S., Brostoff, S., Sasse, M.A.: Too close for comfort: a study of the effectiveness and acceptability of rich-media personalized advertising. In: Proceedings of the SIGCHI Conference on Human Factors in Computing Systems, pp. 579–588. ACM (2012)

30. Meng, W., Ding, R., Chung, S.P., Han, S., Lee, W.: The price of free: privacy leakage in personalized mobile in-apps ads. In: NDSS (2016)

31. Pachilakis, M., Papadopoulos, P., Markatos, E.P., Kourtellis, N.: No more chasing waterfalls: a measurement study of the header bidding ad-ecosystem. In: Proceedings of the Internet Measurement Conference, pp. 280–293 (2019)

32. Papadopoulos, P., Kourtellis, N., Rodriguez, P.R., Laoutaris, N.: If you are not paying for it, you are the product: how much do advertisers pay to reach you? In: Proceedings of the 2017 Internet Measurement Conference, pp. 142–156 (2017)

33. Pochat, V.L., Van Goethem, T., Tajalizadehkhoob, S., Korczyński, M., Joosen, W.: Tranco: a research-oriented top sites ranking hardened against manipulation. arXiv preprint arXiv:1806.01156 (2018)

34. Rastogi, V., Shao, R., Chen, Y., Pan, X., Zou, S., Riley, R.: Are these ads safe: detecting hidden attacks through the mobile app-web interfaces. In: NDSS (2016)

35. Reznichenko, A., Francis, P.: Private-by-design advertising meets the real world. In: Proceedings of the 2014 ACM SIGSAC Conference on Computer and Communications Security, pp. 116–128 (2014)

36. Speicher, T., et al.: Potential for discrimination in online targeted advertising (2018)

37. Springborn, K., Barford, P.: Impression fraud in on-line advertising via pay-per-view networks. In: Presented as part of the 22nd USENIX Security Symposium (USENIX Security 2013), pp. 211–226 (2013)

38. Thomas, K., et al.: Ad injection at scale: assessing deceptive advertisement modifications. In: 2015 IEEE Symposium on Security and Privacy, pp. 151–167. IEEE (2015)

39. Venkatadri, G., et al.: Privacy risks with Facebook's PII-based targeting: auditing a data broker's advertising interface. In: 2018 IEEE Symposium on Security and Privacy (SP), pp. 89–107. IEEE (2018)

40. Xing, X., et al.: Understanding malvertising through ad-injecting browser extensions. In: Proceedings of the 24th International Conference on World Wide Web, pp. 1286–1295 (2015)

41. Yu, H., Wei, E., Berry, R.A.: Analyzing location-based advertising for vehicle service providers using effective resistances. Proc. ACM Meas. Anal. Comput. Syst. 3(1), 1–35 (2019)

42. Zarras, A., Kapravelos, A., Stringhini, G., Holz, T., Kruegel, C., Vigna, G.: The dark alleys of madison avenue: understanding malicious advertisements. In: Proceedings of the 2014 Conference on Internet Measurement Conference, pp. 373–380 (2014)

Author Index

Adarsh, Vivek 141
Aggarwal, Shivang 513
Akhavan Niaki, Arian 427
Akiwate, Gautam 57
Akiyama, Mitsuaki 39
Ammar, Mostafa 337
Ariemma, Lorenzo 213
Ashiq, Md. Ishtiaq 161

Bajpai, Vaibhav 192
Barbette, Tom 319
Belding, Elizabeth 141
Borgolte, Kevin 444
Bronzino, Francesco 20

Candela, Massimo 213
Carlsson, Niklas 175
Chen, Xunxun 93
Chiba, Daiki 39
Chiesa, Marco 319
Chung, Jae 499
Chung, Taejoong 161
Claffy, K. C. 230
Claypool, Mark 499
Claypool, Saahil 499

Davids, Marco 460
Davis, Jacob 302
Deccio, Casey 302
Demir, Nurullah 76
Di Battista, Giuseppe 213
Dietzel, Christoph 284
Doan, Trinh Viet 192
Durairajan, Ramakrishnan 247

Ermakov, Alex 141

Farhoodi, Sahand 427
Feamster, Nick 20, 444
Feldmann, Anja 547
Flores, Marcel 355

Gasser, Oliver 547
Ghasemisharif, Mohammad 390

Ghoshal, Moinak 513
Gill, Phillipa 427
Gupta, Arpit 141

Heinrich, Tiago 269
Hesselman, Cristian 460
Hohlfeld, Oliver 284
Hooft, Emilie 247
Hounsel, Austin 444
Hu, Y. Charlie 513

Jansen, Rob 481
Johnson, Aaron 481

Kanich, Chris 390
Kärkkäinen, Ljubica 406
Katsikas, Georgios P. 319
Kawaoka, Ryo 39
Keshvadi, Sina 111
Kong, Zhaoning 513
Kopp, Daniel 284
Korzhitskii, Nikita 175
Kostić, Dejan 319
Koutsonikolas, Dimitrios 513
Kristoff, John 390
Kunze, Ike 3

Levchenko, Kirill 57
Levin, Dave 161
Li, Ruidan 531
Li, Vector Guo 57
Liotta, Simone 213
Liu, Shinan 20
Lopez-Pacheco, Dino Martin 128

Ma, Wenrui 564
Maghsoudlou, Aniss 547
Maguire Jr., Gerald Q. 319
Marczak, William 427
Marder, Alexander 230
Mayer, Juno 247
Maziero, Carlos A. 269
McGregor, Andrew 427
McNiece, Matthew R. 531

Mislove, Alan 161
Mori, Tatsuya 39
Moura, Giovane C. M. 460
Müller, Moritz 460

Nekrasov, Michael 141

Obelheiro, Rafael R. 269
Olson, Karl 373
Omolola, Olamide 161
Ott, Jörg 406

Paul, Udit 141
Pohlmann, Norbert 76
Polakis, Jason 390

Raman, Prathy 355
Reaves, Bradley 531
Roberts, Richard 161
Roubia, Soufiane 128
Rüth, Jan 3

Saeed, Ahmed 337
Sahakian, Valerie 247
Sander, Constantin 3
Sarkar, Ishani 128
Savage, Stefan 57
Scaife, Nolen 373
Schmitt, Paul 20, 444

Shen, Fan 373
Snoeren, Alex C. 230

Toomey, Douglas 247
Torkamandi, Pegah 406
Tsang, Haiwei 93
Tsareva, Irina 192

Urban, Tobias 76
Urvoy-Keller, Guillaume 128

Vigil-Hayes, Morgan 141
Voelker, Geoffrey M. 57

Wampler, Jack 373
Watanabe, Takuya 39
Weaver, Nicholas 427
Wehrle, Klaus 3
Williamson, Carey 111
Wittek, Kevin 76
Wullink, Maarten 460

Xu, Haitao 564

Zang, Tianning 93
Zegura, Ellen 141, 337
Zeng, Yuwei 93
Zhao, Yimeng 337